Readings in Adolescent Psychology: Contemporary Perspectives

1977-1978 edition

edited by
Thomas J. Cottle

Harper & Row's
CONTEMPORARY PERSPECTIVES READER SERIES
Phillip Whitten, Series Editor

Harper & Row, Publishers

New York   Hagerstown   San Francisco   London

Sponsoring Editor: George A. Middendorf
Project Editor: Robert Ginsberg
Production Supervisor: Kewal K. Sharma
Printer & Binder: The Murray Printing Company

Cover photo: Tim Egan, Woodfin Camp & Associates

Readings in Adolescent Psychology: Contemporary Perspectives

Library of Congress Cataloging in Publication Data
Main entry under title:

Readings in adolescent psychology.

    (Harper & Row's contemporary perspectives reader
series)
    1. Adolescent psychology—Addresses, essays,
lectures. I. Cottle, Thomas J.
BF724.R37   155.5'08   77–1515
ISBN 0–06–047057–7

ACKNOWLEDGMENTS

I. THE ADOLESCENT: CHARACTERISTICS
ADOLESCENCE IN AMERICA: FROM IDEA TO SOCIAL FACT by David Bakan is reprinted by permission of DAEDALUS, Journal of the American Academy of Arts and Sciences, Boston, Massachusetts, Fall 1971.
Photograph by Elizabeth Hamlin, Stock Photo, Boston.
ADOLESCENCE IN HISTORICAL PERSPECTIVE by John Demos and Virginia Demos. Copyright © 1969 by National Council on Family Relations. Reprinted by permission.
Photograph by Charles Gatewood.
MEMORANDUM ON YOUTH by Erik H. Erikson is reprinted by permission of DAEDALUS, Journal of the American Academy of Arts and Sciences, Boston, Massachusetts, Spring 1976.

II. ADOLESCENT DEVELOPMENT: MIND AND BODY
REQUIREMENTS FOR HEALTHY DEVELOPMENT OF ADOLESCENT YOUTH by Gisela Konopka. Copyright © 1973 ADOLESCENCE.
Photograph by Jean Claude LeJeune
Photograph by permission from Phillip Whitten.
ADOLESCENCE AS A DEVELOPMENTAL DISTURBANCE by Anna Freud, Chapter 1 in ADOLESCENCE: PSYCHOLOGICAL PERSPECTIVES by Gerald Caplan and Serge Lebovici, Editors, © 1969 by Basic Books, Inc., Publishers, New York.
ONE OF THOSE SPECIAL STUDENT TYPES by Thomas J. Cottle is reprinted by permission from the author, Children's Defense Fund of the Washington Research Project.

III. THE SELF: PRIVATE AND PUBLIC
PSYCHOSEXUAL DEVELOPMENT by William Simon and John Gagnon is published by permission of Transaction, Inc. from TRANSACTION, Vol. 6 #5, copyright © 1969 by Transaction, Inc.
Photograph by George Gardner.
SEX DIFFERENCES IN ADOLESCENT CHARACTER PROCESSES by Elizabeth Douvan is reprinted by permission of the author and the MERRILL-PALMER QUARTERLY OF BEHAVIOR AND DEVELOPMENT.
THE TERROR OF LIFE—A LATENT ADOLESCENT NIGHTMARE by Stephen J. Goldburgh and Charles D. Rotman. Copyright © 1973 ADOLESCENCE.
ADOLESCENT APPEARANCE AND SELF CONCEPT by Kathleen E. Musa and Mary Ellen Roach. Copyright © 1973 ADOLESCENCE.
Photograph by Charles Gatewood.
THE PRIVATE GENERATION by Jeffrey K. Hadden is reprinted by permission of PSYCHOLOGY TODAY Magazine. Copyright © 1969 Ziff-Davis Publishing Co.

IV. THE FAMILY
OF YOUTH AND THE TIME OF GENERATIONS by Thomas J. Cottle. From TIME'S CHILDREN, Little Brown, 1971. Copyright © 1971 Thomas J. Cottle.
Photograph by Virginia Hamilton.
PARENTAL POWER LEGITIMATION AND ITS EFFECT ON THE ADOLESCENT by Glen H. Elder is reprinted by permission from the American Sociological Association and the author.
Photograph by Charles Gatewood.
ADOLESCENCE, MARRIAGE, AND SEX by Cora DuBois from THE PEOPLE OF ALOR: A SOCIAL-PSYCHOLOGICAL STUDY OF AN EAST INDIAN ISLAND. University of Minnesota Press. Minneapolis, copyright 1944.
THE RUNAWAY GIRL: A REACTION TO FAMILY STRESS by Ames Robey, Richard J. Rosenwald, John E. Snell, and Rita E. Lee is reprinted by permission from the AMERICAN JOURNAL OF ORTHOPSYCHIATRY and the author.
KIDS WITH KIDS by Leslie Aldridge Westoff. Copyright © 1976 by The New York Times Company. Reprinted by permission.
Photograph by Vicki Lawrence, Stock Photo, Boston.

V. EDUCATION
THE NIGHT WORLD OF PREADOLESCENCE by Donald McNassor is reprinted by permission from CHILDHOOD EDUCATION, April/May 1975.
Photograph by Virginia Hamilton.
WHAT THE PUBLIC SCHOOLS SHOULD TEACH by Walter P. Reuther. Copyright © 1957 by President and Fellows of Harvard College.
THE SAINTS AND THE ROUGHNECKS by William J. Chambliss is published by permission of Transaction, Inc. from SOCIETY, Vol. 11 #1, Copyright © 1973 by Transaction, Inc.
SOME DISADVANTAGED YOUTHS LOOK AT THEIR SCHOOLS by Beatrice M. Hill and Nelson S. Burke is reprinted by permission from the JOURNAL OF NEGRO EDUCATION.
Photograph by Michael Dobo, Stock Photo, Boston.
THE EQUALLY GOOD OFF, THE EQUALLY BAD OFF by Thomas J. Cottle is reprinted with the permission of the Center for Law and Education, Cambridge, Mass.

VI. FRIENDS
ADOLESCENT CHOICES AND PARENT-PEER CROSS-PRESSURES by Clay V. Brittain is reprinted with permission from the American Sociological Association.
Photograph by George Gardner.
BRAINWASHING: PERSUASION BY PROPAGANDA by Max Gunther is reprinted with permission from TODAY'S HEALTH Magazine © February 1976. All rights reserved.
Photograph by Charles Gatewood.

CONTENTS

PREFACE

A well-known psychologist was once asked to describe his major areas of interest, the topics that really interested him most. The psychologist looked puzzled as though he had never before been asked this question. Then he responded: "I have no topics of special interest. All you can say is that I seem to be interested in people who range in age from about ten to 20." Then he grinned, not without some embarrassment. "I guess that makes me a student of adolescence."

Indeed it does. For as theories about human behavior and methods of studying human behavior have evolved, and as scientists attempt to make order of what they understand and don't yet understand about human behavior, the subject of adolescence has emerged as a very significant "topic of inquiry." Quite a large number of men and women, in fact, have become interested in people from ten to 20, in how they mature physically and psychologically, what they do, how they lead their lives, and how this period of the life cycle called adolescence touches upon the periods of childhood and young adulthood. With all that is written on adolescence, it is hard to believe that the study of adolescence is a relatively new field for social scientists. It is hard to know, exactly, why this should be, but perhaps it reflects society's interest in young people generally. Or perhaps it reflects adults' attitudes toward their own adolescence. Whatever the reasons, the fact is that we now have a greater understanding of the richness and complexity of this period of the life cycle than we did 25 years ago, and far better ways of exploring adolescence.

This book, as its title indicates, attempts to give the reader various perspectives on adolescence. In preparing such a book, one could select innumerable topics and innumerable examples of work to represent each of these topics. But as always, choices must be made, and so we have settled on 12 sections, each of which examines a different facet of adolescent life. Before beginning, one word of caution might be offered. There is always a temptation to generalize about human behavior. For some, this is one of the goals of social science. Some people, however, fight against generalization. They argue that when one generalizes, one loses sight of the individual, and indulges not only in the act of depersonalization, but misses out on the exceptional aspects of human life. The debate on this subject is far from over. In this book, we have tried to give examples of work where more general or theoretical statements are offered, as well as examples of work which focus on individual or group behavior, and leave generalization to the reader. By presenting these different examples, we hope to suggest that adolescence, both as a concept and period of the life cycle, and the individual adolescent, the young man or young woman, are all worthy of study. They all demand our attention.

One difficulty in our inquiry into adolescence is that cultures and people are constantly changing. Styles, social roles, the very definition of an adolescent will change in time and from culture to culture. Similarly, as every human being changes, it is a difficult task to hold people still long enough merely to describe them, much less understand their movements and behavior. With the young, this is especially true. Still, we do know a great deal and have recorded a great deal about adolescence, a small sample of which is presented in the following pages.

Acknowledgments

I wish to thank Phillip Whitten, his administrative assistant Leslie Palmer, and our colleagues at Harper & Row. All of them have worked enormously hard on this project. Also, let me thank, Ann Hird, Sharon Liburd, Michael I. Kessler, Sandra Becket, and always Kay M. Cottle.

Reader Response

This anthology will be revised every two years to include outstanding new articles, and in response to changes in the study of adolescent psychology, important new research findings, and the feedback we receive form you—the students and instructors who use the book.

At the back of this book is a Reader Response Card, requesting your evaluation of READINGS IN ADOLESCENT PSYCHOLOGY: CONTEMPORARY PERSPECTIVES. Please take a few minutes to fill the card out and mail it to Harper & Row. Thank you.

THOMAS J. COTTLE

I. The Adolescent: Characteristics

One of the most treacherous tasks any social scientist faces is attempting to list the characteristics of a huge group of human beings. How, really, does one begin to characterize boys and girls, young men and women of all races, all cultures, who range in age from . . . well, do we even agree on the commencement and conclusion dates of adolescence? If all this were not complicated enough, and if we could agree that adolescence is a term referring to people from say, twelve to about eighteen or nineteen—and these are arbitrary temporal guideposts—what are we to say about social, cultural and historical aspects of adolescence? That is, we must realize from the beginning that people at all ages, not merely those we classify as adolescents, are influenced not only by the society and culture in which they live, but by the history of the peoples of that society and those cultures. The very definition of adolescence, moreover, no matter what it may be, will also be influenced by the patterns of human behavior in cultures other than the one a particular person calls his or her own.

All of this sounds rather fundamental, a bit like elementary sociology or psychology. Yet it is remarkable how in speaking about adolescence, or young people, remarks are made that indicate that we actually believe people create their own behavior and are governed strictly by what is in their mind at a particular time. But consider the remark, "She's just a typical twelve year old!" Ironically, the remark means enough that we rarely challenge the person who made it. But if one reads closely the selections in the first section, one sees just how fatuous such a remark can be.

The section makes something else clear to us. When we deal with a period of the life cycle, in this instance adolescence, we are essentially dealing with a phenomenon whose boundaries are marked by time. More precisely, we are overlooking childhood, that which has gone before, just as we are overlooking young adulthood, that period of time which is to follow. While it is fair to concentrate our attention on people of a particular age, we had best not believe that the people we are studying are themselves concentrating only on the present. Adolescents think plenty about the past and future, their historical antecedents, and the eventualities of their own lives and the lives of their families and friends. Too many people have characterized adolescents as being "present-oriented" to the point of being self-centered, even narcissistic. They forget, these particular observers, about the enormous range of so-called adolescent behavior, and, as one of the authors of the section points out, the difficulty in predicting a person's adulthood on the basis of that person's adolescence.

One last point. The reader might wish to explore these first sections with the thought that according to some theorists, the human personality is formed well before a child reaches the period of adolescence. Growth, according to these theorists, surely takes place between the ages of ten and twenty, but the foundations of character are fixed long before then. Fortunately, not all theorists of human behavior feel this way. And indeed, no one yet has spoken the last words on the characteristics of adolescents.

DAVID BAKAN

Adolescence in America: From Idea to Social Fact

The Idea of Adolescence

OFTEN A technical term is invented in order to create a social condition and a social fact; such has been true with respect to the term "adolescence." The idea of adolescence as an intermediary period in life starting at puberty and extending to some period in the life cycle unmarked by any conspicuous physical change but socially defined as "manhood" or "womanhood" is the product of modern times. The *Oxford English Dictionary* traces the term to the fifteenth century. Prior to that, if we follow the thought of Philip Aries,[1] the notion of childhood hardly existed, let alone the idea of the prolongation of childhood beyond puberty, as the term adolescence suggests.

Meaningful ascription of serious role characteristics for this period of life occurs, perhaps for the first time, in Rousseau's *Émile*, in which he characterized the period of adolescence as being beyond the earlier period of weakness of childhood and as a second birth. "We are born, so to speak, twice over; born into existence, and born into life; born a human being and born a man."[2] His aim was explicitly to prolong childhood, including the condition of innocence, as long as possible.

Although *Émile* has had considerable influence since its publication, the conversion of the idea of adolescence into a commonly accepted social reality was largely associated with modern urban-industrial life. Rousseau may have *invented* adolescence, as maintained by Musgrove,[3] but the notion as it is commonly understood in contemporary thought did not prevail prior to the last two decades of the nineteenth century and was "on the whole an American discovery."[4] The idea received an important stamp of reality from G. Stanley Hall in his monumental two-volume work on *Adolescence*, which he proudly presented to the reader as "essentially the author's first book" in 1904.[5] In point of fact he had introduced the idea as a special stage of development earlier.[6] In *Adolescence* he complained that we in America, because of our history, "have had neither childhood nor youth, but have lost touch with these stages of life because we lack a normal developmental history . . . Our immigrants have often passed the best years of youth or leave it behind when they reach our shores, and their memories of it are in other lands. No country is so precociously old for its years."[7] The giving of social reality to adolescence would, as it were, youthen the nation.

By reviewing some of the history, I will attempt to show in this

essay that the invention or discovery of adolescence in America was largely in response to the social changes that accompanied America's development in the latter half of the nineteenth and the early twentieth century, and that the principal reason was to prolong the years of childhood. Adolescence was added to childhood as a second childhood in order to fulfill the aims of the new urban-industrial society which developed so rapidly following the Civil War.

Historical Background

From the days of the early settlement of America to the second half of the nineteenth century, America suffered a chronic labor shortage. It sought to overcome this labor shortage through slavery, the encouragement of immigration, and industrialization. The incompatibility of slavery and industrialization plagued America during much of its early history, and that incompatibility remained until the Civil War, the Emancipation Proclamation, and the Thirteenth Amendment resolved it in favor of industrialization. But with the development of urban-industrial society, the nation became possessed of new contradictions characteristic of modern technological society, most serious among them the presence of a large number of persons who were mature by historical standards but immature in the new context.

The country changed dramatically during the second half of the nineteenth century. In 1880 the railroad network was completely integrated; there was no longer a frontier; the number of cities that had populations of more than 8,000 almost doubled in the decade from 1880 to 1890. By the year 1900 more than a third of the population was living in cities and more than half the population of the North Atlantic area lived in cities of more than 8,000 persons. In 1890 more than a third of the American population were people of foreign parentage. The question of property was becoming increasingly salient, as testified to by the proliferation of criminal laws designed to protect property rights—a not unimportant fact when we consider the question of juvenile delinquency, because most juvenile crimes are crimes against property, such as burglary, larceny, robbery, and auto theft.

The low level of "morality" of the new occupants of the burgeoning cities was a matter of frequent comment. Drinking, sexual immorality, vagrancy, and crime were not only intrinsically threatening to orderliness, but were also particularly distressing influences on the young. The rapid breeding, the continuing threat of "street Arabs," evoked a strong cry that the state intercede in restraining and training the young. In an address before the American Social Science Association in 1875, the influential Mary Carpenter said that if the parents of the young fail in their duty, then the whole society suffers; it was therefore the duty of the state to intercede and "stand *in loco parentis* and do its duty to the child and to society, by seeing that he is properly brought up."[8] Not the least of the dangers was the presence of un-American ideas and ideologies brought by the new immigrants, which were considered threatening to the basic fiber of American life. Even private education, as compared with public education, was regarded as a threat, the fear being that the children would not be sufficiently socialized and "Americanized." The Ku Klux Klan, for example, took a firm stand against private education.

As a result of these conditions, three major social movements developed, all of which conspired to make a social fact out of adolescence: compulsory (and characteristically public) education, child labor legislation, and special legal procedures for "juveniles." By the explicit citation of a precise chronological age, the legislation associated with these three areas essentially removed the vagueness of all previous ideas of the time at which adolescence terminates. Thus adolescence became the period of time between pubescence, a concrete biological occurrence, and the ages specified by law for compulsory education, employment, and criminal procedure.

There is no doubt that these movements were strongly motivated, at least on the conscious level, by humanitarian considerations. The rhetoric in defense of these three types of law was always cast in terms of the benefit and the saving quality that they would have for the young. The presumption that the various child welfare laws were principally created for the benefit of youth must, however, be confronted with the fact that there has been only a small degree of legal attention to the serious problem of child abuse in our society. The so-called "battered child" was not discovered until the late 1940's and early 1950's, and to this day appropriate protective and social support legislation is still quite negligible in contrast to the magnitude of the problem and the frequency of cases of cruelty to children.[9] The confluence of humanitarian considerations with the major economic, social, and political forces in the society needs to be clearly recognized. Indeed, the recognition of these underlying forces may help us to understand some of the failures to fulfill humanitarian aims and the disabilities which currently prevail with respect to that period of life that we call adolescence.

Compulsory Education

In the late nineteenth century, public compulsory education for children between six and eighteen, characteristically to age sixteen, was introduced widely in the United States. English common law had given parents virtually complete control over the education of the child, a principle prevalent in colonial America and throughout most of our early history. However, the general legal position later became that: "The primary function of the public school . . . is not to confer benefits upon the individual as such." Rather "the school exists as a state institution because the very existence of civil society demands it. The education of youth is a matter of such vital importance to the democratic state and to the public weal that the state may do much, may go very far indeed, by way of limiting the control of the parent over the education of his child."[10]

In the case of a father who had violated the compulsory attendance law, the court stated in its opinion:

The course of study to be pursued in the public schools of our state is prescribed either by statute or by the school authorities in pursuance thereof. These schools include not only elementary schools, but high schools as well . . . A parent, therefore, is not at liberty to exercise a choice in that regard, but, where not exempt for some lawful reason, must send his child to the school where instruction is provided suitable to its attainments as the school authorities may determine.[11]

It has been held that even a competent parent may not engage in domestic education on the following grounds:

We have no doubt many parents are capable of instructing their own children, but to permit such parents to withdraw their children from the public schools without permission from the superintendent of schools, and to instruct them at home, would be to disrupt our common school system and destroy its value to the state.[12]

At the same time the school authorities have been granted virtually complete discretionary powers with respect to suspension, expulsion, and punishment.[13] Such power rests in the hands of school authorities even in cases where the pupil has violated no rules. In one case, for example, a pupil was expelled for general misbehavior. In holding that the board of education had power to expel the pupil, the court said:

It matters not whether rules have been announced by either the directors or teachers. If the conduct of the pupil is such as reasonably to satisfy such school officers that the presence of that pupil is detrimental to the interests of the school, then the power of expulsion is conferred.[14]

Thus, it has turned out that the power of the state in America is such that it can, through its officials, not only compel school attendance, but also bar a pupil access to educational resources. Certainly there have been numerous legislative acts and court actions which would qualify particular cases. However, the total thrust of the various steps that have been taken since the middle of the nineteenth century has been in the direction of increasing the power of the state rather than protecting the rights of young people and their parents.

At the same time as the legal power of school authorities over pupils and their parents has been great, the schools have been derelict in the teaching of law—instruction which some regard as essential for people living in a democracy. In a society that is heavily dependent for its functioning on law, it is important that an appreciation of law, how it works, and its limits be taught in the public schools. One critic of this aspect of American education, in discussing the matter of education on due process, indicates that it is taught as though it applies only to criminals and that it fails to reflect itself in procedural fairness in school disciplinary matters. The idea of freedom of the press is characteristically not brought to bear in connection with school newspapers. "One of the difficult problems," he laconically comments, "is whether [proposed] law courses will be permitted to ventilate these issues, given the anxiety about them."[15]

Although from time to time there have been steps to increase the knowledge of law among educators, the emphasis has been on the kind of legal knowledge that an educator might require to deal with relationships of the school to outside institutions and individuals rather than on teaching law to students. One article along these lines, for example, deals with the legal structure of education, pupil personnel policies, control of pupil conduct, staff personnel policies, curricula, and liability. Illustrations are that: physical education coordinators should be expert in the law of liability for pupil injuries; guidance teachers should be familiar with compulsory education laws and their enforcement; curriculum coordinators should understand the legal position of parents in relation to school studies and activities; business administrators should understand contract law; personnel administrators should understand the legal aspects of employing and discharging teachers; and teachers of the history or philosophy of education should be acquainted with the relevant judicial opinions.[16]

Child Labor

The movement to restrict child labor in the United States also provided a definition of the termination of adolescence. Though there is a considerable amount of variation from state to state, the laws with respect to employment give specific minimum ages for definitions of maturity of different kinds: eighteen, minimum age for work in "hazardous occupations"; under eighteen, eight-hour day and forty-hour week; under eighteen, employment certificate required; under sixteen, limited hours of night work; sixteen, minimum age for factory work and employment during school hours; fourteen, minimum age for work outside of school hours. These are fairly typical laws governing age and employment.

The regulation of child labor has been one of the most controversial issues in this country since the nineteenth century. The harm to children from work in factories has been stridently declaimed. On the other hand, the virtues of work, the harm associated with idleness, and even the economic discriminatory effect of such legislation have also been consistently indicated. As an example, Senator Alexander Wiley, in questioning the representative of the American Federation of Labor before a Senate subcommittee to investigate juvenile delinquency said: "To me when I see the youth of this country in idleness, walking the streets of the cities, [I feel] we are meeting a challenge to our common sense because we know idleness breeds not only crime but everything else."[17] There have been repeated charges that the legal regulation of child labor is partly responsible for the widespread unemployment among young people, particularly Negroes.[18]

Adolescents in the labor force were a common occurrence

throughout American history. In 1832 about 40 per cent of the factory workers in New England were children. Starting a few years after the Civil War the major historical trend of a chronic labor shortage began to reverse itself, with ever-increasing evidences of labor surplus. With the changes in the kinds of work needed in the growing cities in the second half of the nineteenth century, an increasing proportion of females sought gainful employment. Indeed, the possibility of a close relationship between the various movements in connection with "child saving" and female employment has been seriously suggested.[19] Labor began to organize. The Knights of Labor, the precursor of the American Federation of Labor, was founded in 1869. In 1885 it had a membership of 100,000; a year later it could boast a membership of 730,000. Virtually from its founding, the Knights of Labor began its campaign for the prohibition of child labor. In spite of its efforts, child labor increased. The participation rate of youth between the ages of ten and fifteen in the labor force increased until 1900 and then began to decline. Indeed, in the decade which ended in 1900, the number of child laborers in the canneries, glass industry, mines, and so forth in the South tripled. The effort to control the labor supply in the United States was evident also in legislation to restrict immigration. In 1882 the Chinese Exclusion Act, barring immigration of Chinese laborers, was passed and was followed by other laws which severely restricted immigration.

Among employers there was a polarization. On the one hand there were certainly those employers who were in favor of having access to the cheap labor of young people and new immigrants; on the other hand the nature of industrial requirements was changing rapidly in favor of more skilled, and especially more reliable, workers. One of the most serious interferences with the reliability of labor was alcohol, and the prohibition movement grew simultaneously with the efforts to remove young people from the labor market and to restrict immigration. The prohibition movement gained increasing support from industrial leaders, "who were not unaware of the economic implications of the trade in intoxicants."[20]

The belief, common during the early part of the nineteenth century, that the children of the poor should work and that education of the children of the poor was filled with social danger tended to decline in the course of the century. The enlightened leaders of industry, taking ever longer views of history, recognized the dependence of industry on the existence of a reasonably educated labor force, educated not only with respect to knowledge and skill, but also with respect to bureaucratic subordination and reliable work habits.[21] At the same time, organized labor sought not only reforms in the conditions of child labor, but also education for their own children, to increase the likelihood of vertical social mobility. The continuing interest of both industry and labor in the education of the young is evidenced by the clear agreement on this on the part of both the National Association of Manufacturers and organized labor.[22]

One of the classic conflicts in connection with child labor was that between the textile manufacturers of the North and those in the South. The northern manufacturers charged that the South had a competitive advantage from its greater use of young workers.[23] Among the factors that eventually led to a resolution of the conflict was the later discovery, resulting in part from the changed nature of manufacture and experience of some restrictive legislation, that, as the *Textile World Journal* in 1918 put it: "The labor of children under fourteen years of age is not only inefficient in itself, but tends to lower the efficiency of all departments in which they are employed; also children of fourteen to sixteen years, worked on a short time basis, are scarcely less efficient and have a disorganizing effect in the departments where they are utilized. Because of these facts, and entirely apart from humanitarian considerations, large numbers of southern mills will not re-employ children of these ages."[24]

Juvenile Delinquency

Quite analogous to the "invention of adolescence," as Musgrove put it, was the "invention of delinquency," as Anthony M. Platt puts it in his book on the history of the notion of delinquency in the United States.[25] The humane motivation associated with the development of the notion of the juvenile delinquent was the desire to remove young people from the rigidities and inexorabilities associated with criminal justice and to allow wider discretionary powers to authorities in dealing with juveniles. The new legal apparatus was intended to separate young offenders from older offenders, and to provide corrective rather than punitive treatment. The first Juvenile Court Act was passed by the Illinois legislature in 1899 and brought together for single consideration cases of dependency, neglect, and delinquency. The hearings under the act were to be informal, the records were to be confidential, the young people were to be detained separately from adults. The aims were to be investigation and prescription rather than the determination of guilt or innocence. Lawyers were to be unnecessary. The definition of the "juvenile delinquent" in the various laws which multiplied after the model legislation in Illinois now vary for the upper limit from sixteen to twenty-one. The United States Children's Bureau had recommended nineteen, and this has been followed in about two-thirds of the states.[26]

Although the juvenile acts tended to free the courts from the obligation of imposing punishments associated with the criminal codes, they also had the effect of suspending the fundamental principle of legality, that one may not be punished for an offense unless a definite law in effect at the time when the act in question was committed has been broken. Considerations of due process were not obligatory. Guilt did not have to be established beyond a reasonable doubt. Among the acts reported under the heading of juvenile delinquency may be found the following: immoral conduct around schools, association with vicious or immoral persons, patronizing public pool rooms, wandering about railroad yards, truancy, incorrigibility, absenting self from home without consent, smoking cigarettes in public places, begging or receiving alms (or in street for purposes of).[27] As Harvey Baker of the Boston juvenile court put it in 1910:

> The court does not confine its attention to just the particular offense which brought the child to its notice. For example, a boy who comes to court for such a trifle as failing to wear his badge when selling papers may be held on probation for months because of difficulties at school; and a boy who comes in for playing on the street may . . . be committed to a reform school because he is found to have habits of loafing, stealing or gambling which can not be corrected outside.[28]

Questions have been raised as to whether the procedures of such courts adequately protect the rights of young offenders and whether they are consistent with constitutional rights.[29] In some states corrective legislation has been attempted by providing for legal defense of persons who come under the jurisdiction of the juvenile courts. However, the evidence is that this is not common. Indeed, treatment by officials tends to be more kindly toward young persons who admit guilt and indicate that they will mend their ways than toward those who are defensive or those whose parents are defensive.[30] The failure of the juvenile court to achieve its avowed objectives is notorious.

Suggestions that the aim of the juvenile court is to introduce a middle-class child-rearing orientation to the courtroom are apparent in the opinion of Judge Ben Lindsey of Denver, one of the pioneers in the juvenile court movement, and in the findings of Melvin L. Kohn. In an introduction to a book called *Winning the Boy* by Lilburn Merrill, Lindsey stressed the importance of "character," rather than the act itself.

You have not really a safe citizen until there comes into the boy's heart the desire to do right because it is right . . . I ask the boy why he will not steal again and he invariably replies, "Because I will get in jail." He is afraid of jail; he is not afraid to do wrong . . . Conscience is the moral director; without it character is impossible, and character is the greatest need, for it means that the pure in heart shall see and know and act the truth, as surely as they shall see God.[31]

Kohn has been able to show, on the basis of comparative data which he has collected, that there are differences in corrective actions between working-class and middle-class parents. Working-class parents tend to punish the external consequences of an action, as contrasted with middle-class parents who tend to punish on the basis of intention, rather than the action itself.[32] The latter mode is clearly suggested in Judge Lindsey's comment. Thus one way of interpreting the development of juvenile delinquency practices is as an effort to bring middle-class child-rearing practices into play, even when they involved the suspension of the principle of legality.

The legal disability of those who come under the juvenile laws is not limited to a small minority of youth in our society. "Statutes often define juvenile delinquency so broadly as to make virtually all youngsters delinquent . . . Rough estimates by the Children's Bureau, supported by independent studies, indicate that one in every nine youths—one in every six male youths—will be referred to juvenile court in connection with a delinquent act (excluding traffic offenses) before his 18th birthday."[33] As soon as the young person gains what may be called the animal sufficiency that comes with puberty, and may enter public places without an attendant, he becomes subject to extraordinary powers of the state until the legal definition of his maturity comes into being. This power of the state differs dramatically from the power of the state over adults in our society. The great discrepancy between adult justice and juvenile justice and the legal vulnerability of juveniles has been one of the major factors associated with the conversion of the idea of adolescence into the social fact of adolescence.

The Study of Adolescence

Starting with the work of G. Stanley Hall, adolescence became the subject of a considerable amount of investigation. There can be no doubt about the value of such investigation—indeed, this may be attested to by the essays in this volume. Nonetheless, this body of literature articulated with the cultural forces in the society at large. Although the intention of people like Hall to draw attention to an extremely important age period significant to the history of civilization generally, and the United States in particular, and thereby to create greater concern with proper development at that stage, was meritorious, there was another effect which needs to be pointed out. By stressing, for example, the presumptive emotional instability and unformed nature of people of that age—the work of Margaret Mead and others suggests that such phenomena of adolescence may be extrinsic rather than intrinsic[34]—Hall and others tended to put a gloss of psychopathology on this age period. Since it has long been a principle in our society that persons regarded as psychologically pathological are to be relieved of rights,[35] the effect of this literature has been to serve the general disability of persons under legal ages. In this way, the workers in the field of adolescence have tended to conspire, certainly unwittingly, with some of the forces depriving adolescents of their rights.

The Promise

A major factor which has sustained the social fact of adolescence in our society has been the belief, so pervasive in our success-oriented culture, in "the promise." The promise is that if a young person does all the things he is "supposed to do" during his adolescence, he will then realize success, status, income, power, and so forth in his adulthood.

A study by Arthur L. Stinchcombe[36] may help us to understand the operation of the promise. He studied the attitudes, behavior, and perceptions of the labor market among high school students, and found a direct and dramatic relationship between the images of the future that the students have and their rebellious attitudes and behavior. His data bear out the hypothesis "that high school rebellion, and expressive alienation, are most common among students who do not see themselves as gaining an increment in future status from conformity in high school."[37] In elaborating on the dynamics of the hypothesis, he writes: "When a student realizes that he does not achieve status increment from improved current performance, current performance loses meaning. The student becomes hedonistic because he does not visualize achievement of long-run goals through current self-restraint. He reacts negatively to a conformity that offers nothing concrete. He claims autonomy from adults because their authority does not promise him a satisfactory future."[38] Stinchcombe's hypothesis is derived from considerations of the legitimacy of bureaucratic authority as developed by Max Weber. Among the interesting derivations Stinchcombe makes from the hypothesis is an explanation of the difference between the sexes in various categories of expressive alienation. Girls are less likely to be rebellious because they perceive at least the possibility of marriage as a viable "career." He points out that the relatively high delinquency rate among Negroes is associated with the perception of the employment discrimination against Negro adult males.

As the credibility of the promise declines, the willingness of young people to accept the varieties of disabilities of adolescence equally declines. The profoundly pervasive metaphor of appropriate behavior in adolescence as a form of capital investment for the realization of returns in the future necessarily falters in cogency as the likelihood of such returns declines. The problems of order in the schools, juvenile delinquency, and other forms of expressive alienation cannot readily be solved by making small changes in the schools, Stinchcombe says.[39] It would appear that the schools cannot promise much because the society cannot promise much.

A study by William Westley and Frederick Elkin[40] of young people in an upper-class suburb of Montreal in 1951 attempted to explode the notion of the adolescent period as being one of storm and stress, nonconformity, gang formation, struggle for emancipation, and the like. The data collected in that place and time indicated considerably greater harmony and positive social adjustment by conventional standards than one might expect. However, the characterization of these young people would clearly indicate that they expected that the promise would be fulfilled. The typical youth in the study "internalizes aspirations for a professional or business career; he learns the expected patterns of language and breeding; he learns to resolve disputes by peaceable means; he learns to defer many immediate gratifications for the sake of future gains."[41]

The major question in our society today is whether, for youth of *all* social classes, the promise has continued credibility. Unemployment among manual workers is increasingly patent. The public service advertisements directed at potential drop-outs to remain in school in order to get better jobs later are met with increasing cynicism.[42] The poor acceptance rates of college students into the labor market predicted in the early sixties[43] are rapidly materializing. Even for scientists with Ph.D.'s the possibilities for employment are extremely dismal.[44] And few young people are ignorant of the fact that a career in "free enterprise" is virtually impossible without access to capital.[45] The idyllic vision of Erik Erikson that adolescence "can be viewed as a *psychosocial moratorium* during which the individual through free role experimentation may find a niche in some section of his society, a niche which is firmly defined and yet seems to be uniquely made for him,"[46] must increasingly be viewed cynically if that niche in life is contingent upon an appropriate niche in the labor force.

One of the likely consequences of these trends will be a strong move on the part of youth and their parents to dissolve the social fact of adolescence and to remove the historical disabilities which have been created by the state and sustained by the promise. Albert K. Cohen, in 1965, indicated that he thought it was sad that youth accepted their disabilities without protest.[47] The picture soon changed. Jerry Farber's critique of what he calls America's "Auschwitz" educational system, "The Student as Nigger," originally published in 1967 in the Los Angeles *Free Press,* quickly became one of the most widely distributed underground documents in history—reprinted, reduplicated, recopied many times by student groups all over America and Canada.[48] A national clearing house of anti-public school thought has been formed in Washington, D.C., which puts out a regular biweekly newsletter called *FPS* (*the letters don't stand for anything*). Ellen Lurie has written what is fast becoming a standard manual for parents seeking to reduce state control over their children's education in the public schools.[49] This book is consistent with the United Nations Universal Declaration of Human Rights, adopted in 1948, that "Parents have a prior right to choose the kind of education that shall be given to their children."[50] The crime statistics mount at an exponential rate. Demonstrations become ever more strident. The "underground revolution"[51] gets new recruits daily.

The future? My assignment was to discuss history. The future must be left to time and other occasions.[52]

REFERENCES

1. P. Aries, *Centuries of Childhood* (New York: Knopf, 1962).

2. Jean Jacques Rousseau, *Émile*, trans. Barbara Foxley (New York: Dutton, 1966; originally published 1762), pp. 128, 172.

3. F. Musgrove, *Youth and the Social Order* (Bloomington, Ind.: Indiana University Press, 1964). Musgrove titles one of his chapters "The Invention of the Adolescent," pp. 33-57.

4. John Demos and Virginia Demos, "Adolescence in Historical Perspective," *Journal of Marriage and the Family*, 31 (1969), 632-638, 632.

5. G. Stanley Hall, *Adolescence: Its Psychology and Its Relations to Physiology, Anthropology, Sociology, Sex, Crime, Religion, and Education* (New York: D. Appleton and Company, 1904).

6. G. Stanley Hall, "The Moral and Religious Training of Children," *Princeton Review* (January 1882), pp. 26-48.

7. Hall, *Adolescence*, p. xvi.

8. As cited in Grace Abbot, ed., *The Child and the State* (Chicago: University of Chicago Press, 1938), II, 372.

9. See M. G. Paulsen, "The Law and Abused Children," in R. E. Helfer and C. H. Kempe, *The Battered Child* (Chicago: University of Chicago Press, 1968), pp. 175-207; and D. Bakan, *Slaughter of the Innocents: A Study of the Battered Child Phenomenon* (San Francisco: Jossey-Bass, 1971; Toronto: Canadian Broadcasting Corp., 1971).

10. Newton Edwards, *The Courts and the Public Schools: The Legal Basis of School Organization and Administration*, rev. ed. (Chicago: University of Chicago Press, 1955), p. 24.

11. *Miller v. State*, 77 Ind. App. 611, 134 N. E. 209, as cited by Edwards, *The Courts and the Public Schools*, p. 524.

12. *State v. Counort*, 69 Wash. 361, 124 Pac. 910, 41 L.R.A. (N.S.) 95, as cited by Edwards, *The Courts and the Public Schools*, p. 522.

13. Edwards, *The Courts and the Public Schools*, pp. 601ff.

14. *State v. Hamilton*, 42 Mo. App. 24, as cited by Edwards, *The Courts and the Public Schools*, p. 603.

15. Alex Elson, "General Education in Law for Non-Lawyers," in The American Assembly, Columbia University, *Law in a Changing America* (Englewood Cliffs, N.J.: Prentice-Hall, 1968), pp. 183-191, 189.

16. E. E. Reutter, Jr., "Essentials of School Law for Educators," in Harold J. Carter, ed., *Intellectual Foundations of American Education* (New York: Pitman Publishing Corporation, 1965), pp. 216-225.

17. *Juvenile Delinquency: Hearings before the Subcommittee to Investigate Juvenile Delinquency*, Senate, 1955 (New York: Greenwood Press, 1968), p. 86.

18. See, for example, the effort to counter these charges by H. M. Haisch of the U.S. Department of Labor: H. M. Haisch, "Do Child Labor Laws Prevent Youth Employment?" *Journal of Negro Education*, 33 (1964), 182-185.

19. "Although child saving had important symbolic functions for preserving the prestige of middle-class women in a rapidly changing society, it also had considerable instrumental significance for legitimizing new career openings for women. The new role of social worker combined elements of

an old and partly fictitious role—defender of family life—and elements of a new role—social servant. Social work and philanthropy were thus an affirmation of cherished values and an instrumentality for women's emancipation." Anthony M. Platt, *The Child Savers: The Invention of Delinquency* (Chicago: University of Chicago Press, 1969), p. 98.

20. John Allen Krout, *The Origins of Prohibition* (New York: Russell and Russell, 1967), p. 302.

21. For an analysis of relations between education and industry see John Galbraith, *The New Industrial State* (Boston: Houghton Mifflin, 1967).

22. See Charles R. Sligh, Jr., "Views on Curriculum," *Harvard Educational Review,* 4 (1957), 239-245; Walter P. Reuther, "What the Public Schools Should Teach," *Harvard Educational Review,* 4 (1957), 246-250.

23. Stephen B. Wood, *Constitutional Politics in the Progressive Era: Child Labor and the Law* (Chicago: University of Chicago Press, 1968), p. 9.

24. Cited by Wood, *Constitutional Politics,* p. 172.

25. Anthony M. Platt, *The Child Savers: The Invention of Delinquency* (Chicago: University of Chicago Press, 1969).

26. Robert W. Winslow, ed., *Juvenile Delinquency in a Free Society: Selections from the President's Commission on Law Enforcement and Administration of Justice* (Belmont, Calif.: Dickenson Publishing Company, 1968), pp. 119-120.

27. Winslow, *Juvenile Delinquency,* pp. 166-167.

28. Cited in Platt, *The Child Savers,* p. 142.

29. See Lewis Mayer, *The American Legal System* (New York: Harper and Row, 1964), pp. 146-149.

30. Winslow, *Juvenile Delinquency,* pp. 140, 150.

31. Cited in Bernard Wishy, *The Child and the Republic: The Dawn of Modern American Child Nurture* (Philadelphia: University of Pennsylvania Press, 1968), p. 134.

32. M. L. Kohn, "Social Class and Parent-Child Relationships: An Interpretation," *American Journal of Sociology,* 68 (1963), 471-480; M. L. Kohn, "Social Class and the Exercise of Parental Authority," *American Sociological Review,* 24 (1959), 352-366; M. L. Kohn, *Class and Conformity: A Study in Values* (Homewood, Ill.: Dorsey Press, 1969).

33. Winslow, *Juvenile Delinquency,* p. 2.

34. Margaret Mead, *Coming of Age in Samoa* (New York: W. Morrow and Co., 1928).

35. See Thomas S. Szasz, *Law, Liberty and Psychiatry* (New York: Macmillan, 1963).

36. Arthur L. Stinchcombe, *Rebellion in a High School* (Chicago: Quadrangle Books, 1964).

37. *Ibid.,* p. 49; see especially chaps. 3 and 4, pp. 49-102, titled "The Labor Market and Rebellion I; II."

38. *Ibid.,* pp. 5-6.

39. *Ibid.,* passim.

40. William A. Westley and Frederick Elkin, "The Protective Environment and Adolescent Socialization," in Martin Gold and Elizabeth Douvan, eds., *Adolescent Development: Readings in Research and Theory* (Boston: Allyn and Bacon, 1969), pp. 158-164; reprinted from *Social Forces,* 35 (1957), 243-249.

41. *Ibid.,* p. 158.

42. See, for example, the stress on the employment advantages of school in the *National Stay-in-School Campaign Handbook for Communities* (Washington, D.C.: Government Printing Office, 1957). The campaign was spon-

sored jointly by the Department of Labor, Department of Health, Education and Welfare, and Department of Defense.

43. J. Folger and C. Nam, "Trends in Education in Relation to the Occupational Structure," *Sociology of Education*, 38 (1964), 19-33; R. Havighurst and B. Neugarten, *Society and Education*, 2d ed. (Boston: Allyn and Bacon, 1962).

44. Allan Cartter, "Scientific Manpower for 1970-1985," *Science*, 172 (1971), 132-140.

45. Such has been the case at least since 1885 when Andrew Carnegie, the great exponent of the idea that any able and energetic young man could "rise to the top," told a group of students that "There is no doubt that it is becoming harder and harder as business gravitates more and more to immense concerns for a young man without capital to get a start for himself." Cited in H. J. Perkinson, *The Imperfect Panacea: American Faith in Education, 1865-1965* (New York: Random House, 1968), p. 120. Ironically, one of the few spheres in which "free enterprise," with relatively little capital and high returns on investment, is still possible is in the illegal merchandising of drugs.

46. Erik H. Erikson, "The Problem of Ego Identity," in Gold and Douvan, *Adolescent Development*, p. 19; reprinted from *Identity and the Life Cycle* (New York: International Universities Press, 1959).

47. In his foreword to Musgrove, *Youth and the Social Order*, p. xix: "Do they really believe that all preparation for life must, in the nature of things, take for its model the process of becoming a thirty-second degree Mason?"

48. Jerry Farber, *The Student as Nigger* (New York: Pocket Books, 1970).

49. Ellen Lurie, *How to Change the Schools: A Parents' Action Handbook on How to Fight the System* (New York: Vintage Books, 1970).

50. Article 26-3.

51. Naomi Feigelson, ed., *The Underground Revolution: Hippies, Yippies and Others* (New York: Funk and Wagnalls, 1970).

52. Since the time that I wrote this the amendment reducing the voting age to eighteen has been ratified. I am of the opinion that it will have important consequences bearing on the considerations in this essay.

2

Adolescence in Historical Perspective

JOHN DEMOS AND VIRGINIA DEMOS

Adolescence, as we know it, was barely recognized before the end of the last century. An examination of various written materials from the period 1800-1875 uncovers (1) almost no usage of the word and (2) only a limited degree of concern with the stage (and its characteristic behaviors). About 1900, however, G. Stanley Hall and his students made adolescence the focus of a new current of psychological study. Their work evoked a broad popular response, though in subsequent years it was discredited in academic circles. The "discovery" of adolescence can be related to certain broad changes in American life—above all, to changes in the structure of the family as part of the new urban and industrial order.

THE idea of adolescence is today one of our most widely held and deeply imbedded assumptions about the process of human development. Indeed most of us treat it not as an idea but as a *fact*. Its impact is clear in countless areas of everyday life—in newspapers, magazines, and books; in various forms of popular entertainment; in styles of dress and of language. Its causes and meaning have been repeatedly analyzed in the work of psychologists and sociologists. Its effects are endlessly discussed by teachers, social workers, officers of the law, and parents everywhere.

Yet all of this has a relatively short history. The concept of adolescence, as generally understood and applied, did not exist before the last two decades of the nineteenth century. One could almost call it an invention of that period; though it did incorporate, in quite a central way, certain older attitudes and modes of thinking. It will be our purpose in this paper to describe the roots and the growth of the concept, to the point in the early twentieth century when it had become well established in the public consciousness. We shall limit our attention to developments in the United States, since adolescence was on the whole an American discovery.

We shall begin with a sketch of some common ideas about childhood and "youth" during the period 1800-1875, as revealed in two kinds of sources: (1) a rapidly developing literature of child-rearing advice, and (2) a large body of books and pamphlets directed to the young people of the country and bearing especially on their "moral problems." Then we shall summarize the activities of the "child-study move-

John Demos is Assistant Professor in the Department of History, Brandeis University. Virginia Demos is a doctoral candidate in the Program of Human Development at Harvard University.

ment" (beginning in about 1890) and in particular the work of the psychologist G. Stanley Hall, for there the concept of adolescence can be examined at its source. And finally we shall propose a hypothesis for drawing together these various types of material and above all for explaining the relationship between the *idea* of adolescence and the social phenomena to which it was a response. It is here that questions of family life will come most fully into view, since adolescence was, we believe, profoundly related to certain fundamental changes affecting the internal structure of many American homes. But this matter of the connection between "ideas" and "facts," between major cultural assumptions like adolescence and the social realities in which they develop, presents extremely tricky problems. It lurks as an uncomfortable presence behind most serious study that bears in one way or another on the history of the family. The difficulty lies in the nature of the evidence available to historians, which comprises for the most part a variety of written materials. It is much easier, therefore, to construct a history of ideas *about* the family than of the family as such.

The present paper cannot pretend to resolve such problems; indeed it may serve chiefly to illustrate them. But it is at least our intention to keep sight of the important distinctions. And if the bulk of our efforts are directed toward the realm of "ideas," it is only because this seems the logical way to begin.

The literature of child-rearing advice is one of the most revealing, and least exploited,[1] sources for the history of the American family.

[1] We know of only three attempts to confront this material directly: Bernard Wishy, *The Child and the Republic*, Philadelphia: University of Pennsylvania Press, 1968; Robert

Its beginnings can be located in the early part of the nineteenth century; and it has been growing steadily, and changing in character, ever since. Before about 1825 relatively few books on child-rearing could be found in this country, and those that were available came chiefly from England.[2] In general, they were mild in tone and full of simple moral homilies strung endlessly together. They do not, in short, seem to have been directed to any very pressing needs or problems in the lives of their readers.

After 1825 the situation, for this country at least, changed rapidly. Child-rearing books by American authors began to appear, some of which went through numerous editions and sold many thousands of copies.[3] This development was owing to several different factors. In the first place it was related to a deepening interest in the fact of childhood itself as a distinct period of life and one which was little comparable to the years of maturity. Secondly, it expressed the broad impulse of nationalism that engulfed the country at this time. English books on child-rearing could no longer be regarded as suitable to American conditions. Finally, the new and authentically "native" literature on this subject reflected deep anxieties about the quality of American family life.[4]

Most of the concern which was evident in these books related to problems of authority. In one form or another they all imparted the same message: the authority of parents must be established early in a child's life and firmly maintained throughout the years of growth. Even the smallest infant reveals a "willfulness" that "springs from a depraved nature and is intensely selfish."[5] This must be suppressed by strict training in obedience, or it will rapidly develop beyond the possibility of control with dire implications for the later (adult) personality.

These injunctions seemed all the more necessary because—so many people thought—parental authority was steadily on the wane. In describing the average home, the writers of the child-rearing books repeatedly used words like "disorder," "disobedience," "licentiousness," and above all "indulgence" (i.e., of the children). Statements such as the following were typical:

> It must be confessed that an irreverent, unruly spirit has come to be a prevalent, an outrageous evil among the young people of our land. . . . Some of the good old people make facetious complaint on this. . . . "There is as much family government now as there used to be in our young days," they say, "only it has changed hands."[6]

This seeming change in the traditional family pattern had other dimensions as well. Thus many authors noted the growth of a kind of "child-centered" attitude and condemned it out of hand. More and more parents, for example, appeared to feel compelled to show off their children before any and all guests. Similarly, there was in many households far too much concern with efforts to amuse and entertain the young.[7] Children who were often made the center of attention in this manner would inevitably become conceited and selfish. Another alarming development was the increasing tendency of children to seek social satisfactions outside of the family, among groups of their own peers. Mrs. Lydia Child, whose *Mother's Book* went through many editions, returned again and again to the theme that "youth and age are too much separated."[8] She and many of her contemporaries decried the "new custom" of holding parties exclusively for young people[9] and urged

---

Sunley, "Early Nineteenth-Century American Literature on Child-Rearing," in *Childhood in Contemporary Cultures*, ed. by Margaret Mead and Martha Wolfenstein, Chicago: University of Chicago Press, 1955, pp. 150-167; and Elaine V. Damis, *The History of Child-Rearing Advice in America from 1800-1940*, unpublished honor's thesis, Radcliffe College, 1960.

[2] See, for instance, Juliana Seymour, *On the Management and Education of Children*, London, 1754; and Miss Appleton, *Early Education*, London, 1821.

[3] Parallel to this increase in books on child-rearing, there developed at this time a new kind of magazine directed specifically to "mothers." *Mother's Magazine* and the *Mother's Assistant* were prominent examples. Both seem to have achieved a wide circulation within a very few years. The magazines, in turn, were closely related to the movement for "maternal associations." These societies, operating at the local level and devoting their energies largely to the discussion of child-rearing problems, became quite a vogue in the 1820s and 1830s. All of this demonstrates further the heightened interest in motherhood—and thus childhood—that characterized the period.

[4] These anxieties were a matter of great complexity and wide ramifications. Indeed they must be understood as relating not only to conditions internal to the family but also to the wider social climate of the time. For some useful discussion of all this, see Bernard Wishy, *The Child and the Republic*.

[5] H. W. Bulkeley, *A Word to Parents*, Philadelphia: Presbyterian Board of Publication, 1858, p. 12.

[6] Warren Burton, *Helps to Education*, Boston: Crosby and Nichols, 1863, pp. 38-39. Similar observations can be found in the writings of foreign visitors to this country. See Arthur W. Calhoun, *A Social History of the American Family*, New York: Barnes and Noble, 1945, pp. 17-19, for some extensive discussion of this travel literature. See also Max Berger, *The British Traveller in America*, New York: Columbia University Press, 1943.

[7] On this matter see, for example, Lydia M. Child, *The Mother's Book*, Boston: Carter, Hendee and Babcock, 1835, p. 94; and Burton, *op. cit.*, pp. 74-75, 92.

[8] Child, *op. cit.*, p. 95.

[9] See *ibid.*, p. 138; also *Mother's Magazine*, 1, pp. 42-45.

that parents should always be the closest friends and confidants of their children.

Lest it be imagined that Americans of the nineteenth century had no special concern whatsoever for the period which we now call adolescence (and which in their day was simply termed "youth"),[10] we must turn to another category of books that were written specifically *for* the "youth" of the time and about their particular problems. The general nature of these writings is implicit in their titles: *A Voice to Youth; How to be a Man; Papers for Thoughtful Girls; The Young Lady's Companion; On the Threshold; Lectures to Young Men.*

From all of these works there emerges quite clearly a sense of "youth" as a critical transition period in the life of nearly everyone. It is a time, first of all, when people are extremely impressionable, extremely open to a wide range of outside influences. It is—to quote from Joel Hawes's *Lectures to Young Men* (1832)—

pre-eminently . . . the forming, fixing period. . . . It is during this season, more than any other, that the character assumes its permanent shape and color.[11]

Words such as "pliant," "plastic," and "formative" appear again and again in the discussions of youth.

Because of this characteristic openness, young people are vulnerable to many kinds of "danger." To begin with, boys and girls entering their teens experience a sudden and sharp upsurge of the "passions." They become highly emotional; their mood fluctuates unpredictably from exuberance to melancholy. Henry Ward Beecher, whose *Lectures to Young Men* were among the best known examples of the genre, declared:

A young man knows little of life; less of himself. He feels in his bosom the various impulses, wild desires, restless cravings he can hardly tell for what, a sombre melancholy when all is gay, a violent exhilaration when others are sober.[12]

In keeping with their Victorian conventions, these writers never directly mentioned the physiological changes that occur at puberty, in par-

ticular the strong new charge of sexual energy and tension. Occasionally one finds an allusion to "internal revolutions" and "occult causes, probably of a physical kind"[13]; but for the most part people were content to define youth in the above terms, that is, as a vast outpouring of the emotions.

As if to complement these disruptive changes within the personality, the world at large was full of "seductive temptations," of inducements to all manner of wicked and ruinous behavior. As Beecher said,

These wild gushes of feeling, peculiar to youth, the sagacious tempter has felt, has studied, has practiced upon, until he can sit before that most capacious organ, the human mind, knowing every step and all the combinations.[14]

Here, then, was the wider, social dimension of the problems which confront the young person. The world lies in wait for him, and "ardent, volatile, inexperienced, and thirsting for happiness," he is

exceedingly liable to be seduced into the wrong paths —into those fascinating but fatal ways, which lead to degradation and wretchedness.[15]

There are, at this stage of life, dangers both within and without.

Most of the material considered so far has been drawn from the period 1825-1850. As the years passed and the century neared its end, the picture of youth that we have been describing was embellished somewhat in certain important respects. Thus, for example, the sexual factor began to receive some attention.[16] And some writers were struck by a kind of aimlessness and indecision that seemed increasingly common among American young people. Theodore T. Munger, whose book *On the Threshold* was published in 1881, declared that

Young men of the present years . . . are not facing life with that resolute and definite purpose that is essential both to manhood and to external success. . . . [They] hear no voice summoning them to the appointed field, but drift into this or that, as happens.[17]

Moreover, towards the end of the century, many

---

[10] The word "adolescence" was known in the nineteenth century, but we have found only a very few cases of its use in the literature on child-rearing and "youth."

[11] Joel Hawes, *Lectures to Young Men*, Hartford, Connecticut: Cooke & Co., 1832, p. 35. See also Child, *op. cit.*, p. 125.

[12] Henry Ward Beecher, *Lectures to Young Men*, Boston: J. P. Jewett & Co., 1844, p. 21. Beecher actually delivered these lectures to an audience of young people in Boston before publishing them. Such was also the pattern for many of the other works of this kind. For a similar comment on the turmoil characteristic of youth, see Henrietta Keddie, *Papers for Thoughtful Girls*, Boston: Crosby and Nichols, 1860, p. 1.

[13] Isaac Taylor, *Home Education*, New York: D. Appleton & Co., 1838, p. 131.

[14] Beecher, *op. cit.*, p. 21.

[15] John M. Austin, *A Voice to Youth*, New York: J. Bolles, 1838, p. 1.

[16] See, for example, Elizabeth Blackwell, *Counsel to Parents on the Moral Education of Their Children*, New York: Brentano's Literary Emporium, 1879.

[17] Theodore T. Munger, *On the Threshold*, Boston: Houghton Mifflin & Co., 1881, p. 5. See also William A. Mowry, *Talks with My Boys*, Boston: New England Publishing Company, 1885, pp. 30 ff.; and Philip S. Moxon, *The Aim of Life*, Boston: Roberts Brothers, 1894, pp. 11-29.

writers identified the "dangers" and "temptations" which threatened youth directly with urban life. Something of this had been implicit from the beginning, but now it came clearly into the open.[18] The city loomed as the prime source of corrupting influences for the young. Its chaotic social and economic life, its varied population, its frenzied commercial spirit, and its dazzling entertainments were all sharply antagonistic to proper growth towards adulthood.

At roughly the same time, meanwhile, the formal concept of adolescence was receiving its first public expression. The immediate context of this development was a new movement for systematic "child study," inspired and guided by G. Stanley Hall. Hall was, of course, one of the major figures in the early history of American psychology. After a lengthy period of study in Germany, he became in 1881 a professor at Johns Hopkins, and six years later he accepted the presidency of Clark University. There he remained for the rest of his life, presiding over a wide range of research and teaching activities.

The aim of the child-study movement was to enlist large numbers of ordinary citizens in a broad effort to deepen both public and scientific understanding of human development. The mothers who belonged to the various local organizations were encouraged to keep detailed records of the behavior of their children and to participate in regular discussions about such records. They were also exposed to, and themselves reflected back, the major themes in Stanley Hall's own work—not least, his theory of adolescence.

The essentials of Hall's view of adolescence appeared in one of his earliest papers on psychology: "The Moral and Religious Training of Children," published in 1882 in the *Princeton Review*. The great point of departure, then as later, was the idea of "storm and stress," of severe crisis characterized by

lack of emotional steadiness, violent impulses, unreasonable conduct, lack of enthusiasm and sympathy. . . . The previous selfhood is broken up . . . and a new individual is in process of being born. All is solvent, plastic, peculiarly susceptible to external influences.[19]

The suggestions contained in this article were subsequently elaborated in much greater detail by some of Hall's students at Clark. Efforts were made to link the adolescent "crisis"

with a wide range of personal and social phenomena—with religious conversion, for example,[20] and with the rising rate of juvenile delinquency.[21] Hall himself provided the capstone to this whole sequence of activity, with the publication in 1904 of his encyclopedic work *Adolescence: Its Psychology, and Its Relations to Physiology, Anthropology, Sociology, Sex, Crime, Religion, and Education*. It is impossible to summarize here the many ideas and vast assortment of data embraced therein, but certain underlying themes can at least be singled out. From the very start Hall's thinking had been profoundly influenced by Darwinism, and the psychology he proposed was explicitly bound to an evolutionary, or "genetic," model. He urged a kind of "archaeology of the mind," in which all the various stages in the development of human consciousness would be rediscovered and understood in their proper order.[22] A key link here was the theory known as "recapitulation," which affirmed that every individual "lives through" each of the major steps in the evolution of the race as a whole. Adolescence assumed a special importance in this scheme, for it represented (and "recapitulated") the most recent of man's great developmental leaps. The adolescent, Hall believed, reveals truly enormous possibilities of growth and "is carried for a time beyond the point of the present stage of civilization."[23] This is not, however, an easy situation, for it encompasses a variety of contradictions and "antithetic impulses." Among the impulses which Hall paired in this context were hyperactivity and lassitude, happiness and depression, egotism and self-abasement, selfishness and altruism, gregariousness and shyness, sensitivity and cruelty, radicalism and conservatism. Caught in the midst of so much change and conflict, the adolescent was bound to experience "storm and stress" more or less continuously.

Hall's work on adolescence quickly exerted a considerable influence in many different directions. Its impact was clear in general texts on psychology,[24] studies of education,[25] the new

[18] See, for example, George H. Hepworth, *Rocks and Shoals*, Boston: American Unitarian Association, 1870; and Mowry, *op. cit.*

[19] G. Stanley Hall, "The Moral and Religious Training of Children," in *Princeton Review* (January, 1882), pp. 26-48. This essay was later republished in a slightly revised form in *Pedagogical Seminary*, 1, pp. 196-210.

[20] See E. D. Starbuck, *The Psychology of Religion*, New York: Ginn & Co., 1899; and an essay by the same author, "A Study of Conversion," in *American Journal of Psychology*, 8, pp. 268-308.

[21] See Edgar J. Swift, "Some Criminal Tendencies of Boyhood: A Study in Adolescence," in *Pedagogical Seminary*, 7.

[22] See G. Stanley Hall, *Adolescence*, New York: D. Appleton & Co., 1904, Vol. 2, pp. 61, 69.

[23] See the "epitome" of Hall's theories by G. E. Partridge, *The Genetic Philosophy of Education*, Boston: Sturgis & Walton Co., 1912, p. 31.

[24] For example, James R. Angell, *Psychology*, New York: H. Holt & Co., 1904. See especially p. 358.

[25] See George H. Betts, *The Mind and Its Education*, New

literature on child-rearing,[26] and a variety of books on child labor, religious training, vocational guidance, and the like.[27] Even critical comments showed the extent to which the idea of adolescence had captured the public imagination: there were those who complained that "we are today under the tyranny of the special cult of adolescence."[28]

Hall's reputation was, however, relatively short-lived. From the very beginning his theories of adolescence aroused at least some criticism. Men like E. L. Thorndike (himself an important figure in the history of American psychology), Charles H. Judd, and Irving King charged him with many forms of exaggeration and overstatement.[29] And after 1925 his work went rapidly into eclipse. Many scholars came to feel that it was unreasonable to view growth in terms of set "stages" of any kind whatsoever. Margaret Mead, in her famous study of Samoan children, tried to show that adolescent "storm and stress" are a function of certain *cultural* determinants.[30] By contrast, Hall was seen as the representative of an outmoded, wholly physiological orientation.[31] Moreover, his fervent, almost missionary approach to his subject, his florid writing, his long-range goal of race improvement—all this came to seem irrelevant, or even offensive, to later generations of psychologists.

Thus G. Stanley Hall has been largely forgotten, if not rejected outright. Yet, we suggest, he has left his mark all the same. Hall's critics denied the validity of considering personal growth in terms of "stages"; but we still regard adolescence in just such a context. His critics accused him of having greatly exaggerated "storm and stress" phenomena, and yet today more than ever we view adolescence in exactly those terms. In fact, the "special cult of adolescence" seems to have lost no strength at all. And it was Hall, more than anyone else, who fixed it in our imagination.

It would be easy to overstate the element of innovation in Hall's thinking. If we compare the kind of adolescence that he was describing with some of the ideas that were current just before his time,[32] we find a considerable degree of continuity. His achievement lay in reshaping certain aspects of popular belief about youth, combining them with some of the most exciting new ideas in science (i.e., evolution), gathering data on a large scale, and presenting the whole in a persuasive and meaningful fashion.

Yet certain questions about the rise of the concept of adolescence remain. What larger developments in American society did it reflect? To what popular attitudes, or needs, or anxieties, did it minister? We offer, in conclusion, the following very tentative suggestions—some of which we have simply lifted from contemporary thinking about adolescence in the fields of psychology and sociology.[33]

We propose, as a starting point, the long-term transformation of the United States from an agricultural into an urban and industrial society; for this change—which has, of course, been basic to so much of our history during the last 150 years—has exerted a profound influence on the structure of American families. Consider that most farm families are characterized by a high degree of internal unity. Children and adults share the same tasks, the same entertainments, the same friends, the same expectations. There is a continuum between the generations. The child appears not so much as a child per se but as himself a potential farmer; he is, then, a miniature model of his father.

York: D. Appleton & Co., 1906; P. M. Magnusson, *Psychology as Applied to Education*, New York: Silver, Burdett and Company, 1913; and Arthur Holmes, *Principles of Character-Making*, Philadelphia: J. B. Lippincott Company, 1913.

[26] See William McKeever, *Training the Boy*, New York: Macmillan Company, 1913; and *Training the Girl*, New York: Macmillan Company, 1914; also W. B. Forbush and Catherine M. Burrell, *The Mother's Book*, New York: The University Society, Inc., 1919.

[27] See George B. Mangold, *Child Problems*, New York: The Macmillan Company, 1910; George A. Coe, *Education in Religion and Morals*, New York: F. H. Revell Company, 1904; and Meyer Bloomfield, *The Vocational Guidance of Youth*, Boston: Houghton Mifflin Company, 1911.

[28] Frank O. Beck, *Marching Manward*, New York: Eaton & Mains, 1913, p. 38.

[29] See E. L. Thorndike, *Notes on Child-Study*, in *Columbia University Contributions to Philosophy, Psychology, and Education*, 8:3-4, p. 143; also Thorndike's article, "Magnitude and Rate of Alleged Changes at Adolescence," in *Educational Review*, 54, pp. 140-147. See too Charles H. Judd, *The Psychology of High School Subjects*, Boston: Ginn & Company, 1915; and Irving King, *The Psychology of Child Development*, Chicago: University of Chicago Press, 1903, pp. 222 ff.

[30] Margaret Mead, *Coming of Age in Samoa*, New York: W. Morrow and Company, 1928.

[31] On this point Hall was somewhat misrepresented. It is true that he regarded the critical changes of adolescence as proceeding from within; but he also spent much effort in analyzing various factors in our *environment*—which, he felt, greatly accentuated adolescent distress. See Hall, *Adolescence, op. cit.*, Vol. 1, pp. xv, 321 ff., 348 ff., 376 ff.; and Vol. 2, pp. 59-60.

[32] *Ibid.*, pp. 5-8.

[33] We have tried to draw together ideas from several different sources, chief among them: Kenneth Keniston, "Social Change and Youth in America," *Daedalus* (Winter, 1962), pp. 145-171; Erik H. Erikson, "Youth: Fidelity and Diversity," *Daedalus* (Winter, 1962), pp. 5-27; Ruth Benedict, "Continuities and Discontinuities in Cultural Conditioning," in *Psychiatry*, 1, pp. 161-167; Kingsley Davis, "The Sociology of Parent-Youth Conflict," *American Sociological Review*, 5, pp. 523-535.

Such, we would argue, was the prevalent situation in nearly *all* the families of this country before the nineteenth century.

But when Americans began to move to the city, all this changed. City children, for example, do not often have a significant economic function within the family as a whole. (Or alternatively—as in the case of poor children employed as factory hands—their work is likely to be quite different from that of their parents.) Moreover, they are thrust into close proximity with other families and have the opportunity to form numerous contacts among their own peers. Thus there develops in the urban setting an important "discontinuity of age-groups."[34] Children and adults are much more obviously separated from each other than is ever the case in a rural environment.

This second configuration was starting to show itself in some American families during the early part of the nineteenth century, and perhaps it helps to explain the material presented in our opening section. Now—i.e., with the new, typically urban family structure—childhood as such is "discovered"; it is no longer feasible to regard children simply as miniature adults. Now, too, "child-centered" families become possible. The behavior of the young is increasingly seen as bizarre and also as appropriate to their particular time of life. A new tolerance for such behavior develops, and parental authority appears to weaken.[35] Finally, there is an obvious place for a literature on child-rearing.

Most cultures with sharp discontinuities of this kind possess a system of "age-grading," which defines the various steps in the transition from childhood to adulthood.[36] In many cases there are elaborate initiation rites to dramatize this change. But our society lacks such rites; ceremonies like confirmation and graduation exercises are losing whatever significance in this regard they once had. It is in such situations, as Kenneth Keniston has suggested, that a "youth culture" is likely to develop. "Youth culture" may be defined, somewhat carelessly, as institutionalized adolescence. It refers, of course, to the special way of life characteristic of large groups of young people of approximately the same age. It is more than a simple substitute for formal age-grading and initiation rites. It is not, Keniston writes,

so obviously transitional . . . [but is] . . . more like a waiting period . . . a temporary stopover in which one can muster strength for the next harrowing stage of the trip.

Its pattern is "not always or explicitly anti-adult, but it is belligerently *non*-adult."[37] In many respects adulthood looks rather forbidding when compared with the life of a child, and youth culture reflects some reluctance to bridge this gap.

It is pertinent to recall at this point the deep concern of many nineteenth-century Americans about the growth of peer-group contacts. We suggest that these people were witnessing the rudimentary beginnings of a youth culture. Of course, there were none of the artifacts so prominent in our own modern-day youth culture (e.g., "rock 'n roll," "teen magazines," special kinds of dress, and so forth). But the very fact of "wanting to be with and for [their own] kind"[38] was significant. By about 1900 the situation had become more clear. The many and varied writings on "gangs," on juvenile delinquency, and on vocational guidance all show some feeling for the special characteristics of a youth culture.

Keniston argues that a second kind of discontinuity—that between specific generations—is also important in the formation of youth culture. By this he means a clear separation between the parents and the children within an individual family. In such cases the situation of the parents offers no viable goal at which their children may aim. Intra-family conflict is likely to become chronic, and the adolescent is on his own in the formation of an identity. This pattern is characteristic of societies with a high rate of social change and a plurality of alternatives in regard to careers, moral codes, and life styles. The young person shrinks from such a bewildering array of choices and becomes part of the youth culture, where a clear-cut, if temporary, identity comes ready-made.

All of this seems to describe nineteenth-century America fairly well, especially the new life of the cities. Social and economic change was everywhere apparent; ambitions were high; there was an astonishing diversity of people, ideologies, occupations. The disparity between

[34] The phrase is Kenneth Keniston's. See his article cited above.

[35] This may have been *only* a matter of appearance. The reality may have been quite different; indeed parental authority seems, if anything, stronger in the nineteenth century than in the eighteenth. But the fact that children were now more visible and more often approached on their own terms was interpreted by many observers as a symptom of decadence and loosened family bonds.

[36] Ruth Benedict, "Continuities and Discontinuities in Cultural Conditioning," *Psychiatry*, 1, p. 165.

[37] Keniston, *op. cit.*, p. 161.

[38] William B. Forbush, *The Boy Problem*, Chicago: The Pilgrim Press, 1901, p. 20.

generations was assumed; it became, indeed, a part of the national mythology. Immigrant families presented an especially dramatic case in point; likewise those families in which the children of uneducated parents had the chance to go to school. Thus, once again, there was the youth culture.

The growth of the concept of adolescence was the final step in this long and somewhat devious process. It was the response to an observable *fact*—the fact of a youth culture, of many young people seemingly in distress (or at least behaving in ways that distressed their elders). Americans needed some means of understanding the problems of, and the problems created by, these young people. We have tried to show them groping toward such an understanding through much of the nineteenth century. And we have located, chiefly in the work of G. Stanley Hall, a kind of culmination of these efforts: the first comprehensive theory of adolescence in modern history.

3

ERIK H. ERIKSON

Memorandum on Youth

I

IN RESPONDING to the inquiry of the Commission on the Year 2000, I will take the liberty of quoting the statements put to me in order to reflect on some of the stereotyped thinking about youth that has become representative of us, the older generation. This, it seems to me, is prognostically as important as the behavior of the young people themselves; for youth is, after all, a *generational phenomenon,* even though its problems are now treated as those of an outlandish tribe descended on us from Mars. The actions of young people are always in part and by necessity reactions to the stereotypes held up to them by their elders. To understand this becomes especially important in our time when the so-called communications media, far from merely mediating, interpose themselves between the generations as manufacturers of stereotypes, often forcing youth to live out the caricatures of the images that at first they had only "projected" in experimental fashion. Much will depend on what we do about this. In spite of our pretensions of being able to study the youth of today with the eyes of detached naturalists, we are helping to make youth in the year 2000 what it will be by the kinds of questions we now ask. So I will point out the ideological beams in our eyes as I attempt to put into words what I see ahead. I will begin with questions that are diagnostic and then proceed to those that are more prognostic in character.

I would assume that adolescents today and tomorrow are struggling to define new modes of conduct which are relevant to their lives.

Young people of a questioning bent have always done this. But more than any young generation before and with less reliance on a meaningful choice of traditional world images, the youth of today is forced to ask what is *universally relevant* in human life in this technological age at this junction of history. Even some of the most faddish, neurotic, delinquent preoccupation with "their" lives is a symptom of this fact.

Yet, this is within the context of two culture factors which seem to be extraordinary in the history of moral temper. One is the scepticism of all authority, the refusal to define natural authority (perhaps even that of paternal authority) and a cast of mind which is essentially anti-institutional and even antinomian.

I do not believe that even in the minority of youths to whom this statement is at all applicable there is a scepticism of *all* authority. There is an abiding mistrust of people who act authoritatively without authentic authority or refuse to assume the authority that is theirs by right and necessity. Paternal authority? Oh, yes— pompous fathers have been exposed everywhere by the world wars and the revolutions. It is interesting, though, that the word *paternal* is used rather than *parental*, for authority, while less paternal, may not slip altogether from the parent generation, insofar as a better balance of maternal and paternal authority may evolve from a changing position of women. As a teacher, I am more impressed with our varying incapacity to own up to the almost oppressive authority we really do have in the minds of the young than in the alleged scepticism of *all* authority in the young. Their scepticism, even in its most cynical and violent forms, often seems to express a good sense for what true authority is, or should be, or yet could be. If they "refuse to define natural authority"—are they not right if they indicate by all the overt, mocking, and challenging kinds of "alienation" that it is up to *us* to help them define it, or rather redefine it, since we have undermined it—and feel mighty guilty?

As to the essentially anti-institutional cast of mind, one must ask what alternative is here rejected. It appears that the majority of young people are, in fact, all too needy for, trusting in, and conforming to present institutions, organizations, parties, industrial complexes, super-machineries—and this because true personal authority is waning. Even the anti-institutional minority (whom we know better and who are apt to know our writings) seem to me to plead with existing institutions for permission to rebel— just as in private they often seem to plead with their parents to love them doubly for rejecting them. And are they not remarkably eager for old and new uniforms (a kind of uniformity of non-conformity), for public rituals, and for a collective style of individual isolation? Within this minority, however, as well as in the majority, there are great numbers who are deeply interested in and responsive to a more concerted critique of institutions from a newer and more adequate ethical point of view than we can offer them.

The second factor is an extraordinary hedonism—using the word in the broadest sense—in that there is a desacralization of life and an attitude that all experience is permissible and even desirable.

Again, the word *hedonism* illustrates the way in which we use outdated terms for entirely new phenomena. Although many young people entertain a greater variety of sensual and sexual experiences than their parents did, I see in their pleasure seeking relatively little relaxed joy and often compulsive and addictive search for *relevant* experience. And here we should admit that our generation and our heritage made "all" experience relative by opening it to ruthless inquiry and by assuming that one could pursue radical enlightenment without changing radically or, indeed, changing the coming generations radically. The young have no choice but to experiment with what is left of the "enlightened," "analyzed," and standardized world that we have bequeathed to them. Yet their search is not for all-permissibility, but for new logical and ethical boundaries. Now only direct experience can offer correctives that our traditional mixture of radical enlightenment and middle-class moralism has failed to provide. I suspect that "hedonistic" perversity will soon lose much of its attractiveness in deed and in print when the available inventory has been experimented with and found only moderately satisfying, once it is permitted. New boundaries will then emerge from new ways of finding out what really counts, for there is much latent affirmation and much overt solidarity in all this search. All you have to do is to see some of these nihilists with babies, and you are less sure of what one of the statements as yet to be quoted terms the "Hegelian certainty" that the next generation will be even more alienated.

As for the desacralization of life by the young, it must be obvious that our generation desacralized their lives by (to mention only the intellectual side) naïve scientism, thoughtless scepticism, dilettante political opposition, and irresponsible technical expansion. I find, in fact, more of a search for resacralization in the younger than in the older generation.

At the same time society imposes new forms of specialization, of extended training, of new hierarchies and organizations. Thus, one finds an unprecedented divorce between the culture and the society. And, from all indications, such a separation will increase.

Here, much depends on what one means by the word *imposes.* As I have already indicated, in much of youth new hierarchies and organizations are accepted and welcome. We are apt to forget that young people (if not burdened with their parents' conflicts) have no reason to feel that radical change as such is an imposition. The unprecedented divorce we perceive is between *our* traditional culture (or shall I spell it *Kultur?*) and the tasks of *their* society. A new generation growing up with technological and scientific progress may well experience technology and its new modes of thought as the link between a new culture and new forms of society.

In this respect, assuming this hypothesis is true, the greatest strains will be on the youth. This particular generation, like its predecessors, may come back to some form of accommodation with the society as it grows older and accepts positions within the society. But the experiences also leave a "cultural deposit" which is cumulative consciousness and—to this extent I am a Hegelian—is irreversible, and the next generation therefore starts from a more advanced position of alienation and detachment.

Does it make sense that a generation involved in such unprecedented change should "come back to some form of accommodation with the society"? This was the fate of certain rebels and romantics in the past; but there may soon be no predictable society to "come back to," even if coming back were a viable term or image in the minds of youth. Rather, I would expect the majority to be only too willing to overaccommodate to the exploiters of change, and the minority we speak of to feel cast off until their function becomes clearer—with whatever help we can give.

II

Having somewhat summarily disavowed the statements formulated by others, I would now like to ask a question more in line with my own thinking, and thereby not necessarily more free from stereotypy: Where *are* some of the principal contemporary sources of identity strength? This question leads us from diagnosis to prognosis, for to me a sense of identity (and here the widest connotation of the term will do) includes a sense of anticipated future. The traditional sources of identity strength—economic, racial, national, religious, occupational—are all in the process of allying themselves with a new world-image in which the vision of an anticipated future and, in fact, of a future in a permanent state of planning will take over much of the power of tradition. If I call such sources of identity strength *ideological*, I am using the word again most generally to denote a system of ideas providing a convincing world-image. Such a system each new generation needs—so much so that it cannot wait for it to be tested in advance. I will call the two principal ideological orientations basic to future identities the *technological* and the *humanist* orientations, and I will assume that even the great politico-economic alternatives will be subordinated to them.

I will assume, then, that especially in this country, but increasingly also abroad, masses of young people feel attuned, both by giftedness and by opportunity, to the technological and scientific promises of indefinite progress; and that these promises, if sustained by schooling, imply a new ideological world-image and a new kind of identity for many. As in every past technology and each historical period, there are vast numbers of individuals who can combine the dominant techniques of mastery and domination with their identity development, and *become* what they *do*. They can settle on that *cultural consolidation* that follows shifts in technology and secures what mutual verification and what transitory familiarity lie in doing things together and in doing them right—a rightness proved by the bountiful response of "nature," whether in the form of the prey bagged, the food harvested, the goods produced, the money made, the ideas substantiated, or the technological problems solved.

Each such consolidation, of course, also makes for new kinds of entrenched privileges, enforced sacrifices, institutionalized inequalities, and built-in contradictions that become glaringly obvious to outsiders—those who lack the appropriate gifts and opportunities or have a surplus of not quite appropriate talents. Yet it would be intellectual vindictiveness to overlook the sense of embeddedness and natural flux that each age provides in the midst of the artifacts of organization; how it helps to bring to ascendance some particular type of man and style of perfection; how it permits those thus consolidated to limit their horizon effectively so as *not* to see what might destroy their newly won unity with time and space or expose them to the fear of death—and of killing. Such a consolidation along technological and scientific lines is, I submit, now taking place. Those young people who feel at home in it can, in fact, go along with their parents and teachers—not too respectfully, to be sure—in a kind of *fraternal identification*, because parents and children can jointly leave it to technology and science to provide a self-perpetuating and self-accelerating way of life. No need is felt to limit expansionist ideals so long as certain old-fashioned rationalizations continue to provide the hope (a hope that has long been an intrinsic part of an American ideology) that in regard to any possible built-in evil in the very nature of super-organizations, appropriate brakes, corrections, and amendments will be invented in the nick of time and without any undue investment of strenuously new principles. While they "work," these super-machineries, organizations, and associations provide a sufficiently adjustable identity for all those who feel actively engaged in and by them.

All of us sense the danger of overaccommodation in this, as in any other consolidation of a new world-image, and maybe the danger *is* greater today. It is the danger that a willful and playful testing of the now limitless range of the technically possible will replace the search for the criteria for the optimal and the ethically permissible, which includes what can be given on from generation to generation. This can only cause subliminal panic, especially where the old decencies will prove glaringly inadequate, and where the threat or the mere possibility of overkill can be denied only with increasing mental strain—a strain, incidentally, which will match the sexual repression of the passing era in unconscious pathogenic power.

It is against this danger, I think, that the nonaccommodators put their very existence "on the line," often in a thoroughly confounding way because the manifestations of alienation and commitment are sometimes indistinguishable. The insistence on the question "to be or not to be" always looks gratuitously strange to the consolidated. If the question of being oneself and of dying one's own death in a world of overkill seems to appear in a more confused and confusing form, it is the ruthless heritage of radical enlightenment that forces some intelligent young people into a seemingly cynical pride, demanding that they be human without illusion, naked without narcissism, loving without idealization, ethical without moral passion, restless without being classifiably neurotic, and political without lying: truly a utopia to end all utopias. What should we call this youth? *Humanist* would seem right if by this we mean a recovery, with new implications, of man as the measure, a man far grimmer and with much less temptation to congratulate himself on his exalted position in the universe, a self-congratulation that has in the past always encouraged more cruel and more thoughtless consolidations. The new humanism ranges from an *existential* insistence that every man *is* an island unto himself to a new kind of humaneness that is more than compassion for stray animals and savages, and a decidedly *humanitarian* activism ready to meet concrete dangers and hardships in the service of assisting the underprivileged anywhere. Maybe *universalist* would cover all this better, if we mean by it an insistence on the widest range of human possibilities—beyond the technological.

But whatever you call it, the universalist orientation, no less than the technological one, is a *cluster* of ideas, images, and aspirations, of hopes, fears, and hates; otherwise, neither could lay claim to the identity development of the young. *Somewhat* like the "hawks" and the "doves," the technologists and the universalists seem almost to belong to different species, living in separate ecologies. "Technological" youth, for example, expects the dominant forces in foreign as well as in domestic matters to work themselves out into some new form of balance of power (or is it an old-fashioned balance of entirely new powers?). It is willing, for the sake of such an expectation, to do a reasonable amount of killing—and of dying. "Humanist" youth, on the other hand, not only opposes unlimited mechanization and regimentation, but also cultivates a sensitive awareness of the humanness of any individual in gunsight range. The two orientations must obviously oppose and repel each other totally; the acceptance of even a part of one could cause an ideological slide in the whole configuration of images and, it follows, in the kind of courage to be—and to die. These two views, therefore, face each other as if the other were *the* enemy, although he may be brother or friend—and, indeed, oneself at a different stage of one's own life, or even in a different mood of the same stage.

Each side, of course, is overly aware of the dangers inherent in the other. In fact, it makes out of the other, in my jargon, a negative identity. I have sketched the danger felt to exist in the technological orientation. On the "humanist" side, there is the danger of a starry-eyed faith in the certainty that if you "mean it," you can move quite monolithic mountains, and of a subsequent total inertia when the mountain moves only a bit at a time or slides right back. This segment of youth lacks as yet the leadership that would replace the loss of revolutionary tradition, or any other tradition of discipline. Then there is the danger of a retreat into all kinds of Beat snobbishness or into parallel private worlds, each with its own artifically expanded consciousness.

III

As one is apt to do in arguing over diagnosis, I have now overdrawn two "ideal" syndromes so as to consider the prognosis suggested in a further question presented to me:

Is it possible that the fabric of traditional authority has been torn so severely in the last decades that the re-establishment of certain earlier forms of convention is all but unlikely?

I have already indicated that I would answer this question in the affirmative; I would not expect a future accommodation to be characterized by a "coming back" either to conventions or to old-fashioned movements. Has not every major era in history been characterized by a division into a new class of *power-specialists* (who "know what they are doing") and an intense new group of *universalists* (who "mean what they are saying")? And do not these two poles determine an era's character? The specialists ruthlessly test the limits of power, while the universalists always in remembering man's soul also remember the "poor"—those cut off from the resources of power. What is as yet dormant in that third group, the truly under-privileged, is hard to say, especially if an all-colored anticolonial solidarity that would include our Negro youth should emerge. But it would seem probable that all new revolutionary identities will be drawn into the struggle of the two ideological orientations sketched here, and that nothing could preclude a fruitful polarity between these two orientations—provided we survive.

But is not the fact that we are still here already a result of the polarization I have spoken of? If our super-technicians had not been able to put warning signals and brakes into the very machinery of armament, certainly our universalists would not have known how to save or how to govern the world. It also seems reasonable to assume that without the apocalyptic warnings of the universalists, the new technocrats might not have been shocked into restraining the power they wield.

What speaks for a fruitful polarization is the probability that a new generation growing up with and in technological and scientific progress as a matter of course will be forced by the daily confrontation with unheard-of practical and theoretical possibilities to entertain radically new modes of thought that may suggest daring innovations in both culture and society. "Humanist" youth, in turn, will find some accommodation with the machine age in which they, of course, already participate in their daily needs and habits. Thus, each group may reach in the other what imagination, sensitivity, or commitment may be ready for activation. I do not mean, however, even to wish that the clarity of opposition of the technological and the humanist identity be blurred, for dynamic interplay needs clear poles.

What, finally, is apt to bring youth of different persuasions together is a change in the generational process itself—an awareness that they share a common fate. Already today the mere division into an older—parent—generation and a younger—adolescing—one is becoming superannuated. Technological change makes it impossible for any traditional way of being older (an age difference suggested by the questions quoted) ever to become again so institutionalized that the younger generation could "accommodate" to it or, indeed, resist it in good-old revolutionary fashion. Aging, it is already widely noted, will be (or already is) a quite different experience for those who find themselves rather early occupationally outdated and for those who may have something more lasting to offer. By the same token, young adulthood will be divided into older and younger young adults. The not-too-young and not-too-old specialist will probably move into the position of principal arbiter, that is, for the limited period of the ascendance of his speciality. His power, in many ways, will replace the sanction of tradition or, indeed, of parents. But the "younger generation," too, will be (or already is) divided more clearly into the older- and the younger-young generation, where the older young will have to take over (and are eager to take over) much of the direction of the conduct of the younger young. Thus, the relative waning of the parents and the emergence of the young adult specialist as the permanent and permanently changing authority are bringing about a shift by which older youth will have to take increasing responsibility for the conduct of younger youth—and older people for the orientation of the specialists and of older youth. By the same token, future religious ethics would be grounded less in the emotions and the imagery of infantile guilt, than in that of mutual responsibility in the fleeting present.

In such change we on our part can orient ourselves and offer orientation only by recognizing and cultivating an age-specific *ethical* capacity in *older* youth, for there are age-specific factors that speak for a differentiation between morality and ethics. The child's conscience tends to be impressed with a moralism which says "no" without giving reasons; in this sense, the infantile super-ego has become a danger to human survival, for suppression in childhood leads to the exploitation of others in adulthood, and moralistic self-denial ends up in the wish to annihilate others. There is also an age-specific ethical capacity in older youth that we should learn to foster. That we, instead, consistently neglect this ethical potential and, in fact, deny it with the moralistic reaction that we traditionally employ toward and against youth (*anti-institutional, hedonistic, desacralizing*) is probably resented much more by young people than our dutiful attempts to keep them in order by prohibition. At any rate, the ethical questions of the future will be less determined by the influence of the older generation on the younger one than by the interplay of subdivisions in a life scheme in which the whole life-span is extended; in which the life stages will be further subdivided; in which new roles for both sexes will emerge in all life stages; and in which a certain margin of free choice and individualized identity will come to be considered the reward for technical inventiveness. In the next decade, youth will force us to help them to develop ethical, affirmative, resacralizing rules of conduct that remain flexibly adjustable to the promises and the dangers of world-wide technology and communication. These developments, of course, include two "things"—one gigantic, one tiny—the irreversible presence of which will have to find acknowledgment in daily life: the Bomb and the Loop. They together will call for everyday decisions involving the sanctity of life and death. Once man has decided not to kill needlessly and not to give birth carelessly, he must try to establish what capacity for living, and for letting live, each generation owes to every child planned to be born—anywhere.

One can, I guess, undertake to predict only on the basis of one of two premises: Either one expects that things will be as bad as they always have been, only worse; or one visualizes what one is willing to take a chance on at the risk of being irrelevant. As I implied at the beginning, a committee that wants to foretell the future may have to take a chance with itself by asking what its combined wisdom and talent would wish might be done with what seems to be given.

II. Adolescent Development: Mind and Body

If the process of living is itself a process of growth and development, as well as eventual deterioration, so too is the period of adolescence a period of growth and development, and in some cases deteriorations as well. It is not superficial to observe that some of the major changes taking place during adolescence occur in the body. Fabulous growth takes place in these ten years, along with equally startling cognitive and emotional maturation. A body may increase 25 percent in this period, an intellectual capacity may grow as much as, well, no one can really say. Indeed what we will notice throughout this book is the difficulty many writers have in trying to describe what it is precisely that makes adolescents what they are.

Understandably, a host of psychiatrists and psychologists have focused a great deal of attention on the minds and psychological well-being, and not so well-being, of adolescent boys and girls. It is not only a fascinating topic, it is a compelling one, for many professionals are confronting young people who are in deep distress about their lives everyday. Predictably, one sees characteristic forms of distress or disturbance in younger and older adolescents, and from the lives of these troubled people, we are able to learn much about so-called normal behavior as well. We can, perhaps, rightly criticize some writers and critics on the grounds that when the question of psychological development arises, they jump too quickly into discussions of sickness, aberration, disease. "How come nobody talks about good old fashioned healthy kids?" a young woman once remarked to me. Her point is well taken. Yet one cannot overlook too quickly the severe problems faced by many young people. Suicide is no stranger to adolescents. Severe psychological disturbance is not a one in a million finding. The source of these problems may be outside the person originally, but still there is the adolescent with his or her intense unhappiness and the strength and the will to do something about that unhappiness.

In this section, we examine some of the issues connected with the adolescent's physical and psychological development. The section begins with a discussion of requirements for health, turns next to discussions of the developmental disturbances of people of this age, and concludes with the more serious physical and psychological problems that young people experience. And let us underscore the fact that while a great many adolescents survive, choose to survive, with pain, others choose to end their lives when they are less than two decades old. *Development*, generally, is another one of those complex and mysterious terms. We use it because life is a temporal process, because changes do occur and we are today slightly different from how we were yesterday. The irony of development, and adolescent development in particular, is that ten years can be, simultaneously, such a long period of time, and such a short period of time. If one doesn't believe this, one might ask people about how they perceive the passage of their lives in adolescence.

4

Requirements for Healthy Development of Adolescent Youth

Gisela Konopka

INTRODUCTION

In the spring of 1973 the Office of Child Development of the Department of Health Education and Welfare asked Gisela Konopka and the Center for Youth Development and Research, University of Minnesota to develop a statement on their concept of normal adolescence and impediments to healthy development. The statement was viewed as a possible base for national policy.

The following is the statement developed in a most interesting process: Gisela Konopka presented her ideas derived from many years of study and experience to the Center staff in three 2-hour sessions. Each point was then discussed by this able staff, consisting of people of various backgrounds, disciplines, and ages. The presentations and discussions were taped and summarized by the editor. Dr. Konopka then reviewed the text with the assistance of Dr. Normal Sprinthall. Editing was done by Lillian Jensen.

The Office of Child Development (HEW) graciously permitted the publication of this document.

PURVIEW OF THIS STATEMENT

We are talking about adolescent youth in the cultural context of the United States of America in the 1970's. Our objectives are:

- to present a positive developmental model of adolescence by describing what we regard as the key concepts and qualities of adolescence;
- to set forth some of the conditions for healthy development of adolescent youth;
- to discuss specific obstacles to such development.

Within this framework we offer a few recommendations concerning programs and research that could facilitate healthy development of adolescent youth.

It should be noted at the outset that whatever is said in this statement (1) never applies totally to one individual because individuals differ; (2) never applies totally to a group or subgroup because ours is a pluralistic culture embodying an infinite variety of subcultures and subgroups; (3) is distinctly intended to be fluid because ours is a culture in transition.

ADOLESCENCE DEFINED

Adolescence is defined here as that span of a young person's life between the obvious onset of puberty and the completion of bone growth. We chose a biological definition; others frequently are used. In the cultural context, the age set by a given society for the rites of transition to adulthood could be perceived as marking the end of adolescence. In the United States of the 1970's that age, for the most part, is set at 18. In general, we apply no rigid age limits. We think of the period of 12 to 15 years as early adolescence and 15 to 18 years as middle adolescence. The period of 18 to 22 years might possibly be considered late adolescence. This statement is directed predominantly to early and middle adolescence.

Two other definitions of adolescence should be mentioned. "Sociologically, adolescence is the transition period from dependent childhood to self-sufficient adulthood. Psychologically, it is a 'marginal situation' in which new adjustments have to be made, namely those that distinguish child behavior from adult behavior in a given society."[1] We do not adhere to either of the two.

Our view of adolescence is eclectic, psychosocial, and goes beyond current existing theories. Central to our concept is this: We do not

[1] Rolf E. Muuss, *Theories of Adolescence.* New York: Random House, 1962, 2nd ed., p. 4.

see adolescence exclusively as a stage that human beings pass through, but rather as a segment of continuing human development. We reject the common conception that adolescence is solely preparation for adulthood, except in the sense that everything in life can be considered to be preparation for what follows. We believe adolescents are persons with specific qualities and characteristics who have a participatory and responsible role to play, tasks to perform, skills to develop at that particular time of life. The degree or extent to which an adolescent experiences such responsible participation will determine and maximize his human development.

CULTURAL CONTEXT

Since we are talking about adolescent youth in the cultural context of the United States, it seems important to set out a few specific attributes of that culture which we consider particularly relevant to this statement. The list obviously is not intended to be exhaustive.

Pluralism

Perhaps the word that best characterizes the United States is "variety." Its people fit no common mold. They reflect a broad mix of racial, national, religious, cultural, and socio-economic backgrounds. Their life styles and interests are diverse. They hold various views on what constitutes the "good life."

Acceptance of Difference

Since ours is a heterogeneous society we must be accepting of difference, or at least work toward that goal. We embrace egalitarianism as an ideal. We reject all forms of discrimination, again ideally. The general development of an increasing capacity on the part of each person to respect others and to be respected is seen as a necessary trend.

Participatory Democracy

Inherent in the representative democratic form of government under which we live is the responsibility of citizens to participate. Every citizen possesses limited political power. Organized groups have greater power. To make democracy work, citizens should be reasonably well informed and be persons of good will—that is, concerned with the common good as well as with the individual, and acting on their concern. Those are not qualities people are born with; they are developed as part of the socialization process.

Human Rights

Ideologically, ours is an open, free society based on the proposition that the purpose of government is to advance and protect basic human rights. Those rights are presumed to be inalienable—that is, natural, irrevocable, and nontransferable. Society is obligated to create the conditions under which human rights can be secure. Among those that we believe lie closest to the healthy development of youth are:

- the right of the individual to be himself, to think his own thoughts and to speak them, consistent with the rights of others;
- the right to grow and to develop his abilities to their full potential;
- the right to air his grievances and to seek redress;
- the right to make mistakes without unreasonable punishment;
- the right to justice.

What course society will take in the 1970's with respect to supporting the basic rights of individuals and groups remains to be seen. We assume the direction will be positive.

Human Responsibilities

The enjoyment of rights carries with it the obligation to take responsibility. In our society, concern for one another with alertness toward handicap-producing circumstances is a basic human responsibility. Informed decision making is also a basic responsibility, since roles and opinions are not authoritatively prescribed.

Change

Attitudes toward change come in all colors of the rainbow. Some people embrace any change simply for the sake of change. Others fight it persistently. Technological change or change in the material sense seems to be generally more acceptable than change in terms of social values, beliefs, morals, ethics, and life styles. We assume change in all social domains will continue to be an important element in our culture, though at times its direction may be pendular. Significant changes in the world of work can be anticipated. Institutional change will perhaps continue to be gradual, incremental, and disjointed.

Competition and Upward Mobility

Emphasis on job advancement and increasing earnings seems to be a durable aspect of our culture. Young men and women entering the labor force may have even higher economic and social expectations than those of a generation ago; they may also be more militant in seeking middle class income and status.[2] The 1971 White House Conference on Youth report, on the other hand, said college age youth give top priority to finding work that addresses critical social problems rather than to jobs that offer the most money and security.

The key consideration here is the social structural availability of choices.

Economy

Trends to note are (1) the widening gap between the economically well off and the poor—that is, the maldistribution of income and

[2] Irving Kristol, "Job Satisfaction: Daydream of Alienation?" *AFL-CIO Federationist*, Feb. 1973.

material goods; (2) the increasing concentration of economic power and the growing powerlessness to influence the economy's direction through the economic system; (3) the accumulating evidence that impact on or participation in economic growth, development, and consequences is achieved increasingly by political means.

Urbanization

Ours is predominantly a complex, organization prone, urban society. Formally organized groups and voluntary associations, focused on a great variety of causes and interests, abound. They create a bewildering maze, but they also provide a means of socialization and constructive activity. Along with increasing urbanization we see a rather unrealistic romanticization of rural living and an enormous nostalgia for the rural environment.

Communication

The media have enlarged greatly the vision of "the good life" and, because of their persuasive power, have added an increasing burden on the human capacity to distinguish propaganda from facts. Their influence is global, ranging from economics to politics to "heroes" to music to modes of dress. The control of content and style seems to be narrowly constructed. The viewing-listening-reading audience, for example, receives the same selection of national and international news in the same style, though there are some exceptions, of course. The pervasiveness and immediacy of modern communication can turn eccentricities into fads, incidents into movements. The notion of a "generation gap," for instance, has been accentuated by the pronounced attention it has received. That youth are affected in many ways by the media goes without saying.

VIEW OF MAN UNDERLYING THIS STATEMENT

"Every man is in certain respects
(a) like all other men,
(b) like some other men,
(c) like no other man."[3]

That is to say: All human beings have qualities in common that make them human. The biological endowments of human beings, the physical environment in which they live, and the societies and cultures in which they develop, have some common features. Members of subgroups have additional qualities in common. Similarities exist, for example, among people in a certain socio-cultural group, among professional groups, among people belonging to the same economic stratum. But no one person is exactly like another. Each individual inherits a unique combination of biological characteristics. His environment is made up of a unique combination of factors. From birth onward he is shaped by countless, successive actions between his developing self and his environment. A given sequence of critically determining situations is

[3] Clyde Kluckhohn and Henry A. Murray, *Personality in Nature, Society and Culture.* New York: Alfred A. Knopf, Inc., 1949, p. 35.

never duplicated. Hence every man is in certain respects like no other man. It is important that the marvel of infinite variation among human beings never be forgotten. No general view of man fits any single individual.

Man is a holistic being. One may emphasize the physical, mental, emotional, and spiritual components of his makeup, but these components are not discrete. The whole is the synthesis of the parts.

Man is a social being. He is a product of the interplay of the environment and the individual—not exclusively of one or the other. Neither is supreme. Gesell left too much up to a random "magical" unfolding, while Skinner goes too far in the other direction by assuming an empty box, the old idea of man born as a "tabula rasa". Healthy growth occurs through appropriate interaction between man and the environment.

Man has a range of choices, but his choices are not unlimited. Total free will is an impossibility. Particular people, by virtue of their membership in a given population group or subgroup, have a broader or narrower range of choices in specific domains. At different times they have different choices.

Man is a developmental being, moving toward self-realization. Every person wants to be significant. The developmental process is never-ending. In it we see the totality of human life. No developmental stage is static. Each stage is related to other stages and builds toward other stages. Each stage is seen as having its own significant aspect. Each is characterized by stresses and exhilarations. The degree of stress and exhilaration in adolescence is enormous because of the great number of new experiences encountered in adolescence. The attainment of sexual maturity and the upsurge of tremendous physical and intellectual capacity are examples.

Man influences and is influenced by a variety of complex systems and subsystems. He acts and is acted upon. Throughout his life he has the capacity to grow, to change, to modify his behavior in accordance with his values. Value formation within the individual is a continuing process, partly emotional, partly intellectual. It is born out of interaction between the individual and the systems that touch him.

VIEW OF ADOLESCENCE UNDERLYING THIS STATEMENT

The concept of adolescence emerges as part of the view of man. Historically it is a comparatively new concept. Our own view of adolescence, while it embodies some features of those theories, comprehends our experience in working with youth and our reflective thinking upon those experiences.

Once more we emphasize that we do not see adolescence purely as preparation for adulthood. Rather we see it as one part of the total developmental process—a period of tremendous significance distinguished by specific characteristics. *Basic to our view is the concept that adolescents are growing, developing persons in a particular age group—not pre-adults, pre-parents, or pre-workers, but human beings participating in the activities of the world around them.* In brief, we see adolescence not only as a passage to somewhere but also as an important stage in itself.

In setting down what we consider to be the significant characteristics or key concepts of adolescence, we call attention again to the fact that they will not apply *in toto* to any person, group, or subgroup. Circumstances and timing, combined with individual differences, make for an infinite variety of behavior patterns, interactions, and outcomes.

Key Concepts of Adolescence

Experience of physical sexual maturity. A phenomenon particular to adolescence that never occurs again in the life of the individual is the process of developing sexual maturation, different from the state of accomplished sexual maturation. Biologically this is a totally new experience. Its significance is due partly to its pervasiveness and partly to the societal expectations surrounding it. It creates in adolescents a great wonderment about themselves and the feeling of having something in common with all human beings. It influences their whole relationship to each other, whether male or female. Entering this part of maturity also stimulates them to newly assess the world. Indicative of the importance attached universally to maturation of the sex organs are the puberty rites and initiation rituals that mark the transition from childhood to adulthood in many cultures, including present day USA.

Experience of withdrawal of and from adult benevolent protection. Along with biological maturity attained in adolescence come varying degrees of withdrawal of and from the protection generally given to dependent children by parents or substitutes. We know that some young people were never protected, even as children, but we assume a modicum of protection as a healthy base. Whatever the degree of previous protection, the adolescent is moving out from the family toward interdependence (not independence, but *inter*dependence) in three areas: (1) with his peers, his own generation; (2) with his elders, but now on an interacting or a rebellious level instead of a dependent level (adults often increase their attempt to control and direct adolescents, which tends to promote active rebellion); and (3) with younger children, not on a play level but on a beginning-to-care-for-and-nurture level. This process of moving away from dependency creates tensions and emotional conflicts.

Consciousness of self in interaction. The development of self and the searching for self starts in childhood, but the intellectual as well as the emotional consciousness of self in interaction with others is particularly characteristic of adolescence. It is a time when personal meaning is given to new social experiences. The young person defines for himself what he is experiencing in his relationships with others. His "meaning" may be different from that of those with whom he is interacting, but so long as it makes sense to him he can grow and move forward. The kind of categories he used as a child to figure out the world begin to break down. What may have been clear and explicable may suddenly become inexplicable.

Re-evaluation of values. Though the formation of values is a lifelong developmental process, it peaks in adolescence. It is related to both thinking and feeling, and is influenced by human interaction. In our culture where young people are likely to be exposed to a variety of contradictory values, questioning begins even in childhood. The adolescent engages in re-evaluation of values that have been either accepted at an earlier age or simply rejected because of individual resistance. He moves beyond simple perception (if I burn my hand it hurts) and sees things in a moral framework as "good" and "bad." He is consciously searching for value clarification. He becomes a moral philosopher concerned with "shoulds" and "oughts." Given the inconsistency of a society whose institutions frequently do not follow the general intent of the ideological system, value confrontations are inevitable. The young, because of the intensity of their total being, tend to be uncompromising. They may opt clearly for a thoroughly egalitarian value system, or they may give up and become cynics. The wish of each generation to start over again is not new. What is new in our time, however, is the intensity and the worldwide drive to translate this wish into reality.

Again, the younger child is constantly developing mastery of the outer world, but the adolescent encounters his world with a new intellectual and emotional consciousness. He meets his world less as an observer and more as a participator who actually has a place to fill.

Experimentation. The young are possessed of greater physical, mental, and emotional capacity and therefore of a great thirst to try out those capacities. Experimentation is writ large—as important as eating or sleeping. Human beings learn through experimentation from childhood on. The child explores, for instance, by touching, putting things into his mouth, etc. Adolescents need to experiment with wider circles of life—meet various kinds of people, see other cultures. They need to experiment with their own strength and value systems—lead a group, try out intimate relationships, engage in some form of adventure. The experimentation necessary to adolescents usually includes a feeling of *risk*. It is their way of learning about their own and the surrounding reality.

This need is fraught with danger because adolescents are not as cautious as adults, yet it must have some outlet. It can become a major form of positive healthy development of the young.

Qualities of Adolescence

Linked inseparably with the major phenomena of adolescence outlined above are a number of qualities or characteristics peculiar to this period; at least they are present in heightened form. We look on them as healthy and normal, not as detrimental or negative. A few of the more significant ones are highlighted here.

The drive to experiment is coupled with a mixture of *audacity* and *insecurity*. The audacity is related to not being experienced enough to envision the harmful consequences of a given action; the insecurity is related to the uncertainty that accompanies inexperience and the lessening or withdrawal of protection.

A deep sense of *loneliness* and a high degree of *psychological vulnerability* are two other specific qualities of adolescence. Every attempt at experimentation, and reaching out is new and very intense. If the outcome is negative it is exceedingly painful because youth do not have a "bank" of positive experiences to draw from when defeats occur. Adults can say, "Oh well, you'll get over it," but such remarks annoy more than they comfort.

Enormous *mood swings* are usually cited as characteristic of adolescence. Many factors contribute to the swings. Physiological changes are related to emotional changes. Moving from dependence to interdependence creates a whole series of tensions and conflicts. The impact of peers is magnified. Ambivalence is common. The yearning to jump into the next stage of development co-exists with the desire to have things stay as they are. The feeling of omnipotence tangoes with the feeling of helplessness and inadequacy. The cocksure conviction that "it won't happen to me" plays hide and seek with the fear that it will. Being expected to act like an adult one minute and being treated like a child the next is experienced as confusing. How can one be too young to do almost everything one wants to do, and adult enough to behave as "they" think one should? Seeing parents as mere humans with frailties can be terrifying after having depended on them as all-wise.

Adolescents have a strong *peer group need*. They stress cooperation with that segment of the group with which they identify. The sub-groups they form are often very tightly knit. To gain group acceptance the individual seems to relegate his personal competitive drives to second place, at least temporarily. The emphasis is on cooperation, whether the goal is positive or negative—manning a hotline emergency service, for example, or "ripping off" a certain store.

Finally, adolescents need to be *argumentative* and *emotional* since they are in the process of trying out their own changing values and their own relationships with the outer world.

* * * * * *

Summarizing the attributes of adolescence into *one* concept is difficult and may be an oversimplification. Erik Erikson gave us the concept of the age of identity-seeking; therefore his stress on provision of a moratorium as condition for healthy development.

I (Konopka) prefer to think of adolescence as the AGE OF COMMITMENT. It is the move into the *true interdependence of men*. The struggle between dependency and independence—so often described in the literature—is an expression of this entrance into interdependence.

Commitment includes the search for oneself, as Erikson stressed, but it also points toward the emotional, intellectual, and sometimes physical reach for other people as well as ideas, ideologies, causes, work choices.

This move toward *commitment* is so serious and so significant that providing healthy conditions to let it unfold becomes just as crucial for human development as providing healthy conditions for growth in early childhood. It elevates adolescence from a stage frequently regarded as one that must be endured and passed through as rapidly as possible to a stage of earnest and significant human development.

CONDITIONS FOR HEALTHY DEVELOPMENT OF YOUTH

Looking back now on our view of man and adolescence in the cultural context of the United States in the 1970's, we begin to see clusters or constellations of associated imperatives, skills, and tasks that—taken together—create a climate conducive to healthy development of youth.

A pluralistic society with egalitarianism as an ideal demands

participation of people. Therefore it is quite clear that creation of conditions that facilitate healthy adolescent development begins with the encouragement of equal and responsible participation by youth in the family or other societal units.

Because we are living in a complex society, *choice-making* becomes increasingly important. It cannot be based on instinct. Therefore youth must develop the capacity to make decisions in many areas: school interests, work interests, use of discretionary time, the kind of friends they want to cultivate, and so on. Practical learning opportunities are essential.

As the protections normally associated with childhood are withdrawn and adolescents move toward wider interdependence, particularly with their peers, they need to have a sense of *belonging* to their own age groups and to adults as well. They need to find ways to interact with peers—both male and female. They need to acquire the skills to handle their sex drives, to develop and maintain friendship, to experience intimacy. They may choose to join a youth organization or a gang, take up a "cause," concentrate on dancing or listening to records in a group, or adopt some other activity—and they should have the opportunity to do so.

Because of the conflicting values adolescents encounter in a rapidly changing world, they should have the opportunity to thrash out their reactions, consider the pluses and minuses, and try to determine where they themselves stand so that they will be better able to deal with ideas of all shades—including demagoguery. Those working and living with youth can foster healthy value formation by *encouraging open discussion* and refraining from trying to superimpose their values upon them.

Although "Who am I?" is a question that recurs throughout life, the search for identity becomes more conscious and highly emotional during adolescence. Therefore the young need a *chance to reflect on self* in relation to others (some use their peers as mirrors) and to test self in a variety of settings. The process is a healthy one so long as it does not consist entirely of looking inward.

In recent years people in the helping professions, and laymen as well, seem to have become engrossed in a very individualistic approach to healthy psychological development. Value clarification is discussed in terms of one person examining his own values; participants in therapy groups delve endlessly into themselves; books on self-analysis keep rolling off the presses. While we believe it is a condition of growth to be able to discover who one is, we also believe that inordinate preoccupation with self in the search for identity can become very unhealthy. Hence we emphasize the importance of looking outward as well as inward.

Since experimentation is essential to learning, adolescents should have the opportunity to discover their own strengths and weaknesses in a host of different situations, to experience success and also learn how to cope with adversity and defeat. These skills are usually acquired through active participation. Therefore adolescents should have a genuine *chance to participate as citizens, as members of a household, as workers—in general, as responsible members of society.*

Experimentation involves risks. With audacious but inexperienced youth doing the experimenting, the risks are magnified. If experimentation is essential to learning, as we have said, then it can be argued that adolescence should be a period in which youth can experiment without suffering disastrous consequences when they fail or make mistakes; in other words, that the means for a psychosocial moratorium should be provided. It can also be argued that learning and growth will not occur unless youth are held responsible for their actions, and that participatory activity without such responsibility becomes tokenism.

Our view is that some allowance for experimentation is important for healthy development, but that the "moratorium" should not be total. Adolescents should be *allowed to experiment with their own identity, with relationships to other people, and with ideas, without having to commit themselves irrevocably.* They should be able to *try out various roles* without being obligated to pursue a given course—in school or in the world of work, for example. They should also have the opportunity to practice with limited hurt if they fail, because while their inexperience does not make them inferior to adults, it does make them different. On the other hand, youth should understand that genuine *participation* and genuine *responsibility go hand in hand;* that a basic tenet of our social system is: for every right or set of rights there is a corresponding responsibility or set of responsibilities. To illustrate: young or old, a bona fide voting member of a governing board or some other decision-making body is responsible for his vote. Also we believe that youth should be helped to develop a feeling of *accountability* for the impact they have on other human beings—accountability not in a hierarchic sense, but *in the context of a relationship among equals.*

Finally, a climate that facilitates healthy development should provide opportunities to cultivate the *capacity to enjoy life*, to be creative, to be frivolous, to do things on one's own, and to learn to interact with all kinds of people—people of different races, different interests, different life styles, different economic and cultural backgrounds, different ages.

* * * * * *

To recapitulate, conditions for healthy development should provide young people with opportunities

- to participate as citizens, as members of a household, as workers, as responsible members of society;
- to gain experience in decision making;
- to interact with peers and acquire a sense of belonging;
- to reflect on self in relation to others and to discover self by looking outward as well as inward;
- to discuss conflicting values and formulate their own value system;
- to experiment with their own identity, with relationships to other people, with ideas; to try out various roles without having to commit themselves irrevocably;
- to develop a feeling of accountability in the context of a relationship among equals;
- to cultivate a capacity to enjoy life.

Given these conditions, adolescents will be enabled to gain experience in forming relationships and making *meaningful commitments.* They are not expected by the adult world to make final lifelong commitments; the expectation is related to their own need for interdependence and humanity's need for their commitment to others without losing themselves.

OBSTACLES TO PROGRESS OF NORMAL DEVELOPMENT

Having looked at some of the conditions that facilitate healthy development, we now look at the other side of the coin: obstacles to the progress of normal development. Both the presence of unfavorable factors and the absence of favorable factors constitute obstacles.

The factors selected for discussion here are closely related to the key concepts and qualities of adolescence described earlier. Those that impede normal development of all human beings—such as *lack of nutrition, inadequate housing, poverty in general, racial discrimination—are exceedingly important and are acknowledged here as basic.* In addition, we wish to underline the following specific obstacles to healthy development of adolescent youth.

Violation of Adolescents' Self-Respect by Adult World

Violation of self-respect is detrimental to all human beings. In adolescence, because of increasing self-consciousness and interdependence with peers, anything that violates self-respect—such as racial discrimination, or being disregarded as a significant human being, or being labeled a failure—is taken with special hurt. It may result in withdrawal, complete destruction of self, mental illness, drug abuse, or enormous hostility. The adolescent sees many inconsistencies in the adult world which were less definable in childhood. He often perceives simple criticism as a demeaning "put-down." To ignore or to laugh off his hurt and frustration is to violate his self-respect in a very real way.

Society's View of Adolescence as Preparatory

The prevailing cultural view that adolescence is only a time of preparation for adulthood is harmful because it places youth in an ambivalent situation where they are neither children nor adults. It causes expectations to be extremely confused: in one instance, "You're too old to behave like that;" in another, "You're still a child, you know." The very rhetoric that adolescence is transition may be an obstacle in itself.

Prolonged Economic Dependence of Youth

Youth's bursting energy, thirst for adventure, and yearning for a productive role in society make it difficult for some to accept prolonged economic dependence. School dropouts, especially in the middle class economic bracket, often are motivated by wanting to make it on their own. A sense of violation of self-respect, inflicted by school or community, contributes to dropouts at all economic levels, perhaps more so at the lower level. While modern technology has increased the need for the more extensive knowledge and training that long schooling makes possible, educational requirements for many jobs are "standard" rather than job-related. They should be less rigid.

Limited Outlet for Experimentation by Youth

Urbanization and population density diminish possibilities for experimentation. Though mobility increases at adolescence, space and places to go are limited. Opportunities for part time work experience are limited by the inability or unwillingness of business and industry to accept large numbers of young people into their operations and by the desire of labor organizations to lock up jobs and entrance to jobs.

Mistrust is another basis for many restrictions on experimentation. Some restrictions are warranted on the grounds of reasonable protection, but others—such as some youth-serving organizations now allowing 16- and 17-year-olds to go on hikes without an adult present—are exaggerated.

Popular Acceptance of the Generation Gap Concept

In recent years the concept of a generation gap has been widely accepted as inevitable—a notion reinforced by the media. Worse, the so-called gap has been acted out as hostility by both adults and young people, each placing the other in the role of adversary. This state of affairs is an obstacle to the healthy development of adults as well as youth, since they are interdependent.

Influences That Encourage Adolescent Egocentricity

An outcome of increased personal alienation and separation from responsibilities and participation has been the problem of adolescent egocentricity. The lack of effective interpersonal competencies, both within the teenage generation and across teenage and adult generations, escalates the tendency toward a narrow individualism. The relativism inherent in the fad to "do your own thing" too often leads to further withdrawal and separation. Such experience can act as an effective negative barrier by preventing the development of needed interpersonal competency.

Lack of Opportunity for Moral Development

It is important to note that many adolescents stabilize their value system at levels well below universal values of social justice. Society's failure to provide for significant experience and careful examination/reflection of that experience for most teenagers literally stunts their moral development. Simple precepts are no more acceptable. Critical to our statement is the finding that there is almost no increase in the level of moral maturity beyond that reached during adolescence. Clearly, according to Kohlberg[4] and Konopka[5], the time to stimulate maximal psychological and moral maturity is during this stage.

Society's Confusion About Sex

A conspiracy of silence about sex or banal exchange on the level of advertising cliches are still characteristic of the wider society. Such practice prevents young people from clarifying their own attitudes about one of the most forceful drives at this age. It pushes them into clandestine experimentations that often frighten or demean them. Such ignorance has helped to increase the incidence of venereal disease in young people.

Society's Belief That Family is the Only Place for Youth

For certain young people the fact that the traditional family (father, mother, children) is considered the only unit conducive to healthy growth, with no alternatives, is damaging. With no legitimate substitute available they are forced into runaway episodes, hiding, drugs.

Dominance of Youth Organizations by Adults

Organizations are instruments of our society. Causes are fought and won by organizations. Yet when the young organize they are seldom permitted to run their own show. Adult needs often supersede the healthy development of youth. Adult leaders of youth organizations tend to view teenagers as minds to be molded and

[4] L. Kohlberg and R. Kramer, "Continuities and Discontinuities in Childhood and Adult Moral Development," *Human Development*, 1969, 12: pp. 93-120.

[5] Gisela Konopka, "Formation of Values in the Developing Person," *American Journal of Orthopsychiatry*, 43(1), January 1973.

shaped as if they were young children. Governing boards are dominated by adults who make policy, "know what is best." Adult "advisers" engineer subtle (and sometimes not so subtle) roadblocks to action. Formal organizations which presumably exist to serve youth become top-heavy bureaucracies impervious to the suggestions youth offer. Such tactics prevent youth from gaining experience as genuinely functioning citizens and breed cynicism.

Denial of Equal Participation to Youth

In almost every aspect of society—family, school, civic organizations, political groups, social and religious groups—youth are usually not permitted equal participation. They may not even be allowed free passage into the organizations. This denial is inconsistent with the notion that people learn and develop by doing.

Uneven Laws Pertaining to Youth

Laws pertaining to youth vary from state to state. Some are outmoded; some are ambiguous; all are variably administered. For those youngsters who run into legal difficulties the obstacles to healthy development are multiplied tenfold. If the offenders are institutionalized they are cut off from normal interaction with their associates and their development is stunted—contrary to the philosophy of the juvenile court which was established so that young persons could be protected and rehabilitated instead of being punished. "Juvenile status offenses" (truancy, chronic absenting, and incorrigibility, for example) are offenses only if committed by the young. Teenagers are punished for behavior often necessary at that age. Laws making it impossible for young people to get medical care without parental consent are obstacles to physical health, and to mental and emotional health as well.

RECOMMENDATIONS

Several considerations influenced our approach to recommendations concerning the kind of programs and research endeavors we believe would facilitate the healthy development of adolescent youth.

The fact that this statement is addressed to a governmental agency led us to direct our suggestions primarily toward action that could be instituted by government.

We do not adhere to the simplistic view that by government action alone or by individual action alone will healthy development of youth be assured. At best it can only be facilitated, and that pursuit will require the best efforts of both worlds—public and private.

It is understood that the fulfillment of basic needs is the foundation on which facilitation of any kind of human development rests. This statement is concerned for the most part with the psychosocial aspects of healthy development. Our recommendations are directly related to our previously stated view of adolescence, taken as a whole.

Two approaches to recommendations were considered: (1) giving attention individually to each system in which adolescents live and move—educational, family, work, discretionary time, correctional, and governmental; (2) looking at the total picture and thinking in terms of remedial or rectifying programs and research efforts. The second approach was agreed upon, chiefly because each system is so closely related to other systems that any program, to be effective, necessarily would have to involve more than one system. The pivotal position of the *educational system* should be specially noted. In the life of adolescent youth the schools are of critical importance. Unless they are supportive of programs aimed at reform in other areas, those programs are likely to fall short.

We begin with some general observations that apply to all systems.

Priority Concerns Related to All Systems Serving Youth

We assign top priority to actuating a major effort to *educate adults who work with youth* about conditions that facilitate healthy development, and how such conditions can be created. Envisioned is an interdisciplinary focus on youth in formal and informal educational programs designed to improve the skills, insight, and understanding of persons involved with youth—teachers, parents, counselors, social workers, recreation directors, correction officers, health professionals, and other youth-serving personnel.

We also urge greater emphasis on the *education of youth* (1) to improve their competency and self-confidence in using the resources and power to which they have access, and (2) to develop in each individual the strength or courage to cope with the system as it affects him.

Changes in structure and program are recommended wherever required *to facilitate significant input by youth.* Experience with federal programs such as Model Cities, Housing, and Community Action could provide direction. In the educational system, for example, consideration might be given to student membership on the school board or on key committees, or the development by students of student rights statements, or the legitimization of organizations run by youth for youth. This is not, however, to suggest the development of a professional group of adolescents who are presumed to speak for the adolescent community. Adolescents, like any other population group, are not all of one mind.

Criteria for Programs and Systems Serving Youth

The effectiveness of programs and systems serving youth can be judged by the opportunities they offer youth and the credibility they enjoy. We believe those which merit support are distinguished by:

• Provision of opportunity for youth to have experience in (1) making choices; (2) making commitments; (3) experimenting with a variety of roles to "try out" the choices and commitments they make.

• Credibility: validity of the program in the eyes of those served.

* * * * * *

Unless real options are available, choice-making becomes an empty phrase. Pseudo decision-making does not promote developing commitment. Therefore, *intervention* logically should be focused on the removal of limiting factors.

Carrying this line of reasoning further, *law* should be used to support healthy development rather than as it is now, presumably to curb socially disapproved behavior (often including behavior that actually has become more common.)[6] The formulation and use of *policy* should be guided by the same principle.

Greatest Urgency

It can always be said (and all too often is) that progress on this or that front cannot be made until such and such changes are made on some other front. While we are well aware of the complex interrelationships that make remedial action difficult, we believe an intensive national effort must be made to rectify conditions in areas where youth are being most cruelly battered and mangled.

1. We have singled out the correctional system as the greatest offender because it is the one in which youth are most powerless, once they enter it. A total and concerted effort should be made to:

(a)   Close mass juvenile institutions;
(b)   Develop substitute living situations for young people who cannot live at home;
(c)   Provide access of juveniles to legal aid.

2. We suggest support of programs to make education (formal and informal) a base for healthy growth instead of humiliation and frustration. We recommend:

(a)   Creation of options and alternatives within and outside of existing school systems. The deliberate promotion of pluralistic learning environments staffed by adults from a variety of backgrounds would provide for greater learning experience and participation by a larger segment of teenagers. These options would include the development of adolescents as teachers and counselors—staff participants—in schools. Prior in-service (or other) education of participating teachers would be essential.
(b)   Provision of experiential education for young people through community participation.
(c)   High priority given to programs which educate teachers and other youth workers to genuinely respect and work effectively with adolescents from various backgrounds.

3. Our final suggestion is the creation of significant employment opportunities for youth. Our concern here is for underemployed and unemployed youth in need of meaningful job opportunities as well as educational and vocational counseling.

We have refrained from making detailed proposals for programs because that must be done by the people who will carry them out.

We suggest that the Office of Child Development convene a small conference to develop priorities and exchange ideas for additional projects.

---

[6] The population of delinquency institutions for girls consists in the majority of girls whose "crime" is involvement is sexual experimentation.

Research and Data Gathering

Support should be given to research focused on *barriers* to opportunities for choice-making, experiencing commitments, and experimenting with many different social roles; that is, barriers to accomplishing that which we said all program changes should be designed to accomplish. We also believe:

• The combined efforts of youth and adults should be employed in research.

• Youth-initiated projects should receive serious consideration, and youth should be encouraged to come forward with ideas for investigation.

•In projects undertaken, youth should provide documentation and monitor all processes, rules, norms, and points of contact with youth organizations.

•Particular attention should be given to field research studies instead of basic laboratory research; that is, to examination of programs in natural environments.

• Data on youth should be gathered uniformly throughout the United States and reported periodically for each state. Findings should be analyzed and implications for national trends printed out.

• It is noted that at present no major office of the federal government carries a title with specific reference to adolescence or youth. It is highly recommended that such a reference be carried in the title of a governmental office responsible for coordinating and facilitating research and experimental programs concerned with youth development.

The Children's Bureau, by tradition, has carried this responsibility, but its major focus has been on the development of the young child. It has done superbly in improving health and emotional conditions for small children.

Yet too little attention in either research or experimental efforts has been given to youth. Youth in poverty (often of minority status) suffer not only from childhood deficiencies but carry the additional burden of adult hostility directed toward them. Furthermore, all their adolescent needs are thwarted in the extreme: no hope for social or geographic mobility, no opportunity for legitimate adventure, no possibility for accepted social involvement. Middle class youth also often feel so alienated that their hostility mounts and is vented on other groups of youth, the adult world or things.

As a country, we know little in hard facts of the aspirations, hopes, and wishes of all our youth. The experience of other countries has shown that an office for youth affairs in the central government can perform a valuable function without becoming dictatorial. Use of the term "adolescence" or "youth" in the title of the office would call attention to the importance of promoting the healthy development of persons in that age group. (The Center for Youth Development and Research at the University of Minnesota may present a working model for such a governmental organization.)

EPILOGUE

"How can I establish a figure, even the crudest outline, if I don't know what I'm doing?. . .What do I know of the causes? The vital structure of a man that lies beneath the surface, and that my eye can't see? How can I know what creates from within, the shapes I see from without?"[7]

Those are always the questions artists, scientists, educators, and finally all people must ask. They ask them all their lives, but especially in adolescence. The preceding statement raises the questions of deeper understanding of one age group related to our present day culture. It is set within the value system of a democratic society with all its possible advantages and its desperate search for realization.

It is my conviction that each life period has its sorrows and exhilarations for the individual who experiences them as well as for those surrounding him and that each period has its significance for the continuous development of the human race. Youth is neither golden nor rotten. It has the potential of all human experience. Only—the adult generation is still partially responsible for helping youth to be healthy, sturdy, able to cope with its own problems and also with the problems of the total society. And all human beings have a responsibility neither to demean others nor to hinder others from developing. Observation alone is never sufficient. It leaves the door open to negative forces sweeping over us. We must take the initiative first, to eliminate the destructive forces impinging on our youth and second, to strengthen those forces that will enhance their health and thus the fate of all of us. The world may never be perfect, but much can be done!

5

Adolescence as
a Developmental Disturbance

Anna Freud

THE PSYCHOANALYTIC VIEW
OF MENTAL HEALTH AND ILLNESS

Our psychoanalytic investigations of individuals have convinced us that the line of demarcation between mental health and illness cannot be drawn as sharply as had been thought before. Especially so far as the neuroses are concerned, neurotic nuclei are found in the minds of normal people as regularly as large areas of normal functioning are part of the makeup of every neurotic. Also, people cross and recross the border between mental health and illness many times during their lives.

There is the further point that the concept of health as it is derived from the physical field cannot be taken over to the mental side without alteration. Physically, we are healthy so long as the various organs of the body function normally and, via their specific action, contribute to an over-all state of well-being. Mentally, more than this is needed. It is not enough if each part of the mind, as such, is intact, since the various parts of our personality pursue different aims and since these aims are only too often at cross purposes with each other. Thus, we may be healthy so far as our instinctual drives are concerned; or our sense of reality plus adaptation to the environment may be well up to the mark; or our ideals may be considered admirable by other people. Nevertheless, these single items do not yet add up to the result of mental health. To achieve this, all the agencies in our mind—drives, reasonable ego, and ideals—have to coincide sensibly and, while adapting to the external world, resolve the conflicts inherent in the total situation. To say it in other words: mental health depends on workable compromises and on the resulting balance of forces between the different internal agencies and different external and internal demands.

THE CONCEPT OF DEVELOPMENTAL
DISTURBANCES

It is implied in the view above that this balance and these compromises are precarious and easily upset by any alteration in the internal or external circumstances. It is obvious also that such changes are as inevitable as they are continuous and that they occur especially frequently on the basis of

development. Every step forward in growth and maturation brings with it not only new gains but also new problems. To the psychoanalyst this means that change in any part of mental life upsets the balance as it had been established earlier and that new compromises have to be devised. Such change may affect the instinctual drives, as happens in adolescence; or it may occur in the ego, that is, in the agency whose function it is to manage and control the drives; or what undergoes change may be the individual's demands on himself, his aims and ideals or his love objects in the external world or other influences in his environment. Changes may be quantitative or qualitative. Whatever they are, they affect the internal equilibrium.

Developmental disturbances of this type are frequent occurrences, for example, in the area of sleep and food intake in early childhood. Infants may be perfect sleepers in the first half-year of life, that is, drop off to sleep whenever they are tired and when no stimuli from inside or outside their bodies are strong enough to disrupt their peace. This will alter with normal further growth when the child's clinging to the people and happenings in his environment make it difficult for him to withdraw into himself and when falling asleep thereby is turned into a conflictful process. Likewise, the disturbing food fads of childhood are no more than the impact on eating of various infantile fantasies, of dirt, of impregnation through the mouth, of poisoning, of killing. These fantasies are tied to specific developmental phases and are transitory accordingly, as are the feeding disorders based on them. In fact, in clinical practice with children, the concept of transitory developmental disturbances has become indispensable to us as a diagnostic category.

It is worth noting here that developmental change not only causes upset but can also effect what is called spontaneous cures. A case in point here is the temper tantrums that serve young children as affective-motor outlets at a time when no other discharge is available to them. This is altered by the mere fact of speech development that opens up new pathways and by which the earlier turbulent and chaotic behavioral manifestation is rendered redundant.

THE ADOLESCENT REACTIONS AS PROTOTYPES OF DEVELOPMENTAL DISTURBANCES

Let us return to the problems of adolescence that, in my view, are the prototypes of such developmental upsets.

Although in the childhood disorders of this nature we are confronted usually with alterations in one or the other area of the child's personality, in adolescence we deal with changes along the whole line. There are, as a basis on the physical side, the changes in size, strength, and appearance. There are the endocrinological changes that aim at a complete revolution in sexual life. There are changes in the aggressive expressions, advances in intellectual performance, reorientations as to object attachments and to social relations. In short, the upheavals in character and personality are often so sweeping that the picture of the former child becomes wholly submerged in the newly emerging image of the adolescent.

A. Alterations in the Drives

So far as the sexual drive in adolescence is concerned, I have found it useful to differentiate between quantitative and qualitative changes. What we see first, in the period of preadolescence, is an indiscriminate increase in drive activity that affects all the facets which have characterized infantile sexuality, that is, the pregenital, sexual-aggressive responses of the first five years of life. At this juncture, the preadolescent individual becomes, as a first step, hungrier, greedier, more cruel, more dirty, more inquisitive, more boastful, more egocentric, more inconsiderate than he has been before. This exacerbation of the pregenital elements is followed then, shortly after, by a change in the quality of the drive, namely the changeover from pregenital to genital sexual impulses. This new element involves the adolescent in dangers which did not exist before and with which he is not accustomed to deal. Since, at this stage, he lives and functions still as a member of his family unit, he runs the risk of allowing the new genital urges to connect with his old love objects, that is, with his parents, brothers, or sisters.

B. Alterations in the Ego Organization

It is these temptations of giving way, first to sexual-aggressive pregenital behavior and, next, to incestuous fantasies or even actions that cause all those ego changes which impress the observer as the adolescent's personal upheaval and also as his unpredictability. Serious attempts are made by the preadolescent to keep the quantitative drive increase under control as drive activity has been controlled in earlier periods. This is done by means of major efforts on the side of the defenses. It means bringing into play more repressions, more reaction formations, more identifications and projections, sometimes also more determined attempts at intellectualizations and sublimations. It means also that the entire defensive system of the ego is overstrained and breaks down repeatedly and that therefore the frantic warding off of impulses alternates with unrestrained upsurges of drive activity. When we approach a young adolescent at this stage, we never know which of these two aspects we are going to meet: his overstrict, highly defended personality or his openly aggressive, openly sexual, uninhibited primitive self.

C. Alterations in Object Relations

What serves the preadolescent as some protection against the quantitative pressure of the drives proves wholly inadequate against the qualitative change to a primacy of the genital urges, that is, adult sexuality proper. Nothing helps here except a complete discarding of the people who were the important love objects of the child, that is, the parents. This battle against the parents is fought out in a variety of ways: by openly displayed indifference toward them—by denying that they are important—by disparagement of them since it is easier to do without them if they are denounced as stupid, useless, ineffective; by open insolence and revolt against their persons and the beliefs and conventions for which they stand. That these reactions alternate also with returns to helplessness and dependence on the part of the young persons does not make it any easier for the parents. Obviously, the task imposed on them is a double one: to be thick-skinned, self-effacing, and reserved, but also to change over at a moment's notice to being as sympathetic, concerned, alert, and helpful as in former times.

The closer the tie between child and parent has been before, the more bitter and violent will be the struggle for independence from them in adolescence.

D. Alterations in Ideals and Social Relations

The adolescent's change in social relationships follows as the direct consequence of his stepping out of his family. He is not only left without his earlier object ties. Together with the attachment to his parents, he has thrown out also the ideals that he shared with them formerly, and he needs to find substitutes for both.

There is a parting of the ways here which, I believe, produces two different types of adolescent culture. Some adolescents put into the empty place of the parents a self-chosen leader who himself is a member of the parent generation. This person may be a university teacher, a poet, a philosopher, a politician. Whoever he may be, he is considered infallible, Godlike, and is followed gladly and blindly. At present, though, this solution is comparatively rare. More frequent is the second course where the peer group as such or a member of it is exalted to the role of leadership and becomes the unquestioned arbiter in all matters of moral and aesthetic value.

The hallmark of the new ideals as well as of the new emotionally important people is always the same: that they should be as different as possible from the former ones. In the remote past, when I myself was adolescent, there had come into being in central Europe the so-called Youth Movement, a first attempt at an independent adolescent culture. This was directed against the bourgeois complacency and capitalistic outlook of the parent generation of the period, and the ideals upheld by it were those of socialism, intellectual freedom, aestheticism, and so on. Poetry, art, and classical music were what parents did not believe in, although adolescents did. We know how far the tide has turned in the last two generations. At present, adolescents are hard put to set up new ideals—constructive or disastrous—which can serve to mark the dividing line between their own and their parents' lives.

CONCLUDING REMARKS

To the abbreviated summary of the main theme given above, I add a few concluding remarks that concern more general issues.

First, it has struck me always as unfortunate that the period of adolescent upheaval and inner rearrangement of forces coincides with such major demands on the individual as those for academic achievements in school and college, for a choice of career, for increased social and financial responsibility in general. Many failures, often with tragic consequences in these respects, are due not to the individual's incapacity as such but merely to the fact that such demands are made on him at a time of life when all his energies are engaged otherwise, namely, in trying to solve the major problems created for him by normal sexual growth and development.

Second, I feel that the obvious preponderance of sexual problems in adolescence is in danger of obscuring the concomitant role of aggression that, possibly, might be of great significance. It is worth noting that countries which are engaged in a struggle for existence, such as, for example, Israel, do not report the same difficulties with their adolescents as we do in the Western world. The main difference in their situation is that the aggression of the young people is not lived out within the family or community but directed against the enemy forces that threaten the state and therefore usefully employed in socially approved warlike activities. Since this is a factor outside the sphere of sexual growth, this should extend our thinking into new directions.

Third and last, it seems to me an error not to consider the details of the adolescent revolt in the light of side issues, disturbing as they may be. If we wish to maintain the developmental point of view, it is of less significance how the adolescent behaves at home, in school, at the university, or in the community at large. What is of major importance is to know which type of adolescent upheaval is more apt than others to lead to a satisfactory form of adult life.

6

One of Those Special Student Types

by Thomas J. Cottle

For ten years I have been speaking with students, teachers, and administrators in various schools in the Boston area. Almost every day, as part of my conversational research, what some call oral history and what others call simply, friendship, I am in touch with a group of people who have some special interest, some special investment in school. It's hard to believe that a decade has passed, and that the children I have met have grown so much. Some of them, who weren't even old enough to speak with me when I first visited their homes, now are thinking about high school.

One such person is thirteen-year-old Delores Patterson, whose classmates call her Del or the Big D. She was tall for five years old, on the thin side, quiet, but certainly not lacking in energy. Her parents watched her development quite closely, I remember. Indeed, on leaving the Patterson home in a working class neighborhood of Boston, I used to think that perhaps they watched Delores a bit too closely. Perhaps they were hoping to hold on to her because she was the only girl in the family, the last child at that. Still, their concern with her emerging capacities seemed excessive.

In time, their concern came to be shared with many people, for Delores, as her parents knew when she was very small, was afflicted with some form of dystrophy, a mysterious and evil disease that would slowly but inevitably cut into her muscles, until finally she would be without the use of her legs, and possibly later on, her arms as well. And so Barbara and Ted Patterson's attention to their only daughter was not excessive at all. They were merely hunting for the signs of the illness that grew in their child's body and would transform her from what we often unthinkingly call a normal child, to what we unthinkingly call a handicapped child.

Delores Patterson, thirteen, an eighth grade student in a Massachusetts junior high school, always smiles when we meet. Her look is one of pleasure and surprise with just a trace of good natured irritation. It's as if she is asking, now, why would you come back to see *me*? What about my life could possibly interest anyone? In fact, she has said these very words. I remember one conversation on a lovely April afternoon. Delores was wearing jeans and a bright red sweatshirt with the words, New England Patriots, written across the front of it. Her long black hair shone in the light as it fell behind the green leather back of her wheelchair. She had asked me to push her along a path in a park near her home. The excursion, which involved lifting her up and down stairs, was to be a test for me, she said happily, but I sensed her feeling sad and embarrassed.

"I like school," she said that afternoon. "Sometimes I feel I like it too much, more than the other kids in my class. Maybe it's 'cause I feel all I *can* do is school. When they're outside running around, I have to be here, I can't go anyplace. It's just as easy to be reading or doing my work. So it turns out I start doing better in school than some of them. It's not that I'm smarter; it's only 'cause I work harder, I have more time. They do many things and I can only do a few. So it's only right that I'm a little bit better than them. It's another thing that makes me feel embarrassed too."

"Another thing?" I wondered.

"I do have my days when I'm embarrassed about being like this. Nobody says anything, but I hear some of the kids joking every once in a while. 'Look out, here comes Ironside,' they'll say. Or, one of the boys is always talking about me pulling into a filling station for gas and oil. Lots of times I'm embarrassed just being the person I am. And then, like, maybe I'll do real well in class, maybe even get the highest grade, and that's just embarrassing all over again. See what I mean? Either they're feeling sorry for me or making fun of me, in a good way I mean, or rooting hard for me to do well." Delores pounded the armrest of the wheelchair and looked straight ahead. "When you have this tagging along with you, there's no way people treat you like you were normal. *I* know I'm not normal. Anyone who's seen as many doctors as I have knows they're not normal. My God, the first ten years of my life, I spent more time in doctors' offices than all the kids in my class combined."

"They've really examined you top to bottom, haven't they, D?"

"Everywhere. I'm like a walking experiment." Delores heard the words as I had. She looked at me with an expression that could only be read as, pretty pathetic, eh? "I talked to a little boy a few days ago. He was telling his teacher no matter what anybody said and no matter how hard they tried, he couldn't learn to spell. He either couldn't see the words in his head or didn't like the alphabet. I don't know which. I was there 'cause I work with the little kids while my class is at gym. So I told him, 'Roland, you can learn to do anything you want. Some things are hard to do and some things are easy. Most of us don't like to do the hard ones. But you got to learn how to spell. And you will if you just start working at it like your teacher's trying to tell you.' So what does little Roland say? He looks at me like I'm a monster, which I suppose I am for him, for other people too, and he says, 'Can you learn to walk if you want to?' I mean, I was stunned. I didn't know what to say. So I didn't say anything, hoping he'd start talking about something else, but he wanted an answer. So I said to him, 'I'll never learn how to walk. It's not 'cause I don't want to, I just can't. All the wanting in the world won't let me walk.' So he said, 'And all the wanting in the world won't let me spell,' and he started to walk away. Miss Michaelson was there. I could tell she was ready to give up on him. But I called him back. 'You think I can't learn to walk, right? And you think you can't learn to spell, right? And you think they're the same, right? But here's where you're wrong. Once upon a time I *could* walk. I *did* walk. But once upon a time you *never* could spell. So you have to learn. When you do, you have the right to forget it, like I have the right not to walk again.'

"What'd he say to that?"

"Nothing. He seemed to be interested in what I was telling him. Miss Michaelson took him away as fast as she could. She thanked me for trying. I could tell she was starting to cry. That's another one of the times when I'm embarrassed about all this." As we sat silently glancing about the small park, I heard Delores pounding the arm of the wheelchair.

Ted Patterson had wasted no time negotiating with schools when he realized his daughter required special attention. One of the neighborhood public schools turned him down when he requested aid. Another school said it wanted to help but didn't have the facilities. A third school indicated that there was no problem for Delores attending if she could navigate the stairs. In time, the Pattersons learned that in many areas of America so-called handicapped children are not automatically granted the right even to attend school. According to *Children Out of School in America*, a report issued by the Children's Defense Fund of the Washington Research Project, in 1972 only 31% of the almost 6,000 labeled handicapped students in Richland County, South Carolina, were being served by special programs. In Montgomery, Alabama, in that same year, less than 25% of labeled handicapped children were being served with special programs. The severity of exclusion was similar in areas of Massachusetts, Maine, Iowa, Colorado, and Georgia.

Still, the Pattersons persisted, exploring schools, interviewing teachers and administrators involved in special education programs. At last a school accepted Delores and even encouraged her parents to participate in their program.

"We were lucky," Delores told me in the park when we spoke of the difficulty of finding a school. "No matter what anybody says, a handicapped child is a pain in the neck for anybody who spends time with them. Even you, Cottle." She pointed her finger at my nose. " 'Member how you were groaning lifting me up those stairs?"

"I was only teasing," I protested with embarrassment.

"I know, but it's a sign I'm a burden. Maybe not a whole burden but part of one. How about when you lifted me out of the car before? You couldn't have liked that. People are always doing things for me and I'm not supposed to feel sorry for myself. All the TV shows on handicapped people, that's all they ever say, don't feel sorry for yourself. But still, I guess we were lucky. I know kids from the hospitals I was in who are blind and deaf who've never even been in school. Maybe they started but they stopped 'cause they couldn't get special help. God, I don't know how you could go to school and not see. And if you couldn't hear," she shuddered, "it'd be awful. I'm lucky 'cause all I need is ramps or elevators or somebody to lift me up once in a while."

"Were there special schools you could have gone to?"

"I suppose so, but I don't see myself as, like, sick, like I belong in a *whole* special school. There's nothing wrong with my brain. You know what?" she interrupted herself. "When I was about, maybe seven, this woman my mother talked to wanted to put me in a school for handicapped kids. I guess my mother was interested 'cause they couldn't find any other place for me. So they took me out to this school in the country which turned out to be part of a mental hospital. The school was for brain damaged children. People still think if you have one handicap you have them all.

"Sometimes when I talk with people in my school, even some of the teachers, I can tell they're trying not to mention my being in a wheelchair. But then I imagine they're looking at me like they're trying to find out whether I'm also blind or deaf, or whether something's wrong with my brain. Once I saw this assistant principal looking at me real funny. So I said to him, 'There's nothing wrong with my brain. I'm not retarded.' He said he wasn't thinking that. He was thinking about his own baby who was just born, like two days before, and the baby was in one of those special things, you know . . ."

"An incubator?"

"Yes, and he was worried because he had just read a story about how some baby in an incubator hadn't gotten enough air to breathe and went blind. He asked me if I knew anything about that. He was really upset. I told him I was never in that part of the hospital. I don't think he heard me."

It is only natural that whenever I ask Delores about her plans for some upcoming event, it becomes an occasion for her to tell me how she sees time unraveling in her life. In these moments I feel her working hard to put aside thoughts of what the future might bring. The matter came up during our conversation in the park that one afternoon:

"I don't want people at school to think of me only as a handicapped girl, the kid in the wheelchair. I want them to see me as a person too. I know that sounds corny, everybody says that. But I'm not really a whole person, to *them*, I mean. To *me* I am. I don't think about what I am and the problems I have which most people don't have, but I *am* a whole person. They try at school, but it's hard for them. Or sometimes, like when I need help, it's like I'm reminding them I'm not really a whole person 'cause I can't get out of this." She gripped tightly to the arms of the chair. "What I'm saying is that I want them to see me as a whole person even though *I* know and *they* know there are times I need help. It *is* like that boy Roland who thought he couldn't spell. It didn't mean he wasn't a whole person though.

"Maybe I was once. Maybe when I could walk and run I didn't think about anything being in the past or future. Now I feel I have to hurry up and do things. Like, I can worry about the past but I have to, like, race the future. What's going to be first, my illness or my learning everything in school? I always want to say, give me everything you can, I don't know how much time I have. You can fool yourself, you know, by thinking things could be worse. My father always tells me that. 'Things could be worse, Delores.' Maybe he's right. Can you imagine if I was like this, and didn't have school?" Delores looked about at a scene of children playing, running, climbing on jungle gyms, working intently in a large sandbox. "I can't run, but I can use my brain. Nobody can change that. And I have school, and my studies . . ."

"Your friends . . ."

"My friends."

During the years of Delores' confinement in the wheelchair, I have been aware of some of the problems she has experienced with friends. When she was younger, many children were confused by her illness and chose to ignore her or pretend they didn't see anything wrong with her. Others laughed at her or made jokes and grotesque impersonations of her, but none of these children broke her spirit. What hurt her more was the natural constraints being imposed on close friendships. Perhaps it is a group of girls talking excitedly together after class and someone suggests that the group run down stairs and continue the conversation outside. Then suddenly they're gone, and in their enthusiasm they have forgotten Delores and her difficulty in navigating stairs. Or perhaps a group of boys and girls are strolling together after school. Gradually they begin to pair off, moving about not far from her, but momentarily unaware of the intimacy from which she is excluded. When I once asked her about these moments, she seemed, naturally enough, reluctant to answer.

"I carry a book with me; always prepared. They don't mean it. You get caught up in your own thoughts and you forget sometimes. My God, I forget my parents' birthday sometimes. Besides, how many times have I gone on talking in class or helping someone with homework and they don't even know what I'm talking about. I'm so interested in *my* interests I don't think about what they might be interested in. I don't blame anyone for forgetting me and my stupid ugly wheelchair."

One draws strength talking with people like the young woman I now was pushing through the small park. It is trite, sentimental, this feeling, but it is very real. This child makes me feel strong and ashamed about many things, hopeful and sad all at the same time, and she recognizes the moods and feelings she evokes in me and in the other people she befriends. She knows when her parents are trying to hide their bitterness about her condition, or when a teacher is frustrated by something she has done or more likely, is unable to do. On some occasions, Delores has even told a teacher, "Go ahead, say what you're thinking. *I* hate this wheelchair more than you do!"

She knows too what the children her age think about her. She sees the expression in the eyes of the little ones like Roland, whose look of wonderment practically screams out the words, why can't you stand up and be like the rest of us? She knows the shame that follows the inadvertent thoughtlessness of her friends. She once told me how several boys accidentally forgot to pick her up after school and left her sitting on a stoop with her wheelchair fifteen feet away. It was an hour before someone came for her.

One of our most common responses to children like Delores Patterson is, how are they doing? We ask their doctors and teachers and parents, how are they doing? To listen to Delores is to convince me that she is doing marvelously well. But in hearing this young woman speak, no one should believe that there are no setbacks, no tears and pain, no denials. She admits to days when the discouragement and fright about her condition makes her so weak she cannot go to school. She refuses to eat, and speaks with no one. On one such day I nonetheless chose to visit her, hoping to cheer her up. Delores lay in her bed, her hair pulled back, her skin a faded white color I had never seen, her eyes lifeless. She saw me but made not the slightest effort to acknowledge my presence. I closed her bedroom door quietly.

On other occasions, Delores suddenly may become enraged to the point of having a violent tantrum. It happened when I joined her family at a restaurant. Embarrassed, her parents took her home where she broke down and sobbed for hours. Similar problems have arisen at school. Frustration over not being able to catch on to some mathematical problem once drove her into a frenzy. She cried bitterly and banged on the spokes of the wheelchair. Her teacher ran to get the school's guidance counselor. The next day Delores apologized to everyone, but the mathematics teacher had her transferred to a different class, claiming that he was not trained in special education. Upon hearing of this transfer, Delores fell into a depression and stayed out of school for a week.

Mr. and Mrs. Patterson, both deeply religious, have their own moments of sadness and anger. Both have had their outbreaks, both have given speeches of damnation and defiance, made pledges to put their daughter in a home, give her up for adoption, move away from the whole mess. Then when the fury lifts, they are back at it, lifting their daughter into the car, scanning the newspapers for interesting summer programs that might accept Delores; classes in swimming, instructions in chess, weaving, needlepoint, foreign language tutors. And in the night, they cry too, in guilt, in exhaustion, in humiliation.

The unspoken goal is days of calmness and resoluteness. The Pattersons have help from others, but mainly they are alone, content that a day has passed without mishap or especial sadness, but troubled by the lingering questions: How many more days, how rich still is the source of strength they together and alone draw upon. Delores' feet have grown and she needs new shoes. That is a good sign, a reason to celebrate at dinner with orange cake, Delores' favorite. Her dentist finds a large amount of decay. It is not that unusual, he reports, but it could be an indication of a more general deterioration. Delores cries as the dentist treats her until finally he cannot work at all.

Everyone hunts for clues, the texture of hair and nails, Delores dropping a spoon at breakfast, increased or decreased frequency of urination, stiffness in the neck, shoulders, upper arms. It's probably nothing, her mother always advises. But it is enough to make Delores weak with fright, and in these moments no one has the power to comfort her.

We had reached my car and I began preparing to lift Delores into the front seat. A man offered to help. We reached down and quickly had her comfortably in the car.

"You two guys are really good at this. Don't forget my wheels, Cottle," she reminded me. "Maybe I ought to take you with me wherever I go. You could be like my private bodyguards."

Then we were driving toward her home. On the way, we went past the high school where in a year she would be enrolling.

"That's the big goal, right there," she said calmly. "That's what I'm pushing for. Then college. I don't even know whether there are ramps in that building. I'm afraid to find out. My luck, I won't be able to go there. But I'll find someplace, even if I have to go to Hawaii."

"Now *that* wouldn't be bad."

"It would be good, they don't have winters there. I hate winters. Mrs. Thurmond, my sixth-grade teacher, promised me I'd get into high school."

"What's your worry?" I asked unthinkingly.

"Don't forget, Cottle, I'm one of those special student types, I don't just automatically pass from one grade to the next, especially one building to the next. Everything has to be checked out, all those little things people like you take for granted. Like, is there a girl's lavatory that doesn't have sixty million steps to climb? We're a problem, we special students, haven't you heard? Even if we're in the top of our class, we're a problem. Nobody likes special students if special means different."

For several minutes Delores and I drove on in silence. She looked out at the neighborhood she knew so well as if she were seeing it for the first time. Everything, it seemed, caught her attention.

"I think you're going to make it," I said at last. "Fact is, I don't have the slightest doubt."

"I do too, Cottle," she answered smartly. "Fact, I know I will, if enough people in the school give me a chance."

I turned right on Medford Street. The Patterson home was in the middle of the block. "They will," I said.

"We'll see," she replied softly. "We'll see."

III. The Self: Private and Public

The title of this section could refer to practically any period of the life cycle. There is nothing inherently special about adolescence that makes it *the* period when one discovers one's self, much less the private and public components of it. Little children know full well the meaning of their inner world and the public world around them. But there is something special about adolescence in regard to the public and private components of the self, if only because there is such a flourishing—though not the birth—of sexuality at this time, and such a special emphasis placed on behavior according to one's gender. Said differently, if adolescence is a period of psychological, physical, emotional, and cognitive growth, then it is most assuredly a period during which the most primitive human components are married to some of the most complex social and cultural forms of behavior. The result is the continuing emergence of that which we call the self.

We must watch carefully that when speaking about such issues as the development of the self—even the most seemingly private issues—we never forget the historical and cultural facets of these issues. It is hard to believe, we discover, that we are not the first to have thoughts about sex, or the first even, to make solemn promises that we will never divulge these thoughts. Similarly, it is hard to believe that so many patterns of action that, seemingly, we adopt as if we were in total control of them are in fact patterns that the culture has laid down for us, that our elders expect us to reveal, even if they never mention anything to us about these patterns.

Surely adolescence is a period when one discusses a great deal about his or her own sexual drives and needs. It is also a time when one's gender becomes especially salient for assessing oneself and others. Like it or not, insidious or not, cultures lay down styles of so-called characteristically masculine and feminine patterns of behavior and, perhaps, thinking as well. While, sadly, values are placed on these patterns, the fact remains that being a boy, or being a girl, matters greatly to people of this age as they set about to reconstruct and reconceptualize that which we call the self. The stimuli from the outside, the pressures and influences, the bullying even that will affect one's deliberations are intense, so intense that some of us who observe adolescents come to believe they have just about forfeited their hold on a private life. But those who watch the young, who listen to them and are able to recall their own adolescence, know well the private world that excites and haunts, exhilarates and terrifies the young man and young woman. Indeed, the great balance the young must maintain lies between the stimuli and pressures of the public and the private: the social and intimate on the one hand, the selfish individualism on the other. And again, let us keep in mind that the resolutions of these tensions have their effects not only during adolescence, but during the rest of one's life as well. For the reality of the self begins at birth, if not before, and ends only at the instant of death.

7

Psychosexual Development

Men and women play the sexual drama according to a post-freudian script

WILLIAM SIMON & JOHN GAGNON

Erik Erikson has observed that, prior to Sigmund Freud, "sexologists" tended to believe that sexual capacities appeared suddenly with the onset of adolescence. Sexuality followed those external evidences of physiological change that occurred concurrent with or just after puberty. Psycho-analysis changed all that. In Freud's view, libido—the generation of psychosexual energies—should be viewed as a fundamental element of human experience at least beginning with birth, and possibly before that. Libido, therefore, is essential, a biological constant to be coped with at all levels of individual, social, and cultural development. The truth of this received wisdom, that is, that sexual development is a continuous contest between biological drive and cultural restraint should be seriously questioned. Obviously sexuality has roots in biological processes, but so do many other capacities including many that involve physical and mental competence and vigor. There is, however, abundant evidence that the final states which these capacities attain escape the rigid impress of biology. This independence of biological constraint is rarely claimed for the area of sexuality, but we would like to argue that the sexual is precisely that realm where the sociocultural forms most completely dominate biological influences.

It is difficult to get data that might shed much light on the earliest aspects of these questions: Adults are hardly equipped with total recall and the pre-verbal or primitively verbal child does not have ability to report accurately on his own internal state. But it seems obvious—and it is a basic assumption of this paper—that with the beginnings of adolescence many new factors come into play, and to emphasize a straight-line developmental continuity with infant and childhood experiences may be seriously misleading. In particular, it is dangerous to assume that because some childhood behavior appears sexual to adults, it must be sexual. An infant or a child engaged in genital play (even if orgasm is observed) can in no sense be seen as experiencing the complex set of feelings that accompanies adult or even adolescent masturbation.

Therefore, the authors reject the unproven assumption that "powerful" psychosexual drives are fixed biological attributes. More importantly, we reject the even more dubious assumption that sexual capacities or experiences tend to translate immediately into a kind of universal "knowing" or innate wisdom—that sexuality has a magical ability, possessed by no other capacity, that allows biological drives to be expressed directly in psychosocial and social behaviors.

The prevailing image of sexuality—particularly that of the Freudian tradition—is that of an intense, high-pressure drive that forces a person to seek physical sexual gratification, a drive that expresses itself indirectly if it cannot be expressed directly. The available data suggest to us a different picture—one that shows either lower levels of intensity, or, at least, greater variability. We find that there are many social situations or life-roles in which reduced sex activity or even deliberate celibacy is undertaken with little evidence that the libido has shifted in compensation to some other sphere.

A part of the legacy of Freud is that we have all become remarkably adept at discovering "sexual" elements in nonsexual behavior and symbolism. What we suggest instead (following Kenneth Burke's three-decade-old insight) is the reverse—that sexual behavior can often express and serve nonsexual motives.

No Play Without A Script

We see sexual behavior therefore as *scripted* behavior, not the masked expression of a primordial drive. The individual can learn sexual behavior as he or she learns other behavior—through scripts that in this case give the self, other persons, and situations erotic abilities or content. Desire, privacy, opportunity, and propinquity with an attractive member of the opposite sex are not, in themselves, enough; in ordinary circumstances, nothing sexual will occur unless one or both actors organize these elements into an appropriate script. The very concern with foreplay in sex suggests this. From one point of view, foreplay may be defined as merely progressive physical excitement generated by touching naturally erogenous zones. The authors have referred to this conception elsewhere as the "rubbing of two sticks together to make a fire" model. It would seem to be more valuable to see this activity as symbolically invested behavior through which the body is eroticized and through which mute, inarticulate motions and gestures are translated into a sociosexual drama.

A belief in the sociocultural dominance of sexual behavior finds support in cross-cultural research as well as in data restricted to the United States. Psychosexual development is universal—but it takes many forms and tempos. People in different cultures construct their scripts differently; and in our own society, different segments of the population act out different psychosexual dramas—something much less likely to occur if they were all reacting more or less blindly to the same superordinate urge. The most marked differences occur, of course, between male and female patterns of sexual behavior. Obviously, some of this is due to biological differences, including differences in hormonal functions at different ages. But the significance of social scripts predominate; the recent work of Masters and Johnson, for example, clearly points to far greater orgasmic capacities on the part of females than our culture would lead us to suspect. And within each sex—especially among men—different social and economic groups have different patterns.

Let us examine some of these variations, and see if we can decipher the scripts.

Childhood

Whether one agrees with Freud or not, it is obvious that we do not become sexual all at once. There is continuity with the past. Even infant experiences can strongly influence later sexual development.

But continuity is not causality. Childhood experiences (even those that appear sexual) will in all likelihood be influential not because they are intrinsically sexual, but because they can affect a number of developmental trends, *including* the sexual. What situations in infancy—or even early childhood—can be called psychosexual in any sense other than that of creating potentials?

The key term, therefore, must remain potentiation. In infancy, we can locate some of the experiences (or sensations) that will bring about a sense of the body and its capacities for pleasure and discomfort and those that will influence the child's ability to relate to others. It is possible, of course, that through these primitive experiences, ranges are being established—but they are very broad and overlapping. Moreover, if these are profound experiences to the child—and they may well be that—they are not expressions of biological necessity, but of the earliest forms of social learning.

In childhood, after infancy there is what appears to be some real sex play. About half of all adults report that they did engage in some form of sex play as children; and the total who actually did may be half again as many. But, however the adult interprets it later, what did it mean to the child at the time? One suspects that, as in much of childhood role-playing, their sense of the adult meanings attributed to the behavior is fragmentary and ill-formed. Many of the adults recall that, at the time, they were concerned with being found out. But here, too, were they concerned because of the real content of sex play, or because of the mystery and the lure of the forbidden that so often enchant the child? The child may be assimilating outside information about sex for which, at the time, he has no real internal correlate or understanding.

A small number of persons do have sociosexual activity during preadolescence—most of it initiated by adults. But for the majority of these, little apparently follows from it. Without appropriate sexual scripts, the experience remains unassimilated—at least in adult terms. For some, it is clear, a severe reaction may follow from falling "victim" to the sexuality of an adult—but, again, does this reaction come from the sexual act itself or from the social response, the strong reactions of others? (There is some evidence that early sexual activity of this sort is associated with deviant adjustments in later life. But this, too, may not be the result of sexual experiences in themselves so much as the consequence of having fallen out of the social main stream and, therefore, of running greater risks of isolation and alienation.)

In short, relatively few become truly active sexually before adolescence. And when they do (for girls more often than boys), it is seldom immediately related to sexual feelings or gratifications but is a use of sex for nonsexual goals and purposes. The "seductive" Lolita is rare; but she is significant: She illustrates a more general pattern of psychosexual development—a commitment to the social relationships linked to sex before one can really grasp the social meaning of the physical relationships.

Of great importance are the values (or feelings, or images) that children pick up as being related to sex. Although we talk a lot about sexuality, as though trying to exorcise the demon of shame, learning about sex in our society is in large part learning about guilt; and learning how to manage sexuality commonly involves learning how to manage guilt. An important source of guilt in children comes from the imputation to them by adults of sexual appetites or abilities that they may not have, but that they learn, however imperfectly, to pretend they have. The gestural concomitants of sexual modesty are learned early. For instance, when do girls learn to sit or pick up objects with their knees together? When do they learn that the bust must be covered? However, since this behavior is learned unlinked to later adult sexual performances, what children must make of all this is very mysterious.

The learning of sex roles, or sex identities, involves many things that are remote from actual sexual experience, or that become involved with sexuality only after puberty. Masculinity or femininity, their meaning and postures, are rehearsed before adolescence in many nonsexual ways.

A number of scholars have pointed, for instance, to the importance of aggressive, deference, dependency, and dominance behavior in childhood. Jerome Kagan and Howard Moss have found that aggressive behavior in males and dependency in females are relatively stable aspects of development. But what is social role, and what is biology? They found that when aggressive behavior occurred among girls, it tended to appear most often among those from well-educated families that were more tolerant of deviation. Curiously, they also reported that "it was impossible to predict the character of adult sexuality in women from their preadolescent and early adolescent behavior," and that "erotic activity is more anxiety-arousing for females than for males," because "the traditional ego ideal for women dictates inhibition of sexual impulses."

The belief in the importance of early sex-role learning for boys can be viewed in two ways. First, it may directly indicate an early sexual capacity in male children. Or, second, early masculine identification may merely be an appropriate framework within which the sexual impulse (salient with puberty) and the socially available sexual scripts (or accepted patterns of sexual behavior) can most conveniently find expression. Our bias, of course, is toward the second.

But, as Kagan and Moss also noted, the sex role learned by the child does not reliably predict how he will act sexually as an adult. This finding also can be interpreted in the same two alternative ways. Where sexuality is viewed as a biological constant which struggles to express itself, the female sex role learning can be interpreted as the successful repression of sexual impulses. The other interpretation suggests that the difference lies not in learning how to handle a pre-existent sexuality, but in learning how to *be* sexual. Differences between men and women, therefore, will have consequences both for *what* is done sexually, as well as *when*.

Once again, we prefer the latter interpretation, and some recent work that we have done with lesbians supports it. We observed that many of the major elements of their sex lives—the start of actual genital sexual behavior, the onset and frequency of masturbation, the time of entry in sociosexual patterns, the number of partners, and the reports of feelings of sexual deprivation—were for these homosexual women almost identical with those of ordinary women. Since sexuality would seem to be more important for lesbians—after all, they sacrifice much in order to follow their own sexual pathways—this is surprising. We concluded that the primary factor was something both categories of women share—the sex-role learning that occurs before sexuality itself becomes significant.

Social class also appears significant, more for boys than girls. Sex-role learning may vary by class; lower-class boys are supposed to be more aggressive and put much greater emphasis on early heterosexuality. The middle and upper classes tend to tolerate more deviance from traditional attitudes regarding appropriate male sex-role performances.

Given all these circumstances, it seems rather naive to think of sexuality as a constant pressure, with a peculiar necessity all its own. For us, the crucial period of childhood has significance not because of sexual occurrences, but because of nonsexual developments that will provide the names and judgments for later encounters with sexuality.

Adolescence

The actual beginnings and endings of adolescence are vague. Generally, the beginning marks the first time society, as such, acknowledges that the individual has sexual capacity. Training in the postures and rhetoric of the sexual experience is now accelerated. Most important, the adolescent begins to regard those about him (particularly his peers, but also adults) as sexual actors and finds confirmation from others for this view.

For some, as noted, adolescent sexual experience begins before they are considered adolescents. Kinsey reports that a tenth of his female sample and a fifth of his male sample had experienced orgasm through masturbation by age 12. But still, for the vast majority, despite some casual play and exploration that post-Freudians might view as masked sexuality, sexual experience begins with adolescence. Even those who have had prior experience find that it acquires new meanings with adolescence. They now relate such meanings to both larger spheres of social life and greater senses of self. For example, it is not uncommon during the transition between childhood and adolescence for boys and, more rarely, girls to report arousal and orgasm while doing things not manifestly sexual—climbing trees, sliding down bannisters, or other activities that involve genital contact—without defining them as sexual. Often they do not even take it seriously enough to try to explore or repeat what was, in all likelihood, a pleasurable experience.

Adolescent sexual development, therefore, really represents the beginning of adult sexuality. It marks a definite break with what went on before. Not only will future experiences occur in new and more complex contexts, but they will be conceived of as explicitly sexual and thereby begin to complicate social relationships. The need to manage sexuality will rise not only from physical needs and desires, but also from the new implications of personal relationships. Playing, or associating, with members of the opposite sex now acquires different meanings.

At adolescence, changes in the developments of boys and girls diverge and must be considered separately. The one thing both share at this point is a reinforcement of their new status by a dramatic biological event—for girls, menstruation, and for boys, the discovery of the ability to ejaculate. But here they part. For boys, the beginning of a commitment to sexuality is primarily genital; within two years of puberty all but a relatively few have had the experience of orgasm, almost universally brought about by masturbation. The corresponding organizing event for girls is not genitally sexual but social: they have arrived at an age where they will learn role performances linked with proximity to marriage. In contrast to boys, only two-thirds of girls will report ever having masturbated (and, characteristically, the frequency is much less). For women, it is not until the late twenties that the incidence of orgasm from any source reaches that of boys at age 16. In fact, significantly, about half of the females who masturbate do so only after having experienced orgasm in some situation involving others. This contrast points to a basic distinction between the developmental processes for males and females: males move from privatized personal sexuality to sociosexuality; females do the reverse and at a later stage in the life cycle.

The Turned-On Boys

We have worked hard to demonstrate the dominance of social, psychological, and cultural influences over the biological; now, dealing with adolescent boys, we must briefly

reverse course. There is much evidence that the early male sexual impulses—again, initially through masturbation—are linked to physiological changes, to high hormonal inputs during puberty. This produces an organism that, to put it simply, is more easily turned on. Male adolescents report frequent erections, often without apparent stimulation of any kind. Even so, though there is greater biological sensitization and hence masturbation is more likely, the meaning, organization, and continuance of this activity still tends to be subordinate to social and psychological factors.

Masturbation provokes guilt and anxiety among most adolescent boys. This is not likely to change in spite of more "enlightened" rhetoric and discourse on the subject (generally, we have shifted from stark warnings of mental, moral, and physical damage to vague counsels against nonsocial or "inappropriate" behavior). However, it may be that this very guilt and anxiety gives the sexual experience an intensity of feeling that is often attributed to sex itself.

Such guilt and anxiety do not follow simply from social disapproval. Rather, they seem to come from several sources, including the difficulty the boy has in presenting himself as a sexual being to his immediate family, particularly his parents. Another source is the fantasies or plans associated with masturbation—fantasies about doing sexual "things" to others or having others do sexual "things" to oneself; or having to learn and rehearse available but proscribed sexual scripts or patterns of behavior. And, of course, some guilt and anxiety center around the general disapproval of masturbation. After the early period of adolescence, in fact, most youths will not admit to their peers that they did or do it.

Nevertheless, masturbation is for most adolescent boys the major sexual activity, and they engage in it fairly frequently. It is an extremely positive and gratifying experience to them. Such an introduction to sexuality can lead to a capacity for detached sex activity—activity whose only sustaining motive is sexual. This may be the hallmark of male sexuality in our society.

Of the three sources of guilt and anxiety mentioned, the first—how to manage both sexuality and an attachment to family members—probably cuts across class lines. But the others should show remarkable class differences. The second one, how to manage a fairly elaborate and exotic fantasy life during masturbation, should be confined most typically to the higher classes, who are more experienced and adept at dealing with symbols. (It is possible, in fact, that this behavior, which girls rarely engage in, plays a role in the processes by which middle-class boys catch up with girls in measures of achievement and creativity and, by the end of adolescence, move out in front. However, this is only a hypothesis.)

The ability to fantasize during masturbation implies certain broad consequences. One is a tendency to see large parts of the environment in an erotic light, as well as the ability to respond, sexually and perhaps poetically, to many visual and auditory stimuli. We might also expect both a capacity and need for fairly elaborate forms of sexual activity. Further, since masturbatory fantasies generally deal with relationships and acts leading to coitus, they should also reinforce a developing capacity for heterosociality.

The third source of guilt and anxiety—the alleged "unmanliness" of masturbation—should more directly concern

the lower-class male adolescent. ("Manliness" has always been an important value for lower-class males.) In these groups, social life is more often segregated by sex, and there are, generally, fewer rewarding social experiences from other sources. The adolescent therefore moves into heterosexual—if not heterosocial—relationships sooner than

Many males elaborate exotic fantasy lives while masturbating, which may play "a role in the processes by which middle-class boys catch up with girls in measures of achievement and creativity."

his middle-class counterparts. Sexual segregation makes it easier for him than for the middle-class boy to learn that he does not have to love everything he desires, and therefore to come more naturally to casual, if not exploitative, relationships. The second condition—fewer social rewards that his fellows would respect—should lead to an exaggerated concern for proving masculinity by direct displays of physical prowess, aggression, and visible sexual success. And these three, of course, may be mutually reinforcing.

In a sense, the lower-class male is the first to reach "sexual maturity" as defined by the Freudians. That is, he is generally the first to become aggressively heterosexual and exclusively genital. This characteristic, in fact, is a distinguishing difference between lower-class males and those above them socially.

But one consequence is that although their sex lives are almost exclusively heterosexual, they remain homosocial. They have intercourse with females, but the standards and the audience they refer to are those of their male fellows. Middle-class boys shift predominantly to coitus at a significantly later time. They, too, need and tend to have homosocial elements in their sexual lives. But their fantasies, their ability to symbolize, and their social training in a world in which distinctions between masculinity and femininity are less sharply drawn, allow them to withdraw more easily from an all-male world. This difference between social classes obviously has important consequences for stable adult relationships.

One thing common in male experience during adolescence is that while it provides much opportunity for sexual commitment, in one form or another, there is little training in how to handle emotional relations with girls. The imagery and rhetoric of romantic love is all around us; we are immersed in it. But whereas much is undoubtedly absorbed by the adolescent, he is not likely to tie it closely to his sexuality. In fact, such a connection might be inhibiting, as indicated by the survival of the "bad-girl-who-does" and "good-girl-who-doesn't" distinction. This is important to keep in mind as we turn to the female side of the story.

With the Girls

In contrast to males, female sexual development during adolescence is so similar in all classes that it is easy to suspect that it is solely determined by biology. But, while girls do not have the same level of hormonal sensitization to sexuality at puberty as adolescent boys, there is little evidence of a biological or social inhibitor either. The "equipment" for sexual pleasure is clearly present by puberty, but tends not to be used by many females of any class. Masturbation rates are fairly low, and among those who do masturbate, fairly infrequent. Arousal from "sexual" materials or situations happens seldom, and exceedingly few girls report feeling sexually deprived during adolescence.

Basically, girls in our society are not encouraged to be sexual—and may be strongly discouraged from being so. Most of us accept the fact that while "bad boy" can mean many things, "bad girl" almost exclusively implies sexual delinquency. It is both difficult and dangerous for an adolescent girl to become too active sexually. As Joseph Rheingold puts it, where men need only fear sexual failure, women must fear both success and failure.

Does this long period of relative sexual inactivity among girls come from repression of an elemental drive, or merely from a failure to learn how to be sexual? The answers have important implications for their later sexual development. If it is repression, the path to a fuller sexuality must pass through processes of loss of inhibitions, during which the girl unlearns, in varying degrees, attitudes and values that block the expression of natural internal feelings. It also implies that the quest for ways to express directly sexual behavior and feelings that had been expressed nonsexually is secondary and of considerably less significance.

On the other hand, the "learning" answer suggests that women create or invent a capacity for sexual behavior, learning how and when to be aroused and how and when to respond. This approach implies greater flexibility; unlike the repression view, it makes sexuality both more and less than a basic force that may break loose at any time in strange or costly ways. The learning approach also lessens the power of sexuality altogether; all at once, particular kinds of sex activities need no longer be defined as either "healthy" or "sick." Lastly, subjectively, this approach appeals to the authors because it describes female sexuality in terms that seem less like a mere projection of male sexuality.

If sexual activity by adolescent girls assumes less specific forms than with boys, that does not mean that sexual learning and training do not occur. Curiously, though girls are, as a group, far less active sexually than boys, they receive far more training in self-consciously viewing themselves—and in viewing boys—as desirable mates. This is particularly true in recent years. Females begin early in adolescence to define attractiveness, at least partially, in sexual terms. We suspect that the use of sexual attractiveness for nonsexual purposes that marked our preadolescent "seductress" now begins to characterize many girls. Talcott Parsons' description of how the wife "uses" sex to bind the husband to the family, although harsh, may be quite accurate. More generally, in keeping with the childbearing and child-raising function of women, the development of a sexual role seems to involve a need to include in that role more than pleasure.

To round out the picture of the difference between the sexes, girls appear to be well-trained precisely in that area in which boys are poorly trained—that is, a belief in and a capacity for intense, emotionally-charged relationships and the language of romantic love. When girls during this period describe having been aroused sexually, they more often report it as a response to romantic, rather than erotic, words and actions.

In later adolescence, as dates, parties, and other sociosexual activities increase, boys—committed to sexuality and relatively untrained in the language and actions of romantic love—interact with girls, committed to romantic love and relatively untrained in sexuality. Dating and courtship may well be considered processes in which each sex trains the other in what each wants and expects. What data is available suggests that this exchange system does not always work very smoothly. Thus, ironically, it is not uncommon to find that the boy becomes emotionally involved with his partner and therefore lets up on trying to seduce her, at the same time that the girl comes to feel that the boy's affection is genuine and therefore that sexual intimacy is more permissible.

In our recent study of college students, we found that boys typically had intercourse with their first coital partners one to three times, while with girls it was ten or more. Clearly, for the majority of females first intercourse becomes possible only in stable relationships or in those with strong bonds.

"Woman, What Does She Want?"

The male experience does conform to the general Freudian expectation that there is a developmental movement from a predominantly genital sexual commitment to a loving relationship with another person. But this movement is, in effect, reversed for females, with love or affection often a necessary precondition for intercourse. No wonder, therefore, that Freud had great difficulty understanding female sexuality—recall the concluding line in his great essay on women: "Woman, what does she want?" This "error"—the assumption that female sexuality is similar to or a mirror image of that of the male—may come from the fact that so many of those who constructed the theory were men. With Freud, in addition, we must remember the very concept of sexuality essential to most of nineteenth century Europe—it was an elemental beast that had to be curbed.

It has been noted that there are very few class differences in sexuality among females, far fewer than among males. One difference, however, is very relevant to this discussion —the age of first intercourse. This varies inversely with social class—that is, the higher the class, the later the age of first intercourse—a relationship that is also true of first marriage. The correlation between these two ages suggest the necessary social and emotional linkage between courtship and the entrance into sexual activity on the part of women. A second difference, perhaps only indirectly related to social class, has to do with educational achievement: here, a sharp border line seems to separate from all other women those who have or have had graduate or professional work. If sexual success may be measured by the percentage of sex acts that culminate in orgasm, graduate and professional women are the most sexually successful women in the nation.

Why? One possible interpretation derives from the work of Abraham Maslow: Women who get so far in higher education are more likely to be more aggressive, perhaps to have strong needs to dominate; both these characteristics are associated with heightened sexuality. Another, more general interpretation would be that in a society in which girls are expected primarily to become wives and mothers, going on to graduate school represents a kind of deviancy —a failure of, or alienation from, normal female social adjustment. In effect, then, it would be this flawed socialization—not biology—that produced both commitment toward advanced training and toward heightened sexuality.

For both males and females, increasingly greater involvement in the social aspects of sexuality—"socializing" with the opposite sex—may be one factor that marks the end of adolescence. We know little about this transition, especially among noncollege boys and girls; but our present feeling is that sexuality plays an important role in it. First, sociosexuality is important in family formation and also in learning the roles and obligations involved in being an adult. Second, and more fundamental, late adolescence is when a youth is seeking, and experimenting toward finding, his identity—who and what he is and will be; and sociosexual activity is the one aspect of this exploration that we associate particularly with late adolescence.

Young people are particularly vulnerable at this time. This may be partly due to the fact that society has difficulty protecting the adolescent from the consequences of sexual behavior that it pretends he is not engaged in. But, more importantly, it may be because, at all ages, we all have great problems in discussing our sexual feelings and experiences in personal terms. These, in turn, make it extremely difficult to get support from others for an adolescent's experiments toward trying to invent his sexual self. We suspect that success or failure in the discovery or management of sexual identity may have consequences in personal development far beyond merely the sexual sphere —perhaps in confidence and feelings of self-worth, belonging, competence, guilt, force of personality, and so on.

Adulthood

In our society, all but a few ultimately marry. Handling sexual commitments inside marriage makes up the larger part of adult experience. Again, we have too little data for firm findings. The data we do have come largely from studies of broken and troubled marriages, and we do not know to what extent sexual problems in such marriages exceed those of intact marriages. It is possible that, because we have assumed that sex is important in most people's lives, we have exaggerated its importance in holding marriages together. Also, it is quite possible that, once people are married, sexuality declines relatively, becoming less important than other gratifications (such as domesticity or parenthood); or it may be that these other gratifications can minimize the effect of sexual dissatisfaction. Further, it may be possible that individuals learn to get sexual gratification, or an equivalent, from activities that are nonsexual, or only partially sexual.

The sexual desires and commitments of males are the main determinants of the rate of sexual activity in our society. Men are most interested in intercourse in the early years of marriage—woman's interest peaks much later; nonetheless, coital rates decline steadily throughout marriage. This decline derives from many things, only one of which is decline in biological capacity. With many men, it is more difficult to relate sexually to a wife who is pregnant or a mother. Lower-class adult men receive less support and plaudits from their male friends for married sexual performance than they did as single adolescents; and we might also add the lower-class disadvantage of less training in the use of auxiliary or symbolic sexually stimulating materials. For middle-class men, the decline is not as steep, owing perhaps to their greater ability to find stimulation from auxiliary sources, such as literature, movies, music, and romantic or erotic conversation. It should be further noted that for about 30 percent of college-educated men, masturbation continues regularly during marriage, even when the wife is available. An additional (if unknown) proportion do not physically masturbate, but derive additional excitement from the fantasies that accompany intercourse.

But even middle-class sexual activity declines more rapidly than bodily changes can account for. Perhaps the ways males learn to be sexual in our society make it very difficult to keep it up at a high level with the same woman for a long time. However, this may not be vital in maintaining the family, or even in the man's personal sense of well-being, because, as previously suggested, sexual dissatisfaction may become less important as other satisfactions increase. Therefore, it need seldom result in crisis.

About half of all married men and a quarter of all married women will have intercourse outside of marriage at one time or another. For women, infidelity seems to have been on the increase since the turn of the century— at the same time that their rates of orgasm have been increasing. It is possible that the very nature of female sexuality is changing. Work being done now may give us new light on this. For men, there are strong social-class differences—the lower class accounts for most extramarital activity, especially during the early years of marriage. We have observed that it is difficult for a lower-class man to acquire the appreciation of his fellows for married intercourse; extramarital sex, of course, is another matter.

In general, we feel that far from sexual needs affecting other adult concerns, the reverse may be true: adult sexual activity may become that aspect of a person's life most often used to act out other needs. There are some data that suggest this. Men who have trouble handling authority relationships at work more often have dreams about homosexuality; some others, under heavy stress on the job, have been shown to have more frequent episodic homosexual experiences. Such phenomena as the rise of sadomasochistic practices and experiments in group sex may also be tied to nonsexual tensions, the use of sex for nonsexual purposes.

It is only fairly recently in the history of man that he has been able to begin to understand that his own time and place do not embody some eternal principle or necessity, but are only dots on a continuum. It is difficult for many to believe that man can change, and is changing, in important ways. This conservative view is evident even in contemporary behavioral science; and a conception of man as having relatively constant sexual needs has become part of it. In an ever-changing world, it is perhaps comforting to think that man's sexuality does not change very much, and therefore is relatively easily explained. We cannot accept this. Instead, we have attempted to offer a description of sexual development as a variable social invention—an invention that in itself explains little, and requires much continuing explanation.

8

Sex Differences in Adolescent Character Processes

ELIZABETH DOUVAN

University of Michigan

According to psychoanalytic theory, adolescence represents a recapitulation of the Oedipus conflict. The relative calm and control achieved during latency suffer a disruption at this point because of the re-emergence of intense sexual impulses, and the child is plunged once more into Oedipal conflict.

Several critical new features mark this re-enactment of the Oedipal drama, however, and distinguish it from its earlier counterpart. The ego of the puberal child, enriched and articulated during latency, is in a more advantageous position in relation to the impulses than it was in the Oedipal phase. For during its struggle with impulses the ego has gained an ally in the agency of the super-ego. And the fact of genital capability opens for the child new possibilities for resolving conflict. The male child need not simply repress his love for the mother and gain mastery of his ambivalence and fears through identification. He may now seek substitutes for the mother, substitutes who are suitable love objects. Though he may identify with the father in a more or less differentiated fashion, he need not use identification as a global defense against overpowering fear of the rival father, since the father is no longer his rival in the same crucial way.

Part of the outcome of the adolescent struggle is the renegotiation of the ego—super-ego compact: that is, a change in character. As part of the process of remodeling his original identifications, the child establishes a set of values and controls which are more internal and personal than earlier ones and which reflect his new reality situation as an adult.

This is the developmental task and context facing the adolescent boy. But what of the task confronting the girl at this period? With what resources and what history does she enter adolescence? Analytic theory, though wanting in specificity, gives us some broad clues about this development, its unique characteristics, and the ways in which it differs from development in the male child.

First, we expect that super-ego is less developed in women (and in adolescent girls). Since the little girl has no decisive motive force comparable to the boy's castration anxiety, she does not turn peremptorily against her own instinctual wishes nor form the same critical and definite identification with the like-sexed parent. Her motives for internalizing the wishes of important adults are fear of loss of love and a sense of shame. According to Deutsch (1), an important step in the socialization of girls occurs when the father enters an agreement with the little girl whereby he exchanges a promise of love for her forfeiture of any direct expression of aggressive impulses.

A significant difference may be noted at this point: the boy who has accomplished the Oedipal resolution now has an *internal* representative of the parents which he must placate and which serves as a source of reinforcement for his acts. The little girl, on the other hand, continues to look

to the parents as the source of reward and punishment since her identifications are only partial and primitive.

At adolescence this difference has a critical significance: the boy enters the adolescent contest with an ego that is reinforced by a strong ally, a vigorous super-ego. And in reworking the relation between the ego and the impulses, there is an internal criterion by which the boy judges the new arrangement. His new values and controls are an individual accomplishment and are judged, at least in part, by individual standards. The girl meets the rearoused instincts of adolescence with an ego only poorly supported by partial identifications and introjects. She still needs to rely heavily on externally imposed standards to help in her struggle with impulses.

With this formulation as a starting point, we made a number of predictions about sex differences in character development and looked at data from two national sample surveys of boys and girls in the 14 to 16 year age group for tests of our predictions.[2] Specifically, we explored the following conceptions:

---

[2] The studies were conducted at the Survey Research Center of the University of Michigan. Respondents were selected in a multistage probability sampling design, and represent youngsters of the appropriate age in school. Each subject was interviewed at school by a member of the Center's Field Staff; interviews followed a fixed schedule and lasted from one to four hours. For details about the studies, and copies of the complete questionnaire, readers may refer to the basic reports (2, 3).

1. Adolescent girls will show less concern with values and with developing behavior controls than will boys; that is, character will show rapid development in boys during adolescence, while girls will be less preoccupied with establishing personal, individual standards and values.

2. Personal integration around moral values, though crucial in the adjustment of adolescent boys, will not predict adjustment in girls. Rather, sensitivity and skill in interpersonal relationships will be critical integrative variables in adolescent girls and will predict their personal adjustment.

Our studies yield substantial support for the first speculation. Girls are consciously less concerned about developing independent controls than boys are. They are more likely to show an unquestioned identification with, and acceptance of, parental regulation. They less often distinguish parents' standards from their own, and they do not view the parents' rules as external or inhibiting as often as boys do. Boys more often tell us they worry about controls—particularly controls on aggression; when we ask them what they would like to change about themselves, the issue of controls again emerges as an important source of concern. More important, perhaps, as evidence of their greater involvement in building controls, we find that boys tend to conceive parental rules as distinctly external, and, to some extent, opposed to their own interests. So when we ask why parents make rules, boys underscore the need to control children (e.g., to keep them out of trouble). Girls reveal an identification with the parents when they say that parents make rules to teach their children how to behave, to give them standards to live by, to let children know what is expected of them. Boys think of rules as a means of restricting areas of negative behavior, while girls more often see them as a means of directing and channeling energy.

In answer to all of our questions about parental rules, boys repeatedly reveal greater differentiation between their own and their parents' standards.[3]

One of the most impressive indications of the difference between boys and girls in their stance toward authority comes from a series of projective picture-story questions. At one point in this series a boy or girl is shown with his parents, and the parents are setting a limit for the child. We asked respondents to tell what the child would say. A quarter of the boys questioned the parental restriction—not with hostility or any sign of real conflict, but with a freedom that implies a right to question—while only 4 per cent of the girls in the same age group responded in this way. On the other hand, a third of the girls reassured the parents with phrases like "don't worry," or "you know I'll behave, I'll act like a lady"; the boys almost never gave answers comparable to these.

Both of these response types reveal a respect for one's own opinions. They both indicate autonomy, but very different attitudes toward parental rules: the boy openly opposes; the girl not only acquiesces to, but reinforces the parents' regulation.

Girls are more authority reliant than boys in their attitudes toward adults other than their parents. And we find lower correlations among internalization items for girls, indicating less coherence in internalization for them than for boys.

These are examples of differences that support the claim that boys are actively struggling with the issue of controls, that they are moving in a process of thrust and counterthrust toward the construction of personal, individuated control systems more conscious and rational than previous

---

[3] In the full series, we asked respondents why parents make rules, what would happen if they didn't, when a boy might break a rule, whether the respondent himself had ever broken a rule, and what kind of rule he would never break. For exact phrasing and order of questions, the reader may refer to the basic study reports (2, 3).

global identifications; and that girls, on the other hand, are relatively uninvolved in this struggle and maintain a compliant-dependent relationship with their parents.

The second hypothesis suggested at the beginning of this paper deals with the significance of progress in internalization for the personal integration and adjustment of boys and girls. Having found that girls are less urgently struggling for independent character, we wonder what this means about their general ego development and integration. Are girls relatively undeveloped in these areas as well as in independence of character?

The analysis we have done to date indicates that the second alternative is at least a viable hypothesis. In an analysis of extreme groups, we find that the well-internalized boy is characterized by active achievement strivings, independence of judgment, a high level of energy for use in work and play, and self-confidence combined with realistic self-criticism. He is well developed in the more subtle ego qualities of organization of thought and time-binding. The boy who has not achieved internal, personal controls and who responds only to external authority is poorly integrated, demoralized, and deficient in all areas of advanced ego functioning (Table 1).

TABLE 1

EXTREME GROUPS ON AN INTERNALIZATION INDEX COMPARED ON MEASURES OF OTHER EGO VARIABLES (BOY SAMPLE)

Selected Measures of Ego Variables	Internalization Index		Chi Square	P Level
	High	Low		
I. ACHIEVEMENT				
a. prefer success to security	.64	.47	8.140	<.01
b. choose job aspiration on achievement criteria	.78	.62	9.331	<.01
c. choose job aspiration because of ease of acquiring job, minimum demands	.01	.13	13.758	<.001
d. upward mobile aspirations	.70	.53	7.158	<.01
II. ENERGY LEVEL				
a. high on index of leisure engagements	.49	.40	2.729	<.10>.05
b. belong to some organized group	.77	.65	5.50	<.05
c. hold jobs	.63	.42	12.576	<.01
d. date	.66	.52	6.007	<.05
III. AUTONOMY				
a. rely on own judgment in issues of taste and behavior	.40	.20	12.786	<.01
b. have some disagreements with parents	.67	.49	12.804	<.01
c. choose adult ideal outside family	.23	.14	4.547	<.05
d. have no adult ideal	.07	.16	8.621	<.01
e. authority reliant in relation to adult leaders	.23	.54	28.544	<.001
IV. SELF-CONFIDENCE				
a. high on interviewer rating of confidence	.43	.22	11.213	<.01
b. low on interviewer rating of confidence	.16	.35	14.205	<.001
c. high on rating for organization of ideas	.65	.43	9.861	<.01
d. low on rating for organization of ideas	.08	.28	19.006	<.001

TABLE 1 (*Continued*)

Selected Measures of Ego Variables	Internalization Index		Chi Square	P Level
	High	Low		
V. SELF-CRITICISM				
a. wish for changes that can be effected by individual effort	.36	.12	16.22	< .001
b. wish for changes that cannot be effected by individual effort	.14	.30	12.613	< .01
c. no self-change desired	.27	.42	7.498	< .05
VI. TIME PERSPECTIVE				
a. extended	.44	.28	7.604	< .05
b. restricted	.14	.33	15.721	< .01

Note.—The Internalization Index is based on responses to three questions: (a) What would happen if parents didn't make rules? (b) When might a boy (girl) break a rule? (c) one of the picture-story items: What does the boy (girl) do (when pressed by peers to ignore a promise to parents)? External responses are those which see children obeying only out of fear, breaking rules when they think they will not be caught, relying exclusively on externally imposed guides. Internal responses, in contrast, reveal a sense of obligation or trust about promises given, consider rules unbreakable except in emergencies or when they are for some other reason less critical than other circumstances, and think that children would rely on their own judgment were parental authority no longer available. Subjects who gave internal responses to two or three questions are included in the High category; those who gave two or more external responses are grouped in the Low Internalization category.

Again, we ask, what does girls' relatively common reliance on external controls mean about their ego integration? We find when we analyze extreme groups of girls that internalization of individual controls is no guarantee of ego development, and that girls who are dependent on external controls do not show the disintegration and demoralization that mark the noninternalized boy. In short, internalization of independent standards is not an efficient predictor of ego organization or ego strength in girls.

There are several possible explanations for this absence of significant association in girls. High internalization in girls may not reflect independence of standards. Deutsch (1) has observed girls' greater capacity for intense identification, compared to boys; and we may have in the girls' apparently well-internalized controls a product of fusion with parental standards rather than a differentiated and independent character. Moreover, dependence on external standards is the norm for girls in adolescence. Parents are permitted and encouraged to maintain close supervision of the growing girl's actions. Under these circumstances, compliance with external authority is less likely to reflect personal pathology or a pathological family structure.

To this point, then, we have seen that girls are less absorbed with the issue of controls, and that the successful internalization of controls is less crucial for their integration at this age than it is for boys.

We speculated that the critical integrating variable for the girl is her progress in developing interpersonal skill and sensitivity. A striking continuity in feminine psychology lies in the means of meeting developmental crises. In childhood, adolescence, and adulthood the female's central motive is a desire for love, and her means of handling crises is to appeal for support and love from important persons in her environment. This contrasts with the greater variety of methods—of mastery and withdrawal— that the male uses in meeting developmental stresses. The girl's skill in pleading her cause with others, in attracting and holding affection, is more critical to her successful adaptation.

We designed a test of the importance of interpersonal development in boys and girls. Again, taking extreme groups, those who reveal relatively mature attitudes and skills in the area of friendship and those who are impressively immature, we compared performance in other areas of ego development. With girls we found clear relationships between interpersonal development and the following ego variables: energy level, self-confidence, time-perspective and organization of ideas, and positive feminine identification (Table 2).

Interpersonal skill in boys is not significantly related to activity level, time-binding, self-confidence, or self-acceptance. In short, it does not assert the same key influence in the ego integration of boys that it does in feminine development.

What significance do these findings have? What are the sources of the differences we have observed, and what do they mean about the later settlement of character issues in the two sexes in adulthood?

Differences in character processes in boys and girls probably reflect both basic constitutional and developmental differences between the sexes and also variation in the culture's statement of character crises for boys and girls.

Perhaps the most crucial factor leading to boys' precocity in moral development is the more intense and imperious nature of the impulses they must handle. The sexual impulses aroused in the boy at puberty are specific and demanding and push to the forefront the need for personal controls which accommodate his sexual needs. Acceptance of parental standards or maintenance of the early identification-based control would require denial of sexual impulses, and this is simply not possible for the boy after puberty.

TABLE 2

EXTREME GROUPS ON AN INTERPERSONAL DEVELOPMENT INDEX COMPARED ON
MEASURES OF OTHER EGO VARIABLES (GIRL SAMPLE)

Selected Measures of Ego Variables	Interpersonal Development Index			
	High	Low	Chi Square	P Level
I. ENERGY LEVEL				
a. high on index of leisure engagements	.41	.27	9.335	< .01
b. belong to some organized group	.97	.75	37.012	< .001
c. hold jobs	.60	.51	2.444	< .10 > .05
d. date	.81	.66	10.98	< .01
II. SELF-CONFIDENCE				
a. high on interviewer rating of confidence	.47	.32	9.071	< .01
b. low on interviewer rating of confidence	.17	.30	11.522	< .01
c. high on interviewer rating for poise	.38	.14	29.613	< .001
d. low on interviewer rating for poise	.14	.29	15.072	< .001
III. TIME PERSPECTIVE				
a. extended	.50	.37	8.621	< .01
b. restricted	.04	.13	12.714	< .01
IV. ORGANIZATION OF IDEAS				
a. high on interviewer rating	.51	.34	12.401	< .01
b. low on interviewer rating	.14	.28	13.168	< .001
V. FEMININE IDENTIFICATION				
a. high on index of traditional feminine orientation	.37	.11	37.93	< .001
b. choose own mother as an ideal	.48	.30	14.14	< .001

Note.—The Interpersonal Development Index is based on responses to three questions: (a) Can a friend ever be as close as a family member? (b) What should a friend be or be like? (c) What makes a girl (boy) popular with other girls (boys)? Answers counted highly developed are those that stress intimacy, mutuality, and appreciation of individuality and individual differences. Our High category consists of subjects who gave such answers to all three questions. The Low group comprises youngsters who gave no such answers to any of the three critical items.

The girl's impulses, on the other hand, are both more ambiguous and more subject to primitive repressive defenses. She has abandoned aggressive impulses at an earlier phase of development and may continue to deny them. Her sexual impulses are more diffuse than the boy's and can also more readily submit to the control of parents and to the denial this submission may imply.

The ambiguity of female sexual impulses permits adherence to earlier forms of control and also makes this a comfortable course since their diffusion and mystery implies a greater danger of overwhelming the incompletely formed ego at adolescence. Freud noted the wave of repression that occurs in females at puberty and contrasted it to the psychic situation of the boy (5).

Additional factors leading to postponement of character issues in girls are their greater general passivity and their more common tendency toward intensive identifications in adolescence and toward fantasy gratification of impulses.

I would like to mention one final point which, I think, has critical implications for character development in girls. Building independent standards and controls (i.e., settling an independent character) is part of the broader crisis of defining personal identity. In our culture there is not nearly as much pressure on girls as on boys to meet the identity challenge during the adolescent years. In fact, there is a real pressure on the girl *not* to make any clear settlement in her identity until considerably later. We are all familiar with the neurotic woman who, even in adulthood, staunchly resists any commitment that might lead to self-definition and investment in a personal identity, for fear of restricting the range of men for whom she is a potential marriage choice. This pattern, it seems, reflects forces that are felt more or less by most girls in our culture. They are to remain fluid and malleable in personal identity in order to adapt to the needs of the men they marry. Too clear a self-definition during adolescence may be maladaptive. But when broader identity issues are postponed, the issues that might lead to differentiation of standards and values are also postponed. I do not, then, feel with Pope that most women have no character at all. I do think that in all likelihood feminine character develops later than masculine character, and that adolescence—the period we ordinarily consider *par excellence* the time for consolidation of character—is a more dramatic time for boys than for girls.

REFERENCES

1. Deutsch, Helene. *The psychology of women.* New York: Grune and Stratton, 1944. 2 vols.
2. Douvan, Elizabeth, and Kaye, Carol. *Adolescent girls.* Ann Arbor, Mich.: Survey Research Center, University of Michigan, 1956.
3. Douvan, Elizabeth, and Withey, S. B. *A study of adolescent boys.* Ann Arbor, Mich.: Survey Research Center, University of Michigan, 1955.
4. Fenichel, O. The pregenital antecedents of the Oedipus complex. *Int. J. Psychoanal.,* 1931, **12,** 141-166.
5. Freud, S. Female sexuality. *Int. J. Psychoanal.,* 1932, **13,** 281-297.

9

THE TERROR OF LIFE–A LATENT ADOLESCENT NIGHTMARE

Stephen J. Golburgh, Ed.D. and Charles B. Rotman, Ed.D.

INTRODUCTION

In certain male patients who are in their late teens and early twenties, we have noted a common group of symptoms which have taken on the composition of a clinical latent adolescent syndrome that we have called the "Terror of Life." The symptoms specifically involve this group of patients' fear of aging as characterized by: (a) their painful and apprehensive perception that the normal physical changes that take place as one gets older is in reality the deterioration of the body, (b) the terror that they feel because of the rapid passage of time, and (c) their absolute panic over the realization of eventual death.

When listening to these patients one hears them pleading with the therapist to slow up the passage of time, to protect them from growing older, and above all to do something to assure them that they will never die. These patients are not psychotic and their suffering is very real, deep and painful. They are generally quite anxious and depressed, usually not active in living a full life, have few meaningful social relationships, have confused sexual lives, are extremely angry, quite shy, fearful, lonely and continually anticipate disaster. They are quite passive, remarkably dependent upon their therapist and although they may improve very significantly in psychotherapy, their progress is very slow, and working out their problems can take a great many years. Let us make clear that in this paper it is not our intention to discuss the dynamics or treatment of these patients directly but merely to delineate and illustrate the syndrome.

Physical Concerns

This group of patients manifest a great variety of physical symptoms which, when medically evaluated, have no organic basis. These patients are terrified of the most minor physical ailment. They see the physician quite frequently for routine examinations, spend long and frightening periods of time studying their bodies and the normal changes that take place in it with age, take unneeded vitamins and frequently become involved in various food fads. They feel upset quite frequently and often overuse both tranquilizers and energizers. Yet when it comes to really important issues such as giving up cigarette smoking and getting sufficient exercise they find themselves unable to behave in their own best interests and in a realistic manner.

These are the patients who sit in terror waiting for a "heart attack." Frequently, while waiting, they develop blatant anxiety attacks which assures them that they in fact are having a "heart attack." Such patients in their early twenties have electrocardiograms two or three times a year. Some buy stethescopes and blood pressure cuffs so that they can check their own blood pressure "at regular intervals" (like daily). Often they take their temperature (daily) and sometimes more frequently. They avoid hospitals and worry endlessly as to what would happen if they needed to have an appendix removed (they feel that they will be put to sleep and never wake up). Often they request local anesthesia should they actually require an appendectomy or a herniotomy. Also, they usually do very well while going through the actual surgery and the period of recovery. The episode they dreaded for so long takes place, they live through it superbly and forget it rapidly. Of course, they always tell others about their "operation."

They may be concerned with their body over satisfactory defecation, urination, amount of sweating, dandruff and their hair being combed just right. Shaving is also a major problem to these patients. It frequently takes them a full hour to shave each morning. While shaving, they examine each blemish and pore on their faces. They feel that they notice day-to-day changes which indicate the deterioration of their bodies. They often will ask the therapist, "Do I look older than I did last month or last year?" and wait in terror for his response or lack of response. A gray hair or the loss of a few hairs produces absolute panic. One such patient when told at age 22 by his pediatrician that he should, in the future, consult an internist, called his therapist in great turmoil because it meant to him, on the surface, that he was old and had to see an old person's doctor.

Time Considerations

Patients with this syndrome, although some aspects appear in many disorders, often make such comments to the therapist as, "Dr., it was just Wednesday and now it's Wednesday again and I don't know what happened in between. The time just disappeared." A patient of five years continued for several years to relate that he had been in therapy for about a year and that he was allowing the therapist two more years to "cure" him."

Time is a major problem to these patients, as is sleep. They generally feel that must have 8, 9, or 10 hours sleep each night or they will be totally unable to function the next day. They worry so about falling asleep that they are, of course, unable to and thus feel that some physical calamity will overtake them the next day. They feel they must guard their bodies so carefully, and at all times, that they have little time to do much else. These are the patients who often brush their teeth after every single meal, beverage, or snack.

They are afraid to sleep at night for fear they won't wake up. Sometimes they keep the radio on while in bed because they find it reassuring. Almost always when they were children, they kept a light on while sleeping. One patient, when he woke up in the middle of the night, had to pinch himself in order to feel the pain which reassured him that he was alive.

These patients suffer tremendously from constant anticipated anxiety. They are never comfortable because they are worried about what will happen in two hours, or the next day or week. Yet, in reality, they generally manage to deal adequately, though uncomfortably, with the events that terrify them. It is also interesting to point out that in an actual crisis situation they almost inevitably deal with it in a remarkably mature and realistic fashion.

Growing Older

While generally quite likeable, they feel that they are very special and that life owes them more than it owes others. They feel that growing older is something that happens to others and next to impossible that it should happen to them. Death is for others and they cannot accept that they too will die. Becoming old, developing gray hair, having dental problems should not, they believe, be a part of their experience. One patient recently told of his shock at being informed by his dentist that, "As we become older and physically age we need to pay more attention to proper gum stimulation and massage in order to minimize complicated dental procedures and to keep our own teeth."

These patients tend to idolize youth. If the person is young he is good—"he is beautiful" regardless of his actual physical characteristics. One patient recently related that he wanted to buy the house he had lived in as a child and move in there with his family. Very often, to fight off the fear of aging and death, these patients establish themselves in occupations where they work almost exclusively with adolescents or young adults. One generally finds that their friends are either quite a few years younger than they are or are considerably older. The friends appear either as father or son figures. They frequently enjoy nurturing the son figures in the manner they wished they had been nurtured by their own parents. Sometimes they have a friend of their own age but the relationship may be a pathological one. Still, those patients cannot terminate the relationships. They are frightened of any change in their style of existing because it would destroy them. The motto they live by is "the devil you know is safer than the devil you don't know." What they fail to realize is that the devil you don't know might turn out not to be a devil at all.

The Therapist

Patients who suffer from this syndrome invariably attach themselves to older male figures whose presence or availability makes living more bearable for them. Any separation from one of these figures often results in a severe depressive reaction and a feeling that they may lose control, become psychotic and require hospitalization. We have never seen this happen. They tell the therapist again and again that they cannot continue to function—yet they do; that they are falling apart—which they don't; that they fear suicide—which they don't commit. They complain endlessly yet they are aware that merely complaining accomplishes nothing for them.

Such patients will readily accept the "old" therapist if he does not behave toward them in the same way their parents did. If the therapist's ideas are young and creative and if he pays careful attention to what lies beneath what the patients say, these patients can work out their problems with him. Although these patients idolize youth, they still realize the importance of having lived in the world a while. This is why we feel that these patients end up in the office of the "old" therapist.

Such patients are astounded by the therapist's lack of concern with aging and eventual death. They often feel the therapist is being kind to them by occasionally saying, "Well, 37 or 50 isn't that old." They fear that the therapist will become upset if they explore what to *them* is dangerous ground and that *must* be dangerous ground for the therapist too. They will ask the therapist what they should do if he dies. Will he leave a list of names for them? They tell the therapist they would never continue treatment with someone else were he to die, yet they can, and so far as we know, usually do.

Environment

These patients are generally very upset by weather phenomena. Summer is too hot; winter is too cold. In the summer they worry because they feel it is passing rapidly and it will soon be stormy and cold. Generally, they do a bit better in the spring and summer but they are terribly upset during fall in anticipation of winter. The best period seems to be the very end of winter. They can then look forward to both spring and summer. Generally they're more comfortable when there are longer periods of daylight and frequently become quite frightened when it becomes dark early. As summer passes, they watch apprehensively as day by day it becomes darker earlier.

Almost always they claim that they are most comfortable in their own bedrooms. There, they feel, is true security. They can lie down on the bed and rest, thus restoring what they feel to be the loss of strength of earlier effort. They are restoring their bodies "to health" by resting. When they don't have to go to work they will frequently sleep until 2 or 3 in the afternoon feeling that they are regaining strength and protecting themselves from disease and conscious living. It is little wonder they do not know where the times goes. They rest or sleep it away. It is little wonder they fear death; they are afraid of living life. "What is the point of it all, they say. I am going to die anyway." So preoccupied with dying, they have little time for living. They either read the obituary columns regularly or assiduously avoid noticing that such a listing does appear in the newspaper.

Conclusion

Those who experience the terror of life are very much involved with the fear of physical aging (deterioration), the rapid passage of time and the eventual certainty of death—as evidenced in certain young adult male patients. These concerns are seen individually in other psychoneurotic disorders, however, when they manifest themselves together they make the life situation of the subject most difficult, uncomfortable and frightening.

Stephen J. Golburgh, Ed.D.
Senior Staff Psychologist
Boston VA Hospital
Boston, Massachusetts

Clinical Assistant Professor of Psychiatry
Tufts University School of Medicine
Boston, Massachusetts

Charles B. Rotman, Ed.D.
Associate Professor of Psychology
Babson College
Wellesley, Massachusetts

Counseling Psychologist
Bedford VA Hospital
Bedford, Massachusetts

Adolescent Appearance And Self Concept

10

Kathleen E. Musa, Ph.D. and Mary Ellen Roach, Ph.D.

Early social structure theorists such as George Herbert Mead, Charles Cooley, and John Dewey are credited with setting the stage for research concerned with self concept. These theorists developed a type of theoretical framework within which man is perceived as a social being who sees himself and the world through others' eyes. Thus each human being forms an evaluation of himself and a personal value system using society as his yardstick and reference point.

Employing the basic theoretical framework of self concept theory, investigators at the University of Wisconsin hypothesized that an adolescent's total self concept, or constellation of self-feelings, would be related to his self concept of personal appearance. In hypothesizing thus, the researchers investigated a relationship between appearance and self concept that has had theoretical support (1, 2, 3, 4, 5), but, except for a study by Secord and Jourard (6), little research support.

A type of instrument incorporating the "social reference point" aspect of self concept was developed and tested to measure

self-evaluation of personal appearance. In this measure each subject's evaluation of his own appearance was scored in relation to his evaluation of his peers' appearance.

Hypotheses

The main null hypothesis was:
1. Self-evaluation of personal appearance is not related to total self concept.

Previous research has investigated relationships between total self concept and the variables of personal adjustment (7, 8, 9), academic achievement (10, 8), and socioeconomic class (11, 12). In the present study these variables were investigated in relation to one aspect of total self concept, self-evaluation of personal appearance, by testing the following null hypotheses:

2. Self-evaluation of personal appearance is not related to personal adjustment.
3. Self-evaluation of personal appearance is not related to grade point average.
4. Self-evaluation of personal appearance is not related to socioeconomic class.

The Subjects

High school juniors, 119 boys and 83 girls attending school in a middle-sized midwestern industrial city, constituted the sample for the study. According to the measure utilized in determining socioeconomic class, 78 percent of the major wage-earners in the subjects' families were of lower-middle class or lower, with the largest proportion rated as upper-lower class.

Measuring Self-Evaluation of Personal Appearance

Self-evaluation of personal appearance was defined as the subject's rating of his own appearance as compared to his rating of his peers' appearance. Thus the factor of social comparison was inherent in the measurement. The instrument used to measure how the subject compared his own appearance to that of his peers was a ladder device based upon one developed by Cantril (13)* for use in a cross-cultural study of values. Subjects were told on a questionnaire that the ladder, shown in Figure 1, represented all the ways that students their age dress. The top "step" of the ladder, number ten, was said to represent "ideal appearance." The bottom step, number one, was said to represent the least desirable appearance for students. "Ideal appearance" was purposely left undefined, so that the standard used in the comparison would be composed of each subject's personal conception of "ideal appearance." The subjects were asked to indicate which step represented most of the students in their class, and which step they themselves would probably stand on. Subjects were then scored according to whether they rated their appearance as less desirable, equally desirable, or more desirable than that of their peers.

*The ladder as conceived by Cantril represents "the spectrum of values a person is occupied or concerned with and by means of which he evaluates his own life."

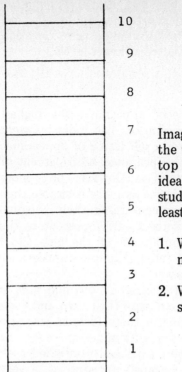

Imagine that this ladder represents all of the ways that students your age dress. The top step represents what you think of as an ideal, most desirable appearance for students. The bottom step represents the least desirable appearance for students.

1. Which step do you think represents most of the students in your class?

2. Which step do you think you probably stand on?

Other Measures

The Personal Adjustment half of the California Test of Personality (14), a paper and pencil instrument widely used in psychological testing, was administered to measure *Personal Adjustment*. The test is designed to measure evidence of six components of adjustment: self reliance, sense of personal worth, sense of personal freedom, feelings of belonging, withdrawing tendencies, and nervous symptoms. The "sense of personal worth" component of the California Test of Personality was used in the study as the measure of *Total Self Concept*. Information for *Grade Point Average* was obtained from school records. The McGuire-White Index of Social Status (15) was used to determine *Socioeconomic Class*.* *Satisfaction with Appearance* was indicated by the subject's response to the question, "If you could change anything you wanted to about your appearance, what would you like to do?" The subject could respond in one of two ways: (a) by writing down his desired changes on lines provided on the questionnaire, or (b) by check-marking the response, "Would change nothing."

Obtaining and Analyzing the Data

Data on socioeconomic class, self-evaluation of personal appearance, and satisfaction with appearance were obtained by use of a questionnaire. The questionnaire and California Test of Personality were administered on the same day. All juniors present the day data were gathered participated. Information was coded on coding sheets and then punched on computer cards.

---

*Three dimensions of socioeconomic class were measured for the main wage-earner in the subject's family: occupation, source of income, and level of education.

Cross-tabulations between the research variables were made, and the chi-square test was applied to determine the significance of relationships. A significance level of .05 was set as basis for rejection of the null hypotheses, but trends were noted at lower levels.

Findings

No subject gave his own or his peers' appearance the highest rating, that is, a rating of "Ideal" appearance. The most frequent response among both boys and girls was a self-rating of appearance equal to that of the rating given peers' appearance; 41.5 percent of the boys and 43.4 percent of the girls did so. However, boys more often than girls rated their own appearance as more desirable than their peers'. Among the boys, 34.7 percent rated their personal appearance as more desirable, as compared to 27.7 percent of the girls. By the same token, a larger proportion of the girls (28.9 percent) than the boys (23.7 percent) rated their own appearance lower than they rated their peers' appearance.

These findings suggested a difference between boys and girls in feelings of social adequacy when they compare their own and their peers' appearance. A boy-girl difference in these feelings was also suggested in findings relating to satisfaction with appearance. Among the boys a substantial 43.7 percent were sufficiently satisfied with their appearance that they desired no change. In contrast, a very small proportion of the girls (12.2 percent) had no desire to change anything about their appearance. Girls who desired appearance changes most often wanted changes relating to hair, weight, clothes, or figure, in that order. Boys who desired change most often referred to clothes, facial characteristics, hair, or weight in that order.

The null hypothesis of "no relationship between self-evaluation of personal appearance and total self concept" could not be rejected for either sex. Visual examination of the data revealed no trends.

Testing of the relationship between self-evaluation of personal appearance and personal adjustment did, however, result in rejection of the null hypothesis for girls. As can be seen from Table 1, 47.2 percent of the girls who rated their appearance as equal to their peers' fell into the high range of personal adjustment. And 62.5 percent of the girls who rated their appearance as less-desirable than peers' were found to be in the low range of adjustment. These findings suggest that for the girls rating one's appearance as equal to peers' appearance was associated with the most favorable adjustment. And rating one's personal appearance as less-desirable than the other girls' was associated with low adjustment. The relationship between self-evaluation of personal appearance and personal adjustment was not significant for the boys. The only discernible trend found for boys was a tendency for rating one's own appearance as less-desirable than peers' to be associated with low personal adjustment.

The null hypothesis of "no relationship between self-evaluation of personal appearance and grade point average" was not rejected for either boys or girls. However, a trend toward a direct relationship was apparent for boys (see Table 2). Boys with the highest self-evaluation of appearance were the most likely to have high grades, and boys with low self-evaluations of personal appearance were most likely to have low grades.

Testing the hypothesis concerning self-evaluation of personal appearance and socioeconomic class also revealed trends in the data for boys: first, a tendency for upper socioeconomic class boys to perceive their own appearance at least equally as desirable as their peers', and second, the tendency for perceiving one's appearance as less-desirable than peers' to increase as social standing decreases. In the case of the latter tendency, Table 3 shows that 9.7 percent of upper class, 28.6 percent of middle class, and 32.5 percent of lower class boys perceived their appearance as less-desirable than their peers'. This trend is consistent with Brogger's findings in an earlier study (16). Brogger also found a significant relationship between girls' self-evaluations of personal appearance and socioeconomic class. This is in contrast to findings of the present study, where no significant relationship or trend was discovered for girls.

Table 1

Self-Evaluation of Personal Appearance
As Related to Personal Adjustment for
Girls

	Rated Self Above Peers	Rated Self Same as Peers	Rated Self Below Peers
Low Range of Personal Adjustment	39.1 (9)	22.2 (8)	62.5 (15)
Middle Range of Personal Adjustment	30.4 (7)	30.6 (11)	16.7 (4)
High Range of Personal Adjustment	30.4 (7)	47.2 (17)	20.8 (5)
TOTALS	100.0% (23)	100.0% (36)	100.0% (34)
(N=83)	$x^2 = 10.35$	.02 $<$ p $<$ .05	

Table 2

Self-Evaluation of Personal Appearance
As Related to Grade Point Average for
Boys

	Rated Self Above Peers	Rated Self Same as Peers	Rated Self Below Peers
G.P.A. Below 2.00	29.3 (12)	35.4 (17)	42.9 (12)
G.P.A. Between 2.00 and 3.00	41.5 (17)	45.8 (22)	53.6 (15)
G.P.A. 3.00 and Above	29.3 (12)	18.8 (9)	3.6 (1)
TOTALS	100.0% (41)	100.0% (48)	100.0% (23)
(N = 117)	$x^2 = 7.25$	.10 $<$ p $<$ .20	

Table 3

Self-Evaluation of Appearance As Related
to Socio-Economic Class for Boys

	Upper Socio-Economic Class	Middle Socio-Economic Class	Lower Socio-Economic Class
Rated Self Above Peers	35.5 (11)	35.7 (15)	27.5 (11)
Rated Self Same as Peers	54.8 (17)	35.7 (15)	40.0 (16)
Rated Self Below Peers	9.7 (3)	28.6 (12)	32.5 (13)
TOTALS	100.0% (31)	100.0% (42)	100.0% (40)
(N = 113)	$x^2 = 6.17$	.10 $<$ p $<$ .20	

Summary and Conclusions

Although the relationship between girls' self-evaluation of personal appearance and personal adjustment was the only statistically significant finding, the additional evidence of several trends suggests the need for further investigation in the area of teen-age appearance and self concept. Results also indicate that the instrument measuring self-evaluation of personal appearance is a useful data-gathering device in studying the appearance aspect of self concept.

Desire to change appearance was widespread among the girls; this was not the case for boys. Sex differences were also revealed in two other findings: (a) the relationship between self-evaluation of personal appearance and personal adjustment was significant for girls; the relationship did not approach significance for boys; and (b) girls more often than boys rated their appearance as less-desirable than peers', and girls less often than boys rated their appearance as more desirable than peers'.

These sex differences could be interpreted as reflections of differential societal emphases placed upon males' and females' appearance in America. Morrison and Holden (17) illuminate this sex difference by suggesting that important respect-and-approval rewards accruing to American females in relation to their appearance act as substitutes for the more direct sources of self-esteem enjoyed by American men, in the form of high-paying, high-status jobs, promotions, control over others, and decision-making power. Furthermore, studies by Stone (18) and Pitcher (19) suggest the differences in emphasis on appearance for boys and girls begins early in the socialization process; little girls learn that dresses and "being pretty" are sources of attention-getting, whereas boys learn that it is not "masculine" to be over-concerned with appearance. Thus these differences are well-developed by adolescence.

The mutual reinforcement of significant findings and trends in the direction of boy-girl differences suggests the need for further research. More specifically, a need for two types of more precise measuring instruments is indicated: more reliable measures of the concepts of personal adjustment and total self concept, and an instrument designed for more precise study of the nature of teen-age dissatisfaction with appearance. Secord and Jourard (6) have developed an instrument that measures degrees of satisfaction-dissatisfaction with many body parts and their functioning. A version of this instrument could be developed that would measure degrees of satisfaction with clothing and accessories as well as satisfaction with the body.

REFERENCES

1. Hall, G. Stanley. "Some Aspects of the Early Sense of Self," *American Journal of Psychology*, IX, April 1898, 337-367.

2. James, William. *The Principles of Psychology*. Vol. I. New York: Henry Holt and Company, 1890.

3. Cooley, Charles Horton. *Human Nature and the Social Order*. New York: Charles Scribner's Sons, 1922.

4. Ellis, Albert. *The American Sexual Tragedy*. New York: Grove Press, 1962.

5. Goffman, Erving. *The Presentation of Self in Everyday Life.* New York: Anchor Press, 1959.

6. Secord, Paul F. and Jourard, Sidney M. "The Appraisal of Body-Cathexis: Body-Cathexis and the Self," *Journal of Consulting Psychology,* XXII, No. 5, 1953, 343-347.

7. Engel, Mary. "The Stability of the Self Concept in Adolescence," *Journal of Abnormal and Social Psychology,* LVIII, No. 2, 1959, 211-215.

8. Reeder, Thelma A. "A Study of Some Relationships Between Level of Self Concept, Academic Achievement, and Classroom Adjustment," *Dissertation Abstracts,* XV, No. 12, 1955, 2472.

9. Reckless, W.C., Dinitz, S. and Kay, Barbara. "Self Concept as an Insulate Against Delinquency," *American Sociological Review,* No. 9, 1956, 744-766.

10. Fink, Martin B. "Self Concept as It Relates to Academic Underachievement," *California Journal of Educational Research,* XIII, No. 2, 1962, 57-62.

11. Mason, Evelyn P. "Some Factors in Self-Judgments," *Journal of Clinical Psychology,* No. 10, 1954, 336-340.

12. Havighurst, R.J. and Taba, Hilda. *Adolescent Character and Personality.* New York: Wiley, 1949.

13. Cantril, Hadley. *The Pattern of Human Concerns.* New Brunswick: Rutgers University Press, 1965.

14. Thorpe, Louis P., Clark, Willis W. and Tiegs, Ernest W. "California Test of Personality," New York: McGraw-Hill, Inc., 1953 Revision.

15. McGuire, Carson and White, George D. "The Measurement of Social Status," Unpublished research paper in Human Development, Department of Educational Psychology, University of Texas, March, 1955.

16. Brogger, Kaye. "The Relationship of Adolescent Appearance to Self Concept and Patterns of Conformity," Unpublished Master's thesis, University of Wisconsin, 1969.

17. Morrison, Denton, and Holden, Carlin Paige. "The Burning Bra: The American Breast Fetish and Women's Liberation," in Peter K. Manning (ed.), *Deviance and Change.* Englewood Cliffs, N.J.: Prentice Hall, 1971.

18. Stone, Gregory P. "Appearance and the Self," in A.M. Rose, (ed.) *Human Behavior and Social Processes: An Interactionist Approach.* New York: Houghton-Mifflin Company, 1962.

Kathleen E. Musa, Ph.D.
Assistant Professor
Human Environment and
Design, College of Human
Ecology
Michigan State University
East Lansing, Michigan

Mary Ellen Roach, Ph.D.
Professor, Textiles
and Clothing
School of Family Resources
and Consumer Sciences
University of Wisconsin
Madison, Wisconsin

11 THE PRIVATE

Absolute priority on the personal: a major new study charts students' withdrawal into the self.

Like others who study the student generation, I have been reluctant to be critical and at times reluctant to be honest with myself. Adults in our teen-worshipping culture want to swing, baby, perhaps to fight the threat of creeping age by identifying with young people and the future. But more importantly, our despair over the failures of our own generation has led us to make wistful heroes of youth. Having crowned them as the saviors we withdraw from judgment and sit back to watch them play—until they happen to step on a sensitive toe.

The result is demeaning to both young and old. Intellectuals patronize young people, much as civil-rights workers once patronized black people, by refusing to analyze their attitudes and behavior with the same standards and rigor that they use on any other topic. So the literature of the generation gap is vast, poorly seasoned and highly sentimental. Analysis and insight have come to a dead end, and with them the realistic prospect for moving with the young from what is to what might be.

Remarkably little attention has been paid to the most distinctive and obvious trait that is emerging: *privatism*.

Some social critics have been reporting, often reluctantly, on the habit of privatization or the cult of personalism—that is, student withdrawal from institutions into the self—but the coined word *privatism* recognizes the whole ideology that is now so important. This generation rejects meaning or authority outside of the self. If the organization slave or other-directed man saw his existence in harmony with social institutions, the new style of privatism not only cries for freedom from established institutions, it fundamentally rejects their legitimacy. Privatism's ideology is altruistic, for it acknowledges the privileges of private existence—as rights—to all men. But in practice this concession is less than heroic; true concern for others is diametrically opposite to the ethic of privatism at its logical extreme—self-indulgence, or a relatively simple form of old-fashioned romanticism.

Here are some striking paradoxes that turned up this year in a national poll of college seniors:

Seventy-six per cent say that they feel morally obliged to do what they can to end racial injustice in this society. At the same time, nearly half are unwilling to reject the most blatant stereotype in our culture—that of the irresponsible and carefree Negro.

Eighty-five per cent say that the most important things in life can be understood only through involvement. Yet, only a third report participating with any regularity in discussion programs dealing with national problems; 16% report participating in a demonstration; 12% sent a letter or telegram to a public official; and 5% had a leadership role in some political cause.

Seventy-three per cent believe that the exodus of whites from the central city has contributed to the ghetto crisis. Eighty-nine per cent say that the problems of cities are personally important to them. Still, 78% believe that suburbia is a style of life that combines the advantages and opportunities of both big cities and small towns, and by their responses to other questions they give every indication that they will join the exodus.

I have agonized over this assessment for several months. It was not what I expected to find a year ago when CRM, Inc.—Communications|Research|Machines, publishers of *Psychology Today* —asked me to construct the first comprehensive student survey since the National Opinion Research Center study in 1960. Working with students, we selected 246 questions to put to a national sample of 2,000 college seniors. We presented most of the questions as statements and asked respondents to mark their views on a five-point scale: *strongly agree, mildly agree, no opinion, mildly disagree, strongly disagree*. For convenience, I am reporting on the percentage of agreement, combining *strongly* and *mildly*, except where the spread along the continuum is important.

Almost two-thirds of the seniors in the sample responded to the questionnaire, and the responses came from every type of campus. The early returns indicated that the overall student body did not fit into either the liberal scheme of reality or the radical one, but it was also clear that they did not fit into any conservative's dream either. Five conclusions now stand out for me:

First, today's students are indeed idealistic and socially aware, maybe more so than any previous generation.

by Jeffrey K. Hadden

GENERATION

DO NOT FOLD,

Second, their idealism often takes the form of contempt for the older generation's hypocrisy, its failure to break out of institutional restraints and to act upon its stated ideals in personal life.

Third, their rejection of existing institutions, however, is much less total than the mass media tend to indicate. Students are hesitant, sometimes quixotic. Depending upon their personal experience, and upon fulfillment of the privatism ethic, they affirm certain existing institutions strongly—and see in them the prospect for creative growth.

Fourth, for all their abstract altruism, students lack a realistic sense of what their ideals imply in terms of social and public action. It is not clear, in fact, that they are fully committed to the ideals they talk about, especially when action may conflict with privatism.

Fifth, their privatism ethic is ambiguous in all its implications. While it tends to be self-centered and anti-institutional, and assumes a high level of materialistic comfort, it develops in many cases an acute sensitivity to others and a determination to conduct their own lives so as to contribute personally to their ideal of a decent society.

The prospects are both ominous and promising. If turning inward to discover the self is but a step toward becoming a sensitive and honest person, our society's unfettered faith in youth may turn out to be justified. However, privatism's present mood and form seems unbridled by any social norm or tradition and almost void of notions for exercise of responsibility toward others. On campus, as in their outside-world judgments, students react to any threat to the private preserves of their existence.

Liberals and conservatives of the older generation are making silly mistakes because of their failure to understand the ethic of privatism. For example, conservatives in Congress want to put Federal marshals on campus as well as require applicants for student loans to sign pledges that they have not participated in demonstrations and will not. This further invasion of personal freedom will drive student moderates and conservatives into the hands of the radicals. By such stupidities, confused conservatives

are likely to radicalize the next generation of young people. The side effect will be further withdrawal into romantic self-centeredness.

Generalized idealism comes through. Ninety per cent hope to live in a way that will make some contribution to man's understanding of man and help build a more tolerant, just world. For most, both men and women, this is more than a pledge of allegiance to motherhood, the flag and apple pie. Only one in five (22%) agrees with this statement of personal despair: "I'll probably never accomplish anything very important."

They believe in their generation as well as themselves. Almost seven in 10 (68%) believe that their generation is going to make a better world. But their optimism is tempered; only 13% believe that their generation "will create the first society that is truly free of prejudice."

Students (60%) doubt that their elders have "the intelligence and moral sensitivity" to deal with the urban crisis. An identical majority believe we have little hope for survival if institutions don't become more sensitive to human needs.

Since the first thrust of the youth rebellion has been directed at the universities, the anatomy of discontent with campus institutions is perhaps prophetic. More than half feel that the college classroom is seriously lacking in relevance to the real problems of the world. Three out of four wish that the universities would develop programs that would involve students in urban problems. Almost as many students agree as disagree with the argument that the universities have abdicated their responsibility to deal with the vital moral issues.

This critical mood, however, does not mean that they have written off the university—or the faculty. Almost three out of four (73%) believe that the university is one important symbol of hope in a troubled world. Only one in five feels that his professors don't really care about the problems of the society, and still fewer feel that what they are learning in class is "silly, wrong or useless."

They feel that where the institution fails, they make up the difference by themselves. Almost half (49%) say that they are learning a great deal *in spite of*

89

"For all the efforts to radicalize the campus . . . a vast majority refused to reject the political process that had just served up two limp disappointments."

the university, and two-thirds (65%) feel that "college has changed my whole view of myself." In the true spirit of privatism, most appreciate college as a period of self-discovery, and a majority say that they are not in college to improve their prospects for fitting into society's jobs.

Here are a few of the statements on which students reveal their intensely personal feelings about education:

Per Cent Agreeing

Significant learning takes place only if the student knows that the teacher fully accepts and is seriously interested in him as a person.	**49**
Today's freshmen and sophomores are much more critical of society than my class.	**40**
The ideal of scientific objectivity or detachment falsifies the inevitably personal nature of all inquiry.	**32**
Most of my professors are too liberal.	**8**
I can't talk to my parents about the things I am learning in school.	**40**
College courses have too much theory, not enough practical training that will help me later on.	**63**
College presents a dilemma of choosing between a major that is interesting and one that leads to a good job.	**61**
I have learned more in a bull-session with other students than I have in class.	**38**

So why the protest? There's a don't-tread-on-me righteousness. College administrators brought on the rebellion, say 59%, by being indifferent to student needs. And the punishment inflicted by students, they feel, has helped educate the administrators. Seventy-nine per cent are sympathetic with the goals of protest, though not always the methods, and 95% insist that they are as concerned with university reform as the protest leaders are. The student majority may hate hippies and radicals at the student union but will defend them against discipline. Though 57% feel that the protest leaders "give the rest of us a bad name," a bigger majority (68%) do not want these fellow students kicked out of school.

If protest against the university is focused, perhaps heightened, by love, no such emotion seems to affect students'

views of government and politics. Sixty per cent look upon politicians as mere maintainers of the status quo. A massive 70% agree with the harsh judgment that "the welfare state has failed in the inner city." Still more (87%) believe that most people would rather just vote about a problem than do something about it.

By design, this student survey was conducted during last year's presidential campaign, when political awareness and action was at a four-year high. Students overwhelmingly rejected the nominees of both parties: 13% had favored Richard Nixon before the convention and only 4% had favored Hubert Humphrey. Three-fourths picked one of the reform-style candidates regardless of party: Senator Eugene McCarthy, Governor Nelson Rockefeller or the late Senator Robert F. Kennedy.

Yet, even at its peak, discontent did not turn into outrage. For all the efforts to radicalize the campus, especially by the students who were brutalized in Chicago last year, a vast majority refused to reject the political process that had just served up two limp disappointments. Only 14% agreed with the gentlest possible statement of radicalism's basic premise: "There is no point in trying to change existing political structure. If one is interested in change he must work outside these structures."

The Students for a Democratic Society, the radical corps who in the past have been able to organize much of the campus protest, have now moved leftward toward hard-line anti-capitalism. Their target is "capitalism's military-educational-industrial complex." My data suggest that the S.D.S. will find far less campus sympathy for its anti-capitalism than it has previously found for its attack on the war, the political process, and the university itself. In fact, this generation's privatism generalizes into a stronger affirmation of business as a system than has been apparent on campus for several decades.

Consider this statement: "The free-enterprise system is the single economic system compatible with the requirements of personal freedom and constitutional government." I included it because I had found, in a nationwide study of Protestant ministers and laymen, that

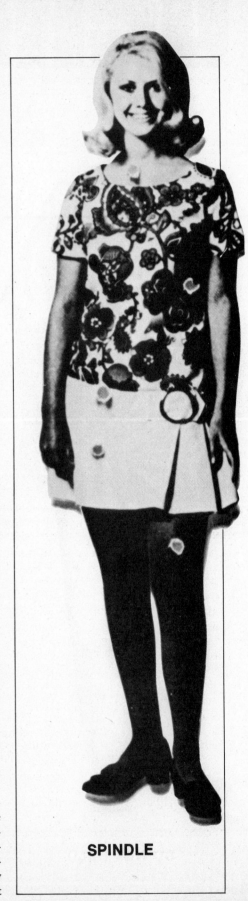

SPINDLE

"Students tend to look down upon businessmen the way the middle-class English look down on tradesmen."

it splits liberals and fundamentalists. Liberals reject, fundamentalists agree. To my surprise, only 8% of the students disagree strongly, 17% disagree mildly and 14% have no opinion. But 61% agree with the statement, 23% of them strongly. Their affirmation is greater than I found among conservative Lutherans.

Students confirm their pro-business attitude on many other questions. More of them have hope for business than for churches as instruments of reform. A clear majority say that private enterprise is capable of solving any problem it puts its mind to, including poverty. And only 40% disagree with a statement that business is already more deeply involved than government in creative urban programs. A majority regard profit and the public interest as compatible. More agree than disagree with the thought that the basic assumptions and goals of business are changing very rapidly.

However, before the Chamber of Commerce goes dancing in the street, let's consider a specific example of the privatism ethic. Students tend to affirm business in the abstract but to suspect its incursions upon the inner self. And nearly two-thirds (61%) say that they don't plan to take jobs in business if they can do something more worthwhile.

Almost half believe that business expects more conformity than they can give; many suspect that corporations still want only organization men in gray-flannel suits. Their suspicions are not ideological, as might be the case among older liberals, for they see no special virtue in business' chief competitor, the Federal Government. "The kind of work I do," say 86%, "matters more than whether I do it for government, business, a university or an independent organization." Nearly 40% expect to work in educational or research organizations, 29% in companies or self-employment, 5% for the Federal Government, 3% for state and local government and 9% for hospitals, churches or welfare organizations.

In short, students tend to look down upon businessmen the way the middle-class English look down on tradesmen. This attitude holds even among students who plan to go into business but it is most pronounced among Ivy Leaguers and the children of "job-rich" parents.

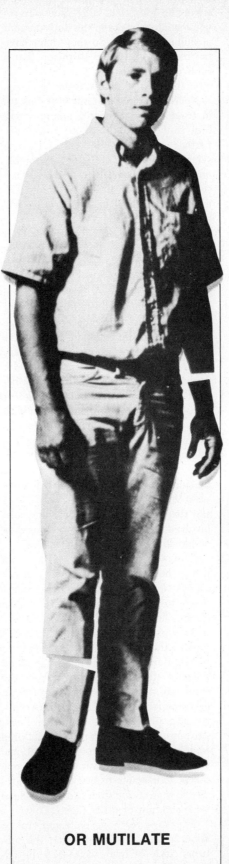

OR MUTILATE

Here are some personal attitudes toward business and other institutions:

Per Cent Agreeing

Those who knock free-enterprise misunderstand what made this a great nation.	67
The churches in America have been hopelessly slow in joining the struggle for social justice.	65
You have more freedom working in business than in government.	46
Business provides little opportunity today for anyone who cares about what happens in the world.	25
The decisions I might make inside a corporation would influence the society more than my votes.	47
The advantage of intellectual work for a corporation is that you get to test your theories in action.	62
I'm bugged by the prospect of working for an organization where I'll have to carry out policies I think are wrong.	65
I would like to work for an organization where the boss wouldn't be upset if I were involved in unpopular causes.	72
Many friends would lose respect for me if I go into business.	7
I'd never work for any part of the military-industrial complex.	21
I would like to work for a company that would give me the opportunity for further education.	86
I prefer a secure job to a high-paying one where I might be fired.	42
I'd like spending a year or two in voluntary service such as the Peace Corps.	49
White backlash poses the most serious threat to American society.	39
Theoretically, the beauty of the city is that it's a center of optimum freedom and choice for the individual.	49
Black Power is an example of participatory democracy that needs to be reawakened in society.	30
The rate of social change is so great that it frightens me.	27
Our society is going to be torn apart by rising tension and unrest.	52

The student attack upon hypocrisy has forced a re-definition of racial hang-ups in very personal terms. "I feel morally obliged," say 76%, "to do what I can to end racial injustice in this country." Applying this conviction to private life, 86% would not mind having a member of a different racial group represent them in Congress. Some 77% are not bothered by the prospects of working for a black boss; and 72% say OK to living next door. On each of these questions, only 5% take clear racist positions.

When the questions shift from personal morality to attitudes that affect public policy, however, it becomes clear that young people do not understand the implications of their altruistic views. Fifty-four per cent believe that most people who live in poverty could do something about it if they really wanted to. A resentful 56% expect to pay a lot of taxes in their lifetimes because many people would rather live on welfare than work. And, as noted in the introduction, 42% accept the oldest stereotype of all: "Negroes could solve many of their own problems if they would not be so irresponsible and carefree about life." Here's privatism reduced to the absurd.

In place of overt prejudice, students adopt a simplistic view of the complex social forces that perpetuate the second-class status of black people and hold down the average Negro—even though the lucky few Negroes benefit from higher education and opening doors. Fifty-one per cent of the seniors think that sensational news coverage has made urban and racial problems seem more severe than they are. Nearly half (48%) imagine that the condition of the average Negro is improving rapidly. And, while defending student protest, 55% suggest that black people ought to take advantage of their opportunities rather than spend so much time protesting.

The absence of an integrated value system becomes apparent in their overall thinking about the urban crisis. On this point, I have to admit a specific partisanship of ideas. I designed the CRM poll with an eye toward the emergence of what might be called an urban theology. The city is an environment created by man, very different from the rural world in which man inhabits an environment that was made by God or nature. The value system demanded for survival in the urban age that is now upon us has to include a number of obvious factors. Among them perhaps would be a willingness to embrace the city in all its dirt and turmoil, to be sensitive to necessary institutional change and to be willing to use technology for humanistic purposes rather than fight it.

Part of the attitudes I had hoped to find are indeed emergent. Sixty-two per cent enjoy being in the middle of a large city where all types of activities go on

in close proximity; 78% reject the view that cities have little to offer than can't be found in small communities; and 73% reject the idea that large cities are an unfortunate mistake in the development of human societies. So they don't have the basic hostility and suspicion that a rural culture once felt toward the big city, that center of revolution and sin.

Nearly all agree that our big cities are in trouble, and a near-unanimous 94% feel that white racial attitudes are partly responsible. Nine out of 10 consider the troubles of cities personally important to themselves. Only 15% see these problems as insoluble, though 75% are not sure that their generation will solve the problems.

There's also a positive attitude about the use of science and technology for re-creating the human environment. The rhetoric about man's alienation from the machine has had very little impact on the student generation. More than half (53%) deny that science and technology are dehumanizing man. Only one in three doubts that technology is a very positive force creating opportunity for man to be truly free. A strong 72% believe that science makes it possible for people to go beyond preoccupation with survival into concern with intellectual attainment, friendship and participation in civic life. And a similar majority believe that we have the economic and technical capacity to do anything we want with our cities. Almost half (45%) say that as business creates new jobs involved in solving urban problems they would like to get in on the action.

However, the commitment to an urban theology on an abstract or hypothetical level loses force when we get down to specifics. Some 85% tend to accept the shibboleth that riots are the handiwork of outside agitators. But 47% believe that agitators are not solely to blame. Few understand the fragmented political structures left over from the rural age; only 39% feel that organizing urban regions into effective political bodies is a particularly difficult problem. An edgy 54% don't want their children to grow up in the city, and an additional 16% are uncertain about this. Only one out of four wants to live in the central city so that his children can go to school with children of other races.

Most are ready, even eager, to be suburbanites; 78% believe that the suburban style of living combines the advantages and opportunities of the city and small town. Getting down to which

city, if any, they would like to live in, we found an intriguing contrast: only one in four would like to live in New York, but almost half (48%) want to live in the country's leading non-city, San Francisco. All in all, it seems fair to infer that the student majority, though it now joins Pete Seeger in protesting life's "Little Boxes," will soon join their parents in suburbia's little boxes.

Even the contempt for the older generation operates on an abstract level, not much on the specific and personal. There's no general alienation from parents. More than 78% deny—55% of them strongly—that "all my parents care about is how much money I make when I get out." Though 43% have parents who feel that college teaches wild ideas, 83% say that their parents would be terribly hurt if they did not finish school.

The irony of the students is not their rebellion but their docile conformity to the stated ideals, if not the example, of their parents and teachers. They have worked hard, often ploddingly, at more years of study than any large group ever known. They have had it impressed upon them that prejudice and discrimination are untenable. They have grown up believing that our society has the technological capability to wipe out poverty. They are aware of war's destructive potential and take for granted the necessity to end war. But, they find themselves in a society where racism abounds, poverty remains, and cities burn. And war drags on, making through the draft one more institutionalized demand about which they have not been consulted. Yet, 67% believe it is "a young man's duty to serve his country when called," and only 18% say they will "use any means necessary to avoid serving in Vietnam."

Their response is to retreat into privatism and there to resist further inroads into their personal domain. Their predominant mood, then, takes the form of rejection of authority and the desire to follow their own modes of conduct. When student radicals get pushy, they are treated as one more set of pressures, unless an administrator overreacts with police authority. As singer Bob Dylan said when he turned from protest toward his folk-rock style, "I don't want to write *for* people any more. I want to write from inside me." Here are a few examples of the don't-tread-on-me attitudes:

Per Cent Agreeing

Universities should not try to control student life outside the classroom.   **79**

The most important thing about college is that it provides the student some time to discover himself and think about what he wants to do with his life. **78**

Whether I work for government or business, I would like a job where I will more or less be my own boss. **85**

My private life will not be sacrificed even if it means making less money. **82**

I would like to work for an organization where the boss wouldn't be upset if I were involved in unpopular causes. **72**

Students should have an option between serving in the Peace Corps and the military. **71**

Nearly two-thirds of the students feel that they were forced to pick a college major before they were ready to, and now they feel pushed on career deci-

sions. Fully half feel that most students will have to "sell out" when they leave the university, and nearly the same proportion don't expect jobs to let the persons who hold them be creative. "I take it for granted that I will make a good income," say 82%. "I'm much more concerned about finding a job where I will do things that matter." Nearly 68% say that they look at work as a way of life and not simply as a way of making a living. But, uncompromising, 82% say that they will not sacrifice their private lives even if it means making less money.

Out of these many and seemingly contradictory views, as out of the last few years with students, I have come to see the danger of a privatism ethic that turns into a kind of romantic withdrawal. Like the drug trip into the self, retreat into the totally personal world can be an escape from responsibility to

others and to the society. The panic of the riot, which leaves its mark only in the mind, is less a sign of strength than a symptom of helplessness,

"I carry my adornments on my soul," said Cyrano de Bergerac, the purest romantic figure of the 19th Century. "I do not dress up like a popinjay; But inwardly, I keep my daintiness." The romantics of today's student generation are understandably put out with those of us who are over 30 because the world they must inherit is in turmoil. The critical question is whether their social idealism, though abstractly stated and daintily enforced in private life, will be molded into a commitment to transform society toward their goals. Or will it become the hypocrisy of the present generation raised to a higher level of rhetoric?

IV. The Family

When we think of adolescence, we tend to think of young people with their families. No matter how much we know of adolescents and their friends at work or school, somehow the word *adolescence* calls up images of families. To be sure, the large majority of adolescents do live with their parents, or with one parent. One point we can make about the period known as adolescence is that it represents a time span during which people undergo radical shifts in their attitudes toward marriage and family. In the course of a few years, a child who never even thinks of marriage may become a parent.

Any discussion of adolescence and the family necessarily is incomplete. Where does one even begin to confront this topic? The relationship between parents and children, and more generally the nature of interaction between generations, is one starting point. There are, after all, culturally legitimate forms of parental behavior, even though many young people may dislike these forms. Power is part of the relationship between generations. More exactly, the nature of the traditional family is that authority lies with the elders. While part of this legitimate use of authority is beneficial for children, it causes troubles for them as well. Power, as we know, becomes a major aspect in the relationships between men and women and between friends of similar age range. It lurks in the fabric of sexual relations and the institution of marriage, even when there are no children. So despite the call among some adolescents for an end to human oppression, adolescents find themselves in a host of involvements and entanglements where power and authority become salient influences on their behavior.

In a culture like our own, we tend to focus on issues of psychopathology, rather than health. The so-called normal adolescent or normal family receive far less attention than the so-called disturbed adolescent or family under stress. In this section we find selections which encompass both perspectives. We examine the natural relationship between generations. We look at the connections, too, between friendships within the family and outside the family. It seems peculiar at first glance, to say that a young person may be friends with his or her parents, but surely in many families this is the case. It is also true that this special friendship, or lack of it, may cause adolescents a great deal of stress, so much so that they run away from their families, despite the often dire consequences of such an act.

The section ends with a reminder: namely, that adolescents may well be parents. Despite the fantastic social changes occurring in our society, the drop in the frequency of marriage, the postponement of having children, we must recall that the median age of a woman getting married is still 20. That is, for each woman who marries beyond the age of 20, there is a woman younger than 20 getting married. If we accept the nomenclature of the day, then 50 percent of American brides are adolescents.

12

Of Youth and the Time of Generations

by Thomas J. Cottle

In the long enslavement of childhood I knelt on hard wood in
cold churches, striking my breast at each mea culpa, and
resolved to confess my sins, do penance, and amend my life; and
so I do; I have forgiven my parents all their care in rearing me.
What I pray for this year is not the remission of my sins, but the
wit to remember them when they come back to me as my
offspring's, and grace to see the luminescence of things lost in
things present. The breath I want now is simpler, only to live,
which is to be hurt, which is to love. . . .
William Gibson, A Mass for the Dead

The action of the secret passes continually from the hider of
things to the hider of self. A casket is a dungeon for objects. And
here is a dreamer who feels that he shares the dungeon of its
secrets. We should like to open it, and we should also like to
open our hearts.
Gaston Bachelard, The Poetics of Space

Not too long ago, an attractive college senior gently
asked whether she might speak with me a few minutes. Her manner was marked by that timorous politeness that symbolizes how
ably school systems instruct students to avoid pestering their elders.
The contractual acknowledgment "only a few minutes" always
seems so sad, implying, as it must, an unforgivable presumption
and a taking one away from activities so unalterably more important.

Jenny sat across from me, her hiked up miniskirt, her youth, a
sorrow in her eyes all compelling me to attend to her. She had
come with "no particular problem." She spoke about her courses,
her job, the few hours each week left for schoolwork, and her two
male involvements. One, she explained, was a boy from the mountains of Utah, someone who knows of the poet's world, yet someone at present dreadfully caught in the scary, exhilarating ca-
cophony of the "drug scene." The second, a young man, "straight,"
good head, "my parents like him," "his father is a noble man."

Although Jenny concluded almost every other sentence with the
words "it's funny," nothing she said was ever funny. She had
known sadness; indeed, as she continued I felt as if she were speaking as the burdened parent, herself as her own child. "It's difficult
to stay healthy here . . . I don't know if I can pull my life together. . . . I don't know if I can make it. I hope so . . . I'm not
sure."

We spoke quite a lot more. Periodically she would ask whether
I was sure I had the time. I tried to convince her of my commit-

ment and interest, but somehow her perception of the teacher's role, together with the institutionalization of "office hours," screened a deep concern.

Then, suddenly, Jenny produced the kind of frightened confession I have heard from nearly every young person who has come to me not necessarily for help but for some hoped-for strength in friendship: "When I was thirteen, I became my father's confidante. He was having an affair with a twenty-year-old girl, and I was the only one he could speak to. . . . Later I went to the prep school she had gone to. He thought I'd like it there."

The moments with Jenny resembled so strongly other hours spent with students troubled by their experiences with drugs. Often with these students I found an absence of any fundamental strength; it just seemed as though some last-ditch power to fall back on was gone. Like Jenny, these other young people were not sure they were going to make it.

Months before, in a hospital therapy session, John, a fourteen-year-old boy living with his mother and his four brothers and sisters in a low-income Boston housing project, had spoken of his parents' divorce, a damaging separation that had been preceded by his mother seeking his counsel. Although only eleven at the time, John was, after all, the eldest of her five children. She had been thinking of getting a divorce and wanted his advice. John looked away from me before he spoke. He rubbed his forehead so that I could barely see his eyes. It was difficult to understand him through the nasal sounds, the sniffing, the Boston-scented words which remain for me an accent. "Why did she ask me? Children don't want to know about things like that! Why did she have to ask me?"

Will is a tall, very pale young man, a high school drop-out. He lacks poise but shows honesty along with despair. His very gait is a plea for help. At the time I met him, he was inextricably dependent on Methedrine, pot, LSD, cough syrup, anything that could be popped, dropped, sniffed, smacked, anything that could produce that coveted ecstasy, "the high." My first and only meeting with him lasted for about an hour. No therapeutic or ritualized rules of time had stopped us; however, Will had opened himself, perhaps too quickly. Having plunked down several chapters of his life, he had begun to frighten himself. There had been his questioning of homosexuality; was he wrong not to want to "make it" with girls; his poetic sophistication about the inexorable realities of lower-class life styles and dreams; his lack of anger, his domination by anger, and a missing father: "When my father left, my mother turned to me in a special way. It was as though she wanted my help. It's like she wanted me to take his place. She made me sleep in the same bed." He held his head in his hands and turned toward me with a look some mistakenly call a smirk. But it is not a smirk. Time and the supreme awareness of this "new" youth have transformed both the context and meaning of expression and expressiveness and what sociologist Erving Goffman has called "face work": "I guess I must have an Oedipal thing, huh?"

One last person. Janet, a college student and a friend of a friend of a friend, somehow "found herself," as she said, in my office. She had been "busted," and the court had placed her under the care of one of their psychiatrists. Because the relationship had become perfunctory, Janet now refused to see him for even the prescribed once a month. "He's not interested in me." And soon the blame had shifted inward: "How can he be? I don't spend enough time with him. I'm just another 'monthly.'" Four years before, when she was fourteen, Janet tried to commit suicide. She swallowed all varieties of pills, a total of more than eighty: "I wanted to go to sleep." The precipitating causes were many, but for her the most fearful event occurred three days before the attempt, when her mother took her into the kitchen and closed the door so that her father and brothers would not hear. "'I know you're young,' she said to me, 'but maybe you can help. Your father and I are not having sex. Have you learned anything that might help me?' I swear to you, these were her words." At the sound of her own words she wept.

The theme of young people's involvement with adult authority is an old theme, hammered to life almost daily in studies published on parents of adolescents, hippies, drop-outs, druggies, militants, etcetera. Recently I have noted that some writers "on youth" have openly chastised parents for failing to assume assertive roles with their children. Even some psychiatrists now argue for parental toughness, perhaps as a reaction to an oft-blamed emphasis on permissiveness.

Authority implies an inequality, or what some prefer to call an asymmetry, between the old and the young. The term asymmetry is rather telling as it implies quite unequivocally that there is no even exchange between generations, nor for that matter is there ever a possibility for it. Parents are by definition not peers, and their concern for children does not even imply that "good" families yield loyal colleagues. Yet the asymmetric structure of authority is not all bad, although parents and children are more than a bit ambivalent about it. Longing for the taste of adolescence, parents in many instances overstep the bounds which the asymmetry purports to guard. In some cases, as in those described above, their intrusions turn out to be nothing short of disastrous. For some young people, a quiet inner strength vanishes when their parents trespass on the property of time belonging strictly to youth and destroy the very same asymmetry which they themselves once wished to destroy.

The theme of authority is complicated, therefore, because the young and old alike often wish to tamper with the time defining generational separations but come to realize the potentially devastating results of such an escapade. The asymmetry means restraints on behavior, and the young, being today so profoundly aware of the facts of life, recognize these restraints as well as anyone. Generally, the young seem more open than ever before, or is it that social reality seems more translucent? Perhaps there are fewer secrets today than yesterday, and perhaps too our society presently honors revelation, and the supposed absolution it yields, more than confidential trust.

To a great extent, my concern here is with the breakdown of asymmetric authority and the effects and meaning of parents trespassing upon the property of the young. For there are quite a few highly sensitive young persons, mostly students, not necessarily "disturbed" (that ubiquitous word), who have experienced the rattling of their very souls when a parent chose not to preserve the asymmetry quite possibly required in authority relations. Often I think of the troubled pasts and equivocal futures of these persons living in a society so riddled with thoughts of death and insanity that the spirit of death and the fear of and fascination with insanity pervades their explorations into sex and drugs. But our topic is not *all* young people or the universal causes of mental illness, drug taking or school problems. One cannot generalize about "youth" from a few encounters, nor indeed would one dare generalize about all the hours in another's lifetime on the basis of but a few hours of friendship. Still, from even these few hours, a few pictures, a few concepts however dim, emerge and they seem worth remarking on.

There is little doubt that young people extend, prolong, or simply react to their parents' demands, be they uttered or silently passed on. As Erik Erikson has said, one generation revives the repressions of the generation before it. But equally important, adolescents have become brilliant readers of parental intentions. Or perhaps adults generally — and I include here parents, teachers, ministers, deans and psychotherapists — have too frequently become predictable or transparent in their dealings with young people. High school students now portray with ease the "shrink scene." They anticipate with frightening accuracy the words and moods of churlish school administrators. A fifteen-year-old Negro boy told me that he could not get help from his school guidance counselor: "I wouldn't say this to his face, but he doesn't like Negroes. He may not even know this, but we know it." I spoke to the counselor in question. Not only had the student correctly interpreted the man's attitude; his impersonation of the man's behavior, right down to the speech patterns, was perfect.

All of this suggests to me that the cat of the authority relationship is out of the bag. The young understand and appreciate more of adult motivations and, significantly, the sociological rationalizations for so-called adult action in authority contexts. While they may protest against school principals and programs, the young will also confess a sympathy for their elders' plight of being trapped in the policies of some greater bureaucratic establishment, the "system." Yet they can recognize what they call a "sell-out" or "game player" a mile away, and a heady college freshman, if the matter concerns him at all, can learn to differentiate between the "authentic" liberal and the "institutional" brand from the last row of a lecture hall. Their language simplifications like "smarts," "head," "cool," "cop-out," are illustrations of an almost social-scientific terminology, and, more significantly, they function in reducing complex action patterns to levels succinct and manageable, at least for them. Their language shows, moreover, the swiftness and clarity with which they can first interpret and then act upon personal and institutional demands. (Many students recognize that their parents' social class is still the best predictor of their own school success, and that the poor and particularly the poor blacks cannot hope to compete even with the omnipresent mediocrity found among the "advantaged." Hence, while their understanding of local school competition and the mobility channels school generally offers may be profoundly true or totally incorrect, greater society seems to become more and more disillusioning and uninspiring.)

Perhaps the best illustration of language reflecting social sophistication and the apparent translucency of social reality is the expression "psyche out." A college junior assured me: "It's so easy to know what a teacher wants, or what he'll ask on a test. They never change. Give 'em what they want. You make them happy and you win." Even modest Phi Beta Kappa students claim they have "psyched out" their teachers and their college programs and have emerged superior merely because they were the better game players. The fact remains that to "psyche out" something or someone is to stay one slender step ahead even of expectation. It seems to be the ability to perceive the expression on the face of the future.

While it is progressively more difficult for young people to be duped by authority figures, it is as easy as it always has been to be damaged by them, a result so common when the superordinate, the elder, the parent, the teacher wants to equalize and make perfectly equitable what might better remain as an asymmetric proposition and relationship. Again, asymmetry refers to relationships wherein the commodities exchanged are of unequal and therefore incomparable content; hence the behavior of one person is not a call or demand for the identical behavior in the other. In its most fundamental form, asymmetry describes relationships in which one of the members represents unquestioned authority in a particular context, and thus it refers to interactions engaging parents with children, teachers with students, doctors with patients.

Several years ago, while leading what some of us call a self-analytic group, something not unlike the popular T-group, I was invited to a party given by the members of this group. As it was early in their history, it seemed reasonable to them that an informal evening together might loosen up and simplify all relationships. I was sorely tempted to go, but a wiser man suggested that I not. The asymmetry, he urged, ultimately must be preserved by the person holding authority. I may have lost something by finally declining, but I probably protected a valuable tension in the leader-member relationship, a tension which added to the learning and enhanced the members' chances to attain a sense of autonomy in the group. The symbolic nature of my refusal, moreover, reaffirmed the asymmetry, or inequality, which some of us working in groups feel is essential, and which members in their way often confess is preferred, especially during the early hours of the group's evolution. The leader (or father) must in some sense forever remain the leader, and while this angers many, particularly those in groups, kindness, gentleness and care are in no way automatically precluded by such a philosophy and by the strategy which derives from it.

More recently, members of a self-analytic group observed their leader's participation in a political demonstration. At the following meeting they spoke of him with a newly discovered reverence. How good that he shares the same values and that he exhibits the courage to speak out against administrations, local and national. But they spoke, too, of a disgust for their mothers wearing miniskirts and for parents generally who act like kids. Anna, a mature young woman, told of a feeling of actual nausea that came over her when her roommate's mother discussed the college courses she, the mother, was attending. Upon returning to her dormitory, Anna made a long-distance phone call home and luxuriated in the relief that her own mother still was pursuing what she called "mother-type" activities: luncheons, museum visits, and food budgeting.

The ambivalence is evident. Young people want to attack authority and I suppose this is probably the way it must be, and always has been. But in matters of human dealings, although not in issues of strict ideology, authority is not to "come down" to the child's level, as parents once so perceptively felt it necessary to kneel down, if only to attain a spatial equality between the generations. Authority is not to give in; it is to remain firm in its commitment to preserve, among other things, that essential asymmetry and the corresponding indelible generational separation, even if this means being seen as a "square" or "straight-arrow." This last statement, however, must not be construed as my suggesting that only authoritarian authority is functional or practical or healthful. This is not what I have in mind.

When a small child orders his parents out of his bedroom, he necessarily fears the enormity of the act. So, in a tearful rage, he can only pray that the parents will go no farther than the living room. Similarly, when members express the intense desire to kick out the leader of self-analytic groups (in symbolic reenactment of the primal horde story, perhaps), invariably they want to know if, should they be successful, he would really go, and if he would return.

There is, then, a primitive core that develops out of interactions with parents, a core that pleads for the overthrow of authority. Yet there is also a hope that one will be unable to do just this. There is a hope, in other words, that the superordinate's strength will resist any attempts to be overthrown. This notion, of course, is paramount in Freud's explication of the Oedipal relationship. Parents simply cannot break down or retreat. They must prevail, and no one wants this more than the child himself. In terms of this infantile core that stays with us, parents are perfect, without problems, immortal. Relationships with them, therefore, preclude both equality and peership. A college student said it this way: "No matter what I do in the face of authority, I end up a child. It happens even when I don't know the authority. Are we forever children to older or more powerful persons?"

When children are born a series of events almost ceremonial in nature takes place, whenever possible, in which the mother's mother lives with her daughter for the first weeks of the newborn's life. Though serving a highly functional purpose, this ceremony tends to reinforce, at more latent levels, the new mother's bond with her own mother. Thus in no way does the arrival of the infant place the mother and grandmother on an equal plane. In a sense, the birth reaffirms the existence and concept of not only generations but history as well, for regardless of one's activities as a parent in one's most recent family, the family one has created, one forever remains a child in that other family, one's first family, the family into which one was born. And this causes more than a few problems.

For example, for children to outachieve their parents, an event not uncommon among college students (and let us not forget, as some would urge us to, that women are confronted with career aspirations and the ensuing competitions as much as men), means that they, the younger, must delicately initiate revisions in parental relationships so that the older generation will not interpret the younger ones' accomplishments as indicators of their own dismal and unprogressing ineptitude. What an incredible task it is for these young and talented students to return during Christmas and summer vacations to the rooms and persons of their childhood; to return where all of us know we cannot again return, then to battle the very essence of what seems to be an unjust but still unstopping passage of time.

Why is it in these times that each of us believes in the development, yes, even in the successes of our surging expectations, but sees only aging in our parents? Perhaps the eternal danger of the immediate future is that while it guarantees reports on the outcome of our most present investments, it brings first our parents and then us closer to some inexplicable end. But for the handful of "right nows" that constitute our involvement with the present, our youthful preoccupations make only our own movement in the life space visible. All the rest, parents and teachers included, remain unchanged, timeless: "It's like they've all stood still. They bring me back to my childhood 'hang-ups.' They know I've grown up, they know I'm at college; but they're used to me as I was when I was last there."

These last expressions and sensations are so clearly not the sensations of regression. Although we all have fought back urges to feel once more, for even a bittersweet interval, the winds of childhood, returning or wishing to return must not be mistaken for regressing. On the contrary, returning is often resuming. This is what is meant by bringing one back to childhood "hang-ups." It seems like regression, for only in our direct involvements with our family does "family time" again move ahead. In our separations from a family, that certain time stops, and the stillness augurs death. But the student returns and the time of the family altogether jolts forward again, alive, just as the family itself becomes vitally alive, although life now becomes a bit more cumbersome. The sensation is precisely the same as seeing someone we haven't seen in years. Almost at once we pick up our conversation exactly as it was at the moment of our separation. Now, because both of us have experienced so much in the interim, we cannot really fill in the spaces, and so we are obliged to disregard the interim and the maturation and change it obviously contains and seek a resumption of those earlier days. Whereas we may feel that we are regressing, in fact we are following reality's dictates right down the line, and doing our level best to resume prior action. And while it is stupendously exhilarating in the first few minutes, or hours, or even days, it sometimes becomes dreadfully cumbersome and, even more, discouraging and unbearable. The time of separations may be that significant, for people once so closely knitted together may find that apart they drift in different directions toward different experiences.

The predicament confronting the child at these times is to help his parents resolve some of the problems that occur when the young outachieve their elders. Variations in accomplishment must be reconciled in ways that legitimately reinforce parents' ultimate authority and special superiority. Irrespective of attainments, son and daughter want to remain in the child's role, at least in this one context and at least in this one home. The parents know the child's task and, like the vaudeville joke, the child knows the parents know, and the parents know the child knows they know.

It is in interpersonal dilemmas and gestures of this sort, gestures made and carried out in such public yet at the same time secretive ways, that families reaffirm health. The gestures imply the mutual recognition and trust of which Erikson has so poetically and firmly spoken. By these gestures, the social and temporal gaps between people, even those who share a treasured intimacy, are preserved, sociologic and psychologic genes are somehow passed from one generation to the next, and one is, in Erikson's words, able "to see one's own life in continuous perspective both in retrospect and in prospect." [1] The division made first by time permits the evolution of the adult and sanctifies the appropriateness and truth of the confirmation and the Bar Mitzvah. For sociological reasons, the gap between the generations stays open. But it is all right because distance need not be construed as distrust, nor separateness as desertion.

There are no such gaps, presumably, in the family histories of those young people presented at the outset of this chapter. In their lives, sociology has been tricked, and time has been placed, as it were, behind itself. By being shoved into unbearable roles, these certain persons were asked to overlook generational intervals which must appear to them to be at least as long as eternity. As the parents despairingly sought to haul in the nets of time in order to make the space between the generations smaller and smaller, they thoughtlessly or impetuously or unwittingly coerced their children into caricatures of marriage counselor, therapist, and, worse, buddy. Jenny *is* the burdened parent; she is as herself, her own child. Her father's confession, the information, the content were all unwanted by her, absolutely and desperately unwanted. In what vessel does one possibly store such information? Time alone should have prevented such utterances, but a "proper sociology" would have guarded against such a "friendship."

In a highly speculative vein, the unquestioned obligation to live sanely through these provocative, seductive and terrifying engagements in which the generations are nakedly slammed together is perhaps the first exposure to what later on becomes the psychology of the drug experience and the basis or content of the drug reaction. The searching for advice, the confessions, and, importantly, the collision with revelations, are without doubt experiences to "blow one's mind." They are the inevitable contact of ageless and recurring dreams and unshakably psychotic moods. They remain almost as a cause of the cerebral explosion pre-LSD and speed. They are "freak-outs" par excellence, and grade school flirtations with insanity.

For two years I saw a girl who is now thirteen in a hospital therapy setting. Kathy's language and psychological test performance indicated a possible psychotic diagnosis. Her recurring dream and one which, truthfully, intrigued us both was of her in a forest being chased by a large bear. Up on its hind legs, it pursued her and quite regularly caught her. The dream had become so terrifying that Kathy had resorted to magical powers invoked through some ritualized bedtime behavior, just to prevent the bear from appearing. How terribly symbolic the content of this is: the personification of impulses at the same time sexual and aggressive. Yet, with more examination, how literal is the content. Kathy's father, an alcoholic for all of Kathy's life, returns home at night from work pitifully drunk and staggers toward her, his shirt off, the hair on his chest, his muscles and his skin exposed, with his smell, with his pants open. Pleading for sex at a locked bedroom door, he is continually rejected by his wife until he promises to "grow up and behave like a man." And so he falls on the sofa, and in the dim light, and with heavy breathing, he masturbates as a little girl watches, bewildered and horrified. Thus the dream evolves, appears and reappears, and never fails to produce an agonizing fright.

Like Kathy, too many children have been "freaked out" by some form or some speech of the family's drama. Now, the strategy of many of these children, although nascent and unconscious, is to get out of their homes, get out of their own lives and out of their minds. What a miracle it is that some do stay, conjuring up reasons for the necessity of their remaining close to suffering parents and a damaged family unit whose mechanism is shattered. But the muffled aggression in their renewed loyalty is unmistakable. The children and their parents are like the envied lovers in the old story who never stopped holding hands until just once, whereupon they beat each other to death. Holding on to a mother's skirt, after all, may be more than a wish to remain near and in touch. It may be playing the boxer who by staying in a clinch prevents himself and his opponent from manning battle stations at arm's length. The act of caring, as gracious and humane as it is, often masks a desire to destroy and cause pain.

When a thoughtless and angry Cambridge mayor's purge on young people led him to chastise "hippies" for having run away from home, I reacted by thinking that on the contrary maybe the parents ran away first, in some fashion, hence the children merely followed suit. Now, after examining life stories like those of Jenny, John and Will, I wonder whether, like the most domesticated of pets, some young people, "pre-hippies," ran away because their parents rushed them, frightened them, and got too close in an uncomfortable way too soon. I wonder whether it was the feeling of being emotionally crowded by their parents that caused them to "split." Or maybe it does in fact have to do with parental and school rejection or derogation, or the constant threat of parents getting a divorce. Maybe the rejection, the running away from children, is more powerful and disruptive than the running toward them. Still, even in unabandoned escape and angered protestation children may be responding to or fulfilling some communicated need or directive of an authority somewhere. Maybe outbursts of anger and "misbehavior" are the only things some parents and some teachers feel comfortable dealing with, as their response to them appears so clear-cut and reasonable. Perhaps they provoke the very outbursts they claim they are seeking to avoid in order to bring about these interactions. How curious the thought, therefore, that protest and escape by the young represent an obeisance of older people turned upside down.

Equally curious is the observation that the familiar need-to-forget-or-escape-from-it-all explanation of alcoholism returns in serious drug taking as a desire to repress. My friend Mickey is a handsome young high school drop-out with an exceptional literary talent. When Mickey was eleven, his parents fought so savagely that he would find his mother lying in pools of blood. Becoming the man of the family, Mickey would have to call for the ambulance, and days later, as it always turned out, after nursing his mother back to health, he would turn his attention to reuniting his parents. This very same pattern was repeated at least six different times in one year.

During one cryptic account of a drug experience, Mickey practically went into a swoon. Then he caught himself, along with the heels of another truth: "But when you come down, man, you come down hard, and that taking each moment one by one dissolves into that rotten other present, the one where you say, I gotta go back to my job. And you ask yourself, why do I do it, and you know, you gotta feel responsible. But it's O.K. because you think about the next high." I suggested to Mickey that coming down means having to think about tomorrow. "Wrong, man," he smiled, for he had one on the shrink. "It's the past; it's on your back like you know what! . . . You say why did it have to happen to me? Fuck tomorrow, baby. It's yesterday I've got to beat!"

In speaking with Mickey and young men like him, one senses an ironical and twisted searching for, most amazingly, what seems to be insanity. While the shocks of childhood were merely flirtations with craziness, by sixteen they have reappeared as an open willingness to consider steady dating with it. At first only a couple of times a week; later on, every day and every night, then all the time. The apparent psychotic quality or "way-out-ness" of the drugs is at once terrifying and exhilarating. The downs hurt but serve to affirm the lingering presence of sanity, or at least the ability to call upon it one more time. Then, if the user is sure it's still there, he goes back up on top all over again. Or so it seemed to me once.

Not ironically, the very same strategy of "blowing one's mind" is sometimes used as a way of keeping out of memory or consciousness the mind-blowing experiences which might have urged persons toward this intimacy with drugs in the first place. But just as drinking fails to induce forgetfulness, drugs seem to be failing many persons in their efforts to "repress" the past and keep it off their backs, or so say many students. If Timothy Leary is right, the next state may just be electronic brain stimulation, hence when pharmacological repression fails, attempts may be made to actively engage in a fantasy of total memory ablation. At that time, a metaphysical present will evolve, free of any recollections and expectations; free of all regrets and despair. At least some might wish this as they commence a new era of experimentation.

Failing to understand these complicated and gifted people, I often forget myself and remind them of their futures as adults and as parents. It's not that easy. For one thing, their very sense of future differs from mine. The option to "start again," moreover, as in marriage and career is highly problematic. Many fear they will repeat the desecrating scenes of their childhood: "I'll ruin my kid a helluva lot more than the drugs I take will"; "Are you kidding man, can you see me as a father? You gotta be nuts! And you a shrink!" "A freak kid's gotta better chance than I did!"

If starting again were possible, some, assuredly, would opt for total recommencement. Knowing full well that their parents never wanted them in the first place, some almost cannot go back far enough to reach a time when their own histories might have started off on good footing. Few admit it, however, for this would be to proclaim absolutely one's non-being. It would be to break the slim and delicate threads that now barely hold the generations pridefully together. Kathy told me that her mother was informed by doctors that she could have no more children after the birth of Kathy's nearest older sister. In fact, two more children were born. The mother admitted that she had not wanted either one. Her "not wanting" became the daughter's description of herself as the "unexpected surprise." Kathy and I knew that she understood the conditions of her origins and the facts of her life. Indeed, I felt that her rather tardy inability to comprehend human anatomy and how children are born might have symbolized an even more profound reluctance and self-protection, a very understandable self-protection to be sure.

But there is even more, for, regrettably, the concept of insanity pervades the worlds, however expansive, of many young people. What many want to know is utterly predictable: "Just tell me one thing man, am I crazy? I mean, you know, am I crazy?" The word "crazy" is ubiquitous. It has lost some of its primeval jolt, perhaps, but it holds on to an unmodifiable message. There is so much insanity in television scripts and movies and newspaper accounts. Insanity is even feared when one is witnessing the inexplicable behavior of those around us as they do nothing more than fight aggressively for social and private rights too long in coming. The blacks are called insane, the poor are insane, the "kids" for sure are insane. It it also feared when one is witnessing those well-meaning men who seek to control persons who protest. The cops and the National Guard and soldiers are insane. The young hear the President called mad and the war insane, and they puzzle over insanity's bewildering function in excusing murderers in jury trials. Partly because of this the young may even seek insanity as a way of getting out of the draft. Insanity or a belief in it seems to be able to immobilize some, liberate others. It's a natural resource to be harnessed.

In my day, not so long ago, a "joking" admonition for guaranteed military deferments was simply this: when the army doctor examines you, kiss him. Now it's insanity. Naturally, the worry exists for these young men that they might carry forever the brand of insanity on their sleeves just about where the private stripe might have gone; but still, to be crazy is to avoid military service. Like kissing the doc, it is also the ineluctable avoidance of maleness. An often cruel society rubs this in: a real man fights for his country. Ideologies and spirit react against this of course, but the doubt, however slight, stays. American socialization patterns, normally instituting strict sex role differentiations, take care of that. There will be a lingering doubt, although in much of their questioning and concern, perceptions and anguish the young find older persons who will support them. Many of the "knowing class," they come to learn, now prefer to think of "business as usual" as the real insane course, and jail as an undesirable but still honorable and healthy way out.

Earlier I spoke of a resistance to bearing children and the feeling that one could not successfully assume responsibilities of parenthood. In some cases it seems as though the diffidence some young people display in "going on" masks a wish to start anew. The present urge to keep the cycle from repeating and the intention to keep fresh life from beginning must be considered from the point of view of sexuality. Although the language remains unchanged, actions of "procuring" and "scoring" today refer to drugs. The prophylactic, its slick package dirtied by months in the seams of an old wallet, has been replaced by the nickel bag: "Always be prepared." A funny reversal, furthermore, concerns sex role functions in a new economic market, as girls now solicit funds to pay for their boyfriends' stuff. I was stopped by one of these girls in the street on a beautiful October afternoon: "Excuse me, sir," she began her proposal, "how about a quarter for a cup of God knows what?"

One cannot be certain of the sexual habits of the persons of whom I speak. But anyway, it's no one's business until they mention it. The subject, however, is close to the conversational surface. It is as intimate as it ever was, but seemingly beginning to be freed of its irrational ties to some mysterious and primordial secrecy. As with much of their behavior, many of the young merely make overt what their elders do covertly. In so doing, they seem much more honest and far less foolish. The conspicuous consumption of products and styles by other youngsters, however, is often little more than a mimicry of their parents.

Like Will, many young men on drugs confess their apprehensions about homosexuality. It is not simply that they fear their impulses. This pattern, ironically, seems to be more common among those actually engaged in heterosexual relationships. Instead, they tell of a lack of sexual impulses and a concern that perhaps hard drugs have destroyed the sex drive. Because of their sophistication, they comprehend the possibility that their activities generally could be interpreted as homosexual, but about this they manifest little panic. Some admit that they are able to "make it" with girls only when "high." They confess to fright, but it does not compare to the fear that they may be (going) crazy.

This is the supreme danger, as it suggests again, the complex reversal of not only competence in drug work and sex work but the associated interchange between the organs of sex and the "organ" of drugs, the mind. One almost wants to assert that a phallic phase of development has been temporarily supplanted or postponed by a "cephalic" phase. All life comes to be fixated in the mind, and Leary spoke for the generation at least once when he advertised that each brain cell is capable of brilliant and repeating orgasms. Whether scientific or metaphoric, Leary's words were not forgotten.

Is it then too farfetched to draw parallels, first between the act of getting high and sexual foreplay or the eventual sexual excitement; and next between the actual mind-blowing experience with its visions and thresholds of exhilaration and the orgasm in which the person is exquisitely primed by his own powers; and finally between the depressing down, the returning to time and reality, and the detumescence and resumption of normalcy and normal size? To be sure, the reasoning is dangerous in its analogical foundation, but the symbolic orgasm of the drug state as occult sex seems to have both homosexual and heterosexual aspects.

This then leaves one issue, namely, going mad from a drug experience, the "freak-out," the ultimate reward, the ultimate punishment. It builds to total destruction, at once implosion and explosion. In students' own words, it is brain damage and disintegration. Simultaneously, it is conception, pregnancy, childbirth, castration and death. Some continue to believe that from the womb of the mind a new child, a freak child is born, and it all is supposed to happen in the longest-shortest instant that time ever knew.

By some students' own admission, the freak-out is also a premeditated "cop-out." To take drugs is to willingly step out of the natural flow for a moment or two. In a way, it has much of the quality of living with a sexual partner unmarried, for there is an anticipation of an end coupled with the preparation for some later recourse. Demanding no commitment, or less than common commitment, drug taking is an out permitting the luxury of retiring as undefeated champion. No one can fault the last-minute term paper writer or the patient hospitalized with an overdose or from a bad trip. Both have their excuses and reasons for being remiss and, like little children, excuses for being out of school. Yet both wonder, presumably, about what their competence might be like void of recourse, void of excuse. Both wonder, too, about the lack of preparations for an equivocal future shrieking death, and the minimal confidence already displayed in present endeavor.

Depicted in so many of these notions is the mass communicative society in which we survive. The accomplishments by so many are so great; the knowledge and awareness so swift in arrival and so deep in meaning that in a way we leave the young no excuse for failure other than severe illness and total collapse. Adlai Stevenson once confessed relief that career decisions were behind him. It *is* hard to be young today as so many good people are already so advanced in practically any area that one might choose for himself. And so many new areas have already become crusty. Perhaps this is a reason for so many "dropping out," if only temporarily.

In sexual relations, the excuse that probably maintained the sanity of frightened generations of men no longer exists. Girls have "the pill" or other devices, and aggressive action now swings both ways. Students offer apologies for not smoking pot and agonize over an inability to get excited, much less involved, in political enterprises. To be straight is to be square, and like it or not the straight become defensive and tempted.

Our televised and instant replay society also allows few secrets. We see the war; we see men murdered; and we become frustrated when we cannot discover the exact frame on which is recorded a President's death. And as if that were not enough, our newspapers pry and reveal, our movies reveal, and so too, apparently, do some parents. While many children fantasize that the secrets they safeguard for their parents preserve some mysterious family integrity, others are, in fact, maintaining this very integrity by keeping all family secrets safe and locked away. It is these persons who sometimes bite a quivering lip in fear that exposure of their treasured secrets will cause their families to unravel.

In truth, there *are* young people responsible for the knit of adult involvements, a knit that sometimes fails to include even themselves. In the long run, Jenny's silence helped to keep her parents together, but she has paid a price. It has taken one great effort! For her, living moment to moment is not the medium in which experience fits. Living through the day is both the medium and the experiential essence. Day work matters. One must keep the glue of sanity from softening and walk on, no matter what.

So one keeps in his head or in his diary what he heard Daddy say to that woman, or what he saw Mommy doing in the restaurant, or what he heard Mommy and Daddy say to each other on those nights when their anger exploded so suddenly that no one took the precaution of closing the bedroom door, as if that really made a difference. This is the stuff that stays inside, sealed over until it pops out in a doctor's office, in a creative writing course short story, or in those first poems written for no reason during a Thanksgiving or Christmas vacation.

Then, while all of this goes on, performance demands shriek for attention. One must compete and succeed often enough, make it on one's own, and react to the war and the fact that he or a boy friend will soon be drafted and, not so unlikely, killed! One must be good in school, good at home, good at sports, good at pot and good in bed. Life becomes unmanageably meaningful. It is enough to make one (want to) go insane.

Most make it through, however, even with the knowledge that their culture warns of belligerent Chinese, overkill, communism, and an equivocal future. One cannot know when the next and final war will come, nor when past experience with drugs will suddenly reerupt in the form of a grotesque child or one's own psychotic demise. But most make it through, and ten years later they look in disbelief on their own pasts. "I couldn't do it again," they often will say.

Unmistakably near, death becomes a real reality. Less fuzzy than ever before, its shape and sound hover about self-analytic groups, rap sessions and coffee dates. Damn the future and the inevitable! It was better in the 'Thirties when gravelly throated heroes sang into megaphones. It was better, too, in the last century when men wore frock coats, beards and long hair. It was better and easier because it was the past, and perception of the completed proves the validity of survival, if not of achievement. At very least, the past means having gotten this far. It also means the seat of much of the trouble that many just cannot shake.

Some young people reveal a peculiar attitude about the past. It is not merely that chunk of time that was, but the series of events that once were and yet somehow continue to remain as a lining to the present. Not exactly recalled or retrieved, the past has become the stuff of moment-to-moment encounter and the routine of day work. The past has not yet become past, therefore, in the sense of being over, because its foundation, like a child's body, remains soft and unfinished. There are no completions yet, no triumphs, no guaranteed deferrals or subsistence.

To be sure, youth cries. Sometimes it is out of sadness for its own past, sometimes in reaction to the two societies, the one encountered and the one held as prospect. Some observers insist that more often than not in much of its activities youth cries to be heard, or for help. It is too difficult to know for certain whether this is true, particularly because out of the concern, guilt and solipsism of an older generation grows the presumptuous pride that youth, when it speaks, must always address itself to parents and elders, or that speaking means crying or begging. This simply is not true. Attacks on society are not merely hatreds of parents which have gone productively astray. To the contrary, it often seems as though the questionings of those who *precede* us are simultaneously pleas for recognition and directives intended to justify prior decisions and behavior. Adults want a bit of attention and do a little crying and begging themselves.

No one as yet has studied the notes written by parents to their runaway children in New York's East Village or San Francisco's Haight Ashbury district, a district which seems to have faded. These pitiful missives document so well the lack of generational space and the confession of failure in parenthood and adulthood. They could almost be the letters of children who, wishing to come home, promise never again to misbehave. If they did not cause guilt or confusion in the recipients, the young people who screen them would have little need to prevent them from reaching the runaway children. (Those people, young and old, whose self-appointed life task it is to maintain the separation and lack of communication between parent and child must fear, I would think, the fruits of love's temptation, the very philosophy they often profess or at least once professed. Moreover, they are reminiscent of professional mourners who continually remind the congregation or family of the recent loss by crying and collapsing when others attain momentary composure. It is almost as though reconciliation, equanimity and peace are destructive to their sense of a social order.)

The "Come back home — all is forgiven" notes stand as a testament to what must be seen by the young as a crumbling structure or a tragic reversal of intentionality and interpersonal competence. They reflect adults' pleas for help and forgiveness, and as such they represent a far worse social fact than "hippie" farm colonies or pot parties. The notes only document what the poets know so well: of all rewards, youth is a supreme ideal. The old might wish to be young, but the young seem happy exactly where they are. This, too, is an asymmetry.

Few parents are able to accept the passing of adolescence, especially when their own children dramatize more vibrantly than ever the former gratifications and projected incompleteness of their own lives. It is inconceivable to think that young people have ever been simultaneously idolized and despised, worshiped and envied as they are presently. But without doubt, the problem of age grading is now of paramount significance in the United States. It is one of *the* dimensions: whether it is good or bad, the old are preoccupied with the young, and the young so often seem preoccupied with themselves. Another asymmetry.

The period, moreover, has become so erotic. Previously, when the activities of the young were more secretive, adults were compelled to deal with their own imaginations. Now, when sexuality in particular screams at us from advertisements, fashions, television, movies and magazines, it becomes increasingly difficult to decline youth's unintended invitation and accept the process and reality of aging. We almost forget that many of these invitations in fact do not originate among the young. Nonetheless, adults must work hard to avoid the eternal seductions of the young, for these affairs simply do not work out. Time inevitably chaperones such liaisons, and the primordial strain which comes about through the separation of generations never does permit a successful consummation of these two hearts, the young and the old.

The seduction does not stop with parents, however, for the succulence of youth is dreamed of each day by teachers, counselors, therapists, ministers, etcetera. A most dangerous tack for any of these persons is to be uncritically won over by youth's stated demands and ideologies or interpretations of them. Let me give an example of this point.

We are emerging from an unfortunate era during which time psychotherapy was viewed as either panacea or black magic. Psychotherapists themselves finally have undertaken critical self-examination, and for the most part attacks on theory and procedure have resulted in clarifying statements for the practitioners and their clients. Still, there are some critics who expend a suspiciously great amount of energy communicating to youth the evils of psychotherapy and, even more, the harmfulness of any benign adult interventions. By acting this way, these people purportedly signify their "stand with youth," a stand normally introduced by some phrase which seems an apologia, but which in truth is more of a boastful pledge to be like the young, or even younger.

Frequently these critics demonstrate a striking accuracy in their realignment of youth's goals, ambitions and philosophies. Just as often their arguments are indecorous and evil. Many young people in fact do find illness in themselves and do seek help. They despise the proverbial "shrink scene" and rightly so, but in their quest of a "hip shrink" they wish for a modification or, better, modernization of the psychotherapeutic relationship, but not its annihilation. They know it is no panacea, but in anticipation they feel it has worth and are willing to try. And that's a lot. The best adults may be able to do, therefore, is experiment with the helping apparatus and not discourage the trying.

So those of us who aspire to speak for or understand youth must be aware of the seductive nature of our interests so that we will not reach the point where speaking for youth means no longer needing to listen to it. Genuine representation, after all, does not require reliving; it requires recalling.

One final point regards the heightened sophistication of the young, their eagerness to speak, their facile access to recesses of an experienced childhood, and their poignant observations of adulthood.

While longevity statistics indicate that with each generation human beings may expect to live longer, much of society, as Erikson points out, demands that individuals be allotted less time for youth. Earnest young protoprofessionals, especially, uphold this ethic. Scattered not so infrequently about, however, are those whose parents have denied them even this minuscule tenure. For Jenny, the kid stuff ended at fourteen and was succeeded by what appears to her as an anachronistic awareness. For most, the awareness is simply a function of a precocious curiosity and creative need to experience. For the ones knowingly in trouble, the most immediate and pressing action resembles an attempt to complete some poorly understood mission started long ago by someone else.

That time repeats itself is but a comforting saying. The concept of a family cycle, moreover, is misleading, as it tends to slur over the individual cycles unwinding at various tempi within it. Individual cycles never repeat themselves, for in progressing or carrying on in any guise, "healthy" or "sick," the young, as ingenious as they often are, do little more than obey the wishes of others and the demands that time imposes. Typically, the directions given by those who were here before us are to wait patiently and not walk so fast.

Sociologists have written that a major function of social structures is to direct its members to appropriate goal states, means of attaining them, and attitudes that are best assumed in evaluating goals and means. The desire to become a doctor or lawyer, indeed the need to achieve, does not come from out of the blue. It is learned. So too is the desire to rebel, make love, take drugs, escape and even "freak out." In their way, all of these actions are creative because they develop out of social forms of, as well as private needs for, expression. But they have not "sprung up"; like instincts, they have evolved.

For many today, the evolution is not satisfying, and the internal excursions and elaborations have become (and probably started out as), in David Riesman's terms, "other-directed" movements. Knowing exactly this, many young persons continue, nonetheless, in their other-directed patterns, and thereby show themselves most willing to listen outward and upward. And considering much of our adult behavior, this fact is remarkable.

13

Parental Power Legitimation and Its Effect on the Adolescent

by Glen H. Elder, Jr.

Research has shown that the assertion of legitimate power engenders feelings of liking and lowers resistance to conformity with respect to the power agent and his rules. However, the effects of different amounts of power exercised by the influencing agent on the above relationships have been left largely unanswered. The objective of this research was to investigate the relationship between the frequency of parental explanations, employed as an index of the degree of power legitimation, and adolescent (1) desire to model parents, (2) compliance with parental requests, and (3) autonomy in program solving and decision making, on three levels of parental power in a sample of Ohio and North Carolina adolescents. The effects of the frequency of parental explanations on adolescent behavior were found to vary substantially in relation to levels of power.

When a child requests a reason or explanation concerning a particular restriction, at least two responses are open to the parent. On the one hand, the parent may fulfill the request and demand compliance; on the other, the parent may ignore the child's inquiry. From the child's perspective, this is essentially the difference between the expression of legitimate and coercive power.

The results of small group research suggest the following inferences: adolescents who perceive their parents as asserting coercive rather than legitimate power over them should be less highly attracted to their parents,[1] and less likely to conform to rules of conduct in the absence of parental surveillance,[2] than other adolescents. Research reveals that adolescents have less favorable attitudes toward coercive than legitimate power,[3] and that coercive power expression by mothers promotes the development of hostility and power needs among children of nursery school age.[4] These findings suggest that the legitimation of power by parents leads to a strengthening of affective relations between parents and the adolescent, and tends to encourage behavioral conformity to parental rules.

The effects of legitimate and coercive parental power on adolescents are less clear when the legitimacy of different levels of parental power is considered. Since the effects of different levels of power on adolescent affection for parents vary substantially, it follows that the effects of legitimate and coercive power may also differ by the level of parental power.[5] For instance, the autocratic parent who, as a rule, does legitimize his demands and restrictions by explaining them, is apt to evoke different kinds of reactions from adolescents than is the permissive parent who offers frequent explanations. Similarly, infrequent explanations at these two levels of power are apt to have different effects on adolescent behavior. Building upon experimental and survey findings regarding the differential effects of legitimate and coercive power, this research is concerned with determining how such effects, as revealed in adolescent behavior and reactions to parents, vary in relation to three levels of parental power.

In an earlier study, seven types of parent-adolescent interdependence in the child rearing relationship were delineated.[6] Five of these structures are condensed in this research to measure high, moderate and low parental power.

Autocratic. The parent does not allow the adolescent to express his views on subjects regarding his behavior nor permit him to regulate his own behavior in any way.

---

[1] Bertram H. Raven and John R. P. French, Jr., "Group Support, Legitimate Power and Social Influence," *Journal of Personality*, 26 (December, 1958), pp. 400–409, John R. P. French, Jr., H. William Morrison, and George Levinger, "Coercive Power and Forces Affecting Conformity," *Journal of Abnormal and Social Psychology*, 61 (January, 1960), pp. 93–101.

[2] Bertram H. Raven and John R. P. French, Jr., "Legitimate Power, Coercive Power and Observability in Social Influence," *Sociometry*, 21 (June, 1958), pp. 83–97.

[3] Anatol Pikas, "Children's Attitudes toward Rational Versus Inhibiting Parental Authority," *Journal of Abnormal and Social Psychology*, 62 (March, 1961), pp. 315–321.

[4] Martin L. Hoffman, "Power Assertion by the Parent and Its Impact Upon the Child," *Child Development*, 31 (March, 1960), pp. 129–143.

[5] Adolescents with highly dominant parents in contrast to democratic parents were much more likely to feel unwanted by their parents, to be low on affectional orientation toward parents, and to consider their child rearing policy to be unreasonable. See Glen H. Elder, Jr., "Structural Variations in the Child Rearing Relationship," *Sociometry*, 25 (September, 1962), pp. 241–62; and *Family Structure and the Transmission of Value and Norms in the Process of Child Rearing*, unpublished Ph.D. Dissertation, University of North Carolina, 1961, Chapters IX and X.

[6] Elder, "Structural Variations in the Child Rearing Relationship," *op. cit.*

Democratic. The adolescent is encouraged to participate in discussing issues relevant to his behavior although the final decision is always made or approved by the parent.

Permissive. The adolescent has more influence in making decisions which concern him than does his parent. The laissez-faire and ignoring types of interdependence are included in this level of power.

The effects of frequent and infrequent explanations of rules of conduct at the three levels of parental power will be examined on (1) the attractiveness of parents—the desire of adolescents to be like or model their parents; (2) compliance with parental requests—conformity to parental wishes regarding peer associations; and (3) autonomy—adolescent independence in decision making and feelings of self-confidence in personal goals and standards of behavior. First, however, the relationship between parental explanations and level of parental power will be investigated. Let us state some general expectations concerning each of the dependent variables (as well as parental explanation) in the order in which they are considered in the subsequent analysis.

Hypotheses

A parent may shrug off a child's inquiry by heatedly exclaiming, "You do it, I don't need to explain," or, in contrast, meet the request with an explanation which seems reasonable.[7] Autocratic parents totally exclude

their children from participating in the formulation of decisions which concern them while the children of democratic and permissive parents have much more freedom in self-direction. These differences lead us to predict that *the frequency of explanation is inversely related to parental power*.

Since research indicates that positive sentiment toward a power agent increases as the perceived legitimacy of his power increases, it is likely that modeling is positively related to the frequency of parental explanations.[8] However, this relationship is apt to vary by level of parental power, since a recent study shows affection toward parents to be related to parental power in a curvilinear manner.[9] Adolescents of autocratic and permissive parents tended to be low on affection. From these results we hypothesize that *modeling is most common among adoles-*

___

[7] The legitimation of rules of conduct was consistently a major function of parental explanations in an earlier exploratory study of a number of child rearing variables. In lengthy focused interviews with 60 ninth and twelfth grade adolescents who represented the extremes in social adjustment and in social class status, we found that the control wielded by parents who explained their rules was in practically all cases viewed as right and reasonable. As one youth put it, "They explain why it's right and it's right, that's all." Very few youths who received frequent explanations could think of times when "false or made up" explanations were offered. The rarity of this practice may be due to the fact that pseudo-reasons seldom fooled or satisfied these adolescents. One girl revealed that she "just tossed them back" at her parents. For the most part, the data from this study indicate that frequent explanations of rules and demands definitely tended to make the regulations seem right in the eyes of adolescents.

[8] For example, see Raven and French, "Group Support, Legitimate Power, and Social Influence," *op. cit.*

[9] Elder, "Structural Variations in the Child Rearing Relationship," *op. cit.*

cents with democratic parents who frequently provide explanations for their rules.

Miller and Swanson found that parental explanations were strongly associated with resistance to temptation in their sample of adolescent boys.[10] While explanations may be directly related to obedience, it is apparent that this relationship is likely to vary substantially by level of power. For instance, we know that autocratic and permissive parents are apt to be less accepting and supportive than the democratic parent[11] and that parental warmth is instrumental in facilitating the adoption of parental standards.[12] Hence, we predict that *conformity to parental rules is most typical of adolescents with democratic parents who frequently provide explanations.*

The possible effects of non-explaining parents on the autonomy of the child are considerable. According to Hoffman, the arbitrary, threatening nature of rules and demands left unexplained ("unqualified power assertion," in his terminology) requires from a child the "unconditional surrender of his own interests and involvements," tends to "frustrate his momentary need for task completion," and "constitutes an assault on his autonomy as well."[13] Miller and Swanson labelled a mother who does not explain requests as *arbitrary.*

> If she is arbitrary, he must obey without understanding. His world soon consists of high fences bounding many little spaces from which he can escape only by risking her disapproval. In new situations he cannot afford the risk of arriving at his own judgments. Because he often does not understand the purposes of his mother's regulations, he cannot tell whether she will condemn the actions he takes on his own initiative. He can be sure only that following directions, whether or not they make sense, is the best way to keep out of trouble and win approval.[14]

The non-explaining parent is thus apt to undermine the self-confidence of the adolescent in his ability to make his own decisions as well as weaken his desire for such independence. While adolescent autonomy may be positively related to the parental practice of explaining rules and requests, it is likely to be inversely related to parental power. By definition, the autocratic type of parent-child interdependence severely limits opportunities for adolescents to acquire wisdom and confidence in independent decision making. Assuming that adolescent autonomy is positively related to the frequency of parental explanations and is negatively related to parental power, we hypothesize that *autonomy is most common among adolescents of permissive parents who explain their requests*

and is least characteristic of autocratically reared adolescents who seldom receive explanations concerning rules of conduct.

Method

The data for this investigation were obtained from a larger project on adolescence in the Institute for Research in Social Science at the University of North Carolina. This larger study is concerned with determining the affectional, associational, and value orientations of adolescents in grades seven through twelve. Slightly more than half of these respondents were obtained from public schools in central North Carolina, and the rest from both public and parochial school systems in central Ohio. The data were collected in April and May, 1960, with a structured questionnaire administered by teachers in the classroom. The data for this present study were obtained from a 40 per cent sample of the seventh through ninth grade students and 60 per cent of the tenth through twelfth graders, randomly drawn from the 19,200 white adolescents from unbroken homes.

The frequency of parental explanation is measured by two five-response category items which are similar in wording except for the referent.

> When you don't know why your (mother/father) makes a particular decision or has certain rules for you to follow, will (she/he) explain the reason?
> Unexplained power expression (low legitimation) (1) Never. (2) Once in a while. (3) Sometimes
> Explained power expression (high legitimation) (4) Usually. (5) Yes, always

The seven types of parent-adolescent interdependence are measured by two seven-response category items, one referring to mother and the other to father. The three levels of parental power are measured by response categories (1) autocratic, (3) democratic, and (5, 6, and 7) permissive, to the following question.

> In general, how are most decisions made between you and your (mother/father)?
>
> AUTOCRATIC
> 1. My (mother/father) just tells me what to do.
>
> DEMOCRATIC
> 3. I have considerable opportunity to make my own decisions, but my (mother/father) has the final word.
>
> PERMISSIVE
> 5. I can make my own decision but my (mother/father) would like for me to consider (her/his) opinion.
> 6. I can do what I want regardless of what my (mother/father thinks.
> 7. My (mother/father) doesn't care what I do.

Parental Power and the Frequency of Explanations

Differences between autocratic, democratic, and permissive parents are examined with age, sex, and social class of the adolescent controlled (Table 1).[15] The data

[10] Miller and Swanson found that boys who received explanations of parental requests were more likely to write stories in which heroes resist temptation than were boys of parents who seldom offered explanations. Daniel R. Miller and Guy E. Swanson, *Inner Conflict and Defense*, New York: Holt-Dryden & Co., 1960, p. 172. Reasoning with the child, which is another method of making parental regulations seem reasonable and legitimate, is highly related to the development of conscience. See Robert Sears, Eleanor Maccoby, and Harry Levin, *Patterns of Child Rearing*, New York: Row Peterson & Co., 1957, p. 393.

[11] Elder, *Family Structure and the Transmission of Values and Norms in the Process of Child Rearing, op. cit.*, Chapter XI.

[12] See, for example, Paul Mussen and Luther Distler, "Masculinity, Identification, and Father-Son Relationships," *Journal of Abnormal and Social Psychology*, 59 (November, 1959), pp. 350–356.

[13] Martin L. Hoffman, "Power Assertion by the Parent and Its Impact upon the Child," *op. cit.*, pp. 131–132.

[14] Miller and Swanson, *op. cit.*, p. 80.

[15] Younger and older adolescents are those in grades seven through nine and ten through twelve, respectively. Adolescents and their families were placed in middle and lower class categories by assigning the youths' fathers' occupations to occupational categories employed by the U. S.

TABLE 1

Frequent Parental Explanations by Autocratic, Democratic, and Permissive Parents:
Age, Sex, and Social Class Controlled

Parent	Level of Parental Power	Frequent Parental Explanations Per Cent of Adolescents							
		Older Males		Older Females		Younger Males		Younger Females	
		Middle Class	Lower Class	Middle Class	Lower Class	Middle Class	Lower Class	Middle Class	Lower Class
Mother	Autocratic	(18) 31.6	(35) 42.7	(10) 16.7	(19) 22.5	(25) 31.2	(62) 43.4	(16) 36.4	(50) 37.9
	Democratic	(232) 75.6	(239) 73.8	(243) 79.2	250) 76.2	(266) 82.1	(218) 72.9	(276) 87.3	(262) 74.6
	Permissive	(190) 73.1	(208) 70.3	(215) 84.0	(228) 76.0	(121) 74.7	(118) 63.4	(144) 79.1	(144) 76.6
Father	Autocratic	(23) 18.7	(36) 19.5	(32) 23.4	(38) 19.0	(39) 34.2	(78) 36.3	(31) 29.8	(64) 27.2
	Democratic	(224) 74.7	(217) 73.8	(285) 79.2	(187) 73.6	(250) 81.7	(176) 64.7	(253) 83.5	(197) 71.4
	Permissive	(130) 75.6	(139) 63.8	(143) 72.2	(168) 70.6	(85) 65.4	(96) 66.7	(108) 72.0	(109) 63.4

reveal that democratic and permissive parents are from two to four times as likely to explain their rules and expectations frequently than are autocratic parents.[16] Democratic parents are slightly more likely to explain than are permissive mothers and fathers. These differences are most evident among middle class parents. Generally, class differences are greatest among autocratic mothers and democratic and permissive parents; lower class autocratic mothers and middle class democratic or permissive mothers and fathers are more likely to explain their rules and policy. Mothers are more likely to explain frequently to younger than older adolescents and to girls rather than boys. Age and sex differences are inconsistent for fathers.[17]

Within each age, sex, and class sub-group frequent explanations are least common among autocratic parents and are most common among democratic parents. In most categories, more than 70 per cent of democratic and permissive parents frequently provide reasons for their actions when asked to do so, whereas this is true for generally less than 40 per cent of the autocratic parents. Thus autocratic parents are inclined to resist explaining their rules and thereby impose coercive controls and demands.

Bureau of the Census. "Clerical and kindred workers" and above were classified as middle class. "Farmers, farm managers, and farm laborers" were treated as unclassified. The sample is largely urban.

[16] Nonetheless, the reasonableness of the autocratic parents' child-rearing-policy is strongly enhanced when explanations are frequently provided. The evaluations of two groups of autocratically reared adolescents were compared with respect to the fairness of their parents' child rearing policy. One group frequently received explanations when requested and perceived greater freedom in decision making during the past two years, whereas the other group of adolescents was low on both parental explanations and decision-making freedom. The former group of adolescents was more than twice as likely as the latter youths to consider their parents to be usually or more often fair (for older males toward their fathers, 68.7 versus 30.3 per cent). See Elder, *Family Structure and the Transmission of Values and Norms in the Process of Child Rearing*, pp. 637–643.

[17] Tests of significance have not been employed in the evaluation of results due to the nature and size of our sample and to our interest in the general pattern of relationships.

The Desire to Model

As a measure of the attractiveness of parents, we asked the following questions with respect to each parent: "Would you like to be the kind of person your (mother/father) is?" The five responses to this item ranged from "Yes, completely," to "Not at all." The responses, "Yes, completely," "In most ways," and "In many ways," are considered as indicating the desire to model, i.e., to be like mother and/or father. This item taps the degree to which the adolescent values the attributes and behavior of a parent and is not restricted to sex-appropriate behavior.

In accord with our hypothesis, modeling is most typical of democratically reared adolescents who often receive explanations.[18] Non-explaining autocratic and permissive parents are least apt to be modeled. Boys are generally more apt to model their fathers and girls their mothers, regardless of level of power and frequency of explanation.

Explaining parents are in all instances more likely to be modeled than are parents who seldom explain. By removing the control on age and sex and computing mean percentage differences between the proportions of youths who desire to model explaining and non-explaining mothers and fathers by each level of power, we find little variation in the differences—five of the six mean percentage differences fall between 22.5 and 27.2 per cent. Thus, adolescent attraction to parents is increased to a similar degree at most levels of parental power by the frequent explanation of rules.

Democratically reared adolescents are more likely to model their mothers and/or fathers than are adolescents of either autocratic or permissive parents who are com-

---

[18] Both the types of parent-adolescent interdependence and the frequency of parental explanations vary in relation to social class. Given a certain level of parental power along with high or low power legitimation, the effects as manifest in adolescent behavior appear similar among middle and lower class youths. The principal variation by social class is in the contrasting distribution of middle and lower class parents by these two variables.

TABLE 2

Levels of Parental Power and Frequency of Explanations in Relation to Desire of
Adolescents to Model their Parents: Age and Sex Controlled

Parent	Age and Sex	Per Cent of Adolescents Who Would Like to be the Kind of Person Their Mothers/Fathers Are in Many, Most, or All Ways					
		Autocratic		Democratic		Permissive	
		Freq.	Infreq.	Freq.	Infreq.	Freq.	Infreq.
Mother	OM	(41) 77.4	(38) 45.2	(391) 83.4	(100) 62.5	(283) 71.5	(74) 48.1
	YM	(69) 81.1	(66) 48.9	(418) 86.7	(91) 65.5	(136) 57.6	(36) 32.4
	OF	(22) 88.0	(30) 29.7	(499) 93.4	(107) 70.8	(392) 88.2	(68) 59.6
	YF	(57) 85.0	(61) 56.0	(512) 95.0	(90) 69.2	(266) 92.4	(53) 64.6
Father	OM	(42) 71.2	(113) 45.7	(405) 91.8	(119) 76.8	(220) 82.4	(57) 47.5
	YM	(92) 80.0	(123) 58.0	(399) 94.8	(118) 78.7	(164) 90.6	(63) 68.5
	OF	(81) 62.8	(141) 42.0	(243) 78.4	(54) 43.9	(340) 89.9	(58) 64.4
	YF	(43) 45.3	(55) 22.7	(291) 64.1	(50) 39.7	(24) 57.4	(33) 31.1
Mean Per Cent							
Mother	Boys	79.3	47.0	85.1	63.0	64.6	40.3
	Girls	86.5	42.9	94.2	70.0	90.3	62.1
Father	Boys	75.6	51.9	93.3	77.8	86.5	58.0
	Girls	54.1	32.4	71.3	41.8	73.7	47.8
Mean Per Cent Difference between Freq. and Infreq. Explanations							
Mother		38.0		23.2		26.3	
Father		22.7		22.5		27.2	

parable in frequency of explanation. Since the democratic type of interdependence facilitates greater parent *and* adolescent involvement in decision making concerning the adolescent than the other two types, this result appears to support the Meadian conception of role learning through interaction.[19] The greater the parent-adolescent interaction, the greater the likelihood that the adolescent will desire to be like his parent. This probability of role imitation seems enhanced considerably when the parent, in addition to frequently interacting with the child, frequently explains the reasons for restrictions and demands which may not be understood.

Compliance With Parental Rules

The economic and educational changes in American society have fostered the emergence of what Coleman describes as adolescent subcultures ". . . with values and activities quite distinct from those of the adult society."[20]

The significant effects of peers upon an adolescent's values, academic motivation, and achievement is convincingly documented by the findings of Coleman's study. A stringent test of the degree to which an adolescent would comply with parental rules and requests might be represented by a situation in which his parents objected strongly to some of his friends. The way in which these cross-pressures are resolved—in favor of parents or peers—would reflect the salience of each group relative to the youth's behavior and indicate to some extent the nature of the youth's system of values and moral standards. As an occasion of parent-peer conflict, the following question was asked: "If your parents were to object strongly to some of the friends you had, would you: (1) Stop going with them, (2) See them less, (3) See them secretly, (4) Keep going with them openly?" The first two responses indicate a measure of compliance with parental wishes; the last two represent resolution in favor of peers.

Similar to the results on the modeling of parents, compliance is most common among adolescents with democratic parents who explain their rules frequently (Table 3).[21] However, variations in the likelihood of compliance

[19] See Orville G. Brim, Jr., "Family Structure and Sex Role Learning by Children: A Further Analysis of Helen Koch's Data," *Sociometry*, 21 (March, 1958), pp. 1–16; and "Personality Development as Role Learning," in I. Iscoe and H. Stevenson (eds.), *Personality Development in Children*, Austin, Texas: University of Texas Press, 1960.

[20] James S. Coleman, "The Adolescent Subculture and Academic Achievement," *American Journal of Sociology*, 65 (January, 1960), p. 337.

[21] Since compliance to parental wishes and autonomy represent aspects of a child's behavior, it is essential to analyze simultaneously the joint effects of maternal and paternal power and explanations. In order to do this and yet have sufficient cases for analysis, we are forced to limit the

TABLE 3

*Levels of Parental Power and Frequency of Explanations as Related to Adolescent
Compliance with Parental Wishes: Sex of Adolescent Controlled*

| Sex | Level of Parental Power | Parental Explanation | N | Per Cent of Adolescents Who in Response to Strong Parental Objections to Some of Their Friends Would: | | Total Per Cent |
				Stop Going with Them or See Them Less	See Them Secretly or Openly	
Boys	Autocratic	Freq.	85	70.6	29.4	100
		Infreq.	123	35.0	65.0	100
	Democratic	Freq.	604	74.2	25.8	100
		Infreq.	110	60.9	39.1	100
	Permissive	Freq.	341	66.0	34.0	100
		Infreq.	100	44.0	66.0	100
Girls	Autocratic	Freq.	54	79.6	20.4	100
		Infreq.	107	43.0	57.0	100
	Democratic	Freq.	626	85.0	15.0	100
		Infreq.	84	77.4	22.6	100
	Permissive	Freq.	385	79.8	21.2	100
		Infreq.	75	53.3	46.7	100

by level of power are pronounced only under conditions of infrequent explanations. Hence, the frequency of parental explanations seems to be more crucial in inducing conformity than level of power. This suggests that level of power may be a more significant factor in regulating observable behavior, while the rationalization of rules by explanations is strongly related to the child's adoption of parental rules. Although no meaningful variations in these results were observed by age, girls are in all instances more likely to claim that they would obey their parents than are boys.

Variations in the frequency of parental explanation have relatively little effect on the likelihood of adolescents' conforming in democratically structured relationships. Presumably an authority structure of this kind engenders mutuality of respect, understanding and trust and reduces the necessity for explanatory efforts. It appears that as structural asymmetry increases in parent-child relations toward either autocratic control or permissiveness, obedience to parental rules becomes increasingly contingent on explanatory efforts by parents. In addition to the factor of parental affection and explanations, extreme asymmetry in the structure of the child-rearing relationship may be associated with general communication failures in the transmission of rules and values. Under such conditions parents may simply say little and rigorously control their children or detach themselves completely in child rearing.

Autonomy

One indication of an adolescent's ability to direct his own behavior is the degree to which he feels confident that his ideas and opinions about what he should do and be-

analysis to parents who correspond in both level of power and in frequency of explanations.

lieve are right and best for him. A youth who expresses confidence in his own values, goals, and awareness of rules is presumably more capable of operating effectively on his own. A second aspect concerns the degree of adolescent self-reliance in problem solving and decision making. When faced with a really important decision about himself and his future, the adolescent who seeks ideas and information from others but makes up his own mind exhibits a high degree of autonomy in problem solving. Two items which measured these two aspects of autonomy were dichotomized and the responses were cross-tabulated to provide four empirical types of dependence-independence; adolescents who have or lack confidence in their own ideas, values, and goals may either be relatively dependent or independent in decision making.

An analysis of the three levels of power and the frequency of parental explanation in relation to these four types of dependence and independence behavior is shown in Table 4. The results partially confirm our hypotheses. As predicted, autonomy (both confident and independent) is most typical of adolescents with parents who are both permissive *and* frequent explainers. On the other hand, we find that youths who seldom receive explanations are least apt to exhibit autonomy, and this result does not vary by level of power.

An examination of variations in the two aspects of autonomy reveals that adolescents with autocratic parents who explain are more apt to feel *self-confident and dependent* in decision making than are children of autocratic parents who seldom explain (a difference of 17.1%), and are more likely to express confidence in their adequacy for self-direction, whether dependent or independent in decision making (a mean difference of 7.5%). There is practically no percentage difference between the proportions of self-confident and independent youths with explaining and non-explaining parents at this level of power. Thus,

TABLE 4

*Levels of Parental Power and Frequency of Explanations in Relation to Types of
Adolescent Dependence-Independence Behavior*

Level of Parental Power	Parental Explanations		Types of Adolescent Dependence-Independence Behavior[a]				Total Per Cent
			Lack of Confidence		Confidence		
			Dependent	Independent	Dependent	Independent	
Autocratic	Freq.	139	27.3	6.5	37.4	28.8	100
	Infreq.	231	34.2	14.7	20.3	30.3	100
Democratic	Freq.	1233	10.5	6.7	37.6	45.2	100
	Infreq.	194	22.7	9.8	35.6	31.9	100
Permissive	Freq.	729	13.2	7.2	29.8	49.8	100
	Infreq.	177	28.2	13.6	24.9	33.3	100

a The degree of self-confidence in personal ideas and values was measured by the following item: How confident are you that your own ideas and opinions about what you should do and believe are right and best for you? [Lack of confidence] (1) Not at all confident, (2) Not very confident, (3) I'm a little confident. [Confidence] (4) I'm quite confident, (5) I'm completely confident.

Self-reliance in problem-solving and decision making was measured by the following item: When you have a really important decision to make, about yourself and your future, do you make it on your own, or do you like to get help on it? [Dependent] (1) I'd rather let someone else decide for me. (2) I depend a lot upon other people's advice, (3) I like to get some help. [Independent] (4) Get other ideas then make up my own mind, (5) Make up my own mind without any help.

among adolescents with autocratic parents, those who receive frequent explanations are most likely to report a dependent type of self-confidence in their ideas and values. As the power of parents decreases, explanations have a different effect on adolescent autonomy; they seem to foster a sense of self-confidence and independence in their children.

About fifteen percent of the adolescents with parents who are both autocratic and non-explaining report that they lack confidence in their ideas yet prefer to make important decisions on their own. It is plausible that these adolescents feel the need to depend on their parents but find them rejecting and unsympathetic concerning their problems. Hence they function independently in decision making but do so reluctantly. When age and sex were introduced simultaneously as controls, variations by age were observed; younger adolescents were inclined throughout to be less confident and more dependent. However, this age difference did not appreciably alter the above results.

The application of behavior controls which are seldom explained and hence not understood is likely to appear very arbitrary and unpredictable. Under such circumstances, there is apt to be little security for a child in interaction with a powerful parent.[22] Among adolescents who seldom receive explanations of parental requests, autonomy shows a curvilinear relation to level of power. Youths with democratic parents are more likely than adolescents with autocratic or permissive parents to express confidence in and preference for governing themselves. Infrequent explanation is more negatively related to adolescent autonomy on the autocratic than on the permissive level of power.

The effects of parental explanations on adolescent autonomy vary considerably by level of power. Although frequent explanations of rules tend to make them more meaningful and acceptable, they do not encourage autonomy unless accompanied by moderate or low parental power. Freedom to experiment in self-direction and to learn by assuming the responsibilities of decision making appear to be necessary experiences for children to desire and feel confident in self-government. Given this allowance of behavioral freedom, frequent parental explanation of requests and regulations seems to increase markedly the likelihood of adolescent self-confidence and independence in decision making.[23] While autonomy is less probable among youths who seldom receive explanations, it is most common under these conditions among adolescents with democratic parents.

The implications of these results seem particularly relevant to academic motivation and aspiration. If the explanation of autocratic control seems to amplify feelings of dependency in decision making, is this type of power assertion related to low adolescent educational goals and to low aspirations regarding the attainment of these goals? Since a restrictive autocratic regime in child rearing does not encourage a strong achievement orientation,[24] it is probable that frequent explanations on this level of power induce acceptance of such power and heighten passivity and indifference toward scholastic achievement. On the other hand, frequent explanations of rules along with some freedom in self-government are likely to augment a youth's desire to achieve scholastically by giving him a sense of emotional security, by providing him with opportunities to operate on his own, and by strengthening his self-confidence with respect to his ability to be independent.

22 An adolescent's feeling of security might be expressed in terms of a power ratio in which his perception of the magnitude of his own power *plus* all friendly or supportive power he can count upon from other sources is in the numerator, and with the adolescent's perception of the magnitude of all hostile power than may be used against him in the denominator. See Dorwin Cartwright, "Emotional Dimensions of Group Life," in *Feelings and Emotions,* Martin L. Reynert (ed.), New York: McGraw-Hill Book Co., Inc., 1950, pp. 441–442.

23 Cf. Lois W. Hoffman, Sidney Rosen and Ronald Lippitt," Parental Coerciveness, Child Autonomy and Child's Role at School," *Sociometry,* 23 (March, 1960), pp. 15–22, especially p. 20.

24 See Bernard C. Rosen and R. D'Andrade, "The Psychosocial Origins of Achievement Motivation," *Sociometry,* 22 (September, 1959), pp. 185–218; and Fred L. Strodtbeck, "Family Interaction, Values and Achievement," Chapter V in *Talent and Society,* David McClelland (ed.), New York: D. Van Nostrand, 1958.

An examination of data bearing on these possibilities revealed that the frequency of explanations was positively related to adolescent commitment to completing high school and to a desire to go to college if the opportunity were provided, on each level of power. A comparison of the proportions of college-oriented boys in the "explaining" and "non-explaining" categories by level of power revealed the following percentage differences: 7.1, autocratic; 19.0, democratic; and 15.1, permissive. These differences are similar in each of the four age and sex groups. Thus, it appears that the scholastic impetus provided by autocratic parents, compared to that provided by democratic and permissive parents, is not heightened appreciably by frequent explanations. As in its effects on adolescent autonomy, the level of parental power appears to be the crucial factor.

The relationship between level of power and educational goals and aspirations is curvilinear in form with the frequency of explanations controlled. This relationship is illustrated by the percentage of college-oriented boys who frequently receive explanations from their parents; the respective percentages from autocratic to permissive are 57.1, 78.8 and 69.6. Similar results were obtained for girls. Adolescents with democratic and explaining parents are thus most likely to have high educational goals.

About one-half of the boys and girls in grades seven through nine who have autocratic parents who seldom explain are not sure that they will finish high school. The implications of this result seem relevant to the drop-out problem, particularly in view of findings concerning the character of a group of drop-outs from Chicago schools. In a three year treatment study of 105 drop-outs, Lichter *et al.* found that, "about two-thirds of the boys and one-half of the girls were dependent children who were unwilling to assume any self-responsibility. The boys generally expressed their dependency in open helplessness and the girls by angry demands for gratification."[25]

These findings suggest that the effects of variations in the legitimacy of parental power are altered considerably by level of power. We have observed that explanation on the democratic level has an entirely different effect on adolescent autonomy and educational aspirations than it has on the autocratic level. In comparison, the effects of frequent explanations on adolescent desire to model and obey parents vary much less by level of power. Given infrequent explanations of rules and requests, adolescent modeling and compliance tend to decrease sharply as parental power increases.

By assuming that frequent explanations are an indication of a high degree of parental warmth and that level of power is an indication of both parental warmth and the degree of adolescent freedom in decision making, we are able to see why a child's autonomy in decision making and his educational goals are strongly contingent upon the type of parent-adolescent interdependence. Moderate or low parental power appears to be essential in fostering ambitions and effectiveness outside of the family. With opportunities to develop an instrumental orientation, frequent explanations operate as a positive reinforcement.

Since parental attractiveness and obedience to parental rules have been shown to be heavily dependent on the

warmth of parents, it is understandable that the effects of explanation are much greater than the effects of level of power on these two variables. Thus, while adolescents who receive frequent explanations from autocratic parents are inclined to model their parents and to obey them, they are most likely to be dependent on them in decision making and to be indifferent concerning school and college. In conclusion, parental explanation is related to a strong parent orientation, while the level of parental power determines whether the child is over-protected and over-contolled.

SUMMARY

The frequency of parental explanations, employed as a measure of the degree of power legitimation, was analyzed in relation to adolescent desire to model parents, obedience to parental rules, and autonomy in decision making on three levels of parental power. Previous research on the effects of legitimate versus coercive power has generally overlooked the significance and potential modifying effects of levels of power. Data for this investigation were obtained from a structured questionnaire administered to white adolescents who lived with both parents in the states of Ohio and North Carolina.

We find that adolescents are more likely to model their parents and to associate with parent-approved peers if their parents explain their rules frequently when asked to do so. The attractiveness of parents as models is less among autocratic and permissive parents than among democratic parents regardless of the frequency of explanations. Variations in compliance by level of power are evident only when explanations are seldom explained—here we find that adolescents with democratic parents are most apt to abide by parental objections to some of their friends.

With the exception of autocratic parents and their adolescents, we find similar results with respect to adolescent autonomy. Generally, adolescents with democratic or permissive parents are much more likely to be confident in their ideas and opinions and to be independent in decision making if their parents explain their rules often than if they do not explain. However, frequent explanations on the autocratic level of power were more related to dependency, which may or may not be of a self-confident type. Infrequent explanations by autocratic parents were related to both low confidence and independence in decision making. Thus, the legitimizing of parental dominance has the effect of making this power more acceptable, and, in doing so, heightens dependency needs as well as self-confidence.

The implications of these results were explored for scholastic motivation and college aspirations. The strongest commitment to high school graduation and to obtaining a college education was evident under conditions of frequent explanations and moderate or low parental power. The effects of level of power appeared to be stronger than the effects of parental explanation.

In summary, the effects of parental explanations on adolescent behavior are generally modified by the level of parental power—whether the parent is autocratic, democratic, or permissive. Thus, any appraisal of the relationship between parental power legitimation and adolescent adjustment and development should include the effects of variations in parental power.

25 Solomon Lichter, Elsie Rapien, Francis Seibert and Morris Sklansky, *The Drop-Outs*, Glencoe, Illinois: The Free Press, 1962, p. 249.

14

Adolescence, Marriage, and Sex

by Cora DuBois

Tattooing for Girls

Among the people on the East Indian island of Alor, the time for girls to be tattooed is on the first day of the four-day communal pig hunt at the end of the dry season, when most of the boys and men leave the village. There is no implied sex segregation in the choice of this time, since any man who has failed to go hunting may be present during the tattooing process. In fact, men also may be tattooed, but this is done casually by some friend at any time during the year, and later in young manhood. Tattooing is rarer among men than among women. Almost all women are tattooed, whereas only an occasional man is.

The men set off for the hunt shortly after dawn, accompanied by a group of women who may not go beyond the crest of the hill. The women then return and are required to be quiet and avoid unduly vigorous activity until the men come back. Girls whose breasts are beginning to develop take this opportunity to be tattooed, but they must wait until a black column of smoke rises from the grass fired by the men for the pig drives. If they do not wait, the tattoo designs will be light and impermanent. Each girl herself expresses the wish and collects the necessary materials. These are a thorn and finely pounded coconut-shell charcoal mixed with the juice of banana bark. Some grown woman who feels that she has a certain skill in the matter will volunteer to perform the operation. The girl lays her head in the operator's lap; a design is first traced on her forehead or cheek and is then pricked in with a thorn dipped in charcoal. The procedure usually draws a number of girls and adult women, all of whom discuss animatedly which of a limited number of simple designs will be used. Often a little girl who has taken no initiative in the matter will be urged by a friend or adult to undergo the operation. Beauty is the only objective.

It is a tradition to insist that the operation does not hurt, and when I asked a girl who had just had the task completed whether it was painful, older women answered before she was able to, assuring me that it was not. On one occasion some older women, by way of teasing the child's grandmother, urged a little girl of seven to let herself be tattooed. The grandmother arrived just in time to prevent the scheme from being carried out. She was very indignant that her grandchild should have been cajoled into it when she was obviously so young. In relation to a discussion of skills and craftsmanship, it should be stated that the tattooing process is often very crude and usually impermanent, so that traces of designs are rarely distinguishable on the faces of middle-aged women.

Growing Up For Boys

Whereas girls are tattooed from approximately ten to fourteen, the comparable badge of adulthood for boys, i.e., long hair, does not come until somewhat later, at ages I should estimate from sixteen to eighteen. When boys begin to let their hair grow long, they also begin borrowing or acquiring male accouterments. These are dwelt upon in loving detail in many myths and consist of a sword, a front shield, a back shield, a parrying shield, a bow, a wide belt of woven rattan that serves as a quiver, an areca basket with bells, and the tubular, areca-bark hair cylinder with the accompanying combs and head plumes. Naturally, a young man rarely succeeds in borrowing or acquiring all these articles at first, but he gets as many as he can and struts about in them, often followed by the half-admiring, half-derisive comments of older women and girls. There is a special expression for the type of laughter that women direct toward a young man, which I can translate only by our word *hoot*. Its character is as unmistakable as the laughter that accompanies the telling of smutty jokes in our culture. A young man of about twenty himself described in the following words this attitude and the associated courting interests of both boys and girls.

"When a lot of women get together to work in the fields or to fetch water, they talk and talk. When you hear them hoot, that means they are talking about a man. Maybe one girl says she likes a certain man and intends to sleep with him. When a young man ties up his long hair and walks with bells on his basket, women watch until he has passed by, and then they say, 'Isn't that a fine man!' and begin to hoot. If he wears a big white shawl from the coast, women will say, 'There goes my white chicken!' and then they hoot. The young man feels glad but also a little ashamed. Also, when a young man begins to versify at a dance and his voice rings out clear and strong, the next day the women will say, 'Don't we have a fine man in our village!' and then they will hoot. When there is a dance, the young man will hunt for areca and betel the day before so as to fill up his basket. When he reaches the dance place on the night of the dance, all the young women will crowd around him and hold out their hands for areca. If one woman comes back again and again for more areca, it is a sign that they already want each other, and soon they will go off and make an agreement. Then the girl says he must go find her bride-price."

This comment sets, better than any outsider could, the pattern of masculine vanity, which often persists through life and which is recognized as a male trait. Consistent with this newly developed swagger, other changes occur in young men's lives. In the course of a few months they break away from the irresponsible free-roving play groups of growing boys and become far more solitary and sedentary. They imitate the indolence of older wealthy men. At the same time, they begin to speculate about the possibilities and the means for entering the financial system of the adults and about ways of ingratiating themselves with men of influence who may be of assistance to them.

One significant detail concerning food should be noted in connection with the coming of age in boys. The picture so far of the development of masculine vanity and the good-natured teasing that it involves is thoroughly familiar to us. There is another and comparable source of teasing. Boys who are beginning to show open interest in girls and to visit the village of someone they find attractive will be teased by older people with comments like the following, "Padama has gone to visit his wife in Karieta. When boys grow up, the food their mother cooks no longer tastes good. They have to go to the house of a young woman to eat." This kind of teasing makes the younger boys squirm with embarrassment much as it would in our society. A few years later a young man will insist on a midday meal, even if he has to cook it himself, as a symbol of the adult status he is struggling to acquire. The extent to which food and courting ideas can be linked is also exemplified in the following instance. Langmai, who was courting Kolmani by helping her with the storage of her harvest, suggested that they had better marry, by saying, "Who will eat this corn I am stacking? I had better come and eat it myself."

Tooth Blackening

It is during this period of adolescence that both boys and girls have their teeth blackened and filed. Again the matter is optional, but since shiny black teeth are much admired and long uneven ones are considered very ugly, practically every young person has his blackened and probably half have them filed. The process is more or less in the nature of a prolonged picnic, free from adult supervision. It is without doubt also a period of license for many of the young people, although adults vigorously contradicted my phrasing it so.

The best indication of the sexual liberty current at this time is that stricter parents forbid their daughters to remain in remote field houses overnight and insist upon their staying at home or near by in the house of some responsible elder kin. Further, when I visited such a group one evening at sundown just as the strips of dye were being passed out, the young man in charge of procuring and mixing the paste used to darken the teeth said sternly to the children, "Now, no intercourse tonight"—a comment that produced a ripple of giggling among the boys and girls.

The actual procedure is as follows: In July or August some young unmarried man, perhaps in his early twenties, announces that he will blacken teeth for the children of the community and designates the field house where it will be done. This is the slack season agriculturally, so that girls can be spared from the fields. He purchases from some friend in the village of Bakudatang a particular type of soil found there. This investment rarely exceeds five cents. With the earth he mixes a fruit resembling a small green fig. The resulting paste is smeared on a strip of banana bark which each child cuts to fit the size of his mouth. The preparation of each day's supply takes the better part of an afternoon. For at least seven nights, and often ten, the children sleep together in a field house, with the paste held against their teeth by the flexible bark strips. During the day boys assiduously hunt rats, and girls go to their fields to collect vegetable foods. The children all eat together, being careful to place small bits of food far back in their mouths in order not to spoil the dye. With the same objective a length of thin bamboo is used as a drinking tube during the period. Surplus rats are smoked to preserve them for a feast on the last day.

The whole procedure reminds one very much of "playing house." It is a carefree time for all the young people. There are no taboos associated with the period except that attending a dance will interfere with proper dyeing and that if small children loiter too near the older group they will fail to grow up rapidly. For his services the young man is paid a nominal sum of an arrow, or nowadays a penny, per child. He seldom makes more than twenty or thirty cents for a week's work. When I asked why a young man undertook such a task when the reward was so small, the answer was, "Because he likes to be near young girls."

On the last day or two of the period those who are to have their teeth filed go through the ordeal. The same person who prepared the dye usually does the tooth filing. The subject's head is laid on the thigh of the operator and wedged against his side with his elbow. The jaws are propped open with a piece of corncob. The six upper and six lower front teeth are then filed to half their length with an ordinary knife blade which has been nicked to resemble a saw. Apparently experience makes it possible to avoid the root canal, which occupies only the upper half of the incisors. The whole operation takes about two or three hours, and for this the operator is paid the equivalent of about five cents. It is undoubtedly painful but, as in tattooing, it is bad form to admit it. The result of this filing means that even when the back teeth are occluded, the tongue will show pinkly between the gaping front teeth when a person smiles. This is considered definitely attractive.

The complete informality of this ceremony is manifest by the fact that some of the young people return two or three years in succession if the first attempt at blackening was not successful. Also, anyone, at any time, may have his teeth filed down to a straight, even line for appearance's sake. The range of ages is also wide. Boys may be from about fourteen to twenty and girls from twelve to eighteen. There is no regulation against young married people joining the group. The married people, however, are most likely to be girls, since marriage comes early for them.

Tattooing, the beginning of masculine vanity, courting, and tooth blackening are all preliminaries to marriage for young people.

15

THE RUNAWAY GIRL: A Reaction to Family Stress

by Ames Robey, Richard J. Rosenwald, John E. Snell, and Rita E. Lee

Running away and its associated behavior is one of the few ways in which an adolescent girl may act out. In a treatment-oriented Court Clinic, a study was made of runaway girls from an essentially middle-class area. The suggested dynamics revolved around family interaction, in which there was a threatened unconscious incestuous relationship with the father incited by the mother. Subsequent acting out of the unresolved Oedipal conflict through running away represents an attempted solution.

Running away from home is one of the most common forms of serious acting out in the adolescent girl. Despite its frequency, it has received little attention in the psychiatric literature. Most papers deal primarily with boys' running away and are predominantly statistical, although several discuss some of the pathogenic elements involved.[1-4, 7, 11, 12, 14-16, 20-22] Rosenheim[16] in 1940 was the first to postulate the importance of the unresolved Oedipal conflict as a cause of running away in boys. Other studies have since shown that the Oedipal conflict and the threat of an incestuous relationship also play an important role in the etiology of running away in girls.[4, 22]

Legally a form of delinquency, the act of running away itself is often treated lightly by the parents, the police and even the courts, unless it becomes chronic or appears in conjunction with severe stubbornness and disobedience at home, sexual acting out, unauthorized use of motor vehicles or other associated delinquent behavior. It should be emphasized, however, that running away, far from being a childish escapade, is almost always indicative of some severe individual or family pathology and may result from a wide variety of intolerable home situations. The cause most frequently observed in this study was the unconscious threat of an incestuous relationship with the father, the fear of the resultant dissolution of the family and the concurrent depression.

This study was made at the Framingham Court Clinic, which serves an essentially middle-class suburban population. The primary function of the Court Clinics is to provide a threefold service in supplying direct and immediate psychiatric evaluations for the Court, advice and assistance to Probation Officers in their handling of offenders, and psychotherapy for appropriate cases within the setting of the Court, where judicial controls and authority are readily available.[17, 19]

Of the entire caseload of 293 adolescent girls brought before the Court during the past ten years, 162 or 55 per cent, had run away. Forty-two of these girls and their families were referred to the Clinic for more study and treatment. The girls' ages ranged from 13 to 17 years and 6 months, with a mean of 15 years and 3 months. We have included only those girls who were living with both parents or one parent and a stepparent. Our definition of running away excludes those who had not stayed away overnight and those who denied the intent to run away. When a case was seen in the Clinic, an attempt was made to interview the parents and the girl at least three times, and some cases continued in treatment for as long as two years. Close co-operation between the Probation Department and the Clinic staff was invaluable in setting up and carrying out treatment programs. Frequently the father refused to be interviewed by a psychiatrist, and we had to rely on the Probation Officer for an evaluation of him, as well as for other information not readily obtainable by the Clinic staff.

In evaluating and treating these 42 runaway girls, we saw a consistent pattern of family interaction that we feel is basic to the etiology of running away. This pattern includes a disturbed marital relationship, inadequate control by the parents over their own and the girl's impulses, deprivation of love of the mother and subtle pressure by her on the girl to take over the maternal role.

This role is managed well in most cases by the girl prior to the onset of adolescence. At this time, however, with the breakdown of the prepubescent defenses, the girl becomes involved in an increasingly bitter attitude of rebellion against her role and finally runs away. The superficial conflict from which the girl runs is between herself and her father. What is perhaps not so clear is the disturbed mother-daughter relationship and the role it plays in this conflict. Kaufman,[10] in his paper on overt father-daughter incestuous relationships, described the strong dependent wishes of both parents and their search for a mother figure. It was his feeling that the girl reacted to the mother's wish to place her in the maternal role by developing a pseudo maturity and then, under pressure from mother, by getting involved in an incestuous relationship with the father in search of oral gratification. According to Kaufman, the lack of parental controls and of assistance by the parents in reality testing and superego development was essential to the development of the situation. In our series, we noted a striking similarity to his cases, although we failed to see the depth of pathology in any member of the family. There were only three instances of alleged incest in the entire group of 145 cases. Indeed, it is our contention that it is because of the girl's strength that, when she is given the choice of taking over the mother's role or running away, she chooses the latter as a method of fighting off the incestuous wishes unconsciously shared by all members of the family.

In reviewing the family histories, we found the fathers usually do well at work but outside their jobs tend to be rather passive and inadequate. They show poor control over their aggressive and sexual instincts and are given to violent temper outbursts, usually when drinking. In many cases, they indulge in extramarital affairs. The mothers are usually better educated and clearly the dominant force in the family structure; underlying this, however, one finds a significant level of depression, verbalized feelings of rejection by their own mothers, often a history of running away or early marriage, and feelings of maternal inadequacy. Though they are frequently seductive toward their husbands, a history of long-term unsatisfactory sexual adjustment is usually found.

We see difficulties arising quite early in the parent-child relationships. The mother does not provide her daughter with sufficient warmth and affection. Instead, by offering material incentives, she tends to force the girl into a position of increased responsibility and gradual assumption of the maternal role. In addition to rejecting her husband sexually, the mother also encourages a warm, close, eroticized father-daughter relationship from which all three derive considerable satisfaction. In this setting, the girl develops into what appears superficially as a hypermature individual, in her struggle to meet her mother's demands. With only material rewards for her efforts, she turns to her father to meet her needs for love, and quite early learns to use seductiveness to gain her ends. Men become objects to be controlled and used, but, as with the mother, the goal is oral gratification.

The family balance achieved during the girl's latency is disturbed by the onset of her physical maturation. The mother pushes her daughter into premature dating and sexual sophistication in an attempt to work out her own poorly resolved Oedipal conflicts. At the same time, she not only rejects her husband further, but continues to foster the close relationship between him and the daughter. With few effective controls demonstrated by either parent, the fear of overt incest comes uncomfortably close to consciousness, and the intimate relationship between the father and the daughter now becomes extremely threatening to both. The father reacts by becoming angry and restrictive. He projects his own sexual feelings onto the girl and

accuses her of sexual misbehavior, thereby justifying his extreme restrictiveness. The girl, angry and rebellious, flouts her father's authority and, with mother's encouragement, attempts to solve her Oedipal conflicts by seeking outside objects. Because of her underlying feelings of worthlessness, she chooses boys who are themselves degraded or emotionally disturbed. The mother now finds herself caught in the middle, wanting unconsciously to continue encouraging her daughter's behavior, but aware of the realistic dangers. The father, upon seeing these boys, becomes more restrictive, the girl more rebellious, and finally, with the increasing tension in the home, the girl begins to fear that she will cause family dissolution. At this point she sees no alternative to impulsive running away.

It is clear from this brief presentation that the family dynamics are extremely complex and in some cases may be sufficiently subtle to escape the notice of the casual observer. It could hardly be considered abnormal for a father to wish to protect his daughter from the clutches of an emotionally disturbed, poorly educated, delinquent boy, nor can it be considered unusual for the girl to rebel against a large number of restrictions. Contemporary society encourages early dating and sexual maturity. It is not unreasonable for the mother to expect help from her daughter with the household duties and care of the younger children. Yet all these factors take on a more sinister significance in a setting of oral deprivation and misdirected, inadequate controls. For the girl to run away under these circumstances becomes not only comprehensible but almost predictable.

Without treatment, the girls tend to leave school, frequently continue to run away, and occasionally become involved in prostitution.[15] More often, however, they contrive to get married either by falsifying their age or by becoming pregnant. From the mothers' histories, we have some indication that, if the girl's marriage endures, her daughter will in turn repeat the runaway pattern. Placement in a foster home or institution, frequently the only solution available to the Court, is usually inadequate to control the girl's behavior unless it is combined with treatment or includes a carefully tailored program that takes into consideration the dynamics and needs of the girl.[9] Severe acting out in terms of further runaway attempts, flouting of authority despite disciplinary action and occasionally homosexual activity may occur in an institutional setting,[8] or acute depression, often with suicidal gestures, may be seen. Where placement does result in improvement, a return home will almost invariably reactivate the previous situation. Even with treatment, the prognosis for successful adult adjustment is guarded. When attempted by a private psychiatrist or a clinic not affiliated with the Court, treatment may be completely impossible due to lack of adequate controls and inability to enforce attendance. Even in a Court Clinic setting, with the Probation Officers and the Judge immediately available to supply the necessary control and authority, treatment may fail because a relationship cannot be established. Invaluable in this connection is a female probation officer who can provide the warmth and control not supplied by the mother.

It should be emphasized that successful treatment of the girl necessarily includes simultaneous treatment of the mother. Here the major goal is an improvement in her relationship with her daughter, which can frequently be effected quite rapidly by extremely direct interpretation of the girl's underlying dynamics.[22]

The girl, when first seen, is usually hostile and uncommunicative. Gradually she begins to talk more freely and, as she does, her depression becomes quite apparent. In an attempt to control the treatment situation, she then becomes seductive.[6] This behavior requires interpretation, with tacit reassurance that she does not need to be seductive to be cared for. It is at this point in treatment that we usually find rapid and striking improvement. Maintenance of this improvement, however, is dependent upon a continuing therapeutic relationship with both the mother and the daughter. Too often we found that, with improvement in the girl, probation would be terminated, and she would then refuse to attend the Clinic any longer. This usually resulted in prompt deterioration of the home situation.

We seldom found the fathers willing to come regularly to the Clinic, but our results so far support our feeling that they are not essential in the treatment process.

In conclusion, we feel that running away is the result of a complex neurotic interaction between the parents and the daughter in a "triangle" situation, and its seriousness as a symptom calls for far greater concern than is presently given by most parents and law enforcement officials.

Because the material on which this study is based consists of only 42 cases, or about one-fourth of the total number of girls who had run away in the ten years covered by this study, we feel strongly that more complete understanding of the runaway girl and the underlying dynamics warrants further study in this and other clinics.

REFERENCES

1. ARMSTRONG, C. P. 1937. A psychoneurotic reaction of delinquent boys and girls. J. Abnorm. Psychol. 32: 329.
2. ———. 1932. 660 Runaway Boys. R. G. Badger. Boston, Mass.
3. BALSER, B. H. 1939. A behavior problem: runaways. Psychiat. Quart. 13: 539.
4. COUNTS, R., T. LEVENTHAL, J. WEINREB AND M. SHORE. Running away as an attempted solution to a family problem. Unpublished manuscript.
5. DEUTSCH, H. 1944. Psychology of Women, Vol. 1. Grune & Stratton. New York, N. Y. Chs. 2 and 3.
6. EISNER, E. A. 1945. Relationships formed by a sexually delinquent adolescent girl. Amer. J. Orthopsychiat. 15(2): 301.
7. FOSTER, R. 1962. Intrapsychic and environmental factors in running away from home. Amer. J. Orthopsychiat. 32(3): 486.
8. HALLECK, S. AND M. HERSKO. 1962. Homosexual behavior in a training school for girls. Amer. J. Orthopsychiat. 32(5): 911.
9. HERSKO, M., S. HALLECK, M. ROSENBERG AND A. PACHT. 1961. Incest: a three-way process. J. Soc. Therapy 7(1): 22.
10. KAUFMAN, I., A. L. PECK AND C. K. TAGUIRI. 1954. The family constellation and overt incestuous relations between father and daughter. Amer. J. Orthopsychiat. 24(2): 266.
11. LEVENTHAL, T., A. M. GRIDLEY, R. M. COUNTS AND M. GLUCK. Preliminary report on the seriousness of running away in childhood and adolescence. Presented at the Annual Meeting of the American Orthopsychiatric Association, New York, N. Y. March, 1958.
12. LOWREY, L. G. 1941. Runaways and nomads. Amer. J. Orthopsychiat. 11(4): 775.
13. O'KELLY, E. 1955. Some observations on relations between delinquent girls and their parents. Brit. J. Med. Psychol. 28(1): 59.
14. RIEMER, M. D. 1940. Runaway children. Amer. J. Orthopsychiat. 10(3): 522.
15. ROBINS, L. N. AND P. O'NEAL. 1959. The adult prognosis for runaway children. Amer. J. Orthopsychiat. 29(4): 752.
16. ROSENHEIM, F. 1940. Techniques of therapy. Amer. J. Orthopsychiat. 29(4): 651.
17. RUSSELL, D. H. AND J. DEVLIN. 1962. The Massachusetts Court clinic program. Juvenile Court Judges J. 13(3).
18. SLOANE, P. AND E. KARPINSKI. 1942. Effects of incest on the participants. Amer. J. Orthopsychiat. 12(4): 666.
19. Special Massachusetts Court Clinic Issue. 1960. J. Assn. Psychiatric Treatment of Offenders. 4(2).
20. STAUB, H. 1943. A runaway from home. Psychoanal. Quart. 12(1): 1.
21. STENGEL, E. 1939. Studies on the psychopathology of compulsive wandering. Brit. J. Med. Psychol. 18: 250.
22. WYLIE, D. C. AND J. WEINREB. 1958. The treatment of a runaway adolescent girl through treatment of the mother. Amer. J. Orthopsychiat. 28(1): 188.

16

Kids with kids

More and more, white, middle-class, teen-age girls
are having babies out of wedlock—and keeping them. Few
are prepared for what comes after.

By Leslie Aldridge Westoff

"How come all the other mothers are women, and you're only a little girl?" a wide-eyed boy demanded in his soprano innocence. He had made one of those stunning observations of which only the pure are capable, darting instantly to the heart of the truth. His mother was, in fact, only a child herself. She was one of a growing number of white, middle-class unmarried girls who reject abortion and adoption and decide to have and keep their babies.

Less than five years ago, when a single, middle-class, white teen-ager became pregnant, she had no choice. Her parents dragged themselves up out of the shock, shame and anger she had plunged them into, and covertly shipped her off to the abortion factories of less restrictive countries, or got an underground abortionist's number from a friend at the hairdresser's, or whisked her away to a maternity home where she secretly had her baby. The newborn infant was left there for adoption, sometimes being sold to pay the expenses, and the girl returned home from her "trip" abroad or her "visit" with a distant relative whom no one could recall ever meeting.

Today, this girl is no longer in disgrace, except perhaps in scattered areas where people still cling to more rigid moralistic judgments. Usually now, the girl can be seen at home, shopping in the supermarket, going about her daily chores, her belly gradually rising like a warm bread dough. Her friends, her family, her neighbors, are all aware that she is still in her teens, still unmarried, still a dependent child, and very much about to become a mother.

More than 200,000 teen-agers (85,000 whites and 121,000 blacks) gave birth to out-of-wedlock children in 1974. This accounts for more than half of all the illegitimacy in the country. And the numbers are rising, even though the over-all teen-age birth rate is dropping. Between 1971 and 1974, there was a 12 percent increase in illegitimate births to white girls aged 15 to 19 (with a corresponding increase of 5 percent among black teen-agers). And in this same three-year period, illegitimate births to white girls under 15 increased by 32 percent (for blacks it was only 3 percent). If not for quite a number of quickie marriages to turn premarital conceptions into legitimate births, these figures would be even higher.

In the past, most black teen-agers kept their babies, and most white girls aborted or gave them up to a hungry adoption market. In recent years, however, the trend has been reversed. Many black girls, with more options open to them, are either having legal abortions or considering adoption. And more white teen-agers who have children out of wedlock have begun to keep them. Thus, in 1966, an estimated 65 percent of white illegitimate babies were given away for adoption; in 1971, Dr. John F. Kantner and Dr. Melvin Zelnik of Johns Hopkins put the estimate at 18 percent. In other words, 10 years ago, only one out of three white girls who had their babies decided to keep and raise them; five years later, four out of five chose that alternative. Today, the proportion is doubtless even higher.

□

Laura (that is not her name) was 18 and just starting college away from home when she became pregnant. She had been taking the pill, but had gained weight and suffered from migraines, so she stopped using it. She thought of trying a different brand of pill, but didn't make the necessary effort.

"I guess it was just plain laziness. I hadn't been using anything for a year. In the back of my mind I thought I was sterile because I'd had intercourse without getting pregnant. Also it cost a lot of money to go to a private doctor, and Planned Parenthood was an hour away."

She and her boyfriend were talking of getting married, but after she became pregnant, he wanted her to have an abortion. "I believed in abortion in general," she says, "but I always knew I could never have one."

"I felt like crying, 'I want my Mommy.' I phoned home and mother said, 'We'll figure it out. We'll handle it. Whatever you decide, we'll support you.' I didn't know if I had the strength to go through with it. People were saying, 'Oh, you're too young. You're not mature enough to have a baby.' Then my boyfriend drove me home to my parents and went away. I felt bitter, as though I'd been conned. He said he was going to marry me, then he left me."

At home, there was criticism. "My obstetrician told me I was dumb not to have been using contraception. My older sister was angry and told me to think of the baby without a father."

Laura wrote to her three favorite teachers, but none of them answered. "I was frightened and wanted someone to talk to. But there was no one. I finally went to a psychiatrist, though I had my mind set. I really didn't want help, I wanted someone to agree with me."

Once it was decided, her mother went to natural-childbirth classes with her. (Other women went with their husbands.) Several months later, she saw her baby being born. "I didn't consider adoption. After nine months, I couldn't have handled it. If my parents hadn't helped me, I would have scraped to keep the baby."

Instead of being surrounded by a cozy group of college friends, Laura is much more isolated now that she lives at home. She commutes to a nearby college, where she is studying to be an art teacher, while her mother takes care of the baby. She hopes to go on to graduate school some day. "My biggest problem is no time for social life. I'd like to go out, but I want to spend more time with the baby. Sometimes I'll go if I can take him with me."

Her mother enjoys caring for the baby. Her engineer father, who feels violent anger when the subject of the baby's father is brought up, looks forward to the day when he can take his grandson hunting. Her pediatrician, Dr. Benjamin K. Silverman, says Laura and her baby have done surprisingly well. All the same, she wishes she were able to live alone. "My mother and I have only small conflicts, but it's a matter of pride. I keep thinking, 'Gee, I'm soaking up an awful lot of money.'"

Laura insists, with persuasive sincerity, "There is nothing I regret about keeping the child. I love him. It's a glowing, warm feeling. Sometimes I stare at his eyes, and have the sense of a vast amount of knowledge behind them."

Yet, for all the pleasure she takes in her child, the pathos of a child-mother trapped by circumstances shows through. "Sometimes I'd like to call somebody and do something. . . ."

□

Why, in this best of all contraceptive worlds, are so many teen-age girls becoming pregnant?

To begin with, sex is a bigger factor in teen-age behavior than it used to be. And that, according to Betty A. Schwartz, director of the Florence Crittenton Services of Baltimore, is the direct result of society's current preoccupation with sex. "Sex is the basic selling medium on TV. They sell toothpaste on the basis of sex. Kids have grown up in a world where sex is a status symbol in the environment. The only thing that counts is how you make it sexually. 'If he kisses you once, will he kiss you again?' We've programmed them this way."

Charlotte Andress, executive director of New York's Inwood House, a service for young mothers and their babies, says, "There has been an almost overnight reversal in teen-age behavior because of the change in social mores. Parents don't disown their pregnant daughters now. It's the breath of air of the 70's."

This change has come about at a time when there are more teen-agers in the population, and when teen-agers are becoming sexually more active earlier. Because of better nutrition, the age of menarche is falling by three or four months every decade. In 1850, it was 16½ years. Today it is 12½ years. Thus there are more teen-age years when a girl can become pregnant—and, with the swing away from early marriage, more years when she can have an illegitimate child.

There are sex-education courses available in some high schools, but they are usually superficial, and most teen-agers don't yet seem able to cope with their emerging sexuality. Three out of four unmarried pregnant girls questioned in a 1971 study by Dr. Kantner and Dr. Zelnik said they had not wanted to become pregnant, but only 13 percent of them had been motivated enough to use contraception. Most of them didn't know

at what time of the month they could become pregnant, and many of them believed nothing would happen because they were too young or did not have sex frequently enough.

Several girls told me they were afraid that if they went to their family doctor, he would tell their parents, who wouldn't understand. Others said they were afraid of getting cancer from the pill. Many don't understand how it works. If they forget to take their pills for four days, for example, they'll take all four at once. Doctors who prescribe don't always have time to explain.

Many teen-agers knowingly take chances: Whatever happens, happens. With others, unconscious drives may be at work. Dr. David D. Youngs, who spent three years as director of the Johns Hopkins Center for Social Studies in Human Reproduction, says that a girl may pick pregnancy, rather than drugs or alcohol, to solve some problem in her family life—in a "primitive attempt to split off from her own mother," for instance; or to replace her father as an object of affection; or in a search for identity. Dr. Virginia Abernethy, a Vanderbilt University anthropologist, suggests that a teen-ager

may allow herself to become pregnant if there is a distant or hostile relationship between her parents: She may resent her mother for fighting with her father, and without a likable mother as a role model she may turn to boys for a love relationship, while denying to herself that the boy may have a sexual motive. Teen-age girls may have always had these feelings; today, when society seems to be saying "O.K., go ahead," it may be more acceptable to let these feelings come forward.

If these are some of the reasons more middle-class white teen-agers get pregnant, why do more of them decide to have and keep their babies?

Again, the answer has a lot to do with the change in social climate. Many of the moralistic prohibitions that governed life-styles in the past have evaporated. Parents and society will very often help the young mothers financially, rather than disown them. To many teen-agers, living outside of marriage with a child does not seem very different from the lives of many single women or divorcées who also live alone with children.

At any rate, after having carried the fetus for nine months, felt the kicking

signs of a new life, gone through the pain and exultation of childbirth—perhaps even observed it herself—a girl is very unlikely to want to give up her baby. To do that would be a violation of her deepest maternal feelings. There is little doubt that most girls always felt this, but in the past the fear of banishment from society was enough to numb them into submitting to adoption.

Now, even rock lyrics celebrate having and keeping one's baby. Adoption has become unfashionable—a cop-out. And the girl's peers back her up. Perhaps some of the sensitivity to pure, beautiful love and concern for all living things that were part of the flower-children culture of the 60's have rubbed off on the next generation.

One girl told me, "If I knew there was a child of mine

on this earth, it would haunt me if I gave it up." Another asked, "How could I give away my own flesh and blood?" A boy said, "Anyone who'd give up a kid is rotten."

It certainly seems very likely that girls who decide to have and keep their babies have a desperate sense of alienation and a need for closeness and love, something that not all parents seem able to offer. For these girls it

would be unimaginable to give up a warm, loving baby who can fill this need, the way no one else in their lives seems to have done. In a world where so many things have become possible for the young, where there is so much choice, they figure this will be possible too.

But, as Janet Forbush, director of the Washington-based National Alliance Concerned with School-Age

Parents, puts it, "They have the baby and then . . . whammy. Two years down the road, or even sooner, it hits them. Some are managing very well, but they are the exception, not the rule."

□

After the enchantment phase, the girls are left with the hard realities. Often too hard. Dr. Janet Hardy, professor of pediatrics at Johns Hopkins, says that, in her experience, "whites and blacks are not very different. Their social problems may be different, but their basic needs, and the underlying factors behind their pregnancies, are not different."

The most supportive situation is for the young daughter and her infant to live with her parents, if they agree to it. If she can't or doesn't want to live at home, she might find it possible to live with the child's father's parents; or to place her baby in a foster home temporarily; or to find another single woman to live with, so they can pool their welfare checks; or to live with the child's father.

Without financial help from her parents, she is usually dependent on getting a job, but since she probably has not finished school, her chances of earning enough money are slim. She can get some welfare money from Aid to Families With Dependent Children (A.F.D.C.), but not enough. (There are 53,000 white girls under 19 on welfare, and 70,000 blacks.) An immature teen-ager burdened with a baby is hardly fit to cope.

Take the case history of a girl I call Sally. She became pregnant at 16. Her middle-class parents were ashamed and tried to pressure her into arranging for an adoption. But Sally wanted to keep the baby because, she reasoned, "he's part of me." The teachers in school did not like a pregnant girl mixing with the other students; it was vaguely immoral, and they gave her a hard time. She finally dropped out.

When the baby was born, her parents called it a "child of sin," and doubted that Sally could handle the responsibility of taking care of it. Sally's mother told her, "You'll have to go back to school if you're going to live with us." She decided not to go and took an apartment with a girl friend who worked. She applied to A.F.D.C., and got $89 a month. After three or four months, Sally decided this wasn't what she wanted. "Just caring for a baby, housework, cooking and shopping . . . no way." She was finally able to locate a welfare day-care center and went back to a different high school to try to prepare for a job. She barely survives on welfare, food stamps and the occasional check her mother sends.

er centered around dating, fun and basketball games. There is often a dreadful sense of dislocation. "I wondered where in the world I fitted in," said one teen-age mother. "With the baby, I felt I no longer belonged with others my age. I lived in the only cheap apartment I could find near my job, and there were middle-aged people all around me. People my age were still in school. I had nothing to talk about to friends who were going to parties. I was into baby things."

Though most teen-agers don't consider it wrong to have produced an illegitimate child, they are aware that society has not fully agreed with them. They are no longer scorned, except perhaps in rare instances, but it can happen. (Recently, a West Virginia judge ordered an unmarried pregnant girl and two unmarried girls with children arrested for promiscuity.) And they often worry about what the effects of illegitimacy will be on their children, what others in school will say, how it will burden them for the rest of their lives.

For many child-mothers whose parents don't take over the major share of responsibility for the new infant, the worries of money, child-care, school, work, housing, adequate food, medical care and finding the available social services (if they exist) are too much. They become saturated with a sense of desperation and alienation. Rather than seeking each other out, they remain aloof and suspicious.

Aside from housing and financial problems, there are the social concerns. A young mother's interests are no longer. One girl couldn't cope any longer and just dropped her baby down a two-flight stair well. Fortunately, he landed on something soft and survived. Some mothers just give up and commit suicide.

Young people are more impulsive than mature adults. Says Miss Schwartz, "If they are expressing loving feelings, they are great. If not, it can be tragic. They are more apt to slap, hit and shake their babies." Cases of child abuse, of battered and neglected children, are closely related to the age of the mother. According to Douglas Besharov, of the Department of Health, Education and Welfare, "it is our impression that a major proportion of young mothers are responsible for all the child abuse." (There are one million cases of child abuse a year; of this number, about 2,000 end in deaths.)

As social problems multiply, they are often joined by a variety of medical complications. Dr. Hardy and her associates at Johns Hopkins conducted a child-development study of 550 black and white children who were 16 or under. They found that among children who were below grade level in school, 75 per cent had teen-age mothers. Among children who had started major fires, 70 percent had young mothers. Dr. Hardy also found that young mothers had more premature babies and more fetal and newborn deaths, and were more susceptible to toxemia, a condition which causes hypertension and high blood pressure.

There are 600 to 700 programs around the country that try to help pregnant teen-agers and their babies. Most of them are inadequate, but there are some exceptions. One of these is the Center for Teen-Age Mothers and Their Infants at Johns Hopkins, established last November with a $300,000 grant from the Joseph P. Kennedy Foundation, with Dr. Hardy as its director. The new center, certainly the most comprehensive of its kind, is meant to be a model for future clinics. Here, the staff will evaluate the pregnant girl and help plan for the delivery and care of her baby. A psychiatrist will offer intensive help with practical and emotional problems; others will give her a better understanding of her own body and of what her baby's needs will be. A social worker will help her fit into her family situation. Nearby Dunbar School will offer courses toward her high-school degree, and will provide a day-care center where she can feed her baby between classes. Getting a girl back to school has been shown to develop college and career interests and prevent repeat pregnancies until they are wanted.

□

It should be clear from all this that while the trend may be one of increasing social acceptance of the out-of-wedlock family, while more neighbors may be polite and helpful and more parents may take it to their bosom, the price paid by the teen-age mother is still a high one. And that raises the question of the parents' responsibilities to their daughters—and of the responsibility of schools.

Though most middle-class white teen-agers are no longer taught by overbearing parents that sex before marriage is evil and forbidden, it seems that no other caution has taken its place. Contraception is something even careful teen-agers don't like, because it deprives them of the spontaneity and romance that sex is supposed to have, and makes the whole act seem calculated. Only early and continued education—and this means schools as well as parents—will ingrain the concept of precaution, making it as automatic as brushing one's teeth every morning.

Someone, somewhere, has to communicate to these teen-agers that the tragedy of unplanned sex can mess up a lot of lives. However broadminded parents may wish to remain, they have in many instances failed their children in this regard because of their own ignorance or embarrassment, leaving this delicate area for their children to muddle through as best they can.

It is difficult for parents to understand how quickly today's children grow up—that from age 12 on (or sometimes even 10) they have the capacity to create life. Because emotionally and intellectually these children are still only children, parents tend to ignore their bursting physical maturity. It is too painful for them to admit that *their* little girl would ever do anything wrong.

Once a teen-ager becomes pregnant, there is again the awkward question of the parents' role. Believing that children now are supposed to decide for themselves, many parents, with endless reserves of understanding, suggest that their daughters make the decision. Since a girl at such a time is under great psychological strain, is confused and has no experience to fall back on, her vision of what child-raising entails probably bears no resemblance to reality. In trying to be modern, such parents may well be leaving too much up to their immature daughters.

Taking a strong position, however, puts parents on tricky ground. They obviously don't want their daughters to be handicapped by a baby while they are still children themselves. On the other hand, if they are adamant in pressing for abortion or adoption, and the girl badly wants the baby, as most do, they are likely to create psychological problems that could ruin her life in quite another way. It may be, nevertheless, that a girl in such a situation would welcome a strong, guiding voice.

Besides the inevitable disadvantages for the young mothers and their babies, middle-class parents who haven't the heart to throw their daughters out, and who see no other choice but to help them, take on an enormous burden—financial, emotional and physical. This is particularly hard on the girl's mother, who, now in her 40's or 50's, has finished raising her family but has to suddenly begin all over again.

There are no easy answers, probably not even any satisfactory ones. There is no question, though, that schools should offer sex-education and family-education courses from the early grades on. And there is no question about the need for communities to offer more counseling services and make them easily available, so that teen-agers and their parents who must make quick and crucial decisions can at least comprehend exactly what the odds are.

'Someone has to communicate to teen-agers that unplanned sex can mess up their lives. . . . Trying to be modern, many parents may be leaving too much up to their daughters.'

V. Education

The danger of a section titled education should be obvious. Textbooks, theories, everyday conversations reinforce the notion that the important instruction, the "real" knowledge of life is received only in school, in the presence of teachers. Let us recognize therefore, as we turn to this section, that people are constantly learning, surely in school, and just as surely out of school as well. They are learning things which may be of immediate use, and no use at all. They are learning things which excite them irrespective of whether these things seem relevant, and they are learning things which utterly bore them.

Adolescents, as much as people in any other age group, are also learning about school. Whereas most young children accept the everyday realities of their school life without question, the adolescent has become rather sophisticated about the institution he or she attends. Indeed, some people believe that no matter what the adolescent learns in school, he or she inevitably is getting training in psychology and sociology. For example, with all the language and mathematics, history—whatever the formal subject—the adolescent is also learning about individual cognitive differences, social groupings of students, the relationship of one's position in the society and the type of school and formal education one can expect. Psychologically, no one completes a formal education without becoming an expert on anxiety, achievement values, intimidation, competence. One learns, in other words, an enormous amount in the process of attending school, even though there aren't examinations on all the "subjects" and no academic credit is given for becoming an expert in them.

Some social scientists have classified adolescence as a period when realistic career choices become codified for the first time. Clearly, adolescents fantasize about their future, but when it comes to making their important decisions they usually reveal an understanding of what we still call the ways of the world. A second characteristic of adolescents, these experts suggest, is the genuine recognition of the world of other people, and the realization that others, whom one will never know, lead their lives very differently from oneself. School, actual classroom work, but even more the out of classroom work, provides a fund of knowledge about the society in which the adolescent is growing up. Merely to know about the rich school several miles away, or the broken down building in the next community where it seems it would be dangerous for children to go to school, affects the adolescent's concept of the role of education. Let no one think that the adolescent doesn't understand the link between his or her school and the future life being shaped directly and indirectly by that school.

We return to a notion discussed in the first section of this book. It is almost laughable to think that one can accurately define the characteristics of adolescence. Again, if one has doubts about this, one need only try to list the variations in types of school and education that, say, 14-year-old children experience. Region of the country will make a difference, as will the size of one's city, one's parents' background, one's sex, the social class of the community, the racial and ethnic composition of a neighborhood. The list is endless. But that is how it should be, for its richness is a reminder not only of the potential richness of school, but of the fact that valuable learning takes place outside of school.

17

The Night World of Preadolescence

What are today's middle-school children like? Here is a warm, insightful analysis of the cognitive, psychic and social changes characteristic of their growth. Donald McNassor is Professor and Chairman, Faculty in Education, Claremont Graduate School, Claremont, California.

Donald McNassor

YOUNG PEOPLE in the "middle school" time of life enter a night world. Daybreak for them will come several years later during high school after a delicate union of biological maturation and experience. Fundamental biological changes make them very different people than their parents knew as third- and fourth-graders. Overnight, it seems, they have leaped from the more stable physiological and psychological world of childhood into a realm of uncontrolled psychic energy, impulse-flooding, powerful new cognitive capacity, and a stubborn sense of self-determination that often dismays parents and teachers. Middle-school children have acquired a powerful new machine. The drivers are not sure how to manage it. Their world is a night world because this time is when people feel most alone, when they live on the border of reality and unreality, when the shackles to imagination are loosened, and when terror mounts. In the night world the self is absorbed with itself. The practical responsibilities, social obligations and objects of the day world fade away.

The middle-school years mark a new stage in psychological growth. Biological developments have prepared the child for changes in cognitive style, interests and behavior. Mechanisms still a mystery alter the child's psychic competence so that he is able to react to events, tasks and people in new ways. If fundamental biological and psychic changes result in a person radically different from what she/he was just a short time before, it is sensible to conclude that modes of education and inter-

personal relationships with adults should be congruent with the needs and problems of the newly acquired energy system. The early adolescent should not be treated like a child of nine, or like an older high school student who has competently integrated biological changes with experience into a more workable unity. The early adolescent requires teaching, counseling and experiences that are not like what is developmentally proper in the elementary school or in the later years in high school. No wonder parenthood is such a worry during these years. Parents can't change gears fast enough.

Middle-school-age youth have long been the center of concern, misunderstanding and frustration for parents and school people alike. How often parents have said or thought, "He has changed so much in one year, it frightens me," or "I don't know how to talk with her anymore," or "He is aloof; I don't know what he's thinking." And how often the unprepared junior high teacher has come to wit's end, yearning to be back with younger children who trust adults and accept their view of the world or with older youth who are more predictable, more in control of their energy system, less brash in asserting their growing power. I have heard it said that the majority of teachers who leave teaching for good are from the junior high schools. Whether or not this assertion is based on fact, it is quite believable.

We have yet to fully appreciate the need for a special kind of teacher in the classrooms of

early adolescents. Effective teachers must truly like to be around these children and find them the most interesting if most unpredictable people in the world. The teachers must like them, be intrigued by them, appreciate and find humor in all sorts of absurdities in human behavior. They must not be threatened by the vacillations between infantile and mature acts; they must not mind disorganized personalities. Most of all, they must appreciate the growing

cognitive power of these children. The early adolescent is fully competent to function in the adult cognitive styles and tasks of his culture. A teacher who sticks to the syllabus of predetermined subject matter, who cannot generate involvement with ideas and projects that match the new powers of the students, will harvest weeks of boredom and trouble. The good junior high teacher is a special breed, no question about it. The arrangements for learning must convey structure and plan but with ample room for improvisation. It is the lack of the latter where teachers fail.

THE NATURE OF THE NEW COGNITIVE COMPETENCE

The early adolescent, unlike the young child, as Jerome Kagan explains in a very noteworthy article, is not confused by the fact that initial premises violate former notions of what is real.* He is gaining ease in dealing with hypothetical premises that may violate reality. The thirteen-year-old, says Kagan, will accept and think about the problem—"All three-legged snakes are purple; I am hiding a three-legged snake; guess its color." The seven-year-old is confused by data concerning what is real, and he will not cooperate in this problem. He does not appreciate the discontinuity between the self-contained information in the problem and the egocentric information inside him (Kagan, p. 92). The younger child's perceptions of the world and of values are fixed, inflexible, simplistic. The world is in one dimension. Right is right, and wrong is always wrong. The early adolescent, on the other hand, can deal with incongruities. He can think relativistically. In short, he thinks like adults. "To appreciate that problems can be self-contained entities solved by special rules is a magnificent accomplishment that is not usually attained until early adolescence" (Kagan, p. 93).

Thinking in Multiple Dimensions

Other attributes of the new-found competence include inducing rules from events with multiple and even inconsistent attributes. The adolescent can deal with multiple attributes simultaneously. He is not limited to one-at-a-time kind of analysis. He knows that events have multiple dimensions, that there is always a network of causes to events or behavior. Simplistic explanations that satisfied the child he now regards as silly. He can differentiate between the act and the intention behind it.

Searching for Inconsistencies

One of the fascinating developments that classroom pedagogy often ignores is the desire and the ability of these children to search for what

Kagan refers to as inconsistencies in sets of beliefs. The beliefs of human beings and analysis of data depend much on interconnected sets of propositions and beliefs and the discovery and removal of inconsistency. When one major idea in the proposition fails, all of them may be vulnerable. The maturing person not only finds the process of belief-building pleasurable, he actively searches for inconsistencies. Early adolescents endlessly engage in peer conversation for this purpose; and they pounce with glee on the disconnected, inconsistent suppositions of adults.

Younger children regard many things as permanently valid. They think that the world as they perceive it will never change. In the middle years, what was permanently valid has become tentative and suspect. Here is one example, from Kagan's data (p. 94), of this revolutionary development in the child. Consider this complex problem:

1. Parents are omniscient.
2. My parent has lost a job, or doesn't understand me, or has behaved badly.
3. If my parents were omniscient, they would not fail and be vulnerable.

Kagan notes that in dealing with this set of beliefs as a whole, the adolescent eventually works his way through to denial of the first premise and the consequent weakening of the whole set. Consider the implications of the search for inconsistencies for teaching in the social sciences, English, sciences. How bored young adolescents must become with teaching based on thinking about things as permanently valid, or hearing adults under the pretense of consistency advance propositions that can be pulled apart! The boredom is relieved only by the fun of catching teachers making incompatible assertions.

New Thoughts . . . Fresh Patterns

I need not develop further this theme of the new cognitive power of junior high students to illustrate how ridiculous middle-school education must seem to students when it is not geared to relativistic thinking, searching for inconsistencies, and questioning and rearranging old beliefs.

Interconnected with biological change components, the hallmark of middle-school behavior is the "rush of new thoughts, their evaluation, and their arrangements in a fresh structure" (Kagan, p. 97). Whether these thoughts conform to the dogmas of parents

* Jerome Kagan & Robert Coles (Eds.), *Twelve to Sixteen: Early Adolescence* (New York: W. W. Norton, 1972), pp. 90-106. (In this section of the paper, the author has drawn heavily from Kagan's examples.) Reprinted by permission.

and teachers is not of primary concern to the preadolescent. Think of junior high education as a process of helping people who have given up the certainties of childhood to explore uncertainties of all kinds in order to learn how to deal with life's incongruities. What a different school this one would be compared with one based on fixed, immutable sets of rules and of subject matter to be assimilated! Nowhere has the idea of teacher as a learning facilitator rather than one who *instructs* greater applicability than in the middle school.

Another consequence of biological changes in sexuality is body awareness, with a good measure of anxiety and guilt, self-consciousness, and at times unrealistic suspicion about the intentions of others. This unpleasant state of affairs produces in some middle-school children either withdrawal signs or their opposite—touchiness, anger, rashness, brashness. Much time may go into silent brooding. Then, failure to get along, to get things done, destroys self-confidence further. Their most pressing need is for adults who like them, help them get things done despite the anarchy within, and aid them in understanding the normative aspects of what is happening to them.

Developing Individual Interests
The rush of new thoughts in middle-school children has been mentioned, new thoughts about self, "I and thou," cause-and-effect in the object world and in human affairs. Imagination, skepticism, questioning formerly held truths, sharply differentiate the early adolescent from younger children. These new forces quite naturally are accompanied by a marked rise in individual interests. This is a period when most children explore a new interest so intensely that daily chores or responsibilities are thoroughly neglected. Their need is to find out what they can do well, what they can be really good at. Hobbies of all sorts consume more and more time: how to do something, how to put something together. All sorts of materials are collected. The child's pockets, purses and room at home are a secondhand store of bits and pieces.

The new-found interests, regardless of their inconstancy, should be known and fostered by middle-school teachers in all subjects. A significant part of the curriculum in the middle school should be EXPLORATION. Some individual interests remain active for a short time, then are replaced by new ones. Others will be the kernel of a permanent development, the core of a future identity. Because early adolescents

are beginning to think like adults, the pursuit of individual interests should be regarded as an important base for the general expansion of self, not just as something to do in a one-hour-a-week "enrichment" period or as a carrot for those who "get their lessons done."

SEARCHING FOR NEW RELATIONSHIPS

Children who are questioning the beliefs and the structure of the world they came to accept in childhood will actively try on new faces and new ideas with adults who are not parents. The parent no longer is an exclusive model for life. The middle-school child actually seeks a close relationship with a few teachers who will allow him to share and test out tentative ideas, interests and feelings. Being unsure about his responses to everything, however, he does not want total freedom. Anarchy in the classroom cannot be accepted by the middle-school child in his unsettled state. She/he is highly amenable to guidance.

Teachers as Friends
He thrives on getting acquainted and sharing ideas and activity with teachers who hopefully will be his friends. It is noteworthy that symbolic love affairs develop at this time so easily between students and teachers—boys for both teacher sexes, and likewise girls. The quality and intensity of this love and friendship toward an adult are entirely different in an eight-year-old or in a seventeen-year-old person. Early adolescents will often remember with pleasure, or with a deep resentment, some junior high teachers long after they have only misty memories of their high school teachers. The ones they remember with affection are teachers with whom they became friends at a time when the world came unglued and they found themselves unstuck in time, as in *Slaughterhouse Five,* and when they first engaged in genital manipulation. These teachers were guides during a development storm and were friendly when the student's world was in turmoil. The guides had a sense of humor that made the tempest in a situation seem to be only one in a teapot; they encouraged exploration of ideas and beliefs that were taboo in childhood; they took a very personal interest in a newfound hobby or skill; they took you places outside the classroom, introduced you to new adults and community life formerly closed to you. When you misbehaved grossly they stood firm, unthreatened and reasonable.

And occasionally they were able to communicate that they had made fools of themselves.

You came to see them, through their openness, as real people with interests, with homes and children; as people who sleep in beds and have dirty laundry; and as people with lifestyles, political ideas and outside interests different from those of your parents. These fondly remembered teachers were your new cultural heroes. Though they had defect and taint, they were mature enough to permit you to explore and test the adult world of thought and activity in your own hesitant and bumbling way. And somehow they forgave you all of your false starts, for each day and each week were full of false starts and blind alleys.

Other Adults "Outside"

The early adolescent also actively seeks contact with adults outside of school and home. This seeking is a matter of necessity, not just of ordinary interest. As their earlier childhood world of beliefs, of right and wrong, and conceptions of the way the world moves begins to crumble, they must reorganize their perceptions without turning into skeptics and weakening self-confidence and the capacity to live well in the world where innocence ends. They have, then, a desire to meet and get into the minds and ways of new adults. They want contact with all kinds of people with varying backgrounds, work interests and values, thus establishing a further proving ground for bringing seemingly incongruent perceptions of life into a harmonious relationship.

In the long distant past, children had such experiences with adults in the natural course of community life. Now, the school has to be the agent for planned experience with adults outside. To do justice to the need, a twelve- to fourteen-year-old child today should have planned contact and mutual-interest experience with at least as many adults outside of school each year as he has inside.

Mutual Peer Testing

This requirement is not to negate the importance of intimate encounter with peers who hold different beliefs and are experimenting with new skills and identities. The early adolescent needs many friends his age. He needs them to help him shape his beliefs and test their validity. The middle school can provide the student all of this he needs, providing there is a sufficient breadth of activity and range of groupings for different purposes. The totally ungraded middle school with a wide base of exploratory interest activity, beyond some basic core educational activity, can afford the mutual peer interaction required. The mostly graded school, with its overemphasis of subject matter, and its hierarchy of groups based strictly on academic capability, provides the most barren environment for peer encounter and self-evaluation.

THE GENERATION OF EARLY ADOLESCENTS TO COME

If we extrapolate the revolutionary changes in the knowledge, beliefs and values that have occurred in the last twenty years and carefully read the signs of new attitudes in children, we can foresee a very different group of early adolescents just a little way down the line. Hopefully the middle school is changing itself to be a more hospitable place for the new generations than was found in the old junior high that was fashioned after the high school.

Tomorrow's School: Obsolescent or Regenerative?

Education at all levels has come dangerously close to being obsolescent. A school is obsolescent when it can be shown that the child's beliefs and especially his skills and knowledge are derived primarily from sources outside the school curriculum and school life. Urgently important in a world of accelerated and unpredictable change is the need for schools truly to become theatres of life, staging grounds for involvement with the activities and the emerging new problems of life in the society. In a society of gradual change and of tradition, there is no such need, for the school can be the same place for child that it was for parent or for older brother and sister. We must now operate the enterprise so that the school is certain to be *different* for the child than it was for slightly older brother or sister. Otherwise obsolescence will certainly have occurred; life will long have outdistanced the dogmas to which children are subjected in school classrooms.

The middle-school child, because of biological change and new psychic energy, will always be closely tuned to the emerging new music, beliefs and values of the times. So the middle school must remain flexible and regenerative—in its organization for learning, in its curriculum of study options, and in interpersonal relations between students and teachers.

Signs of the Future

As to the generation of early adolescents to come, the following are some of the things we may expect:

☐ The students will be less concerned about grades. Grades are becoming less and less of a motive for study. Students want to learn something because it seems vital, or necessary, or useful; or because it excites their search for inconsistency; or because it satisfies curiosities. The decline of trust in authority throughout the world has weakened grades as a motivation to study. Besides, knowledge today is very tentative and children are acutely aware of this.

☐ Students will seek encounters with teachers who are honest. An honest teacher is one who does not profess things to children that he believed as a child but no longer really believes as an adult in the world as it is. Adolescents will seek contact with adults who will not shield from them the real world of man's activity. They will avoid persons who assume a too righteous posture, or anything as permanently valid except perhaps the need for love, respect and care for all living things.

☐ The early adolescent to come will be a natural learner in the inquiry method. From early childhood he will be stimulated in a fast changing world to ask questions, to find things out for himself, to weigh options on the basis of evidence. He will learn early in life that adults cannot supply the answers to complex questions, either in the realm of value or technology. Adults can only join him in the pilgrimage to reconceive things in a new light. Think of the implications here for evaluating some present-day courses in history, civics, or home economics and art.

The trend of more independent inquiry that has gotten into colleges and now high schools will be extended into the middle school. The early adolescent of the future will be less satisfied with structures that permit little leeway for individual exploration.

☐ The age we have fallen into, with disillusionment concerning power, wealth, legitimized corruption, and value of possessions, an age of the loss of heroes, will produce more children who turn to value-seeking, philosophy and art, if the school and its facilities can foster the setting for it. Our new generations of youth will be seeking a kind of knowledge formerly sought only by people in later life, if at all: self-knowledge, personal integration, and the building of community.

The children of the night world need better schools than we now have in order to mature into people who have themselves together and can put truly human communities together.

Suggested Readings

Alexander, William M. *The Emergent Middle School.* New York: Holt, Rinehart & Winston, 1968.
————. "The New School in the Middle." Phi Delta Kappan 50 (6, 1969):356.
Ansubel, David P. *Educational Psychology: A Cognitive View.* New York: Holt, Rinehart & Winston, 1968. Pp. 219-24. (On early adolescent cognitive development.)
Association for Supervision and Curriculum Development, NEA. *Educational Leadership* 31, 3 (Dec. 1973): 195-245. (Most of the issue is devoted to articles about "Middle School in the Making.")
Jacobsen, A. G. "Inductive Processes in Embryonic Development." *Science* 152 (1966): 25-34.
Kagan, Jerome. "A Conception of Early Adolescence." *Daedalus,* Fall 1971, pp. 27-35. Reprinted by permission of *Daedalus,* Journal of the American Academy of Arts and Sciences, Boston, MA. Fall 1971, *Twelve to Sixteen: Early Adolescence.*
Kagan, Jerome, & Robert Coles (Eds.). *Twelve to Sixteen: Early Adolescence.* New York: W. W. Norton, 1972. Pp. 352. (Fourteen articles by biologists, sociologists, psychoanalysts, psychologists.) Reprinted by permission.
Shuttleworth, F. K. "The Adolescent Period." A Graphic Atlas (growth trends in boys and girls). *Monograph of the Society for Research in Child Development,* Vol. 14, 1951.

18

What the Public Schools Should Teach

WALTER P. REUTHER

In this article, Mr. Reuther brings into sharp focus some of the central questions concerning curriculum in the public schools, and takes a consistent and clear stand on these questions. There are many arguments in this statement which should be considered seriously by every member of the educational enterprise.

Mr. Reuther has long been interested in the secondary school system of this country. As president of the UAW International Union, and vice president of the AFL - CIO, it may be said that he is, in this article, speaking for the organized labor movement.

Perhaps it is too much to expect that our current national preoccupation with costs of school construction will open a new inquiry into the more fundamental question of what to teach.

Americans have been impatient with basic questions. We solved them, presumably, long ago, and have merely been living very well, so to speak, on our original investment.

Yet the era of uncritical optimism and self-confidence is drawing to a close. Whether its formal ending came with the explosion of the first atomic bomb by the United States or the recognition by both this nation and Russia, when they agreed to meet at the summit conference of Geneva, that peace is an absolute condition of survival, is a matter for debate among historians.

The fact is we are already living in a new period, and there is a great lag between old assumptions that have hardened into venerable practice and the changing actualities of our lives.

Nowhere is this more true than in the field of education. So while it may seem academic, in the worst sense of that term, to raise fundamental questions about what to teach — which is very close to raising ultimate questions about our views of man — at a time when the financial crisis of our schools is so acute as to involve the viability of the very system, such as it is, there may be a very practical connection between the basic questions and the current financial dilemma.

There is always a smouldering debate, of course, over curriculum, not only among professional educators but also among lay advocates of various attitudes toward retrenchment and reform. The weakness of this debate, in my view, is two-fold.

Among educators, first, the debate seems to lose itself too quickly in considerations of method. Method, of course, is vitally important. It can affect the substance of what is taught to the point of changing it significantly. Yet it cannot replace it, as some educators seem to believe.

The basic question remains: what to teach. No elaboration of method can evade this question. All the elaboration of method in the world, for example, will not convert a course in business administration into a history of trade-unionism. It is the commitment of our culture at its most articulate and influential levels to a business view of society that accounts for the availability of schools of business administration and for the lack of similar opportunity for study of the nature and purposes of the labor movement.

Proponents of the various views on curriculum, secondly, are in effect quarreling over the distribution of educational scarcity rather than coming to grips with the underlying lack of educational means.

Take, for example, the debate over the education of the so-called gifted child. How, from the standpoint of the average competent and well-intentioned school administrator, can a genuine program specifically devoted to the gifted child be foisted upon a community the majority of whose children are forced, by the current regime of educational scarcity, to submit to part-time schooling by over-worked and underpaid teachers?

The gifted-child approach to curriculum is as much an evasion of the full dimensions of our educational crisis as is the professional obsession with technique. In a regime of educational abundance, where there were enough teachers, enough schools, enough classrooms, where we spent as much on learning as we did on plumbing, the problem of what to teach would not disappear but it would become manageable.

Only under such a regime of educational abundance, as a matter of fact, would it be possible to develop sensible and real programs for gifted children, for only under educational abundance will we be able to pay attention to each child, to recognize the variety of growth patterns, to draw out the latent capacities of children who are not academic front-runners but who may finish strong, to their own and the community's advantage, when we can afford to lavish upon them the attention they will deserve, whatever their record on the I. Q. and aptitude tests.

The subjective bias and cultural preconceptions that permeate these testing devices are considerable, as most educators surely know. A smaller classroom population, leading to more understanding between the teacher and the dullard or eccentric in the corner, will shatter the latest reading of the tests beyond recognition. Each child is unique, we tell each other in our finer democratic moments. Let us believe that enough to create an educational system dedicated in practice as well as in theory to the discovery and cultivation of that uniqueness.

The current advocacy of special programs for the gifted child, when unaccompanied by a concern for the gross lack of educational means, is, it seems to me, an intrusion into the realm of educational discourse of a general view of democracy characteristically held by short-sighted businessmen.

I have myself advocated, and still advocate, a comprehensive federal scholarship program which would have the purpose of developing a civilian corps of men and women trained as technicians and scientists. I believe that such a program is urgently needed to end the senseless pirating of skilled manpower by industry and to put us, domestically, and in terms of our world commitments, in a competitive position to meet the long-term Russian threat.

Yet I do not believe that such a program should be conceived or operated within the present framework of penury and lack. I do not believe in robbing Peter to pay Paul, which is what such a program would amount to if it were not developed as part of a comprehensive federal-state-local program to make public education as central in our budgets as it seems to be in our democratic daydreams and professional doctrine.

Yet the notion of plunging, as it were, on the education of the gifted child is wholly compatible with the current effort of the National Association of Manufacturers and the American Chamber of Commerce to block adequate federal aid to our schools. In this context, the notion is clearly the old class notion of education. The short-sighted businessman is typically interested in two kinds of learning: the best that money can buy for his own children, and a smattering of ignorance mixed with vocational training for other people's children, who will grow up to work for him. Anything else is "frills," or subversive or both, while any departure from use of the local property tax to support public education (except for those vocational supports already forthcoming from the federal government) is anathema, since it would involve the federal taxing power.

The whole nation, of course, ultimately suffers from this niggardly view of our national educational responsibilities. There is a growing awareness now of the domestic and world consequences of the skilled manpower shortage, but it is mostly limited to a concern with this particular shortage; it has not reached the point at which the general insufficiency of our schools will be confronted. To talk of curriculum seriously now is to anticipate that juncture. What to teach must, nevertheless, it seems to me, be seriously discussed now in order that the wisest answers will be available — and in order to hasten the day when the wisest answers may be generally applied. And the leading question, I should say, should be something like the following: How does a technological, business-oriented society, wedded to a utilitarian, vocational concept of education's role, yet willing, despite ingrown anti-intellectualism, to make allowances for subordinate excursions into the liberal arts providing that such flights from "reality" do not divert us from the acquisition and proliferation of material goods — how does such a society cultivate both the necessary special skills and the necessary general culture which alone can save us from the centrifugal pull of specialization?

How do we save, in all its richness and complexity, the general fund of human experience, together with the running commentary on that experience whose continuing availability is our only guarantee of an open society, while at the same time building barriers of specialization across which our most highly trained men and women are finding it increasingly difficult to communicate with each other and with the generality of citizens?

This is not strictly an educational problem; if we ever solve it, it will be solved outside of the schools, in the arenas of our common life. Yet the schools must have their great part in helping to solve it. It will not be solved by timidity, by a stubborn insistence on the life-giving virtues of the local property tax.

I should say that perhaps our first step in solving it would be to understand that all of our particular problems, educational, economic, military, and the rest, are subsumed in the root problem of what man has done to man.

For what man has done to man, once the lament of a poet, has become the basic datum of our situation. Anything we think or do about what to teach must have this moral datum as a point of departure and arrival. Of course, we must "facilitate growth." But we are dealing with human beings, not livestock or hybrid corn. We have to be sure about whether we are facilitating the growth of perfectly-adjusted consumers, sitting ducks for the skilled technicians of motivation research, whether we are facilitating the growth of perfectly-adjusted profit-and-loss reckoners, who know the price of everything and the value of nothing, whether we are facilitating the growth of perfectly-adjusted wage-earners, who will be so coddled and numbed by the personnel department that they will live their lives to its tempo — or whether we are fostering the growth of men and of man.

In the latter case, we must look to much more than the critical shortage of skilled manpower. We must do much more than send the upper percentiles to college, while we shunt the lower percentiles into the vocational schools. Such a course is cynical and defeatist, and what we fondly call the free world can die of it.

I think that we must look to the general disciplines, to the human or humanist disciplines, to the liberal arts. I think we must look to English, to history, to foreign languages, to a study, from what might be called the inside, of other cultures than our own.

I think every American child should learn a second language as well as he learns American English, that this study should begin in the primary grades. I believe that the studies of other countries should be pursued to some extent from the viewpoint of those countries as well as from our viewpoint, while we push the UNESCO and any other fruitful efforts to write histories that are not blinded or misshapen by narrow nationalism.

I think we should teach the history of science as a branch of the humanities, trying to make as much of it as possible available to as many students as possible as early as possible in the primary and secondary grades.

It is my view that the study of the humanities must rank with the vocational and technical studies in our public schools. I think no current or future pressure for skilled manpower should push us into forgetfulness that these general disciplines constitute our long-range hope that, whatever the complexities of a technological society, men will still be knitted together in the creative and truly democratic fellowship of a common awareness of the human record.

These are some of the broad lines along which, in my opinion, the curriculum of our public schools can be strengthened. I am sure, though, that all discussion of curriculum is and will remain "academic" as far as its wholesome effect on most of our children is concerned, as long as we timidly accept the current stranglehold upon education of the penny-wise, democracy-foolish viewpoint fostered by the National Association of Manufacturers and the United States Chamber of Commerce.

19

Black and white, male and female, rich and poor, American teenagers have the herding instinct. On streetcorners, in shopping centers, in the ghetto and in the suburbs, the boys and the girls hang out. Sometimes the kids get together for fun, sometimes for trouble, sometimes for political purposes. Mostly, they crave recognition, companionship and excitement. Gangs are a way of life for many adolescents—part of the ritual of growing up.

The Saints and the Roughnecks

William J. Chambliss

Eight promising young men—children of good, stable, white upper-middle-class families, active in school affairs, good pre-college students—were some of the most delinquent boys at Hanibal High School. While community residents and parents knew that these boys occasionally sowed a few wild oats, they were totally unaware that sowing wild oats completely occupied the daily routine of these young men. The Saints were constantly occupied with truancy, drinking, wild driving, petty theft and vandalism. Yet not one was officially arrested for any misdeed during the two years I observed them.

This record was particularly surprising in light of my observations during the same two years of another gang of Hanibal High School students, six lower-class white boys known as the Roughnecks. The Roughnecks were constantly in trouble with police and community even though their rate of delinquency was about equal with that of the Saints. What was the cause of this disparity? the result? The following consideration of the activities, social class and community perceptions of both gangs may provide some answers.

The Saints from Monday to Friday

The Saints' principal daily concern was with getting out of school as early as possible. The boys managed to get out of school with minimum danger that they would be accused of playing hookey through an elaborate procedure for obtaining "legitimate" release from class. The most common procedure was for one boy to obtain the release of another by fabricating a meeting of some committee, program or recognized club. Charles might raise his hand in his 9:00 chemistry class and asked to be excused—a euphemism for going to the bathroom. Charles would go to Ed's math class and inform the teacher that Ed was needed for a 9:30 rehearsal of the drama club play. The math teacher would recognize Ed and Charles as "good students" involved in numerous school activities and would permit Ed to leave at 9:30. Charles would return to his class, and Ed would go to Tom's English class to obtain his release. Tom would engineer Charles' escape. The strategy would continue until as many of the Saints as possible were freed. After a stealthy trip to the car (which had been parked in a strategic spot), the boys were off for a day of fun.

Over the two years I observed the Saints, this pattern was repeated nearly every day. There were variations on the theme, but in one form or another, the boys used this procedure for getting out of class and then off the school grounds. Rarely did all eight of the Saints manage to leave school at the same time. The average number avoiding school on the days I observed them was five.

Having escaped from the concrete corridors the boys usually went either to a pool hall on the other (lower-class) side of town or to a cafe in the suburbs. Both places were out of the way of people the boys were likely to know (family or school officials), and both provided a source of entertainment. The pool hall entertainment was the generally rough atmosphere, the occasional hustler, the sometimes drunk proprietor and, of course, the game of pool. The cafe's entertainment was provided by the owner. The boys would "accidentally" knock a glass on the floor or spill cola on the counter—not all the time, but enough to be sporting. They would also bend spoons, put salt in sugar bowls and generally tease whoever was working in the cafe. The owner had opened the cafe recently and was dependent on the boys' business which was, in fact, substantial since between the horsing around and the teasing they bought food and drinks.

The Saints on Weekends

On weekends the automobile was even more critical than during the week, for on weekends the Saints went to Big Town—a large city with a population of over a million 25 miles from Hanibal. Every Friday and Saturday night most of the Saints would meet between 8:00 and 8:30 and would go into Big Town. Big Town activities included drinking heavily in taverns or nightclubs, driving drunkenly through the streets, and committing acts of vandalism and playing pranks.

By midnight on Fridays and Saturdays the Saints were usually thoroughly high, and one or two of them were often so drunk they had to be carried to the cars. Then the boys drove around town, calling obscenities to women and girls; occasionally trying (unsuccessfully so far as I could tell) to pick girls up; and driving recklessly through red lights and at high speeds with their lights out. Occasionally they played "chicken." One boy would climb out the back window of the car and across the roof to the driver's side of the car while the car was moving at high speed (between 40 and 50 miles an hour); then the driver would move over and the boy who had just crawled across the car roof would take the driver's seat.

Searching for "fair game" for a prank was the boys' principal activity after they left the tavern. The boys would drive alongside a foot patrolman and ask directions to some street. If the policeman leaned on the car in the course of answering the question, the driver would speed away, causing him to lose his balance. The Saints were careful to play this prank only in an area where they were not going to spend much time and where they could quickly disappear around a corner to avoid having their license plate number taken.

Construction sites and road repair areas were the special province of the Saints' mischief. A soon-to-be-repaired hole in the road inevitably invited the Saints to remove lanterns and wooden barricades and put them in the car, leaving the hole unprotected. The boys would find a safe vantage point and wait for an unsuspecting motorist to drive into the hole. Often, though not always, the boys would go up to the motorist and commiserate with him about the dreadful way the city protected its citizenry.

Leaving the scene of the open hole and the motorist, the boys would then go searching for an appropriate place to erect the stolen barricade. An "appropriate place" was often a spot on a highway near a curve in the road where the barricade would not be seen by an on-coming motorist. The boys would wait to watch an unsuspecting motorist attempt to stop and (usually) crash into the wooden barricade. With saintly bearing the boys might offer help and understanding.

A stolen lantern might well find its way onto the back of a police car or hang from a street lamp. Once a lantern served as a prop for a reenactment of the "midnight ride of Paul Revere" until the "play," which was taking place at 2:00 AM in the center of a main street of Big Town, was interrupted by a police car several blocks away. The boys ran, leaving the lanterns on the street, and managed to avoid being apprehended.

Abandoned houses, especially if they were located in out-of-the-way places, were fair game for destruction and spontaneous vandalism. The boys would break windows, remove furniture to the yard and tear it apart, urinate on the walls and scrawl obscenities inside.

Through all the pranks, drinking and reckless driving the boys managed miraculously to avoid being stopped by police. Only twice in two years was I aware that they had been stopped by a Big City policeman. Once was for speeding (which they did every time they drove whether they were drunk or sober), and the driver managed to convince the policeman that it was simply an error. The second time they were stopped they had just left a nightclub and were walking through an alley. Aaron stopped to urinate and the boys began making obscene remarks. A foot patrolman came into the alley, lectured the boys and sent them home. Before the boys got to the car one began talking in a loud voice again. The policeman, who had followed them down the alley, arrested this boy for disturbing the peace and took him to the police station where the other Saints gathered. After paying a $5.00 fine, and with the assurance that there would be no permanent record of the arrest, the boy was released.

The boys had a spirit of frivolity and fun about their escapades. They did not view what they were engaged in as "delinquency," though it surely was by any reasonable definition of that word. They simply viewed themselves as having a little fun and who, they would ask, was really hurt by it? The answer had to be no one, although this fact remains one of the most difficult things to explain about the gang's behavior. Unlikely though it seems, in two years of drinking, driving, carousing and vandalism no one was seriously injured as a result of the Saints' activities.

The Saints in School

The Saints were highly successful in school. The average grade for the group was "B," with two of the boys having close to a straight "A" average. Almost all of the boys were popular and many of them held offices in the school. One of the boys was vice-president of the student body one year. Six of the boys played on athletic teams.

At the end of their senior year, the student body selected ten seniors for special recognition as the "school wheels"; four of the ten were Saints. Teachers and school officials saw no problem with any of these boys and anticipated that they would all "make something of themselves."

How the boys managed to maintain this impression is surprising in view of their actual behavior while in school. Their technique for covering truancy was so successful that teachers did not even realize that the boys were absent from school much of the time. Occasionally, of course, the system would backfire and then the boy was on his own. A boy who was caught would be most contrite, would plead guilty and ask for mercy. He inevitably got the mercy he sought.

Cheating on examinations was rampant, even to the point of orally communicating answers to exams as well as looking at one another's papers. Since none of the group studied, and since they were primarily dependent on one another for help, it is surprising that grades were so high. Teachers contributed to the deception in their admitted inclination to give these boys (and presumably others like them) the benefit of the doubt. When asked how the boys did in school, and when pressed on specific examinations, teachers might admit that they were disappointed in John's performance, but would quickly add that they "knew that he was capable of doing better," so John was given a higher grade than he had actually earned. How often this happened is impossible to know. During the time that I observed the group, I never saw any of the boys take homework home. Teachers may have been "understanding" very regularly.

One exception to the gang's generally good performance was Jerry, who had a "C" average in his junior year, experienced disaster the next year and failed to graduate. Jerry had always been a little more nonchalant than the others about the liberties he took in school. Rather than wait for someone to come get him from class, he would offer his own excuse and leave. Although he probably did not miss any more classes than most of the others in the group, he did not take the requisite pains to cover his absences. Jerry was the only Saint whom I ever heard talk back to a teacher. Although teachers often called him a "cut up" or a "smart kid," they never referred to him as a troublemaker or as a kid headed for trouble. It seems likely, then, that Jerry's failure his senior year and his mediocre performance his junior year were consequences of his not playing the game the proper way (possibly because he was disturbed by his parents' divorce). His teachers regarded him as

"immature" and not quite ready to get out of high school.

The Police and the Saints

The local police saw the Saints as good boys who were among the leaders of the youth in the community. Rarely, the boys might be stopped in town for speeding or for running a stop sign. When this happened the boys were always polite, contrite and pled for mercy. As in school, they received the mercy they asked for. None ever received a ticket or was taken into the precinct by the local police.

The situation in Big City, where the boys engaged in most of their delinquency, was only slightly different. The police there did not know the boys at all, although occasionally the boys were stopped by a patrolman. Once they were caught taking a lantern from a construction site. Another time they were stopped for running a stop sign, and on several occasions they were stopped for speeding. Their behavior was as before: contrite, polite and penitent. The urban police, like the local police, accepted their demeanor as sincere. More important, the urban police were convinced that these were good boys just out for a lark.

The Roughnecks

Hanibal townspeople never perceived the Saints' high level of delinquency. The Saints were good boys who just went in for an occasional prank. After all, they were well dressed, well mannered and had nice cars. The Roughnecks were a different story. Although the two gangs of boys were the same age, and both groups engaged in an equal amount of wild-oat sowing, everyone agreed that the not-so-well-dressed, not-so-well-mannered, not-so-rich boys were heading for trouble. Townspeople would say, "You can see the gang members at the drugstore, night after night, leaning against the storefront (sometimes drunk) or slouching around inside buying cokes, reading magazines, and probably stealing old Mr. Wall blind. When they are outside and girls walk by, even respectable girls, these boys make suggestive remarks. Sometimes their remarks are downright lewd."

From the community's viewpoint, the real indication that these kids were in for trouble was that they were constantly involved with the police. Some of them had been picked up for stealing, mostly small stuff, of course, "but still it's stealing small stuff that leads to big time crimes." "Too bad," people said. "Too bad that these boys couldn't behave like the other kids in town; stay out of trouble, be polite to adults, and look to their future."

The community's impression of the degree to which this group of six boys (ranging in age from 16 to 19) engaged in delinquency was somewhat distorted. In some ways the gang was more delinquent than the community thought; in other ways they were less.

> Through all the pranks, drinking and reckless driving the Saints managed miraculously to avoid being stopped by the police. No one was ever seriously injured despite all the carousing and vandalism.

The fighting activities of the group were fairly readily and accurately perceived by almost everyone. At least once a month, the boys would get into some sort of fight, although most fights were scraps between members of the group or involved only one member of the group and some peripheral hanger-on. Only three times in the period of observation did the group fight together: once against a gang from across town, once against two blacks and once against a group of boys from another school. For the first two fights the group went out "looking for trouble"—and they found it both times. The third fight followed a football game and began spontaneously with an argument on the football field between one of the Roughnecks and a member of the opposition's football team.

Jack had a particular propensity for fighting and was involved in most of the brawls. He was a prime mover of the escalation of arguments into fights.

More serious than fighting, had the community been aware of it, was theft. Although almost everyone was aware that the boys occasionally stole things, they did not realize the extent of the activity. Petty stealing was a frequent event for the Roughnecks. Sometimes they stole as a group and coordinated their efforts; other times they stole in pairs. Rarely did they steal alone.

The thefts ranged from very small things like paperback books, comics and ballpoint pens to expensive items like watches. The nature of the thefts varied from time to time. The gang would go through a period of systematically shoplifting items from automobiles or school lockers. Types of thievery varied with the whim of the gang. Some forms of thievery were more profitable than others, but all thefts were for profit, not just thrills.

Roughnecks siphoned gasoline from cars as often as they had access to an automobile, which was not very often. Unlike the Saints, who owned their own cars, the Roughnecks would have to borrow their parents' cars, an event which occured only eight or nine times a year. The boys claimed to have stolen cars for joy rides from time to time.

Ron committed the most serious of the group's offenses. With an unidentified associate the boy attempted to burglarize a gasoline station. Although this station had been robbed twice previously in the same month,

Ron denied any involvement in either of the other thefts. When Ron and his accomplice approached the station, the owner was hiding in the bushes beside the station. He fired both barrels of a double-barreled shotgun at the boys. Ron was severely injured; the other boy ran away and was never caught. Though he remained in critical condition for several months, Ron finally recovered and served six months of the following year in reform school. Upon release from reform school, Ron was put back a grade in school, and began running around with a different gang of boys. The Roughnecks considered the new gang less delinquent than themselves, and during the following year Ron had no more trouble with the police.

The Roughnecks, then, engaged mainly in three types of delinquency: theft, drinking and fighting. Although community members perceived that this gang of kids was delinquent, they mistakenly believed that their illegal activities were primarily drinking, fighting and being a nuisance to passersby. Drinking was limited among the gang members, although it did occur, and theft was much more prevalent than anyone realized.

Drinking would doubtless have been more prevalent had the boys had ready access to liquor. Since they rarely had automobiles at their disposal, they could not travel very far, and the bars in town would not serve them. Most of the boys had little money, and this, too, inhibited their purchase of alcohol. Their major source of liquor was a local drunk who would buy them a fifth if they would give him enough extra to buy himself a pint of whiskey or a bottle of wine.

The community's perception of drinking as prevalent stemmed from the fact that it was the most obvious delinquency the boys engaged in. When one of the boys had been drinking, even a casual observer seeing him on the corner would suspect that he was high.

There was a high level of mutual distrust and dislike between the Roughnecks and the police. The boys felt very strongly that the police were unfair and corrupt. Some evidence existed that the boys were correct in their perception.

The main source of the boys' dislike for the police undoubtedly stemmed from the fact that the police would sporadically harass the group. From the standpoint of the boys, these acts of occasional enforcement of the law were whimsical and uncalled for. It made no sense to them, for example, that the police would come to the corner occasionally and threaten them with arrest for loitering when the night before the boys had been out siphoning gasoline from cars and the police had been nowhere in sight. To the boys, the police were stupid on the one hand, for not being where they should have been and catching the boys in a serious offense, and unfair on the other hand, for trumping up "loitering" charges against them.

From the viewpoint of the police, the situation was

quite different. They knew, with all the confidence necessary to be a policeman, that these boys were engaged in criminal activities. They knew this partly from occasionally catching them, mostly from circumstantial evidence ("the boys were around when those tires were slashed"), and partly because the police shared the view of the community in general that this was a bad bunch of boys. The best the police could hope to do was to be sensitive to the fact that these boys were engaged in illegal acts and arrest them whenever there was some evidence that they had been involved. Whether or not the boys had in fact committed a particular act in a particular way was not especially important. The police had a broader view: their job was to stamp out these kids' crimes; the tactics were not as important as the end result.

Over the period that the group was under observation, each member was arrested at least once. Several of the boys were arrested a number of times and spent at least one night in jail. While most were never taken to court, two of the boys were sentenced to six months' incarceration in boys' schools.

The Roughnecks in School

The Roughnecks' behavior in school was not particularly disruptive. During school hours they did not all hang around together, but tended instead to spend most of their time with one or two other members of the gang who were their special buddies. Although every member of the gang attempted to avoid school as much as possible, they were not particularly successful and most of them attended school with surprising regularity. They considered school a burden—something to be gotten through with a minimum of conflict. If they were "bugged" by a particular teacher, it could lead to trouble. One of the boys, Al, once threatened to beat up a teacher and, according to the other boys, the teacher hid under a desk to escape him.

Teachers saw the boys the way the general community did, as heading for trouble, as being uninterested in making something of themselves. Some were also seen as being incapable of meeting the academic standards of the school. Most of the teachers expressed concern for this group of boys and were willing to pass them despite poor performance, in the belief that failing them would only aggravate the problem.

The group of boys had a grade point average just slightly above "C." No one in the group failed either grade, and no one had better than a "C" average. They were very consistent in their achievement or, at least, the teachers were consistent in their perception of the boys' achievement.

Two of the boys were good football players. Herb was acknowledged to be the best player in the school and Jack was almost as good. Both boys were criticized for their failure to abide by training rules, for refusing to come to practice as often as they should, and for not playing their best during practice. What they lacked in sportsmanship they made up for in skill, apparently, and played every game no matter how poorly they had performed in practice or how many practice sessions they had missed.

Two Questions

Why did the community, the school and the police react to the Saints as though they were good, upstanding, nondelinquent youths with bright futures but to the Roughnecks as though they were tough, young criminals who were headed for trouble? Why did the Roughnecks and the Saints in fact have quite different careers after high school—careers which, by and large, lived up to the expectations of the community?

The most obvious explanation for the differences in the community's and law enforcement agencies' reactions to the two gangs is that one group of boys was "more delinquent" than the other. Which group *was* more delinquent? The answer to this question will determine in part how we explain the differential responses to these groups by the members of the community and, particularly, by law enforcement and school officials.

In sheer number of illegal acts, the Saints were the more delinquent. They were truant from school for at least part of the day almost every day of the week. In addition, their drinking and vandalism occurred with surprising regularity. The Roughnecks, in contrast, engaged sporadically in delinquent episodes. While these episodes were frequent, they certainly did not occur on a daily or even a weekly basis.

The difference in frequency of offenses was probably caused by the Roughnecks' inability to obtain liquor and to manipulate legitimate excuses from school. Since the Roughnecks had less money than the Saints, and teachers carefully supervised their school activities, the Roughnecks' hearts may have been as black as the Saints', but their misdeeds were not nearly as frequent.

There are really no clear-cut criteria by which to measure qualitative differences in antisocial behavior. The most important dimension of the difference is generally referred to as the "seriousness" of the offenses.

If seriousness encompasses the relative economic costs of delinquent acts, then some assessment can be made. The Roughnecks probably stole an average of about $5.00 worth of goods a week. Some weeks the figure was considerably higher, but these times must be balanced against long periods when almost nothing was stolen.

The Saints were more continuously engaged in delinquency but their acts were not for the most part costly to property. Only their vandalism and occasional theft of gasoline would so qualify. Perhaps once or twice a month they would siphon a tankful of gas. The other costly items were street signs, construction lanterns and the like. All of these acts combined probably did not quite average $5.00 a week, partly because much of the stolen equipment was abandoned and presumably could be recovered. The difference in cost of stolen property between the two groups was trivial, but the Roughnecks probably had a slightly more expensive set of activities than did the Saints.

Another meaning of seriousness is the potential threat of physical harm to members of the community and to the boys themselves. The Roughnecks were more prone to physical violence; they not only welcomed an opportunity to fight; they went seeking it. In addition, they fought among themselves frequently. Although the fighting never included deadly weapons, it was still a menace, however minor, to the physical safety of those involved.

The Saints never fought. They avoided physical conflict both inside and outside the group. At the same time, though, the Saints frequently endangered their own and other people's lives. They did so almost every time they drove a car, especially if they had been drinking. Sober, their driving was risky; under the influence of alcohol it was horrendous. In addition, the Saints endangered the lives of others with their pranks. Street excavations left unmarked were a very serious hazard.

Evaluating the relative seriousness of the two gangs' activities is difficult. The community reacted as though the behavior of the Roughnecks was a problem, and they reacted as though the behavior of the Saints was not. But the members of the community were ignorant of the array of delinquent acts that characterized the Saints' behavior. Although concerned citizens were unaware of much of the Roughnecks' behavior as well, they were much better informed about the Roughnecks' involvement in delinquency than they were about the Saints'.

Visibility

Differential treatment of the two gangs resulted in part because one gang was infinitely more visible than the other. This differential visibility was a direct function of the economic standing of the families. The Saints had access to automobiles and were able to remove themselves from the sight of the community. In as routine a decision as to where to go to have a milkshake after school, the Saints stayed away from the mainstream of community life. Lacking transportation, the Roughnecks could not make it to the edge of town. The center of town was the only practical place for them to meet since their homes were scattered throughout the town and any noncentral meeting place put an undue hardship on some members. Through necessity the Roughnecks congregated in a crowded area where everyone in the

community passed frequently, including teachers and law enforcement officers. They could easily see the Roughnecks hanging around the drugstore.

The Roughnecks, of course, made themselves even more visible by making remarks to passersby and by occasionally getting into fights on the corner. Meanwhile, just as regularly, the Saints were either at the cafe on one edge of town or in the pool hall at the other edge of town. Without any particular realization that they were making themselves inconspicuous, the Saints were able to hide their time-wasting. Not only were they removed from the mainstream of traffic, but they were almost always inside a building.

On their escapades the Saints were also relatively invisible, since they left Hanibal and travelled to Big City. Here, too, they were mobile, roaming the city, rarely going to the same area twice.

Demeanor

To the notion of visibility must be added the difference in the responses of group members to outside intervention with their activities. If one of the Saints was confronted with an accusing policeman, even if he felt he was truly innocent of a wrongdoing, his demeanor was apologetic and penitent. A Roughneck's attitude was almost the polar opposite. When confronted with a threatening adult authority, even one who tried to be pleasant, the Roughneck's hostility and disdain were clearly observable. Sometimes he might attempt to put up a veneer of respect, but it was thin and was not accepted as sincere by the authority.

School was no different from the community at large. The Saints could manipulate the system by feigning compliance with the school norms. The availability of cars at school meant that once free from the immediate sight of the teacher, the boys could disappear rapidly. And this escape was well enough planned that no administrator or teacher was nearby when the boys left. A Roughneck who wished to escape for a few hours was in a bind. If it were possible to get free from class, downtown was still a mile away, and even if he arrived there, he was still very visible. Truancy for the Roughnecks meant almost certain detection, while the Saints enjoyed almost complete immunity from sanctions.

Bias

Community members were not aware of the transgressions of the Saints. Even if the Saints had been less discreet, their favorite delinquencies would have been perceived as less serious than those of the Roughnecks.

In the eyes of the police and school officials, a boy who drinks in an alley and stands intoxicated on the street corner is committing a more serious offense than is a boy who drinks to inebriation in a nightclub or a tavern and drives around afterwards in a car. Similarly, a boy who steals a wallet from a store will be viewed as having committed a more serious offense than a boy who steals a lantern from a construction site.

Perceptual bias also operates with respect to the demeanor of the boys in the two groups when they are confronted by adults. It is not simply that adults dislike the posture affected by boys of the Roughneck ilk; more important is the conviction that the posture adopted by the Roughnecks is an indication of their devotion and commitment to deviance as a way of life. The posture becomes a cue, just as the type of the offense is a cue, to the degree to which the known transgressions are indicators of the youths' potential for other problems.

Visibility, demeanor and bias are surface variables which explain the day-to-day operations of the police. Why do these surface variables operate as they do? Why did the police choose to disregard the Saints' delinquencies while breathing down the backs of the Roughnecks?

The answer lies in the class structure of American society and the control of legal institutions by those at the top of the class structure. Obviously, no representative of the upper class drew up the operational chart for the police which led them to look in the ghettoes and on streetcorners—which led them to see the demeanor of lower-class youth as troublesome and that of upper-middle-class youth as tolerable. Rather, the procedures simply developed from experience—experience with irate and influential upper-middle-class parents insisting that their son's vandalism was simply a prank and his drunkenness only a momentary "sowing of wild oats" —experience with cooperative or indifferent, powerless, lower-class parents who acquiesced to the laws' definition of their son's behavior.

Adult Careers of the Saints and the Roughnecks

The community's confidence in the potential of the Saints and the Roughnecks apparently was justified. If anything, the community members underestimated the degree to which these youngsters would turn out "good" or "bad."

Seven of the eight members of the Saints went on to college immediately after high school. Five of the boys graduated from college in four years. The sixth one finished college after two years in the army, and the seventh spent four years in the air force before returning to college and receiving a B.A. degree. Of these seven college graduates, three went on for advanced degrees. One finished law school and is now active in state politics, one finished medical school and is practicing near Hanibal, and one boy is now working for a Ph.D. The other four college graduates entered submanagerial, managerial or executive training positions with larger firms.

The only Saint who did not complete college was Jerry. Jerry had failed to graduate from high school with the other Saints. During his second senior year, after the other Saints had gone on to college, Jerry began to hang around with what several teachers described as a "rough crowd"—the gang that was heir apparent to the Roughnecks. At the end of his second senior year, when he did graduate from high school, Jerry took a job as a used-car salesman, got married and quickly had a child. Although he made several abortive attempts to go to college by attending night school, when I last saw him (ten years after high school) Jerry was unemployed and had been living on unemployment for almost a year. His wife worked as a waitress.

Some of the Roughnecks have lived up to community expectations. A number of them were headed for trouble. A few were not.

Jack and Herb were the athletes among the Roughnecks and their athletic prowess paid off handsomely. Both boys received unsolicited athletic scholarships to college. After Herb received his scholarship (near the end of his senior year), he apparently did an about-face. His demeanor became very similar to that of the Saints. Although he remained a member in good standing of the Roughnecks, he stopped participating in most activities and did not hang on the corner as often.

Jack did not change. If anything, he became more prone to fighting. He even made excuses for accepting the scholarship. He told the other gang members that the school had guaranteed him a "C" average if he would come to play football—an idea that seems far-fetched, even in this day of highly competitive recruiting.

During the summer after graduation from high school, Jack attempted suicide by jumping from a tall building. The jump would certainly have killed most people trying it, but Jack survived. He entered college in the fall and played four years of football. He and Herb graduated in four years, and both are teaching and coaching in high schools. They are married and have stable families. If anything, Jack appears to have a more prestigious position in the community than does Herb, though both are well respected and secure in their positions.

Two of the boys never finished high school. Tommy left at the end of his junior year and went to another state. That summer he was arrested and placed on probation on a manslaughter charge. Three years later he was arrested for murder; he pleaded guilty to second degree murder and is serving a 30-year sentence in the state penitentiary.

Al, the other boy who did not finish high school, also left the state in his senior year. He is serving a life sentence in a state penitentiary for first degree murder.

Wes is a small-time gambler. He finished high school and "bummed around." After several years he made contact with a bookmaker who employed him as a runner. Later he acquired his own area and has been working it ever since. His position among the bookmakers is almost identical to the position he had in the gang; he is always around but no one is really aware of him. He makes no trouble and he does not get into any. Steady, reliable, capable of keeping his mouth closed, he plays the game by the rules, even though the game is an illegal one.

That leaves only Ron. Some of his former friends reported that they had heard he was "driving a truck up north," but no one could provide any concrete information.

Reinforcement

The community responded to the Roughnecks as boys in trouble, and the boys agreed with that perception. Their pattern of deviancy was reinforced, and breaking away from it became increasingly unlikely. Once the boys acquired an image of themselves as deviants, they selected new friends who affirmed that self-image. As that self-conception became more firmly entrenched, they also became willing to try new and more extreme deviances. With their growing alienation came freer expression of disrespect and hostility for representatives of the legitimate society. This disrespect increased the community's negativism, perpetuating the entire process of commitment to deviance. Lack of a commitment to deviance works the same way. In either case, the process will perpetuate itself unless some event (like a scholarship to college or a sudden failure) external to the established relationship intervenes. For two of the Roughnecks (Herb and Jack), receiving college athletic scholarships created new relations and culminated in a break with the established pattern of deviance. In the case of one of the Saints (Jerry), his parents' divorce and his failing to graduate from high school changed some of his other relations. Being held back in school for a year

and losing his place among the Saints had sufficient impact on Jerry to alter his self-image and virtually to assure that he would not go on to college as his peers did. Although the experiments of life can rarely be reversed, it seems likely in view of the behavior of the other boys who did not enjoy this special treatment by the school that Jerry, too, would have "become something" had he graduated as anticipated. For Herb and Jack outside intervention worked to their advantage; for Jerry it was his undoing.

Truancy for the Roughnecks meant almost certain detection. The Saints' technique for covering truancy was so successful that teachers did not even realize that the boys were absent from school much of the time.

Selective perception and labelling—finding, processing and punishing some kinds of criminality and not others—means that visible, poor, nonmobile, outspoken, undiplomatic "tough" kids will be noticed, whether their actions are seriously delinquent or not. Other kids, who have established a reputation for being bright (even though underachieving), disciplined and involved in respectable activities, who are mobile and monied, will be invisible when they deviate from sanctioned activities. They'll sow their wild oats—perhaps even wider and thicker than their lower-class cohorts—but they won't be noticed. When it's time to leave adolescence most will follow the expected path, settling into the ways of the middle class, remembering fondly the delinquent but unnoticed fling of their youth. The Roughnecks and others like them may turn around, too. It is more likely that their noticeable deviance will have been so reinforced by police and community that their lives will be effectively channelled into careers consistent with their adolescent background. □

Beatrice M. Hill and Nelson S. Burke

Some Disadvantaged Youths Look at Their Schools

Background

Equality of Educational Opportunity,[1] a report recently issued by the U.S. Office of Education, stated that "American Public Education remains largely unequal in most regions of the country, including all those where Negroes form any significant proportion of the population." To come to grips with these inequalities and the obvious crisis in American schools, especially schools in depressed areas, there has been a rash of legislation which has produced a proliferation of new educational programs both in the regular school establishment and in the anti-poverty programs.

The National Defense Education Act of 1958, The Elementary and Secondary Education Act of 1965, and the Higher Education Act of 1965, are examples. In addition to these, The Economic Opportunity Act of 1964 created many programs which contain an educational focus. Among these are the Neighborhood Youth Corps and the Job Corps. It also created Community Action Agencies which are authorized to administer some programs that have an educational focus.

Since the improvement of educational competence among disadvantaged youth is one program objective of NYC, Job Corps, and some Community Action Programs, the NYC sponsored a Workshop for Teachers of Youth With Special Needs on May 18, 19, and 20, 1966, in San Francisco, California, in cooperation with these agencies and the Office of Disadvantaged and Handicapped, U.S. Office of Education. To understand the role of education in the NYC, it is appropriate to have a clear understanding of its goals and objectives.

What is NYC?

Title I of the Economic Opportunity Act authorized the Neighborhood Youth Corps (NYC). This program is designed to provide work experience for youth from low income families which will enable them to (1) stay in school, (2) return to school if they have dropped out, or (3) obtain work experience and develop good work habits if they are out-of-school and out-of-work. NYC projects are operated by State and local governments, private and public nonprofit agencies and private profit-making agencies on contract with the NYC of the U.S. Department of

Labor. The projects employ youth in a wide variety of jobs where they will help meet unmet needs and will not displace present workers. NYC operates three kinds of programs—in-school, out-of-school, and summer. The in-school projects operate during the school year and are designed for full-time students who are in the ninth through twelfth grades of school and who, through their NYC work experience, will be able to maintain their school attendance. The out-of-school projects, operating year-round, are designed for unemployed youth between ages 16 and 21 who are out of school but who need work experience in order to prepare them for further education, training or a job. The summer projects are designed to make it possible for students on vacation to earn the income and receive the counseling that will enable them to return to high school in the fall.

An Important Mission of the Workshop

One of the purposes of the May 1966 workshop was to discover some of the critical issues and approaches to educating disadvantaged youth. Two of the more provocative issues emerging from the workshop were: How can the schools be made more attractive to deprived young people and how can we sensitize teachers to work more effectively with deprived young people?

The significance of these issues has been mentioned by Kenneth B. Clark who states . . .

> the clash of cultures in the classroom is essentially a class war, a socioeconomic and racial warfare being waged on the battleground of our schools, with middle class and middle class aspiring teachers provided with a powerful arsenal of half-truths, prejudices and rationalization, arrayed against hopelessly outclassed working class youngsters.[2]

Approach to the Problem

To discover some of the feelings and attitudes of young people about their schools, their teachers and their NYC and Job Corps experiences, a special workshop was established solely for the 15 NYC and Job Corps enrollees. This workshop provided an excellent opportunity to secure information which would help to solve the issues

---

[1] U.S. Department of Health, Education and Welfare, Office of Education, *Equality of Educational Opportunity*, U.S. Government Printing Office, Washington, D.C., 1966.

[2] Kenneth B. Clark, *Dark Ghetto* (New York: Harper and Row, 1965), p. 1.

relating to making the schools for disadvantaged youth more attractive and sensitizing their teachers. This procedure represented a departure from the usual approach of searching for answers to educational problems in schools in depressed areas by analyzing the culture of the disadvantaged and assessing the disadvantaged child.

Although enrollee representation from a wide variety of ethnic groups was desired, all enrollee participants except two were Negroes. Both of these were females—one white, the other, Mexican-American. Consequently, the opinions expressed here are heavily weighted with the feelings of the Negro youth.

Some Feelings and Thoughts of Enrollees

The enrollees concluded that their schools had been disappointing to them. The curriculum was inadequate, especially for Negro students, who concluded that it was designed "to prepare white children to live in a white society." The textbooks were white-oriented. In fact, they concluded that the books were written in such a way as to make the Negro student feel inferior. The slanted texts and biased teachers made the Negro child feel crushed psychologically; he feels that he does not belong.

All of the quoted statements presented here from the youths of the workshop were made by Negro enrollees.

Commenting on the textbooks used in public schools,

an enrollee observed:

I remember when I entered school, and I can remember the little books, "Sally and Jane," all these in it, and all I would see would be white faces in all my books, and I would see this glamorous mother cooking, and my mother didn't look like that, and it seemed as if it was a white image and by the time I was in the third grade, I was ready to hang up the whole thing.[3]

The Negro enrollees felt that the Negro has no historical identity and that schools were not helping him to acquire information about his past. They felt that Negro history should have been offered in their schools. In general, the enrollees felt that school was unbearable to them. The Mexican-American enrollee, however, felt that what one gets out of life depends on the individual. When asked if Negro history had been taught in her school, an enrollee responded:

No, no more than George Washington Carver and his peanuts, I mean, that is true. You can count the Negroes that we actually learn about. You can hold what they told you about them in the palm of your hand. He, (Carver) took peanuts and made cold cream and junk like that. They had an overflow of peanuts and didn't know

[3] Neighborhood Youth Corps, U.S. Department of Labor, Unpublished Proceedings of the San Francisco, California Workshop for Teachers of Youth With Special Needs, May 1966, p. 106.

what to do with them . . . I am sick of George Washington Carver and his damn peanuts![4]

Referring to his teachers reactions when he became knowledgeable about Negro history, an enrollee stated:

After I started learning about Negro history in school a lot of the teachers didn't like me . . . because after you get it and you get some dignity about yourself, you get suspended from school. I got suspended one day and the teacher said I was arrogant . . . He said if I was going to leave school, I had better leave it in the right direction. He said I wasn't going to achieve anything without the white people. It is time they found out you have some dignity or something . . . By the time you stand up on your own two feet, that is when they are ready to knock you down.[5]

The enrollees, especially the Negroes, felt that their teachers had shown racial prejudice toward them. Moreover, they thought that the teachers taught subject matter only, not people. The young people felt that (1) the teachers and counselors in the public schools had been oppressive and dictatorial, (2) they had been pushed out of school, (3) their teachers had just been babysitters and, (4) they had not really learned anything in school.

Queried about his feelings regarding teachers in public schools, a teenage enrollee made the following observation:

The worst thing a teacher can do is to make a boy feel like he is losing his pride, something like that. They've done that to me lots of time. And there is nothing like it. I tell you, if I didn't have more self control, I would probably beat up the teacher or knife him.

They can kill your pride. They make you feel like dirt and it's nothing nice to feel like. O.K., so you don't know something, you don't know it. But if you *do* know something, they give you an argument so good on it that they make you feel wrong even about what you know.[6]

A youth who had attended a Harlem school made the following observation about his school experiences.

Discrimination was in the school I attended. I know my teacher was very prejudiced because I had certain questions that had to be answered for my knowledge, but he would never answer. I told him one night to his face, that if he didn't want to answer my questions, just tell me and I would leave. There are always other teachers. He didn't say anything. He just looked at me and figured I was going to . . . so he said, "well maybe next time." There is no next time . . . this is the time and I am not taking second best from any white man.[7]

Speaking of non-acceptance by public schools, an eighteen year old enrollee explained it this way.

I think you know that after these kids have been in the schools and they see that teachers talk over a fence, and they see the schools won't accept them, either they will give the whole thing up or they are going to start to really hate. I think that often white people don't realize that Negroes, too, have feelings, and when these things happen, and they are not accepted, they can begin to hate.[8]

These are the voices of some of the dropouts and the pushouts, the difficult 30 per cent, and members of minority groups and the poor reflecting their invisibility in public schools and their rejection by a middle-class educational structure. There is much in the literature to suggest a basic incompatability between the schools and deprived young people. Jack Goldberg[10] puts it this way.

It is now an accepted fact that there is a considerable lack of fit between the culturally deprived child and the public school system. This mismatch results in a high rate of school dropouts and a high rate of underachievement.

Goodwin Watson[11] speaking of the relationships between public schools and deprived young people makes this observation

The starting point is respect. Nothing else that we have to give will help very much if it is offered with a resentful, contemptuous or patronizing attitude. We don't understand these neighborhoods, these homes, these children, because we haven't respected them enough to think they're worthy of study and attention.

The young people felt that the Neighborhood Youth Corps and Job Corps had improved their learning ability. They now have a greater desire to learn and to achieve. They have acquired a renewed interest in achieving in spite of their socioeconomic status or race. Being in their new environment has provided them with contacts with others who have suffered similar deprivations and causes them to become more determined to overcome their deprivation. It has helped the Negro enrollees achieve a sense of identity and personal worth.

Referring to his experience in the NYC educational programs, an enrollee remarked:

. . . they devoted most of their time showing us what the Negro had done, and I have learned an awful lot from that. I was surprised. This is what I was told there. Like when Christopher Columbus come over, they considered him as white, Caucasian, you know; he wasn't. He was Spanish or some other nationality, but he wasn't that, you know. And just like there was a Negro who guided him across. There is a lot of things. . . .[12]

Some Suggested Approaches for Program Improvement

To accomplish the drastic reforms necessary to transform ghetto schools into meaningful educational institutions and to eliminate human wastage and despair will require first of all, an unyielding commitment to the concept of the equality of man and vigorous, determined and honest appraisal and action by national, State and local education authorities to implement this commitment.

---

[4] *Ibid.,* p. 124.
[5] *Ibid.,* p. 130.
[6] *Ibid.,* p. 133.
[7] Neighborhood Youth Corps, U.S. Department of Labor, Unpublished Proceedings of the San Francisco, California Workshop for Teachers of Youth With Special Needs, May 1966.

[8] *Ibid.,* p. 118.
[10] Jack Goldberg and others, *Washington Action for Youth,* Washington, D.C., United Planning Organization, p. 430.
[11] Goodwin Watson, "Foreword" in Frank Riesmann, *The Culturally Deprived Child,* New York: Harper and Row, 1962), p. XI.
[12] Neighborhood Youth Corps, *op. cit.,* p. 84.

Teacher training institutions across the Nation should require prospective teachers to be thoroughly grounded in courses in Negro history which present a truthful and complete account of the outstanding achievements of Negroes to American civilization. This will provide a fund of information to be transmitted to students. An honest and objective presentation of Negro history and the use of multiracial instructional materials should begin early in elementary schools. A real awareness of the historical contributions of Negroes and visibility of minority youth in instructional materials should tend to foster attitudinal changes among teachers, better self-images among Negro youth, and better racial attitudes among white youth.

The recruitment of teachers and school administrators must cut more across culture lines and be more representative of the populations they serve. Racial minorities in many parts of the country are often missing from the classroom as teachers and from administrative posts when there are integrated student bodies. Models for minority groups are necessary.

There is an obvious urgency for teacher sensitization programs to orient teachers to work with youth with special needs. If this is to be done meaningfully and effectively, administrators, teachers, and other school personnel who work in depressed areas should boldly and diligently develop programs designed to encourage truthful and constructive dialogue between educators and deprived young people. In this way, many of the problems in human relations can be identified and significant sensitization programs developed.

Concluding Statement

There is need for more assessment in the schools in the areas of human relations and curriculum. Perhaps this enrollee workshop sponsored by the Neighborhood Youth Corps, will encourage more dialogue between educators and deprived young people across the nation so that some of the problems relating to race, and self-image can be more fully understood and more effectively resolved.

21

THE EQUALLY GOOD OFF,

THE EQUALLY BAD OFF

by Thomas J. Cottle

Ever since I met them, I have thought of them as a pair. Perhaps it is their physical appearance, their age or their goals, or the way our respective friendships have evolved that makes me see them as being somehow related.

Mitchell Walker and Edward Kelly are tall young men, strongly built, with large hands that suggest they are nowhere near finished growing. At fifteen their interests are similar, with sports and girls and school keeping them busy, and in a way, rather fulfilled. Both are attractive, popular in their schools, and interestingly too, concerned with the welfare of younger boys and girls. Both have spent time working with children in after-school programs and during the summer in day camp activities. Their involvement with children no doubt began at home where each has younger brothers and sisters. There are six children in Mitchell's family, five in Edward's. They are each the first born son, being preceded by a sister. Only now are they getting close to these older sisters whom they see as possessing valuable information about girls in general, and about some special girls in particular.

Among the similarities, however, loom some profound differences. Mitchell's family lives in a section of Boston that some call working class; in fact the families in this neighborhood are poor. His parents have known many years of illness, and although they are in their middle forties, their capacity for work has been reduced by disease. Mr. Walker is employed as a part time bookkeeper in a small trucking firm. Mrs. Walker occasionally helps

Thomas J. Cottle is affiliated with the Children's Defense Fund of the Washington Research Project, Inc. His recent books include The Voices of School *and* Black Children, White Dreams.

out in the kitchen of a downtown Boston hotel. Mitchell and his older sister Sally have taken part-time jobs, but their parents worry that their school work has been affected by these additional responsibilities. The children insist that contributing money to the family is more important than their education and besides, they aren't slighting their school work all that much. Actually their grades dropped noticeably when they began working three years ago. Sally Walker hopes to finish high school. Once she thought of becoming a nurse, but recently that idea has disappeared. Mitchell wants to go to college. He feels he has a chance. His presence at college, he believes, would encourage his younger brothers and sisters to study.

For Edward Kelly the matter of money has never been a problem. Since the time he was ten he has wanted to work, but there has never been a serious need for him to gain employment. His father Edward Kelly, Senior, an attorney with a large Boston firm, has worked his way from what he calls "humble beginnings" to a handsome house in a wealthy suburb. Mrs. Kelly was for several years a secretary in the firm her husband entered upon graduating from law school twenty years ago. She thinks of taking a job now and again, but at present is satisfied in her role as mother to five children and wife to a man she feels has not yet attained the stature he deserves. She speaks of moving to a larger home in a suburb even farther out ten years from now. Perhaps when the last child graduates from grammar school to high school, the Kelly's will take this next step. In the meantime, their present suburban home and rustic New Hampshire cabin which they use during the summer suits her well enough.

There is little doubt among the senior Kellys

155

that their children will go to college. Young Ed has his eye on Ivy League schools and thinks that his academic record combined with his athletic abilities will earn him a place in a fine school. He speaks about the matter regularly with his father and is well aware of the financial burden of having two children in college at the same time. His father has advised him to apply for an athletic scholarship since any money he might bring in would help. Both parents feel Ed should work during the summers and save the money for personal expenses at college. He is doing exactly that. One afternoon a week and two months in the summer he works as a general assistant and delivery boy in a local pharmacy. The work has started him thinking about a possible career in medicine, quite a change from years ago when it seemed natural that he would follow his father into law.

"I think alot about my future," he has said, "even though I've got a couple of years left of high school. But these days you have to think about it. There's so much competition that you can wreck your chances when you're as young as I am. I've already sent away for college catalogues. Last week a group of us went into Boston to the library to work on term papers for English. I was looking around in their shelves and I saw they had *all* the catalogues. That's all I read for three hours. I saw alot of West Coast schools that really look good too. Up to now I was thinking of staying around here, but I'm not so sure anymore.

"I'm in a pretty good position out here. Everybody expects you to do good. I mean, they're pretty shocked when kids like me don't do well, don't go to college, you know. Like all these kids who take drugs? That surprises alot of people. Everybody reads in the papers about the suburbs, people getting divorced and all the rich kids on drugs, but at school everybody's expecting us to be smart. I'm not talking about the kids in the bottom tracks. I'm talking about kids in the college "prep" programs. 'Course the honor kids, there's no way they're going to fail. But my group's the one that has to fight it out. We're not the top of the top. We'll get in, you know, but we're not going to get our first choice. That's why I'm counting on basketball and baseball. The guidance counselor told me that alot of the really good schools like to hide their interest in athletics, but they need us. He said if I get B's I'll probably get into an Ivy League school. 'Course, making All League one of these years wouldn't hurt any.

"Must sound strange hearing me talk like this, huh? Some guys I know, they're taking their life easy. They just go along not letting anybody

see what's bothering them. But I talk to my folks more than alot of guys do. My dad's really taught me alot. Like, how a man's really got to work, and if he does how the rewards come. I saw where he grew up. Man, you can't believe a guy could accomplish so much, and what the heck, he's only forty-something now. He could still get a whole lot more. 'Course it's not the same for me since I'm starting off way better than him. But still, I'd hate to see my life be nothing more than throwing away lots of good chances. Some guys don't care. They know their old man is loaded so they keep on spending it. But I see how he has to work for it so I've got a better sense of what money's all about. I'm not going to be any failure. Too many people are counting on me. Not only in my family, but at school too. Later on in life, like my dad always says, there are people waiting around, watching you, hoping maybe that you'll fail. But right now, it's like this whole town is out to make life good for us. I don't mean school's that great. It could be a whole lot better, but they sure want us to go to college. Anybody who doubts that hasn't been around here too long, I can tell you that.

"There's something else about the school too that's pretty good. Lots of the teachers spend time talking about places where kids are growing up. Not kids like us, I mean, poor kids. Some of them are black but not all. Lots of these kids are just as smart as anyone out here. They could be doing just as good as anyone of us and getting ready to go to college, except they don't have the opportunities we have. That's about the only difference between us. Our fathers have money but their fathers don't. It's not their fault. It all comes down to just where you were born.

"That's the funny part, like we were talking about yesterday in social studies. Mr. Hamblin told us to imagine how our lives would be five, ten years from now. We wrote these papers for him and then talked about them. Everybody was a success. College and jobs, and people making money and getting married and taking trips. We really sounded like we were big shots. But then we talked about competition for the *best* schools and the *best* jobs and everybody started to laugh a little, you know. But the interesting thing was how all that competing came about because we were born pretty well off. Those kids who go to school in Boston, lots of them are going to compete with each other the same way as us, but the chances just aren't there. Some of those kids, even the ones who do the best, won't be as well off in the end as some of us who do lousy. Boy, if that's the way it worked in sports, trying out for a team and making it but still, you know, not making it, I'd be just as angry as those kids probably are."

Mitchell Walker lives among those "other kids." He is very much aware of the world where Ed Kelly lives. He speaks about it, even follows it as one might follow the progress of a baseball team, but recognizes that the opportunities "out there," fifteen miles away, will never befall him. College is a dream. There is a chance, although it fluctuates from month to month, and the possibility of the career that might ensue from it seems even more vague. The idea of becoming a doctor stays alive in the mind of this young man, but he is careful about telling the dream to certain people. Some laugh at him, others look at him with pride. His father always says, "We'll just have to wait and see," as if he were afraid that his response might spoil his son's chances.

Mitchell receives little encouragement at school. The two guidance counselors work mainly with the seniors; the athletic coaches tell the boys that thinking of the future is fine, but nothing substitutes for good old everyday work. According to Mitchell, the administration seems concerned only with making certain students behave. And as for the teachers, they have taken an interest in Mitchell, but he wonders whether they have picked him out, along with several other students, because he is charming and speaks well. He is not convinced they believe in his intelligence. Few take his medical school dream seriously.

"I can't always be sure what they're saying when they tell me to stop worrying about the future," he said once. "Maybe it's good advice. If you worry too much about the future you won't get tonight's homework done. But sometimes I think they're trying to tell me to forget it. I think what they'd like to say is that the old Walker kid doesn't have the smarts to make it. I got the smarts all right, the question is, is there a college I can get into? I could always go to some junior college or a community college somewhere, but from what I hear you kind of pass through those places and come out the other end looking like you did when you went in. And anyway, there's always the money problem. That's the root of all the evil, right?

"What happens, say, if I do get in and we can't get the money to let me go? I'd have to keep working 'cause it isn't going to get any better at home. My father's pretty sick already. He'll be earning a whole lot less by the time I'd be ready to go. So maybe if I went to college it would only make him feel worse. You know what I mean?

Maybe he'd feel pressured to work harder so I could get through, and maybe that extra work would kill him. Or my mother too. Even if I go to school around here it ends up costing alot of money. And you can't work too much, otherwise your grades fall down. I've already seen that happen.

"Hell, you'd think my school would help, but they only care about the real smart kids. They just want to pass the rest of us and not have any trouble. If you're a real brain they treat you special. But if you're like me, not all that smart, you know, but willing to make it up with alot of work, they don't care as much. They tell us hard work's the best thing, but I see the way they treat us. You got to be born smart before the teachers care about you. Like the coaches, they talk about how we should be scholars as well as athletes. But they don't ever talk to us about school. All they worry about is that we might flunk something and be ineligible or something like that. Don't get me wrong. Sports are maybe the most important thing in my life, but sometimes when you hear those guys talk, you forget you're in a school. They act like we were professionals or something. Going on to college, or what we're going to do with our lives, they couldn't care less. Oh yeah, going to college might matter to them 'cause if any of us get famous they get some of the glory. You know, Mitchell Walker's high school basketball coach was none other than Arnold Kuyper. That's what old Kuyper really wants too.

"I'll tell you another thing about sports. You remember I said I didn't think lots of people in the school really wanted to help some of us non-brains get into college? Well, there are kids like that too. Like, I have friends who don't want me to study. They think all we should do is mess around. They know they aren't going to get much out of school; they always tell me I'm wasting my time trying. They probably think they're doing the best thing for me, but they're only making it tougher. Lot of kids, you know, they stop liking you if you start doing better in school than they think you're supposed to be doing. Like, they'll say, 'ain't we good enough for you no more, man?' They put the choice to you: stick with them, which means be the way they are, or leave. But I don't want to leave them. You can't be friends with alot of people, especially around here. Like, the black kids aren't friendly with us, except some of the ones we play ball with. And the brains, they aren't about to let people like me in. So I've got my friends. I have to stay tight with them. I don't want to be alone, all by myself. My brothers got their friends and I got mine, only some of mine have a narrow way of seeing the world.

"It puts me in a strange position, though. I can't leave them, and I can't get myself to believe that school doesn't matter. I'm afraid to tell people around here when I like a subject. Like, I think social studies is all right. I don't mind reading the books she gives us. I don't even mind preparing for the tests, and they give us alot of tests too. But I don't let anybody know this. I make believe everything sucks so the kids my age won't dump on me. There are other kids like me, but we're a minority. I don't even tell the teachers I like it. They'd think I'm just sucking up to them. And you couldn't prove too much with my grades.

"The way I see it, those kids are just acting the way the school wants them to act. If you're really smart, everyone helps you to get smarter. But everyone knows there are lots of kids who aren't smart. Just to make sure they give us tests. Then they divide us up into the real smart, the not smart and the retarded kids. But those kids don't count since they're, like, sick in a way. Then they work real hard to get the best out of the smart kids, like they were athletes, and forget the really dumb kids, which leaves us. We're their problem. We aren't brains, but we also aren't ready for a hospital. So, what can they do? The best thing is to make sure we don't give them any trouble, so they teach us, kind of, not to like school and not to want to go to college. Vocational school is what they want us to do. The brains go to college and we're supposed to learn how to fix cars. And the girls go to cooking and nursing classes, things like that. Everytime someone like me wants to go to college it's like it messes up their plans. When we get older they'll tell us don't apply to college, but some of us do anyway. We know some older kids who tell us what we have to do to apply. But now, the teachers are happy if we pass. They don't want anything for us. They're even worse on the black kids, which isn't fair, 'cause those kids, you know, they got it worse than we do.

"Then on the other end you got all those fancy kids going to school in the suburbs. They can't fail. There's no way their schools are going to let them fail. If they have to, they'll drag every kid out there into college even if the kid doesn't want to go. 'I don't want to go. I don't want to go,' the kid will be crying. 'You're going, kid!' the school will say. 'You're going. What do you think all this money we've been spending on you has been for?'

"They have it all right out there. I mean, it's no paradise with all those people drinking all the time, and the kids messing around with drugs 'cause they don't have anything else to do. You don't hear alot about that. It's always *our* school that's supposed to be filled with heads and drinkers. But they got their share out there too. They got plenty of sickness out there. But see, it doesn't matter in the long run 'cause the whole damn community can help those kids. First off, they got more money than they do around here. If you read those figures about how much those communities spend on each student, it's no wonder they got swimming pools and these great big gyms, while all we got are buildings that would probably fall over if people made enough noise. You bang your locker too loud and a wall falls over.

"But they got everybody organized to where they're protecting the students. Not just in school but all over the town. Say, like, we see a policeman walking around. You know that guy's going to bust you, he doesn't care that you're a student. You break a law, you're just another criminal to him. What's he care? He earns more than your old man, and he's got superiors telling him to look for crime and track it down. So there he is prowling around in the bathrooms, in the girls' bathrooms too, like some dog. Sniffing around, you know, like we were running the big crime syndicates right here in the school. I'll tell you, man, I see those guys and I go the other way. All they have to do is pick me up once, even if it turns out to be a mistake, and I'm through. I'll go to college with some correspondence course in the penitentiary. They're looking for us to do something, you know what I mean? You ask the black kids. They'll tell you everything you want to know about the police and how the administration, instead of cutting down the number of cops, keeps telling us we need more of them.

"Out there, though, in the fancy schools, the police are supposed to help the kids. They're not going around hoping they can arrest somebody. They're trying to help. They better too, since the people out there have just about hired them to do it. Our families don't have any power like those families do. One yell and we go to court. Those kids get away with alot more. Hell, the way they have it set up, police pick you up and drag you off to college. They don't mix the students up with the criminals. Maybe that's why they don't throw them in jail out there.

"Rich kids got their problems. They got pressure on them, but they don't know how good they got it. When one thing falls down they've got something else. If their family falls apart, they got their school. If they do bad in school, they got their friends. If their friends leave them, like I was saying before, well, at least the homes are pretty. Here, when things go they really go. You start out bad, you end up bad. If you're family breaks up, all you got are lousy schools and no place to go where you can get yourself together. It's like we're in jail over here. They don't even have to put us in jail; we're already in there. Classrooms are jail, cafeterias are too. And the halls, man, they really are jail. You talk too loud and they send you off to see the warden. They're looking for us to make mistakes. The teachers, the principals, the cops, they got their eyes on us. If I told a cop I was going to college, he'd say, 'Who you trying to kid? You're only a dumb punk.'

"That's the difference between the kids here and the kids in those fancy schools in the country. They don't have punks out there. All the punks go here. You never even hear the word punk out there. They got kids who accidentally misbehave, but no one over there is a punk. You got to be poor to be a punk. I'll bet even if I go to college, and then medical school after that, people will still call me a punk. 'Hey, Doctor Punk, come over here and look at my kid's broken face.'

"Everybody goes around telling us about how great America is. I want to believe them all right, but when they start shoving that stuff about people being equal I'd like to cram it down their throats. No two people in the world are equal. My old man sure isn't equal to any old man in the suburbs. Even if a guy there was sick like my old man, they'd never be equal. That guy would have insurance. He'd find a high paying job. Hell, he could probably find a job that would pay as much in one day as both my folks and me and my sister put together earn in a week. They got the schools, they got the cops, they got all the good jobs, they got all the good streets, they got everything that's good. And everything they left behind, that's what we got. You ever wonder how come they don't send their kids to our schools?

"What gets me is that they have it so good there's no way one of their kids is going to end up here. And they fix it so none of us kids get to go there, unless we marry one of them. The way I see it, my education is only a ticket out of here. If it's really good, I'll take my whole family with me. If not, I'll go by myself. Maybe go find a rich girl. When I was a kid, I thought the most important thing was to stay around here and help my folks. But when I see what those fancy neighborhoods got, I tell myself, *I* come first. The first thing is to get *me* out of here. I won't end up anywhere if I stay here, but here. And here is nowhere, man. Here is nothing. It's just hanging around getting ready to get yourself a crumby job and a wife so you can have lots of children so they can go to the same crumby school you went to so they can hang around going nowhere. Then everybody will talk about me like I talk about my old man. Him, me and my kids, all those years and nobody's moved more than ten blocks.

"And they go around in our school telling us people are equal. They're right. All of us living here are equally bad off. That's what they really ought to be telling us. We're all equally bad off and the kids out there are equally good off. I guess they figure that us being equally bad off and them being equally good off makes everybody equal. Seems to me they better count again."

VI. Friends

In the preceding section, we mentioned that our culture tends to focus more on the problematic ways of adolescents than on the normal course of daily events. In this section, the issue again becomes salient. Our focus here is more on the tensions in friendship than on the normal, positive, life-affirming aspects of friendship. These aspects, however, are addressed in various selections throughout the book. For the moment, we take up the issue of the pressures inherent in some of the friendships engaged in by adolescents. In this context, we explore one of the most delicate factors of friendship, namely, the pressure that people put on one another, for all sorts of reasons, but ultimately just to get their way in that particular association.

If the pressure in friendships is the first topic, the second topic relates to the problems of just who can be friends with whom. Again, while a spirit of egalitarianism and freedom emanates from young people, it is foolish to romanticize adolescents or to ignore their often exclusionary tactics in friendship and the salience to them of inclusion and exclusion of human beings from certain rights and opportunities. There are always people who shove other people around, convince them of what they see as the right way to be, the right way to act. Conversely, there are always people who seem to be shoved around, even "brain-washed," by those who seem to them stronger or more impressive. One can preach all one likes about the dangers of these phenomena occurring in friendships, but they do exist, and adolescents know about them only too well.

There is another aspect of friendship that each of us has confronted. To have a friend, or group of friends, is to know the tension between the public and private self, a matter with which we dealt earlier. How much of ourselves do we wish to reveal? How closely allied to another person do we want to become, and will this alliance affect what we think about ourselves? As a related matter, whom we chose to be with, especially during adolescence, is partly a function of our relationship with our families. Is it not our families after all, in their role as agents of socialization, who teach us, either overtly or covertly, who we are "meant" to have as friends and who we are "meant to steer clear of?" We can smirk at those who lay down laws of inclusion and exclusion in friendship, but who among us has escaped the sting of these laws?

One last point. While all of us pride ourselves in being able to master problems or initiate creative and productive acts, we also like to believe that the trouble in which we find ourselves was in fact caused by someone else. A boy is sent home from school for fighting and his parents ask him who started it. Surely there was someone else who caused the difficulty. To a certain extent, this hunt for the real culprit is not an invalid approach. Wholly innocent or naive people get enmeshed in situations which lead them in uncomfortable directions. So it is a genuinely legitimate concern of all parents that their children, as we say, have not fallen in with the "wrong kind of people," the neighborhood gang, the "tough bunch" in the school. How many adolescents become infuriated at their parents for watching too closely who they choose as friends? And how many adolescents become disenchanted with their parents for *not* watching their friendship selections closely enough?

Adolescent Choices And Parent-Peer Cross-Pressures

22

CLAY V. BRITTAIN

Emory University

The hypothesis explored held that the extent to which adolescents are peer-conforming when confronted with parent-peer cross-pressures depends upon the nature of the content alternatives presented to them; i.e., they tend to be peer-conforming in making certain kinds of choices and parent-conforming in making other kinds of choices. Adolescent girls responded to hypothetical dilemmas involving conflicting parent-peer expectations. Their choices were consistent with the hypothesis. From these results and from interview data inferences were drawn about factors predisposing adolescents toward peer-conforming or parent-conforming choices.

As they are commonly portrayed, adolescents confronted with parent-peer cross-pressures tend to opt in favor of the peer-group. But to what extent and under what circumstances does this image square with reality? [1] Does the tendency toward peer-conformity vary as a function of the type of choice to be made by the adolescent?

The concept of reference group is useful in attacking this problem. Following Shibutani's [2] formulation that a reference group is one whose perspective constitutes the frame of reference of the actor, both peers and parents might be thought of as reference groups; i.e., as groups each provides perspectives in terms of which adolescents make choices. Does the extent to which adolescents tend to adopt these different perspectives vary systematically across situations? We hypothesized that in making certain kinds of choices, adolescents are inclined to follow peers rather than parents; in making certain other types of choices, the opposite is true.

From "Parents and Peers As Competing Influences in Adolescence" (unpublished Ph.D. dissertation, University of Chicago, 1959). The writer gratefully acknowledges the guidance of Professors Robert D. Hess, Jacob W. Getzels, and Robert J. Havighurst.

[1] There is controversy about the legitimacy of this image. For contrasting views see Frederick Elkin and William A. Westley, "The Myth of the Adolescent Peer Culture," *American Sociological Review,* 20 (December, 1955) pp. 680–684; and James S. Coleman, *The Adolescent Society,* New York: The Free Press, 1961, Ch. 1.

[2] Tamotsu Shibutani, "Reference Groups as Perspectives," *American Journal of Sociology,* 60 (May, 1955), pp. 562–569.

PROCEDURE

Situations involving conflict between parent-peer expectations were described to the subjects—girls in grades 9 through 11. Each situation was structured around an adolescent girl who was trying to choose between two alternatives, one of which was favored by her parents and the other by her friends. The following item illustrates the procedure:

A large glass in the front door of the high school was broken. Jim broke the glass. But both he and Bill were seen at the school the afternoon the glass was broken and both are suspected. Bill and Jim are friends and they agree to deny that they know anything about the broken glass. As a result, the principal pins the blame on both of them. Nell is the only other person who knows who broke the glass. She was working in the typing room that afternoon. She didn't actually see the glass broken, but she heard the noise and saw Jim walking away from the door a few moments later. Nell is very much undecided what to do. The three girls she goes around with most of the time don't think Nell should tell the principal. These girls hate to see an innocent person punished. But they point out to Nell that this is a matter between Jim and Bill and between Jim and his conscience. Nell talks the matter over with her mother and father. They felt that Jim is unfairly using Bill in order to lighten his own punishment. Her parents think Nell should tell the principal who broke the glass.
Can you guess what Nell did when the principal asked her if she saw who broke the glass?
—— She told him that she didn't see it broken.
—— She told him who broke the glass. [3]

Two versions of 12 items each were con-

[3] Item number 4 on the instrument used in the study.

163

structed to make up two forms (A and B) of the present instrument, which will be called the Cross-Pressures Test, or CPT. The two forms were identical in all respects except for the opinions and preferences attributed to parents and friends. These were reversed from one form to the other. The parent-favored alternatives on Form A were the peer-favored alternatives on Form B, and vice versa.[4] The instructions accompanying the CPT were:

> The following stories are about young people like your friends and the people you know. These people are in situations where they are not sure what to do. We would like to have you read each story carefully and tell us which one of the two things the person in the story is more likely to do. Do *not* tell us what the person should do, but what she is *likely* to really do. We hope you will enjoy doing this.

The CPT was administered to an experimental group and a small control group. The experimental group responded to one form and then to the other; the control responded twice to the same form. Both were divided into subgroups and tested as follows:

Experimental Group	First Testing	Second Testing
Group AB	Form A	Form B
Group BA	Form B	Form A
Control group		
Group A	Form A	Form A
Group B	Form B	Form B

One to two weeks intervened between the testing dates. The subjects were not told that they were to be tested a second time.

As can be seen from the specimen item, the dilemmas described on the CPT were double-barrelled (as well as double-horned). There is the dilemma embodied in the content of the alternatives (e.g., telling who broke the glass in the door of the high school versus not telling; or going steady with a

boy having certain personal qualities versus going steady with a boy having other personal qualities), and, on top of this, the dilemma posed by the cross-pressures from parents and friends. The subjects could respond to either dilemma or to both. We anticipated that they would respond to both; i.e., the tendency to choose the parent-favored or the peer-favored alternative would depend upon what the dilemma was about. Hence, there would be marked inter-item variation in the frequency of parent-conforming and peer-conforming choices.

The experimental group data were analyzed for differential preferences for the parent-favored and peer-favored alternatives. In response to each item there were three possibilities: (1) The subject, responding to the content of the dilemma, chooses the same content alternative on both forms of the CPT. (2) The peer-favored alternative is selected on both forms. (3) The parent-favored alternative is selected on both forms. In event of 2 or 3, the choice of content alternative shifts from the first testing to the second. The data, then, were analyzed for shifts in choice of content alternatives from one form of the CPT to the other.[5] The control group was used to help establish that the shifts in the experimental group were due to differences in the forms of the test and not simply to the tendency to respond randomly.

Items on which peer-conforming response shifts were more frequent and those on which parent-conforming shifts were more frequent were identified. From the content of these items inferences were drawn about the bases of preferences for peer-favored and parent-favored alternatives.

Following the second testing, 42 girls in grades 9 and 10 were individually interviewed.[6] The interview data help to clarify the above analysis of responses to the CPT.[7]

---

[4] The alternate version of the item given above read as follows: "The three girls she goes around with most of the time feel that Jim is unfairly using Bill in order to lighten his own punishment. They think that Nell should tell the principal who broke the glass. Nell talks the matter over with her mother and father. They don't think Nell should tell the principal. Nell's parents hate to see an innocent person punished. But her father points out to Nell that this is a matter between Jim and Bill and between Jim and his conscience." There are obviously many situations for which this type of reversal would not be plausible.

---

[5] Biases toward parent-favored or peer-favored alternatives showed up also as differences in first test responses between experimental subgroups AB and BA. A comparison of these groups, not reported here, reveals substantially the same trends as shown in the present analysis.

[6] Both the interviewing and the testing were done by the writer.

[7] Sociometric data were collected in one of the schools included in the study, but only brief reference is made to them in this paper.

TABLE 1. PROPORTION OF CONTROL GROUP AND EXPERIMENTAL GROUP SHIFTING RESPONSES

Item	Experimental Group N=280	Control Group N=58	Difference $P_E - P_O$	Chi Square [1]
1. Which course to take in school	.52	.23	.29	15.60**
2. Which boy to go steady with	.50	.28	.22	12.71**
3. How to get selected for a school honor	.33	.28	.05	.94
4. Whether to report boy who damaged school property	.35	.14	.21	13.57**
5. Whether to enter beauty contest or be cheerleader	.44	.16	.28	22.52**
6. How to dress for football game and party	.51	.19	.32	26.42**
7. Whether to be beauty contestant or appear on TV program	.39	.14	.25	18.56**
8. Which dress to buy	.58	.19	.39	39.39**
9. Which one of two boys to date	.49	.16	.33	29.00**
10. Which part-time job to take	.34	.16	.18	10.66*
11. Whether to report adult who damaged public property	.38	.19	.19	10.23*
12. How to let boy know she is willing to date him	.36	.21	.15	6.66*

[1] Chi square computed from frequencies. df=1, * p<.1 ** p<.001.

SUBJECTS

The subjects were girls [8] from high schools in Alabama and Georgia. The 280 girls in the experimental group came from an urban high school, a high school in a small city, and three small rural high schools. Analysis of the data did not reveal any rural-urban differences. The 58 control respondents were from a high school in a small town and a rural high school.

RESULTS

Comparison of the experimental and control groups indicates that the findings reported below were not due to the tendency to respond randomly, but that changes in form did elicit changes in choice of content

alternatives. The data are given in Table 1. On item one, for example, 23 per cent of the control subjects, who responded twice to the same form, shifted content alternatives from the first testing to the second as compared to 52 per cent in the experimental group. On each of the 12 items, shifts in choice of content alternative occur more frequently in the experimental group. On 11 of the items the experimental-control differences were significant at the .01 level or better.

An analysis of the experimental group data is given in Table 2. The responses to each item were first broken down in terms of the following two categories: (1) The choice of content alternatives did not shift from one form to the other. (2) The content choice did shift; i.e., the peer-favored or parent-favored alternative was consistently chosen. (See columns NS and S.) The second category was then broken down into peer-conforming and parent-conforming

---

[8] This imposes an important qualification in generalizing the findings. If a sample of adolescent boys were studied in similar manner, the findings would undoubtedly diverge at some points from those presented here.

20

TABLE 2. FREQUENCY OF SHIFTS IN CHOICE OF CONTENT ALTERNATIVES FROM ONE FORM TO THE OTHER

Item	Not Shifting Content Alternatives (NS)	Shifting Content Alternatives			Chi Square [1]
		Total (S)	Alternative Selected Parent(P)	Peer(F)	
1. Which course to take in school	135	145	48	97	16.56***
2. Which boy to go steady with	141	139	70	69	.01
3. How to get selected for a school honor	187	93	63	30	11.70***
4. Whether to report boy who damaged school property	182	98	58	40	3.30
5. Whether to enter beauty contest or be cheerleader	156	124	93	31	28.26***
6. How to dress for football game and party	138	142	47	95	16.22***
7. Whether to be beauty contestant or appear on TV program	170	110	83	27	31.00***
8. Which dress to buy	118	162	59	103	11.92***
9. Which one of two boys to date	143	137	81	56	4.56*
10. Which part-time job to take	184	96	69	27	18.37***
11. Whether to report adult who damaged public property	174	106	73	33	15.09***
12. How to let boy know she is willing to date him	180	100	64	36	(7.84)**
Column totals	1908	1452	808	644	—

[1] Chi square for differences between columns P and F computed on the basis of 50/50 assumption. df=1. * p<.05; ** p<.01; *** p<.001.

choices. (See columns P and F.) As can be seen from this break-down, items 1, 6, and 8 tended more strongly to elicit peer-conforming choices; items 3, 4, 5, 7, 9, 11, and 12 tended to elicit parent-conforming choices. All of these differences except that for item 4 are significant at the .05 level or better. Parent-conforming and peer-conforming choices were distributed equally on item 2.

Before interpreting these findings, note the following observations. They suggest the results were not dictated simply by the method.

(1) The subjects responded naively. Of the 42 girls individually interviewed soon after the second testing, only two were able

to tell how the two forms of the CPT differed.

(2) Responding to the CPT seemed to be accompanied by anxiety. In informal group discussions immediately following the second testing there were expressions of irritability at having to make the choices called for. This suggests that the subjects did tend to become emotionally involved in the hypothetical situations themselves.

(3) Groups of subjects differentiated on the basis of their responses to the CPT were also differentiated on the basis of sociometric data. For example, subjects who most frequently chose peer-favored alternatives tended not to be well accepted by their peers.

(4) At least some of the response trends

were consistent with what informal observation of adolescent behavior would lead one to expect. For example, choices relating to dress were especially likely to be peer-conforming.

DISCUSSION

The findings, as reported in Table 2, are consistent with the hypothesis that responses of adolescents to parent-peer cross-pressures are a function of the content of the alternatives and that peer-conformity in adolescence, rather than being diffuse, tends to vary systematically across situations. The response variation across items supports the hypothesis.

More specific interpretations of the response trends are now in order. Why were the peer-favored alternatives more commonly selected in response to some of the hypothetical situations and parent-favored alternatives in response to others? This question relates to the more general problem of understanding the processes involved in coming to terms with conflicting pressures, which, as Merton [9] has pointed out, is salient for reference group theory.

From the content of the hypothetical dilemmas, viewed against the response trends shown in Table 2, the following hypotheses are offered:

1. The responses reflect the adolescent's perception of peers and parents as competent guides in different areas of judgment.

The general social orientation of adolescents is of a dual character. Choices tend to derive meaning from either of two general references groups, or both: the peer society in which many status and identity needs are gratified, and the larger society in which the status positions which one can aspire to as an adult are found. When choices pertain to the latter, parents are perceived as the more competent guides. In response to the hypothetical situation involving choice of part-time jobs (item 10), for example, preferences commonly were for the parent-favored rather than the peer-favored alternatives.

2. The responses reflect concern to avoid being noticeably different from peers. Two of the items to which responses showed clearcut peer-conforming trends involved a choice of dress; i.e., item 6—how to dress for a football game and party, and item 8 —which one of two dresses to buy.

3. The responses reflect concern about separation from friends. Peer-conforming choices were predominant in response to item 1—which one of two courses to take in school, where the consequence of a peer-defying choice would have been some degree of separation from friends.[10]

4. A fourth hypothesis overlapping but different from those above is that the choices reflect perceived similarities and differences between self and peers and self and parents. Adolescents, for example, perceiving themselves to be more like peers in regard to tastes in clothes and in regard to feelings about school, find peer-favored alternatives in these areas psychologically closer and more acceptable. But in other areas the greater perceived similarity is between self and parents. For example, with respect to values involved in the difficult choice whether to report a person who has destroyed property (items 4 and 11), the parent-favored alternatives are closer and more acceptable.[11]

The interviews referred to above provided a source for further inferences. According to one hypothesis derived from the interview data, responses to the CPT were a function of the perceived difficulty of the content choices. Parent-conformity was more prevalent in response to dilemmas posing what were perceived to be the more difficult choices. The 42 subjects interviewed soon after the second testing were asked to rank the content choices according to difficulty. The items from the CPT, with the parent-versus-peer aspect deleted, were typed on small cards; the subjects were asked to select from among them, first the situation in which the girl would have the greatest difficulty making up her mind, then the sit-

[9] Robert K. Merton, *Social Theory and Social Structure.* Revised and Enlarged Edition, New York: The Free Press, 1957, p. 244.

[10] An example identical on both forms concerned which one of two high schools to attend. Responses to it were predominantly peer-conforming.

[11] This hypothesis holds, in effect, that there is a close interrelationship between what Merton refers to as normative type and comparison type reference groups. Merton, *op. cit.*, p. 283.

uation in which she would have the least difficulty. This was repeated until the choices were ordered from most to least difficult. Median ranks were computed. The items eliciting predominantly peer-conforming trends fell at the least difficult end of the resulting rank order. Hence, the tendency toward parent-conformity was directly related to the perceived difficulty of the choice.

A second inference was suggested by a discrepancy between the interview data and CPT responses. Interviewees were asked to select from among the content dilemmas, as presented on the cards, the two about which a girl would most likely talk to her friends rather than her parents. Neither of the two items most frequently selected had elicited predominantly peer-conforming CPT response shifts. Choices in response to one of them (item 9—which one of two boys to date) were more frequently parent-conforming; while in response to the other (item 2 —which one of two boys to go steady with) parent-conforming and peer-conforming choices were equally· frequent. No such discrepancy was found when the girls were asked to select the two dilemmas about which a girl was most likely to talk to her parents rather than her friends. The three items most commonly selected (i.e., 4, 10, and 11) had all elicited predominantly parent-conforming response shifts.

This divergence of interview and test data may indicate that the latter lead to an overestimate of parent-conformity. But it also suggests a device used by adolescents in coping with parent-peer cross-pressures, namely, avoiding communication with parents. This would be likely to occur in areas in which parent-peer conflict is most acute. If this is the case, such discrepancies as those reported here could be used to identify points at which adolescents tend to be most disturbed by cross-pressures from parents and peers.

Let me note one other aspect of the data. Despite the greater overall incidence of parent-conformity, there was greater convergence relative to peer-conforming choices. As shown in Table 2, a majority of the items elicited a preponderance of parent-conforming over peer-conforming choices. On each of the items where there was a reversal of this trend (i.e., items 1, 6, and 8) there were,

however, more peer-conforming choices than parent-conforming choices on any single item. This suggests the following possibility: Analogous trends in the social behavior of adolescents create the impression that peer-conformity in adolescence is more diffuse than actually is the case. Lack of parent-adolescent communication about certain types of choices contributes to this impression.

SUMMARY AND FURTHER APPLICATIONS

The study explored the hypothesis, suggested by reference-group theory, that adolescent choices in response to parent-peer cross-pressures are dependent upon the character of the content alternatives presented. Hypothetical dilemmas were described to adolescent girls. In each dilemma a girl was confronted with a complex choice where one course of action was favored by parents and another by peers. The respondents were asked in each case to indicate what the girl would probably do. With the situations remaining otherwise unchanged, peer-favored and parent-favored alternatives were interchanged and the hypothetical dilemmas again presented to the respondents. Comparison of responses to the two forms of the test revealed that peer-conforming choices were more prevalent in response to certain of the dilemmas and parent-conforming choices in response to others. These results were taken to support the hypothesis.

The content of the items suggested additional specific hypotheses as partial explanations of the trends toward peer-conforming and parent-conforming responses: (1) The responses reflect the adolescent's perception of peer and parents as competent guides in different areas of judgement. (2) The responses reflect a concern to avoid being noticeably different from peers. (3) The responses reflect concern about separation from peers. (4) The choices reflect perceived similarities and differences between self and peers and self and parents.

Additional data were collected by interviewing a number of the respondents. From the interview data and from discrepancies between test and interview it was hypothesized that: (1) The tendency toward parent-conformity is directly related to the perceived difficulty of the choices. (2) Adolescents attempt to come to terms with parent-peer cross-pressures by simply not communicating with parents.

The present study argues the value of the approach exemplified here in exploring an important facet of adolescence. What considerations predispose adolescents toward peer-conformity in situations where they are confronted with parent-peer cross-pressures? What are the persisting cognitive schemata against which choices in such situations are made? We believe that through applications of the present method or adaptations of it, hypotheses relating to these questions could be investigated. For example:

1. Stability of social values: Adolescents are more strongly given to peer-conformity in making choices in areas in which social values are changing rapidly, than making choices in areas in which social values are relatively stable.

2. Time perspective: Adolescents are more strongly disposed toward peer-conformity in making choices where immediate consequences are anticipated than in making choices where the emphasis is on long term effects.

In addition, the present procedure might be used to assess individual differences in predispositions toward peer-versus parent-conformity. Although the study did not deal with the problem, the subjects were found to differ from one another in their tendencies to make parent-conforming or peer-conforming choices. At the extremes four groups were indentified: (1) subjects manifesting relatively strong tendencies toward parent-conformity; (2) subjects manifesting relatively strong tendencies toward peer-conformity; (3) a mixed-conformity group composed of subjects making parent-conforming choices and peer-conforming choices with relatively great and about equal frequency; and (4) subjects making very few responses of either type; i.e., subjects whose responses were mostly consistent by content. The stability of these response biases and their possible correlates remain a problem for further study.

23

Brainwashing: Persuasion By Propaganda

Why are our young people open prey for cults that seek to rob them of their old loyalties and beliefs?

By Max Gunther

"**Brainwashing?**" says James J. Sheeran. "Yes, that's what a lot of people call it. I call it *menticide*—killing a part of someone's mind."

"Brainwashing is an apt enough term for it," says Robert C. Cardais. "There isn't usually any physical force involved, but that's the only missing element. It's a deliberate attempt to erase someone's old loyalties and former ways of looking at the world."

Both men are fathers, both are angry, and both are talking about the tactics of peculiar religious cults that recently claimed their college-age daughters. In each case, the young women seemed to undergo a sudden, radical change in personality. Each abruptly rejected her family and their values; withdrew into the fenced-off world of the cult; and became an unquestioning disciple of its religious, mystical, political, and social teachings.

There have been many such cases in recent years: strange cases in which an apparently happy, stable, middle-class young man or woman drifted into an odd religious cult or extremist political group and abruptly, inexplicably, seemed to become somebody else. The story of Patricia Hearst is probably the most notorious at the moment. A seemingly contented young woman, certainly one with enviable material advantages and prospects for a bright and rewarding future, she was abducted early in 1974 by a group calling itself the Symbionese Liberation Army. Unaccountably, in a short time, she seemed to make a 180° turn from kidnap victim to disciple; from

being angry at the group or frightened by it to adopting its untidy and violent code of values.

What is behind these sudden, puzzling changes in personality and outlook? The word on everybody's lips, including Patricia Hearst's, is "brainwashing." William Sargant, M.D., a British psychiatrist and expert on brainwashing, was brought to California recently to determine the mental condition of Patricia Hearst. Though he hasn't said what his examination revealed, it is expected that her lawyers will use Dr. Sargant's testimony to bolster her defense against a bank robbery charge; claiming that, as Patricia said in an early court statement, her captors used both physical and psychological coercion to force her into accepting their idealogy; that she was unable to think for herself. Dr. Sargant's past writings indicate that, to him, such a state of mind is quite conceivable. In a recent article in the *London Times*, he wrote that the brain can be made "suggestive" through controlled tension and fatigue, and that a man or woman in this state can be made to do things that are inimical to his or her own welfare.

But brainwashing is a word which, by being used too often and too glibly in too many contexts, has lost what sharpness of meaning it once had. What does it really mean? What actually goes on in a brain that is being "washed?"

Seeking answers, *Today's Health* sought people who have been directly and personally involved in recent "brainwashing" episodes. We talked to young

people who were once members of fanatical cults but have since been through a process known in the field as "deprogramming," in which the effects of brainwashing are deliberately undone or reversed. We talked to their parents, to psychiatrists, and to professional deprogrammers. Here is what we found.

* * *

Brainwashing is defined in Webster's Dictionary as "a forcible indoctrination to induce someone to give up basic political, social, or religious beliefs and attitudes and to accept contrasting regimented ideas." The term actually came into popular usage in this country during and after the Korean War in the early 1950s. American men, imprisoned in North Korea, were induced to sign statements and make public appearances in which they repudiated what they had been fighting for. While it is possible that many or most were only faking this apparent change in political belief so their captors would leave them in peace, some actually may have bought the Communist doctrine. It is likely that these men lacked strong beliefs to begin with, or had no real convictions of their own. The Communists' technique relied on a prolonged period of preconditioning; of deliberately induced anxiety, fatigue, confusion, discomfort, and sometimes physical pain. The resulting mentally weakened state caused the prisoners to accept whatever indoctrination their captors gave them.

The tactics used were classic, having been perfected by agents of the Spanish

Inquisition, and passed down to the Soviet secret police (the KGB), the Nazi Gestapo, and the French terrorists in Algeria. What may be new today is that in modern America, for many young people, this preconditioning, or something like it, is evidently accomplished by society itself. In the words of Scott Cardais, brother of an ex-cultist, "the best way to prevent people from joining offbeat groups and getting brainwashed is to give them a clear set of values, including goals they can feel good about. Unfortunately, that is easy to say but not always easy to do—not in the confused world we've got to deal with today."

Scott's family learned this the hard way. The Cardaises of Winnetka, Illinois are of Catholic background. Scott's sister, Alison, today an articulate, dark-haired girl of 20, had lost her religious certainties in her early teens. The loss troubled her. When she went to the University of Iowa as a freshman in 1973, she was in what she calls an "uncertain, groping state of mind . . . I thought I wanted to become a nurse but wasn't sure. I thought Christianity meant a lot to me but I wasn't sure of that either. I guess I was kind of desperately looking for somebody who had firm yes-and-no answers, somebody who was sure about things and could make me sure."

In her sophomore year she encountered a group that was very, very sure: a nomadic religious commune that called itself simply the Body. It consisted of perhaps three dozen men and women, a few in their thirties or forties but most younger. The Body spent its time hiking from one college campus to another, living on handouts and stale or damaged food discarded by stores, preaching an odd gospel, and seeking converts.

"They camped near the school," Alison says. "One of the men preached on the campus. I was attracted by how sure and calm he was, the strength he got from his faith. I was frightened because I'd never known anything like the Body before, but I couldn't stay away. I kept going back and asking them questions, and they always knew the answers—I mean really knew them."

When the Body left the University of Iowa campus, Alison went with them.

The Body required its members to forsake the rest of the world entirely. Contact with parents and former friends, who might turn a member from the path of righteousness, was forbidden as sinful. It was also a sin to read anything but the Bible and a few approved recipe books

and hymnals. "New souls," like Alison, had to walk with heads bowed so that they wouldn't be tempted to commit the sin of reading billboards or looking into store windows. All the members wore long, loose robes, and the two sexes were strictly segregated except for those who were "married" under the Body's auspices. The women were subservient to the men and always walked several paces behind them. Unmarried souls weren't allowed to look at any part of the opposite sex's body but the feet. Every night there were long Biblical readings, teaching, prayers.

"There was no love or laughter, not even any real companionship," says Alison. "It was cold. But it was a world where you had direct, clear, simple rules

to tell you how to find salvation. There were no questions, no confusion—and I guess that's what I'd been looking for."

When Alison had been gone for about a year, her worried family tracked her and the Body to El Paso, Texas. Her father and a friend flew there, rented a car, spotted her sitting in a park, and "kidnapped" her. She fought, kicked, screamed. Finally she quieted and made a pact with her father: She would return home and stay for one week, after which she would be free to rejoin the Body if she still wished to.

"As I understand brainwashing," says her father, "the basic principle is that you isolate the individual. You set up a situation where rewards can only come from one all-powerful source, and the individual gets no rewards unless he or she learns the 'right answers.' That is what happened to my daughter."

"The Alison who came home wasn't the bright, vivacious Alison we used to know," says her brother, Scott, today 24 and an insurance agent. "She walked and sat with her head bowed all the time. She was so subdued that it was eerie. We had only a week to deprogram her, and we began talking to her through every waking hour."

The deprogramming was taken on mainly by Alison's mother, Alice, and her brother, both of whom are devoutly religious. "The main problem," Scott says, "was that the Body had picked certain Biblical passages out of context and ignored all the rest. For instance, they had one teaching that it is sinful to 'lay up treasures'—meaning that the members were supposed to own nothing, live in poverty, grub food out of garbage cans. We showed Alison other passages to contradict that notion. The Bible has nothing against people earning an honest living."

"I heard all these arguments and understood them," Alison recalls. "Some people thought I was in a hypnotic state, where I couldn't grasp what was going on around me, but it wasn't quite like that. I guess you could say I was in a kind of soft hypnosis. I knew what Scott and the others were saying to me, but I could only answer in Biblical platitudes. The Body had taught me it was a sin to do or think anything else. I really thought I'd go to hell if I turned my back on the Body."

But after two days, Scott remembers, she began to ask questions and began trying to refute their arguments on logical grounds. "That's when I knew we had her back," he says.

She not only rejoined her family and the world, but she turned completely against the Body and its strange teachings. She now spends much of her time helping other families deprogram sons and daughters rescued from such sects. The Cardais home has become a minor way station for former Body members, several of whom have lived there temporarily while trying to reconnect themselves with the outside world.

A perplexing story, hard to believe, but by no means unusual. The very existence of full-time, professional deprogrammers suggests that there must be some popular demand for their services, and there is indeed—a large demand. One of the most active deprogrammers is

Joe Alexander of Munroe Falls, Ohio. He estimates that there are perhaps 5,000 religious and mystical cults in America like the one Alison Cardais joined. His guess is that these cults may together claim as many as 3 million members equally divided between males and females, mostly in their teens and twenties.

Not all their stories end as tidily as the Cardais family's, as James Sheeran can testify.

Sheeran, state insurance commissioner of New Jersey, has four daughters and two sons. The three oldest daughters, in their middle and early twenties, have all joined the controversial Unification Church whose chief architect is a mysterious Korean evangelist named Sun Myung Moon. Echoing the words of Robert Cardais, Sheeran says flatly that the Moon sect has brainwashed his daughters (along with an estimated 30,000 other members in America) by a process in which the young people are isolated from family and other outside influences, constantly harangued with religious-political sermons, and denied rewards and gratifications except those that flow down from Reverend Moon himself.

When we spoke with Sheeran he had just been on the phone with his daughters. They live in a communue-like group, and he wanted them to come home for Thanksgiving. "They're resisting," he says. "That's what they've been taught to do: reject their parents and the world they used to know. This cult is obviously afraid of what would happen if I could get them back home for a few days. As for me, I'm not sure their mother and I could deprogram them that fast. The menticide is designed to last. They aren't the girls I brought up. They've changed into mindless robots—all the spontaneity washed out. They don't think for themselves any more. All they do is parrot Moon's sermons."

Reverend Moon's teachings are an odd blend of old-time, fire-and-brimstone Protestantism and right wing politics. He claims to have found religion after a visitation by Christ on a Korean mountain some 40 years ago. Moon's conservatively dressed, studiously polite young disciples call him "Father," and many believe he is Christ in person returned to earth. They reject orthodox churchmen's doubts about him and refuse to hear allegations spread by his antagonists—for example, that the wife he calls his second is in fact his fourth, and that he lives in luxury on money earned and donated by

his flock.

Moon preaches a militant anti-Communism—a fact that James Sheeran finds inconsistent with the sect's practices. "The Unification Church is run much like a totalitarian Communist state," Sheeran says. "The kids are in virtual slavery. They sell merchandise door-to-door, work long hours, turn the money over to the chiefs. The church has to approve the 'mates' they pick. Another analogy to a totalitarian state is that the church doesn't like outsiders poking around inside."

Sheeran charges that when he tried to visit one of his daughters at a seminary run by the sect at Tarrytown, New York, a group of men knocked him down, shoved a gag in his mouth, and held him for almost an hour. A court battle arising from that charge is still in progress.

Moon and his disciples deny that their organization is secretive or sinister. "What's all this talk about brainwashing?" asks a young Connecticut man, George Petrie, who has attended Moon rallies and thinks he will formally join the sect. "I've talked to kids who are in it, and they're like any other kids. They aren't chained and handcuffed. They're free to quit any time they want to. They don't have glassy eyes or walk around like zombies either. They're just people who happen to hold a certain set of beliefs."

Joe Alexander is not convinced. You don't have to have glassy eyes to be brainwashed, he says. "Some of the kids walk with bowed heads, act like robots and zombies, talk in a monotone—but not all do. The key thing to look for is this state of not thinking—blindly clinging to one set of beliefs and refusing to look beyond. Most of these kids are programmed so that they're actually *scared* to look beyond. Somebody like me is an agent of Satan: It's mortally dangerous to listen to me. To doubt is sinful *in itself*. If you're in a state of mind where you're actually afraid to let yourself speculate, wonder, doubt, then I'd say you're brainwashed."

Alexander, a 54-year-old former businessman of Catholic faith, got into this odd business a few years ago when a favorite nephew joined the Children of God (COG). This is a fairly large fundamentalist cult with some resemblances to both Reverend Moon's sect and the Body. Its archenemy is Ted Patrick of San Diego, California, whose first deprogramming venture had been to get his own son out of COG in 1971. With Patrick's help, Alexander deprogrammed his nephew. Other families then started asking for his help, and finally he became a full-time "religious counselor" (a term he prefers to "deprogrammer"). He now spends nearly all his time flying around the country, counseling distraught families, sometimes for a steep fee, sometimes for free, depending on their financial circumstances. He has worked with more than 500 cult members. Of those, he has "lost" only six.

While there is only one way for Alexander to operate—"get them out of the controlled situation, argue with them around the clock until they start to think again"—brainwashing itself can be accomplished in various ways. "Usually it's a situation designed to scare," he explains. "The leader of the group, the messiah, claims he has a direct line to God, and to win God's love you've got to win the messiah's. This means thinking exactly what he says you should think." There may also be an element of physical coercion. The new recruit may have to work hard all day and then be made to stay up half the night while lessons are pounded into him, until his brain's normal thinking processes are fogged with fatigue. "Denial of sleep and denial of food are powerful levers," says Alexander. "I saw one young man who had a plaque hung on his neck with 10 mystical verses on it. He had to recite them from memory each night, or he got no supper."

Physical coercion of this sort may effectively force someone to act in ways that are contrary to his or her basic philosophy, according to Dr. Sargant, the psychiatrist who examined Patricia Hearst. But do actions necessarily imply beliefs? James Brussel, M.D., also a psychiatrist and expert on the subject, thinks not. The former assistant mental hygiene commissioner for the state of New York has worked with police on a number of bizarre cases in which people claimed that brainwashing or hypnotic influences caused them to commit crimes. His attitude to such claims is one of caution, lightly peppered with cynicism.

"The first thing to remember," he says, "is that a state of being 'brainwashed' or 'hypnotized' can be faked. The second thing—and this is my own strong opinion; not all psychiatrists seem to share it —is that you can't be brainwashed into changing your fundamental beliefs. I can force you at gunpoint to perform a certain act, or I can badger you into it, but there's no way I can make you believe it's right if you really believe it's wrong."

Then is brainwashing a fiction? "No, not necessarily. If you're in a state of confusion or uncertainty, not knowing *what* to believe, then it's easy. These kids who join oddball cults are usually in that kind of state. They have no strong beliefs that can be violated—and what's more, they're desperately looking for somebody to tell them what to believe. They want some firm, easy-to-understand code to guide their lives by. Anybody who has such a code to offer, with an assertive personality to back it up, can mold this kind of kid like putty."

Dr. Brussel's words bring into sharp focus Scott Cardais's warning about the "confused world" in which young people today must live. How many of them have come through the era of Vietnam, Watergate, women's liberation, and assaults on the nuclear family structure with a clearcut set of values to cling to? Adolescence itself is a major upheaval in the lives of most individuals of any generation; a time in which the child must abandon familiar patterns of thought and behavior in exchange for an adult role in society; a time of vulnerability.

James Sheeran notes that mystical and religious cults seem to do their most successful recruiting among college freshmen and seniors. "The freshmen are newly uprooted from home," he says. "They're away from their parents for the first time, in a world where they've got to fend for themselves, and a lot of them are scared and bewildered. As for the seniors, they're about to make another kind of transition, out into the world of jobs and responsibilities where they'll have to prove themselves as adults. A lot of them are afraid to face that or don't know how they'll go about it. Both the freshmen and the seniors are ripe for plucking by any cult that seems to offer a cozy, protected home and an all-powerful 'Father' who tells you what to do," he concludes.

Joe Alexander's wife, Esther, who participates in what she calls "rehabilitation" of former cult members, has also noticed that college people drift into fanatical cults most readily in periods when their lives are coming unstuck. "The cults get a lot of kids at exam time," she says. "I've heard this same story from young men and women over and over again. They were depressed and anxious about the exams, afraid they were flunking, so they went away with some mystical group and kind of escaped from the world. Most of these cults, the evangelist ones and also the Eastern-mystical ones, preach exactly what a troubled young person wants to hear. You know: It isn't important to pass exams and get a good job, and so on. The only important thing is to save your soul or find peace. If you were upset about exams, wouldn't that be appealing?"

Another time of particular susceptibility, she says, is the aftermath of painful experiences with sex or drugs. "This is a common kind of triggering event," she says. "The young man or woman is upset, hurt, feeling guilty, feeling just plain bad. The cult seems to offer a way to atone, and also a way to live without having to make hard choices all the time. As Joe says, it offers a way to live without thinking. Thinking can hurt a lot, sometimes."

Somehow we have failed to make the world a place where the privilege of thinking for oneself is precious enough to outweigh the pain. The fault, then, may not be that of a few fanatic leaders, but our own, for having made followers of our children.

24

Teen-age Interracial Dating

Frank A. Petroni

Early in the still unfolding story of school desegregation, many observers were saying that what white opponents of integration were most afraid of was interracial sex. People who had been comforting themselves with such abstractions as "Negroes are OK, but I wouldn't want my daughter to marry one," now, with desegregation, had suddenly to cope (they thought) with a real possibility, not a farfetched hypothesis.

Be this as it may, I doubt there are many Americans who have not, at one time or another had to cope with the question of interracial sex, either in imagination—"what would happen if . . ."—or in fact. Interracial dating and interracial marriage are social realities, however much white racists and black nationalists may deplore it.

A few years ago, while I was with the Menninger Foundation in Topeka, Kansas, my wife and I had an opportunity to study the extent of, and students' feelings about, interracial dating at a desegregated high school. Our procedure was rather unorthodox. Instead of trying to gather a 5 percent random sample of the 3,000-member student body, we began slowly by letting our initial student contacts tell us what they considered to be the principal "types" of student in the school. They distinguished 12 such types: middle-class whites, hippies, peaceniks, white trash, "sedits" (upper-class blacks), elites, conservatives, racists, niggers, militants, athletes and hoods. Then, and again through our initial contacts, we brought in other students and roughly classified them according to "type." In this way, I believe we got a representative cross section of the social world of this high school. We interviewed the boys and girls in groups of three or four, and in time 25 groups came to our house for these conversations. We had two refusals: a black girl canceled her appointment after Martin Luther King was killed, and a boy told us he wouldn't talk to white people.

Few topics demonstrate the multiple pressures students are subject to better than interracial dating. These pressures come from parents, teachers, counselors, school administra-

tors and peers. However, mixed dating is emphatically not a barometer of the amount of "integration" in a desegrated school; that is not the reason we chose to study it.

Needless to say, the students did not all share the same point of view on interracial dating. Yet, most of them—independent of race—did feel that it was none of the school's business: if students wanted to date interracially, the school had no right to stop them.

White Boys and Black Girls

Not one student knew of a case of interracial dating involving a white boy and a black girl. There was considerable speculation about why. A conservative white girl said that white boys are too proud to date blacks. The two white boys with her disagreed: both said that it's because black girls aren't as pretty as white girls. One of the two also suggested that blacks and whites have little in common and so he would not consider dating a black. Note the popular stereotypes in this answer:

Well, there are cultural differences, and their attitudes are different. I think that's what makes the difference. They're easygoing. They like to have a lot of fun. They don't think about the future, about things that are important like getting a job, or supporting a family. They don't try for grades. They're just out to have a good time.

Even when black girls met an individual's standard of physical attractiveness, however, white boys spoke of other obstacles: where to go, how to ignore community disapproval and what to do about family and friends who disapprove. These conflicts are cogently summarized in the response of a white boy who considered dating a black:

I think if you dated a Negro, you would lose a lot of so-called friends. But you would probably gain some Negro friends. I contemplated asking this Negro girl for a date, but I chickened out. I thought, where would I take her? The only place where people wouldn't stare at me would be a drive-in movie, and I don't have a car. If you went to a restaurant, you would get dirty looks from people. I couldn't take her home and introduce her to my mom; she'd probably kill me.

Social obstacles apart, there is some doubt in my mind whether a black girl, in the school we studied, would go out with a white boy even if asked. Each black girl we interviewed was asked, "Suppose a white boy asked you out, how easy would it be for you to accept?" One girl answered: "Any white boy who asked me out, I would know what he wants. For a Negro boy to have a white girl is some sort of status symbol, but if a white boy asked me out, it would be a step down for him. I would think he wants something I'm not about to give him."

Other black girls spoke of the double standard between boys and girls, and how girls were less free to date interracially because their reputations would be ruined. Fear for one's reputation was also a factor among white girls. The students associated interracial dating with sex;

and girls, be they black or white, stood to lose the most. Yet sex was not always associated with dating. There was no reference to sex when respondents talked about dating within one's race. Sometimes the reference to sex in interracial dating was subtle, but nonetheless it was present. A white girl's comment demonstrates this: "When you think of mixed dating, you always think of a colored boy with a white girl. And you always think it is the white girl who is low. If it was a white boy with a colored girl, then it would be the white boy who was low."

When asked for the meaning of low, another white girl said: "Well, generally the public thinks that the girl has low standards and low morals, if she's willing to go out with a Negro."

Particularly among "elite" blacks, parental disapproval of interracial dating also stood between black young women and dates with white boys. Most of the black students in this strata stated that their parents would not tolerate interracial dating. The parents expected their children to compete with white students academically, for school offices, and in extracurricular activities; socially, however, they expected them to stay with blacks.

Still other respondents saw the white boys' reluctance to date blacks as essentially a matter of status considerations. If the belief that *all* whites are better than *all* blacks is general in this society (and it showed up among some of the blacks in our sample as well), then the response of an 18-year-old black girl, who was given the highest academic award the school has to offer, makes sense:

White boys would be scared to ask us out anyway. The Negro boys will ask white girls out, but white boys will never ask Negro girls out. For a Negro boy, going out with a white girl is an accomplishment; it raises his status, even if the white girl is lower-class. All white kids are supposed to be better than Negro kids. If a white boy dated a Negro, even if the white boy was one of the "trashy" kind, and the girl was, say me, his status would drop. They would ask him if he was hard-up or something. White boys would be stepping down if they asked Negro girls for dates.

Aside from the black girl's fear of parental disapproval and loss of her reputation, we were told that few blacks would accept a date from a white boy because of pressures from black young men, who would object if black girls dated whites. However, this pressure doesn't appear to count for much with the elite, college-bound black girl; it was the athletic girl who gave us this answer. Unlike her elite counterpart, the athletic black girl was not preoccupied with achieving what the white man prized for whites: academic achievement, social popularity and a svelte figure. The reference group for these girls was the black community. A star on the girl's track team said:

No Negro girls that I know of have ever been dated by a white guy. There are some that wish they could. In fact, I know some white guys, myself, I wouldn't mind going out with, but the Negro girls are mostly afraid. Even if a white guy asked them out, they wouldn't go out with them. Negro boys don't like for Negro girls to date white guys. Sometimes I see white guys who look nice, and I

stop and talk to them. The Negro boys get upset. They are real screwy. They can date white girls, but we can't date white guys.

The Reaction of Black Males

The black young men in our sample at times disagreed on how they would react to dating between white boys and black girls, but in general their answers fell into one of the categories predicted by the black girls. A boy, who has dated white girls, admitted to the double standard alleged by the girl athlete. He told us:

You know, I think that Negro boys would detest having a Negro girl go out with a white boy. They don't want Negro girls to date white boys. They don't like it. I feel like that, and I think I'm a hypocrite. I've been out with white girls, but I don't like it if a Negro girl goes out with a white boy. If I see a colored girl with a white boy, I think, why didn't she date me, or another Negro? What's he got that I ain't got?

Not all blacks who date whites felt this way. The young man whom we just quoted identified positively with the black community. But another young man, with a steady white girl friend, and who prized white over black, had this to say: "I don't think most of the white boys would ask Negro girls out. Maybe I shouldn't say this, but I think any Negro girl would consider it a privilege to have a white boy ask her out. I feel if a colored girl is good enough to get a white boy, they should go out together."

It was easier for most of the students, white or black, to talk about interracial dating in which the girl is white. This is the kind of dating most of them have seen. Some students, however, had seen black girls with white boys at the state university and in larger communities. One black spoke frankly of his reactions when he first saw a white man with a black woman:

You see this at the colleges [white boys with Negro girls]. You know, it's a funny thing now that you mention it, you never see Negro girls with white boys here. I was in New York once. It was kind of funny; I saw this Negro girl with a white guy. I was shocked. You know, I looked, and it seemed kind of funny to me. I mean you see white girls with Negro boys, but you never see a Negro girl with a white guy; it kind of shocks you at first.

Black Males and White Girls

The pressures from parents, teachers, counselors, peers and the community are also brought to bear on the black boy and white girl who cross the barrier against interracial dating. As one student poignantly put it, "For those who violate this convention, the tuition is high." Just how high is exemplified by the white girl in the most talked about relationship involving an interracial couple.

Around Christmas time, I got to know this colored guy real well and wanted to date him. There was a big mix-up; my parents didn't like it. My parents put a lot of pressure on me not to go out with him. They are the type people, like Dad, who says he's not prejudiced. He even has *them* working in his office, but he wants them to stay in their place. At school there was a lot of talking behind my back and snickering when I walked down the hallway. I tried to tell myself it didn't matter what people thought, but it still hurt. It hurt an awful lot. My parents made me feel so guilty. They made me feel so cheap. They were worried about what people would say. They made me feel like two pieces of dirt. You know, I never thought interracial dating was a good idea, but when I met this colored guy, it changed me. I never went with anyone I really liked before. I think this changes your outlook. It gives you hope, when you find someone you really like.

Sex and Dating

That sexual intercourse is associated with interracial dating is indicated by the fact that one reaction to such dating is to question the girl's moral standards. We heard this frequently from both white girls and boys, but particularly the latter. Prior to dating a black, however, the girl's personal conduct is rarely mentioned. It seems as if the disbelief among the white community that a white girl would date a black is softened by the rationalization that she "'must be immoral." One white girl found it hard to accept this student reaction: "I got kind of sick of the kids throwing her to the dogs. There were times when you had to take a stand. You either turned the other cheek, or you fought back for her. They thought she was cheap, and they said nasty things about her. Even the guy I'm dating, he's that way, too."

However, a white girl doesn't have to date a black to have others question her morality. Just talking to a black student can result in the same labeling process. A liberal white girl, identified as a hippie, told us: "One day we were talking to some black power students in front of school. Some adults going by in cars made some filthy remarks. You can imagine what they think of white women, hanging around talking to Negroes. They shot it right out as they drove by. These are the good, white middle-class people."

A very articulate black youth described a similar incident in which he was talking to a white girl: "One time I was walking down the stairs outside school. I was standing with this white girl, and we were talking. About six white kids drove by and yelled, 'White trash, you're nothing but white trash.' I guess because she was white and I'm black, and we were talking, she was white trash."

Other blacks, aware of the white community's reaction to white girls who date or talk in public with blacks, were prevented from asking white girls out because they did not want to ruin the girls' reputations. The son of a prominent black professional, who was a football letterman, in the student government and extremely popular, refused to date a white girl for this reason.

In general, I would say that just the fact that I was taking out a white girl, the imaginations would go wild. They think the moral standards are lower in interracial dating. There's this one white girl I goofed around with a lot. It's gone beyond the friendship stage, but we never dated. If I did go out with a white girl, it would be hard to take her anyplace. I would have to think about it for a while before I took out a white girl, because I feel she would be downgraded. I wouldn't want to ruin her reputation.

White girls who date across the color line find themselves unacceptable to white boys. Most of the students agreed that to date interracially limited a girl's field of potential dates. For many white girls, knowledge of this reaction on the part of white boys served as a deterrent to interracial dating. Nevertheless, a number of white girls told us they were attracted to certain black young men. One of the girls who did defy her society reported this also. She said, "When I was dating him, I was surprised at how many girls wanted to date colored guys. They would come up to me and ask me things. They really wanted to date colored guys, but they were afraid."

White "Boycott"

We found, too, that the white boycott (as it were) persisted after the interracial couple no longer dated, albeit only among white boys still in school. Girls who broke off their relationship with blacks were dated by older whites in the community. But to regain admission as an acceptable date among the high school boys, a girl would have to move to a new community to lose the pejorative label, which is part of the price for dating interracially.

The black male who dates a white girl does not escape criticism from his own race, particularly the black girls. Part of their disapproval is motivated, again, by the lack of reciprocity: black girls were not dated by whites. When a high status black, generally an athlete, dated a white girl, he was replaced by neither a high status nor low status white. The black girls' resentment is summarized in the answer of one of our respondents, identified as a "militant."

Well, in junior high, the Negro girls resented the fact that I went out with a white girl, and they really got onto me. They feel inferior. The white girls get all the guys. Some hostility between the Negro girls and white girls comes from this. The Negro girls kind of feel left out. She doesn't have white guys to date, and she doesn't have Negro guys to date. She says, "Hey, gal, you dating that Negro, and I can't get a date with him." This kind of builds up a resentment in her.

Pressure on the black male comes in two forms. First, his racial identification may be questioned. Often he is accused of thinking he is white. Second, retaliation by black girls can be more direct and swift. There were reports of boys physically beaten for dating a white girl. However, this response was the exception; it was more common for girls to spread the rumor that a boy is an "Uncle Tom."

Parental Pressures

The double threat of losing one's reputation and losing favor among the white boys prevented many white girls from dating blacks. Yet the pressures do not end there. Interracial dating is a test of the white liberal's commitment to civil rights—a test that few have passed. A number of white students spoke of their disappointment in their parents who gave lipservice to "liberalism" but in the final analysis were prejudiced. White girls reported this more often than white boys. However, white girls *tested* their parents more often. A white girl who sensed this in one of her parents said:

This Negro friend of mine gets along beautifully with my mother, but not my father. He senses this, too. After meeting my father, he said my father didn't like him. This is something new for me because my father and mother have always been liberal. Now that he has been over to my house a couple of times, my father is acting strange. I guess I'm learning something about him I didn't know before.

Sometimes the parental reaction isn't as subtle as the feeling that one's father doesn't approve of interracial dating. A rather tough black girl, who admitted that at one time she was a hood, told us what happened to a white girl, who used to date her ex-boy friend:

For many Negro boys, dating white girls is their way of showing their superiority, their way of trying to hurt the white man. This boy I used to date went with a white girl once. She went through hell with her parents and everyone else to go out with him. But he didn't really care. He was just showing off. Her father even spit in her face. Her parents attacked her; they beat her and called her a slut.

Parental disapproval of interracial dating is not restricted to whites. The blacks reported a generation gap between themselves, their parents and their grandparents on this issue. In general, they reported that the intensity of the disapproval varied directly with age. Thus, grandparents showed more disapproval than parents. By and large, however, the black students agreed that the mixed couple that chooses to go out together should have that choice without interference from members of the adult community, be they parents, teachers, counselors, school administrators or anonymous members of the community.

The sample included few Mexican-Americans; those interviewed, however, reported the same phenomenon: Mexican parents, like white and black parents, objected to interracial dating. An outspoken Mexican-American girl related the Mexican parents' position. Her answer reveals the confusion parental inconsistencies can create for a young person.

Mom always said have your fun as long as you're young, and as long as you marry a Mexican. I don't feel that way. If I fall in love with a Negro, I'll marry him. If I fall in love with a white, I'll marry a white. My parents would frown on us dating a Negro, even if he has higher standards than the Mexicans we date now: even if the Negro's father was a lawyer or a doctor, and he was a better person than many of the lower-class Mexicans we date now. I don't understand it. They would rather see us go out with white people, who aren't as good, just because of skin color. They say they want the best for us; if the best meant going out with a Negro, they would say no!

The School

As if the pressures of peers, parents and community were not enough, those who try to break down the barrier against interracial dating, or who ignore it, must also cope with teachers, counselors and school administrators, who, by and large, are united on this issue. In a word, boy-girl relationships should be white-white, or black-black, but not black-white.

It became apparent to us that when we discussed the school's position on interracial dating, the students' objections to interference became more emotionally charged. This suggested to us that the students perceived the school and its functionaries as having less legitimacy than either parents or peers in attempting to control and dictate norms for their social life.

The hostility was increased by the fact that both black and white students perceived a selective interference by the school. The teachers, counselors and school administrators did not interfere with interracial dating per se. Their interference increased in direct proportion to the white girl's social status. A black girl described this selective process to us.

I think it's their business, not the school's. She was crazy about him, and he was crazy about her. They went to school to get an education, and that's what the school should be concerned with: giving them an education. Instead, they threatened him, they said he wouldn't get an athletic scholarship. I felt this was entirely wrong for the school to interfere. It's not the school's affair to concern itself with whether or not the students have companionship. It's their business to teach. These kids aren't the only couple at school. But she was somebody. With some of the other couples, the girls aren't important. In fact, one of the other girls is just white "trash." They don't say too much to these others; it's the important ones they want to save.

Another girl left little doubt of the painful slur implicit in this attitude of the school functionaries: "If you're a low white person, the administration could care less, but if you're a higher white person, they're worried that you might be dragged down by a Negro."

Although we cannot be certain, there is a possibility that the school's policy in these matters is dictated by the reality of the situation. There was little that the school could do to low status students who dated across the color line; the school did not have an effective lever to stop them from continuing except to inform the parents, and most parents already knew. The only other course open to them was to expel the students for the slightest infraction of the rules. Among high status students, however, the school could threaten removal from the very positions the students worked to achieve. Black athletes were called in and ordered to desist or forfeit their chances for an athletic scholarship; others were threatened with removal from the team. And white girls were told they could not run for a school office, they were not eligible to become cheerleaders and they would receive no assistance in obtaining a scholarship.

Summary and Conclusions

Interracial dating was one of the most emotionally charged subjects in our discussions with these young people. Although we have not cited all our respondents in this brief presentation, all of them had opinions on the issue. There was complete agreement on the type of interracial dating that occurred. In no case was the male white and the female black. Generally the black male, who dated a white girl, was a high status athlete; however, by high status we are not referring to his father's socioeconomic position in the community. This may, or may not, have been high; in most cases it was not.

The fact that black students with prestige took up with white girls was a source of tension between black and white girls. More than her male counterpart, the black girl preached black separatism. Some students felt that this was because the girls did not share a sports experience such as that shared by black and white boys. On the surface, that may appear to be right. However, since there was little camaraderie between black and white athletes off the field or court, direct competition for high status blacks in the dating-mating complex seems to be a more plausible explanation for the friction between white and black girls.

While interracial dating was not commonplace, it did exist, and those who did it paid a heavy price. Payment was exacted from peers, parents, the community, teachers, counselors and other school administrators. In short, the entire social world of these teen-agers was united against them. There was no citadel to protect them. When school and peers were allied against them, there was no comfort from their parents. The couple had each other, and a small enclave of "friends," but even among the latter, the attrition rate was high.

Join this to the implication that their moral standards were lower if they dated interracially, and it is small wonder that few felt strong enough to weather all these assaults.

25

The informal world of reform school girls is the world of the adolescent girl on the outside, modified to fit the formally structured world of the institution.

Reform School Families

Barbara Carter

Inmate culture in a girls' reform school is best understood as a complex of meanings through which the girls maintain continuity between their lives inside and outside of the institution; and as social forms established to mitigate and manage the pains of confinement and problems of intimate group living. The informal world of reform school girls is one of make-believe families, homosexual courting relations and adolescent peer group culture. It is the world of the adolescent girl on the outside, imported into the institution and appropriately modified to fit the formally structured world of the institution.

Love and Romance: Going with Girls

Adolescent concern with boy-girl love relationships is no less intense for girls in the institution than it is for adolescents in the world outside of the institution. But for these girls, many of whom have gotten into trouble because of their associations with boys, there are no boys around with whom to explore courtship, romance and love. To fill the painful void created by the total absence of boys, the girls turn inward to each other and create their own world of love relationships.

"Going with girls" is a relationship which attempts to capture the characteristics and qualities of the traditional adolescent boy-girl relationship. Girls in the institution go with girls for much the same socio-emotional reasons that boys and girls in the society at large go with each other: they seek recognition, companionship and emotional involvement.

Courtship in the reform school allows a girl to ac-

knowledge a romantic and symbolically heterosexual attachment to another girl. While in part a state of mind and a world of fantasy, this acknowledgement is objectively concretized, like its outside counterpart, by pleas for and declarations of love, flirting and jealousy; by the exchange of letters and verbal messages; and generally, by seeking out a present or prospective courting partner in a variety of informal settings. These courting relationships, like boy-girl relationships in the external world, provide the substance for everyday social conversations.

Smiles, stares, glances, pushes, pats and name-calling take on important and exaggerated meaning for the conversational and romance lives of the training school girls. Physical contact per se is a relatively minor component of the courting relationships and is most often manifested in hand-holding, touching and, to a lesser extent, by kissing. For most girls more extensive physical contact appears to be both undesirable and/or unattainable. The vast majority of the courting relationships are emotional and symbolically sexual rather than physical.

Generally, informal group pressure encourages but does not demand that one go with girls. The decision to do so is entirely voluntary. The threat of force, or its actual use, is neither a socially accepted nor practiced way of inducing girls to participate in the courtship system.

Despite the absence of overt coercion and in the presence of formal restrictions against it, somewhere around 70 percent of the girls participate in the courtship system. This estimate is based on my own counting and familiarity with the declarations and activities of the girls. Girls participating in courting activities estimate that close to 90 percent of all girls go with girls. The specific estimates of the noncourting girls cluster around 50 percent. The few staff estimates elicited tended to be considerably lower and most often characterized as "not many." It is clear that estimates about the extent of participation in the courting system are influenced by one's relationship to that system.

Courtship Roles

"Butch" and "femme" are the two pivotal roles in the courtship system. Auxiliary roles are the "stone butch," the "half-ass butch," the "jive butch" and the "stone femme."

The butch is that position in the courtship system assigned to the girl who assumes the masculine role in the courting relationship. An important part of being a "good butch" is learning to look the part. In a setting where real sex differences are nonexistent, nuances of dress, hair style, carriage and posture take on great social significance.

In summary, then, to be a butch simply means to "act the part of a boy." However, a butch may still show interest in some traditionally feminine activities like knitting, crocheting and sewing. Also she may, like the other girls, decorate her room with dolls, stuffed animals and bric-a-brac. The butch is permitted to play a role without assuming an identity which implies a "real" or permanent commitment. She is permitted to maintain an image of herself as female. It is this permissiveness which gives rise to the distinction between the butch and the stone butch. The butch plays a role while the stone butch purports to have accepted an identity.

A girl may be a butch for the duration of her stay in the institution, or she may be a butch one day and a femme the next—a butch in one relationship and a femme in a concurrent relationship. Most of the terms used by girls in describing roles in the courtship system are terms taken from black culture. That this is so reflects the dominance of the soul orientation in reform

school life. For example, the label "half-ass butch" is applied to the girl who calls herself a butch but generally fails to play the part. The black societal counterpart is "half-ass nigger."

The term "jive butch" is most frequently used to describe the butch who courts many girls at once without being "serious" about any. Its equivalent on the outside is the playboy. To call a butch jive is at once to offer a compliment and a criticism; to be jive means that one is popular; but to openly exploit that popularity is bad. The black societal counterpart is "jive nigger."

The female counterpart of the butch is the femme. Within the reform school culture the femme affects in an exaggerated fashion behavioral patterns culturally associated with femininity. Most girls perceive this as just acting "natural." A femme is expected to take pride in her personal appearance and to wear jewelry, make-up and lipstick to make her attractive to butches. The femme is expected to be submissive or, as the girls say, "to do what the butch tell her." She is expected to "obey" her butch.

At any given moment in the courting system femmes probably outnumber butches by at least two to one. This uneven distribution, of course, contributes to the internal

---

Love Is Here and Now You're Gone, I'm Your Puppet, Hello Stranger, Respect, Ain't No Mountain High Enough, Reach Out

Time — To pen you
Place — My lonely room
Thought — Of you
Reason — I love you
Desire — To be with you
Hope — We meet on the outs
Wish — You were here now!
Want — You and your loving
Need — You and your loving
Care — For you
Hurt — By love
Love — You
Hate — I hate —— (I hope she drops dead)
Happy — Not now
Sad — Yes
Mood — Confused
Songs — I Do Love You, Stand by Me, Since I Lost
My Baby

Say Love,

Time plus pleasure permits me to write you these few sweet lines. Hon I hope I did not upset you but I just had to tell you. And if I did not tell you when I did decide to tell you which I probably would you would have either been angry or hurt because I didn't tell

you before. Paula I do love you and I mean it but hon I don't know how to prove it to you but believe me I'll do anything to prove it to you. Hon, I want you to go to board and go home why should you suffer because of me oh sure you'll say you're not suffering but I'll know and deep down you will too. And if you go home and behave I'll probably be able to see you in June or even on my Xmas weekend and remember one thing even if we don't meet on the outs or for that matter ever see each other again remember there will always be someone else that you will love and be happier with than me.

You may not think that now but when you do meet that someone you'll look back and say Pony really knew what she was talking about and then after a while you'll forget me and then it will be hard for you to think that we were more than friends but I hope that doesn't happen to us but if it does, well that's life and boy life sure is hard. Isn't it?

Well I got to go see you tomorrow sometime I hope

1 4 3
6 3 7
Little Miss Supreme

P.S. But promise me never again as long as you live to touch that Dope! and I mean it hear?
Well good night and   1 4 3
6 3 7

This love note is typical of those which the girls regularly write to each other. 1 4 3 means "I love you" and 6 3 7 means "always and forever."

dynamics of "going with girls" by further allowing butches—as scarce commodities—to assume a role of dominance by defining the terms of the courting relationship. The *single* most important factor determining this distribution is race. Within the context of the institution, race becomes a highly visible constant for imagined sex differentiation. Blacks, grossly disproportionate to their numbers in the institution, become butches, and whites, equally disproportionately, become femmes. The most common and desirable arrangement is a relationship consisting of a black butch and a white femme.

Whether black girls become butches because they have been socialized to be more aggressive than white girls, or are more aggressive because they have become butches, is unclear. I am inclined to believe that the two are mutually reinforcing: the black girls are in fact "tougher" than the white girls but their toughness is made acceptable and manageable to white girls by having the blacks become the symbolic masculine figures in a social context which is microcosmic of a society that assigns toughness and power to males and not females.

A second argument is that the purpose of creating symbolic males in an all-female population is to permit the vast majority of girls to continue to maintain their pre-institution identities as "feminine people." One might then argue that due to past and present position in society, black girls are more willing to temporarily give up their female roles for certain high-status rewards.

The Dynamics of Courtship

Courting relationships in the reform school, like teen-age courtships on the outside, are highly charged emotionally and often short-lived. Girls frequently estimate that during the course of nine to 12 months in the institution, the typical girl may go with anywhere from five to ten girls, with five or six girls being the most common estimate given.

Despite, and maybe because of the relatively short duration of most courtships, going with girls is one of the most alive, emotionally intense and conversationally consuming experiences of the girls. These relationships are the source of considerable anxiety for many girls. Girls talk about, dress for, "show-off" for and look forward to seeing each other, even momentarily and at a distance. Girls are excited and joyous when things go well and sometimes angry or sad when things go badly.

Daily courtship relations revolve around the exchange of written and verbal messages; the sharing of "goodies" and the exchange of small gifts; the arranging and engaging in momentary and public rendezvous; hand-holding, smiles, glances, kisses, petty jealousies and continually recapturing these moments in conversations with friends.

The single most prominent feature of going with girls is the regular exchange of "pen notes." These illegal written communications are saved, hidden and treasured by the girls who receive them. The themes of loneliness, frustration and a need for love are common to most of the letters.

A code for various phrases is used. Presented below are some of the most common phrases.

1 4 3	I love you
2 1 6	As a sister
2 2 6	As my mother
2 2 3	As my man
2 4 3	Go fuck off
2 2 4	Go to hell
2 2 5	As my woman *or* It is quits
2 1 8	As a daughter
1 3 3	I dig you
3 2 4	Pen me back *or* Pay me back
6 3 7	Always and forever
2 6 8	We belong together
2 1 7	As a brother
4 4 6	True love always
4 2 3	Kiss my ass
4 2 4	Take me back

The codes reflect the sense of a need for secrecy, but also seem to create some emotional distance. For example, in face-to-face encounters girls are far more likely to say, "1 4 3" than "I love you."

A common pattern observable at recreational activities is the informal sorting of femmes and butches into separate groupings. These groupings are often seen as some combination of the sorting of symbolic males and females to discuss their respective partners and activities and as an informal grouping of blacks (butches) and whites (femmes). In first discussing this phenomenon with the observer, one femme vividly recalled how she had been told to leave an informal grouping of butches, some of whom were her close friends, because the conversation was to be about things which she, as a femme, should not hear. With respect to the second basis for groupings (race), the observer notes that a considerable portion of conversation content for butches centers around the recounting of pre-institution experiences, events and places known to the blacks coming from common urban area ghettos.

The dynamics of the courtship system can be elaborated further by describing the everyday language of courtship. Girls talk about "digging" girls, and this is their way of saying that one girl is attracted to another and would like to enter into or continue a courting relationship. Talk about who is "digging" whom is very common. A girl may communicate this particular attraction for another girl by penning a note or more informally by a variety of nonverbal gestures such as stares, smiles, winks, pushing or hitting. Presented below is one girl's description of how the observer could identify when one girl is "digging" another. "If that name keeps popping up. They keep bringing it up and you get suspicious. That's what Lee did with Helen. We were talking about cars and she said, 'Don't Helen look cute today.' " To accuse a partner of "digging" another girl is to charge her with unfaithfulness. Such accusations of jealousy are common and lively features of the courtship drama. These accusations, often true, lead to many break-ups. While butches and femmes probably make an equal number of accusations, butches are more likely to take the initiative in ending relationships. This is so because femmes are more numerous than butches and consequently, it is easier for butches to find new partners than for femmes to do so. Then too, femmes are less likely to end relationships when partners are suspected of being unfaithful because there is a general consensus that butches, like males, are to some extent "jive." That is, butches, like men, are expected to be playboys.

Girls also talk about "rapping." Girls "rap" to each other, but especially butches to femmes. Rapping is variously described as, "You make a girl think you like her," "You talk bull," or "Play up to her." "Rapping" is the act of artistically persuading one to believe the impossible or improbable. Historically, it is similar to the art of making the master believe that he is loved by his slave.

"Slobbing" is the local and graphic vernacular for "French" kissing. Though frequently described as a "natural" feature of courting relationships, this activity seems to occur as frequently, if not more so, between non-courting partners as it does between courting partners. "Slobbing" is perceived as one of the "big" things that girls can engage in. It certainly carries a greater penalty from the school's administration than writing pen notes. Physical contact for most courting partners seldom goes beyond "slobbing." Most girls say that this limitation is imposed by the girls themselves, but a small number do see it as an expedient reflecting the absence of opportunities for more extensive contacts. The actual amount of "slobbing" occurring in the institution is open to debate. Some girls estimate that it is a frequent activity and say that about three-quarters of courting partners slob each other; others place the figure higher and some estimate that it is an activity in which as few as one-third of the courting girls are engaged.

While the dominant relationship in the romance complex is the courting relationship, marriage relationships are also acknowledged. Except for the name, and a ceremony which accompanies it, it is usually impossible to distinguish between courting and marriage. Girls, however, say that marriage relationships, like those relationships in the external world, imply a degree of permanence, stability, faithfulness and commitment not necessarily implied by a courting relationship.

Most courting girls do not get "married." "Mar-riage" relationships last no longer than the more common courting relationships, and girls may get married one day and divorced several days later. Many girls involved in courting simply refuse to get married on the grounds that it, unlike courting, is "too unrealistic."

One girls summed up the meaning of marriage by saying, "It means that they like each other a whole lot more than kids just going together. They have to stay together or get a divorce. The girl takes the last name of the butch."

Marriages, like most other activities, take place during recreational periods in the presence of other girls. Like marriages on the outside, they are performed by preachers. Any butch may become a preacher simply by performing a marriage. (There are few female preachers in the outside world and none in the institution.) The marriage ceremony varies both with the style of the preacher, the setting, the risk of discovery, and the amount of time available for performing the ceremony. It may be as simple or as embellished as the preacher desires, but always consists of the lines "Do you (*pen name*) take (*pen name*) to be your lawfully wedded butch/femme." Each marriage must be witnessed by at least two people, but more are usually present, often standing as camouflage or lookouts.

Divorces most often seem to occur because partners lose interest in each other, though it is reported that some girls simply get divorced before they leave the institution, maybe to denote a real end to a symbolic existence. Below is a brief description of how one girl described her divorce and the circumstances surrounding it.

She quit me for no reason at all. I wasn't going with anybody. At first I thought she was jealous or something, but she wasn't. She just said that she wanted to go with Thelma. [Have you had other break-ups like this?] No we haven't. We quit each other before but usually we were back together in five minutes. . . . Yet we got a divorce. A preacher divorced us. [Did you have to stand together?] No. It was a one-way divorce. I didn't want to get it. She told me that she wanted a divorce and I said no. I thought she would just forget all about it but she didn't. Then the girl who divorced us told me that we were divorced. [What did you do when told about the divorce?] I turned in her dirtiest pen note. She lost her weekend and everything. But I don't care. I'm glad. She hurt me.

New girls learn the language and etiquette of courting by talking with, listening to and observing their peers as they act out the daily courtship drama. These girls learn that it is a voluntary activity which "gives you something to do" and which "helps to pass the time." But, too, they learn of the verbal ambivalence of even those girls who participate in the system: that going with girls is "fun" and "exciting" but also "wrong," "crazy," "sick" and "stupid"—and that one can get in trouble for it. They learn that the staff officially and usually informally disapproves of it and that one can really get in trouble for a "dirty pen note" if it is discovered. They learn that some matrons who are otherwise accepting get really upset when they hear girls talking about going with girls and that a few staff members also see it as a "game" and will laugh or smile when they overhear girls talking about it. Mostly they learn that it's best to try to keep going with girls a secret.

Most girls stop going with girls when they leave the institution, for they know that "it's only something you do up here," and "once you leave you forget all about this place." After all, almost everybody prefers life on the outs to life inside, and boys to girls.

Having a Family

In recreating life on the outside, the girls do not stop at boy-girl relations. Just as they miss having boyfriends, they long for their mothers, fathers, sisters and brothers. The following is a typical letter written by one of the girls to her family at home.

Dear Ma and Dad
I hope this letter finds you in the best of health.
Ma and Dad I lonely and blue and I need you very much. more than I did before. because I know How much you & the kids mean to me now. I never knew how much yous mean tell now. So I am asking for yours and Dad forgives. Please! take me back I need you and I need your love.
I know you say she only fooling around so she can come home. but am not I mean every word I am saying to you. Ma please take me in your arms and love me like you do the other kids. Please! Rock me and hold me in your arms Ma. Someone said to me (You can have a lot of fathers but you can only have one mother. Cause she the one who brought you in this world. I believe that if only you would let me love you and you love me. Ma please understand what I am trying to say. Well thats all for now. Please forgive me.
I already forgave you and ready to try again.

Love & Kisses & Hugs
Dena

Dena writes from the heart and paints a plea for love, acceptance and affection. Her letter, unfortunately, is typical of many I read during my fieldwork at the Girls' Reform School.

Dena, like many girls at the school, is estranged from her family and feels an intense loneliness for them. Families, both loved and hated, are everyday topics of conversation for the girls, their visits anticipated and letters anxiously awaited.

Girls in the institution talk about and long for their families. Yet there is little that one can do about families on the outside except write to them, wait for their visits, hope for an infrequent weekend, send apologies, and ask for forgiveness and acceptance. Perhaps this is the reason that girls create their own make-believe familial relationships within the institution.

Girls use kin terminology to describe a variety of close relationships between them and other girls in the institution and speak of having "sisters," "brothers," "mothers," "fathers" and "daughters." Kin relationships generally lack the tone of emotional excitement so characteristic of the courting relationships, and the vast majority of girls acknowledge not just one but several make-believe relatives on the grounds. This commonly ranges from a low of two or three relatives to a high of 14 or 15. Girls most typically have about four to seven family relations. Having family relations distinguishes courting from non-courting friends and thus reduces feelings of jealousy, suspicion and distrust among courting partners involved in multiple relationships.

I have found it convenient to divide kin relationships into two broad categories: macro- and microfamily groupings. Girls speak of the macrogroupings as "grounds families," meaning that these families are institution-wide. The most popular of these large groupings at the time of my research were the Robinsons and the LaMonts. Girls simply identified themselves as belonging to one of the "grounds families" and often took the family name as their pen note surnames. Belonging to a large family grouping seemed to convey some positive status on girls. The major function of these groupings presently seems to be to provide a sense of social rather than emotional integration.

When asked about the history of the two dominant macrofamilies the responses ranged from "don't know" to constructions of a recent past. Many times I was told that the Robinson family, the larger of the two families, was started up in the fall of 1966 by two girls who were "married" to each other. Others reported that the Robinson and LaMont surnames have been used by the girls for many years. Thus the girls have attempted to create a past and legitimate the families and interrelationships.

One becomes a member of a family grouping simply by being asked or so identified by someone who is already a member. Getting out of a family is as simple as getting into it. A girl simply declares that she no longer wants to be in that family.

From the perspective of the girls the large grounds family groupings are seemingly less important on the level of day-to-day interaction than are the smaller, comparatively more closely knit nuclear and sibling groups into which the girls also organize themselves.

A sizable number of girls are mothers or daughters,

and an even larger number of girls acknowledge sister or brother relationships. (Interestingly, there are no "sons." A girl assuming a butch role in a courting relationship will usually become a brother to another girl or even a daughter. In most cases it seems that a girl identifying herself as a butch will not have a parent unless she has alternated between the roles of butch and femme.) It is not uncommon that a girl will be a mother or father in one relationship, a sister or brother in another, and a daughter in still another.

In general, girls who acknowledge kin relations regularly write pen notes to each other, send verbal messages, share with each other and exchange small gifts. These girls seek out each other and talk together at recreational activities, hold hands, exchange affectionate hugs and kisses, and often move in the same circle of friends. In terms of observable content, these relationships are practically indistinguishable from courting relationships. Importantly, however, these relationships lack the talked-about glamour and excitement of the courting relations. Of course in the outside world adolescent girls take families for granted and talk, instead, about boyfriends.

A sister or brother, most commonly a sister, is frequently the first kin relation to be acknowledged by a girl on the grounds and this tie is frequently established within a week or two of a girl's arrival at the institution. Some girls establish these ties within a few days after their arrival but others do not choose or are not chosen until much later. One girl, for example, reported that she was at the institution for five months before she acknowledged a kin relation. At the time of our conversation she acknowledged five sisters, several brothers, an aunt and uncle (both unusual since the term "aunt" is usually reserved for matrons) and a host of "good friends" described as "not worthy" of being called sisters and brothers. Another girl, however, reported that on her first day at the institution she received six pen notes with several of them containing requests for a sister relationship. At present this girl is in the Robinson grounds family and acknowledges a mother, two daughters, four sisters and two brothers.

Mother-daughter relations are less common than sibling associations, and the girls seemed at a loss to describe the parent-child relationship. In explaining why she had chosen a particular girl as her daughter, one girl said it was, "because I like her. She's little. I don't know, I like little people. If they're smaller than me they can be my daughter." Mothers are nearly always older than their daughters. Girls typically describe those who become mothers as "more mature girls."

Mothers give advice, provide a sense of security and help meet material needs. Parents assume some responsibility for socializing their children into the informal culture of the institution. When asked to describe the relationships which commonly exist between parent and child on the grounds, the girls almost always say that the parent tells the child what to do, how to behave and how to avoid trouble. One in fact frequently hears parents, as well as girlfriends and relatives, telling the girls to "be good" or "You'd better make A-Party" (for girls who have adhered to all school rules for the week) or to obey the matrons.

Family members on the grounds, like the idealized concept of families on the outside, "like" and "care" for each other. The girls themselves see the parental role as being one which provides the child with a sense of emotional security, social direction and physical protection. The parent fulfills the desire to nurture; the child has her need to be nurtured fulfilled. These are intensely personal needs which cannot be fulfilled by the formal structure of an institution.

The child-parent relationships are effective channels for socializing recruits into life on the grounds: it is an informal but powerful channel of social control. The girls want to protect their social system and to maintain a comfortable social order where staff discipline is minimal. To the extent that parents (and other kin and friend relations) express concern about the behavior of their children by telling them to "be good" or "make A-Party" and children obey these commands, the child-parent unit becomes an important informal source of support for the formal structure's emphasis on discipline and order. To the extent that the entire enterprise is successful, parents become informal social control agents of the formal institutional structure.

Families—parents, daughters, sisters and brothers—are important to adolescents both inside and outside the institution. For these adolescent girls on the inside, plagued by real family conflicts and often social and emotional estrangement and certainly physical separation, make-believe families function to fill a void not otherwise filled by the institution. There is some interaction between girls and matrons characteristic of child-parent interaction, and though girls may develop special attachments for certain matrons, these attachments clearly do not erase the need for make-believe families. In the final analysis, say the girls, even most of the "nice" matrons are people who just *work* at the institution. Furthermore, not even the matrons themselves feel equipped to provide the 25 girls in their cottages with the "love and affection" they are perceived as needing.

These reform school girls have attempted, consciously and subconsciously, to affect their restricted environment, finding ways to compensate not only for their incarceration but also for deprivation in their lives outside of the institution. Make-believe boyfriends, girlfriends and families provide, at least temporarily, the romantic, sibling and parental relationships that these girls crave.

VII. Work and Career

Ask people to characterize adolescents and one typically receives images that relate to young people and school, at home with their families, or just messing around somewhere, listening to the radio or perhaps going to the movies. References to work and career are made very infrequently, despite the fact that millions of adolescents work at part and full-time jobs. While in the United States and Canada we are accustomed to the notion of children finishing high school, it is common for people as young as 16 in Great Britain to leave school and begin their search for full-time employment. And, of course, the majority of adolescents in the world have long finished whatever formal schooling they may have had and are engaged in the adult world of work.

Another image of the working adolescent is the temporary nature of the job. Surely no one as young as 15, we might think, is serious about what he or she is doing. They wouldn't really try to form it into a career. In fact, a great many adolescents are doing at 15 and 16 exactly what they will be doing for the rest of their lives. They are engaged in full-time work, drawing their weekly or biweekly checks, and settling into life styles that will change very little as time goes on. Again, we must be alert to the patterns of growth and development of all adolescents, from all regions of a country, from all walks of life, and not merely focus on our own adolescence, or the lives of the few young people we happen to know. To be sure, some adolescents are merely trying on work for size with their weekend or summer jobs. But many adolescents, both in rural and urban areas, are contributing to the well-being of their families and communities, and beginning to know the burdens and boredom of certain work, as well as the gratifications that might derive from what they do.

One aspect of work that adolescents experience is the feeling of competence in what they do. We underestimate the importance of a person believing he or she can effect some outcome, perform some task. We underestimate, too, the significance of working, of holding down a job, of believing that one is financially independent and able to make his or her way in the world. Let us respect the cautionary word about romanticizing young people. At the same time, let us remind ourselves of the stereotyped vision of nonworking people, roaming around like hordes looking for something to do with their lives.

Sigmund Freud held that the signs of health are the capacity to love and to work. While this observation may seem simplistic, as shorthand it actually turns out to be profound. Everyone probably has his or her own definition of health, but surely these two capacities ought to be part of the definition. There is, however, an important qualification to be made. The term *capacity* would make us believe that working and living are purely psychological abilities, that no social components exist whatsoever. It is hard to love if potential loved ones are constantly abandoning one, just as it is hard to work if one is forever being denied the opportunity. One must examine this section on work and career, therefore, with an eye to the ever-growing number of unemployed people, a high percentage of whom are adolescents.

26

DALE B. HARRIS
Pennsylvania State University
University Park, Penna.

Work and the adolescent transition to maturity

FREEDMAN (*5*) HAS INSISTED that "the successful transition from school to work is central to the process of coming of age in America." Certainly, the 1950's saw a marked shift from social concern with exploitative child labor to social concern with the developmentally constructive aspects of work experience for youth. Increasing proportions of young people —not merely increasing numbers, but increasing proportions—are at gainful work, except during occasional recessions in the nation's business. The hypothesis here is that part-time, casual work experience can be valuable in the socialization of adolescents. In exploring this contention, we shall not be occupied with the social or educational significance of vocational guidance, vocational training, or the need to make career choices. Rather, we shall focus on the young teenager's introduction to the world of work and its psychological significance.

Attitudes Toward Work

The work of several decennial White House Conferences on children has been well done. We have been thoroughly imbued with the notion that children and youth should not be at work, but should be in school. Even in the past decade, one not infrequently met in welfare and labor circles the notion that work is inherently bad for children and that a signal victory is won when some part-time work opportunity is closed to youth. In discussion after discussion, the emphasis has been on the physical, mental, and social hazards of employment to young people, very seldom (until recently) on the possible socializing, training, or educational features of work experience for them.

This emphasis may only be part of the large assumption that work is dull and debilitating, tolerable only because it is necessary to buy leisure and fun, which are what we really want. As David Riesman (*12*), William Whyte, Jr. (*19*), and others have observed, we seem to be reversing the older American ethos with respect to work, the concept of work as intrinsically good, virtuous, and satisfying. There are, of course, other factors involved in eliminating the employment of youth. There is, for example, the wish to eliminate a cheap labor group and to maintain high minimum wages, which have grown steadily as our social awareness has grown.

Yet in recent years we have heard another point of view. We have been warned that idleness in the 'teen years plays directly into the hands of juvenile delinquency. We have heard that the school drop-out problem (which persists in the face of determined efforts to keep all youth in school) indicates that the school and its program are not meeting the needs of a large number of adolescents. Nor will this condition grow less as we return to a more academic emphasis in high schools.

The fact is that the proportion of young people enrolled in high school— and in the last few years their absolute numbers as well—has increased for two decades. Yet in spite of this increase, almost half the youth between the ages of 14 and 17 report some paid employment during the year. The *proportion* of this age group who are both enrolled in school and working has been steadily climbing for 15 years. This fact reflects a shift that arose in the necessities of World War II. It has been temporarily checked by short periods of economic recession, but the trend is clear and seems to be here to stay in spite of laws and court decisions increasingly restrictive to the employment of young people under 18. Adolescents *want* work, paid work. But it is well to remember that we are talking about part-time employment. A sizeable proportion of the under-18 youth who are not in school at all are in the ranks of the unemployed. One study (*13*) showed that those who quit school "to find work" actually took twice as long to start looking for it as those who completed school first!

It should be recognized that this discussion refers to the work experiences of all youth, not just the school-leavers. Indeed, school-leavers, as many studies show (*1, 3, 17*), do not have a hopeful future. More are unemployed than their classmates who finished high school. They earn less, hold lower status jobs and have a greater record of irregular employment. The inference in many studies of the early school-leaver is that remaining in school improves prospects for these youth. Those who leave school, however, are a selected group in other ways. They have a lower academic intelligence and earn poorer grades, the latter factor often being directly or indirectly the reason for early school leaving (*11*). Matching a group of early school-leavers with high school graduates in both intelligence and general socioeconomic status, the author (*8*) has shown that as early as the sixth grade, those destined to drop out early do significantly more poorly on a number of personality and social background indices.

While keeping these youth in school may possibly improve their employment prospects, they evidently do not constitute a significant pool of unrealized abilities of a very high order. Furthermore, with high schools tending toward more academic emphasis, this group is not likely to be better served or to diminish in size.

Adolescent Traits

Let us now turn to some characteristics of the adolescent period which seem to be quite characteristic of youth regardless of time and place. In the first place, adolescents are healthy in a physical sense, with a tremendous capacity for marshalling and expending energy. We may be socially concerned about the health of young people, but the fact remains that the years of early adolescence represent just about the healthiest of one's entire life in resistance to infectious disease and onset of various disabilities.

In the second place, normal healthy adolescents are, by adult standards, notably psychopathic, manic, and schizoid in their psychological makeup and behavior (*10*). A less dramatic statement is that in assent to statements of attitudes which notably characterize adults with psychopathic, manic, or schizoid disorders, the *average* American adolescent is surpassed only by 15% of the total adult population. Such findings suggest psychologically that adolescents are excitable, show a high level of activity and drive, have little regard for official social norms, are iconoclastic, and exhibit marked contrasts and inconsistencies in attitudes and behavior. Anyone who has ever lived with a normal teenager needs not be told this! Coupled with the high energy output of the period, this personality structure gives rise to the behavior which distresses adults so much, creates a so-called youth problem, and, indeed, seems to accentuate the delinquency rate, because this rate falls sharply in age groups past 20 years.

In the third place, adolescents seek to establish roles. The word "quest" has always seemed appropriate to characterize their restless, searching behavior. The adolescent needs to find a sense of identity and a sense of personal worth. He needs to clarify his sex role as a developing young man or young woman. He needs to find social skill, a sense of assurance, and a place with his peers. His desire to conform to the peer standard has been so often remarked that we need not mention it. And, finally, he searches for ways to realize his independence socially, emotionally, financially, and intellectually, changing from his childhood dependency on adults.

All these characteristics occur in persons who live in a very rapidly changing social scene. Mature, stable adults are often bewildered by the loss of familiar behavior norms and landmarks. Institutional and ritual supports to the development of roles which existed in the rural village and extended family have disappeared. In mid-century American society, there is a relative lack of restraint on and supervision of youth's behavior. And we must admit in our culture to a considerable exacerbation of two very powerful drives—the drive toward aggression and the drive toward sexual expression.

Given the characteristics of good health and an amazing capacity for energy mobilization; given in the average youth qualities which in adult life are identified as bizarre or deviant; given a driving need to establish mature roles—place these givens in a rapidly changing social context where the clear guide lines of a stable culture seem to be missing, and it is not surprising that we identify youth problems!

It seems probable that serious study and exploration of the significance of work can assist in the solution of some of these problems. This hypothesis cannot be defended directly by data, either observational or experimental. Rather, one must induce from indirect evidence and deduce from the logic of dynamic psychological theory to develop the case. Although the argument rests on no stronger grounds than these, it may serve to provoke thought and investigation.

Responsibility and Role

We may now turn to a discussion of the elements of a theory of adolescent work experience. First of these is the significance of responsibility. Responsibility, by which we mean dependability and accountability as well as the production of high-quality work, is much valued in society. Industry, business, and the professions all want a steady person—a dependable, self-starting, stable functioning, productive individual. Yet a common complaint about adolescents is their irresponsibility. Most of the problems adults have with youth arise in trying to inculcate dependable, conforming behavior to adult norms or from the failure of youth to realize such behavior.

Research on responsibility (6, 7) indicates that although its roots seem to be sowed early and crucially in parent attitudes and family relationships, this trait increases with age. The learning process is certainly not completed at adolescence, and it seems clear that the learning of responsibility is rooted in the significant interpersonal relations of a responsible adult with the child and youth. One of the few positive findings of these studies indicated that responsibility in children is associated with certain evidences of social responsibility in their parents. It does not seem to be at all associated with particular training or child-rearing techniques that are often thought to inculcate this quality.

Super's (14) study of vocational maturity in ninth grade boys formulated an index of Independence of Work Experience, based on evidence that a boy has obtained paid work on his own initiative, worked for non-family persons, and worked in situations in which he was "on his own," relatively free of supervision. Indications that the work required responsibility for materials, for the satisfaction of persons, and for handling money also enter the index. Super found his measure internally consistent and reliably evaluated, but it did not relate significantly to other measures of vocational maturity, although it did correlate with a measure of Acceptance of Responsibility. Super did not use his index as a *predictor* variable, however, which is the significance the present writer would put upon it. Nor would the variance in the index possible with ninth grade boys be as great as that possible with fifteen- or sixteen-year-olds eligible for working permits. Hence, the index may be more functional above the ninth grade.

The incomplete development of responsibility in the 'teen years suggests, then, that if work experience can be shown to evoke stable and efficient work habits and dependable and accountable attitudes toward work, such experience would be very important. Studies indicate that children more willingly perform around the house those tasks in which they are more nearly equal to adults. They assume readily serious and demanding assignments in contrast to trivial chores which make little demand on ability or interest. Significant work experience should therefore be serious and place performance demands on the person. Super's finding of a correlation between Independence of Work Experience and Acceptance of Responsibility should be followed up in further studies.

A second element of importance is the significance of occupation or work role. Society generally views work role in terms of status or prestige. Jobs are graded along a continuum of "respectability" and give status to the persons holding them. Youth, however, quite generally view occupation in terms of self-development and independence. From the studies of adolescents conducted by both the Boy and Girl Scouts (*15, 16*), it appears that young people regard the post-high-school years in terms of further education, work, or marriage, and interpret all these in relation to self-development and self-realization. Youth, then, perceive the work role in terms of the independence it will give them and the chance to realize abilities and to enhance the self. Hence any work *often* appears desirable and is eagerly sought. Industrial psychologists have noted a pronounced drop in job satisfaction indices as characteristic of workers in their early twenties. It is quite possible that this phenomenon signals a shift from an adolescent to a more mature expectation from the job.

There is a third aspect to the work role in the adolescent years. About half of mid-teenagers work for pay during the school year and about three-fourths work for pay during the summer months. The bulk of this work is done for "strangers," persons outside the immediate family. Indeed, it seems that young people *prefer* to work for pay outside the home. This is not difficult to understand. A child recognizes that though he may be valued by his parents, they *must* support him. Both legally and morally, it is their obligation. To be able to do something someone else will pay for is tangible evidence of worth on a different basis. This realization is by no means unimportant to the adolescent struggling to realize his self-image and a sense of identity while at the same time weaning himself from dependency on his parents.

Moreover, in paying a wage, the employer represents society in its more objective relationships to the teenager. This may be useful in developing a sense of accountability in young people. A child may be expected by family tradition to participate in household chores. Whether they are done well or poorly, willingly or grudgingly, becomes as much a matter of the parents' skill or the amount of irritation they can induce in the child as of the youngster's pride or sense of responsibility. Neither the parent nor the immature child can voluntarily give up the other. In the employer-employee relationship, there is a degree of freedom or option which seems desirable and important for young people to experience and to live with successfully for a time.

Money and Attitudes

There is, of course, also the point that money is important to teenagers. It gives direct access to many social experiences. Studies show that both high school and college students today have much more money for entertainment than similar age groups less than a generation ago. In one study (*18*), this difference is estimated to be in the neighborhood of around 1,000% more cash available for entertainment to post-World War II college students in contrast to pre-World War II students. This is a far greater increase than can be accounted for in terms of a general inflation or a change in general standards of living. It represents a very real change in circumstances for the contemporary adolescent generation. Yet money continues at the head of lists of problems claimed by youth(*9*)!

The fourth element in a theory of adolescent work experience is the significance of attitudes, both self-attitudes and work attitudes. Erickson (*4*) has, perhaps more forcefully than any other, emphasized the teen years as the period of achievement of a sense of identity. The sense of self-worth has been held to be the core of all human values. The ego, as a psychological construct, is important in many theories of personality development. If adolescence truly is a time of achievement of this sense of identity, the age is of peculiar importance in the development of personality. We have seen that being able to do work considered payworthy by an unrelated, objective adult can be important in confirming a child's sense of worth, no matter how significant his parental relationships may have been originally in establishing his self-esteem. Simply being aware that one is learning significant "tricks of the trade" can also be an important reinforcer of this attitude. Discovering that he can make suggestions on the job which others accept is a tremendously reinforcing experience.

Much has been made of early work experience as occasioning floundering and failure. Such experiences need not be devastating to the self-image, provided the individual understands them as exploratory and as necessary in developing the best use of his abilities. Too much floundering and too much failure, as clinicians have amply demonstrated, can have a serious, negative effect on the self, despite firmly laid foundations in childhood experiences of acceptance. Fortunate is the young person who is able to get work experience which reveals his developing abilities adequately, thus providing positive rather than negative reinforcement for his sense of identity.

Work attitudes are also important. While much of the adolescent's adjustment to authority is in relation to parents and teachers, the primary authority symbols, we have seen that the employer also is a significant representative of authority. Industrial and personnel psychologists frequently remind us that two important aspects of work adjustment are the adjustment to authority and adjustment to co-workers. More individuals fail on the job for these reasons than for a lack of specific skills. It has been said that industry interprets docility in the worker as "responsibility." However that may be, the young worker must somehow learn to be willing to take directions and to progress slowly toward goals—that is, to serve his apprenticeship or to "win his spurs." Studies show that the younger worker is often more dissatisfied on the job than the older worker. Somehow, the young worker must learn willingness to go through the training program, to bring his skills to the level of the reward he hopes for. This is not easy when work operations are simple, dull, and intrinsically uninteresting.

Finally, in the formation of work attitudes, the young worker's relationship to a responsible adult is of considerable importance. As jobs become more fragmented and specialized and require less craft or skill, it is harder to locate appropriate work experience which reinforces responsible work attitudes. The teenager who can work as a part-time helper to the craftsman is in a much better position to learn attitudes than the youth who pushes a broom or the errand boy in the large office. The boy who helps load cars at the super-market gets much more direct personal reinforcement than the one who fills shelves in the stock room. In every case, contact with adult models seems to be helpful to the formation of the desired attitudes, and such contact is increasingly hard to get. Both business and industry and organized labor often seek to avoid bothering with the teenager. He is an uneconomical producer, on the one hand, and too economical on the other!

Implications

To implement the point of view affirmed by this paper is not easy for a number of reasons, not least of which is the great dearth of research on work experiences of youth, work attitudes of youth, evaluations of training experiences, and the like. But at the present time two or three general patterns of pre-vocational work experience are available to teenage youth. One of these, in some respects the most hopeful in theory and with definite pre-vocational significance, has proved rather disappointing in practice. This is the work-experience program in the high school, where part-time paid employment is offered under the supervision of the school and related to courses in the regular school curriculum. Only a very small number of young people are reached by this type of program, and there has been a general resistance to developing this program both by industry and labor.

Schoolmen find real problems in the adequate administration and supervision of these programs. They are costly. There is some evidence from one study (2) that such programs are more helpful to individuals lower rather than higher in ability and scholarship. Thus, this program may have some potential value for the school dropout. The effort has not caught on widely, however, and one of the significant challenges to educators is to do something about the development of work attitudes in youth who more and more must stay in school.

Another pattern has been to encourage "job-exchanges" for summer employment. Newspapers, PTA, service clubs, and other agencies sometimes sponsor campaigns to list young people seeking work, or to sponsor job-finding campaigns. The National Committee on the Employment of Youth (NCEY), a division of the National Child Labor Committee, has done pioneer work in this field, stimulating local agencies to undertake projects in specific communities. This is a recent and hopeful development, yet too young to appraise adequately.

Volunteer work programs are becoming increasingly popular with youth-serving groups having character-building or international relations goals. The pattern was set early by the American Friends Service Committee and has been adopted rather widely by church groups. And now we hear of a Peace Corps. These enterprises have been and promise to continue to be very highly selective, taking the youth with the greatest early de-velopment of the qualities they seek to foster. On a lesser scale, and perhaps more meaningful to the average youth, are volunteer service jobs in school, civic or citizenship education assignments in the community or projects in settlement houses, summer playgrounds, and the like. Most of these tasks are unpaid, a drawback from the point of view of the objectives urged here as developmentally important.

Outstandingly successful has been a program of paid summer work combined with recreation in the city parks of Berkeley, California, where particular attention is paid to youth needing both money and group experiences.

In summary, we have argued for the significance to youth of part-time job experience, quite apart from vocational guidance or training objectives. We have tried to show that such experiences are actively sought by youth, are often quite difficult to find, and that providing them as a significant part of the transition to adult status constitutes a real challenge to education and the community.

REFERENCES

1. Adams, L. P. When young people leave school. *I.L.R. Research*, 1958, *4*, 9-11.
2. Brown, W. C. Diversified occupations of graduates of 1952. *Univer. of Missouri Bull.* Education Series, No. 60, 1959.
3. Dillon, H. J. *Early school leavers.* New York: National Child Labor Committee, 1949.
4. Erickson, E. H. *Childhood and society.* New York: Norton, 1950.
5. Freedman, Marcia. Work and the adolescent. In *Children and youth in the 1960's.* Washington, D. C.: White House Conference, 1960. Pp. 137-153.
6. Harris, D. B., et al. The measurement of responsibility in children. *Child Developm.,* 1954, *25*, 21-28.
7. Harris, D. B., et al. The relation of children's home duties to an attitude of responsibility. *Child Developm.,* 1954, *25*, 29-33.
8. Harris, D. B. Psychological and social characteristics of a group of school drop-outs, *Child Developm.,* 1960, *31*, 230-233.
9. Harris, D. B. Life problems and interests of adolescents. *School Rev.,* 1959, *67*, 335-343.
10. Hathaway, S. R., & Monachesi, E. D. *Analyzing and predicting juvenile delinquency with the MMPI.* Minneapolis: Univer. Minnesota Press, 1953.
11. Kitch, D. E. Does retardation cause drop-outs? *Calif. J. Elem. Educ.,* 1952, *21*, 25-28.

12. Riesman, D., Glazer, N., & Denny, R. *The lonely crowd.* New Haven: Yale Univer. Press, 1953.
13. Riches, Naomi. Education and work of young people in a labor surplus area. *US Month. Labor Rev.,* 1957, *80,* 1457-1463.
14. Super, D. E., & Overstreet, Phoebe L. *The vocational maturity of ninth grade boys.* New York: Bureau of Pub., Teachers College, Columbia University, 1960.
15. Survey Research Center. *Adolescent girls.* New York: Girl Scouts of America, 1957.
16. Survey Research Center. *A study of adolescent boys.* New Brunswick, N. J.: Boy Scouts of America, 1955.
17. U. S. Dept. of Labor. *Hunting a career.* Washington, D. C.: Govt. Print. Off., 1949.
18. Williamson, E. G., Layton, W. L., & Snoke, M. L. *A study of participation in college activities.* Minneapolis: Univer. Minnesota Press, 1954.
19. Whyte, Jr., W. H. *The organization man.* New York: Doubleday, 1956.

27

Vocational Choices in College

by
Emanuel M. Berger

Our society presses unreasonably on students to "know" what they want to do vocationally. The pressure is unreasonable, especially when applied to high school seniors and college freshmen, because most of them have not yet learned enough about themselves or about occupations to be able to make a first, satisfying choice. And especially they have not learned enough about the nature of their limitations in college-level work. As a result, many students commit themselves to vocational choices prematurely and then perceive the experience as a "failure." Students should be encouraged to consider any early decision as tentative, *a choice to be tested, confirmed, or disconfirmed. They should be relieved of pressure to "know" what they want to do, and helped to see their task as one of confirming or discovering what they want to do by way of a process of exploration, experimentation, and personal development that may go on through their lifetime.*

The very freedom of our college-bound youth to choose a vocation has become an important problem and task for most of them. More so than in most other countries of the world—and more so than their grandfathers before them—young people in our country today have freedom to decide on how they want to work. At the same time that there is greater freedom to choose, there is greater difficulty in choosing because of the much-enlarged number of possibilities to choose from in an increasingly complex occupational world. This situation requires knowing much more about one's self and about possible occupations if one is to make satisfying choices.

In my work as a counseling psychologist, I see many students who are disturbed to various degrees by not knowing what their vocational goals are. According to the students' reports, this lack of vocational goals is responsible for much anxiety, low motivation in college work, poor grades, and—not just occasionally—for their leaving college until they know what they want to accomplish there. This is not a distinctly local situation, certainly, but one that exists for thousands of college people all over the country. The sheer number of such students can be expected to skyrocket in the next few years as the "babies" of the 1947–50 post-war years come of college age.

And it is not just the students who are concerned, but also their parents. One large part of parental concern, understandably, is that their children be content in the work they choose. Another part, also understandable from their point of view, has to do with using hard-earned money to finance a college education when their children are so confused or uncertain about vocational goals that it seems doubtful that their education will have any practical, vocational value.

EMANUEL M. BERGER *is Associate Professor, Student Counseling Bureau, University of Minnesota.*

These concerns are nourished and aggravated by a general social pressure on students to make a vocational choice before they enter college, or soon thereafter. Other students, parents, relatives, the community in general, and even some teachers, counselors, and advisers in high school and college, are a party to the pressure. In high school, and to an increasing extent in earlier grades, there is likely to be a vocational counselor and prominently displayed occupational information—a general stimulation and prodding of the student to make a vocational choice. When he enters college he is likely to be asked what his vocational choice is, from which it is easy for students to take the implication that they are expected to be able to make one at the outset. Even among some professionals concerned with education and counseling there is a use of language that implies that there is but one grand and lasting choice to be made and that students should be able to make that choice now or very soon. They talk or write of choosing *a* career, of making *a* vocational choice.

Although the high tide of pressure seems to center on students about to begin their college experience, perhaps because this is seen as the beginning of serious professional training, the pressure continues for the more advanced students if they have not been able to make a satisfactory vocational choice.

The pressure is based on an erroneous and misleading assumption, namely, that most college freshmen are able to make a lasting and satisfactory vocational choice as freshmen or soon thereafter. The assumption is erroneous because most college freshmen have not yet learned, and will not learn in a short time, what they need to know about themselves and about occupations in order to make a first, satisfactory vocational choice. The assumption is misleading because it creates the impression that the student's vocational task is merely one of "choosing" a vocation, cafeteria style, rather than a potentially lifelong task of vocational self-discovery which may reasonably include many vocational choices, especially in the process of discovering a satisfactory occupational field. In a sense, the assumption requires that the freshman be omniscient, that he foresee his future experience and development, that he predict what his eventual vocational choice will be before he has had the experience and undergone the development out of which satisfactory choices emerge.

Ill Effects

In response to the pressure to make a definite vocational choice, many students commit themselves prematurely. They tell the world they are going to be engineers or architects or nurses or whatever, before they know whether they can handle the required subjects, before they know whether they have the required talents or special aptitudes, before they know what the training is actually like, before they have any idea of how much they would like the day-to-day work possible in their chosen field. Then, when they discover that their choice was not a good one for some reason or reasons, such as the possibilities just suggested, their tendency is to view the experience as a "failure." They said they were going to become engineers, etc., and they could not do it. And to the extent that people around them share the same assumption, that they should have known better somehow when they made their choice, the feeling of failure will be reinforced. They should not see such experiences as a failure on their part. The fault is in their point of view.

Another unhappy effect of the pressure stems from a sort of corollary of the assumption underlying it. If a student doesn't know as a freshman or shortly thereafter what he wants to do vocationally, the thinking goes, then he should not be in college. How many times I have heard students say that they have no idea of a major, no vocational goals, so they plan to leave college and go into the military service or get a job. They express the vague hope that such experience will help them decide on their vocational plans, and this could be the case. But they assume that it is a waste of time and money, from a vocational point of view, to go to college when one doesn't have any definite vocational plans. It is difficult to assess the extent to which these students delay or distort their vocational development when they act on this assumption.

And when students and parents become anxious because the student has not been able to make a definite, satisfactory vocational choice as a freshman or soon thereafter, that anxiety is needless. It is needless because the assumption on which it is based is in error. Most such students have not yet learned enough about themselves or about occupations to be able to make a definite, satisfactory vocational choice. The fault again is in their point of view.

Discovery—Not "Knowing"

A healthier and more realistic point of view recognizes that students eventually discover and confirm that a vocational choice they made is satisfactory, following experiences that permit them to do so. They cannot know in advance of such experience that they will be able to handle the academic requirements or be able to find a satisfying way of working in some chosen field. And yet, that is apparently just what our society expects of its young college people.

Even those students who eventually realize an early choice with satisfaction did not really "know," but rather discovered and confirmed that the early choice was a good one.

It then follows that every student who has made a choice at all—with little or much confidence—should consider it a *tentative* one rather than a committed one. Then his task becomes one of discovering, testing, confirming whether or not the choice was a good one in much the way a scientist goes about testing a hypothesis. He does not have to defend the presumption that he knew all he needed to know about himself and the field he chose at the time he chose it, before he had any opportunity to confirm his choice by experience. He can avoid a position where he clings unrealistically to a choice mainly because he told the world of his decision as if it were final in response to the social pressure to make a definite vocational choice.

In this perspective, the negative experiences that a student has in his efforts to confirm a choice can be seen in a different light. They can be seen as the "error" part of a trial-and-error process that is necessary and inevitable in any successful solution of a difficult problem. When a student discovers that he lacks the ability, aptitude, or talent that is required to maintain his vocational choice, this is a negative experience in relation to that choice but it has the positive aspect of eliminating an inappropriate choice, thereby narrowing the field of best looking vocational possibilities from which he is trying to make a choice. It brings him closer to a positive choice. Also, a student who sees his task as one of discovering his vocational choice through experience is more likely to accept the discovery of limitations as part of the process he must go through on his way to a satisfactory choice. But the student who has committed himself to a choice on the assumption that he should be able to choose wisely in advance of confirming experience will tend to see the interfering limitations as "incompetence" and the inappropriate choice as a kind of "failure." Of course, not all students react this way, but many do, and in a sense they are beating themselves into a loss of self-esteem because they were not omniscient enough to choose wisely from the beginning.

A broad academic experience can be helpful to a student who has not yet been able to make a first, tentative choice of vocation. Most liberal arts colleges require students to fulfill requirements in a variety of fields—sciences, social sciences, and humanities. The student has an opportunity to follow up interests he has and discover new interests in subject matter and to see how well he can handle different kinds of college courses. Learning about his abilities, limitations, and interests helps him to narrow down the field of best vocational possibilities for him. The point for those students who cannot see the vocational value of broad academic experience is that military service or a job, though they may be valuable experiences in other ways, are not likely to permit a student to learn about his interests, abilities, and limitations in relation to academic subjects. But what he can aspire to educationally and vocationally depends on just that sort of self-knowledge.

While I consider the above to be generally true, it should be recognized here that a student's performance in college sometimes improves greatly with increased maturity. Thus, a period in which he works at a job or is in the military service may contribute indirectly to improved academic performance when he returns to college. This in turn can permit him to raise his vocational aspirations. It is in view of just this sort of possibility that students might, under certain conditions, help their vocational development by leaving college for a while to work or go into military service.

Choice of a specialty within a field is also a matter of discovery and confirmation. The student who feels pretty sure that he wants to be in a certain occupational field is generally misplacing his anxiety if he worries a lot about how he wants to specialize. This is something he either confirms or discovers, something to be learned from experience rather than known in advance of experience.

Abilities and Limitations

One of the primary ways in which a student needs to have learned about himself to some degree before he can begin to choose a field is with respect to his abilities and limitations at the college level. Generally speaking, a student aspires to vocational goals in the belief that he has enough of whatever abilities and talent are required to reach those goals and do well in the field.

But a college freshman's conception of his abilities as he enters college is likely to be based on his high school experience. Although there are some exceptions, most high schools in our country pitch the level of difficulty of subject matter at some medium point so that most students will be able to understand it. Also, the degree of responsibility, initiative, and effort required of students in most high schools in order to "pass" is relatively much less than that required by most colleges.

As a result, many of our high school graduates have little conception of their limitations. They tend to have one or another omnipotent attitude: (1) that they can do well at just about anything in school if they really want to and try hard enough; (2) that they are so bright that they can do well at just about anything in college with only a little effort. It is this state of affairs that I see as accounting in large measure for the unrealistic aspirations of high school students suggested by the data obtained in Project TALENT.

Project TALENT, a large-scale, continuing research on our human resources, has published a report on the American high school student that concludes on several different occasions that the aspirations of our high school seniors appear "unrealistic" (Flanagan, et al., 1964). The conclusions are based on large amounts of data on the aptitudes, interests, and aspirations of our high school students. For example, it was found that 48 per cent of high school senior boys and 40 per cent of senior girls planned to enter a professional field; yet census data show that only about 15 per cent of employed males and 17 per cent of employed females between the ages of 25 and 29 are in professional and technical occupations. And in a study of the plans of those high school seniors who entered college a year after leaving high school, it was found that 37 per cent of those in the bottom quarter on a test of college aptitude planned to obtain an advanced degree!

College freshmen who learned little about their academic limitations from their high school experience are likely to get a jolt if they go to a college with relatively high standards. They will fail courses or do poorly as a result of too little effort or lack of sufficient aptitude in certain subjects. They are then forced to face their academic limitations perhaps for the first time. For some students this can be a serious problem. Their conception of what they can do in college and thereby vocationally is contradicted by their college performance. Unfortunately, many quite capable students interpret this as meaning that they are not competent. They confuse limitations with incompetence, and their self-esteem is damaged.

I believe we should have a high school system where students have an opportunity to learn about their limitations at a level of difficulty closer to that in most colleges without having to be failed out of high school if they cannot handle this level of work. This could be done if we "passed" students at different levels of difficulty, assigning grades to each—1, 2, 3, or whatever—with passage from one level to another being possible as the student's performance merits being raised or dropped from one level to another. This would help students to be realistic about their abilities and limitations earlier, cut down the number of unrealistic vocational plans and consequent emotional hurt that comes with their disruption at the college level, and perhaps avoid the loss of talented youth who give up career goals in scientific fields because of poor performance due to their not having learned earlier the limitations of how well they could do with a minimum or insufficient effort.

Determining what one's specific limitations are is a tricky and uncertain business at best. In an abstract and ideal way one learns about a limitation by doing his "best," making a maximum effort to achieve something, and then evaluating the outcome of his efforts. But one's best efforts in arts or academic subjects at one stage of his development may have very different results five or ten years later when he has become more mature. And, at any particular time in a person's life, a "best" effort is limited by the circumstances of his individual life and his own attitudes about what a maximum effort is.

The question is really one of the nature of limitations. With what degree of effort and at what level of difficulty do the limitations occur? In what specific subject matter? What are the implications of the limitations for the individual's choice of vocational field?

A student's limitations due to level of difficulty may mean that an advanced degree in mathematics is out, but he may still be able to do well enough to become a competent engineer. At a somewhat lower level, he may be able to do well enough to teach high school math or go ahead with training in business.

Also, some students have an either-or attitude, which says in effect: "Either I will be among the best in my field or I won't go into it—I refuse to be mediocre." Then, getting a C in some course in a major field or doing slightly above average work is a sign to them that they cannot possibly be "among the best." They are then ready to look elsewhere to some field where they can be "at the top." They do not recognize that no one excels in every subject in a field all the time or in every way—or that there is a very large segment of people in any field who are quite competent and make a modest contribution most of the time, and some of whom will eventually make an outstanding contribution despite "not being among the best" when they were doing their academic work. Given a degree of accomplishment sufficient to admit a student to an occupational field, it is the willingness to accept the risk that one's continued efforts may not result in an outstanding contribution that I see as the necessary but not sufficient condition for making an outstanding contribution in one's field.

The Developing College Student

The task of the student who is trying to reach a vocational decision about a field of work is a complex one. He must eventually bring together in a harmonious way his conceptions of himself that might in any way be vocationally relevant and his knowledge of occupations. But important changes in his vocational thinking may and do occur during the college years, thus complicating his problem. The student must not only be able to clarify and assess accurately the nature of his abilities, limitations, talents, interests, values, and personal dispositions, he must also be able to cope with changes that may take place in these aspects of himself at the very same time he is trying to evaluate them in relation to ways of working in some occupational field.

Some of the change can be attributed to students' difficulties with courses basic to a field they chose earlier. Would-be nurses have trouble with chemistry, etc. Naturally, such difficulty leads many students to change their vocational plans. It represents a complication due to a change in students' conceptions of their academic or creative abilities and limitations.

Students also change their vocational thinking as a result of the development of their interests and values. In general, social and aesthetic values and interests develop later in adolescence and it seems that the special stimulation of the college esperience spurs their development. Not for all students, certainly, but for many.

There may be changes in students' conceptions of their nonacademic potentialities as a result of experiences they have along with the academic experience or before they complete it. It may be a summer camp experience where the student enjoyed helping young teen-agers, or working on a student newspaper and confirming a commitment to journalism, or being an officer in the service and discovering a potential for management. Many kinds of nonacademic experience can contribute to a student's developing sense of himself as a potential teacher, newspaperman, or manager, or whatever.

Another factor is that of the student's knowledge of occupations—the nature of the training, abilities, and personal qualifications required as well as the specific ways of working possible within the occupation. As things are, some students choose engineering because they want to design airplanes or are mechanically minded, only to discover from experience that engineering training emphasizes mathematics and sciences and theories, and that the design of airplanes will have to come much later, after all that, and that one's mechanical skills may not be important in engineering and certainly not a sufficient basis for choosing it. Even at a much later vocational stage, engaging in the work of an occupation, there are those who discover from that experience that they are not suited to the field in some way—not patient enough to do chemical research, more interested in people problems than they are in engineering problems, etc.

Knowledge of occupations, like other kinds of awareness and information, grows with time and experience, is an aspect of the developing person, and another complicating factor in the process of vocational development and choice.

Reasonable Expectations

Considering all of the potential for change in a student's vocational thinking, when could we reasonably expect a student to be able to make a stable and satisfying vocational decision about a field? There is no simple, general answer to this question although one might say what we could reasonably expect of most students, with qualifications.

We would expect most seniors in college to have matured enough so that their awareness of their abilities, limitations, interests, and values has become stable enough to permit them to make a satisfying choice of an occupational field. Then the matter of how they want to work more specifically within the field can be worked out later as they get more training and experience.

Even then it is not so unusual or necessarily a sign of some special problem if a student majors in one field, graduates from college, and then switches to some quite different field. In my own field of psychology, I can think of at least a dozen acquaintances who switched to graduate work in psychology from undergraduate majors in science, engineering, or mathematics. And in a recent study of the career choices of scholars, Strauss (1965) found that 32 out of 96 university professors changed their field of interest, 14 of them to unrelated fields (such as from natural science to social science or humanities), although one can't tell from the study just when the changes to an unrelated field took place.

Some men manage to make rather radical changes even in their middle years without undue hardship to themselves or others. One acquaintance switched from a career in engineering to one in law in his mid-thirties. And most of us have heard about or read about the lawyer in mid-career who switched successfully to writing or to composing hit musicals or the salesman who switched in his forties to acting, with success and satisfaction.

The Long Look

The opportunity or necessity of making further vocational choices does not end with a satisfactory choice of an occupational field. With experience, what a man enjoys doing most and does best may come more sharply into focus. He may develop new skills, different aspirations.

The physician who has liked his work in general practice for several years may move with equal or greater satisfaction to specializing in internal medicine or psychiatry, to editing a medical journal, to being a hospital administrator. A lawyer may similarly move from general practice to corporation law, to being a judge, to becoming a congressman.

Not that satisfying development and change will be a general matter for all professionals. Some will be content to continue to work in a certain way most of their lives; others may not be content but may not have the freedom or power to choose other ways of working.

Vocational thinking and choices, if we view them in a broad way that goes beyond the matter of earning one's livelihood, may continue throughout one's lifetime, including the retirement period. Then each of us may again consider his values, interests, abilities, and limitations in relation to the question of how he can most satisfactorily engage himself in his later years. Some retirees are content to putter around the house, go fishing, play golf, etc. Others, needing something more akin to "work," take to community projects or writing or painting or turning out fine carpentry.

The point is that as long as we live, develop, and change we can and may think about and evaluate ourselves in relation to how we use our energies in the world much in the same way we did when we made our choice of an occupational field.

REFERENCES

FLANAGAN, J. C., DAVIS, F. B., DAILEY, J. T., SHAYCOFT, M. F., ORR, D. B., GOLDBERG, I., & NEYMAN, C. A., JR. *The American high-school student*. Cooperative Research Project No. 635, U.S. Office of Education. Pittsburgh, Pa.: Project TALENT Office, Univ. Pittsburgh, 1964.

STRAUSS, S. Career choices of scholars. *Personnel and Guidance Journal*, 1965, *44*, 153–159.

28

Work and Families

Great Expectations for College Seniors

DAVID GOTTLIEB

Data based on a survey of graduating seniors focuses on the family and interpersonal relationship patterns and career expectations of the class of 1972. It appears that the work ethic which emerges places a much greater demand upon work, that it be of greater significance to the individual and society, and that it be an integral part of one's life.

Just a few years ago the popular image of the college student was one of political, personal, and social activism. Students were viewed as rebels, alienated, disenchanted, pilgrims, pioneers, and seekers of a new and higher self-consciousness.

Now with the decline in campus based protest and militancy, a contrasting image has emerged, an image which stands in direct and dramatic contrast to the portrait of student as activist. The more contemporary student is viewed as being apolitical, relatively indifferent to the inequities of the system, and if not overly enthusiastic about middle-class life at least willing to go through

DAVID GOTTLIEB *is professor of sociology at the University of Houston.*

A revision of a paper presented at the 68th Annual Meetings of the American Sociological Association, New York City, August, 1973. The research from which this paper is taken was prepared for the Manpower Administration, U.S. Department of Labor, under research and development contract No. 81-11-72-04. A copy of the full final report may be obtained by contacting the National Technical Information Service, Operations Division, 5285 Port Royal Road, Springfield, Virginia, 22151. The report is entitled *Youth and the Meaning of Work.*

the educational process which provides one with the necessary social-mobility credentials.

Unfortunately it is necessary to state what many would say is the obvious, neither image accurately reflects where college students were in the past nor where they are now. As the selective campus disturbances of the past were translated into broad and sweeping generalizations so has the reduction in kinetic student behavior been interpreted as a return to the climate of apathy attributed to colleges and universities of the fifties.

It would be inappropriate here to discuss all of the factors which have contributed to the portrait of college student as activist or as apathetic. For our purposes it is only necessary to identify one critical factor: the tendency of behavioral scientists, university administrators, and the mass media to project to a universe from data obtained from a highly-selective and limited population. Despite empirical data to the contrary, as well as an intellectual awareness that individuals, groups, and institutions do vary, our pronouncements continue to reflect a "you've seen one you've seen them all" posture.

One purpose of the research presented here is to note at least some of the ways in which certain individual, group, and institutional variables are associated with differences and similarities on the expectations, plans, and attitudes of a sample of graduating college seniors. Here specifically our focus is upon the postcollege work and family orientations of our respondents.

The data discussed here are based upon a survey of 1,860 male and female graduating seniors (classes of 1972) from five different colleges and universities in Pennsylvania. The sample schools were selected in order to maximize a student population which would be representative of varying religious, ethnic, racial, regional, and socioeconomic backgrounds.

While we cannot assume that our sample is representative of all college seniors in Pennsylvania, much less all college seniors who graduated in the spring of 1972, whatever general data dealing with the characteristics of college seniors that we have been able to locate leads us to believe that our sample students are not too unlike college seniors in four-year colleges and universities throughout the country. We feel that our sample is sufficiently representative to make tentative generalizations; at the same time we are fully aware of methodological considerations and hence recognize the need for caution in the making of such generalizations (see Appendix).

A paper and pencil survey instrument was utilized in this research. The sample was obtained through a systematic random selection process at the four schools whose population sizes were sufficiently large to be appropriate for this procedure. The fifth school's senior enrollment was so small that all seniors were approached for their participation. It should also be noted that an attempt was made to obtain data from equal numbers of males and females. Our initial goal was a sample of 2,000 students. The return of usable questionnaires from 1,860 students represented a response rate of 86 percent. The lowest return response for an individual school was 82 percent, the highest 97 percent.

SAMPLE CHARACTERISTICS

The vast majority of our respondents had obtained the baccaluareate degree in four years. At the time of graduation more than two-thirds were either 21 or 22 years of age. Eighty-nine percent are white; 9 percent black; and 2 percent of other racial backgrounds. Most, 85 percent, were single. Socioeconomic status (based upon an index utilizing parental income, fathers education and occupation), showed the following distribution:

Very low:	30%	(561)
Middle low:	22%	(416)
Middle High:	19%	(348)
Very High:	29%	(535)
Total	100%	1860

An examination of major fields of study by sex would suggest that despite social change and the rhetoric of sexual liberation, few students seem to cross the traditional sex-field lines. The vast majority of women (79 percent) are found in three fields (education, humanities, and social sciences) with education accounting for half (51 percent) of the females. The males are more evenly distributed with the largest percentage in the social sciences (26 percent) followed by education (18 percent), engineering (13 percent), and business administration (12 percent).

It is also worth noting that in terms of postbaccalaureate educational expectations that males are twice as likely as females to indicate immediate plans for graduate or professional school enrollment. Comparisons with similar data collected in a national survey of 1961 college graduating seniors would support the interpretation that few changes in field of study and postcollege educational plans for males and females have occurred during the past decade.[1]

Prior to the presentation of our discussion dealing with postcollege work and life-style preferences and expectations, it is important to note the impact of three variables: sex, socioeconomic status, and ethnic-religious orientation.

Briefly, sex and socioeconomic status are very much associated with the schools which students attend, the fields of study they enter, and the career and life styles they anticipate. Women, as noted earlier, are highly concentrated in a limited number of fields. Generally, they anticipate working as school teachers, social workers, guidance counselors, nurses, and health profession technicians. Men are more evenly distributed, more likely to anticipate immediate entrance into graduate school, expect higher salaries and more rapid occupational advancement.

Students of lower socioeconomic backgrounds are most likely to have been enrolled in colleges with the fewest academic offerings; they are more likely to enter fields which offer terminal baccalaureate degrees; and they are most likely to express the more traditional views with regard to work attitudes familial relationships, and sex-role equality.

We find that low-income, first-generation college students in general, and black students more specifically, expect careers in relatively few fields. Very few Blacks aim for careers in law, medicine, science, or business.

Similarly, we find that many young people of blue-collar working class backgrounds expect careers which are at the bottom of the white-collar, professional ladder. Further, we can conclude from this research that there is a greater discrepancy between occupational preferences and expectation for lower-income students than is the case with more affluent students.

The students' current ethnic-religious affiliation is yet another dimension which contributes to variations in expressed attitudes, values, and expectations. In a number of instances ethnic-religious orientation is a more powerful

---

[1] James A. Davis. *Great Aspirations: Career Plans of America's June 1961 College Graduates.* National Opinion Research Center, September, 1961.

predictor of career and life-style preferences than are sex, socioeconomic status, or field of study. Just how this factor operates and the stages in the life span in which ethnic-religious orientation takes hold we cannot say. We do know, however, that there are significant differences in a number of career- and life-related variables which seem to be best explained by ethnicity and religiosity. In general, those students who see themselves as having no current religion identification stand in greatest contrast to all other students. The "no religion" students are more likely than all other students to see themselves as alienated, least accepting of the traditional work ethic and of the belief that work builds character or makes you a better person. Significant differences are also found between Irish and Italian Catholics even when we control for sex, socioeconomic status and field of study. Similarly, the degree of religiosity also plays an important part in preferences and expectations.

The impact of these intervening variables are mentioned here in order to add emphasis to the need for maintaining a nonmonolithic view of our respondents even though they might have in common certain experiences and characteristics.

We turn now to the findings dealing with postcollege work and familial expectations. Again the reader is cautioned to keep in mind that our purpose here is to present an overview—a feeling for the general mood or direction of the attitudes expressed by our respondents.

In attempting to understand the data which deals with expected and preferred postcollege life styles, it is important to differentiate between the form and content of student responses. The form or surface data suggest that most students anticipate life styles very much like those lived by most middle-class adults. There is little evidence of nontraditional marital or family forms. Only a handful of students anticipate a family structure different from that of the conjugal or nuclear. Less than 10 percent anticipate living with a member of the opposite sex without going through the formalities and rituals of some kind of marriage licensing and ceremony. The form picture does give the impression that the male will be the outside breadwinner and goal-attainment facilitator, while the female will be the child caretaker and hold responsibility for the day-to-day activities of the home.

When, however, we go beyond the presentation of data which deal with family and sex-role relationship patterns and deal with the content of the expected and preferred relationships between men and women, parents and children, and the individual and others, we get a somewhat different impression. For example, although only a few students indicate a preference for communal living itself, many are very much in favor of developing relationships which one would expect to find within a commune or some other type of extended kin system. The quality of human relationships is clearly a salient factor to the majority of these people. Openness and freedom in relationships is another important ingredient of desired life styles. A "happy family" is in fact the dimension of life most frequently referred to by most college graduates. Work is important, but work can be sacrificed if the needs and demands of the job will come at the expense of family and family relationships.

While traditional expectations of sex-role relationships and responsibilities have not been abandoned, there certainly is more than sufficient evidence to indicate that many people are willing to explore alternatives. The traditional norms dealing with the sex role division of labor, both within and outside of the family, are questioned. The students in this research, if not yet convinced, are at least willing to recognize that times are changing and that there is a need to redefine and reassess the relationships between men and women and between husband and wife. Similarly, there is a willingness to examine and modify how one rears and relates to one's children. Our impression is that many young people will attempt to interact with and socialize their children in ways different from those in which they themselves were reared.

Again, the surface form may look no different from that which we now see or think we see as being representative of the American middle class. The contrast will be found in the more private and less visible aspects of families. There is emphasis upon the equality, rights, and individual needs of the family members regardless of age or sex. Respondents express the need for much more in the way of open relationships and a willingness to deal with the many problems which arise when people live in constant and close proximity to one another.

The greater emphasis upon the importance of family and human relationships within families is the result of a number of factors. Obviously the current popular concern, both on and off campus, with sex roles, interpersonal relationships, and families does enhance discussion of such matters. As others have noted, growing technology and rapid social change, as well as large scale, impersonal dimensions of our society, contribute to feelings of loneliness, isolation, and powerlessness. The nation-state and the various social institutions which have provided a source of identification and association in the past seem less satisfying and fulfilling now. Finally, the experience of seeing the relative ineffectiveness of the efforts of young people who have sought to influence the policies of the college and the nation is yet another factor contributing to the emphasis upon privatism and concern with the family and family relationships.

Our data show that in comparison to a study of 1961 graduating seniors, a growing number of students have moved away from the religion in which they were reared and many more indicate that they have no single political orientation or ideology. Both of these changes appear to represent a shift away from more traditional associations and identifications. The shift appears to be inward toward more private and more restricted positions. This turning inward does in some ways represent a form of "splendid isolation." At the same time, it does not necessarily represent an indifference to the problems of the society.

What many students seem to be saying is, "Before I can really help others, I have to 'get myself together.'" Rather than seeking to take on the entire social system and its shortcomings, these students believe they must first build a more wholesome, meaningful, and workable smaller social system. That smaller social system is limited to their spouse, children, kin, and perhaps a select group of friends. Within this smaller social system it is expected that there will be greater opportunity for maintaining control over one's destiny to live the way one wishes, to express one's ideals and feelings, to feel that one is a person with unique needs and desires, and for self-exploration and self-development.

The expressed expectations of these respondents would suggest that this generation of college seniors does not expect to neglect the problems of others or the problems of the society. At the same time their first priority is with self, family, and closest associates. The emphasis upon self and a small group of others is not, we believe, the result of self-indulgence, denial of the needs of others, or the single-minded pursuit of affluence. Rather this turning inward represents what many people, particularly young, see as the only effective and efficient way of retaining a feeling of self-worth and actualization.

With regard to career expectations we begin with the observation that the vast majority of our students express favorable attitudes toward work. Many in fact believe that their feelings about work are more positive than are the work attitudes held by others, particularly parents. Regardless of their feelings about work, the majority of respondents expect to enter the job market either within a year of college graduation or at the time they complete their graduate school training. Very few expect to be self-employed and very few expect to find employment outside of the conventional job market.

Despite expressed concern about the current job market, most students assume that they will eventually find employment and that it will be the kind of employment which will provide them with a reasonable income. The major concerns do not seem to be with matters of income, economic security, or social prestige. Rather, the major concerns are with finding careers and work settings which will allow the individual to do relevant things, which will facilitate self-growth and development, which will enhance the use of unique skills and ideas, which will encourage creativity and learning, and, of primary importance to many, work settings which will enable the individual to help others and to contribute to the quality of the society.

The majority of the respondents believe that work is a good builder of character. At the same time there is far less commitment to the belief that hard work alone makes one a better person. To be a better person one must find relevance and meaning both within and outside of the work setting.

Not unlike other members of our society, the graduating seniors view work as a critical necessary part of adult life. Few students have ever seriously believed that they could escape at least some type of work involvement. The difference between these college seniors and others is found, we believe, in what they expect from their work and in the intrinsic nature of the connection they seek to make between work and other important parts of their lives.

From the information provided by the respondents we would have to reject the position of those who maintain that the work ethic is dead or dying. Rather, we would maintain that we are witnessing the emergence of a new and in many ways much improved work ethic. It appears to be a work ethic which reflects the expectation that work is more than a means to an end, more than a means of earning a livelihood; it suggests that one works not only because of societal expectations, family responsibilities, or religious ideology. The changing work ethic reflects beliefs that work can and should be nonexploitive; that it can and should be relevant and useful; that it should provide the individual with opportunities to interact with others; and at least to some extent that it should allow the individual some opportunity to influence the policies, goals, and procedures of the work setting.

This emerging work ethic de-emphasizes the importance of money, power, and social prestige. An adequate salary is of course assumed, but the accumulation of wealth is not a salient goal. Money itself is not seen to represent success or happiness. These students' work attitudes reflect a concern with the consequences of their work activities; that is, they do not want to be involved in work efforts which contribute to the production of inferior products or the pollution and deterioration of the physical environment.

In conclusion, there appears to be an emerging work ethic which places a much greater demand upon work. The expectation is that work can and should be of greater significance to the individual and of greater value to the society. As there are higher and different expectations for the content and form of work, there is also a change, we believe, in the expected fit between work and other life activites. Work for many of these seniors is not seen as an activity which should be separate or isolated from one's family or private life. Work is viewed as being an integral part of one's total life. Again, work is not considered to be a means to an end, but rather as a potential source for enhancing self-sufficiency and family relationships. At the same time work and career needs are not expected to take priority over family relationships. Occupational mobility will be sacrificed if it must come at the expense of family needs and desires.

APPENDIX

A brief description of each of the five participating schools follows. One of the schools requested that it not be identified by name in our final report. It was our decision to substitute names for all five schools as well; nevertheless, basic descriptions and demographic data are accurate.

Latham University:　Located in a small town, Latham has a total of 2,696 undergraduates, 564 of whom are in their senior year. Latham is a private school primarily enrolling white, fairly affluent youth from a number of states along the eastern seaboard and in the midwest. Although the emphasis is on undergraduate training, there are several graduate programs. Field of study alternatives are numerous and include majors such as Business Administration, Engineering, Physical Sciences, and Biological Sciences. Many of these students have parents who have attended college and are therefore second generation college-goers. A large number of Latham graduates go on for advanced degrees.

Fletcher State College:　Also located in a small town, there are 3,856 undergraduates including 575 seniors enrolled at Fletcher State College. The majority of students come from rural communities or from the moderately large cities nearby. The student body consists primarily of white, first-generation college students from working-class homes. Most anticipate entering the full-time job market upon graduation as teachers in elementary or secondary schools.

State University:　Located in a small college community in the rural center of Pennsylvania, State University enrolls approximately 19,000 undergraduates, 5,091 of whom are members of the 1972 senior class. Although the majority of students are from Pennsylvania, they represent a fairly heterogeneous student population. Many are from the major metropolitan areas of the state. Based on demographic data provided by the university, we know that about one fourth come from families where one or both of the parents have completed college, and the majority come from middle income homes. About 5 percent are Black and 30 percent come from rural or middle-sized communities. The university has a variety of graduate and professional programs.

University of Metro:　Located in one of the large metropolitan cities of Pennsylvania, there are 10,542 undergraduates at the university of whom 2,966 are seniors. Many of the undergraduates are either residents of the city itself or of the nearby surrounding communities. The school has a fairly heterogeneous population of urban and suburban students. The student body includes minority group members and students representing different socioeconomic and religious backgrounds. The University of Metro, like State University, has a large number of professional and graduate school programs.

Reeves State College: Located in a small town within close proximity to a large urban center, there are 2,100 undergraduates at Reeves State College, of which 300 are members of the senior class. The student population is approximately 85 percent Black and most are from working-class families. Very nearly all of the undergraduates are city residents and half of them live at home while attending Reeves. The college offers several undergraduate programs, however most of the students major in Elementary or Secondary Education, and the Social Sciences.

29

The image of young people communicated by the mass media is misleading. Poverty—of spirit as well as pocket—characterises many.

NON-SWINGING YOUTH

by Bernard Davies

Watching *Top of the Pops* in one of Lancashire's dockland youth clubs. On the screen, swaying bodies, gay and fashionable clothes, space-age decor, music to match. The weekly ritual confirmation of youth's popular image. Freedom, wealth, confidence, unconventionality—all unmistakably symbolised.

Around me, a different scene. Fashion caricatured. Skirts short and revealing, but not truly mini—only turned up at the hem. Hair, both boys' and girls', long but simply straggling, without style, sheen or grooming. No bell-bottoms or frills, snappy waistcoats or high-necked shirts. Just tired and shapeless sweaters (not even Marks & Spencer) and stained blue-denim jeans. Faces pale, drawn, probably undernourished. Movement lethargic, without spark, without conviction. A microcosm of Lancashire's imprisoned youth.

Of course, the comparison may not be altogether fair. For the studio visitors to *Top of the Pops*, this was at least a big night out; but for the youngsters by my side it was clearly just any night, and in a club, moreover, whose unpainted walls, stone floors, poor heating and rickety furniture were hardly a temptation to dress up.

Yet those young Lancastrians in the youth club cannot in my experience be regarded as exceptional. Theirs is an anti-image in which the supposedly essential traits of present-day youth don't feature. What seems to characterise so many of their lives is not wealth but privation and even outright poverty. These young people are mostly not angry and active, but apathetic and unassertive, especially in the face of "them." Even where few minorities threaten them directly, a deep-seated bigotry often bitterly obtrudes, as they seek to defend the little they do possess. Far from challenging the world around them with an insistent individuality, they seem personally and socially incarcerated; their talents are consistently underrated, their vision constricted, their most personal modes of expression stifled. Each self-image they have created for themselves has been repeatedly deflated, all futures prematurely and permanently foreclosed.

The point of stirring all this to the surface is not to paint one more of those black, outsider's portraits of the north. It is rather to question *in general* how accurately the widespread image of contemporary youth fits with the realities. Lancashire may have triggered off such thoughts, but evidence can be accumulated from much farther afield that everything that is young does not swing.

Take, for example, the tag of affluence. Mark Abrams attached it to young people very firmly, with revelations about the hugeness of teenage consumer spending. This he fixed in 1960 at £950 million, and ever since the bulging teenage wage-packet has simply been taken for granted.

Yet, when one begins to look closely, some contradictions emerge. In the first place, Abrams was concerned with unmarried 15 to 25 year olds. This upper age limit was bound to raise the total spending figure sharply, but it disguises important age differences. Abrams discussed only *total* expenditure and average earnings. He said nothing of how many high-earners were hiding how many low ones. He offered no regional or local differences and so threw no light on how young people in London compare with those from the north or Scotland.

Such discrepancies do exist. It is not just that I feel them when I see youngsters huddling and cuddling in the bus shelters or against the railings of Atherton, Tyldesley, Ince-in-Makerfield and elsewhere. Nor is it just that I hear of them even more personally when I talk with shopgirls, waitresses, factory hands and other young workers. Much more convincing is the research evidence which is now available, drawn from larger groups in other areas.

Cyril Smith, in his Bury study, *Young People at Leisure*, concluded that "the popular picture of affluent teenagers grossly over-simplifies the very real differences in income among them." The amounts of money available to the young people he studied in 1963 varied greatly with age and sex. In general over 90 per cent of his 17 and 18 year olds spent £2 a week or less, and nearly 40 per cent of the 18 year olds spent under 15s.

In Scotland, according to Pearl Jephcott in *Time of One's Own*, the picture is not very different. Despite overtime, bonuses and increases for age, she found that between 1964 and 1966 41 per cent of young people aged 17½ *and over* were earning only £5 to £7, with a further 15 per cent falling below this amount. The wages of girls during the first two years at work rose from £3 or £4 to £5 maximum, while a mere 7 per cent of the whole under-21 group she interviewed had more than £9 a week. Spending money was of course much less: 59 per cent of the 15 to 17½ year olds had less than £1; 81 per cent of the 17½ to 19 year olds had less than £3. Pearl Jephcott's conclusion, inevitably, is that "the popular image of today's adolescent as having money to burn was certainly not true of the great majority of these Scottish boys and girls."

Once one examines the teenage image in this detailed way, one discerns all sorts of other cracks. Take youth's reputation for unconventionality and unorthodoxy. Research findings on teenage values and attitudes do very little to confirm it. In *Youth and the Social Order*, Frank Musgrove's general thesis is that "the broad picture of contemporary youth is not of a population either actually or potentially deviant—or even particularly adventurous." Such chapter sub-headings as "The realism of youth" and "the conservatism of the young" reveal where Musgrove stands. They are supported by his own and other evidence. Thus, he reports that statements like "Boys (or girls) of my age should be allowed more freedom," get very little teenage support. But statements concerned with young people "acting their age" or being "responsible" are approved by a majority.

Inquiries into the specific views and standards held by teenagers tend to reinforce this conservative picture. True, on sexual morals an NOP survey, published in the *Daily Mail* in November 1967, suggested that, in their *attitude* to pre-marital sex, girls are equally divided, while two thirds of the boys are in favour. This, however, says nothing of actual *behaviour*. According to Michael Schofield's authoritative and widely quoted 1965 survey of nearly 1,900 young people (*The Sexual Behaviour of Young People*), this seems to be much more conventional. Only 11 per cent of the 15 to 17 year old boys interviewed, and 6 per cent of the 15 to 17 year old girls, had had sexual intercourse. The corresponding figures for the 17 to 19 year old age-group were 30 per cent and 16 per cent. Thus, by the age of 20, only a third of the boys and one sixth of the girls, were sexually experienced; most of the experience was gained after the age of 16 (the law, of course, may have an effect); and the vast majority of these sexual encounters were with a single partner.

Peter Willmott's conclusion in *Adolescent Boys of East London* (1966) is very similar: "Those we talked to suggested that by 18 something like a third or half of the local boys would have had intercourse"—though many of these, it is clear, had done so either with a small number of highly promiscuous girls, or only with the one girl with whom they were going steady." A more recent study in the midlands, whose comparability with Schofield's or Willmott's work is not clear, suggests some noticeable shift towards permissiveness in the last few years. Yet from the solid evidence available, long after the so-called teenage revolution got under way, it is clear that, far from being one of gay and irresponsible abandon, the path of sexual experience along which young people travel has until now been most striking for its conformism, or at least for the way it would appear to mirror adult morals and behaviour.

Perhaps it is not surprising, therefore, that in what they want and expect from their own future family lives and careers, young people again reveal much that is most noticeable for its resemblance to adult responses. Adolescent aspirations in these areas are only minimally tinged with the fantasy and idealism one might expect. They apparently stay firmly within boundaries which any "sensible" adult might lay down for them.

Professor C. A. Mace noted in 1962, in his introduction to Thelma Veness's study, *School-Leavers: their aspirations and expectations*, that "few young people have the ambition to become millionaires, peers, film-stars, even Lord Mayors of London. They are on the whole realistic, setting their sights to the reasonably attainable." The average boy's "peak ambition lies somewhere in the middle management in industry or similar status in other occupations or professions . . . At 23 he gets married, and his wife bears him two or three children who thereafter are apt to become the centre of his ambitions. The ultimate objective is retirement on an adequate pension." The picture of the "average" girl is, according to Professor Mace, very similar (and this was confirmed in a study reported by Gillian Tindall in NEW SOCIETY, 30 May 1968).

Thelma Veness herself found that over a third of her sample, when asked what they might especially want to be in the future, responded by pointing to an ordinary sort of job. She concludes that "a large number of these boys and girls have tailored their ambitions to fit what they are in fact likely to do." (Some of her results, however, revealed that such realism did not exclude a good deal of day-dreaming or resort to fantasy.)

This absence not only of idealism but even of burning personal ambition—this striking emphasis on pragmatic, traditional values and aspirations so little different from those of their elders—is equally discernible in other spheres of young people's lives. It can be seen, when their views on political, religious and social issues are sought. The NOP survey I quoted earlier also revealed that 68 per cent of the young people interviewed wanted the death penalty restored, so that this emerged as top of a list of "reforms" desired by the young—hardly a rallying cry for social upheaval! As many as 30 per cent would have sent all coloured immigrants back home (even before Powell's Birmingham and Eastbourne speeches), and almost as many were against abortion law reform as were for it. Sixty per cent of the boys and 76 per cent of the girls said they believed in God.

It follows logically that the anti-authority feelings, said to be so prevalent among the young, were little in evidence in the NOP survey. In the list of "most popular personalities." Mother was No. 1 and Father No. 5, the Queen No. 2, Harold Wilson No. 4, President Johnson No. 6 and Prince Philip joint number 10. The footballer Bobby Charlton was the only sportsman to get a mention. The only pop idol, Elvis Presley, cast an unmistakably dated shadow even two years ago.

This only confirmed what E. M. and M. Eppel had found in 1966 in *Adolescents and Morality*. Among the young people they talked with, nearly two thirds were prepared to accept orders either without qualification or provided the person giving the orders had thought about them in advance, was sure they were right, or gave them in a reasonable and humane way. Only a quarter of the sample appeared uncompromisingly hostile to authority.

Whether one is relieved or appalled by this widespread adolescent conservatism depends on one's starting point. To those who read only press reports, or watch only television newscasts, such a portrait of youth may bring relief. The more radical will see it as evidence of repression of the young, their premature moulding according to adult models, their direction into restricting channels.

Both would be right, in a way. But for the purposes

of policy towards youth, quite apart from the question of understanding, the adolescent anti-image must be accepted, once and for all, as a fact. Even among university students, few are active radicals; and students are a tiny minority of youth. A great deal of education, not least in the youth service, still seems to be carried out on the assumption that it is only to greater affluence, independence and alienation among the young that adults must respond. Yet the first need is to help youth out of its straitjacket.

In traditional youth organisations, in youth clubs, in more recent youth work bodies such as the Duke of Edinburgh's Award Scheme and the Young Volunteer Force Foundation, and in the schools themselves, the motives of exploiting what is socially "beneficial" the damming up what is socially "destructive" still predominate. Control remains the first, though rarely the explicit, priority. Genuine teenage self-expression—which, I repeat, at present *we have not got*—is still an undervalued and even feared objective.

The real lesson of the research on young people's condition and philosophy is that we don't need some co-ordinated movement to keep most young people in check, but we do need an enormous programme to release many more of them from the mould (curriculum reform in the secondary schools may be at any rate a first step). For every individual young person who frightens or undermines the established order, many more are going to have only a tiny opportunity to discover what is most individual in their personalities. Penned into a pattern of badly-off homes, run-down schools and poor jobs, they are going to remain poor (emotionally as well as, sometimes, financially), to adopt blind prejudice against any group threatenng their uncertain stability, to be convinced of the inevitability of their own limitations and even failures—and to reproduce this pattern of humble acquiescence in restricted lives in the generations that succeed them.

Behind the headline-snatching students and hippies and swinging kids, the truth of these youngsters' condition may seem difficult to discern and even more difficult to act on. Yet whatever *Top of the Pops* may communicate, those Lancashire teenagers in that youth club exist; and they are far more common than most of us care to admit.

REFERENCES

Mark Abrams, *Teenage Consumer Spending: parts 1 and 2* (London Press Exchange, 1959 and 1961)

Cyril Smith, *Young People at Leisure: a report on Bury* (Department of Youth Work, University of Manchester, 1966)

Pearl Jephcott, *Time of One's Own* (Oliver & Boyd, 1967)

Frank Musgrove, *Youth and Social Order* (Routledge & Kegan Paul, 1964)

Michael Schofield, *Sexual Behaviour of Young People* (Longmans, 1965)

Peter Willmott, *Adolescent Boys of East London* (Routledge & Kegan Paul, 1966)

Thelma Veness, *School Leavers—their aspirations and expectations* (Methuen, 1962)

E. M. and M. Eppel, *Adolescents and Morality* (Routledge & Kegan Paul, 1966)

National Opinion Poll survey, "The Teenagers" (*Daily Mail*, 27–30 November 1967)

VIII. Morality and Spirituality

If one listens to adolescents, one hears many references being made to the moral and spiritual aspects of their lives. The references may emerge somewhat disguised, but they are there. One hears, for example, remarks about good vibes and bad vibes, having one's head turned around by something or someone, or appeals to fairness and unfairness. There are also references to, and intense beliefs in, God and strictly organized religious principles.

In the past, behavioral scientists might have made a mistake in assessing adolescents when they attributed the adolescent's involvement with religion to some displacement of his or her attitudes toward parental authority. Believing in God, in other words, was strictly a transferring of feelings from real parents to an abstract figure. Or perhaps, the theories went, ambiguous family relationships lead to a need for concrete, even dogmatic, religious principles. A certain amount of evidence does exist to partially support such theses, but the issue of adolescent morality and spirituality still is far from settled. It makes sense to say that the emotional and cognitive factors of the adolescent's sense of morality emerge as a function of childhood experiences. But childhood experiences both inside and outside the home hardly account for it all. By the time a person is 12 or 15, a great deal about the world is understood and an appreciation for religion is well-formed, even if this appreciation eventually becomes a rejection of religion.

In addition, the adolescent's growing sense of self, experiences with friends, and a growing awareness of what being a man or woman is about, will contribute to the stuff of moral and spiritual development. No one knows for certain just what attitudes and opinions will become part of a particular moral or spiritual stance. Some belief systems are predicated in great measure on rules governing sexual behavior, marriage, family behavior. And perhaps adolescents, because they are increasingly concerned with sexuality and intimacy, incorporate these feelings and attitudes into their morality and spirituality. Yet again we stress that social and cultural factors play a significant role in the initiation and organization of moral and spiritual forms. Thus, one might say that only certain personality types will be sympathetic to certain religious forms. True enough. But what about the directions taken by a culture generally, say, toward power, materialism, achievement at the cost of human freedom? Might not these elements, too, affect the adolescent's sense of morality and spirituality?

Similarly, while a person, young or old, must work out for himself or herself the private aspects of morality and spirituality, friendships and even loose associations with other people will influence a person's definition of morality and spirituality. We begin to see that while this volume, for the sake of clarity and organization, is divided into 12 different sections, the sections should be seen as interrelated, each shedding light on the others.

LAWRENCE KOHLBERG AND CAROL GILLIGAN

30

The Adolescent as a Philosopher: The Discovery of the Self in a Postconventional World

Those whose exterior semblance doth belie
Thy Soul's immensity;
Thou best Philosopher . . .

Thou little child, yet glorious in the might
Of heaven-born freedom on thy Being's height,
Why with such earnest pains dost thou provoke,
The years to bring the inevitable yoke?
Thus blindly with thy blessedness at strife?
Full soon thy Soul shall have her earthly freight,
And customs lie upon thee with a weight
Heavy as frost, and deep almost as life!

The thought of our past years in me doth breed
Perpetual benediction; not indeed
For that which is most worthy to be blest;
Delight and liberty, the simple creed of childhood . . .
But for those obstinate questionings
Of sense and outward things,
Fallings from us, vanishings;
Blank misgivings of a creature
Moving about in worlds not realized,
High instincts before which our mortal Nature
Did tremble like a guilty thing surprised:

—Wordsworth, *Intimations of Immortality*

THE CENTRAL themes of this essay are first, the definition of adolescence as a universal stage of development; second, the way in which the universal features of adolescence seem to be acquiring unique colorings in the present era in America; and third, the implications of these changes for education.

In turn-of-the-century America, G. Stanley Hall launched developmental psychology with his discussion of adolescence as a stage of development. For the next fifty years, however, most American educators and psychologists tended to think about adolescence not as a stage but as a period in life, "the teens." The teenager was viewed as half-child, half-grown up, with a half-serious peer "culture" or "youth culture" of his own. Textbook after textbook on adolescence was written telling in statistical detail the sort of information which could be gathered from reading *Seventeen* or *Harold Teen*.

Even with the textbook description of the teenager, one could surmise that the central phenomenon of adolescence is the discovery of the self as something unique, uncertain, and questioning in its position in life. The discovery of the body and its sexual drive, and self-conscious uncertainty about that body, is one stock theme of adolescent psychology. The romantic concerns and hopes for the self's future has always been another element of the stock description of the adolescent. The third stock theme implied by the discovery of the self is the need for independence, for self-determination and choice, as opposed to acceptance of adult direction and control. The fourth stock theme implied by the adolescent discovery of self is adolescent egocentrism and hedonism, the adolescent focus upon events as they bear upon his self-image and as they lead to

immediate experiences. (While the child is egocentric and hedonistic, he is not subjective; he focuses upon events, not upon his subjective experience of the events, as what is important.)

While the discovery of the self in the senses just listed has been a stock theme in American discussion of adolescence, it has been subordinated to another theme, the theme of adolescence as a marginal role between being a child and being grown-up. The adolescent sense of self, with its multiple possibilities, its uncertainties, and its self-consciousness has been viewed as the result of a social position in which one is seen and sees oneself, sometimes as adult, sometimes as child. In the marginal role view, the adolescent's need for independence and fantasies of the future are seen as the desire to "be grown-up," his conflicts and instabilities are seen as the conflict between the desire to be grown-up and a role and personality not yet consistent with being grown-up.

This social role view of adolescence, the adolescent as teenager, places the instability of the adolescent self against the background of a stable society. Against the background of the moods and tantrums and dreams of the American teenager lay an unquestioned acknowledgment of the stability and reality of the social order the adolescent was to enter. Underneath the hedonism and rebellion of the teenager lay the conformist. Harold Teen and Andy Hardy's first law was conformity to the norms of the peer group. Beneath this conformity to the peer group, however, was the teenager's recognition that when the chips were down about your future you listened to dear old Dad. An extreme example in reality of the American image of the teenager as cutting up while basically conforming is a group of California suburban high school seniors of the late 1950's. This group celebrated graduation by a summer of well-planned robberies. Their one concern while they engaged in their delinquent activities was that if they were detected, they would not get into the college of their choice.

Conformity to the peer culture, then, was the first theme of the American treatment of the adolescent in the fifties, of August Hollingshead's *Elmtown's Youth*, James Coleman's *Adolescent Society*, Albert K. Cohen's *Delinquent Boys*. The second theme was that this peer culture was itself determined by the realities of adult social class and mobility in which the peer culture was embedded. Whether grind, jock or hood, glamour girl, sex kitten or Plain Jane, the teenager's discovery of self led to the enactment of the stock roles of the adolescent culture. At a different level than the sociology of the teenager, American literature also presented adolescence as accepting unquestioningly the reality of adult society. Adolescence was presented as an imaginative expansion of the innocence of childhood facing the sordid but unquestionable reality of adult life. From *Huckleberry Finn* to *Catcher in the Rye*, the true American adolescent brought the child's innocence to a new awareness of adult reality, leading to a vision of the phoniness and corruption of the adult world, which was, however, unquestioned in its reality. Sherwood Anderson's story of the fourteen-year-old finding his father figure with a prostitute is titled "I Want to Know Why." While

215

the American adolescent might be shocked by the sordid elements of adult life and might "want to know why" there was no question that he would eventually enter and accept "adult reality." Even when he wanted to know why, the American adolescent seldom questioned the American assumptions of progress and upward mobility, the assumption that society was moving ahead. Rather, he questioned the wisdom of his parents because they were old-fashioned. This questioning was itself an expression of faith in the adult society of the future. The adolescent's sense of the superiority of his values to those of his parents was an expression of the adolescent's belief in a greater closeness to the adult society of the future than his parents had; it was a faith in progress.

Today, we are aware of the possibility of a deeper questioning by the adolescent than was true at earlier times. Our image of the adolescent must accommodate to the phenomena of the counterculture, of the hippie and the revolutionary who does not believe in progress and upward mobility. Both the hippie and the New Left reject not only the *content* of adult society but its *forms*. The new radical refuses to organize as his revolutionary predecessors of the thirties did. Unlike the revolutionary of the thirties, he does not want to be a grownup, to really transform and govern the adult society of the future. And beneath a questioning of social *forms* is a questioning of social *functions*. The current radical rejection of adult society seems to be the rejection of any adult society whatever, if an adult society means one including institutions of work, family, law, and government. Radicals have always questioned the social *forms* of authority, of competitive achievement, and of the nuclear privatistic family and have dreamed of a more egalitarian and communal society. The essential realities of the social *functions* of work, child rearing, and of an organized social order were never questioned, however. Since Paul Goodman's *Growing Up Absurd*, we have been aware that the reality of work and making a living has come into question. Now the new ethics of population control and the Women's Liberation Movement leads to the questioning of the supreme reality of adulthood, being a parent and having children. Finally, the reality of social order is in question. When current adolescents talk of revolution, they do not seem to mean merely that adult society is evil and is resistant to rational change. More deeply, they seem to be saying that there is no real social order to destroy anyway. Social order is a myth or illusion in the adult's mind and revolution is not the destruction of an order, whether good or bad. On the optimistic side this is the message of Charles Reich's "revolution in consciousness," the idea that the young can transform society without entering or dealing with it. On the pessimistic side, the popular versions of the counterculture reiterate the theme of *Easy Rider*, the theme that the adult culture is hostile and absurd, that it does not want you to join it but that it envies you and will destroy you in the end no matter what you do.

To summarize, all accounts of adolescence stress both the sense of questioning and the parallel discovery or search for a new self of the adolescent. Usually this questioning and search for self has been seen as the product of the adolescent's marginal role between childhood and adulthood. Usually, too, it has been assumed that there are underlying givens beneath the questioning, that whatever uncertainties the adolescent has, he wants to be a grownup. Recent experience makes real for Americans the much deeper forms of questioning which may characterize adolescence, one which is not merely a matter of roles. The potential for a deeper questioning by the adolescent is implied by the identity conflict central to Erik Erikson's psychohistorical stage theory of adolescence. It is the philosophic doubting about truth, goodness, and reality implied by J. Piaget's epistemological stage theory of adolescence. It is the doubting represented by Dostoevsky's adolescents, not Mark Twain's. Deeper doubting is still a rare phenomenon, for adolescents. Beneath most hippie exteriors is an interior more like Harold Teen than Hamlet or Raskolnikov. But theoretical understanding of adolescence as a stage must stress its ideal type potential, not its "average" manifestations.

The importance of taking adolescent questioning seriously is not only important for psychological theory, it is also central to a successful resolution of the current problems of the American high school. For education, the problem of meaning just raised is the problem of whether the high school has meaning to the adolescent. We said that American psychology placed the adolescent discovery of the self against a stable but progressive social order. It saw the discovery of self within a desire to be "grown up," however confused or vague this image of the grownup was. The high school had a double meaning to the adolescent from this point of view. First, it was the locus of the peer culture in which he found his immediate identity, whether as grind, jock, or hood. Second, on the academic side, it was a point of connection to a place in the adult world. In most high schools these meanings still remain and the questioning of the reality of adulthood is not that deep. In others, however, it is a serious problem and high school is essentially a meaningless place. Before we can solve the problem of the felt meaninglessness of the high school, a clearer view of adolescent questioning is required. For this, we must turn to stage theory of the Erikson and Piaget variety.

The Meaning of the Stage Concept—Illustrated from the Preschool Years

To understand the universal meanings of adolescence as a stage and its implications for education, it will help to examine briefly an earlier stage and its implications for education, one more thoroughly understood than the stage of adolescence. Almost all cultures implicitly recognize two great stages or transformations in development. Adolescence, the second transformation, traditionally terminated compulsory schooling. The first transformation occurring from five to seven years of age initiated compulsory schooling.[1] This five-to-seven shift is termed the "onset of the latency period" by Freudian theory, the onset of concrete logical thought by Piaget. As embodied in educational thought, the Freudian interpretation of the five-to-seven shift implied letting the child grow, letting him work through his fantasies until he had repressed his sexual instincts and was ready to turn his energies into formal learning. This Freudian interpretation of the preschool stage suffered both from lack of confirmation by empirical research and from irrelevance to the intellectual development and everyday behavior with which the schools were concerned. When the Great Society decided to do something for the disadvantaged child, the Freudian "let him work through his oedipus complex" implications of the five-to-seven shift were dismissed as a luxury for the wealthy. Programs of preschool intellectual stimulation and academic schooling were initiated, with the expectation of long-range effects on intelligence and achievement. These programs failed to fulfill their initial hope of changing general intellectual maturity or long-range achievement.[2]

One reason they failed was because they confused specific teaching and learning with the development of new levels of thinking truly indicative of cognitive maturity. The evidence of limitations of these early education programs, together with growing positive research evidence of the existence of cognitive stages, convinced early educators of the reality of the stage transformation at the age five to seven. The stage transformation of the period five to seven is now conceived in quite a different way than in the vogue of Freudian education. In the Freudian view, the preschooler was in a stage of domination of thought by sexual and aggressive fantasies. The new stage which succeeded this was defined negatively as latency, rather than positively. Under the influence of Piaget, more recent thinking sees the preschool child's fantasy as only one aspect of the preschooler's pattern of prelogical thought. In the prelogical stage, subjective appearance is not fully distinguished from "reality"; the permanent identities of things are not differentiated from their momentary transformations. In the prelogical stage view, the preschool child's special fantasy is not the expression of an instinct later repressed but of a cognitive level of thought. The decline of fantasy in the years five to seven, longitudinally documented by R. Scheffler,[3] is not a repression; it is closely related to the positive development of concrete logical patterns of thought.

The child's changed orientation to reality in the five-to-seven period is part of the development of concrete logical operations then. During this period the child develops the operations of categorical classifications, of serial ordering, addition, subtraction, and inversion of classes and relations. This development occurs in the absence of schooling in African and Taiwanese villagers in much the same way that it occurs in the American suburban child.[4]

As a concrete example, Piaget and the writers have asked children if they had had a bad dream and if they were frightened when they woke up from their bad dream.[5] Susie, aged four, said she dreamt about a giant and answered, "Yes, I was scared, my tummy was shaking and I cried and told my mommy about the giant." Asked, "Was it a real giant or was it just pretend? Did the giant just seem to be there, or was it really there?" she answered, "It was really there but it left when I woke up. I saw its footprint on the floor."

According to Piaget, Susie's response is not to be dismissed as the product of a wild imagination, but represents the young child's general failure to differentiate subjective from objective components of his experience. Children go through a regular series of steps in their understanding of dreams as subjective phenomena. The first step, achieved before five by most American middle-class children, is the recognition that dreams are not real events. The next step, achieved soon thereafter, is the realization that dreams cannot be seen by others. The third step is the notion that dreams are internal (but still material) events.

By the ages six to eight children are clearly aware that dreams are thoughts caused by themselves. To say such cognitive changes define stages implies the following things:

(1) That young children's responses represent not mere ignorance or error, but rather a spontaneous manner of thinking about the world that is qualitatively different from the way we adults think and yet has a structure of its own.

(2) The notion of different developmental structures of thought implies consistency of level of response from task to task. If a child's response represents a general structure rather than a specific learning, then the child should demonstrate the same relative structural levels in a variety of tasks.

(3) The concept of stage implies an invariance of sequence in development, a regularity of stepwise progression regardless of cultural teaching or circumstance. Cultural teaching and experience can speed up or slow down development, but it cannot change its order or sequence.

The concept of stage, then, implies that both the youngest children's conceptions of the dream as real and the school age children's view of the dream as subjective are their own; they are products of the general state of the child's cognitive development, rather than the learning of adult teachings.

Cross-cultural studies indicate the universality of the basic sequence of development of thinking about the dream, even where adult beliefs about the meaning and significance of dreams is somewhat different from our own.[6] While the stage of concrete operations is culturally universal and in a sense natural, this does not mean it is either innate or that it is inevitable and will develop regardless of environmental stimulation. In the United States, the doctrine of stages was assumed for sometime to mean that children's behavior unfolded through a series of age-specific patterns, and that these patterns and their order were wired into the organism. This indeed was the view of Gesell and Freud, and Americans misunderstood Piaget as maintaining the same thing. The implications of the Gesellian and Freudian theory for early education were clear; early teaching and stimulation would do no good since we must wait for the unfolding of the behavior, or at least the unfolding of the readiness to learn it.

In contrast, Piaget used the existence of stages to argue that basic cognitive structures are not wired in, but are general forms of equilibrium resulting from the interaction between organism and environment. If children have their own logic, adult logic or mental structure cannot be derived from innate neurological patterning because such patterning should hold also in childhood. (It is hardly plausible to view a succession of logics as an evolutionary and functional program of innate wiring.) At the same time, however, Piaget argued that stages indicate that mental structure is not merely a reflection of external physical realities or of cultural concepts of different complexities. The structure of the child's concepts in Piaget's view is not only less complex than the adult's, it is also different. The child's thought is not just a simplified version of the adult's.

Stages, or mental structures, then, are not wired into the organism though they depend upon inborn organizing tendencies. Stages are not direct reflections of the child's culture and external world, though they depend upon experience for their formation. Stages are rather the products of interactional experience between the child and the world, experience which leads to a restructuring of the child's own organization rather than to the direct imposition of the culture's pattern upon the child. While hereditary components of I.Q., of the child's rate of information processing, have some influence on the rate at which the child moves through invariant cognitive sequences, experiential factors heavily influence the rate of cognitive-structural development.[7] The kind of experience which stimulates cognitive stage development is, however, very different from the direct academic teaching of information and skills which is the focus of ordinary schooling. Programs of early education which take account of cognitive stages, then, look neither like the permissive "let them grow" nursery school pattern nor like the early teaching programs popular in the sixties. They are a new form now coming into being.[8]

Cognitive Stages in Adolescence

The older children get, the more difficult it is to distinguish universal stage changes from sociocultural transitions in development. We said that the core phenomenon of adolescence as a stage was the discovery of the subjective self and subjective experience and a parallel questioning of adult cultural reality. The manifestations of this discovery, however, are heavily colored not only by historical and cultural variations, but also by previous patterns of life history of the child.

In our first section, we discussed one manifestation of the discovery of the self, the discovery of the body and its sexual drives. In part this is, of course, a biological universal, the physical growth spurt marking adolescent puberty and an accompanying qualitatively new sex drive. If there is anything which can be safely said about what is new in the minds of adolescents, it is that they, like their elders, have sex on their minds. These changes, of course, have been the focus of Freudian thinking about adolescence as a stage. If anything, however, Freudian thinking has underestimated the novel elements of sexual experience in adolescence. For the Freudian, early adolescent sexuality is the reawakening of early childhood sexuality previously latent, with a consequent resurrection of oedipal feeling. Although it is true that adolescent sexuality bears the stamp of earlier experience, it is not the resurrection of earlier sexual feelings. Adolescent sexual drive is a qualitatively new phenomenon.[9]

While sexual drives are awakened at puberty, there are vast individual and cultural variations in the extent to which they determine the adolescent's behavior and experience. Sexuality is a central concern for the self of some fourteen-year-olds; it is something deferred to the future for others. What is common for all, however, is an intensified emotionality whether experienced as sexual or not. This emotionality, too, is now experienced as a part of the self, rather than as a correlate of objective events in the world. C. Ellinwood studied the age development of the verbal experiencing and expression of emotion in projective tests and in free self-descriptions. She found that prior to adolescence (aged twelve or so), emotions were experienced as objective concomitants of activities and objects. The child experienced anger because events or persons were bad; he experienced affection because persons were good or giving; he felt excitement because activities were exciting or fun. At adolescence, however, emotions are experienced as the result of states of the self rather than as the direct correlate of external events.[10]

The difference may perhaps be clarified by reference to middle-class drug experiences. Occasionally, a psychological preadolescent may take drugs, as he may drink beer or sneak cigarettes. When he does this, he does this as an activity of an exciting forbidden and grown-up variety. For the adolescent drug-taker, drugs represent rather a vehicle to certain subjective moods, feelings, and sensations. In many cases, the drug experience is a vehicle for overcoming depression, felt as an inner subjective mood. In any case, drug-taking is not an activity with an objective quality; it is a mode of activating subjective inner feelings and states. The same is true of such activities as intensive listening to music, an activity characteristically first engaged in at early adolescence (ages eleven to fourteen). The rock, folk-rock, and blues music so popular with adolescents is explicitly a presentation of subjective mood and is listened to in that spirit.

Associated with the discovery of subjective feelings and moods is the discovery of ambivalence and conflicts of feeling. If feelings are objective correlates of external good and bad events, there can be little tolerance and acceptance of feeling hate and love for the same person, of enjoying sadness and feeling sad about pleasure. Ellinwood's study documents that adolescents are consciously expressing such ambivalence, which is of course the stock in trade of the blues and folk-rock music beamed to them.

We have spoken of the adolescent discovery of subjective moods and feelings as linked to puberty. More basically, it is linked to the universal cognitive stages of Piaget. We have said that the five-to-seven transition is defined by Piaget as the transition to *abstract, reflective* thought. More exactly, it is the transition from logical inference as a set of *concrete operations* to logical inference as a set of *formal operations* or "operations upon operations." "Operations upon operations" imply that the adolescent can classify classification, that he can combine combinations, that he can relate relationships. It implies that he can think about thought, and create thought systems or "hypothetico-deductive" theories. This involves the logical construction of all possibilities—that is, the awareness of the observed as only a subset of what may be logically possible. In related fashion, it implies the hypothetico-deductive attitude, the notion that a belief or proposition is not an immediate truth but a hypothesis whose truth value consists in the truth of the concrete propositions derivable from it.

An example of the shift from concrete to formal operations may be taken from the work of E. A. Peel.[11] Peel asked children what they thought about the following event: "Only brave pilots are allowed to fly over high mountains. A fighter pilot flying over the Alps collided with an aeriel cable-way, and cut a main cable causing some cars to fall to the glacier below. Several people were killed." A child at the concrete-operational level answered: "I think that the pilot was not very good at flying. He would have been better off if he went on fighting." A formal-operational child responded: "He was either not informed of the mountain railway on his route or he was flying too low also his flying compass may have been affected by something before or after take-off this setting him off course causing collision with the cable."

The concrete-operational child assumes that if there was a collision the pilot was a bad pilot; the formal-operational child considers all the possibilities that might have caused the collision. The concrete-operational child adopts the hypothesis that seems most probable or likely to him. The formal-operational child constructs all possibilities and checks them out one by one.

As a second example, we may cite one of Piaget's tasks, systematically replicated by D. Kuhn, J. Langer, and L. Kohlberg.[12] The child is shown a pendulum whose length may vary as well as the number of weights attached. The child is asked to discover or explain what determines the speed of movement (or "period") of the pendulum. Only the formal-operational child will "isolate variables," that is, vary length holding weight constant, and so forth, and arrive at the correct solution (for example, that period is determined by length). Success at the task is unrelated to relevant verbal knowledge about science or physics, but is a function of logical level.

In fact the passage from concrete to formal operations is not an all or none phenomenon. There are one or two substages of formal operations prior to the full awareness of all possibilities just described. These substages are described in table 1, which presents an overview of the Piaget cognitive stages. For simplifying purposes, we may say that for middle-class Americans, one stage of formal operations is reached at age ten to thirteen, while the consideration of all possibilities is reached around fifteen to sixteen. At the first formal-operational stage, children became capable of reversing relationships and ordering relationships one at a time or in chains, but not of abstract consideration of all possibilities. (They are capable of "forming the inverse of the reciprocal," in Piaget's terminology; but not of combining all relationships.) A social thinking example of failure to reverse relationships is shown in concrete-operational children's responses to the question: "What does the Golden Rule tell you to do if someone comes up on the street and hits you?" The typical answer is "hit him back, do unto others as they do unto you." The painful process of the transitional formal-operational child in response to the question is given by the following response: "Well for the Golden Rule you have to like dream that your mind leaves your body and goes into the other person, then it comes back into you and you see it like he does and you act like the way you saw it from there."[13]

We have described Piaget's stage of formal operations as a logical stage. What is of special importance for understanding adolescents, however, is not the logic of formal operations, but its epistemology, its conception of truth and reality. In the previous section we said that the child's attainment of concrete operations at age six to seven led to the differentiation of subjective and objective, appearance and reality. The differentiation at this level was one in which reality was equated with the physical and the external. We cited the child's concept of the dream, in which the unreality of the dream was equivalent to its definition as an inner mental event with no physical external correlate. The subjective and the mental are to the concrete-operational child equated with fantasies, with unrealistic replicas of external physical events. The development of formal operations leads, however, to a new view of the external and the physical. The external and the physical are only one set of many possibilities of a subjective experience. The external is no longer the real, "the objective," and the internal the "unreal." The internal may be real and the external unreal. At its extreme, adolescent thought entertains solipsism or at least the Cartesian cogito, the notion that the only thing real is the self. I asked a fifteen-year-old girl: "What is the most real thing to you?" Her unhesitating reply was "myself."

The lines from Wordsworth introducing this essay represent his own adolescent experience described by him as follows: "I was often unable to think of external things as having external existence, and I communed with all that I saw as something not apart from, but inherent in, my own material nature. Many times while going to school have I grasped at a wall or tree to recall myself from this abyss of idealism to the reality. At this time I was afraid of such processes."[14]

Wordsworth's adolescent solipsism was linked to his awakened poetic sense, to his experience of nature, and to his transcendental religiosity. It seems that for all adolescents the discovery of the subjective is a condition for aesthetic feeling in the adult sense, for the experience of nature as a contemplative experience, and for religiosity of a mystical varity. It is probably the condition for adolescent romantic love as well. This whole constellation of experiences is

Table 1. Piaget's eras and stages of logical and cognitive development.

Era I (age 0-2) The era of sensorimotor intelligence
Stage 1. Reflex action.
Stage 2. Coordination of reflexes and sensorimotor repetition (primary circular reaction).
Stage 3. Activities to make interesting events in the environment reappear (secondary circular reaction).
Stage 4. Means/ends behavior and search for absent objects.
Stage 5. Experimental search for new means (tertiary circular reaction).
Stage 6. Use of imagery in insightful invention of new means and in recall of absent objects and events.

Era II (age 2-5) Symbolic, intuitive, or prelogical thought
Inference is carried on through images and symbols which do not maintain logical relations or invariances with one another. "Magical thinking" in the sense of (a) confusion of apparent or imagined events with real events and objects and (b) confusion of perceptual appearances of qualitative and quantitative change with actual change.

Era III (age 6-10) Concrete operational thought
Inferences carried on through system of classes, relations, and quantities maintaining logically invariant properties and which *refer to concrete objects*. These include such logical processes as (a) inclusion of lower-order classes in higher order classes; (b) transitive seriation (recognition that if a > b and b > c, then a > c); (c) logical addition and multiplication of classes and quantities; (d) conservation of number, class membership, length, and mass under apparent change.
Substage 1. Formation of stable categorical classes.
Substage 2. Formation of quantitative and numerical relations of invariance.

Era IV (age 11 to adulthood) Formal-operational thought
Inferences through logical operations upon propositions or "operations upon operations." Reasoning about reasoning. Construction of systems of all possible relations or implications. Hypothetico-deductive isolation of variables and testing of hypotheses.
Substage 1. Formation of the inverse of the reciprocal. Capacity to form negative classes (for example, the class of all not-crows) and to see relations as simultaneously reciprocal (for example, to understand that liquid in a U-shaped tube holds an equal level because of counterbalanced pressures).
Substage 2. Capacity to order triads of propositions or relations (for example, to understand that if Bob is taller than Joe and Joe is shorter than Dick, then Joe is the shortest of the three).
Substage 3. True formal thought. Construction of all possible combinations of relations, systematic isolation of variables, and deductive hypothesis-testing.

called romantic because it is centered on a celebration of the self's experience as the self enters into union with the self's counterpart outside. The common view of romanticism as adolescent, then, is correct in defining the origins of romanticism in the birth of the subjective self in adolescence.

If the discovery of subjective experience and the transcendental self is one side of the new differentiation of subjective and objective made by the adolescent, the clouding and questioning of the validity of society's truths and its rightness is the other. To consider this side of adolescence we must turn from cognitive to moral stages.

Before we turn to adolescent moral thought we need to note a real difference between the development of concrete operations and the development of formal operations. There are two facts which distinguish the adolescent revolution in logical and epistemological thinking from the five-to-seven revolution in thinking. The first is that the adolescent revolution is extremely variable as to time. The second is that for many people it never occurs at all. With regard to concrete operations, some children attain clear capacity for logical reasoning at five, some at eight or nine. But all children ultimately display some clear capacity for concrete-logical reasoning.[15] This is not true for formal-operational reasoning. As an example, the percentage of 265 persons at various ages showing clear formal-operational reasoning at the pendulum task is as follows:

Age ten to fifteen: 45 per cent
Age sixteen to twenty: 53 per cent
Age twenty-one to thirty: 65 per cent
Age forty-five to fifty: 57 per cent[16]

The subjects studied were lower-middle and upper-middle-class California parents (age forty-five to fifty) and their children (age ten to thirty). The figures indicate that it is not until age twenty-one to thirty that a clear majority (65 per cent) attain formal reasoning by this criteria. They suggest that there is no further development of formal reasoning after age thirty. This means that almost 50 per cent of American adults never reach adolescence in the cognitive sense. The figures should not be taken with too great seriousness, since various tasks requiring formal operations are of somewhat varying difficulty. In the study cited another problem, a "correlation problem," was used which was passed by even fewer members of the adult population. It is possible that easier tasks could be devised which would lead to more people displaying formal reasoning. The point, however, is that a large proportion of Americans never develop the capacity for abstract thought. Most who do, develop it in earlier adolescence (age eleven to fifteen), but some do not reach full formal reasoning until the twenties. We should note, too, that rate of attainment of formal operations is not simply a function of I.Q.: the correlations between Piaget and I.Q. measures are in the 50's. Finally, in simpler cultures—for example, villages in Turkey—full formal operations never seem to be reached at all (though it is reached by urbanized educated Turks).

The high variability in age of attainment of formal operations, then, indicates that we cannot equate a cognitive stage with a definite age period. Puberty, the attainment of formal operations, and the transition from childhood to adult status are all components of adolescence variable in time and in their relations to one another.

Moral Stages in Adolescence and Their Relation to Cognitive Stages

Joseph Adelson, in this volume, documents the way in which the adolescent's thinking about political society is transformed by the advent of formal-operational thought. To understand the adolescent's social thinking, however, we need to be aware not only of logical stages but also of stages of moral judgment. In our research, we have found six definite and universal stages of development in moral thought. In our longitudinal study of seventy-six American boys from preadolescence, youths were presented with hypothetical moral dilemmas, all deliberately philosophical, some of them found in medieval works of causistry.

On the basis of their reasoning about these dilemmas at a given age, each boy's stage of moral thought could be determined for each of twelve basic moral concepts, values, or issues. The six stages of moral thought are divided into three major levels, the *preconventional*, the *conventional*, and the *postconventional* or autonomous.

While the preconventional child is often "well-behaved" and is responsive to cultural labels of good and bad, he interprets these labels in terms of their physical consequences (punishment, reward, exchange of favors) or in terms of the physical power of those who enunciate the rules and labels of good and bad. This level is usually occupied in the middle class by children aged four to ten.

The second or conventional level usually becomes dominant in preadolescence. Maintaining the expectation and rules of the individual's family, group, or nation is perceived as valuable in its own right. There is concern not only with conforming to the individual's social order, but also in maintaining, supporting, and justifying this order.

The postconventional level is first evident in adolescence and is characterized by a major thrust toward autonomous moral principles which have validity and application apart from authority of the groups or persons who hold them and apart from the individual's identification with those persons or groups.

Within each of these three levels there are two discernable stages. At the preconventional level we have: Stage 1: Orientation toward punishment and unquestioning deference to superior power. The physical consequences of action regardless of their human meaning or value determine its goodness or badness. Stage 2: Right action consists of that which instrumentally satisfies one's own needs and occasionally the needs of others. Human relations are viewed in terms like those of the market place. Elements of fairness, reciprocity, and equal sharing are present, but they are always interpreted in a physical, pragmatic way. Reciprocity is a matter of "you scratch my back and I'll scratch yours," not of loyalty, gratitude, or justice.

At the conventional level we have: Stage 3: Good-boy-good-girl orientation. Good behavior is that which pleases or helps others and is approved by them. There is much conformity to stereotypical images of what is majority or "natural" behavior. Behavior is often judged by intention—"he means well" becomes important for the first time and is overused. One seeks approval by being "nice." Stage 4: Orientation toward authority, fixed rules, and the maintenance of the social order. Right behavior consists of doing one's duty, showing respect for authority, and maintaining the given social order for its own sake. One earns respect by performing dutifully.

At the postconventional level we have: Stage 5A: A social-contract orientation, generally with legalistic and utilitarian overtones. Right action tends to be defined in terms of general rights and in terms of standards which have been critically examined and agreed upon by the whole society. There is a clear awareness of the relativism of personal values and opinions and a corresponding emphasis upon procedural rules for reaching consensus. Aside from what is constitutionally agreed upon, right or wrong is a matter of personal values and opinion. The result is an emphasis upon the legal point of view, but with an emphasis upon the possibility of changing law in terms of rational considerations of social utility, rather than freezing it in the terms of Stage 4, law and order. Outside the legal realm, free agreement and contract are the binding elements of obligation. This is the official morality of American government, and finds its ground in the thought of the writers of the Constitution. Stage 5B: Orientation to internal decisions of conscience but without clear rational or universal principles. Stage 6: Orientation toward ethical principles appealing to logical comprehensiveness, universality, and consistency. These principles are abstract and ethical (the Golden Rule, the categorical imperative); they are not concrete moral rules like the Ten Commandments. Instead, they are universal principles of justice, of the reciprocity and equality of human rights, and of respect for the dignity of human beings as individual persons.

These stages are defined by twelve basic issues of moral judgment. On one such issue, Conscience, Motive Given for Rule Obedience or Moral Action, the six stages look like this:

1. Obey rules to avoid punishment.
2. Conform to obtain rewards, have favors returned, and so on.
3. Conform to avoid disapproval, dislike by others.
4. Conform to avoid censure by legitimate authorities and resultant guilt.

5A. Conform to maintain the respect of the impartial spectator judging in terms of community welfare.

5B. Conform to avoid self-condemnation.

In another of these moral issues, the value of human life, the six stages can be defined thus:

1. The value of a human life is confused with the value of physical objects and is based on the social status or physical attributes of its possessor.

2. The value of a human life is seen as instrumental to the satisfaction of the needs of its possessor or of other persons.

3. The value of a human life is based on the empathy and affection of family members and others toward its possessor.

4. Life is conceived as sacred in terms of its place in a categorical moral or religious order of rights and duties.

5. Life is valued both in terms of its relation to community welfare and in terms of being a universal human right.

6. Belief in the sacredness of human life as representing a universal human value of respect for the individual.

We call our types "stages" because they seem to represent an invariant developmental sequence. True stages come one at a time and always in the same order.

All movement is forward in sequence and does not skip steps. Children may move through these stages at varying speeds, of course, and may be found half in and half out of a particular stage. An individual may stop at any given stage and at any age, but if he continues to move, he must move in accord with these steps. Moral reasoning of the conventional or Stage 3-4 kind never occurs before the preconventional Stage 1 and Stage 2 thought has taken place. No adult in Stage 4 has gone through Stage 6, but all Stage 6 adults have gone at least through 4.

While the evidence is not complete, our study strongly suggests that moral change fits the stage pattern just described. Figures 1 and 2 indicate the cultural universality of the sequence of stages which we found. Figure 1 presents the age trends for middle-class urban boys in the United States, Taiwan, and Mexico. At age ten in each country, the order of use of each stage is the same as the order of its difficulty or maturity. In the United States, by age sixteen the order is the reverse, from the highest to the lowest, except that Stage 6 is still little used. The results in Mexico and Taiwan are the same, except that development is a little slower. The most conspicuous feature is that at the age of sixteen, Stage 5 thinking is much more salient in the United States than in Mexico or Taiwan. Nevertheless, it is present in the other countries, so we know that this is not purely an American democratic construct.

Why should there be such a universal invariant sequence of development? In answering this question, we need first to analyze these developing social concepts in terms of their internal logical structure. At each stage, the same basic moral concept or aspect is defined, but at each higher stage this definition is more differentiated, more integrated, and more general or universal. When one's concept of human life moves from Stage 1 to Stage 2 the value of life becomes more differentiated from the value of property, more integrated (the value of life enters an organizational hierarchy where it is "higher" than property so that one steals property in order to save life) and more universalized (the life of any sentient being is valuable regardless of status or property). The same advance is true at each stage in the hierarchy. Each step of development, then, is a better cognitive organization than the one before it, one which takes account of everything present in the previous stage, but making new distinctions and organizing them into a more comprehensive or more equilibrated structure.

What is the relation of moral stage development in adolescence to cognitive stage development? In Piaget's and our view, both types of thought and types of valuing (or of feeling) are schemata which develop a set of general structural characteristics representing successive forms of psychological equilibrium. The equilibrium of affective and interpersonal schemata, justice or fairness, involves many of the same basic structural features as the equilibrium of cognitive schemata logicality. Justice (portrayed as balancing the scales) is a form of equilibrium between conflicting interpersonal claims, so that "in contrast to a given rule imposed upon the child from outside, the rule of justice is an imminent condition of social relationships or a law governing their equilibrium."[17]

What is being asserted, then, is not that moral judgment stages are cognitive—they are not the mere application of logic to moral problems—but that the existence of moral stages implies that normal development has a basic cognitive-structural component.

The Piagetian rationale just advanced suggests that cognitive maturity is a necessary, but not a sufficient condition for moral judgment maturity. While formal operations may be necessary for principled morality, one may be a theoretical physicist and yet not make moral judgments at the principled level.

As noted in the previous section, Kuhn, Langer, and Kohlberg found that 60 per cent of persons over sixteen had attained formal operational thinking (by their particular measures). Only 10 per cent of subjects over sixteen showed clear principled (Stages 5 and 6) thinking, but all these 10 per cent were capable of formal-opera-

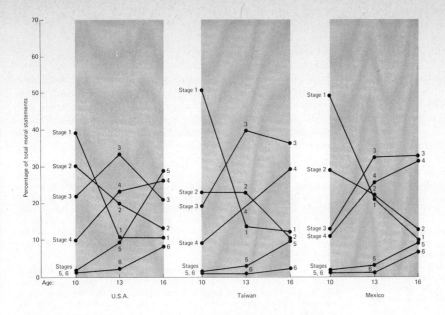

1. Middle-class urban boys in the U.S., Taiwan and Mexico (above). At age 10 the stages are used according to difficulty. At age 13, Stage 3 is most used by all three groups. At age 16 U.S. boys have reversed the order of age 10 stages (with the exception of 6). In Taiwan and Mexico, conventional (3-4) stages prevail at age 16, with Stage 5 also little used.

2. Two isolated villages, one in Turkey, the other in Yucatan, show similar patterns in moral thinking. There is no reversal of order, and preconventional (1-2) thought does does not gain a clear ascendancy over conventional stages at age 16.

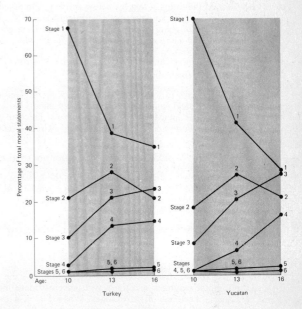

tional logical thought. More generally, there is a point-to-point correspondence between Piaget logical and moral judgment stages, as indicated in table 2. The relation is that attainment of the logical stage is a necessary but not sufficient condition for attainment of the moral stage. As we shall note in the next section, the fact that many adolescents have formal logical capacities without yet having developed the corresponding degree of moral judgment maturity is a particularly important background factor in some of the current dilemmas of adolescents.

Adolescent Questioning and the Problem of Relativity of Truth and Value

The cornerstone of a Piagetian interpretation of adolescence is the dramatic shift in cognition from concrete to formal operations by which old conceptions of the world are restructured in terms of a new philosophy. Piaget defined the preschool child as a philosopher, revolutionizing child psychology by demonstrating that the child at each stage of development actively organizes his experience and makes sense of the physical and social world with which he interacts in terms of the classical categories and questions of philosophers concerning space, time, causality, reality, and so on. It is, however, only in adolescence that the child becomes a philosopher in the formal or traditional sense. This emergence of philosophic

questioning has been studied most carefully in the moral realm.

The transition from preconventional to conventional morality generally occurs during the late elementary school years. The shift

Table 2.   Relations between Piaget logical stages and
Kohlberg moral stages.
(all relations are that attainment of the logical stages is necessary,
but not sufficient, for attainment of the moral stage)

Logical stage	Moral stage
Symbolic, intuitive thought	*Stage 0:* The good is what I want and like.
Concrete operations, Substage 1 Categorical classification	*Stage 1:* Punishment-obedience orientation.
Concrete operations, Substage 2 Reversible concrete thought	*Stage 2:* Instrumental hedonism and concrete reciprocity.
Formal operations, Substage 1 Relations involving the inverse of the reciprocal	*Stage 3:* Orientation to interpersonal relations of mutuality.
Formal operations, Substage 2	*Stage 4:* Maintenance of social order, fixed rules, and authority.
Formal operations, Substage 3	*Stage 5A:* Social contract, utilitarian law-making perspective.
	Stage 5B: Higher law and conscience orientation.
	Stage 6: Universal ethical principle orientation.

in adolescence from concrete to formal operations, the ability now to see the given as only a subset of the possible and to spin out the alternatives, constitutes the necessary precondition for the transition from conventional to principled moral reasoning. It is in adolescence, then, that the child has the cognitive capability for moving from a conventional to a postconventional, reflective, or philosophic view of values and society.

The rejection of conventional moral reasoning begins with the perception of relativism, the awareness that any given society's definition of right and wrong, however legitimate, is only one among many, both in fact and theory. To clarify the issue of moral relativism as perceived by an adolescent, we will consider some adolescent responses to the following dilemma:

In Europe, a woman was near death from a very bad disease, a special kind of cancer. There was one drug that the doctors thought might save her. It was a form of radium that a druggist in the same town had recently discovered. The drug was expensive to make, but the druggist was charging ten times what the drug cost him to make. He paid $200 for the radium and charged $2,000 for a small dose of the drug. The sick woman's husband, Heinz, went to everyone he knew to borrow the money, but he could only get together about $1,000 which was half of what it cost. He told the druggist that his wife was dying, and asked him to sell it cheaper or let him pay later. But the druggist said, "No, I discovered the drug and I'm going to make money from it." Heinz got desperate and broke into the man's store to steal the drug for his wife.

Should the husband have done that? Was it right or wrong? Bob, a junior in a liberal private high school, says:

There's a million ways to look at it. Heinz had a moral decision to make. Was it worse to steal or let his wife die? In my mind I can either condemn him or condone him. In this case I think it was fine. But possibly the druggist was working on a capitalist morality of supply and demand.

I went on to ask Bob, "Would it be wrong if he did not steal it?"

It depends on how he is oriented morally. If he thinks it's worse to steal than to let his wife die, then it would be wrong what he did. It's all relative, what I would do is steal the drug. I can't say that's right or wrong or that it's what everyone should do.

Bob started the interview by wondering if he could answer because he "questioned the whole terminology, the whole moral bag." He goes on:

But then I'm also an incredible moralist, a real puritan in some sense and moods. My moral judgment and the way I perceive things morally changes very much when my mood changes. When I'm in a cynical mood, I take a cynical view of morals, but still whether I like it or not, I'm terribly moral in the way I look at things. But I'm not too comfortable with it.

Here are some other juniors from an upper-middle-class public high school:

Dan: Immoral is strictly a relative term which can be applied to almost any thought on a particular subject . . . if you have a man and a woman in bed, that is immoral as opposed to if you were a Roman a few thousand years ago and you were used to orgies all the time, that would not be immoral. Things vary so when you call something immoral, it's relative to that society at that time and it varies frequently. [Are there any circumstances in which wrong in some abstract moral sense would be applicable?] Well, in that sense, the only thing I could find wrong would be when you were hurting somebody against their will.

Elliot: I think one individual's set of moral values is as good as the next individual's . . . I think you have a right to believe in what you believe in, but I don't think you have a right to enforce it on other people.

John: I don't think anybody should be swayed by the dictates of society. It's probably very much up to the individual all the time and there's no general principle except when the views of society seem to conflict with your views and your opportunities at the moment and it seems that the views of society don't really have any basis as being right and in that case, most people, I think, would tend to say forget it and I'll do what I want.

The high school students just quoted are, from the point of view of moral stage theory, in a transitional zone. They understand and can use conventional moral thinking, but view it as arbitrary and relative. They do not yet have any clear understanding of, or com-

mitment to, moral principles which are universal, which have a claim to some nonrelative validity. Insofar as they see any "principles" as nonrelative, it is the principle of "do your own thing, and let others do theirs." This "principle" has a close resemblance to the "principles" characteristic of younger children's Stage 2 instrumental egoistic thinking. The following examples of a ten-year-old naïve egoist and a college student transition relativistic response are more clearly of this instrumental egoistic form.

Jimmy (American city, age 10): It depends on how much he loved his wife. He should if he does. [If he doesn't love her much?] If he wanted her to die, I don't think he should. [Would it be right to steal?] In a way it's right because he knew his wife would die if he didn't and it would be right to save her. [Does the druggist have the right to charge that much if no law?] Yes, it's his drug, look at all he's got invested in it. [Should the judge punish?] He should put him in jail for stealing and he should put the druggist in because he charged so much and the drug didn't work.

Roger (Berkeley Free Speech Movement student, age 20): He was a victim of circumstances and can only be judged by other men whose varying value and interest frameworks produce subjective decisions which are neither permanent nor absolute. The same is true of the druggist. I'd do it. As far as duty, a husband's duty is up to the husband to decide, and anybody can judge him, and he can judge anybody's judgment. If he values her life over the consequences of theft, he should do it. [Did the druggist have a right?] One can talk about rights until doomsday and never say anything. Does the lion have a right to the zebra's life when he starves? When he wants sport? Or when he will take it at will? Does he consider rights? Is man so different? [Should he be punished by the judge?] All this could be avoided if the people would organize a planned economy. I think the judge should let him go, but if he does, it will provide less incentive for the poorer people to organize.

Relativity, Moral Stages, and Ego Identity

We first came across extreme relativist responses in some of our longitudinal subjects shortly after college entrance in the early sixties.[18] At that time, we interpreted their responses as a regression to Stage 2 thinking. Fifteen per cent of our college bound male students who were a mixture of conventional (Stage 4) and social-compact-legalist (Stage 5) thought at the end of high school, "retrogressed" to an apparent Stage 2 instrumentalist pattern in college.

In terms of behavior, everyone of our retrogressed subjects had high moral character ratings in high school, as defined by both teachers and peers. In college at least half had engaged in anticonventional acts of a more or less delinquent sort. As an example a Stage 2 Nietzschean had been the most respected high school student council president in years. In his college sophomore interview, however, he told how two days before he had stolen a gold watch from a friend at work. He had done so, he said, because his friend was just too good, too Christ-like, too trusting, and he wanted to teach him what the world was like. He felt no guilt about the stealing, he said, but he did feel frustrated. His act had failed, he said, because his trusting friend insisted he lost or mislaid the watch and simply refused to believe it had been stolen.

The forces of development which led our 20 per cent from upstanding conventional morality to Raskolnikov moral defiance eventually set them all to right. Every single one of our "retrogressors" had returned to a Stage 5 morality by age twenty-five, with more Stage 5 social-contract principle, less Stage 4 or convention, than in high school. All, too, were conventionally moral in behavior, at least as far as we can observe them. In sum, this 20 per cent was among the highest group at high school, was the lowest in college, and again among the highest at twenty-five.

In other words, moral relativism and nihilism, no matter how extensive, seemed to be a transitional attitude in the movement from conventional to principled morality.

Cognitive Moral Stages and Ego-Identity

In considering further the meaning of relativism in adolescence, it is helpful to relate logical and moral stages to Erikson's stages of ego-identity. Logical and moral stages are structures of thought through which the child moves sequentially. Erikson's stages are rather segments of the life histories of individuals; they define the central concerns of persons in a developmental period. An adolescent does not know or care that he is moving from concrete to formal thought; he knows and cares that he is having an Erikson "identity crisis."

Cognitive-developmental stages are stages of structure, not of content. The stages tell us *how* the child thinks concerning good and bad, truth, love, sex, and so forth. They do not tell us *what* he thinks about, whether he is preoccupied with morality or sex or achievement. They do not tell us what is on the adolescent's mind, but only how he thinks about what is on his mind. The dramatic changes in adolescence are not changes in structure, but changes in content. The adolescent need not know or care he is going from conventional to principled moral thinking, but he does know and care that sex is on his mind. In this sense cognitive structural stages may be contrasted with both psychosexual and Eriksonian stages.[19]

When we turn to Erikson's ego stages, we are partly dealing with a logical sequence as in logical and moral stages. Within Erikson's stages is the logical necessity that every later disposition presupposes each prior disposition, that each is a differentiation of prior dispositions. Erikson's ego stage centers around a series of forms of self-esteem (or their inverse, negative self-esteem). The first polarity trust-mistrust is one in which self and other are not differentiated. Trust is a positive feeling about self-and-other; mistrust is a negative feeling. The next polarity, autonomy versus shame, involves the self-other differentiation. Autonomy is a trust in the self (as opposed to the other); shame is a depreciation of self in the eyes of another whose status remains intact. Shame, however, is itself a failure to differentiate what one is from what one is in the eyes of the other, a differentiation implied in the sense of guilt. Similarly, initiative (I can be like him, it's all right to be or do it) is a differentiation from autonomy (I can do it). Such sequential progressive differentiations in self-esteem are involved throughout the Erikson stages. While there is an inherent logical (as opposed to biological) sequence to the Erikson ego stages, they are not hierarchical in the way cognitive stages are. Resolutions of identity problems are not also resolutions of trust or initiative problems, that is, each of the earlier problems and dispositions persists rather than being integrated into or being hierarchically dominated by the next. As a result, when we turn to Erikson's stages as defining focal concerns, we have a stage scheme which is so multidimensional as to resist empirical proof in the sense in which Piagetian stages may be proved. Ultimately the Erikson stages are "ideal-typical" in Weber's sense. They are not universal abstractions from data, but purifications and exaggerations of typical life histories. They do not predict regularities in the data, they aid in establishing historical connections in case histories. As Erikson uses his stage schema, it helps to suggest historical connections in a particular life, like Luther's. The truth of the stage schema is not in question; the truth of particular historical connections is. The stage schema helps select and illuminate these historical connections. In this sense, the stage of identity formation is not a step in an abstract but observable universal sequence, but is an ideal-typical characterization for a concrete historical period of adolescence.

As such, it need not have any exact logical relation to logical and moral stages, as they must to one another. While Erikson's stages cannot be defined, measured, or logically handled in the same sense as cognitive-developmental stages, suggestive empirical relations between ego-identity terms and moral stages are found.

M. H. Podd[20] gave an ego-identity interview to 134 male college juniors and seniors as well as the moral judgment interview. Following J. E. Marcia,[21] the identity interview covered occupational choice, religious beliefs, and political ideology. "Crisis" and "commitment" are assessed in each of these areas and serve to define each identity status. When an individual undergoes active consideration of alternative goals and values he is said to have experienced a "crisis." "Commitment" is the extent to which an individual

has invested himself in his choices. The identity statuses operationally defined are: (1) identity achievement—has gone through a crisis and is committed; (2) moratorium—is in crisis with vague commitments; (3) foreclosure—has experienced no crisis but is committed to goals and values of parents or significant others; (4) identity diffusion—has no commitment regardless of crisis.

Subjects in the Podd study could be grouped into three major groups, the conventional (Stages 3 and 4), the principled (Stages 5 and 6), and the transitional. The transitional subjects could in turn be divided into two groups, those who were a combination of conventional and principled thinking and the extreme relativists who rejected conventional thought and used more instrumental egoistic ("Stage 2") modes. Two-thirds of the principled subjects had an "identity achievement" status. So too did about 40 per cent of the conventional subjects, the remainder being mainly in "identity foreclosure" (a status missing among the principled). None of the morally transitional subjects had an identity achievement status, and very few had foreclosed identity questioning.

Essentially, then, morally transitional subjects were in transition with regard to identity issues as well as moral issues. Stated slightly differently, to have questioned conventional morality you must have questioned your identity as well, though you may continue to hold a conventional moral position after having done so.

The impact of the Podd study is that the relativistic questioning of conventional morality and conventional reality associated with logical and moral stage development is also central to the adolescent's identity concerns. As a corollary, morally conventional subjects have a considerable likelihood of never having an identity crisis or an identity questioning at all. Erikson's picture of an adolescent stage of identity crisis and its resolutions, then, is a picture dependent upon attainment of formal logical thought and of questioning of conventional morality. It fits best, then, the picture of adolescence in the developmentally elite and needs further elaboration for other adolescents.

Historical Change in Adolescent Relativism

We have linked adolescent relativism to a transition from conventional to principled morality, associated with identity crisis. This picture emerged most clearly from our longitudinal data from the late fifties and early sixties reported in the Kohlberg and Kramer article (see note 18). In this data only a small minority of college students entered a phase of moral nihilism and relativism in the transition from conventional to principled morality. Typically they attempted to construct or select an ideology of their own in this transitional phase, ideologies which ranged from Nietzschean racism to Ayn Rand objectivism to early S.D.S. New Left formulations. In these college subjects of the early sixties it was possible to see an intense identity crisis, in Erikson's terms. These college relativist-egoists were rare, and they all seemed to have been moralistic and guilt prone in high school. As part of their identity crisis, they seem to have had strong problems in freeing themselves from childhood moral expectations and guilt.

There were two universal developmental challenges to conventional morality to which these "regressors" were also responding: first, the relativity of moral expectations and opinion; second, the gap between conventional moral expectations and actual moral behavior. It is clear that these developmental challenges are universal challenges; the integration of one's moral ideology with the facts of moral diversity and inconsistency is a general "developmental task" of youth in an open society; its solution is the formation of a universal principled morality.

For our extreme relativists or amoralists, there seemed to be an additional task in the need to free themselves from their own early "rigid" morality. In Erikson's terms our retrogressors were living in a late adolescent psychosocial moratorium, in which new and nonconforming patterns of thought and behavior are tried out. Their return to morality or moral thought is the eventual confirmation of an earlier identification as one's own identity. To find a sociomoral identity requires a rebellious moratorium, because it requires liberation of initiative from the guilt from which our retrogressors suffer. At the "stage" of identity the adult conforms to his standards because he wants to, not because he anticipates crippling guilt if he does not.

By the 1970's the extreme doubt and relativism which earlier characterized only a minority of college students appears both earlier and much more pervasively. It is now sometimes found toward the end of high school.[22] In our own Harvard undergraduate course for freshmen and sophomores, about two-thirds of the students assert that there are no such things as valid moral rules or principles, no objective sense in which one thing is morally better than another. It appears that a majority rather than a minority of adolescents now are aware of relativism and of postconventional questioning, though it is still a minority who really attempt postconventional or principled solutions to these questions.

Parallel historical changes seem to have occurred in the relationship of extreme moral relativism to identity issues. Podd's findings from the *late* sixties differed from those of Kohlberg and Kramer in the *early* sixties in one important way. Kohlberg and Kramer found their extreme relativists, the Stage 2 or regressed subjects, in a condition of moratorium, in a state of "crisis" with vague and uncertain commitments. In contrast, Podd found them in a condition of identity diffusion with no sense of commitment and not necessarily a sense of crisis. In other words, extreme relativism no longer appeared to be a temporary ego-developmental maneuver of a small group of subjects in crisis, but rather to represent a more stable, less crisis-like pattern of low commitment. It seems likely to us that the psychological meaning of extreme relativism had changed in the five to ten years between the data reported by Kohlberg and Kramer (1969). Extreme relativism is no longer the struggle for independence from a strongly internal conventional morality in a period of moratorium and crisis in one's identity.

The relativistic rejection of convention, once individuality and spontaneously developed by adolescents in the course of reflecting on their own experience, is now manufactured as a cultural industry called the "counterculture." Further, the adult culture itself offers a very unsteady counter to the counterculture, particularly from the viewpoint of the adolescent to whom it offers a dwindling number of jobs and a world already overcrowded and crying out for less rather than more. It is clearly seen that one result of affluence, technology, and increased longevity has been to decrease the need of the adult community for its adolescents. Instead, it has some stake in keeping them in the youth culture since in one sense they only further threaten an already defensive adult world with fewer jobs and still more people. Thus the adults at once produce and market a counterculture and present themselves as a less than appealing alternative to it.

From the point of view of the adolescent, the counterculture has other meanings. The rejection of the conventional culture can be seen as a rebellion which can either turn into submission spelled backwards, or into the formation of principles. In our terms, the former remains conventional in form with only the content changed by being stood on its head. Although the impetus for the counterculture may have been once either principled or the expression of young people in identity crisis, the manufacture of the counterculture transforms it into yet another conventional system, although one lacking the solidity of the traditional conventional society.

While only a minority of adolescents actually have a postconventional view of morality and society, many more live in a postconventional culture or society. As a specific example, the majority of a sample of Haight-Ashbury hippies[23] emerge as mixtures of preconventional Stage 2 and conventional Stage 3 thinking. While hippie culture appears to be postconventional, it is almost entirely a mixture of Stage 2 "do your own thing" and Stage 3 "be nice, be loving" themes. The hippie culture continually questions conventional morality but on Stage 3 grounds of its being harsh and mean, or Stage 2 grounds of "Why shouldn't I have fun?" rather than in terms of its irrationality. Many hippies, then, belong to a counter-

culture which is largely conventional in its appeal but which lacks the solidarity of traditional conventional society and is not embedded in it. As moral counterculture, the hippie culture differs primarily from the conventional culture in its extreme relativism and consequent fluidity, not in any positive forms of moral thought different from the conventional.

In most eras of the past, the adolescent went through questioning of value, meaning, and truth in a world of adults apparently oblivious to these doubts. Reflective adolescents have always considered adults as benighted for accepting conventional norms and imposing them on youth, for never doubting the truth and goodness of their world. The questioning adolescent has always seen the adult acceptance of the conventional social world as reflecting the hypocrisy, insensitivity, and dreariness of the adult. Equally, the questioning adolescent has always expected to remake the adult world nearer to his heart's desire, and at given moments in history has succeeded. What is new is the creation of a questioning culture providing half-answers to which adolescents are exposed prior to their own spontaneous questioning.

The adolescent is faced then with not one but two cultures offering alternative ideologies and ways to live. Both present resolutions to the postconventional doubt which now appears to be so pervasive. Both may be embraced in our sense conventionally for the set of answers they provide, or may be seen in principled terms, their validity as social systems resting on the principles of justice they more or less successfully embody.

Implications for Education

The extreme relativism of a considerable portion of high school adolescents provides both a threat to current educational practice and a potentiality for a new focus of education.

We said earlier that the five-to-seven shift has been traditionally represented in education by the beginning of formal schooling. The traditional educational embodiment of the adolescent shift has been a different one, that of a two-track educational system dividing adolescents into two groups, an elite capable of abstract thought and hence of profiting from a liberal education and the masses who are not. At first, this division was made between the wealthy and those who went to work. As public high schools developed, the tracking system instead became that of an academic school or lycee leading to the university and a vocational school. The clearest formulation of this two-track system as based on the dawn of abstract thought was found in the British 11+ system. Based on his score on an intelligence test given at the dawn of adolescence, a child was assigned to either a grammar (academic) or a modern (vocational-commercial) high school.

The aristocratic tracking system just described rested on the assumption that the capacity for abstract thought is all or none, that it appears at a fixed age, and that it is hereditarily limited to an elite group in the population. The evidence on formal operational thought does not support these assumptions. However, when democratic secondary education ignored the existence of the adolescent cognitive shift and individual differences in their attainment, real difficulties emerged. Most recently this ignoral occurred in the wave of high school curriculum reform of the late fifties and early sixties in America, the "new math," the "new science," and the "new social studies." These curricula reforms were guided by the notion that more intellectual content could be put into high school and that this content should not be factual content and rote skills, but the basic pattern of thinking of the academic disciplines of mathematics, physics, or social science. The focus was to be upon understanding the basic logical assumptions and structure of the discipline and the use of these assumptions in reflective or critical thinking and problem-solving. Clearly the new curricula assumed formal-operational thought, rather than attempting to develop it. Partly as a result of this ignoral, some of the most enlightened proponents of the new curricula became discouraged as they saw only a subgroup of the high school population engaging with it. The solution we have proposed is that the new curricula be reformulated as tools for developing principled logical and moral thought rather than presupposing it.[24]

Experimental work by our colleagues and ourselves[25] has shown that even crude efforts based on such objectives are challenging and are successful in inducing considerable upward stage movement in thought. Hopefully, our efforts are the beginning of reformulating the "new" high school science, mathematics, social studies, and literature as approaches using "disciplines" as vehicles for the stimulation of the development of thought, rather than making young Ph.D.'s.

The difficulties and failures of the new curricula and of the general movement to democratize higher learning or liberal education, then, is not due to hereditary differences in capacity used to justify the two-track system. They represent, instead, the failure of secondary education to take developmental psychology seriously. When stage development is taken seriously by educators as an aim, real developmental change can occur through education.

In saying this, we return to the thought of John Dewey which is at the heart of a democratic educational philosophy. According to Dewey, education was the stimulation of development through stages by providing opportunities for active thought and active organization of experience.

The only solid ground of assurance that the educator is not setting up impossible artificial aims, that he is not using ineffective and perverting methods, is a clear and definite knowledge of the normal end and focus of mental action. Only knowledge of the order and connection of the stages in the development of the psychical functions can, negatively, guard against those evils, or positively, insure the full maturation and free, yet, orderly, exercises of the physical powers. Education is precisely the work of supplying the conditions which will enable the psychical functions, as they successively arise, to mature and pass into higher functions in the freest and fullest manner. This result can be secured only by a knowledge of the process of development, that is only by a knowledge of "psychology."[26]

Besides a clear focus on development, an aspect of Dewey's educational thought which needs revival is that school experience must be and represent real life experience in stimulating development. American education in the twentieth century was shaped by the victory of Thorndike over Dewey. Achievement rather than development has been its aim. But now the achieving society, the achieving individual, and even the achievement tests are seriously questioned, by adults and adolescents alike. If development rather than achievement is to be the aim of education, such development must be meaningful or real to the adolescent himself. In this sense education must be sensed by the adolescent as aiding him in his search for identity, and it must deal with life. Neither a concern with self or with life are concerns opposed to intellectuality or intellectual development. The opposition of "intellect" and "life" is itself a reflection of the two-track system in which a long period of academic education provided a moratorium for leisurely self-crystallization of an adult role identity by the elite while the masses were to acquire an early adult vocational identity, either through going to work or through commitment to a vocation in a vocational high school.

Our discussion of adolescent relativism and identity diffusion suggests that the two tracks are both breaking down and fusing. Vocational goals are evaded by relativism and counterculture questioning as are deferred goals of intellectual development. An identity crisis and questioning are no longer the prerogative of the elite, and they now occur earlier and without the background of logical and moral development they previously entailed. If the high school is to have meaning it must take account of this, which means it must take account of the adolescent's current notion of himself and his identity. Like most psychologists, most adolescents think the self has little to do with intellectual or moral development. The relativistic adolescent is content to answer "myself" to questions as to the source and basis of value and meaning. Like most psychologists he tends to equate the content of self-development with the ego, with self-awareness, with identity. The other pole of ego or self-

development, however, is that of new awareness of the world and values; it is the awareness of new meanings in life.

We discussed the moral strand of ego development, which is clearly philosophical. We have also noted aesthetic, religious, metaphysical, and epistemological concepts and values born in adolescence. One side of ego development is the structure of the self-concept and the other side is the individual's concept of the true, the good, the beautiful, and the real. If education is to promote self-development, ego development must be seen as one side of an education whose other side consists of the arts and sciences as philosophically conceived. We have pointed to the need for defining the aims of teaching the arts and sciences in developmental terms. In this sense one basic aim of teaching high school science and mathematics is to stimulate the stage of principled or formal-operational logical thought, of high school social studies, the stimulation of principled moral judgment. A basic aim of teaching literature is the development of a stage or level of aesthetic comprehension, expression, judgment. Behind all of these developmental goals lie moral and philosophic dimensions of the meaning of life, which the adolescent currently questions and the school needs to confront. The adolescent is a philosopher by nature, and if not by nature, by countercultural pressure. The high school must have, and represent, a philosophy if it is to be meaningful to the adolescent. If the high school is to offer some purposes and meanings which can stand up to relativistic questioning, it must learn philosophy.

REFERENCES

1. S. H. White, "Some General Outlines of the Matrix of Developmental Changes Between Five to Seven Years," *Bulletin of the Orton Society*, 20 (1970), 41-57.

2. L. Kohlberg, "Early Education: A Cognitive-Developmental Approach," *Child Development*, 39 (December 1968), 1013-1062; A. R. Jensen, "How Much Can We Boost I.Q. and Scholastic Achievement?" *Harvard Educational Review*, 39 (1969), 1-123.

3. R. Scheffler, "The Development of Children's Orientations to Fantasy in the Years 5 to 7," unpublished Ph.D. dissertation, Harvard University, 1971.

4. L. Kohlberg, "Moral Education in the School," *School Review*, 74 (1966), 1-30; Kohlberg, "Early Education."

5. Kohlberg, "Moral Education in the School."

6. *Ibid.*

7. Cognitive stage maturity is different from I.Q., a separate factor, though the two are correlated. (See L. Kohlberg and R. DeVries, "Relations between Piaget and Psychometric Assessments of Intelligence," in C. Lavatelli, ed., *The Natural Curriculum* [Urbana: University of Illinois Press, 1971].) General impoverishment of organized physical and social stimulation leads to retardation in stage development. Culturally disadvantaged children tend to be somewhat retarded compared to middle-class children with the same I.Q.'s in concrete-operational logic. Experimental intervention can to some extent accelerate cognitive development if it is based on providing experiences of cognitive conflict which stimulate the child to reorganize or rethink his patterns of cognitive ordering.

8. Kohlberg, "Early Education."

9. Kohlberg, "Moral Education in the School."

10. C. Ellinwood, "Structural Development in the Expression of Emotion by Children," unpublished Ph.D. dissertation, University of Chicago, 1969.

11. E. A. Peel, *The Psychological Basis of Education*, 2d ed. (Edinburgh and London: Oliver and Boyd, 1967).

12. D. Kuhn, J. Langer, and L. Kohlberg, "The Development of Formal-Operational Thought: Its Relation to Moral Judgment," unpublished paper, 1971.

13. Another example of transitional stage response is success on the question: "Joe is shorter than Bob, Joe is taller than Alex, who is the tallest?" The transitional child can solve this by the required reversing of relations and serial ordering of them but will fail the pendulum task.

14. Wordsworth's note to ode on *Intimations of Immortality* quoted in Lionel Trilling *The Liberal Imagination* (New York: Viking, 1941).

15. Kohlberg, "Moral Education in the School."

16. Taken from Kuhn, Langer, and Kohlberg, "The Development of Formal-Operational Thought."

17. J. Piaget, *The Moral Judgment of the Child* (Glencoe, Ill.: Free Press, 1948; originally published in 1932).

18. L. Kohlberg and R. Kramer, "Continuities and Discontinuities in Childhood and Adult Moral Development," *Human Development*, 12 (1969), 93-120.

19. J. Loevinger, "The Meaning and Measurement of Ego Development," *American Psychology* (1966), 195-206.

20. M. H. Podd, "Ego Identity Status and Morality: An Empirical Investigation of Two Developmental Concepts," unpublished Ph.D. dissertation, 1969.

21. J. E. Marcia, "Development and Validation of Ego Identity Status," *Journal of Personality and Social Psychology*, 3 (1966), 551-558.

22. C. Gilligan, L. Kohlberg, and J. Lerner, "Moral Reasoning About Sexual Dilemmas: A Developmental Approach," in L. Kohlberg and E. Turiel, eds., *Recent Research in Moral Development* (New York: Holt, Rinehart and Winston, 1972).

23. N. Haan and C. Holstein, unpublished data, 1971.

24. L. Kohlberg and A. Lockwood, "Cognitive-Developmental Psychology and Political Education: Progress in the Sixties," speech for Social Science Consortium Convention, Boulder, Colorado, 1970; L. Kohlberg and E. Turiel, "Moral Development and Moral Education," in G. Lesser, ed., *Psychology and Educational Practice* (Chicago: Scott, Foresman, 1971).

25. L. Kohlberg and M. Blatt, "The Effects of Classroom Discussion on Level of Moral Judgment," in Kohlberg and Turiel, eds., *Recent Research in Moral Development*.

26. J. Dewey, *On Education: Selected Writing*, ed. R. D. Archambault (New York: The Modern Library, republished 1964).

John Janeway Conger

31

A New Morality: Sexual Attitudes and Behavior of Contemporary Adolescents

It has been apparent for some years now that the sexual attitudes and values of adolescents have been changing significantly, that a "new morality" has been developing in the United States and other Western countries (**3, 16, 20**). In comparison to their peers of earlier generations, today's adolescents place a greater emphasis on openness and honesty about sex (**4, 16, 29**). In a number of recent surveys (**8, 9, 10, 33, 34**), the majority (85% or more) of American adolescents expressed the view that young people need more and better sex education and that information about sex should be given in the schools—under most circumstances, in coeducational classes.

In one national survey of the confidential opinions of 1500 middle-class adolescent girls aged 13 to 19, 98 percent said they wanted sex taught in school (**10**). When asked what was currently being taught and what *should* be taught, most girls responded that such topics as the anatomy and physiology of the female reproductive system and the menstrual cycle not only *should* be taught, but that they were being covered. Most girls also felt strongly that sex education classes should deal with such philosophical or scientific issues as premarital ethics, abortion, birth control and contraception, male and female sex drives, masturbation, homosexuality, loss of virginity, impotence and frigidity, fertility, and the nature of the orgasm. In *all* of these important areas, however, less than half of the sample reported having had school instruction.

In addition, there is a growing tendency among young people to view decisions about individual sexual behavior as more of a private and less of a public con-

cern (**4, 63**). In part, this appears to reflect a growing sus-piciousness of or disenchantment with established social in-stitutions and their proclaimed values, together with a shift among many young people in the direction of indi-vidual self-discovery and self-expression—of "doing one's thing." But it also reflects a greater emphasis on the im-portance of "meaningful," that is, genuine and sincere, interpersonal relationships in sex as in other areas.

In the view of a majority of contemporary adoles-cents, the acceptability of various forms and degrees of sexual behavior, including premarital intercourse, is highly dependent on the nature of the relationship between the individuals involved (**16, 20, 26, 29**). Eighty percent of adolescent boys and 72 percent of girls in this country agree with the statement, "It's all right for young people to have sex before getting married if they are in love with each other" (**29**). Seventy-five percent of all girls maintain that "I wouldn't want to have sex with a boy unless I loved him" (**29**). While only 47 percent of boys stated this stringent a requirement, 69 percent said, "I would not want to have sex with a girl unless I liked her as a per-son" (**29**). In contrast, most adolescents clearly oppose exploitation, pressure or force in sex, sex solely for the sake of physical enjoyment, and sex between people too young to understand what they are getting into (**16, 20, 29**). Nearly 75 percent of all adolescents concur that "when it comes to morality in sex, the important thing is the way people treat each other, not the things they do to-gether" (**29**).

Despite a growing emphasis among adolescents on openness and honesty, there is little evidence of preoc-cupation with sex, as many parents and other adults seem to think. Indeed, it may well be that the average adoles-cent of today is less preoccupied and concerned with sex than prior generations of young people, including his par-ents when they were the same age. Greater acceptance of sex as a natural part of life may well lead to less preoc-cupation than anxious concern in an atmosphere of se-crecy and suppression. Most contemporary adolescents (87%) agree that "all in all, I think my head is pretty well together as far as sex is concerned" (**29**).

Furthermore, in ranking the relative importance of various goals, younger adolescent boys and girls (13–15) cited as most important: "Preparing myself to earn a good living when I get older," "Having fun," and "Getting along with my parents"; for younger girls, "Learning about myself" was also important. Older adolescents of both sexes (16–19) stressed "Learning about myself" as most important, followed by "Being independent so that I can make it on my own" and "Preparing myself to accom-plish useful things." Among all age groups, "Having sex with a number of different boys (girls)" and "Making out" consistently ranked at or near the top among goals con-sidered *least* important (**29**).

ARE CHANGING ATTITUDES REFLECTED IN BEHAVIOR?

Are the significant and apparently enduring changes in sexual attitudes and values among contemporary ado-lescents reflected in their behavior, and, if so, how? At least until very recently, a number of generally recognized authorities maintained that the overall behavior of today's

adolescents and youth, though more open and in some respects probably freer, did not differ strikingly from that of their parents at the same age (**20, 24, 28**). Conversely, other observers have asserted that, although attitudinal changes may have been the more dramatic, there have also been marked changes in behavior (**17, 20**). What do the available data reveal? As will become evident, the answer appears to depend on *what* behaviors one is referring to, among *which* adolescents, and *how recently.*

Although current data are admittedly incomplete, the available information indicates that there has been rela-tively little if any change in the past few decades in the incidence of male masturbation (**1, 21, 22, 27, 29**); mas-turbation appears to have remained fairly stable over the years, with an estimated incidence of about 21 percent by age 12, 82 percent by age 15, and 92 percent by age 20 (**13, 27**). However, recent data (**9, 29**) indicates that there has been an increase in masturbation among girls at all age levels, with incidences of *at least* 36 percent by age 15 and 42 percent by age 19. In contrast, only about 17 percent of the mothers of today's adolescent girls had en-gaged in masturbation to orgasm by age 15, and by age 20, only about 30 percent (**12**).

One might be tempted to conclude that masturbation would occur most commonly among adolescents lacking other outlets. Interestingly, however, current masturbation experience among contemporary adolescents occurs about three times as frequently among those engaged in sexual intercourse or petting to orgasm as among the sexually inexperienced (**29**).

Petting does appear to have increased somewhat in the past few decades, and it tends to occur slightly earlier (**12, 13, 16, 20, 23, 24, 29**). The major changes, however, have probably been in the frequency of petting, degree of intimacy of techniques involved, the frequency with which petting leads to erotic arousal or orgasm, and, certainly, frankness about it (**2, 4, 16, 19, 28, 29**).

Premarital Intercourse

Currently, the greatest amount of public discussion (and parental and societal apprehension), as well as the most extensive data, deals with the incidence of sexual intercourse among contemporary youth. A favorite assertion among those who have claimed there have been few *recent* changes in adolescent sexual behavior is that, while there has indeed been a sexual revolution in this century, it took place, not among today's adolescents, but among their parents and grandparents. It does, in fact, appear that significant percentage increases in premarital intercourse occurred during this earlier period. For example, Kinsey's data indicate that only 2 percent of females born before 1900 had premarital intercourse prior to age 16, 8 percent prior to age 20, and only 14 percent prior to age 25 (**12**). In contrast, for the mothers of today's adolescents, the corresponding figures are 4 percent, 21 percent, and 37 percent, respectively (**12, 13**).

This, however, leaves unanswered the question of how the incidence of premarital intimacy among today's parents compares with that of their adolescent sons and daughters. Until very recently, relevant data for such a comparison were lacking, except in the case of college students. However, in a representative national study of adolescents aged 13 to 19, published in 1973, Robert Sorenson (**29**) found that 44 percent of boys and 30 percent of girls have had sexual intercourse prior to age 16. These figures increased to 72 percent of boys and 57 percent of girls by age 19. When compared with females of their mothers' generation in Kinsey's investigation (only 3% of whom had engaged in premarital intercourse by age 16 and less than 20% by age 19), this represents a very large increase, particularly at the younger age level. When compared with males of their fathers' generation (approximately 39% of whom had engaged in premarital intercourse by age 16 and 72% by age 19), contemporary adolescent boys as a whole show a much smaller change, mainly a tendency to have first intercourse at a slightly younger age. However, as will become apparent in the following section, these *overall* findings for boys obscure significant changes taking place among boys of higher socioeconomic and educational levels.

DIVERSITY OF SEXUAL ATTITUDES AND BEHAVIOR

Up to this point, our focus has been on *overall* trends in sexual attitudes and behavior among contemporary youth. Such group trends have meaning and usefulness in their own right, but they should not be allowed to distract our attention from an equally important phenomenon,

namely, the diversity of sexual attitudes and behavior in different sectors of the adolescent and youth population. There is increasing evidence that this diversity is currently marked and probably growing (**5, 16, 20, 29**). Such factors as age, sex, socioeconomic and educational level, race, religion, and even geographical area all appear to be related to sexual attitudes, values, and behavior. For this reason, the results of almost any survey dealing with adolescent sexuality will inevitably seem exaggerated to some young people and adults and minimized to others.

What do we know about some of these variations? As we have already noted, Sorenson's recent survey (**29**), shows that for the first time in such studies, a majority (52%) of American adolescents aged 13–19 reported having engaged in sexual intercourse. As significant as this evidence of a trend toward greater sexual freedom clearly is, it should not be allowed to obscure the complementary finding that a very substantial minority (48%) of adolescents had not as yet had such experience. Furthermore, neither of these broad groups was homogeneous. Thus, adolescents in the nonintercourse group ranged from those with virtually no sexual experience to those with a wide variety of experiences short of intercourse itself, including petting to orgasm.

Among the group with intercourse experience, two major subgroups emerge from the findings of this study: *serial monogamists* and *sexual adventurers*. The former "generally does not have intercourse with another during that relationship. We say 'serial' because one such relationship is often succeeded by another" (**29**, p. 121). The latter, on the other hand, "moves freely from one sex partner to the next and feels no obligation to be faithful to any sex partner" (**29**, p. 121). Among nonvirgins, serial monogamy was more frequent overall; it was also more frequent among girls, older adolescents, those from the northeast and west, and those from larger metropolitan areas. The total number of partners was obviously far higher among sexual adventurers, although it is interesting to note that frequency of intercourse was higher among monogamists.

Not surprisingly, the two groups tended to vary significantly in attitudes, as well as in behavior. Most monogamists believe they love and are loved by their partners, believe in openness and honesty between partners, and deny that sex is the most important thing in a love relationship—although they also expressed greater satisfaction with their sex lives. At the same time their code stresses personal freedom and the absence of commitment to marriage, despite the fact that more than half believe they will or may marry their partner eventually. Sexual adventurers, in contrast, are primarily interested in variety of experience for its own sake, do not believe that love is a necessary part of sexual relationships, and feel no particular personal responsibility for their partners, although neither do they believe in hurting others. For many adventurers, sex itself is viewed as an avenue to communication; as one young adventurer stated, "Having sex together is a good way for two people to become acquainted."

As a group, monogamists tended to be more satisfied with themselves and life in general, to get along better with parents, and to be more conventional in social, political, and religious beliefs. Despite their greater emphasis on sex as a goal in itself, female adventurers report having orgasm during intercourse less frequently than monogamists.

In general, and contrary to recent popular impressions, both the attitudes and behavior of younger adolescents still appear more *conservative* than those of older adolescents (**4, 6, 8, 10, 20**). Younger adolescents may possibly, as some have speculated end up less constrained by social mores than their older brothers and sisters. But the fact remains that for the great majority this is not presently the case.

Girls as a group are consistently more conservative than boys, both in attitudes and values and in behavior. In virtually all population subgroups, the incidence of all forms of intimate sexual behavior is less frequent among girls; girls are also more likely than boys to believe that partners in advanced forms of petting or intercourse should be in love, engaged, or married (**9, 16, 20, 25, 29**). Furthermore, girls are more likely than boys to be influenced by parental wishes and community social standards.

In Sorenson's study, 80 percent of the sexual adventurers were male; in contrast, 64 percent of serial monogamists were female. (The implication here is that a significant percentage of female monogamists were involved with males who were over 19, and hence not included in the study; the other possibility is that in some relationships the girl considered herself a monogamist, while the boy did not.) The greater emphasis among girls on love as a necessary component of sexual relationships is consistent with the stronger interpersonal orientation of girls generally. The extent to which a higher level of sexual activity among boys is a function of physiological differences, cultural influences, or (as seems most likely) both is still an unresolved question (**1, 4, 17**).

College youth emerge as consistently less conservative in their attitudes and values than noncollege peers of the same age. For example, in one study of American youth 17 and older (**35**), college youth were significantly less likely to express the view that premarital sexual relations "were not a moral issue." They were also more likely to believe that "sexual behavior should be bound by mutual feelings, not by formal ties," and they were more likely to express a desire for "more sexual freedom" than their noncollege peers.

Within the college population there appears to be considerable diversity in attitudes and values, both among geographical regions and types of schools attended— particularly in the case of girls. In general students from the east and west coasts emerge as less conservative than those from the Midwest (**16, 20, 25**). In a 1969 study more than two-thirds of midwestern students, but only about 40 percent of eastern students (both male and female), responded affirmatively to the question, "Do you feel that ideally it is still true that a man and a girl who marry should have their first full sexual experience together?" Similarly, three-fourths of girls at midwestern schools, but less than a third of those at eastern schools, agreed that "coitus was reasonable 'only if married' for possible participants who would be in the 21- to 23-year-old age group" (**20**, p. 163). Students at permissive, liberally oriented colleges emerged as less conservative than those at more traditional colleges (**6, 16, 20**). Interest-

ingly, the only apparent exception to the tendency for girls to have more conservative attitudes and values than boys occurs among students in some highly permissive, liberal colleges (**16, 20**).

It is also among college youth that the greatest changes in sexual behavior have occurred since their parents' generation (**4, 16, 20, 30, 31**). This trend appears especially pronounced among some demographically distinguishable groups of female students. In the 1940s Kinsey and others (**12, 13, 23**) found that by the age of 21 the incidence of premarital experience among college-educated persons was 49 percent for males and 27 percent for females. In contrast several recent, broadly representative investigations of American college and university students of comparable ages, conducted between 1967 and 1971 (**9, 16, 20, 30, 31**), indicate a substantial upward shift, particularly among girls. Thus, for males, obtained incidence figures in these investigations ranged from a low of 58 percent to a high of 82 percent; comparable percentages for females ranged from a 43 percent to 56 percent. In both cases the highest percentages were obtained in the most recent samples (**9, 30, 31, 36**).

Interestingly, whereas the percentage of male students engaging in premarital intercourse appeared to have reached a plateau (of about 80%) by 1970, among girls the incidence was apparently still increasing in 1971: Fifty-one percent of female students reported having had intercourse in 1970; 56 percent did so in 1971. Premarital relations are likely to be more frequent among those attending eastern colleges and universities than among those attending midwestern institutions (**20**) and among students attending private, "elite" colleges and universities.

Politically conservative youth are more conservative in sexual attitudes and values than "moderate reformers" and far more conservative than left-oriented "revolutionary" youth (**4, 9, 30, 31, 34**). Thus, among older adolescents *in general* (both college and noncollege), only 18 percent of conservative youth stated they would welcome more sexual freedom, as compared with 43 percent of moderate reformers and 80 percent of revolutionaries (**35**). Similarly, nearly two-thirds of conservative youth viewed premarital sexual relations as a moral issue, compared with one-third of moderate reformers and none of the revolutionaries!

Cultural differences are clearly reflected in the wide variations obtained between nations in various studies (**3, 11, 15, 66, 20**). Canada and the United States consistently rank lowest in incidence of premarital intercourse and England ranks highest, followed by the Scandinavian countries.

Even on the basis of the limited data discussed in this essay, it appears clear that adolescent attitudes and values regarding sex and sexual behavior itself are changing, although the extent of the changes varies widely from one segment of the youth population to another. Indeed, as in other areas of social concern, *the differences between some subgroups of youth appear wider than those between youth in general and adults in general*. There is a real and often ignored danger in generalizing too widely from specialized subgroups (e.g., a particular college campus or a particular urban high school) to youth in general. Furthermore, the greatest *relative* changes in both attitudes and behavior since their parents' generation have occurred among middle- and upper class adolescents, particularly girls. Not surprisingly it is among this socio-economically favored, and probably more socially conflicted, segment of the youth population that the "youth culture" of the 1960s took root and found its sustenance.

DISCUSSION

In brief, these findings, combined with general observation, do indicate an emerging new morality among contemporary adolescents. While this new morality has many positive aspects—a greater emphasis on openness and honesty, mutual respect and lack of dissembling or exploitation, and a more "natural" and better-informed approach to sex—it would be a mistake to conclude that the picture is wholly unclouded. Many experienced adolescents, particularly older adolescents, appear able to handle their sexual involvement and their relationships with themselves without undue stress. (Four out of five nonvirgins report getting "a lot of satisfaction" out of their sex lives; two-thirds of all nonvirgins and four out of five monogamists state that sex makes their lives more meaningful.) However, significant minorities report feelings of conflict and guilt, find themselves exploited or rejected, or discover belatedly that they have gotten in over their heads emotionally. Especially after the first experience of intercourse, girls are far more likely than boys to encounter negative feelings. While boys are most likely to report being excited, satisfied, and happy, girls most frequently report being afraid, guilty, worried, or embarrassed after their initial intercourse experience (**29**).

Obviously there are dangers, particularly for girls, with their generally stronger affiliative needs, in believing that sexual involvement is "okay as long as you're in love." Encouraged by such a philosophy among peers, a girl or boy may become more deeply involved emotionally than she or he can handle at a particular stage of maturity (**1, 4**). "An adolescent may also consciously think that his attitudes are more 'liberal' than they actually are, and involvement may lead to unanticipated feelings of guilt, anxiety or depression" (**18**, p. 643).

There also remain very practical problems, such as the possibility of pregnancy. Many girls today express the opinion that "now that science has given us the (birth control) pill, we no longer have to be frightened about pregnancy. We just have to decide what is right" (**4**, p. 254). Noble as this sentiment may be, the facts indicate that only a small percentage of unmarried girls having intercourse have used the contraceptive pill to prevent pregnancy (**7, 14, 29, 32**); a disturbingly high percentage —between 55 and 75 percent—used no contraceptive device whatever, at least in their first experience, and only a minority consistently use such a device thereafter (**14, 29, 36**). Even among monogamists, only two-thirds reported always using contraceptive devices. Furthermore, despite talk of the pill, less than a third of female nonvirgins have used this method.

Such lack of precaution against pregnancy results partly from ignorance or lack of availability of contraceptive devices. Far more often, however, it results from carelessness, impulsiveness of the moment, a magical conviction that pregnancy cannot really happen, a belief that the spontaneity of sex is impaired ("If the girl uses birth control pills or other forms of contraception, it makes it seem as if she were *planning* to have sex"), or a belief that the *other* partner has taken precautions. Furthermore, 40 percent of all nonvirgin girls in Sorenson's study agreed that "sometimes I don't really care whether or not I get pregnant." Rather astonishingly, he found that "10 percent of all American female adolescents and 23 percent of all nonvirgin girls report that they have been pregnant at least once" (**29**, p. 324).

It seems unlikely that the trend toward premarital intercourse as an accepted practice, and especially toward serial monogamy as the most frequent and the most socially approved pattern among sexually experienced adolescents, will be reversed. Of all residuals of the youth culture of the 1960s, greater sexual freedom and openness appear to be the more enduring. What one must hope is that adolescents entering sexual relationships can be helped to become mature enough, informed enough, responsible enough, sure enough of their own identities and value systems, and sensitive and concerned enough about the welfare of others so that the inevitable casualties in the "sexual revolution" can be reduced to a minimum. Sexuality as a vital part of human relationships should promote, rather than hinder, growth toward maturity and emotional fulfillment.

REFERENCES

1. Bardwick, J. *Psychology of women: A study of bio-cultural conflicts.* Harper & Row, 1971.
2. Bell, R. R. Parent-child conflict in sexual values. *J. Soc. Issues,* 1966, *22,* 34–44.
3. Christenson, H. T., & Carpenter, G. R. Value-behavior discrepancies regarding premarital coitus in three Western cultures. *Am. Sociol. Rev.,* 1962, *27,* 66–74.
4. Conger, J. J. *Adolescence and youth: Psychological development in a changing world.* New York: Harper & Row, 1973.
5. Conger, J. J. A world they never knew: The family and social change. *Daedalus,* Fall 1971, 1105–1138.
6. Gallup poll, *Denver Post,* May 12, 1970.
7. Grinder, R. E., & Schmitt, S. S. Coeds and contraceptive information. *J. Marriage Fam.* 1966, *28,* 471–479.
8. Harris, L. Change, yes—upheaval, no. *Life,* January 8, 1971, 22–27.
9. Hunt, M. *Sexual behavior in the 1970s.* Chicago: Playboy Press, 1974.
10. Hunt, M. Special sex education survey. *Seventeen,* July 1970, 94 ff.
11. Karlsson, G. Karlsson, S., & Busch, K. Sexual habits and attitudes of Swedish folk high school students. Research Report No. 15. Uppsala, Sweden: Department of Sociology, Uppsala University, 1960.
12. Kinsey, A. C., Pomeroy, W. B., Martin, C. E., & Gebhard, P. H. *Sexual behavior in the human female.* Philadelphia: Saunders 1953.
13. Kinsey, A. C., Pomeroy, W. B., & Martin, C. E. *Sexual behavior in the human male.* Philadelphia: Saunders, 1948.
14. Lake, A. Teenagers and sex: A student report. *Seventeen,* July 1967, 88.
15. Linner, B. *Sex and society in Sweden.* New York: Pantheon. 1967.
16. Luckey, E., & Nass, G. A comparison of sexual attitudes and behavior in an international sample. *J. Marriage Fam.,* 1969, *31,* 364–379.

17. Money, J., & Ehrhardt, A. A. *Man and woman, boy and girl: The differentiation and dimorphism of gender identity from conception to maturity.* Baltimore: Johns Hopkins Press, 1972.

18. Mussen, P. H., Conger, J. J., & Kagan, J. *Child development and personality.* New York: Harper & Row, 1969 (3rd ed.).

19. Packard, V. . . . and the sexual behavior reported by 2100 young adults. In V. Packard, *The sexual wilderness: The contemporary upheaval in male-female relationships.* New York: Pocket Books, 1970, pp. 166–184.

20. Packard, V. *The sexual wilderness: The contemporary upheaval in male-female relationships.* New York: Pocket Books, 1970.

21. Pomeroy, W. B. *Boys and sex.* New York: Delacorte, 1969.

22. Pomeroy, W. B. *Girls and sex.* New York: Delacorte, 1969.

23. Reevy, W. R. Adolescent sexuality. In A. Ellis & A. Abarband (Eds.), *The encyclopedia of sexual behavior* (Vol. I). New York: Hawthorn, 1961, pp. 52–68.

24. Reiss, I. L. How and why America's sex standards are changing. In W. Simon and J. H. Gagnon (Eds.), *The sexual scene.* Chicago: Trans-action Books, 1970, pp. 43–57.

25. Reiss, I. L. The sexual renaissance in America. *J. Soc. Issues,* April 1966.

26. Reiss, I. L. The scaling of premarital sexual permissiveness. *J. Marriage Fam.*, 1964, 26, 188–199.

27. Simon, W., & Gagnon, J. H. Psychosexual development. In W. Simon & J. H. Gagnon (Eds.), *The sexual scene.* Chicago: Trans-action Books, 1970, pp. 23–41.

28. Simon, W., & Gagnon, J. H. (Eds.). *The sexual scene.* Chicago: Trans-action Books, 1970.

29. Sorenson, R. C. *Adolescent sexuality in contemporary America: Personal values and sexual behavior ages 13–19.* New York: World Publishing, 1973.

30. Student survey, 1971. *Playboy*, September 1971, 118 ff.

31. Student survey, *Playboy*, September 1970, 182 ff.

32. *The report of the Commission on Obscenity and Pornography.* New York: Bantam Books, 1970.

33. What people think of their high schools. *Life*, 1969, 66, 22–23.

34. Wilson, W. C. et al. *Technical report of the Commission on Obscenity and Pornography, Vol. VI: National survey.* Washington, D.C.: U.S. Government Printing Office, 1971.

35. Yankelovich, D. *Generations apart.* New York: CBS News, 1969.

36. Zelnik, M., & Kantner, J. E. Survey of female adolescent sexual behavior conducted for the Commission on Population, Washington, D.C., 1972.

32

**NO DRUGS • NO LIQUOR • NO TOBACCO
NO PREMARITAL SEX • NO HOT PANTS • NO POSSESSIONS**

**They're young, tireless, devout, dogmatic, evangelical
and terribly earnest on this fundamentalist farm in a Western state.
And it's a man's world: the women know their place.**

by Mary White Harder, James T. Richardson, and Robert B. Simmonds

"I know God created us equal. And we're just helpmates for the man. I know that our souls and spirits are equal. But I know that we're weaker vessels. We just have different ministries to fulfill." —a sister at Christ Commune

THE YOUNG MEN ("brothers"), long-haired and bearded, were hoeing the field. A few young women ("sisters") worked alongside them. One sister, wearing a dress with a loose-fitting top, bent over and inadvertently allowed a brother to glimpse her breasts. Later in the day the brother complained to a pastor that the sister had "stumbled" him—she had caused him to have fleshly desires. The hoeing continued; later the brothers and sisters congregated as usual for dinner, the sisters who were not serving food took places at the end of the line, behind the men. That evening after dinner the sisters had a special meeting.

As part of our ongoing study of Christ Commune, one of our female interviewers was permitted to attend the meeting. Sisters who were "older in the Lord" explained that it was necessary for women to dress in a manner that revealed neither ankle nor curve. Cosmetics and jewelry were discouraged for the same reason; sisters were to avoid drawing attention to their bodies. The justification given for these rules was that the male's God-given nature automatically causes him to "stumble" at the sight of certain parts of the female body. The male has little or no control over this, so it becomes the female's responsibility to avoid sexually charged situations. It is also a mark of vanity and pride for the female to call attention to herself through flirtation or dress.

Sexism. This justification, of course, absolves males of responsibility and puts females in the position of agreeing that their bodies cause sin. The episode helped

delineate for us the place of women in the group, as well as the sexism that we believe is inherent in fundamentalist theology.

Our interest in sex roles of the young Christian converts is part of our general interest in the religious organization that operates the commune. Christ Commune is a pseudonym for one branch of what is probably the best-organized, most rapidly growing sect in the so-called Jesus movement. It appears to us the group is more viable than even the much-publicized Children-of-God sect.

The commune is two years old, located in a Western state. During the summer of 1971, and again last summer, its leaders allowed us to visit for several weeks on three different occasions and to interview members. The approximately 100 persons living there during the summers were drawn from the group's year-round houses strung out along the West Coast. At the end of both summers the members returned to their original houses, or continued on to others where they would be trained for leadership and groomed for work in evangelical teams formed to open houses.

Sect. The organization that runs Christ Commune has been in existence four years; it operates, in addition to the commune branch we studied, other agricultural activities, a small fishing fleet, and about 35 other houses across the country. We estimate that the sect has between 600 and 800 members overall, and financial assets of about a million dollars.

In addition to studying sex roles at Christ Commune, and the structure and history of the group, we gathered information about members' backgrounds and personalities, about the theology and values of the sect, and about the techniques used to win conversions and keep com-

**"I do love my brothers,
and I do want the house to
be nice for them, but
I clean it for the Lord."**

mitment. We investigated changes in persons before and after they joined the group, and changes in the operation of the group itself.

Blessing. Among the noticeable changes in the operation of Christ Commune over two summers was a perceptible redefinition of sex roles. During our 1971 visit we often heard sisters exchange comments that summed up woman's role in the group—such as, "Isn't it a blessing to know your place!"

The following summer, although basic sex roles remained intact, there were changes indicating that some sisters were less than satisfied with their "place." The ankle-length, loose-fitting dresses of 1971 had given way to more formfitting and stylish clothes. An occasional sister even wore knee-length shorts. Some sisters had begun to work in the fields, and teams of brothers volunteered to help with the dishes in the evening. We have found no evidence that changed sex-role behavior has meant any change in the group's theology of sex roles.

Submission. Today as in 1971 the women of the group know their place: one of submission to men, just as men are in submission to the Lord. Theoretically, men and women in the group are equal. According to the Word of God as revealed in the scriptures—so goes the group's official theology—all Christians are equal in the eyes of the Lord. But also rooted in the scriptures is the idea that God has provided an appropriate place for all His children, and in order to be a good Christian, one must accept that place.

Sisters recognize their subservience to brothers, but they define themselves in terms of their relationship with God. They appear to gain neither status nor identity through their relationships with men, but instead evaluate themselves in terms of fulfilling their duties as required by the Lord.

One sister explained to us: "At two of the houses I've lived at I've been the only sister the majority of the time, besides the married wife whose ministry is to her husband. So, my ministry was to like patch up the brothers' pants when they tore out. And cook—always cook—breakfast, lunch and dinner. And keep the house clean. 'Cause it's the Lord's house, 'cause I always know that Jesus could come at any time. And I don't want Him to see the house being a mess. Like I'm not on a self-righteous-worker trip, praise God, 'cause I fall into that sometimes. But I just like to keep the house presentable to the Lord, and clean it for the Lord. I do love my brothers, and I do want the house to be nice for them, but I clean it for the Lord. I do it for Him, not for the 10 different brothers that are in the house. It's just the Lord."

Trials. As a result of this male-female hierarchy, no woman at Christ Commune in 1972 is included in the farm's decision-making process. One woman has the title of deaconess, but her authority is limited to other women, primarily to their kitchen duties. Women bow to the authority of all men in the group, especially their fiancés or husbands. Some of the sisters have difficulty accepting their roles. They have had to reject their former life-styles, which often included sexual relations with men, employment and independence, and have had to assume submissive positions. One newly engaged sister we interviewed was having "trials" accepting the authority of her fiancé. She talked with the other sisters about her problems, and they advised her to search her heart for the strength to follow the Lord's will, or to take her trial to the Lord. The older sisters counseled

From the Bible—WOMAN'S PLACE

For after this manner in the old time the holy women also, who trusted in God, adorned themselves, being in subjection unto their own husbands:

Even as Sara obeyed Abraham, calling him lord: whose daughters ye are, as long as ye do well, and are not afraid with any amazement.

Likewise, ye husbands, dwell with them according to knowledge, giving honor unto the wife, as unto the weaker vessel, and as being heirs together of the grace of life; that your prayers be not hindered.

—I PETER, 3:5-7

And Adam said, This is now bone of my bones, and flesh of my flesh: she shall be called Woman, because she was taken out of Man.

—GENESIS 2:23

Also thou shalt not approach unto a woman to uncover her nakedness, as long as she is put apart for her uncleanness.

—LEVITICUS 18:19

A gracious woman retaineth honor; and strong men retain riches.

—PROVERBS 11:16

A virtuous woman is a crown to her husband: but she that maketh ashamed is as rottenness in his bones.

—PROVERBS 12:4

Who can find a virtuous woman? For her price is far above rubies.

—PROVERBS 31:10

And I find more bitter than death the woman, whose heart is snares and nets, and her hands as bands: whoso pleaseth God shall escape from her; but the sinner shall be taken by her.

—ECCLESIASTES 7:26

Be ye followers of me, even as I also am of Christ.

Now I praise you, brethren, that ye remember me in all things, and keep the ordinances, as I delivered them to you.

But I would have you know, that the head of every man is Christ; and the head of the woman is the man; and the head of Christ is God.

Every man praying or prophesying, having his head covered, dishonoreth his head.

But every woman that prayeth or prophesieth with her head uncovered dishonoreth her head: for that is even all one as if she were shaven.

For if the woman be not covered, let her also be shorn: but if it be a shame for a woman to be shorn or shaven, let her be covered.

For a man indeed ought not to cover his head, forasmuch as he is the image and glory of God: but the woman is the glory of the man.

For the man is not of the woman; but the woman of the man.

Neither was the man created for the woman; but the woman for the man.

For this cause ought the woman to have power on her head because of the angels.

Nevertheless neither is the man without the woman, neither the woman without the man, in the Lord.

For as the woman is of the man, even so is the man also by the woman; but all things of God.

Judge in yourselves: is it comely that a woman pray unto God uncovered?

Doth not even nature itself teach you, that, if a man have long hair, it is a shame unto him?

But if a woman have long hair, it is a glory to her: for her hair is given her for a covering.

—I CORINTHIANS 11:1-15

Let the woman learn in silence with all subjection.

But I suffer not a woman to teach nor to usurp authority over the man, but to be in silence.

For Adam was first formed, then Eve.

And Adam was not deceived, but the woman being deceived was in the transgression.

Notwithstanding she shall be saved in childbearing, if they continue in faith and charity and holiness with sobriety.

—I TIMOTHY 2:11-15

For by means of a whorish woman a man is brought to a piece of bread: and the adulteress will hunt for the precious life.

—PROVERBS 6:26

And if they will learn any thing, let them ask their husbands at home: for it is a shame for women to speak in the church.

—I CORINTHIANS 14:35

Even as Sodom and Gomorrha, and the cities about them in like manner, giving themselves over to fornication, and going after strange flesh, are set forth for an example, suffering the vengeance of eternal fire.

—JUDE 7

Nevertheless, to avoid fornication, let every man have his own wife, and let every woman have her own husband.

—I CORINTHIANS 7:2

"Courtship is encouraged, but closely regulated. Close chaperoning guarantees that taboos on petting and premarital sex will be honored."

her in the familiar words: "What a blessing when you finally find your place!"

Women's conversations seem to focus on knowing that "place," instead of on such topics as men, dating and dress. It is assumed that sisters who were "new" in the Lord would experience many trials in their relationships with men. The group encourages these sisters to share their trials with "older" sisters or with pastors (all males). "Older" sisters anticipate these problems and serve as strong intentional socializing agents. They sympathize with the trials but never challenge the correctness of the rules.

We hope to return to Christ Commune next summer to investigate further changes in sex-role definitions, and in the group's operation. We interpret the changes to date in dress and work roles as part of an effort by the group's leaders to attract and keep more females. More sisters mean more brothers. No group without enough females can expect to maintain the interest and commitment of all its male members, especially ones the age of Christ Commune members (average, 21). "Nonbelieving" females would attract males from the group, even though this is strongly discouraged by the social isolation and by directives from pastors in the group.

Courtship. Indirect evidence supporting this interpretation comes from the emphasis that the group places on courtship and marriage. Such emphasis intensifies interpersonal relationships *within* the sect, which is a crucial factor in group maintenance.

Courtship is encouraged, but closely regulated. When a brother or sister develops an interest in a fellow member, he or she is expected to communicate this at first in subtle ways. One sister said that one good way to let a brother know of your interest was to give him extra-large servings of food, or just to smile at him. After the initial hints, the brother or sister openly confesses his or her interest to the other.

If the interest is mutual, the couple talks to a pastor. Then, if they have the pastor's permission, they are engaged for a six-month period that must include a three-month separation. The couple may separate immediately, or they may postpone the parting until the last three months of their engagement.

Separation. The separation is real; one of the two must leave the commune, and go to live at another of the group's houses or farms. During their time apart, each "searches the heart" to discern God's will in the matter. Engaged couples are expected and permitted to spend their free time together during the other three months. There is some hand-holding at Christ Commune, but no other overt signs of affection. Close chaperoning guarantees that taboos on petting and premarital sex will be honored. Members told us that married members interact more and more with engaged couples, thus preparing them for their future roles. Some of the engaged females we interviewed were very conscious that they were being taught the "place" of a woman. After six months, if the couple still wants to marry, one of the pastors, who has counseled them at length on sex relations and family life, performs the ceremony.

After marriage the couple might stay on at Christ Commune (the original farmhouse was used as a couples' building, with a separate bedroom for each couple), or they might go to another house or farm. Most couples move to one of the houses designated by the sect as "couples' houses."

Contraception. The concern for group maintenance evident in courtship and marriage rules carries over to procreation. Married women are expected to have children "as God wills." Even so, we found some sisters very interested in birth-control techniques. The pill is taboo, as is abortion, but the all-male leadership approve other methods including foam, condoms, rhythm, and "trusting the Lord."

At least for the time being, the group seems to have worked out a successful compromise between its theology and the rights of its female members. On our first visit the disproportionate sex ratio at Christ Commune was apparent. Only about 15 percent of the members were female. We concluded that the generally low status of women in the group contributed to this disparity. (Of course, the population from which membership is drawn [street people] has a disproportionately high number of males.) The proportion of females at Christ Commune has increased, perhaps a reflection of relaxed dress and work codes. Early this summer about 25 percent were female, and by late summer female members had increased to about 35 percent.

The members of Christ Commune usually rise at 4:30 a.m. and go to bed at 11 p.m. They meet for meals in a plain room furnished with rough benches and tables. In the room is a bookcase, in which the youthful eaters place their Bibles, and a large, wood-burning stove. In response to a gong, the sisters and the brothers file in quietly and sit at the tables. Then, with no apparent direction, some of them start singing. The songs, nearly always minor-key spirituals, are picked up by the group, which sings them in a subdued, haunting way. After several songs a person stands and offers a long and thoughtful prayer, praising God for the accomplishments of the day, thanking Him for the food (usually soup and homemade bread) and always asking that others (including the observers) be "led to accept Christ." Then the food line forms.

Satisfaction. The brothers and sisters are satisfied with their simple fare (little meat, water to drink, only peanut-butter sandwiches for lunch) and with the strenuous

"There is no talk of football games, dating and sex, politics, drugs, school, or other topics common among 21-year-olds. The talk is of God."

work. For the entire summer they work hard six days a week, hoeing and harvesting crops, repairing machinery, and keeping the profitable agricultural operation going. They do it without complaint and with praise to God for giving them the work. Nearly all the members always have their Bibles at hand. They read their Bibles during brief breaks from work and talk among themselves about the marvelous things that God, through Christ, had done for them. There is no talk of football games, dating and sex, politics, drugs, school, or other topics common among 21-year-olds. The talk is of God.

One day a week is designated as a day of rest. This day was Monday during the past summer. Members relaxed, spent time in prayer, Bible study or just visiting. Occasionally when work on the farm demanded it, teams of "volunteers" work on this day of rest. No special services are held, except for the usual daily evening Bible study.

———————————

Who are these young Christian fundamentalists?

For two years we have worked with the members of Christ Commune to find out. Leaders in the commune have been extremely cooperative throughout our research, taking our appearance as "God's will." They gave us access to members and, because of the group's authority structure, they could encourage members to cooperate in interviews. As a result, we interviewed between 95 and 100 percent of available members during each of our three trips to the farm, and we have nearly 250 interviews.

Interview teams lived in the group during visits, sharing food, entering into conversations, attending nightly Bible study and prayer groups, and taking a close look at life in the group. All members of the interview teams felt extreme pressure to convert. Many members made attempts to convert us during interviews and mentioned interviewers in their extemporaneous prayers at meals and in Bible-study periods. The members were genuinely glad that we were there and went out of their way to help us with our research, even though we plainly did not share the fundamentalist Christian beliefs of the group and were gathering personal data on its members.

Education. We interviewed 88 members during the summer of 1971. Most were between 18 and 24, and the average age was 21. The youngest member was a 15-year-old girl, while the oldest was a 30-year-old male. All were Caucasian. (There was one black male who declined to be interviewed.) Sixty-seven of them had completed at least 12 years of school; the average was 12.2 years. A few had had as little as three years of formal education, while a handful had studied at graduate-school level. Twenty of the 74 males had served in the armed forces. In the two years before he joined the organization that operates Christ Commune, the typical

member had held a variety of low-paying, boring jobs.

The average member comes from a fairly affluent, fairly large family. Although 32 did not know their parents' income, 16 reported that their parents' incomes were $20,000 or more. The average reported family income was over $17,000. Nearly half of the members said that their fathers were professionals, managers, officials, or self-employed businessmen.

Thirteen members said there were six or more children in their families, and only two were only children. The average member's family had about four children. The majority said that they got along well with their mothers, but not so well with their fathers. Only 15 percent said that they felt closer to their fathers than to their mothers, and most of these were females.

Twenty-five percent reported that their parents were divorced or separated. When they were asked how their parents got along together, only 16 percent reported good relationships. Thus there emerges a pattern of fairly affluent, but unhappy homes.

Religion. As a child, the average member attended church regularly, but religion apparently did not play an integral part in his life. Eighty of the 88 reported that their families did not read the Bible at home; 76 said that their families took no part in religious observances except at Christmas and Easter; and 48 said that their parents did not turn to God when they faced crises. Members were most likely to come from Baptist or Roman Catholic homes, although many had been Methodists, Lutherans and Pentecostals.

The beliefs and practices—life-styles—of most members are different today from what they were on the outside. To demonstrate this change, we compared members' behavior and attitudes on drugs, alcohol, tobacco and sex before and after they joined the group. We understand the pitfall in attributing all changes in behavior and beliefs to group influence. For example, some members we interviewed "found Christ" before they joined the group, and their behavior changes may date from their conversion. Others gave up tobacco some time before they joined because they had turned to other drugs. Some had left drugs to go on nature trips. Even with these qualifications, the data are impressive and represent a fundamental shift in behavior.

Drugs. Although 85 percent of the members formerly had used alcohol and 67 percent had used tobacco, only two reported that they continued to use tobacco, and only one said that he used alcohol. None reported using drugs, although 90 percent said they had had previous experience with drugs. Among the former drug users, 45 percent had taken drugs daily for some time. We coded a person according to the hardest drug he or she admitted using. Twenty-one of the 79 users said they had taken opiates or cocaine; 43 others said they had

"Drugs played an important part in the former lives of 51 of the 88 we interviewed."

used hallucinogens. Only seven reported that they used only marijuana.

Drugs played an important part in the former lives of 51 members, and 65 said that most of their friends on the outside were drug users. Many said that they had started using drugs because their friends used them.

Attitudes toward premarital sex also changed dramatically. Eighty-six percent of the members we interviewed said that before joining the group they had approved of premarital sex; today only five percent approve. This change, while it is consistent with fundamentalism's belief that pleasures of the flesh are sinful, has led to difficulties. Members of both sexes say that "marriage trials" (sexual desires) are a major problem.

Sex, Use of Alcohol, Tobacco, and Drugs Before and After Joining Christ Commune (First Visit)

	before	after
premarital sex	76(86%)	5(6%)
alcohol	75(85%)	1(1%)
tobacco	59(67%)	2(2%)
drugs	79(90%)	0(0%)

Mission. Many, for good reason, have applauded the Jesus movement for its success in changing attitudes and behavior concerning drugs, alcohol, sexual promiscuity, and other components of the counterculture. It is apparent that Christ Commune and other segments of the movement have built viable alternative life-styles, which many in our society still seek. The "new life" of the commune members deeply impressed all who worked on the project. Members had been transformed from purposeless, cynical, and self-destructive persons into loving, concerned, productive individuals with a sense of mission. The fellowship and sense of community that we encountered at Christ Commune is rare in today's world. One member summed up the sentiments of many when he said, "If I had not come to the Lord, I would either be in jail or in an institution, or maybe dead by now."

This seems to indicate that Christ Commune (and the Jesus movement in general) may serve a useful function for individuals and for society. At worst it is a deterrent to self-destruction and may often serve as a halfway house on the road back into society. But many, particularly intellectuals, continue to pass negative judgment on the entire Jesus movement. At least some of the bias is, we feel, simply irrational, antireligion sentiment. Some want nothing to do with religion on any terms, and they seem to resent the fact that religion can do some good. However, we would readily admit that some of our findings could substantiate a negative evaluation of the movement and of Christ Commune in particular. Those opposed to the movement could point to the members' political interest, alienation, and personality assessment.

Politics. Before they joined the group, 42 of the members we interviewed in 1971 said they were radicals or liberals (although only two had led political demonstrations). Another 14 claimed to be moderates or conservatives. Only 27 said they had no interest in politics when they lived on the outside. When we asked them to categorize themselves at the time of the interview, only four claimed to be liberals or radicals, and 71 said "nothing" or that they had lost all interest in politics.

We asked them how one could change society if he took no part in politics, and they gave us replies consistent with religious fundamentalism. "The only way to change society is to change men's hearts," said one. "Politics is man's way not God's way, and it (politics) has failed," said another. We often heard references to the Second Coming of Christ, which most members believe to be imminent, making energy spent on politics a waste of time. Our second visit to the group was during the hotly contested 1972 California primary, but not a single member mentioned this crucial contest. No one was interested.

Political Self-Characterization Before and After Joining Christ Commune (First Visit)

Characterize self as:	before joining	after joining	change
conservative	8	6	–25%
moderate	6	5	–17%
liberal	19	1	–95%
radical	23	3	–87%
nothing, don't care	27	71	+ 163%
total	83*	86	

*Totals differ because some information was not ascertained. Eighty eight were interviewed.

Alienation. Such political apathy puts the group (and most other segments of the Jesus movement) in the position of indirectly supporting the political status quo. Members' responses to some items in a preliminary alienation scale (based on Peter Berger's *The Sacred Canopy*) that we used during our first visit confirmed this indirect support.

When we asked, "Do you think that God has a hand in the nomination and election of our country's leaders?" 77 said yes, or yes with some qualifications. Only five said no, or qualified a no answer. When asked, "Do you think that the leaders of our country are guided by God in making decisions?" they gave 50 yes or qualified-yes

" 'I am confident in the Lord, but I am not confident in myself. Therefore I do not have self-confidence.' "

responses, and 27 no or qualified-no responses. When we asked members, "Do you think it is a sin to break a law of the land?" 75 said yes or qualified yes, and only seven said no, or qualified no. When we asked, "Do you think the U.S. generally is an instrument of God in the area of world politics?" 38 said yes or qualified yes, and 43 said no or qualified no. Berger's theory about the alienating effects of religious beliefs predicts that the members of Christ Commune would be likely to answer these questions with a strong yes.

But we found it surprising that so many agreed to this last question, which relates closely to the Vietnam conflict. It is difficult to assess data from the alienation scale. It is possible, of course, that the members were alienated from the institutional structure *before* they joined the Jesus movement, and that their joining simply gave a religious flavor to their alienation. This is information we hope to concentrate on in the future.

Personality. The data that we gathered on the personality patterns of members run into the same objections. We have no way of knowing whether members' personalities changed when they joined, or whether the patterns they reported had been established before they joined the group.

At an evening prayer meeting during our first visit, we administered Gough's Adjective Check List (ACL) which asks a person to choose from a list of 300 adjectives, both positive and negative, those words that he feels best describe him.

We compared our data from Christ Commune with ACL data from a sample of 1,600 college students of similar age, education, and past socioeconomic circumstances. Comparison of standard scores from the two groups suggests that members of Christ Commune are significantly less defensive and less self-confident than their college counterparts. The Christ-Commune group also scored significantly lower on personal adjustment and on all these needs: for achievement, dominance, endurance, order, intraception (a low scorer tends to become bored or impatient when direct action is impossible), affiliation, heterosexuality and change. Group members scored significantly higher than college students on readiness to submit to counseling and on the need for succor and abasement. Per-

sons in the religious group also checked significantly fewer favorable adjectives and more unfavorable adjectives than persons in the college sample did.

Prophecy. Some might say that those ACL results indicate that life in Christ Commune (or in the Jesus movement) leads to maladaptive and deficient personality patterns; however, the results may reflect a greater honesty and frankness in self-evaluation by the commune members than the comparison group showed. Also, the ideology of Christian fundamentalism explicitly suggests that man is sinful and degraded. Thus the commune respondents may have tried to evaluate themselves "the way they were supposed to be," instead of the way they saw themselves. Such attempts at negative self-definition would probably function as self-fulfilling prophecy.

This process seemed to be operating in an interview that took place on the first day of our second visit. An interviewer described one sister's struggle to respond to a question on one of the inventories: "The first person I interviewed was a girl named May Woods. She had an extreme amount of difficulty with one question on the questionnaire: 'I feel self-confident.' She kept talking to herself, trying to figure out what to do about this question. She kept saying things like, 'I'm confident in the Lord, but I'm not confident in myself.' She said this over and over, and she circled and erased her answer several times. Twice she looked up and spoke to me and said something to this effect, 'This is really a tough question. This is really a hard question. I'm having trouble with this question.' And finally she worked it out in a very logical fashion after at least five minutes of fretting over it by saying audibly as she talked to herself, 'I am confident in the Lord, but I am not confident in myself. Therefore I do not have self-confidence.' She circled 'not at all' with reference to that question."

Cooperation. Besides the usual problems of data interpretation another substantial issue must be raised. Some would accept the ACL results as valid and go on to criticize the commune for producing such personality patterns. These same critics propose life-styles that differ from the competitive, aggressive, achievement orientation of our society. We suggest that the Christ Commune might have developed a viable life-style that differs remarkably from what our culture ex-

pects. Perhaps we should congratulate them for developing a way of life that encourages cooperation and self-abasement instead of competition and dominance. We are not ready at this time to take a stand on the issue. The question of the value of such personality patterns is still open. On our two visits there this past summer we again gave members the Adjective Check List and added other personality inventories, but we have not completed analyzing this data.

Mechanism. If, as seems apparent, the brothers and sisters do experience profound changes of personality when they join the sect that operates Christ Commune, interesting questions arise about how the changes occur. We found the thought-reform research of Robert Jay Lifton and others very helpful in understanding the mechanisms of personality change. Lifton's studies of the reform of Chinese intellectuals seem particularly apropos. He developed a three-step model:

1 the great togetherness: group identification;
2 the closing in of the milieu: the period of emotional conflict; and
3 submission and rebirth.

Lifton's analysis comes from an examination of what went on at the Chinese revolutionary universities that were set up between 1948 and 1952. These "universities" were quite large, sometimes involving up to 4,000 persons in highly organized, authoritarian situations. At the start of a session (which lasted approximately six months) administrators warmly greeted participants and told them to spend several days getting to know members of their small groups of about six to 10 persons. Lifton points out that a high *esprit de corps* developed as members openly exchanged personal information and discussed why they were attending the "university."

Thus, we see the development of a new reference group for the persons involved—something similar to what happens upon first contact with some Jesus-movement groups, including Christ Commune. Such groups are friendly and open, and members express genuine concern for the visitor who crashes at the group's residence—they treat him as an important person.

Step 1. Close personal ties begin to develop between prospects and members,

"The prospect either leaves or he submits to group pressures and accepts the group's world view."

strengthening the great "togetherness." Many prospects have come from the dog-eat-dog world of drug-oriented communities or have been moving around the country. Such situations prevent close relationships from developing and the close ties become meaningful. Our data indicate that prospects often stay on at Christ Commune because of the primary relationships that develop; in order to stay successfully, they *must* begin to show interest in the group's ideology.

A prospect begins by studying the Bible, attending prayer groups, and working with the members in the fields. These activities allow him to demonstrate his interest in the group. They also teach him how to act and believe if he wants to remain in the group. The activities affect the prospect as the formal courses and group discussions in the revolutionary universities affected the Chinese intellectuals. In both situations group leaders present acceptable views and help others to rationalize them during the group discussions.

Step 2. The prevailing harmonious situation soon changes drastically. In Lifton's terms, there is a "closing in of the milieu." The group expects the prospect to make progress toward becoming a "committed Christian," and progress follows a fairly rigid timetable. The group brings pressure, both subtle and overt, on the novice, letting him know what kind of belief and behavior the group expects. The leaders at Christ Commune allow an outsider to remain for three or four days without indicating that he is "accepting Christ." After this period, if he still shows no sign that he seriously considers "taking Jesus," they ask him to leave. Commune leaders say that their goal is to bring people to Christ, and that the nonaccepting person would feel uncomfortable unless he shared the beliefs of the others.

Group members explain over and over the value in taking Christ (happiness and, implicitly, acceptance), and the reasons for the difficulty (pride, sinfulness, pleasures of this world, etc.). When a prospect responds there is celebration and the group offers social rewards (warmth, acceptance, addressing the person as "brother" or "sister").

Pressure. The pressure often is successful because the prospect places a high value on the primary relationships that he has developed among the members. The high value members place on such

relationships showed up when 84 percent of members we interviewed on our first visit said that if they had to leave the commune they would miss most the fellowship of the brothers and sisters.

All of us who interviewed members came under such pressure that we felt the need to withdraw at least once a day in order to reaffirm our own world views. If trained and fairly objective observers began to succumb to the group influences, then the effect on participants without strong personalities or alternative reference groups must be great.

A simple way of describing the step of closure is to say that the prospect, after a certain length of time, no longer occupies the privileged newcomer status. He must occupy a new role of interested person which he may hold for an indeterminate period and which eventually leads to the role of "convert."

Step 3. Conversion comes about through "submission and rebirth." The prospect either leaves or he submits to group pressures and accepts the group's world view. This world view contains many elements that aid him in making a proper self-definition and in knowing what actions to take and beliefs to hold as a consequence of his conversion. The new member publicly confesses—submits. (Perhaps he watches members demonstrate the ritual first.) After denying his past and his old self, he commits himself to the future and a new self. This is his rebirth. For some members at Christ Commune, conversion seems to have been a going home—more a reaffirmation of earlier-held values than a learning of things completely new. For these members who have grown up in conservative or fundamentalist churches, the thought-reform process is particularly effective.

Winning converts is the first step. Keeping them is the second.

Here again the organization that runs Christ Commune has been successful. The disaffiliation rate is low; even though the work at the commune is difficult and boring, only about 10 percent of the members drop out.

Christ Commune's emphasis on community is a major element in the group's success. Members must make a total commitment and give up all material things, never to reclaim them. The group encourages members to break their outside ties, and members may not leave or

even make a phone call without receiving a pastor's permission.

The physical isolation of the farm (five miles from a small town) reinforces the social isolation.

Disruption. Communal living and working also builds community. Group leaders structure the daily work so that brothers and sisters toil side by side, never alone. The courtship and marriage rules give needed structure in the troublesome area of sex relations, which might cause group disruption. The organization also has established two schools—kindergarten and elementary—for the 50 to 100 children of members. Thus the group plans to educate their children in the ways of the sect.

While it has developed much elaborate structure, Christ Commune also has shown a willingness to make necessary changes. It has relaxed rules governing sex roles. It has branched out into unknown areas such as farming or fishing as opportunities arose or—they say—"as God guides us."

Recognition. Christ Commune is a successful farming operation that fills its contracts and buys the supplies it needs. The Federal Government has declared it eligible for commodity foods (homemade bread at every meal is made from these). It is a county labor camp (which means that members get free medical care); it is a state-designated conscientious-objector alternative-service center; it has Government-approved nonprofit status, with attendant privileges. The state courts recognize Christ Commune and occasionally remand juvenile delinquents to its custody.

The successful agricultural operation of Christ Commune is a major reason for our confidence in the group's future. It provides a solid financial basis and furnishes money for missionary work. As funds come in, teams go into new areas to establish houses, which serve as recruitment centers.

Another reason Christ Commune will last is the members themselves. They are alienated from institutional society, and are disinterested in it (except as a pool of potential converts). They are noncompetitive, anti-intellectual, and otherworldly. In short, either by accident or design they are unlikely to drift back into ordinary society. Christ Commune and the group it serves will be around for a long time.

IX. Politics

If we have made one mature step in the understanding of young people's involvement with politics, it is that political action is not necessarily equated with adolescent rebellion. One explains little, and at the same time derogates the young by suggesting, as some have, that adolescents' interest in political action stems either from their desire to find safe friendships or rebel against their families, usually their fathers.

One needn't be a historian to know the role of the young in politics over the last few decades. Similarly, one doesn't need to be a behavioral scientist to know that whether or not adolescent political action makes for good news stories, many young people are constantly involved in political action of one sort or another. Indeed, it hardly seems possible that any young person these days can escape from becoming implicated in some political activity, no matter how short-lasting it might be. We have some appreciation for the origins of political interests and attitudes, just as we have some sense of how these attitudes develop into intense political stances and orientations. The problem for observers of adolescent politics, however, is that they rarely get to see the attitude forming, or the political activity getting off the ground. Normally, something of a political nature takes place and then we race to interview the participants, hoping that in their discussions of their lives and their viewpoints, we might make sense of the political world of adolescence. Clearly, we do learn something following this procedure, but to fill out the picture we also need to listen closely to the political activists themselves, as well as to young people who don't see themselves as being particularly political.

In the end, a section on adolescence and politics reminds us that in the study of any human group it is essential that somewhere in our investigation we listen to those we claim to be "studying." Always there will be considerable differences between the way their world appears to them and to us. And, while these differences may not seem to amount to too much, when the topic is politics, the differences may well sizzle. Indeed, even the rise of adolescent sexuality, which we explored briefly in Sections III and VI, doesn't scintillate in the same way that the topic of politics will. It is hard to believe that once adolescent politics meant little to students of human behavior, since now it looms so important as a topic of inquiry.

To be in the world is, at some level, to be political, or at least politicized. While we mustn't be misled by the seeming political sophistication of a young person, we must also not ignore the intensity of feeling generated by that person when political issues are at stake. Adolescents typically know a great deal about politics and good old-fashioned political machinations. They know because an enormous system of communications makes it impossible for them not to know; and they know because they are implicated. And, as we pointed out in the introduction to the section on education, adolescents' involvement with politics cannot be measured by or equated with their knowledge of contemporary and historical political events. Knowledge and the accumulation of information is an essential part of one's political involvements, but it is not the only part. The very definition of "political knowledge" is open to question.

33

Growth of Political Ideas in Adolescence: The Sense of Community

by Joseph Adelson and Robert P. O'Neil

This paper traces the growth of the sense of community during the course of adolescence. Depth interviews were conducted with 120 Ss, 30 each at the ages of 11, 13, 15, and 18. Findings were: (a) Before the age of 13, youngsters are rarely able to transcend personalized modes of discourse in the political realm—they find it hard to imagine the social consequences of political action; (b) younger children, particularly those below 15, find it difficult to conceive the community as a whole—they conceptualize government in terms of specific and tangible services; (c) the idea of the future is incompletely developed in the early years of adolescence—hence it is only in the later period that youngsters can take into account the long-range effects of political action; (d) younger adolescents are usually insensitive to individual liberties and opt for authoritarian solutions to political problems—at the same time, they are unable to achieve a differentiated view of the social order, and thus cannot grasp the legitimate claims of the community upon the citizen; (e) there is a gradual increase with age in the use of philosophical principles for making political judgments.

During adolescence the youngster gropes, stumbles, and leaps towards political understanding. Prior to these years the child's sense of the political order is erratic and incomplete—a curious array of sentiments and dogmas, personalized ideas, randomly remembered names and party labels, half-understood platitudes. By the time adolescence has come to an end, the child's mind, much of the time, moves easily within and among the categories of political discourse. The aim of our research was to achieve some grasp of how this transition is made.

We were interested in political ideas or concepts—in political philosophy—rather than political loyalties per se. Only during the last few years has research begun to appear on this topic. Earlier research on political socialization, so ably summarized by Hyman (1959), concentrated on the acquisition of affiliations and attitudes. More recently, political scientists and some psychologists have explored developmental trends in political knowledge and concepts, especially during childhood and the early years of adolescence; the studies of Greenstein (1965) and of Easton and Hess (1961, 1962) are particularly apposite.

Our early, informal conversations with adolescents suggested the importance of keeping our inquiry at some distance from current political issues; otherwise the underlying structure of the political is obscured by the clichés and catchphrases of partisan politics. To this end, we devised an interview schedule springing from the following premise: Imagine that a thousand men and women, dissatisfied with the way things are going in their country, decide to purchase and move to an island in the Pacific; once there, they must devise laws and modes of government.

Having established this premise, the interview scheduled continued by offering questions on a number of hypothetical issues. For example, the subject was asked to choose among several forms of government and to argue the merits and difficulties of each. Proposed laws were suggested to him; he was asked to weigh their advantages and liabilities and answer arguments from opposing positions. The interview leaned heavily on dilemma items, wherein traditional issues in political theory are actualized in specific instances of political conflict, with the subject asked to choose and justify a solution. The content of our inquiry ranged widely to include, among others, the following topics: the scope and limits of political authority, the reciprocal obligations of citizens and state, utopian views of man and society, conceptions of law and justice, the nature of the political process.

This paper reports our findings on the development, in adolescence, of *the sense of community*. The term is deliberately comprehensive, for we mean to encompass not only government in its organized forms, but also the social and political collectivity more generally, as in "society" or "the people." This concept is of course central to the structure of political thought; few if any issues in political theory do not advert, however tacitly, to some conception of the community. Hence the quality of that conception, whether dim, incomplete, and primitive, or clear, complex, and articulated, cannot fail to dominate or temper the child's formulation of all things political.

The very ubiquity of the concept determined our strategy in exploring it. We felt that the dimensions of community would emerge indirectly, in the course of inquiry focused elsewhere. Our pretesting had taught us that direct questions on such large and solemn issues, though at times very useful, tended to evoke simple incoherence from the cognitively unready, and schoolboy stock responses from the facile. We also learned that (whatever the ostensible topic) most of our questions informed us of the child's view of the social order, not only through what he is prepared to tell us, but also through what he does not know, knows falsely, cannot state, fumbles in stating, or takes for granted. Consequently we approached this topic through a survey of questions from several different areas of the schedule, chosen to illuminate different sides of the sense of community.

Method

Sample

The sample was comprised of 120 youngsters, equally divided by sex, with 30 subjects at each of 4 age-grade levels—fifth grade (average age, 10.9), seventh (12.6), ninth (14.7), and twelfth (17.7). The sample was further divided by intelligence: At each grade level, two thirds of the subjects were of average intelligence (95–110) and one third of superior intelligence (125 and over), as measured by the California Test of Mental Maturity. Table 1 shows the distribution by grade, intelligence, and sex. For each grade, school records were used to establish a pool of subjects meeting our criteria for age, sex, and IQ; within each of the subgroups so selected, names were chosen randomly until the desired sample size was achieved. Children more than 6 months older or younger than the average for their grade were excluded, as were two otherwise eligible subjects reported by their counselor to have a history of severe psychological disturbance.

This paper will report findings by age alone (to the next nearest age) and without regard to sex or intelligence. We were unable to discover sex differences nor—to our continuing

TABLE 1

DISTRIBUTION OF SAMPLE BY GRADE, SEX, AND INTELLIGENCE

	Boys		Girls	
	Average IQ	Superior IQ	Average IQ	Superior IQ
5th grade: N	10	5	10	5
Mean IQ	106.1	127.8	105.1	128.4
7th grade: N	10	5	10	5
Mean IQ	104.1	140.0	104.5	134.4
9th grade: N	10	5	10	5
Mean IQ	106.6	133.2	105.1	134.0
12th grade: N	10	5	10	5
Mean IQ	106.1	140.8	103.8	134.8

surprise—differences associated with intelligence. The brighter children were certainly more fluent, and there is some reason to feel that they use a drier, more impersonal, more intellectualized approach in dealing with certain questions, but up to this time we have found that they attain political concepts earlier than subjects of average intelligence.

The interviews were taken in Ann Arbor, Michigan. We were able to use schools representative of the community, in the sense that they do not draw students from socioeconomically extreme neighborhoods. The children of average IQ were preponderantly lower-middle and working class in background; those of high intelligence were largely from professional and managerial families. Academic families made up 13% of the sample, concentrated in the high IQ group; 5% of the "average" children and somewhat over one quarter of the "brights" had fathers with a professional connection to the University of Michigan. In these respects—socioeconomic status and parental education—the sample, which combined both IQ groups, was by no means representative of the American adolescent population at large. Yet our inability to find differences between the IQ groups, who derive from sharply different social milieux, makes us hesitate to assume that social status is closely associated with the growth of political ideas as we have measured them, or that the findings deviate markedly from what we would find in other middle-class suburbs.

Interview

The aims, scope, and form of the interview schedule have already been described. In developing the schedule we were most concerned to find a tone and level of discourse sufficiently simple to allow our youngest subjects to understand and respond to the problems posed, yet sufficiently advanced to keep our older interviewees challenged and engaged. Another aim was to strike a balance between the focused interview—to ease scoring—and a looser, more discursive approach—to allow a greater depth of inquiry and spontaneity of response. Our interviewers were permitted, once they had covered the basic questions of a topic, to explore it more thoroughly.

The interviews were conducted at the school. There were six interviewers, all with at least some graduate training in clinical psychology. The interviews were tape-recorded and transcribed verbatim. Those conducted with younger subjects were completed in about 1 hour, with older subjects in about 1½ hours.

Reliability

In order to appraise the lower limits of reliability, only the more difficult items were examined, those in which responses were complex or ambiguous. For five items of this type, intercoder reliabilities ranged from .79 to .84.

Results

When we examine the interviews of 11-year-olds, we are immediately struck by the common, pervasive incapacity to speak from a coherent view of the political order. Looking more closely, we find that this failure has two clear sources: First, these children are, in Piaget's sense, egocentric, in that they cannot transcend a purely personal approach to matters which require a sociocentric perspective. Second, they treat political issues in a concrete fashion and cannot manage the requisite abstractness of attitude. These tendencies, singly and together, dominate the discourse of the interview, so much so that a few sample sentences can often distinguish 11-year-old protocols from those given by only slightly older children.

The following are some interview excerpts to il-lustrate the differences: These are chosen randomly from the interviews of 11- and 13-year-old boys of average in-telligence. They have been asked: "What is the purpose of government?"

11A. To handle the state or whatever it is so it won't get out of hand, because if it gets out of hand you might have to . . . people might get mad or something.

11B. Well . . . buildings, they have to look over buildings that would be . . . um, that wouldn't be any use of the land if they had crops on it or something like that. And when they have highways the government would have to inspect it, cer-tain details. I guess that's about all.

11C. So everything won't go wrong in the country. They want to have a government because they respect him and they think he's a good man.

Now the 13-year-olds:

13A. So the people have rights and freedom of speech. Also so the civilization will balance.

13B. To keep law and order and talk to the people to make new ideas.

13C. Well, I think it is to keep the country happy or keep it going properly. If you didn't have it, then it would just be chaos with stealing and things like this. It runs the country better and more efficiently.

These extracts are sufficiently representative to direct us to some of the major developmental patterns in adoles-cent thinking on politics.

Personalism

Under *personalism* we include two related tenden-cies: first, the child's disposition to treat institutions and social processes upon the model of persons and personal relationships; second, his inability to achieve a sociocentric orientation, that is, his failure to understand that political decisions have social as well as personal consequences, and that the political realm encompasses not merely the individual citizen, but the community as a whole.

1. "Government," "community," "society" are ab-stract ideas; they connote those invisible networks of obli-gation and purpose which link people to each other in organized social interaction. These concepts are beyond the effective reach of 11-year-olds; in failing to grasp them they fall back to persons and actions of persons, which are the nearest equivalent of the intangible agencies and ephemeral processes they are trying to imagine. Hence, Subject 11A seems to glimpse that an abstract answer is needed, tries to find it, then despairs and retreats to the personalized "people might get mad or something." A more extreme example is found in 11C's statement, which refers to government as a "he," apparently confusing it with "governor." Gross personalizations of "government" and similar terms are not uncommon at 11 and diminish markedly after that. We counted the number of times the personal pronouns "he" and "she" were used in three questions dealing with government. There were instances involving six subjects among the 11-year-olds (or 20% of the sample) and none among 13-year-olds. (The most striking example is the following sentence by an 11: "Well I don't think she should forbid it, but if they, if he did,

TABLE 2
PURPOSE OF VACCINATION

	Age			
	11	13	15	18
Social consequences (pre-vention of epidemics, etc.)	.23	.67	1.00	.90
Individual consequences (pre-vention of individual illness)	.70	.33	.00	.10

Note.—$x^2(3) = 46.53$, $p < 0.01$. In this table and all that follow $N = 30$ for each age group. When proportions in a column do not total 1.00, certain responses are not included in the response categories shown. When proportions total more than 1.00, responses have been included in more than one category of the table. The p level refers to the total table except when asterisks indicate significance levels for a designated row.

well most people would want to put up an argument about it.")

Although personalizations as bald as these diminish sharply after 11, more subtle or tacit ones continue well into adolescence (and in all likelihood, into adulthood)—the use of "they," for example, when "it" is appropriate. It is our impression that we see a revival of personalization among older subjects under two conditions: when the topic being discussed is too advanced or difficult for the youngster to follow or when it exposes an area of ig-norance or uncertainty, and when the subject's beliefs and resentments are engaged to the point of passion or bitter-ness. In both these cases the emergence of affects (anx-iety, anger) seems to produce a momentary cognitive regression, expressing itself in a loss of abstractness and a reversion to personalized modes of discourse.

2. The second side of personalism is the failure to attain a sociocentric perspective. The preadolescent sub-ject does not usually appraise political events in the light of their collective consequences. Since he finds it hard to conceive the social order as a whole, he is frequently un-able to understand those actions which aim to serve com-munal ends and so tends to interpret them parochially, as serving only the needs of individuals. We have an illustra-tion of this in the data given in Table 2. Table 2 reports the answers to the following item: "Another law was sug-gested which required all children to be vaccinated against smallpox and polio. What would be the purpose of that law?"

A substantial majority—about three quarters—of the 11-year-olds see the law serving an individual end—personal protection from disease. By 13 there has been a decisive shift in emphasis, these children stressing the pro-tection of the community. At 15 and after, an understand-ing of the wider purposes of vaccination has become nearly universal.

Parts and Wholes

Another reflection of the concreteness of younger adolescents can be found in their tendency to treat the total functioning of institutions in terms of specific, dis-crete activities. If we return to the interview excerpts, we find a good example in the answer given by Subject 11B on the purpose of government. He can do no more than mention some specific governmental functions, in this case, the inspecting of buildings and highways. This answer exemplifies a pattern we find frequently among our younger subjects, one which appears in many content areas. Adolescents only gradually perceive institutions (and their processes) as wholes; until they can imagine the institution abstractly, as a total idea, they are limited to the concrete and the visible.

Table 3 is one of several which demonstrates this. The subjects were asked the purpose of the income tax.

TABLE 3

PURPOSE OF INCOME TAX

	Age			
	11	13	15	18
General support of government	.23	.33	.47	1.00*
Specific services only	.23	.17	.23	.00
Do not know	.53	.50	.30	.00

Note.—p level refers to row designated by asterisk.
* $x^2(3) = 9.54$, $p < .05$.

The responses were coded to distinguish those who answered in terms of general government support from those who mentioned only specific government services. (In most cases the services referred to are both local and visible—police, firefighting, etc.) We observe that the percentage of those referring to the government in a general sense rises slowly and steadily; all of the high school seniors do so.

Negatives and Positives

Before we leave this set of interview excerpts, we want to note one more important difference between the 11- and 13-year-olds. Two of the former emphasize the negative or coercive functions of government ("To handle the state . . . so it won't get out of hand"; "So everything won't go wrong . . ."). The 13-year-olds, on the other hand, stress the positive functions of the government— keeping the country happy or working properly. This difference is so important and extensive that we will treat it in depth in a later publication, but it should be discussed at least briefly here. Younger subjects adhere to a Hobbesian view of political man: The citizenry is seen as willful and potentially dangerous, and society, therefore, as rightfully, needfully coercive and authoritarian. Although this view of the political never quite loses its appeal for a certain proportion of individuals at all ages, it nevertheless diminishes both in frequency and centrality, to be replaced, in time, by more complex views of political arrangements, views which stress the administrative sides of government (keeping the machinery oiled and in repair) or which emphasize melioristic ends (enhancing the human condition).

The Future

The adolescent years see a considerable extension of time perspective. On the one hand, a sense of history emerges, as the youngster is able to link past and present and to understand the present as having been influenced or determined by the past. On the other, the child begins to imagine the future and, what may be more important, to

ponder alternative futures. Thus the present is connected to the future not merely because the future unfolds from the present, but also because the future is *tractable*; its shape depends upon choices made in the present.

This idea of the future asserts itself with increasing effect as the child advances through adolescence. In making political judgments, the youngster can anticipate the consequences of a choice taken here and now for the long-range future of the community and can weigh the probable effects of alternative choices on the future. The community is now seen to be temporal, that is, as an organism which persists beyond the life of its current members; thus judgments in the present must take into account the needs of the young and of the unborn. Further, the adolescent becomes able to envision not only the communal future, but himself (and others) in possible statuses in that future as well.

The items which most clearly expose the changing meaning of the future are those dealing with education. When we reflect on it, this is not surprising: Education is the public enterprise which most directly links the generations to each other; it is the communal activity through which one generation orients another toward the future. Several questions of public policy toward education were asked; in the answers to each the needs of the communal future weigh more heavily with increasing age. One item runs: "Some people suggested a law which would require children to go to school until they were sixteen years old. What would be the purpose of such a law?" One type of answer to this question was coded "Continuity of community"; these responses stress the community's need to sustain and perpetuate itself by educating a new generation of citizens and leaders. Typical answers were: "So children will grow up to be leaders," and "To educate people so they can carry on the government." Looking at this answer alone (analysis of the entire table would carry us beyond this topic), we find the following distribution by age (see Table 4).

TABLE 4

PURPOSE OF MINIMUM EDUCATION LAW

	Age			
	11	13	15	18
Continuity of community	.00	.27	.33	.43

Note.—$x^2(3) = 11.95$, $p < .01$.

Another item later in the interview poses this problem: "The people who did not have children thought it was unfair they would have to pay taxes to support the school system. What do you think of that argument?" Again the same category, which stresses the community's continuity and its future needs, rises sharply with age as shown in Table 5.

Finally, we want to examine another education item in some detail, since it offers a more complex view of the sense of the future in adolescent political thought, allowing us to observe changes in the child's view of the personal future. The question was the last of a series on the minimum education law. After the subject was asked to discuss its purpose (see above), he was asked whether he sup-

TABLE 5

Should People without Children
Pay School Taxes?

	Age			
	11	13	15	18
Continuity of community	.10	.10	.47	.60

Note.—$x^2(3) = 18.61$, $p < .001$.

ports it. Almost all of our subjects did. He was then asked: "Suppose you have a parent who says 'My son is going to go into my business anyway and he doesn't need much schooling for that.' Do you think his son should be required to go to school anyway? Why?"

Table 6 shows that as children advance into adoles-

TABLE 6

Should Son Be Required To Attend School
though Father Wants Him To Enter Business?

	Age			
	11	13	15	18
Yes, education needed to function in community	.00	.23	.43	.77***
Yes, education good in itself	.03	.23	.20	.27
Yes, education need in business	.40	.47	.23	.13
Yes, prevents parental coercion	.57	.47	.43	.23

Note.—p level refers to row designated by asterisk.
*** $x^2(3) = 25.54$, $p < .001$.

cence, they stress increasingly the communal function of education. Younger subjects respond more to the father's arbitrariness or to the economic consequences of the father's position. They are less likely to grasp the more remote, more general effects of a curtailed education—that it hinders the attainment of citizenship. Representative answers by 11-year-olds were: "Well, maybe he wants some other desire and if he does maybe his father is forcing him"; and ". . . let's say he doesn't like the business and maybe he'd want to start something new." These children stress the practical and familial aspects of the issue.

Older subjects, those 15 and 18, all but ignored both the struggle with the father and the purely pragmatic advantages of remaining in school. They discoursed, sometimes eloquently, on the child's need to know about society as a whole, to function as a citizen, and to understand the perspectives of others. Here is how one 18-year-old put it:

. . . a person should have a perspective and know a little bit about as much as he can rather than just one thing throughout his whole life and anything of others, because he'd have to know different things about different aspects of life and education and just how things are in order to get along with them, because if not then they'd be prejudiced toward their own feelings and what *they* wanted and they wouldn't be able to understand any people's needs.

Older subjects see education as the opportunity to become *cosmopolitan*, to transcend the insularities of job

and kinship. For the older adolescent, leaving school early endangers the future in two ways. On the personal side, it threatens one's capacity to assume the perspective of the other and to attain an adequate breadth of outlook; thus, it imperils one's future place in the community. On the societal side, it endangers the integrity of the social order itself, by depriving the community of a cosmopolitan citizenry.

Claims of the Community

We have already seen that as adolescence advances the youngster is increasingly sensitive to the fact of community and its claims upon the citizen. What are the limits of these claims, the limits of political authority? To what point, and under what conditions can the state, acting in the common good, trespass upon the autonomy of the citizen? When do the community's demands violate the privacy and liberty of the individual? The clash of these principles—individual freedom versus the public welfare and safety—is one of the enduring themes of Western political theory. Many, perhaps most, discussions in political life in one way or another turn on this issue; indeed, the fact that these principles are so often used purely rhetorically (as when the cant of liberty or of the public good is employed to mask pecuniary and other motives) testifies to their salience in our political thinking.

A number of questions in the interview touched upon this topic tangentially, and some were designed to approach it directly. In these latter we asked the subject to adjudicate and comment upon a conflict between public and private interests, each of these supported by a general political principle—usually the individual's right to be free of compulsion, on the one hand, and the common good, on the other. We tried to find issues which would be tangled enough to engage the most complex modes of political reasoning. A major effort in this direction was made through a series of three connected questions on eminent domain. The series began with this question:

Here is another problem the Council faced. They decided to build a road to connect one side of the island to the other. For the most part they had no trouble buying the land on which to build the road, but one man refused to sell his land to the government. He was offered a fair price for his land but he refused, saying that he didn't want to move, that he was attached to his land, and the Council could buy another piece of land and change the direction of the road. Many people thought he was selfish, but others thought he was in the right. What do you think?

Somewhat to our surprise, there are no strong developmental patterns visible, though we do see a moderate tendency (not significant statistically, however) for the younger subjects to side with the landowner (see Table 7). The next question in the series sharpened the issue somewhat between the Council and the reluctant landowner:

The Council met and after long discussion voted that if the landowner would not agree to give up his land for the road, he should be forced to, because the rights of all the people on the island were more important than his. Do you think this was a fair decision?

The phrasing of the second question does not alter

TABLE 7

WHICH PARTY IS RIGHT IN EMINENT-DOMAIN CONFLICT?

	Age			
	11	13	15	18
Individual should sell; community needs come first	.30	.20	.30	.40
Detour should be made; individual rights come first	.60	.47	.27	.37
Emphasis on social responsibility; individual should be appealed to, but not forced	.10	.17	.17	.07
Ambivalence; individual is right in some ways, wrong in others	.00	.13	.27	.17

TABLE 8

SHOULD LANDOWNER BE FORCED TO SELL HIS LAND?

	Age			
	11	13	15	18
Yes, rights of others come first	.40	.37	.63	.70
No, individual rights come first	.57	.50	.33	07**
No, social responsibility should suffice	.03	.10	.00	.23

Note.—*p* level refers to row designated by asterisk.
** $x^2(3) = 12.17$, $p < .01$.

the objective facts of the conflict; yet Table 8 shows decisive shifts in position. It is hard to be sure why: perhaps because the second question states that the Council has considered the matter at length, perhaps because the Council's decision is justified by advancing the idea of "the people's rights." Whatever the reason, we now see a marked polarization of attitude. The younger subjects—those 11 and 13—continue to side with the landowner; those 15 and 18 almost completely abandon him, although about one quarter of the latter want to avoid coercion and suggest an appeal to his sense of social responsibility.

The final question in the series tightened the screws:

The landowner was very sure that he was right. He said that the law was unjust and he would not obey it. He had a shotgun and would shoot anyone who tried to make him get off his land. He seemed to mean business. What should the government do?

The landowner's threat startled some of the subjects, though in very different ways depending on age, as Table 9 shows: The younger subjects in these cases did not quite

TABLE 9

WHAT SHOULD GOVERNMENT DO IF LANDOWNER THREATENS VIOLENCE?

	Age			
	11	13	15	18
Detour	.60	.63	.37	.10
Government coercion justified	.23	.27	.57	.83

Note.—$x^2(3) = 29.21$, $p < .001$.

know what to do about it and suggested that he be mollified at all costs; the older subjects, if they were taken aback, were amused or disdainful, saw him as a lunatic or a hothead, and rather matter-of-factly suggested force or guile to deal with him. Nevertheless, this question did not produce any essential change in position for the sample as a whole. Those older subjects who had hoped to appeal to the landowner's social conscience despaired of this and sided with the Council. Otherwise, the earlier pattern persisted, the two younger groups continuing to support the citizen, the older ones favoring the government, and overwhelmingly so among the oldest subjects.

These findings seem to confirm the idea that older adolescents are more responsive to communal than to individual needs. Yet it would be incorrect to infer that these subjects favor the community willy-nilly. A close look at the interview protocols suggests that older adolescents choose differently because they reason differently.

Most younger children—those 13 and below—can offer no justification for their choices. Either they are content with a simple statement of preference, for example: "I think he was in the right"; or they do no more than paraphrase the question: "Well, there is really two sides to it. One is that he is attached and he shouldn't give it up, but again he should give it up for the country." These youngsters do not or cannot rationalize their decisions, neither through appeal to a determining principle, nor through a comparative analysis of each side's position. If there is an internal argument going on within the mind of the 11- or 13-year-old, he is unable to make it public; instead, he seems to choose by an intuitive ethical leap, averring that one or the other position is "fair," "in the right," or "selfish." He usually favors the landowner, because his side of the matter is concrete, personal, psychologically immediate, while the Council's position hinges on an idea of the public welfare which is too remote and abstract for these youngsters to absorb. Even those few children who try to reason from knowledge or experience more often than not flounder and end in confusion. A 13-year-old:

Like this girl in my class. Her uncle had a huge house in
————, and they tore it down and they put the new city hall there. I think they should have moved it to another place. I think they should have torn it down like they did, because they had a law that if there was something paid for, then they should give that man a different price. But then I would force him out, but I don't know how I'd do it.

What we miss in these interviews are two styles of reasoning which begin to make their appearance in 15-year-olds: first, the capacity to reason consequentially, to trace out the long-range implications of various courses of action; second, a readiness to deduce specific choices from general principles. The following excerpt from a 15-year-old's interview illustrates both of these approaches:

Well, maybe he owned only a little land if he was a farmer and even if they did give him a fair price maybe all the land was already bought on the island that was good for farming or something and he couldn't get another start in life if he did buy it. Then maybe in a sense he was selfish because if they had to buy other land and change the direction of the road why of course then maybe they'd raise taxes on things so they could get more money cause it would cost more to change directions from what they already have planned. [Fair to force him off?] Yes, really, just because one person doesn't want to sell his land that don't mean that, well the other 999 or the rest of the people on the island should go without this road because of one.

In the first part of the statement, the subject utilizes a cost-effectiveness approach; he estimates the costs (economic, social, moral) of one decision against another. He begins by examining the effects on the landowner. Can he obtain equivalent land elsewhere? He then considers the long-range economic consequences for the community. Will the purchase of other land be more expensive and thus entail a tax increase? Though he does not go on to solve these implicit equations—he could hardly do so, since he does not have sufficient information—he does state the variables he deems necessary to solve them.

The second common strategy at this age, seen in the last part of the statement, is to imply or formulate a general principle, usually ethico-political in nature, which subsumes the instance. Most adolescents using this approach will for this item advert to the community's total welfare, but some of our older adolescents suggest some other governing principle—the sanctity of property rights or the individual's right to privacy and autonomy. In either instance, the style of reasoning is the same; a general principle is sought which contains the specific issue.

Once a principle is accepted, the youngster attempts to apply it consistently. If the principle is valid, it should fall with equal weight on all; consequently, exceptions are resisted:

I think that the man should be forced to move with a good sum of money because I imagine it would be the people, it said the rights of the whole, the whole government and the whole community, why should one man change the whole idea?

And to the question of the landowner's threatening violence: "They shouldn't let him have his own way, because he would be an example. Other people would think that if they used his way, they could do what they wanted to." Even a child who bitterly opposes the Council's position on this issue agrees that once a policy has been established, exceptions should be resisted:

Well, if the government is going to back down when he offers armed resistance, it will offer ideas to people who don't like, say, the medical idea [see below]. They'll just haul out a shotgun if you come to study them. The government should go through with the action.

The Force of Principle

Once principles and ideals are firmly established, the child's approach to political discourse is decisively altered. When he ponders a political choice, he takes into account not only *personal* consequences (What will this mean, practically speaking, for the individuals involved?) and pragmatic *social* consequences (What effect will this have on the community at large?), but also its consequences in the realm of *value* (Does this law or decision enhance or endanger such ideals as liberty, justice, and so on?). There is of course no sharp distinction among these types of consequences; values are contained, however tacitly, in

the most "practical" of decisions. Nevertheless, these ideals, once they develop, have a life, an autonomy of their own. We reasoned that as the adolescent grew older, political principles and ideals would be increasingly significant, and indeed would loom large enough to overcome the appeal of personal and social utility in the narrow sense.

To test this belief we wanted an item which would pit a "good" against a "value." We devised a question proposing a law which, while achieving a personal and communal good, would at the same time violate a political ideal—in this case, the value of personal autonomy. The item ran: "One [proposed law] was a suggestion that men over 45 be required to have a yearly medical checkup. What do you think of that suggestion?" The answer was to be probed if necessary: "Would you be in favor of that? Why (or why not)?" Table 10 shows the distribution of responses.

TABLE 10

SHOULD MEN OVER 45 BE REQUIRED TO HAVE
A YEARLY MEDICAL CHECKUP?

	Age			
	11	13	15	18
Yes, otherwise they would not do it	.50	.07	.00	.03***
Yes, good for person and/or community	.50	.80	.70	.60
No, infringement on liberties	.00	.13	.27	.37**

Note.—*p* level refers to rows designated by asterisk.
** $x^2(3) = 11.95$, $p < .01$.
*** $x^2(3) = 33.10$, $p < .001$.

The findings are interesting on several counts, aside from offering testimony on the degree to which good health is viewed as a summum bonum. The 11-year-olds, here as elsewhere, interpret the issue along familial and authoritarian lines. The government is seen in loco parentis; its function is to make its citizens do the sensible things they would otherwise neglect to do. But our primary interest is in the steady growth of opposition to the proposal. The basis for opposition, though it is phrased variously, is that the government has no business exercising compulsion in this domain. These youngsters look past the utilitarian appeal of the law and sense its conflict with a value that the question itself does not state. These data, then, offer some support to our suggestion that older adolescents can more easily bring abstract principles to bear in the appraisal of political issues. Strictly speaking, the findings are not definitive, for we cannot infer that all of those supporting the law do so without respect to principle. Some of the older adolescents do, in fact, recognize the conflict implicit in the question, but argue that the public and personal benefits are so clear as to override the issue of personal liberties. But there are very few signs of this among the younger subjects. Even when pressed, as they were in a following question, they cannot grasp the meaning and significance of the conflict; they see only the tangible good.

Discussion

These findings suggest that the adolescent's sense of community is determined not by a single factor, but by the interaction of several related developmental parameters. We should now be in a position to consider what some of these are.

1. *The decline of authoritarianism.* Younger subjects are more likely to approve of coercion in public affairs. Themselves subject to the authority of adults, they more readily accept the fact of hierarchy. They find it hard to imagine that authority may be irrational, presumptuous, or whimsical; thus they bend easily to the collective will.

2. With advancing age there is an increasing grasp of the *nature and needs of the community.* As the youngster begins to understand the structure and functioning of the social order as a whole, he begins to understand too the specific social institutions within it and their relations to the whole. He comes to comprehend the autonomy of institutions, their need to remain viable, to sustain and enhance themselves. Thus the demands of the social order and its constituent institutions, as well as the needs of the public, become matters to be appraised in formulating political choices.

3. *The absorption of knowledge and consensus.* This paper has taken for granted, and hence neglected, the adolescent's increasing knowingness. The adolescent years see a vast growth in the acquisition of political information, in which we include not only knowledge in the ordinary substantive sense, but also the apprehension of consensus, a feeling for the common and prevailing ways of looking at political issues. The child acquires these from formal teaching, as well as through a heightened cathexis of the political, which in turn reflects the generally amplified interest in the adult world. Thus, quite apart from the growth of cognitive capacity, the older adolescent's views are more "mature" in that they reflect internalization of adult perspectives.

4. We must remember that it is not enough to be exposed to mature knowledge and opinion; their absorption in turn depends on the growth of *cognitive capacities.* Some of the younger subjects knew the fact of eminent domain, knew it to be an accepted practice, yet, unable to grasp the principles involved, could not apply their knowledge effectively to the question. This paper has stressed the growth of those cognitive capacities which underlie the particular intellectual achievements of the period: the adolescent's increasing ability to weigh the relative consequences of actions, the attainment of deductive reasoning. The achievement of these capacities—the leap to "formal operations," in Piaget's term—allows him to escape that compulsion toward the immediate, the tangible, the narrowly pragmatic which so limits the political discourse of younger adolescents.

5. In turn the growth of cognitive capacity allows *the birth of ideology.* Ideology may not be quite the right word here, for it suggests a degree of coherence and articulation that few of our subjects, even the oldest and brightest, come close to achieving. Nevertheless there is an impressive difference between the younger and older adolescents in the orderliness and internal consistency of their political perspectives. What passes for ideology in the younger respondents is a raggle-taggle array of sentiments: "People ought to be nice to each other"; "There are a lot of wise guys around, so you have to have strict laws." In time these sentiments may mature (or harden) into ideologies or ideological dispositions, but they are still too erratic, too inconsistent. They are not yet principled or generalized and so tend to be self-contradictory, or loosely held and hence easily abandoned. When younger subjects are cross-questioned, however gently, they are ready to reverse themselves even on issues they seem to feel strongly about. When older subjects are challenged, however sharply, they refute, debate, and counterchallenge. In some part their resistance to easy change reflects a greater degree of poise and their greater experience in colloquy and argument, but it also bespeaks the fact that their views are more firmly founded. The older adolescents, most conspicuously those at 18, aim for an inner concordance of political belief.

These then are the variables our study has suggested as directing the growth of political concepts. We must not lean too heavily on any one of them: The development of political thought is not simply or even largely a function of cognitive maturation or of increased knowledge or of the growth of ideology when these are taken alone. This paper has stressed the cognitive parameters because they seem to be so influential at the younger ages. The early adolescent's political thought is constrained by personalized, concrete, present-oriented modes of approach. Once these limits are transcended, the adolescent is open to influence by knowledge, by the absorption of consensus, and by the principles he adopts from others or develops on his own.

A Developmental Synopsis

We are now in a position to summarize the developmental patterns which have emerged in this study. It is our impression that the most substantial advance is to be found in the period between 11 and 13 years, where we discern a marked shift in the cognitive basis of political discourse. Our observations support the Inhelder and Piaget (1958) findings on a change from concrete to formal operations at this stage. To overstate the case somewhat, we might say that the *11-year-old* has not achieved the capacity for formal operations. His thinking is concrete, egocentric, tied to the present; he is unable to envision long-range social consequences; he cannot comfortably reason from premises; he has not attained hypothetico-deductive modes of analysis. The 13-year-old has achieved these capacities some (much?) of the time, but is unable to display them with any consistent effectiveness. The *13-year-olds* seem to be the most labile of our subjects. Depending on the item, they may respond like those older or younger than themselves. In a sense they are on the threshold of mature modes of reasoning, just holding on, and capable of slipping back easily. Their answers are the most difficult to code, since they often involve an uneasy mixture of the concrete and the formal.

The *15-year-old* has an assured grasp of formal thought. He neither hesitates nor falters in dealing with the abstract; when he seems to falter, it is more likely due to a lack of information or from a weakness in knowing and using general principles. His failures are likely to be in content and in fluency, rather than in abstract quality per se. Taking our data as a whole we usually find only moderate differences between 15 and 18. We do find concepts that appear suddenly between 11 and 13, and between 13 and 15, but only rarely do we find an idea substantially represented at 18 which is not also available to a fair number of 15-year-olds.

The *18-year-old* is, in other words, the 15-year-old, only more so. He knows more; he speaks from a more extended aperceptive mass; he is more facile; he can elaborate his ideas more fluently. Above all, he is more philosophical, more ideological in his perspective on the political order. At times he is consciously, deliberately an ideologue. He holds forth.

REFERENCES

EASTON, D., & HESS, R. D. Youth and the political system. In S. M. Lipset & L. Lowenthal (Eds.), *Culture and social character*. New York: Free Press of Glencoe, 1961. Pp. 226–251.

EASTON, D., & HESS, R. D. The child's political world. *Midwest Journal of Political Science*, 1962, 6, 229–246.

GREENSTEIN, F. *Children and politics.* New Haven: Yale University Press, 1965.

HYMAN, H. H. *Political socialization.* Glencoe, Ill.: Free Press, 1959.

INHELDER, B., & PIAGET, J. *The growth of logical thinking from childhood to adolescence*. New York: Basic Books, 1958.

34

ERIK H. ERIKSON

Reflections on the Dissent of Contemporary Youth

I

IT IS not without diffidence that one undertakes to write yet one
more paper on youth. The literature on contemporary "unrest" is
growing by the week, the day, the hour. Much of it reflects a profound unrest among adults—a traumatized state, in fact, that seeks
catharsis in hurried attempts to reassert intellectual mastery over a
shocking course of events. The conclusions reached, therefore, tend
to become outdated during the very period of publication. At this
point, then, only the double promise of some systematic clarification
of the divergent phenomena of dissent and of some gain for the
theory of development justifies writing about dissent at all. My reflections will concentrate on what we have learned about the place
and function of youth in the human life cycle in all its historical
relativity, and about the fateful role of childhood in historical
change.

In writing for a professional journal, one can take the assumption for granted that there is, there must be, a pervasive irrational involvement in any attempt on the part of adults to reorient
themselves in the face of youthful challenges; for youth, almost
by definition, has a presence that defies theorizing. One may also
assume agreement that a historical self-critique of psychoanalysis as
well as other schemata of human development must include an
assessment of the role that their discoveries are playing in the ideological tensions of our time. If rebellious youth in the second part of
this fast-moving century must manage and transcend the revolutionary changes of the first part, the influence of Freud's insights into
unconscious motivation are now part of that burden. True, some
young people can accept the new depth only by displaying it, sometimes passionately and often mockingly, on the very surface, or by
challenging it precipitously with experiences induced by drugs, as
if the new generation had already faced up to all the inner dangers
as well as the outer ones. But if in this stance—as also in that of
much of modern literature and drama—we detect an attempt to
assimilate the insights of psychoanalysis by means of overt enactment of previously repressed urges, then psychoanalysis is faced
with new Hippocratic tasks.

One such task is defined by the fact that today we can no longer,
not even in clinical literature, write *about* youth without writing
for youth. And while a systematic critique of contemporary and

controversial behavior is always beset with grave methodological problems, I do not see how we can take either our students or our field seriously without stating what *prophecy* and what *retrogression* we are able to discern with our methods in today's patterns of dissent. By this I mean that youthful behavior, where it arouses ambivalent fascination, always appears to be both prophetic—that is, inspired by the vigor of a new age—and retrogressive insofar as it seems to insist on outworn simplicities and to display astonishing regressions. I am speaking, then, of the emotional charge of certain patterns of dissent, not of their political utility or detriment. The young reader of a discourse concerned with such alternations, however, will always find himself responding to open or hidden indications as to whether the author seems to be for or against what he attempts to clarify; and if the methodology of the discourse is based on the application of clinical observation, every reference to developmental fixation or retrogression is apt to be understood as a suggestion of weakness, wickedness, or morbid pretense, and thus as an expression of a generational or political prejudice on the part of the author. These difficulties, however, cannot be shunned if and when we concern ourselves with contemporary phenomena, convinced as we are that psychoanalytic insight has a role to fulfill in the critique of the wasteful aspects of cultural and historical change, which mankind as a whole can ill afford. It would seem, in fact, that a few of the leading young revolutionaries of today are aware of some emotional regressiveness in radical undertakings which are already marked by historical retrogression.

In attempting to clarify the emotional roots of youthful dissent, we must concede from the onset that even psychoanalysis—like other once-revolutionary movements—has let itself be drawn into modern attempts to neutralize powerful inner and outer forces by making man more superficially and more mechanically adjustable. Some of the more prophetic concerns of today's youth may, in fact, serve to renew—or, at any rate, to remind us of a liberating vision inherent in the beginnings of psychoanalysis.

II

Before selecting some circumscribed phenomena of active dissent for psychoanalytic scrutiny, I, too, must present a few speculations on the changing ecology of youth in the present stage of history. To the older generation, of course, historical and technological change always seems to be a matter of degree until many related differences have come to amount to a frightening change in over-all quality.

Adolescence has always been seen as an interim stage between an alternately invigorating and confusing sense of an overdefined past that must be left behind and a future as yet to be identified—and to be identified with. Even in a period of rapid change, adolescence seems to serve the function of committing the growing person to the possible achievements and the comprehensible ideals of an existing or developing civilization. In our time, the new requirements of disciplined teamwork and programmed rationality in organizations living in inescapable symbiosis with technological systems seem to offer a satisfying and self-corrective world-image to many, if not most. Most young people, then, see no reason to question "the system" seriously, if only because they have never visualized another.

In every individual, however, and in every generation, there is a potential for what we may call an intensified *adolescence*—that is, a critical phase marked by the reciprocal aggravation of internal conflict and of societal disorganization. Psychoanalysis, for obvious reasons, has primarily studied those more malignant kinds of aggravation that are the result of unresolved infantile conflict and of adolescent isolation. Yet, from Freud's patient Dora on, the case histories of neurotically aggravated young people have also demonstrated a relationship between the epidemiology of a given time and the hidden conflicts of the generations—and thus to history itself. If, on the other hand, another sector of aggravated youth becomes militantly agitated and sets out to agitate on a large scale, it often succeeds way beyond its numerical strength or political foresight because it draws out and inflames the latent aggravations of that majority of young people who would otherwise choose only banal and transient ways of voicing dissent or displaying conflict—and about whom, therefore, psychoanalysis knows so very little. From this point of view, our patients often appear to be the inverted dissenters—too sick for the modish malaise of their time, too isolated for joint dissent, and yet too sensitive for simple adjustment.

What, then, are the quantitative changes that seem to change the quality of adolescence in our time? It is said that there are simply more young people around than ever before; that they now generally mature earlier; and that more of them are better informed about world conditions—and informed both by a common literacy and the common imagery of mass communication—than ever before. But while these shared vocabularies and imageries convey simplified ideals of identity, personality, and competence, such promise becomes forever illusory because of the daily vagaries of technological, legal, and bureaucratic complexities—themselves a result of a variety of quantitative changes. Often, therefore, only to be intensely "with it" and with one another provides a sense of individuality and communality in otherwise paralyzing discontinuities. This, it seems, is expressed vividly and often devastatingly in songs of shouted loneliness underscored by a pounding rhythm-to-end-all-rhythms in a sea of circling colors and lights. Such active and joint mastery of a cacophonous world can be experienced with an emotional and physical abandon unlike anything the older generations ever dreamed of; and yet—especially where compounded by drugs—it can also camouflage a reciprocal isolation of desperate depth.

III

But perhaps an observer learns most as he becomes aware of what social change is doing with (and to) his own conceptualizations of youth. We have, for example, postulated within the stage of youth a psychological moratorium—a period when the young person can dramatize or at any rate experiment with patterns of behavior which are both—or neither quite—infantile and adult, and yet often find a grandiose alignment with traditional ideals or new ideological trends. A true moratorium, of course, provides leeway for timeless values; it takes the pressure out of time—but it must end. If in the past young people (and creative adults) have often mourned the end of the moratorium as an irrevocable loss of potential identities, today young leaders, transient as they are, declare the world beyond youth to be totally void and faceless. But a moratorium without end also disposes of all utopias—except that of an infinite moratorium. The large-scale utopias that were to initiate a new kind of history in the postwar period—the war that would end all wars, the socialism that would make the state wither away, the thousand-year Reich, or the advent of militant nonviolence—they have all been followed by holocausts as coldly planned as were the gas chambers and Hiroshima, or as shockingly planless as mass riots; and they have been superseded by bureaucratic-industrial systems of negligible ideological differentiation. Thus also ended the unquestioned superiority of the fathers whether they had obeyed and died, or survived and thrived. If then, as it always must, rebellious youth borrows roles from past revolutions, it must now avoid the temptation to settle for any previous consolidations. The mere thought of what form the world might take after the next revolution seems in itself counter-revolutionary.

A moratorium without some kind of utopian design, however, can lead only to an ideological promiscuity that both adopts and disposes of the old revolutions. There is, of course, the Marxist model. Some of today's activists like to resemble Marxist revolutionaries in appearance and in vocabulary, but cannot possibly share either their erstwhile hopes or, indeed, their intellectual discipline and political skill. They need a proletariat to liberate, but few groups of workers today could be led for long by intellectual youths with no blueprint. Thus, youth must appoint *itself* a kind of proletariat—and "the people" often comes to mean primarily young people.

Another model is the Gandhian one, anticolonial and nonviolent. There is hardly an item in the arsenal of modern protest—from card-burning to mass marching—that Gandhi did not invent as part of the revolutionary method of militant nonviolence. Originally a revolt of those who happened to be unarmed, it came through him

to mean above all the method of those who *chose* to remain unarmed. Yet today's youth (except for such devotional groups as
the civil rights marchers and the draft-resisting dissenters in
America) has lacked the continuity that could elevate nonviolent
protest to the level of national campaigns. Nor is there much likelihood that the remaining victims of colonialism care to count on
the youth of affluent countries. Therefore, youth has appointed
itself also the corporate victim of colonialism; and the mere dependence on an older generation comes to symbolize a despised
colonial heritage.

Gandhi was by no means unaware of the cathartic function of
violence; the psychiatrist Frantz Fanon was its spokesman. By emphasizing the therapeutic necessity of revolutionary violence, he
forms an ideological link between anti-colonialism and the "Freudian revolution," which has counterpointed the methods of political
liberation with a systematic exploration of man's psychological
bondage. Some of our young people, combining emotional license
with alternately violent and nonviolent confrontation and with both
intellectual and anti-intellectual protest, attempt to combine the
gains of all revolutions in one improvised moratorium and often
succeed only in endangering and even mocking them all.

Out of the combined revolutions of the oppressed and the
repressed, of the proletarians, the unarmed, and the mental suffer-
ers, there seems to have now emerged a *revolt of the dependent*.
That to be dependent means to be exploited is the ideological link
between the developmental stage of youth, the economic state of
the poor, and the political state of the underdeveloped. This, at
least, could partially explain the astounding similarity of the logic
used in the patterns of confrontation both by privileged youth and
by the underprivileged citizenry. And has youth not learned from
psychoanalysis to look at man's prolonged childhood dependence as
an evolutionary fact artificially protracted by adults in order to sub-
vert the radiance of children and the vigor of youth and to confirm
the molds of adult self-images?

The revolt of the dependent, however, directly challenges all
those existing institutions that monopolize the admissions procedures to the main body of society. These confirmations, graduations,
and inductions have always attempted to tie youthful prophecy to
existing world images, offering a variety of rites characterized by
special states of ceremonious self-diffusion. All this, too, dissenting
youth now seeks to provide for itself in newly improvised and ritualized self-graduations, from musical happenings to communal experiment and to political revolt.

I have now indicated a few aspects of the revolutionary inheri-
tance which past generations and especially the charismatic leaders of the postwar period have bequeathed to youth. In the meantime, however, industrialization has changed all basic premises; and
the majority of young people remain engaged in the invention and
perfection of techniques that by their immense practicality could
assure safety, rationality, and abundance, even as the exploration
of space promises a new type of heroic adventure and limitless ce-
lestial leeway. But even technological youth respond at times to
the prophetic quality of the two questions aggravated youth seems
to ask: When if not now, in this post-ideological period in history
and before cosmic technocracy takes over altogether, will man attempt to combine his timeless values, his new insights, and his coming mastery in one all-human outlook and planning? And who if not
they, the young people assembled in the prolonged moratorium of
academic life, will live and rebel for the sake of that outlook?

IV

Freud at one time stressed that society must of necessity act as a suppressor of individuality, genitality, and intellect, and that far from wishing to overcome human violence as such, societies merely insist on the right to control the means and to stipulate the targets of violence. Freud stood for the primacy of insight, but he took state and civilization for granted; he faced the specter of totalitarian societies only toward the end of his life. Since then, psychoanalysis has found a mutual accommodation with societal systems that can claim to offer a maximum of opportunity to the greatest number of their citizens and that promote, together with the comforts of expanding technology, the pursuit of learning and of health—even of mental health. Psychoanalytic ego psychology, in turn, has come to study those adaptive social processes that must protect and support ego development in childhood and give strength and direction to adolescent identity. But while the complementarity of individual and societal processes has been acknowledged and studied, questions in regard to the potential arbitrariness of all systems of power have remained. This questioning has, in fact, been vastly intensified in recent years with the increasing awareness of the use (or misuse) to which large-scale organization puts individual inventiveness and valor. Even the most affluent and progressive systems seem to thrive at the expense of individual values: Their costliness may become apparent in the restriction of spontaneity in the midst of a system extolling individual freedom; in the standardization of information in the midst of a universal communications industry; and, worse, in new and numbing denials in the midst of universal enlightenment.

Modern youth has grown up with the fact that an affluent civilization can learn to become relatively peaceful and neighborly in large areas of its existence and yet delegate the greatest destructive power that ever existed to nuclear monsters scientifically created and loyally serviced by well-adjusted experts and technicians. Not that most young people any more than most adults can keep this paradox in the center of attention for any length of time; but was it not, again, psychoanalysis which taught that man is responsible for what he represses or attempts to remain unaware of? Yet much as we have learned about the consequences of sexual repression, we do not yet possess systematic terms and concepts adequate to deal with the split in human awareness that makes the coexistence of consumer affluence and of minutely planned "overkill" possible, nor with the emotional price exacted for this split.

And yet we must realize that the specter of nuclear war changes the whole ecology of what we have come to view as the over-all instinctual economy of man. As long as wars can (or could) provide ideologically convincing reasons for the massive deflection of hate on external enemies, much interpersonal and intergenerational conflict could live itself out in periodic states of war. As communication makes the enemy appear human, and as technological developments make war absurd, unrelieved self-hate as well as the hateful tension in families and communities may well cause new and bewildering forms of violence.

No wonder, then, that the *legitimacy of violence* becomes the greatest single issue in the ideological struggle of youth today. It can come to sharpest awareness in those young men who must be prepared to see themselves or their friends inducted into a "service" that legitimizes what appears to be the senseless continuation of colonial wars. Most of them decide to fulfill traditional expectations of duty and heroism. Some object conscientiously, and—if they must also conscientiously admit that they do not believe in the prescribed kind of God—must face jail under conditions that negate even a traditional sense of martyrdom. A few turn furiously against the system; but if they seem totally committed to a negative utopia in which the existing world must come to an end before anything can live, one should remember that they have grown up in a setting in which adult happiness-as-usual did not exclude the minute-by-minute potential of a nuclear holocaust—and an end of mankind as we know it.

V

If I should now attempt to throw some methodological light on the range of reactions which youth exhibits in the face of the conditions just sketched, I must begin by clarifying some terms which I have used over the years. Instead of using *identity diffusion* (or ego diffusion) and *confusion* alternately, I would now wish to take account of the fact that the adolescent ego *needs* a certain diffusion. I would, therefore, use this term for experiences in which some boundaries of the self are expanded to include a wider identity, with compensatory gains in emotional tonus, cognitive certainty, and ideological conviction—all of this occurs in states of love, sexual union, and friendship, of discipleship and followership, and of creative inspiration. Such states can, of course, occur within culturally sanctioned affiliations or in self-affirming groups usurping a place on the fringe of society. The question is always whether the cumulative state of diffused selfhood adds up to a potent new vision or to a retrogressive delusion of acting meaningfully. *Identity confusion* would then characterize those states in which there is an impoverishment and a dissipation of emotional, cognitive, and moral gains in a transitory mob state or in renewed isolation—or both.

The difficulty of classifying such states and, above all, of assigning them to given classes of individuals with particular personalities or similar backgrounds is, of course, compounded where the same young individuals and the same groups seem to demonstrate an alternation of prophetic and retrogressive states, being at one time heroically committed and at another cynically disengaged, at one time devastatingly logical and at another quite deliberately irrational, at one time planfully affirmative and at another quite carelessly destructive. The defensive aspects of such alternation are inherent in the mechanisms described by Anna Freud in her classic characterization of puberty. But one could probably take up these mechanisms, one by one, and make explicit the complementary nature of the inner needs of the adolescent individual and the inducements offered not only by spontaneous group formations, but also by ideological movements. The cognitive facts established by Piaget make it plausible enough that youth *thinks* ideologically—that is, with a combination of an egocentric, narcissistic orientation determined to adapt the world to itself and a devotion to idealistic and altruistic schemes and codes, whether or not their feasibility can be proved or disproved with adult logic. Correspondingly, in ideological world images (and I am, of course, not speaking only of the totalitarian kind) such logic is rendered superfluous; the "self-evident" truth of simplistically overdefined alternatives and the omnipotence promised in a radical course of action permit the young to invest their loyalty and to offer their very lives. At decisive moments in history and in the hands of leaders of genius, such prophecy, up to a point, fulfills itself; but in the long intervals of minimized revolutionary potential, youth is led into beliefs and actions in which the borderlines between prank and delinquency, adventure and political drama, are often hard to draw— even as it is often difficult to discern where in the personalities of ideological leaders, hysterics and histrionics blend with true charisma.

All this is well known; but there is much to learn about the developmental position of youthful enactments midway between the play of children and the ritualized aspects of adult society. Infantile play, among other accomplishments, re-enacts experiences and anticipations of a traumatic character in the microcosm of the toyworld, and the promises of its make-believe provide a necessary balance against the combined pressure of an immature conscience, a vague drivenness, and a bewildering social reality. The need for such a balance is multiplied in adolescence when the grown-up body, the matured genital equipment, and a perceptive mentality permit actions on the borderline of mere playfulness and utterly serious reality, of passing prank and irreversible deed, of daring pretense and final commitment. In negotiating these borderlines together, young people may be able to share transient conflicts that might otherwise force each individual to improvise his own neurosis or delinquency, but they obviously also can lead one another into permanent involvements out of line with their self-image, their conscience—and the law. Most "grow out" of this; but it is important to visualize how much the adult world, too, with its ceremonial habituations in areas of the greatest and most lasting relevance continues to express the need for ritual make-believe.

But we are concerned here with the retrogressive aspects of youth re-enactments. I avoid the term *regression* here because of its ontogenetic and clinical implications. Transitory regression can be part both of creativity and of development, as is implied in Kris' term "regression in the service of the ego" and in Blos' "regression in the service of development." Blos, in fact, considers the "capacity to move between regressive and progressive consciousness with . . . ease" the unique quality of adolescence.

And, indeed, I would submit that some of the adolescent processes described so readily as regressive have the distinct adaptive function of reviving and recapitulating the fragmentary experiences of childhood for the sake of recombining them actively in a new wholeness of experience. Such unification must obviously count on the workings of the ego. But it is accompanied by a new sense of "I," as well as a new experience of "we." The fate and function of such a sense and such an experience in the sequence of life stages have so far eluded conceptualization in psychoanalytic terms. At any rate, that a specific wholeness of experience may be irretrievably lost once adolescence has passed is the fear which gives much of adolescent behavior a certain desperate determination. And this, too, is a source of identification with the underprivileged, anywhere, who have missed their chance and must be offered a new one.

VI

I will select for more detailed discussion one strand of development little discussed in psychoanalysis—namely, that of moral and ethical orientation. I will speak of *moral learning* as an aspect of childhood; of *ideological experimentation* as a part of adolescence; and of *ethical consolidation* as an adult task. But as we know from the study of psychosexuality, the earlier stages are not replaced, but—according to the epigenetic principle—absorbed into a hierarchic system of increasing differentiation. If the child learns to be moral, by which I mean primarily to *internalize the prohibitions* of those significant to him, his moral conflicts continue in adolescence, but come under the primacy of ideological thinking. By ideology, in turn, I mean a *system of commanding ideas* held together more (but not exclusively) by totalistic logic and utopian conviction than by cognitive understanding or pragmatic experience. This ideological orientation as well as the moral one are in turn absorbed, but never quite replaced by that ethical orientation which makes the difference between adulthood and adolescence— "ethical" meaning a *universal sense of values assented to* with insight and foresight in anticipation of immediate responsibilites not the least of which is a transmission of these values to the next generation. Such development guarantees to this whole value structure a gradual synchronization with economic-political realities, but it also results in a persistent liability that can always lead to partial retrogressions. In youth, this can be seen in an arrest on the ideological level or a backsliding to infantile conflicts over moral interdicts, wherefore aggravated and especially agitated youth alternately reenacts a *premoral* position that denies any need for morality; in an *amoral* position that flaunts accepted norms; in an *anti-moral* position that militantly negates all authority; and finally, in an *antiauthoritarian* and yet *moralistic* position that condemns the adult world with righteous fervor—all in the context of an insistence that the stubborn vitality of youth must not be surrendered to the existing system.

To begin with the ethical orientation: On October 16, 1967, at the Arlington Street Church in Boston, Harvard student Michael

K. Ferber was one of the leaders of an anti-draft ceremony at which he made a statement entitled "A Time to Say No." He concluded it thus:

But what I want to speak about now goes beyond our saying No, for no matter how loudly we all say it, no matter what ceremony we perform around our saying it, we will not become a community among ourselves nor effective agents for changing our country if a negative is all we share. Albert Camus said that the rebel, who says No, is also one who says Yes, and that when he draws a line beyond which he will refuse to cooperate, he is affirming the values on the other side of that line. For us who come here today, what is it that we affirm, what is it to which we can say Yes?

If Ferber was speaking so ethically for the young who were acting like himself, there were at his elbows a most affirmative university chaplain and a famous pediatrician who had used psychoanalytic insight to make more people say Yes to more babies with more practical awareness than had any doctor before him. Such company, however, only emphasizes the fact that the most ethical sentiments of the young are often synchronized with the most youthful sentiments of concerned adults. Most of all, however, Ferber's statement must serve here as a motto for the ethical leadership of a new generation of *young adults* who, with exhortation by song or slogan, by dramatic action or quiet resistance, have in recent years introduced a new ethical orientation into American life—an orientation already well visible in the concerns of a new generation of students.

I have begun with the Boston Resisters because a group retrogression is least likely to occur where a disciplined civil resistance to a circumscribed nationwide grievance dominates action. I have heard an equally clear Yes by students at Capetown University who reiterated their and their teachers' determination to open the universities to black countrymen. If one should single out a retrogressive danger in this whole area of ethical dissent, it is the arbitrary choosing of rebellious gestures that do not add up to a sustaining Yes, and of methods uncoordinated with the actions of others.

In turning from a consideration of the ethical position to that of the re-enactment of earlier moral conflicts, I will follow the usual method of outlining the childhood stages first subsumed under the theory of pregenitality. In some analogy to the principles of that theory, we will proceed on the assumption that the process of adolescence includes a re-enactment of all the pre-adolescent positions, from infancy on, in order to integrate all the gains of childhood in an individual as well as a collective style of adolescence consonant with the needs of the historical period. On the way, however, each part position can make itself independent in conjunction with an adolescent subculture which specializes in some utopian promises of the position in question and attempts to contribute them to an emerging world order. Such a *totalization* of one set of human potentials can eventually become both regressive and destructive for the person, the "sect," and society at large.

Infancy contributes to all later life, together with some fateful vulnerabilities, an undaunted orality and an unbroken sensory eagerness. What in clinical discussion we have habitually called, for short, "oral" has always been more than a zonal or libidinal emphasis; the original modes of incorporating both food and sensations form a vital basis for an active acceptance of the world. Any clinical or developmental assessment, then, could begin with each of a number of themes and lead inescapably to all the others. I will emphasize here the infant's *mutuality* of responses with the *maternal person,* which leads to the introjection of a benevolent and reliable mother image and thus helps to appease primal anxiety. This, in turn, works for a favorable ratio of *basic trust* over *basic mistrust* that assures that *hope* becomes the fundamental quality of all growth. All this combines to form a first *developmental position* that will become a contributory element to all later stages as it reaches on each stage a higher level of differentiation. This developmental timetable is, of course, also a map of transient and partial regressions in states of crisis, illness, or fatigue, and of an irreversible withdrawal to delusional fulfillment in malignant states.

In adolescence, the quality of fidelity, the capacity to be loyal to a vision of the future, now incorporates infantile trust, while the capacity to have faith emerges as a more focused hope tuned to an ideologically coherent universe. The corresponding totalization we know clinically in the form of massive regression in isolated, addictive, or psychotic individuals. We know it biographically as the special state of a creative recapitulation of sensory awakening in some medium of artistic representation. And we know it sociologically as a utopian or revivalist community life of a markedly childlike, trusting, and mystical spirit.

Returning to today's patterns of dissent, it must be obvious that the group style generally subsumed under the term "hippiedom" is such a totalization of the first developmental position. In the midst of our technocratic world, young men and women encourage one another to live like the proverbial lilies of the field, with trusting love as their dominant demand and display.

In the scheme of moral stages, such a return to the logic of both infancy and paradise can be seen as a re-enactment of the *premoral stage*. These young people seem to convince themselves (and sometimes us) that the fall from grace and the expulsion from paradise were overexertions of divine rigor and that basic mistrust is superfluous baggage for a "human being." This return can be a reaffirmation of the indispensable treasure of experience that our technocratic world is vaguely aware of having sacrificed to the gods of gadgetry, merchandise, and mechanical adjustment; and, up to a point, the world is grateful to or, at any rate, fascinated by this tribe from "another world." But, alas, an existing technology has its own methods of absorbing and neutralizing utopian innovations, and the flower children, too, have suffered—precisely because of their repression of the necessary minimum of mistrust—from combined exploitation by microbes, drugpushers, and publicists.

VII

There could be no greater contrast than that between the ethical and the premoral positions just sketched and the amoral one to be considered next. And yet dissent unites, and the hippies and the motorcycle gangs have on occasion been seen to dwell together like the lambs and the lions. I have also heard of at least one instance when draft resisters linked themselves together around a conscientious deserter with chains handed them by a black-leathered gang. If the amoral position has more obviously sinister trends than the premoral one, however, it is because it champions a sincere belief in the goodness both of physical violence and of "obscenity."

The amoral position is clearly related to the second stage of infantile development (that is, about the second and third year of life). In dogmatic brevity, *anal-urethral* and *muscular* development had a psychosocial corollary in the sense of *autonomy* which in turn outweighed the danger of excessive *doubt* and *shame*. The new, rudimentary strength to emerge from this stage is a sense of free *will*—seasoned with the acceptance of a mutual delineation with the will of others. The psychopathological counterpart of all this is, in fact, a malfunction of the will, either in the form of inner *over-control* manifested in *compulsive* and *obsessive* trends or in that of a willful *impulsivity*.

Identity development in adolescence calls for a revival of the second developmental position too. Tested once more, will can then be subordinated to some order acknowledged as a higher will and willful impulse to communal experience, while blind obedience can become self-chosen discipline—the subjective emphasis always being that the individual chooses freely what proves inescapable. In totalistic rebellion, however, the negative re-enactment of this position can lead to a complete reversal of positions. Far from exhibiting any embarrassment, the dissenters sport shamelessness, obedience becomes defiance, and self-doubt, contempt. These deliberate challenges, in turn, arouse the worst in others, wherefore the militant amoralist finds himself, sooner or later, confronted by uniformed men, paid to do the "dirty work" for nice people, and apt to oblige the amoral phantasy-life by behaving like the externalized version of a brutal conscience while being at times—in terms of their task and training—amoral themselves.

It is well within developmental logic, then, that the retrogression to an amoral state recapitulates—no less compulsively for seeming so obvious and deliberate—such infantile patterns of protest as the deft deposition of feces in places to be desecrated and the use of excrement as ammunition. In this context also belongs the indiscriminate appellation of dirty names to authorities. In the case of "pigs," this certainly shows a strange lack of respect for an innocently muddy animal, and in that of sexual four-letter words, a blatant retrogression from sexual freedom.[1]

This may be the place to discuss briefly the often-heard simplistic assumption that such retrogressive acts on the part of privileged youth are simply overgrown temper tantrums due to their parents' "permissiveness." Authentic permissiveness can probably not be learned in a few generations. In the meantime, there is, rather, an excessive inhibition of parental anger and even of genuine indignation. This leaves the rage of both the parents and the children untested and untrained, and survives as a residual anxious expectation as to when the parents will dare to vent their suppressed rage and prove that they, indeed, can manage their own violence. But problems of child-rearing are always part of an intergenerational climate; and it may not be childhood experience alone that compels young people to test the limits of the dispassionate fairness claimed by authorities as well as by parents. Where such challenge is met with the deployment of a hired force that does not hesitate to vent all the frustrated anger shunned by the privileged, the ethical weakness in delegating violence immediately arouses the solidarity of those larger numbers of students who would not otherwise be attracted by amoral stratagems.

VIII

In the third stage of childhood—that is, the fourth and some of the fifth year of life—the imaginative *anticipation of future roles* is played out with toys and costumes, in tales and games. This, too, is recapitulated after puberty, when youth meets economic reality and historical actuality. What is reawakened, then, is the claim to the right to wield *initiative* of imagination and action—and this without the oppressive sense of *guilt* which at one time deepened the propensity for repression and made the child so amenable to moralistic pressure. In the boy this initiative was (and now is again) *intrusive* and *locomotor,* with an emphasis on invading the domain of the fathers; and it was (and is) for a while intrusive as well as locomotor in girls, sometimes with a competitive fervor surprising to the boys. If the repression of sexual and aggressive thrusts toward parent figures was the negative heritage of the third stage—and this with a marked fear of damage to the executive body parts—it becomes only more plausible that young people should be attracted by charismatic leaders and utopian causes which will sanction and give direction to the re-emergence of vigorous and competitive imagination.

To ward off the worst, the older generation tries, not without condescension, to assign to the young an area of boisterous, promiscuous, and rebellious re-enactment of phallic pursuits for the purpose of "sowing wild oats" or of "blowing off steam" before adult "reality" will force all sportive exuberance back into obedient channels. Higher education, especially, has always cultivated its style of genteel boasting and sportive competition. But in the long run it has also conveyed the power of ideas as embodied in rebellious men and periods of the great past, and it has thus helped to thwart the readiness of aggravated youth to be made subservient to technical and bureaucratic regimentation.

Among the retrogressive trends associated with the revival in adolescence of infantile guilt, there is the *anti-authoritarian, hypermoralistic* stance which is sometimes even stranger to behold than the name I am here attaching to it. Here is a simple and mild example of what I mean. In a college paper, a student took a truly distinguished professor to task for an allegedly illogical and unethical point of view. The issue is not so important here as the stance. The writer scolded: "What truly bothers me is the quality and logic of your justification . . ."; "I find thoroughly naïve your attempt to distinguish between . . ."; "Still more ludicrous is the characterization in your letter . . ."; "Even if I were to grant you this point for the sake of argument . . ."; "What most . . . experts lack is a discernible sense of responsibility. . . ." This total kind of turning against the "authority" of a legendary schoolmaster's posture is typical of the tone sported by many self-appointed revolutionaries, who declare a given man or group to be "guilty" with a fanatic use of the "guilt-by-association" logic. Some young people with the clearest intelligence and the most ethical intentions can talk one another into such retrogression, unaware of the probability that they are hastening the time when they will use it against one another for reciprocal moral liquidation.

In the meantime, fanaticism "dared" by agitators can lead to dangerous confrontations precisely because they are staged in the center of adult male prerogative. Perhaps the re-enactment of the third developmental position is nowhere more obvious than in the emotional and behavioral side effects of those confrontations that center in the occupation of buildings as seats and symbols of established power. The acquisition of a *territorial base* in the heart of the Establishment is, of course, an old revolutionary technique which is as strategic as it is symbolic. In the occupation of a center in the alma mater, however, the retrogressive aspects are underscored because the conquerors claim and count on the protection of academic *extraterritoriality.* And, indeed, their subsequent moodswings seem to vary from an undoubted sense of having accomplished a historically valid communal deed to excesses clearly dramatizing themes of a degradation of father figures as guilty usurpers and of the right of the young to claim license and amnesty, almost before the deed is consummated. And, indeed, faculties tend to make family affairs of such revolts; so that it becomes equally ludicrous to demand or to grant amnesty or to insist on severe punishments for deeds that, in fact, do manage to arouse guilty doubts in the confronted adults and force them to confront one another in prolonged and overdue debate.

IX

We must now, at last, look at that majority of the young who, without such provocation, would be aggravated only latently and would probably never join a revolt. Not that the majority has not always cultivated periodic pranks, raids, and riots which in various cultures have come to be taken for granted. But even though in some countries occasionally lives are lost, these youthful disorders rarely assume the nature of a concerted rebellion, except where most students have reason to feel that the system does not give them their due place *within* it. Students are not necessarily alienated from an industrial world or even a military-industrial complex so long as their studies promise them active participation and advancement in it, and a style of leisure utilizing all the comfort of modern mechanization. It is difficult to ascribe to this majority a tendency to re-enact a previous developmental position, because their aspirations are to a large extent only an extension of the fourth stage, the *school and play* age, into a prolonged period of apprenticeship. In our continuum from premoral to expressly ethical orientations, this great middle range cultivates a post-moral and pre-ethical *pragmatism.* This dominates, above all, the students of occupational specialties which attempt to come to grips with the concrete complexities of modern life, be they production or distribution, transportation or communication, medicine or law: For them, *what works is good,* and it is man's fate to be in motion and to set things in motion in league with a divine engineering power. Teamwork justifies man's trust in the eventual manageability of all modern complexities, including poverty and race relations, war and the conquest of space.

According to this general orientation, morality, ideology, and ethics can all be fitted into the acquisition of techniques, problems of sin or salvation being delegated to a Sunday religiosity which is never in conflict with habit and reason and which rewards those who help themselves. The result is a new technical-cultural consolidation analogous to those that have dominated all previous periods of history.

If there is retrogression in this orientation, it is an all-too-early, all-too-complete adjustment to the dominant modes of production and of success; and while those who can feel at home in it are apt to escape the more disturbing forms of identity confusion, they also must live by a dissimulation of emotions, the cumulative and corporative fate of which in inner or interpersonal life is hard to gauge. The patterns of dissent displayed by those in tune with "the system" differ in countries of different degrees of economic development; and even where the pragmatists occasionally permit themselves to be aggravated or led by radical activists, the latter cannot always foresee whether their temporary supporters want a different system or a more profitable identity within the existing one; for the pragmatists are closer to the power struggles within the political structure than they are to ideological issues as such.

Do moral pragmatists, too, feel "alienated" in a technocratic

world? It is hard to say. But increased contact with humanist intellectuality is apt to breed radical dissent. Otherwise, a retrogression within the logic of the school age takes the form of "dropping
out" for the sake of doing "my thing." Such avoidance of an early
submission to the narrow techniques of limited competencies can
(where the draft laws permit) be of great value especially when
joined to enriching experiences and exercises. But sooner or later
dropouts are apt to erect a communal pretense of superiority over
all those who work and serve—a superiority often only covering
that exquisite *sense of inferiority* which is the subborn shadow of
the school age.

X

One could condense all that has been said about the various
types of dissent by claiming that group retrogressions originate in
the incapacity or the refusal to conclude the stage of identity on the
terms offered by the adult world. But the generational barrier is
always one between future adults and erstwhile adolescents. Today
it is reinforced on the adult side by a pervasive sense of deficiency
in ethical and religious orientation such as would be consonant with
an identity development still promised a generation ago. In fact,
many of the adults most effective in modern transactions have had
the least time to complete, or indeed to renew, their identity development—not to speak of their sense of intimacy or generativity—
under the pressure of technological and historical change. (Is this
the reason why some bearded young men and severe young women
manage to look and act like veterans of life compared to their
successful and boyish-looking fathers and their happy and girlish-
appearing mothers?)

Some militants, of course, refuse to concede any need for identity; to them the very concept is only another attempt to force youth
into roles prescribed by the Establishment. Whether or not this is
partially true, it is important to realize that there is a hidden ideological connotation to all theories concerning man's nature; even
the most carefully verified observations will prove to have been subject to the ideological polarizations of their historical period. This
certainly has been the case with the theory of psychosexuality. Today, when (to paraphrase McLuhan) the mask is so often the
message, we face young people who hide their true identity—in
every sense of the word—behind dark glasses and ubiquitous hair,
while flaunting a negative identity often way beyond their emotional
means. This, too, can be part of courageous living; but it can also
go together with a negation of the three developmental necessities
marking the termination of adolescence: an identity tied to some
competence; a sexuality bound to a style of intimacy; and the anticipation of becoming, before long, responsible for the next generation.

We should acknowledge in passing the advances on the part
of many young people in making genital freedom a central aspect
of greater communal honesty. A vigorous genital culture, however,
depends among other things on contraceptive methods; and while
their invention was fervently anticipated by Freud, it may be
necessary today to be vigilant in the face of an all-too-ready belief
that genital and procreative instinctuality can be divided so neatly
without new kinds of emotional strain. On the other hand, the
freedom of choosing parenthood with a fuller consciousness of what
mankind can and must be able to promise each newborn child,
anywhere, could well become the *sine qua non* of a future ethics

equipped with a clearer knowledge of the all-around needs of a human being.

The future, so I would submit in conclusion, will force on young adults not only new styles of parenthood, but also the responsibility of being, indeed, their younger brothers' and sisters' keepers. After all the remarkable service which some of our young people have rendered to the underprivileged and underdeveloped on the periphery of their lives, they may have to learn that to be a young person under conditions of rapid change means to assume responsibility for younger persons nearby, and this in ways impossible to perform by older people and least of all by parents. This, too, is prophetically anticipated in the transient brotherhoods and sisterhoods of today—even if such caring for one another is at times only a sporadic and romantic phenomenon.

In this mostly "diagnostic" paper I should like to make this one "therapeutic" suggestion which (luckily, as so often) relies on the prognostically obvious: If the older young people could find the courage in themselves—and encouragement and guidance from their elders—to institutionalize their responsibility for the younger young, we might see quite different images of both youth and young adulthood emerge than those we now know. New models of fraternal behavior may come to replace those images of comradeship and courage that have been tied in the past to military service and probably have contributed to a glorification of a kind of warfare doomed to become obsolete in our time; and they may come to continue the extraordinary work, both inspired and concrete, done in the last few decades by pioneering youth groups on a variety of frontiers. This, in turn, would make it possible for adults to contribute true knowledge and genuine experience without assuming an authoritative stance beyond their actual competence and genuine inner authority.

In the definition and defense of such a new generational bond I also see a new role for (well, relatively) young men and women with psychoanalytic training. Beyond their function as healers, they could well serve as interpreters of the conflicts that are aroused in those who—on either side of the barrier—cannot let go of the images and impulses of the "classical" generational struggle. But in supporting this trend, one must also emphasize the Hippocratic obligations implied in it: Diagnostic and therapeutic insights cannot, beyond a certain amount of professed partisanship, be subservient to ideological counter-transferences. In a post-Freudian world, psychological insight must assume a significance and an ethical power of its own.

For adults, too, retrogress under the conditions described. Or rather the manifestations discussed are already the result of acute and yet hidden adult retrogression. We who know so much about the child in the adult know so much less about the fate of the adolescent in him; and yet it is eminently clear that adults of ethical stature retain their irrational ideological involvements as well as their punitive moralism and can fall back on both. That adolescent remnants endure can be seen in quieter times in the ritualized retrogressions of such groups as alumni or veterans; and they are often obvious in the peculiarities of people whose occupation forces (or permits) them to spend their lives with and for youth, not to speak of the adolescents-in-residence on every faculty. Acutely confronted by challenges of aggravated and agitated youth, the adult is apt to suffer a kind of emotional paralysis caused by acutely roused remnants of his own unfulfilled identity fragments and a certain irresistible—punitive or self-punitive—identification with the new brand of youth. Whether the result is generational surrender or renewed generational isolationism, it must sooner or later lead to a display of that brittle dignity which is supposed to protect occupational identity and status. To this, again, the majority of young people react negatively; to them a career that is not worth sacrificing for professed ideals is not worth having.

To share true authority with the young, however, would mean to acknowledge something that adults have learned to mistrust in themselves: a truly ethical potential. To study the psychological foundation of this potential may be one of the more immediate tasks of psychoanalysis. As we have already passed the "century of the child" and are now experiencing, with a vengeance, that of the adolescent, we may well be entering a period in which we must dare to ask: What, really, *is* an adult?

A new generation, for us, always starts again with Oedipus. We take it for granted that King Laius knew what he was doing—for could he not count on the authority of the Oracle when he left his baby boy to die, taking no chances with the possibility that a good education might have proven stronger than the oracular establishment? From what we know today, however, we might be inclined to ask: What could you expect of a little boy whose father felt so bound by phobic traditionalism? Yet theory has confirmed the oracle: Each new child appears to be a potential bearer of the Oedipal curse, and parricide remains a much more plausible explanation of the world's ills than does filicide.

And yet it must be clear that all puberty rites and confirmations as well as all inductions and (yes, all) graduations, besides establishing a reciprocity of obligations and privileges, also threaten with an element of mutilation and exile—if not in the crude form of surgical covenants, then in the insistence that a person's final identity must be cut down to size: the size of a conventional type of adult who knows his place and likes it. Thus we continue to institutionalize generational identifications that serve as built-in solutions for childhood conflicts and yet also guarantee their recurrence from generation to generation.

The discovery of the Oedipus Complex made amenable to conscious critique a generational fate grounded both in phylogeny and ontogeny. Such fate does not become altogether relative through historical change. But it may well be that different periods of history and different epidemiologies open new aspects of man's tragic involvement and of his rare victories to psychoanalytic insight. In this wider sense, it may well be that some of the confrontations in actuality which rebellious youth insists upon and the inner confrontation which is the essence of our method are highlighting the inner and outer consequences of patriarchal moralism and the present necessity for a world-wide new ethics supported by the informed choices of young men and young women.

REFERENCES

1. I cannot discuss here the different significance which deliberate obscenity and profanity assumes among the militants of racial minorities, who for generations and all their lifetimes have been exposed to extralegal "law enforcement."

35

Confessions of a middle-class drifter

The rebels of '70

By James S. Kunen

Times change.

My first car was a political decision. In 1969, a tiny Austin America sedan seemed to conform to the radical line. It was a *rational* vehicle, one designed to meet the needs of The People.

Its little engine could move four people without consuming much gas, therefore without greatly polluting the air, nor greatly depleting the earth's resources, nor requiring me to gather to myself an unseemly amount of wealth to support its appetites. And if hills slowed it up, that gave me the opportunity to relate to my environment. And if after a long journey I felt as though I had walked, it was good to feel something, it added *validity* to my experience.

James S. Kunen is the author of "The Strawberry Statement" and "Standard Operating Procedure."

Now here I am, a one-man energy crisis, behind the wheel of The Dream, a metallic blue '69 Chevy Malibu convertible (white top), 307 cubes to blast me wherever I want to be. Thanks to my installation of a cassette player The Dream has the capacity to shut down radio communication with the outside world while maintaining its internal entertainment function. It is in short, a mobile self-contained modular life support system, and a sleek one.

I'm steaming through the badlands of Montana, near the edge of the white world, so far from anywhere I practically don't exist. The road ahead shimmers into the July sky. I ram in a tape, the captured music recalling events, and places, and people that are not with me now. In this euphoric state there is one cause for which I can conceive of risking my life—The Passing of Trucks. I do it constantly.

Still, one thing bothers me, especially when I pass hitchhikers without picking them up: Have I become one of the people I used to be against?

I'm on my way to California. After 18 months as a conscientious objector, working with juvenile delinquents in the Massachusetts Department of Youth Services, I'm going to "drift around" the country. "You realize, of course, this all comes from the movies," said my friend Phil of the idea. He's right. I'm trying to be a drifter, but by virtue of trying I cannot succeed. I'm a middle-class drifter—a bogus drifter—far too purposeful ever really to cut loose.

In this case my purpose is to gather material for an essay on what my friends are doing these days, to see if it's true that, after shutting down campuses five years ago, they're entering establishment careers—what we used to call "selling out."

I'm not writing about blacks, because I don't know anything about blacks. I'm not writing about women, because when a woman fights her way to status and power, that's a radical act. I'm writing about white prep- and Ivy-educated males, class of '70, who were born to power but looked prime to reject it. I'm writing about the Middle Class Vanguard.

Just before I left on the trip a friend asked me how my new Joe Reporter Tape Recorder was working. I said it seemed to pick up voices very clearly from close up, but I wasn't sure it could pick up a speech at a rally.

"Jim," she said gently, touching my wrist, "they don't have rallies anymore."

"**S**CAB grapes! Scab store! Please don't shop here anymore!"

My prep-school friend Dick Casey and I were picketing, for the United Farmworkers, San Francisco groceries which carried nonunion grapes. It felt good to be good again, out in the streets,

shouting for justice, but it also felt a little awkward. Our half-dozen co-picketers seemed strangely young, and the words of their chants sounded almost foreign. Occasionally, Casey and I would quietly slip in a "Ho Ho Ho Chi Minh . . ." or "Hey Hey L. B. J. . . . "—our language.

In the old days Casey used to battle police around the University of Buffalo. The students would march through the streets chanting, and then the police would shoot tear gas at them and charge them with clubs, and the students would run away, then reassemble and start marching again, until the police would charge them again.

One day in the spring of '70 Casey had been doing this for several hours, until it was time to go home for supper. There, it struck him. "I was just fighting the police, and now I'm eating supper. If I was really serious, why did I go home for supper, and why did the police let me?" He decided he wasn't really "fighting" police, who, after all, had guns. Whatever he did was at their indulgence. So he stopped. As did many others.

Since then, having graduated with a degree in English and a prize for writing, Casey's been a liquor-store clerk, a cabdriver, a house painter, a shingler of roofs and a cook. The last job avowedly was his idea of a meaningful career. "People gotta eat," he used to say, and he still talks fondly of opening a restaurant called "Working Class Heroes." But he moves around a lot—as does everybody; a six-month-old address book is a keepsake—and is often out of work.

In San Francisco he was getting incremental haircuts and going down every day to the "deployment office," as he calls it, looking for a menial job. He and executive positions are not attracted to one another. "What am I supposed to say, 'O.K., I'll *be* vice-president of Coca-Cola'?" More and more he'd like to be something: perhaps a film maker. His latest home effort was a two-minute animated Hamlet.

I told him that our mutual friend John Short had decided to leave his small-town newspaper job and go to law school.

"Dropping out, huh," Casey observed.

"Growers get rich! Farmworkers starve!"

IHAD been surprised when Short called me last May to break the news that he was going to law school. Why, I wanted to know. He sounded apologetic: "Getting licensed to drive your car, that's the whole structure of life," he explained. "Besides, I want to be powerful. I've found that whatever you do, you're going to take crap, and I'd rather take crap from people below me than from people above me."

John Short, Andover '66, Harvard '70, springs from an upper-class background. His family is wealthy and well-connected, and among his forebears was one desperate soul who risked everything on the Mayflower. Short used to be known at Andover for being "in a fog," but he had the moral acuity to help barricade a Dow recruiter in an office at Harvard way back in 1967.

Upon graduation he duly set about not making his fortune and not climbing to power, quietly working on a small-town newspaper, The Provincetown (Mass.) Advocate. He remembers that he "scoffed at the idea" of taking law-school entrance exams as a senior, and was "shocked" at the number of his friends who paused to do so before embarking on their pastoral pursuits. "They were hedging," he says, "and that's what we were against."

I followed Short during his first day of law school this September. Registration at Northeastern University's Gryzmish Law Center was held in a lecture room full of legless black plastic seats attached to long white linoleum-topped tables. The air was conditioned, the windows blinded, the walls cinder-blocked—a law-and-order building. Members of the entering class of '76 looked as though they were there to be booked. Short, an organic if very slightly paunchy 25-year-old in sneakers and permanently unpressed white dungarees, was typical of those shuffling from table to table getting things stamped, except that half of them were women.

"Hello, John!" called a Harvard classmate, Bart Gordon, from a few places back in line.

"Oh God," Short groaned. "I didn't know *you* were going to be here. It kind of cheapens the whole experience."

Gordon was fresh from a commune in Vermont, where he'd lived "till I couldn't handle it anymore—living in a house for four with nine people, seeing people at breakfast every morning that I maybe could have gotten along with if I saw them every three weeks."

I asked Gordon if it were money that had brought him down to school. "No, I don't need money. My wife and the baby and I could live on $3,000 a year, with some help from our parents. But I want a skill. All my jobs in Vermont were unskilled labor. I was an unskilled carpenter, an unskilled farmer, an unskilled teacher. I want a skill —it's the ideal of meaningful labor." He added that it may be "a fantasy" that the law will be "meaningful labor."

When Gordon asked Short his excuse for being there, Short said he wanted to be a D.A., to go after "the real criminals." "The real criminals are sitting in offices, like some people's fathers."

"You're going to be going after people's fathers?" I asked.

"I don't know," Short answered. "What do I know about being a D.A.?"

What does one know about anything after 16 years of school? One knows how to go to school. Short and his classmates completed their computer cards with dispatch, consumed coffee, doughnuts, speeches. The registrar informed them that 2,500 had applied to be in their class of 125.

"Few people here would admit this," Short whispered, "but it feels good in spite of yourself to hear that you're still 'prime material.'"

Afterwards, the freshmen recessed to a nearby room for sherry. Nothing could be more established than sherry. It prompted me to ask John —who, as a Democratic party official helped deliver Provincetown to McGovern—if his commitment to social change was void.

"I'm not committed in the same way I was in college," Short said. "It's such a youthful thing. I thought things then were—not so much *worse*, but—more *disgusting*. Now I just think things *exist*."

A few of Short's classmates brought a bottle of Taylor Cream over and sat down. The revelation that I was writing an article only confirmed their sense that they—going to law school at 25—represented a trend, a trend that might be called Bourgeois Chic.

Short figures he'll be in a position to do more good as a lawyer than as a demonstrator or anything that he was before. 'In college the standard thing to believe was that our parents and even people a few years older than ourselves were incomprehensibly shackled by their occupations. Today I'd say the most important thing in my life is my work."

"And how much would you look to get paid for it?"

"It's hard to say. I've said to friends that my goal is to have a Pontiac with a telephone in it, and that bespeaks a certain amount of income. Pontiacs are basically for *arrivés*, self-made men. That's probably what I want more than the Pontiac—to be known as someone who's really earned his money, because that obviously hasn't been true up to now, being a rich kid, a prepster."

"With a career and a Pontiac you can't help but get married, can you?" I asked.

Short sipped his *n*th sherry. "Fortunately, I retain a power not to look into the future. The civilizing process of going to law school does make the idea more palatable. The thing is, I just don't know any marriages that are successful among people within shouting distance of our age. Everyone fails. It's just horrible. The time to go into it would seem to be after you've settled on what you're going to be doing for the rest of your life."

Or it's settled on you.

"You don't make long-range plans," Dave Warren (Midwood High School '66, Columbia '70) told me. "You find yourself at a point and you take the next step that seems appropriate, which usually turns out to be the path of least resistance."

Proceeding in this fashion, Warren weaved his way into N. Y. U. Law School last year, after two years of "keeping his options open" with the deftness of a juggler. He supported himself as a public school teacher days while taking a full architecture course at night, until he decided he wanted to be better at something than he was going to be at architecture.

When I called him recently, he was too harried with studying to see me. I commiserated. "The essence of happiness," I said, recalling my experience as a happy 40-hour-a-week state employe, "is not having to take home any work."

"That's the essence of law — taking home work," he replied.

"You can do it," I said.

He said he knew he could. It was just a question of organization. "It's organization, man." And inspiration, he might have added. He psychs himself up for studying each night by first sitting down at his upright piano and banging out the theme from "The Defenders" TV show of our youth.

We soon managed to get together, rendezvousing at the sundial at Columbia, the erstwhile podium for innumerable speeches by Mark Rudd (now silent, hiding from the F. B. I.) and the loading platform for the police vans that hauled 400 of us away one night five years ago.

Warren sat down beside me on the stone pedestal. He looked around the broad plaza at the foot of Low Library and observed, "You know, I really think half the reason for everything that went on here was the way this place is laid out. It's a giant theater." On stage that fall day were large numbers of students who managed to walk to and fro without ever congregating. They looked like location footage for a documentary on libraries.

Warren shared my contempt for our successors in college. What do they *do?* It's not that they should be demonstrating, necessarily, though with over 100,000 political prisoners in United States-financed South Vietnam there's plenty to demonstrate about. Maybe that's not their thing, and it has been done. But why don't they do *something?* Swallow goldfish, for instance. Swallowing goldfish is an existential statement, an assertion of the validity of the absurd in an absurd world, an outcry for something meaningful to do. But *these* kids. Waterbed heads.

My Andover friend Stan Olson, who's a teaching assistant at Clark University, tells me that his undergraduates say they're right to be preoccupied with grades and success, that *we* were the aberration. "I think it has something to do with whether Nixon's in high office during your adolescence," Stan explains.

It's a nice feeling, contempt. This way we don't feel that we're over the hill; there has been no succession. We are still what is happening, whatever has happened.

"I knew the times they were a-changin'," Dave said, "when Dylan bought a split-level house." But Warren distinguishes between buying in and selling out. "Back in '68, people were setting up a false dichotomy. Either you joined the establishment and sold out, or you set about fulfilling yourself. But you can work in the establishment and still work for your own ends. Working

with the establishment is confronting the world.

What it comes down to is that Warren sees the establishment as the only game in town. "As established institutions have been losing their meaning, counterinstitutions lose their meaning. Like the Church used to be something to be against. Marriage. But as they lose their vitality, the meaningfulness of opposing them diminishes."

It's true. It used to seem that growing your hair long, setting yourself against the establishment, was a meaningful act. You knew it, because they'd come down on you. You'd be castigated, maybe assaulted. But today, for a middle-class white guy, oppression is very hard to come by.

With meaning in decay on all sides, Warren sees the world in "universal entropy." His reaction is to aim for self-sufficiency and . . . Stability.

"I'd like to set up something that's independent, whether a law firm or a bookstore, just some enterprise I could set up with people I like." As far as money goes, "doing something I like is more important that money," but in 10 years he'd like to be earning $30,000 to $40,000 — in 1973 dollars.

And ultimately, he would like a Relationship, "and you want it to be permanent, and you want it to be exclusive. You want somebody to grow old with."

One stark winter Monday in 1972 I was working the 7 to 3 shift at the Massachusetts Department of Youth Services' Campbell House in Lancaster. I was holding a counseling session, in which I shared my accumulated wisdom in weekly installments with one of the kids. She was telling me that she just could not get along with her father, who would throw her out of the house in the intervals

between her running away. I was trying to show her that this did not necessarily mean that she was as worthless a person as she supposed, that such strained familial relationships were not all that uncommon. "People don't really live like the 'Donna Reed Show', you know," I said.

"They *don't!*" she replied. In her 17 years that actually had never occurred to her.

It had just then occurred to me.

So much of our life is spent perceiving illusions that we tend to measure reality against them instead of the reverse. Instead of dismissing Coke ads as unreal, I'm inclined to feel my life is inadequate in the fun department because it isn't like the Coke ads—"the Real Thing." It doesn't matter that I interpret and resist the ads, that I know what they're up to. Those images are in my mind.

At Columbia we used to joke about the need for a course:

Life 1001x - 1002y FUNDAMENTALS OF REALITY 6 pts.

Fall term: *The Meaning of Life.* Sex, love, work, wealth, leisure and ideology are examined as possible sources of meaning, with attention to the question, What do 70-year-olds know that 19-year-olds don't?

Spring term: *Selected Problems in Living.* Emphasized are taxes, insurance, automotive legal problems, subleases, contracts, credit, birth control, venereal disease, zoning, local government, divorce, social behavior, job-seeking and unemployment.

We felt the need for some such instruction because we felt we had been shielded

from experience by our affluent backgrounds. Having lived in the shadow of destitution, our parents had naturally sought not just to survive but to survive with room to spare. They strove to isolate themselves from suffering by interposing layer on layer of things between themselves and want — pushing suffering ever farther away.

But we grew to feel that perhaps suffering was not all that we were removed from. Reading an account of a childhood of poverty, I would get the feeling that *there* was *authentic* experience, more meaningful and more *real* than my own affluent existence. (As though there were a principle of conservation of value: the greater the monetary value of your milieu, the less the value of your experience). We felt that as characters in novels, we would not be very interesting.

THE goal of middle-class life — from the air inside a Cadillac to the curriculum of a prep school — is insulation and control. Even our "own" youth culture came to us packaged. We had a communal experience, of a sort — though it was not experienced communally — an atomized communal experience. Millions of times in thousands of dorm rooms, the class of '70 heard revolution on the stereo. But however savage the rhythm or radical the words, anything we heard we heard because The Corporation had decided we'd hear it — though its motive be that most innocent of all: making money.

The youth culture was so pervasive because it filled a vacuum. Affluence had given us, luxury of luxuries, four years with nothing to do: college. Unheard of numbers of "kids" were in college; we were unbelievably well set up, regaled with music "systems," diverted by studies, and yet feeling a vague malaise, beginning to suspect that we were not in touch with reality and did not know very much about it, that we ourselves were not *relevant*.

The most important activity among this crowd was drug-taking, the principal purpose of which was, as always, escape. But in this case the students were trying to escape a reality they suspected was unreal, and to probe the depths and heights for a more basic or transcendent Reality, which would inform their actions and allow them to begin to live, at last, after having been suspended in a perpetual state of "preparation."

Browsing through the cosmos we found that there were worlds other than the one our parents perceived, a discovery which eroded our received beliefs and certainties; and one side effect of the drugs was to put us all outside the law.

Meanwhile, our parents' world came up with its war, misrepresented as this and that but obviously — to anyone with the time to look into it, and we, protected by deferments, had time — a cynical imperialist operation. That we were lied to about the war intensified our scrutiny of how much of our given reality was illusion. It set us looking for other lies, which weren't hard to find. Universities not being very portable, many had remained behind after the core cities had turned black and poor. A Columbia student, for instance, didn't have to look very far to see the effects of racism in the land of equal opportunity.

We had concluded, correctly, that we were living in a rotten, corrupt, morally bankrupt, brutally exploitative system, failing to apprehend only that this meant the world was clicking along as usual.

We were outraged. To us the war was a moral offense, not a question of politics, and we reacted to it in moral, rather than political terms. We didn't try to mobilize interest groups, or manipulate one power concentration against another, or do any of those things that politicians know about. And, of course, we didn't have "a program." Insofar as our rhetoric was political, that was a response to the needs of the conceptual framework of older people.

When people used to demand of us, "But what's your program?" we'd dutifully come up with something that could pass for one, talking about taxes and things. We should have said, "Why should we have a program? We're the Scourge of the Earth, we're the Wrath of God, and you're asking us about programs?"

I never knew anyone who, at 19, was seriously interested in running the country. We were trying to *stop* something. We felt ourselves to be a purifying force, the force of life. Somehow by the strength of our youth the nation would be wrenched from the grip of death, cleansed, made new.

"The Movement," we were aptly named. Not the party or the revolution. The Movement — an undirected upheaval of the earth, an inarticulate force of nature. We weren't trying to convince the nation of anything. We were just trying to wake it up. Our "tactic" was an appeal to the nation's conscience, the existence of which we posited, apparently in error.

To our great surprise, we failed — never ending the war. (We had no way of knowing at the time that we had catalyzed Nixon's paranoia, driving him to acts which would bring about his downfall.) Failure was something we had never contemplated. The only question was when we would end the war, not whether we would end it. It didn't occur to us that the war might end because the Indochinese *won* it, nor that it might go on forever (beyond our lifetimes).

Our confidence and resolve had grown from our middle-class backgrounds just as surely as our naiveté. We were raised to believe that we could do anything if we worked hard enough at it, and, conversely, that if we failed to achieve something it could only be because we had not worked hard enough. There was never any mention in our households of the breaks, or fate, or the authorities, or the Will of God. Achievement flowed from effort like interest from principal.

If we wanted bombs to stop falling on Indochina, then bombs would stop falling on Indochina. But they did not. Unable to sustain ourselves in the face of failure, we withdrew. Three years after graduation I could find no one who could say for sure whether any aboveground remnant of S.D.S. exists.

NONE of my friends went to Vietnam. Those of us who were called got out by getting 4-F's or by doing alternative service as conscientious objectors. All you need is to know the rules.

Some of us got involved in counterinstitutions — free schools, communes, co-ops — but, typically, we remained aloof, rejecting all organization and politics, rejecting *abstraction*. After years of dealing in policies and issues, we wanted jobs where you could see what you were doing. We were trying, after graduating from college, to begin to learn what life was like.

We avoided long-term commitments, and spent a lot of time not working at all. We were afraid of losing our selves before finding them. Embarking on a career meant accepting definition, that is, finitude, stasis, the closing of options and narrowing of potential — and it was the same with getting married. Once you decided with whom and where you'd live and what you'd do, it would be a matter of 15 new cars and a hearse.

Since we didn't need to "provide for" a woman in order to enjoy a relationship with her, career and marriage were two things we could do without. To no one did this become more apparent than to those who got married.

Not working toward a career, let alone not working at all, was also a rejection of the System within which success and exploitation, work and war, were of a piece in our minds. ("Work! Study! Get ahead! Kill!" we used to chant at Columbia.) It seemed the country was full of people who subsumed themselves in their work roles, deriving their identities from their functions, abdicating human will and responsibility, leaving the country to be run not by people but by a System, capable of anything.

Of course it was the System that enabled us to reject the System. It gave us time. There was no need — or opportunity — for everyone to be producing all the time. You can bet there aren't a lot of sensitive young intellectuals trying to find themselves in The People's Republic: "You can find yourself right out there in the rice paddies with everybody else, buddy."

We were terrified of working as hard as did our fathers, charter subscribers to the Protestant Ethic: Pay now, fly later. Olson up at Clark University, told me, "When I look at how incredibly difficult it is for me to do very little, then I can't even imagine what it must be like for people to do a lot." He likes to think about the easy fortune he could make marketing draft-evader bracelets, each engraved with the name of an exile, to be worn until amnesty.

By not having any hopes now of finding meaning in a career, he's saving himself from any crushing disillusion later. "The people who freak out at 45 are those who *thought* they were getting somewhere." But not being career-oriented — not building anything to lean on — needs peer-group support. "Me and my friends," says Olson, a grad student in English, "we don't work at careers." But even among Olson's friends the attrition rate is climbing.

Strange to say, we—whose whole sense of "we" was built around being "kids" — are getting older. The other day I looked in the mirror and saw a single gray hair — which I decided not to pull, because it made me look very slightly distinguished — but more alarming is the thinning, no longer deniable. A lot of longhairs have thinning hair.

At 25, you find your own stories boring you. Half the Red Sox are younger than you are. It's easy to get fat. Country and Western lyrics suddenly make sense. And your father faces his mortality, which prompts you to

think about your own.

The pressure mounts to make your deal, some sort of compromise between the quest for authentic experience and the need for identity, between adventure and security.

As I heard one character say to another in a late-night TV movie, "Doing nothing is a very difficult job. It requires a lot of concentration." And an older friend of mine confirms that when you turn 30, "You can relax in ways you couldn't before, because you're no longer plagued by all those options. That's what makes life so difficult in your 20's, all that glorious potential to grapple with."

"It's not easy living the way I do," says my Columbia classmate Larry Lane, now a graduate student of uncertain prospects. "I'm looking for something I can do — it doesn't have to be fun — just something I can *do*, as opposed to *be*. I'd love to *be* a doctor [his father's a dentist] and have everybody respect me, but there's no way I want to put on rubber gloves and *do* doctor things."

Right now he's thinking of writing poetry to be illustrated by his girl friend, but a lot of people wouldn't consider that doing anything, and in occasional chilling moments it appears to him they may be right. "Don't you think I'd like to come home to a big house and bounce a kid on my knee?"

I T'S been three years now that we've been on the outs. The world of the small job, the personal project, inevitably begins to seem constricting. Our middle-class *instinct* (subliminal, unshakable) to "make something of yourself," abetted by our social commitment — also rather hard to shake — drives us

back toward the larger arena. We can't leave the running of the world entirely in the hands of the exec types, can we?

And as we find idealistic gratification hard to come by, materialistic gratification becomes more attractive. I, for instance, used to think I could stop the war; then I thought I'd get realistic and instead save delinquents from lives of crime; finding that beyond my power, I resolved to show them a good time. My success in pursuit of even that modest goal was equivocal. After several months as a supervisor and associate of juvenile delinquents it came to me that I'd feel somehow more *confident* if I had a big car. On May Day of '72, I bought The Dream.

As Dave Warren says, "Whatever else you say about those bourgeois comforts, they sure are comfortable."

I agree with a friend who said, "You don't want to be in the position of not knowing where your next car is coming from." And money can be habit-forming. After the hook, the line and sinker are easy.

Summing up the last three years, John Short said, "People led whatever kind of life they had to in order to convince themselves that they were exercising free will." That done, having gained control of their lives, having insulated themselves from outside pressures, more and more holdouts are becoming late-signers.

The question is: will we, despite the hallucinations and barricades in our backgrounds, become indistinguishable from our parents? We still take drugs, but mostly just grass, and that without any imputation of mystic import. In this period of Post-Mumbo-Jumbo Mate-

rialism the popularity of psychedelics has fallen along with that of transcendence.

Our attitude toward authority is still shaped by the clashes in college. To quote Olson, "Whenever I see a cop on my block I feel like I better flush all my books down the toilet."

Our political views would still look appropriate on leaflets. I spoke with 11 classmates across the country, and most would agree with Casey that "the United States is the world's leading reactionary force." Though everyone enjoys Watergate, no one buys it as the redemption of the System. It's so American — instead of purging a corrupt government we do a TV show on it. And we can't help recalling that there was no uproar when "radicals" were bugged. No one I know has the slightest doubt that the C.I.A. was behind the coup in Chile, but no one has any plans for doing anything about it either, since there are no bumper-stickers out and no organization to send five dollars to. The activists among us are those who volunteered a few hours for McGovern.

In our rowdy days we were told we couldn't change the world. I think we can't help but change the world, one way or another.

I was just talking to a friend of mine, who said, "I'm much happier now that I'm not 'a radical.' I stopped feeling guilty over just being alive in America."

And I said, "My father always held to the belief that young people would eventually abandon their idealistic visions and come around to appreciating the verities — like the overwhelming importance of money."

"Your father sounds like a very wise man," she said.

X. Adolescents in Institutions

When the phrase "adolescents in institutions" is used, it applies normally to young people and their families or schools. While we are aware of the other forms of institutional life among adolescents, we do not address ourselves to these forms often enough. For example, how much do we know about children in jail? Do we know fully what their lives are like in jail, or what they have done that ended up with their being sentenced to jail? Do we know about children in hospitals and the sort of treatment, physical and psychological, that they are receiving? Do we know about those cases in which children in hospitals and jails are used for subjects in various experiments, even when the children and their families have never granted consent?

Then there lurks the question, if we do know little about children in jail and in hospitals, why is this so? Are people keeping information from us? Is there something about the treatment of institutionalized children that we are not meant to know?

Such an approach to the topic of adolescents in institutions sounds conspiratorial, to say the least. Yet the topics of health care and life in jail are serious and very much understudied. Even more, when one goes to explore these topics, information is hard to come by. In the name of protecting the child, certain facts are not revealed, and one is often denied access to the child in the institution as well as his or her family. For that matter, even some schools now make it difficult for the outside investigator. Access to information is denied, and again, in the name of protecting them, students are kept out of sight and earshot of reporters and social scientists.

No one can totally fault this protective stance on the part of institutional custodians. There is a very important need to protect a child's right to privacy, whether that child is in a school, hospital or jail. Moreover, schools in particular have learned that the investigations done of them have not yielded too much information that helps either them or their students. In this regard, therefore, the protective posture is justifiable.

The problem, however, is that without access to the institutions, without being able to speak to students, prisoners, patients, we cannot gain an understanding of what is happening to the children in these institutions. We don't even know whether the children are being well served or damaged by the institutions. Thus, one confronts a delicate balance between the adolescent's right to privacy on the one hand and the guaranteeing of proper medical, legal, and educational attention on the other. The balance is often so difficult to achieve that some people turn their back on the matter altogether. But as the material in this section reveals, adolescents in institutions is not a topic to be ignored or slighted.

36

Children and the Law

Jerrold K. Footlick

Bobby was 9 when he was arrested for shoplifting. As they always do with first offenders, Los Angeles police spoke sternly to him and released him. Three months later, Bobby had graduated to burglary, and was released with a warning. Bobby's sixteenth arrest—he was 12 years old by then—earned him his first jail term, two years at a California Youth Authority Camp, from which he escaped four times. A few days after his release, at age 14, he killed a man. He has been charged with 26 crimes, including murder. But now that he has turned 18, he is, so far as the law is concerned, no longer a juvenile. He is a free man.

Mark's mother was a junkie and he was born in 1965 with heroin withdrawal symptoms. He spent his first six years in a foster home before being returned to his mother, whom he did not know. When she went to work, she regularly tied Mark to a bed. A year later, she told New York juvenile authorities that he was disruptive and uncontrollable, and Mark was institutionalized. Last year he was in court, charged with fighting with his peers and being difficult to control. He is 10 years old.

Bobby and Mark are both products of the American system of juvenile justice. One has compiled an awesome criminal record; the other has never committed a crime. Yet they both have juvenile records and they have been confined in institutions for about the same time. Both are poisoned products of one of the starkest shortcomings of American justice: how to cope with children who fall into trouble with the law. "The system has failed," says veteran Detroit Judge James H. Lincoln. "We do no more than clean the boil without treating the disease." No one is well served—neither the youngsters nor the nation—and no one—not police, judges, legislators or theoreticians—has figured out what to do about it.

MORE CRIME AND MORE FEAR

The statistics on child criminals are awesome. Juvenile crime has risen by 1,600 per cent in twenty years. More crimes are committed by children under 15 than by adults over 25—indeed, some authorities calculate that half of all crimes in the nation are committed by juveniles. Last year, police arrested 2.5 million youngsters under 18. In Los Angeles, juveniles account for more than one-third of all major crimes, and in Phoenix, officials estimate that juveniles are responsible for 80 per cent of law violations. In Atlanta, juvenile arrests for arson have tripled since 1970, and in New York, since 1972, burglary and rape charges against juveniles have nearly doubled.

The headlines cry out the grim news every day. In Florida, a 15-year-old boy is sentenced to death for sexually molesting and murdering a 12-year-old girl. Then two boys, 13 and 15, are accused of murdering a 4-year-old boy—"to have some fun," as they later tell police. Six New York teen-agers, one of them 13, are charged with murdering three impoverished men in their 70s and 80s. In the city's Brownsville section, a gang leader orders the punishment of one of his foot soldiers; the gang burns down the boy's house and six people die. A boy of 12 in Phoenix carries a .38 revolver to school and holds his horrified teacher and classmates at gunpoint for an hour before surrendering.

PINS, CHINS, JINS AND MINS

These crimes—which the law calls "juvenile delinquency"—are no more difficult to understand than a knife at the throat. But they are only part of the story. For fully one-third of the cases that reach juvenile courts are what are termed "status offenses," which means acts that would not be criminal if they were committed by an adult—truancy, running away from home, disobeying parents. These children are called, in different states, PINS or CHINS or JINS or MINS, for persons or children or juveniles or minors "in need of supervision." Status offenders, more often than not, are emotionally beleaguered kids whose home life is so shattered that they will do anything to break free from it. In pathetic contrast to the street-wise young criminals, who often can cite the Miranda decision by heart, the children who

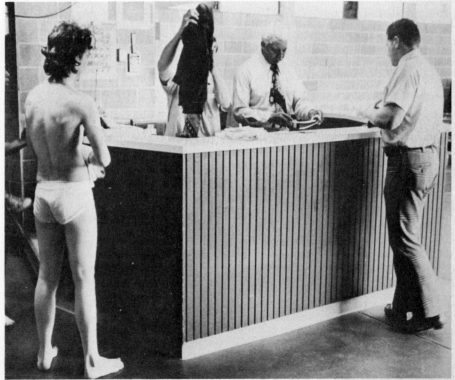

James D. Wilson—Newsweek

Youth stripped down for 'check-in' at San Francisco's Juvenile Hall: Caught in a maze

become status offenders drift helplessly through an endless legal maze.

The reasons for today's high rate of juvenile crime are a familiar litany. Poverty and overcrowding in city slums; soaring rates of unemployment among minority teen-agers that instill in them a "don't give a damn" bitterness; violence that flickers into every home on the television screen; the lure of drugs that can quickly become a dependence, and the easy availability of knives and guns—all contribute to crime at any age level. In the U.S. today, "society seems to be flying apart," Phoenix school psychologist William Hall says. "The kids just feel the vibrations much more than adults."

The juvenile-justice system in the U.S. pivots on an array of human decisions, often made with too little knowledge and too little time. "The system works on the kids like an octopus," says Marian Wright Edelman, director of the Children's Defense Fund, "with lots of arms picking them up and dropping them at different times." Even when the personnel are trained and the decisions are sincere, a series of interlocking bureaucracies has so diffused responsibility that no one has final control—not cops, judges, prosecutors, public defenders, probation officers, social workers, welfare clerks, foster-care centers, adoption agencies or penologists. The buck never stops. "It's like a Shakespearean tragedy," says Milton Luger, the former director of the New York State Division for Youth. "Everybody stabs everybody to the left."

From the moment a youngster becomes caught up in the legal system, humane intentions clash with practical limitations—and nobody wins. "If our goal is to rehabilitate, we're not doing it," says Wayne Mucci, director of the national Juvenile Justice Standards Project, "and if we're supposed to be punishing, we're not doing that either."

OUT THE REVOLVING DOOR

A cop arrests a youngster. It doesn't seem fair to detain him for days or weeks while he awaits a hearing, so he is released almost instantly—perhaps to commit another crime. "The kids get out of Juvenile Hall before the cop gets his report made out," complains San Francisco police Capt. Gus Bruneman. When the hearing date arrives, it seems reasonable to bring the child's parents to court with him. This can mean that a mother may have to give up a day's wages and sometimes must drag along the rest of her brood, which turns juvenile courts into squawling day-care centers. In many New York courts, these hearings average five to seven minutes, and cynical clerks sometimes keep a 25-cent daily pool on how many cases they will dispose of.

Some youngsters repeat this process so often that "it's like an immunization shot—they lose their fear of the law,"

says Atlanta Judge Tom Dillon. "These kids have to be seen to be believed," marvels Brooklyn cop Louis Eppolito. "They have no regard for property or life. In the station house, they dance on the tables like it was 'Soul Train'."

Sometimes months will pass after a criminal act before the social workers, lawyers and a judge decide what to do with a youngster. Usually a delinquent will be released in the charge of an overworked probation officer, who in theory will counsel him thoughtfully and monitor his progress. In Denver, typically, a harried staff of only seventeen probation officers tries to cope with a stream of 1,100 delinquents at any given time. If a youngster commits several offenses, or some particularly serious crime, he may be sentenced to reform school—often called a "training school."

In the best of these, children may attend classes as if they were in school. They will be counseled about their anxieties and the background of their problems. They may be taught a useful trade. But in most juvenile centers, a youngster seldom receives appropriate rehabilitation. What he does learn, says Georgia youth services director John Hunsucker, "is how to break into houses instead of stealing a bag of pecans."

Venality did not bring about these conditions; on the contrary, the juvenile-justice system is a product of noble reform. In 1646, the Puritans of the Massachusetts Bay Colony decreed the death penalty for "a stubborn or rebellious son," and for more than two centuries afterward children were treated by the law more as possessions than as persons. But at the turn of the twentieth century, the same reformers who were plumping for women's rights and the rights of the immigrant poor also discovered children. In 1899, Illinois passed the nation's first juvenile act and by 1925 46 states had set aside special courts and procedures for children.

Rehabilitation was the watchword, and the child was to be protected as he was led through the system. In practice, however, most children were just shoved through it. Finally, in 1967, an Arizona boy named Gerald Gault became one of the historic figures in American jurisprudence. At the age of 15, Gerald had made an obscene telephone call to a woman neighbor, a misdemeanor for which an adult might serve two months in jail. Police offered him no legal counsel, and he was sentenced to reform school until he became 21—a six-year term. But Gerald Gault's case was appealed to the U.S. Supreme Court, which finally ruled that when juveniles face the threat of jail, they are entitled to counsel, to notice of the charges and to the privilege against self-incrimination.

CHALLENGING THE SYSTEM

Even now, no children have an adult's right to trial by jury or to bail. A new

generation of reformers intends to carry kids' legal rights still further. In Washington, D.C., the Children's Defense Fund is challenging the authority of a parent to commit a child to a mental hospital indefinitely without a hearing. In New York, the Civil Liberties Union and the Legal Aid Society have filed a class-action suit on behalf of all black Protestant children, charging that religion-affiliated child-care agencies—which received close to $150 million in public funds last year—systematically discriminate against minorities. In Atlanta, the ACLU is asking a state court to rule that status offenders may be confined only at centers in their own communities instead of being shipped to penal institutions.

In what could become the most significant juvenile decision since Gault, U.S. District Judge William W. Justice last fall condemned the entire Texas institutional structure for its "widespread physical and psychological brutality." Juveniles were not rehabilitated but "warehoused," Justice charged in a 204-page opinion. He said they were beaten and tear-gassed as punishment and given tranquilizers to quiet them without medical supervision. The judge ordered the state to close two of its reform schools and convert the rest to halfway houses and group homes. Texas officials responded that the total cost of such changes makes them impossible, and the state is appealing. Eventually the U.S. Supreme Court will be asked to pronounce a judgment on the conditions of juvenile incarceration that would apply to every state.

But the fact that young offenders are often treated badly is sometimes overwhelmed by anger and fear as violent juvenile crime spreads through the nation. "I don't care what kind of background this kid comes from or how misguided his parents were," says Larry K. Schwartzstein, a prosecutor of juvenile cases for the City of New York. "Why should a person be afraid to walk the streets in broad daylight? Why should the innocent victim be the one removed from the community?" New York Gov. Hugh Carey put the problem succinctly last winter. "A 15-year-old killer may be too young to send to prison," he said, "but he is too dangerous to return to the streets."

TOUGH TACTICS

Many states are searching for a new line between the point at which a teenager can still be rehabilitated and the time when he should be treated like an adult criminal. Most states cut off juvenile treatment at the age of 18, and allow courts to waive youngsters to adult courts at 16 for such serious felonies as murder and rape. Two years ago Georgia decided that capital felons could be tried in adult courts at 13, and this year New Mexico lowered to 15 the age at which defendants could be tried for first-degree murder. In California, the waiver age of 16 for serious crimes is discretionary, but the Los Angeles district attorney's office is pushing to make it mandatory.

But merely lowering the age at which all juveniles become adults in the eyes of criminal law may serve little purpose. "Kids today have a greater wealth of knowledge about adult life than children years ago," says child psychologist Lee Salk, "but this sophistication doesn't mean that youngsters are better able to cope with their impulses."

What most law-enforcement officials would prefer is firmer treatment of the hard-core delinquents, who commit a disproportionate share of all juvenile crimes, especially the violent crimes. In a major study published three years ago, University of Pennsylvania criminologist Marvin Wolfgang and his colleagues found that of 10,000 Philadelphia boys born in 1945, only one in six had ever been arrested for more than one offense. Six per cent of these, however, had committed five or more crimes and that group accounted for 66 per cent of all violent crimes.

Law-enforcement officials contend that the hardened teen-age criminal must learn that he will not be coddled but will pay a quick, sure price for repeated, violent crimes. "I don't put the blame for crime on discrimination or poverty or TV," says Brooklyn assistant police chief Jules Sachson. "I put it squarely where it belongs, on the lack of a deterrent. These kids are getting more violent because they know they can get away with it. We could stop it tomorrow by putting them away to stay."

Tough tactics for the few, however, do not reach the occasional or potential young offenders, and authorities have not given up on them. "If you can't rehabilitate a 13-, 14- or 15-year-old, who can you rehabilitate?" asks Charles Schinitsky, head of the New York Legal Aid Society's juvenile-rights division. At California's Hidden Valley Ranch School, near San Francisco, youngsters are put through a 90-day evaluation period before they are guided into a rehabilitation program. In New York, which like other states has been accused of warehousing its charges, the Division for Youth is attempting to increase preventive counseling. But though local, state and Federal officials are all groping for answers, few have confidence that they will be found soon.

TOURING THE TROUBLE SPOTS

Last year, over stiff opposition from the White House, Congress passed the first comprehensive Federal law to deal with juvenile crime. Chiefly, the act authorizes Federal grants to develop community programs aimed at preventing delinquency. "The only way to deal with the problem is to start early enough," says Indiana Sen. Birch Bayh, whose juvenile-delinquency subcommittee pushed the measure. The Ford Administration, giving the program low priority, has reluctantly committed only $25 million, one-third of the budget request. Juvenile crime costs the U.S. $12 billion annually, responds Bayh, and "if we think we're saving money this way, we're kidding ourselves."

How would a community crime-prevention program work? Detroit has hired 25 civilian youth advisers, all with college experience, who tour potential trouble spots learning to know the kids better. These advisers work with probation officers in counseling first and second offenders and their parents. Cleveland has started a touring panel, made up of a policeman, judge, lawyer and teacher, that discusses the law and answers questions for junior-high-school students. San Francisco last year established a "diversion" plan that treated 77 youthful auto thieves, only four of whom have since committed another crime. Under the plan, the youth and his parents signed a contract enrolling the offender for six months in a community counseling program sponsored by agencies such as the YMCA. The pilot project was successful enough that the city is extending it this year to nearly 300 delinquents. But the money will run out by the end of the year and the program may die.

NO ANSWERS

One simple way to unclog the juvenile courts would be to eliminate status offenders, who are not criminals, from their jurisdiction. "You can't use courts, judges and lawyers to rehabilitate kids," says Patrick T. Murphy, the former director of Chicago's Legal Aid Society juvenile office. "Obviously some are thugs and belong in prison. Why charge youngsters with delinquency, though, just because they got into a fight, ran away or cut school?" But retired Judge Justine Wise Polier, an official of the Children's Defense Fund, contends that many families need a court's help. "These parents file status petitions only when they are at their wits' end," Polier says, "when they are terrified that the children are going to destroy themselves or commit a really serious crime." The issue is now causing fierce debate in the entire juvenile-justice system, but no solutions are in sight, partly because if the courts are no longer to deal with these children, no one really knows who will.

For the moment, no one is sure what to do about almost anything in the juvenile-justice system. "I'm not going to tell you it's not hopeless," says University of Virginia Law School dean Monrad G. Paulsen, "because it may be hopeless." "The juvenile-justice system suffers from lack of a constituency," says New York's Luger. "Nobody gives a damn until some kid commits murder or sodomy in their neighborhood and then there's hell to pay."

On some propositions, everyone can agree. Juvenile crime must be controlled. Violent young criminals must be punished. Children who suffer from forces over which they have no control must be treated. Youngsters must have protection by the law and from the law. Yet down every avenue, so many interests clash—so many factors interplay—that the solutions remain tantalizingly out of reach. "There are no quick answers," warns Justice Joseph B. Williams, chief of New York City's Family Court. "All of a sudden, the juvenile-justice system is supposed to come up with an answer that wipes out all the experience in a child's life and all that has been done to him. I don't think any system can do that." Juvenile justice, troubled as it is by its own failures, is just like the youngsters—as much victim as offender.

37

A Child in Jail— 'Tasting Scared'

By Thomas J. Cottle

According to statistics prepared by the Law Enforcement Assistance Administration, there are approximately 160,000 people in jail throughout the United States on any given day. If one considers turnover rates, as many as 5,500,000 men and women are in jail in the course of one year. Of those persons arrested for violent crimes, about 22 percent are children under the age of 18. Of those arrested for property offenses, 50 percent are children under 18. But the figures for crimes committed by children and the number of children in jail in the United States are far from clear.

It is known that the most common crimes committed by children are vandalism, arson, burglary and running away. Furthermore, if the figures provided in the President's Crime Commission Report are accurate, about 90,000 children were in jail in 1967. An additional 100,000 were held in police lock-ups. In all, more than 400,000 children were detained in a variety of facilities. Like everything else, however, the numbers have changed in the last eight years, so it is possible that annually more than 600,000 children are placed in detention homes. In March of 1970, the State of New York alone reported that 4550 juveniles were in its jails.

To be sure, these are awesome statistics. But as so often in statistical reports, serious problems are masked by rates and percentages. Ignoring the question of what if any good imprisonment does for juveniles,

(Thomas Cottle, affiliated with the Children's Defense Fund of the Washington Research Project, is the author of many books, including A Family Album and Black Children, White Dreams.)

another fundamental issue must be addressed. How is it that children are placed in adult jails, and what effect does this inappropriate — and sometimes illegal — incarceration have on them?

* * *

Robert Martin Gumpert (the name is fictitious) was arrested with two other youths in January of 1974 — one week before his 15th birthday — for burglary. The arrest was made in Rhode Island, but cases such as his occur in Massachusetts and almost every other state. Gumpy, as he is called, is a white boy of medium height for his age and very thin. He wears his hair long, usually hiding it under a cap. His teeth have yellowed from years of neglect — he has not visited a dentist since he was seven — and an obstruction in his nose makes breathing difficult. When he speaks it always sounds as if he has a cold.

After the arraignment and legal negotiations, Gumpy was placed in a county jail for what was supposed to be a maximum 10-day period before his appearance before a judge. Because the arresting officers listed Gumpy as an accessory to the burglary, his case was considered less severe than those of the two others arrested with him, Manny Malzone and Frederic Fritz Gallaher. All three were placed in the same jail but were kept from seeing one another. There was no bail set for any of them. Both Manny and Fritz had prior police records; Gumpy, although he had once been picked up by the police, had never been booked or fingerprinted. Ever since the neighborhood police had first gotten to know him when he was nine, Gumpy was regarded as a loud-mouthed trouble-maker but not thought of as a criminal. It was always said that he was a follower: if his

friends stayed clean, he would stay clean; if they decided to break the law, he'd go along with that, too.

Bobby Gumpert sat in jail over a week awaiting trial. On the morning of the 10th day, he learned that because of a judge's illness, his case would be continued indefinitely, but presumably no more than two weeks. He was still not allowed to be released on bail. In fact, he waited 41 days before trial, one of 15 young men under the age of 18 in a jail holding about 65 prisoners.

During these 41 days I was allowed to visit once a week with Bobby, whom I have known for seven years. His mother, brothers and sisters were allowed three weekly visits, but because they live so far from the jail, they came only once a week. My conversations with the boy were always the same. He was bewildered, angry at the treatment he was getting, and scared. As the days wore on, his terror and outrage increased. Several days before his trial took place — although at the time he did not know that a date had been set — we met in the visiting room of the jail for the last time.

"Do me one favor," he demanded when he sat down. "Promise one favor. Get me out of here. They're driving me crazy in here, man. They got guys locked up in there, man, who shouldn't be in here. I mean, nobody should be in here, but these guys are off the wall, man. They're off the wall. They ought to be in a hospital. All night long I hear 'em talking to each other. They're whispering shit back and forth, man. They don't even make any sense. They're just talking. You can't believe it. There are old guys too. Guys in their 40s, 50s, 60s. Jesus, I haven't seen another kid my age in there. Where the hell they sen-

ding all the juveniles anyway? There's only men in there. Everybody calls me son. 'Hey, son, do this'; 'son, do that.' It gives me the creeps, man. They're going to drive me crazy.

"They got this one guy in there, he really thinks I am his son. Something happened to the guy's real son, I think. Maybe he was in a car accident or something. Somebody said he was electrocuted on the train tracks. Anyway, the first week I was here he decided I was his son. So he keeps yelling at me. Jesus, he gets me with this thing about me being his son. I'm a turn-on for him. So this other guy, he says I ought to yell at him and shut him up, tell him I'm not his son, you know, or walk past him one day and kick him in the nuts. I can't do that, man. I don't know the guy. I don't know what he's been through. I just want out of here. I don't want to make no trouble. I just want to be transferred. If I'm guilty and have to go to prison or some place, you know, then let them send me with guys my age.

"They got queers in here, man. Lot of 'em. Guys must have been straight once, but not now. At night, you know, everybody's in there slapping meat, yelling, whispering. Guy this morning started to come at me from the back. I looked around, man, I couldn't believe this guy. I expected maybe it was Malzone, who I haven't seen all this time. He's a whack — he'd do something like that, too. But Malzone? Hell, it was this old guy, a short little ugly guy. He must have been 70 years old. And he was standing there, holding on to himself, looking up at me like I was some chick. I swear to God, man. This guy was ready to poke it in me. Like getting stiffed by your own goddamn grandfather. Jesus, man, they got me in with these old geezers. I think that's why they want me here. I think it turns these guys on. They don't have no women coming to see them, so they put some kids in there like me and keep pretending the trial gets pushed forward. I'll bet that's it, too, man. I'm the goddamn whore for this jail. Shit, they'd all shove it into me if they had a chance. I told this guard the other day — he wanted me to get outside for exercise. I mean, he's cool. I told him I'm staying in here. Only safe damn place in the city. They'll keep those fags unlocked in their cells. That's what I heard. So when the

Illustration by Ray Rue

guard's not looking, you know, they go in and get it on with each other. I ain't never seen that, but I heard they did. I'll bet they do, too.

"This ain't no place for a kid, man. Shit, this ain't no place for anybody but an animal, and I ain't no animal. I still like girls, man. I ain't ready yet to have no guard molesting me. You hear what I'm telling you? It's me, Gumpy. I can't believe this is happening. It's a fuckin' dream, you and I talking in this place. We're in a jail, man. I'm going back after I talk to you to sit in a goddamn jail cell. I ain't even got no window in that room. I can't look anyplace, man. I just pray they'll let me sleep, but I never felt so healthy. The food here stinks but I'm really healthy, man. I don't want to sleep, man. I mean, I want to sleep but I don't need no sleep."

Bobby looked over his shoulder, then leaned across the table toward me.

"You got to get me out of here. Can't you find out if there's a kid's prison someplace? There's

got to be one, man. I don't care where it is. I'd rather be in with nine-year-old kids than have to go back in there with those guys. They're going to eat me up in there, man. Eat me up or have me jerking them off one by one. I ain't told no one else but my brother, but you know damn well each person has a breaking point. They're going to break me in there, man. There's no one in there to look out for me. One of these days, if I don't behave like they want me to, they'll turn me loose on 'em. I've heard the stories, man. You go in there at 10 o'clock in the morning, and by 10:30 you've heard every goddamn story about every goddamn guy who's ever been in there. Whitey Polansky, this one guy everybody talks about? They said he made it with every chick in the city. Then they got him on this rape charge, you know. So they put him in here, man, and the guy goes A.C. Goes mad, man, and starts raping everybody in sight. I'll bet there were lots of guys in there who dug it, too. So then he goes after

the guard, this new policeman, you know. So the cop takes it for a minute, then turns around and clouts the guy. Foom! I don't even know if he died, or what happened to him after that. Someone said they took him to the South and cut his nuts off. Some sheriff, they said, cut his nuts off and tied them in the guy's pocket so he couldn't get 'em out. You believe that, man? That's what I heard. Maybe it's a lot of bullshit, but that's what I heard. Everybody that's been in there long enough has stories like that, too. Old timers have the most. But I got some stories now, too, which means I've been in there pretty long.

"I saw some guy walking through the halls last night. Guy next to me says he thought it was the sheriff. I never saw the man before — could have been the sheriff, could have been the plumber, for all I know. Little red-faced guy, funny-looking. He kept smiling. I'd smile too if I could walk out of here the way he does. I'd take this whole place if I could come and go like him. And like you. So the guy, this sheriff or whatever he was, he comes walking up to my cell. I can see from the way he's looking in at me that he's surprised somebody young is sitting in on the bed, you know. 'How you doing, son?' he goes. So I goes, 'Terrific! I love it here.' So he goes, 'Cut the shit — what do you need?' So now *I'm* the one who's surprised So I stand up and go over to where he's standing outside the cell, you know. And he knows that maybe I want to tell him something, which I did, only I don't know what I wanted to say. 'You can talk,' he goes. 'Nobody's listening but me.' And when he's talking, he kind of nods at these guards and they walk away. I could see them but they couldn't hear. So I guess he must have been the sheriff, or some big shot.

" 'You got a lawyer?' he goes. I tell him 'Yeah, a shitty one I never see.' 'What's his name?' he goes. 'Mooney,' I goes. 'Arthur the bullshitter Mooney. Mooney like money.' 'He helping you?' he goes. 'Helping me to stay here. Somebody must be doing something super,' I goes. 'I been here six weeks.' 'Bullshit,' he goes. 'You're just waiting trial.' 'Bullshit nothing, baby,' I go.

'You ask 'em. Ask the guards. Six weeks, almost.' The guy was really upset. He was really upset. You couldn't fake the way he looked. I've seen people, like that Mooney, pretend he's interested in what you're saying, but this guy wasn't faking. Oh man, I was standing there so close to him. I could see his freckles, you know, and these funny hairs growing on his head. The cat was bald, you know. So then he puts his hand around the bar holding it, and I'm standing there wanting to touch it. Jesus, maybe I'm queerer than I thought. But I really had this thing just to touch him, like to have contact, you know what I mean? So he goes, 'What do you need?' And he's serious. I mean, I know if I say get me out, that would be silly, but if I asked him for a steak or a different shirt, or to change cells to get away from the creeps, maybe he'd be able to get it for me.

"So I look at the guy and he's really looking serious. He ain't saying nothing, just looking at me, holding on to the bar. So I goes, 'You want to help me, man?' I smiled like I was real tough and I didn't want to be. I couldn't help myself, you know. And I goes, 'If you want to help

me, man, get me Spiro Agnew's lawyer.' It was dumb, man. Real dumb. I felt like a goddamn asshole. I mean, the guy wanted to help, so what do I do? I tell him to fuck off. He knew what I was doing, too. He goes, I'll do my best for you.'

"I blew it, man. The second he let go of that bar — it was like he'd been holding it up — I knew I blew it. I got so mad. And he walked away. I sat down, man, like I was really tough. Big tough kid, you know, and all of a sudden I was crying, and I ain't cried since, I don't even know when. But I was crying, man, and I didn't give a rat's ass if the whole jail knew it. Until that man came up to that cell and held on to that bar the way he did, you know, 'til I saw his hand holding on to that bar, I didn't know how bad off I am, and how scared I am. And I really am scared now, too, man. I'm so scared now I can taste it."

* * *

After 41 days of confinement prior to trial, Robert Gumpert's case went to court. In the end, the judge ruled that he was guilty but suspended his sentence.

38

To Cure One Boy: The Case of Wilson Diver

by Thomas J. Cottle

Wilson Diver is by far the smallest, thinnest and most frail looking of the nine Diver children. At age twelve, he looks younger than his eleven-year-old sister Theresa and his ten-year-old brother Curtiss. On meeting Wilson for the first time, everyone believes he is either on his way to a hospital or has just come out of one. It doesn't help young Wilson's condition any that he and his family are among the poorest families in Massachusetts.

It was very clear to his mother, Mrs. Claudia Diver, that her seventh baby even at birth was not as strong as the other ones. He had a fine disposition; he learned to walk when everybody thinks it's normal to begin walking, and talk when talking's supposed to begin, but he was, somehow, an unwell child. The first sign of illness came when he was about two, when for weeks at a time he would lie in his bed whimpering, having trouble breathing and running abnormally high temperatures. As he grew up these bouts of bronchitis, asthmatic bronchitis as they later were diagnosed, came more frequently—eight, nine times a year. Like all children, Wilson would show the beginning signs of a cold. He would cough a bit, sneeze, and find his nose running. At night, the coughing became unbearable. He might cough without respite for two minutes, until finally his chest would sag and deep rings lined his eyes. By flaring his nostrils and opening his mouth, he barely got sufficient air into his lungs. The cold weather naturally made his life miserable, particularly at night when there was no heat in the Diver apartment. There was no way to keep him warm or provide him any relief. His mother would prop him up in bed and hold him while she and several of his sleepy brothers and sisters would just stare at him, expecting him surely to die at any minute. No one could believe how sick Wilson could get in such a short time. One day he would be fine, the next morning he would show symptoms of a cold, and by that night he would look to be on the brink of death.

Wilson was examined once by a young medical student in the large hospital six miles from the Diver house. The doctor said that he heard nothing in Wilson's chest to indicate a problem. "Some kids," he told Mrs. Diver, "are just susceptible to pulmonary and bronchial complications when they get sick." He did give them some medicine to try the next time Wilson got sick. The medicine seemed to help, at least it gave Wilson some relief in breathing. Strangely though, it also seemed to stimulate him so that he was unable to sleep at night. Mrs. Diver had to decide which was more important, relief in breathing or sleep.

By his twelfth year, Wilson Diver was accustomed to his periodic illnesses. He did his best to avoid catching colds, but he simply was more susceptible to them than anyone he knew. No matter how warmly he dressed or wisely he ate, the infections got to him. Claudia Diver kept promising she would move the family to a warmer climate, for she had relatives in Birmingham, but the shortage of money never allowed for this. And where could she find a job as good as the one she had now in the small factory so near to her home? "Wilson has survived this long," she said, "and he's getting bigger and stronger. He'll survive the rest of the way. He has to."

In February, two months almost to the day before Wilson's thirteenth birthday, he got sick again. All the usual signs were present: the unstoppable coughing at night, the runny nose and eyes, the pains in the sinus areas behind his cheeks and forehead, and the chest aching from strain and fatigue. But this time the infection seemed to hang on longer than before, indeed several days longer, and a new symptom appeared. Early one morning, after he had managed to get back to sleep for a few hours, Wilson became nauseated and began to vomit violently. Even when he had rid his stomach of all its contents, a muscular reflex continued, and he gagged until he felt he would expel his lungs. A bit of blood appeared in the vomit.

Awakened by the sounds of Wilson retching and crying, Wilson's older brother, McCay, found him in the bathroom and promptly awoke everyone. At six o'clock in the morning they decided that, difficult as it would be, they had to take Wilson to the hospital. A portion of the hospital trip was described by Wilson himself several months later.

"First we called the police, you know, and they said they couldn't send nobody around to our house unless we could prove it was an emergency. McCay said I should get on the phone and cough for 'em. He wasn't joking neither. But they would not come out. So we went down to the corner and waited for the bus and, man, it was so cold out there we might as well have frozen altogether. Everybody was standing around me, trying to keep me warm, you know. Must have had ten coats and jackets on me. And I kept up this gagging and choking I was doing too. So maybe after a half hour, the bus comes, and we get on.

"Then we had to transfer to another bus, and finally we got there. We were real early too, and this waiting room they got there was crowded with people, it was like we were going to a bus station or something. Every chair was filled up. An old man gave his seat to my mother, but McCay and me, we sat on the floor. And the place was cold too, man, and there wasn't anything to eat. They had a real nice water fountain, I remember.

"Now here's the truth: we must have got there by eight o'clock, and we didn't talk to no one, no one, man, until eleven, or maybe even later. And then it was this woman who took our names and stuff like that, you know. She wasn't even a nurse! She was just taking our names. And the place is getting more crowded every minute. You should have seen the people coming in there too. Broken legs and bleeding. Then they brought this one guy in on a table with wheels and they said he died. The man died there after the doctors saw him.

"So then, like at twelve, the woman calls our name and we go up to this little desk, and she tells my mother that we don't have the right kind of insurance to get medical help. My mother needed to prove where she worked or something, I don't remember, but anyway, McCay has to go home and get something that proves she can come to the hospital. And 'cause we don't have a telephone we couldn't call up at home, and anyway no one was home 'cause they were all at school.

"So McCay goes and he comes back, this time with the police. He just went there and told him his problem and this cop gave him a ride all the way. Now it's like one, one-thirty, and I ain't seen no one. Finally they get all the stuff straightened out on the paper, oh, here's what it was. They thought it would be better for my mother to say she was on welfare than to say she had a job. Somehow it worked out better for them if they did it like that. So they did. She didn't care, she just wanted me to see the doctor, 'cause I wasn't getting any better. Finally, they call my name and I see this doctor. He tells me to take off my shirt and lie on a table, one of those tables like that other guy died on, only this one had a clean sheet. So I get on the table and I'm thinking the doctor looks real young. And it's cold in this little hall they got me in too, 'cause it's not a room, it's just a hall with a sheet hanging down from the ceiling to kind of hide me, you know. Then the doctor goes out and he don't come back. And I'm lying there with my shirt off, freezing, so finally I get up and walk out and ask somebody can I put my shirt on and he says, 'You can put your hat on for all I care. If you can walk and ask questions like that you ain't sick enough to be in the emergency room!' So I get disgusted and go back to my little sheet room in the hall, you know, but I get dressed.

"Now, while all this is going on, McCay goes home 'cause he's so hungry he can't stand it no more. But he asked someone before he left how come no one's helping *me*, and the woman tells him it's her job to choose which people who come into the room look the sickest. And since I didn't look that sick to her she kept me waiting. So then I go out again and tell someone I'm really hungry. This time it's a doctor and he looks at this little piece of paper they had me carry with me and he says, 'You've been vomiting, so you better not eat yet.' And when I went back again to my sheet room I saw that the clock said five-thirty. And still nobody had come to see me.

"You ain't going to believe that nobody came until six-thirty. Then this other doctor comes, not the first one,

but a different one, and he's looking so tired and he's talking to so many people he looks like he should see a doctor himself. So guess what he says to me?

" 'Take your shirt off Mr. Wilson.' "

"I say, 'My *first* name's Wilson.' He don't hear me. He's got that thing in his ears already and he's starting to listen to my chest and my back. Then he lays me down and pushes his hands so hard on my stomach I thought he was going to kill me 'stead of cure me. Then he asks if I'm hungry. I say I ought to be, haven't eaten since last night. So he gives me this great hard candy and he tells me where he buys it and pats my face. Nice guy.

" 'How you feel,' he says.

"I tell him I want to go home.

" 'You're going to be fine, Wilson my boy,' he says. 'You're going to be good as new. You just got to eat my special candy.'

"Man, did I feel good after that. 'Can I go, doc?' I ask him.

'Hold still a bit longer,' he says.

"All this time he's writing on a sheet of paper.

'You got a phone number?' he says.

"No."

'What's your address?'

"I tell him. 'Now can I go?'

'Hold still.'

"So now I have to wait some more. But when he leaves he promises me he'll come right back. Don't worry! Then he leaves and I hear him tell another man, 'There's a boy in there who is very sick. We got to find him a bed.' I didn't know what he meant at first. But then I figured they want me to go to the hospital 'cause I wasn't fine, and I started to cry. Real soft 'cause I didn't want no one to find me. But when nobody came back I put my shirt on for like the tenth time and went to get my mother, but she was gone. And the room wasn't crowded any more. Then I really got scared. But this new woman had a note saying my mother would come back and that I shouldn't worry. Shouldn't worry, why not? They wanted to put me in the hospital which meant I was sick, real sick, man. I'd been there all day and only one person saw me and he only was there a couple minutes. Course he gave me that candy which was my breakfast, lunch and dinner. They did give me that!

"So then I waited some more.

"Then, like at about ten o'clock in the night, a nurse came in this room where they got the television to say a policeman's outside waiting to take me home. She says I should be in the hospital and they've been waiting for a bed to open up, whatever that means, but since they had no room they were sending me home. But before I left she had to take some blood from me which hurt me, man, like out of natural sight pain! You going to drink it? I asked her. She didn't laugh. 'Too late for that nonsense,' she said. 'I been here all day lady,' I told her. 'Me too,' she said. She was an angry old bitch. Anyway, the cop took me home and had to carry me into the house. Everybody was asleep except my mother and McCay. They had tried to get back to the hospital but the buses weren't running no more. That was the longest day of my life man. Started out with me vomiting up my lungs and ended with a policeman carrying me home. But I knew I had to go back to the hospital. I told my mother couldn't she find a better hospital. She said they were all the same, and anyway, this one now had my records. I was doomed, man. That's what I told McCay the next day. If I go back there I'm going to die, man. Hospital's going to kill me off, just by all the waiting. My mother told me not to talk that way, but McCay, he said, "Wilson's right. What about that man we saw who died on the table like the one they put Wilson on?' My mother told him to shut up, but he was right. Only I didn't want nobody to talk about it like he did. He didn't have to go back there like I did."

Ten days following Wilson's examination, the hospital sent a letter to Mrs. Diver indicating that the results of his blood test suggested that Wilson should enter the hospital for further tests. The hospital would notify the Divers when a bed was free but that it would be helpful if they could return to the hospital before that time for a chest x-ray. It was almost three weeks before the x-ray was taken.

"This time," Wilson said, "I only waited three hours, only I was all by myself. But it was all right 'cause it meant I didn't have to go to school all that day. People were nice to me too. The woman remembered me from before. But one week later they wrote to us saying they had a record of me coming in for x-rays but no record of the x-rays. So I had to go back again. And you got to remember that each trip to the hospital takes about two hours, if you don't have to wait too long for the buses. Each time you got to wait outside in the cold, you know, and you're getting so cold you don't know whether to go

on or go back. One time I went back and told my mother I went. Then I had to cut school another day so I could go. So they did the same x-ray all over. I was noticing then how my chest seemed to be getting smaller. For a while I was thinking so much about going to the hospital and worrying about it, I didn't even think about being ill. Although I near vomited again like I did that one time. But I couldn't shake my cold, you know. It's like it was stuck to me, like I'd have it forever. I don't know. Maybe I will."

Three and one half months after his first examination and the decision to put him in the hospital, Wilson Diver was admitted. He was placed in a ward room with five other young people. New doctors examined him this time; he never saw the same doctor twice. A third chest x-ray was taken and all sorts of medical tests were performed. On the third afternoon of his hospitalization, Mrs. Claudia Diver was called into the doctor's room on the second floor for consultation. Her son was suffering with pulmonary problems, she was told. The x-rays had recorded a rather large spot on his right lung which indicated tuberculosis. Moreover, while the doctors were not certain, several tests suggested the possibility of his also having leukemia, although they hoped it was a mild, treatable form. He was also malnourished. As Claudia Diver reports it, the doctor was about to remonstrate with her for the way she had failed to give her son proper medical attention. Then, she said, he had looked at her, and he stopped himself. She did not have to explain Wilson's circumstances, or her circumstances.

XI. Adolescents and Social Change

No matter how one examines the lives of those people we call adolescents, and no matter what our theoretical orientation, people from the ages of 10 to 20 always are perceived in terms of their development and growth. The very word adolescence has come to imply process: the person in process of changing from a child to an adult. It is almost as if adolescents don't do anything but kill time, in school, on the street, in jobs, at home, hoping that the years will pass so they can call themselves adults. To counteract this viewpoint, some of us protest that, adolescent or not, people of this age are in the military, holding jobs, becoming parents, winning Olympic medals, earning enormous amounts of money. Still, the stereotype remains: adolescence is "merely" a period of transition in the life cycle. Adolescents are "merely" passing from genuinely formative years of childhood to the genuinely productive years of adulthood, and somebody had to make up a name for the decade in which this passing through business takes place, at least in our society.

The three selections chosen for the section on Adolescents and Social Change probably won't dispell the old myths and stereotypes, but they should help to make one point: adolescents can change their society as well as be influenced by the norms, rules, customs, and regulations of their society. Again, let us not romanticize anybody, but let us stress that change can take place because of the presence and activity of young people. This point needs clarification.

When a population of people is large, and that population lives in a culture dominated by economic passion and material success, then that population becomes important, if for no other reason than its extraordinary purchasing capacity. The young buy, they spend money, billions of dollars. Their clothes, books and records, their entertainment and everyday needs are the source of gigantic profits. To be sure, some young people themselves benefit from this endless consumer source, but in the main, the society at large is the beneficiary of the adolescent market. So, by their mere presence in the culture, adolescents will change that society in fundamental ways, if only because their tastes and needs, real and contrived, constantly change.

Yet, as the following selections indicate, adolescents by their actions, political concerns, their tastes, their desire to contribute to the shape of the culture also change the culture in fundamental ways. Adolescents have affected the direction music and dance have taken, just as they have affected the directions schools have taken. Their position, as much as the position of any other group, affects the future of the relationship of various races and ethnic groups within a culture, and as a voting block, they can influence national elections. There are more subtle influences as well, and some courageous stands taken: on college campuses by people in their late teens, in school buses by children still a couple of years away from becoming teenagers.

Once again, that word of warning: newspapers, radio, and television keep us alert to the more sensational stories, literally the newsworthy ones. Often these stories tell us a great deal about the ways of the young and their contribution to social and cultural change. But the people of the media know that the real story in adolescence and social change is the story of the way the young person leads his or her life every day, and this story, inevitably, is too difficult or impractical to tell, and hardly seems newsworthy at all.

Social Change and Youth in America

39

KENNETH KENISTON

Every society tends to ignore its most troublesome characteristics.[1] Usually these remain unfathomed precisely because they are taken for granted, because life would be inconceivable without these traits. And most often they are taken for granted because their recognition would be painful to those concerned or disruptive to the society. Active awareness would at times involve confronting an embarrassing gap between social creed and social fact; at other times, the society chooses to ignore those of its qualities which subject its citizens to the greatest psychological strain. Such pluralistic ignorance is usually guaranteed and disguised by a kind of rhetoric of pseudo-awareness, which, by appearing to talk about the characteristic and even to praise it, prevents real understanding far more effectively than could an easily broken conspiracy of silence.

Such is often the case with discussions of social change in America. From hundreds of platforms on Commencement Day, young men and women are told that they go out into a rapidly changing world, that they live amidst unprecedented new opportunities, that they must continue the innovations which have made and will continue to produce an ever-improving society in an ever-improving world. Not only is social change here portrayed as inevitable and good, but, the acoustics of the audience being what it is, no one really hears, and all leave with the illusory conviction that they have understood something about their society. But it occurs to none of the graduating class that their deepest anxieties and most confused moments might be a consequence of this "rapidly changing world."

More academic discussions of social change often fail similarly to clarify its meaning in our society. Most scholarly discussions of innovation concentrate either on the primitive world or on some relatively small segment of modern so-

291

ciety. No conference is complete without panels and papers on "New Trends in X," "Recent Developments in Y," and "The New American Z." But commentators on American society are usually so preoccupied with specific changes—in markets, population patterns, styles of life—that they rarely if ever consider the over-all impact of the very fact that our entire society is in flux. And however important it may be to understand these specific changes in society, their chief importance for the individual is in that they are merely part of the broader picture of social change in all areas.

Even when we do reflect on the meaning of change in our own society, we are usually led to minimize its effects by the myth that familiarity breeds disappearance—that is, by the belief that because as individuals and as a society we have made an accommodation to social change, its effects have therefore vanished. It is of course true that the vast majority of Americans have made a kind of adaptation to social change. Most would feel lost without the technological innovations with which industrial managers and advertising men annually supply us: late-model cars, TV sets, refrigerators, women's fashions, and home furnishings. And, more important, we have made a kind of peace with far more profound nontechnological changes; new conceptions of the family, of sex roles, of work and play cease to shock or even to surprise us. But such an adaptation, even when it involves the expectation of and the need for continuing innovation, does not mean that change has ceased to affect us. It would be as true to say that because the American Indian has found in defeat, resentment, and apathy an adaptation of the social changes which destroyed his tribal life, he has ceased to be affected by these changes. Indeed, the acceptance and anticipation of social change by most Americans is itself one of the best indications of how profoundly it has altered our outlooks.

Thus, though barraged with discussions of "our rapidly changing world" and "recent developments," we too easily can remain incognizant of the enormous significance, and in many ways the historical uniqueness, of social change in our society. Rapid changes in all aspects of life mean that little can be counted on to endure from generation to generation, that all technologies, all institutions, and all values are open to revision and obsolescence. Continual innovation as we experience it in this country profoundly affects our conceptions of ourselves, our visions of the future, the quality of our attachment to the present, and the myths we construct of the past. It constitutes one of the deepest sources of strain in American life,[2] and many characteristically "American" outlooks, values, and institutions can be interpreted as attempts to adapt to the stress of continual change.

Social Change in America

Many of the outlooks and values of American youth can be seen as responses to the social changes which confront this generation.[3] But merely to point out that society is changing and that youth must cope with the strains thus created is to state a truth so universal as to be almost tautological. Social change is the rule in history: past ages which at first glance appear to have been static usually turn out on closer study to have been merely those in which conflicting pressures for change were temporarily canceled out. Indeed, the very concept of a static society is usually a mistake of the short-sighted, a hypothetical construct which facilitates

the analysis of change, or a myth created by those who dislike innovation.[4] All new generations must accommodate themselves to social change; indeed, one of youth's historic roles has been to provide the enthusiasm—if not the leadership—for still further changes.

And even if we add the qualifier "rapid" to "social change," there is still little distinctive about the problems of American youth. For though most historical changes have been slow and have involved little marked generational discontinuity, in our own century at least most of the world is in the midst of rapid, massive, and often disruptive changes, and these may create even greater problems for the youth of underdeveloped countries than they do for Americans. Thus, to understand the responses of American youth to the problems of social change, we must first characterize, however tentatively and impressionistically, the most striking features of social change in this country.

Social change in America is by no means *sui generis;* in particular, it has much in common with the process of innovation in other industrialized countries. In all industrially advanced nations, the primary motor of social change is technological innovation: changes in nontechnological areas of society usually follow the needs and effects of technological and scientific advances. But though our own country is not unique in the role technology plays, it is distinguished by the intensity of and the relative absence of restraint on technological change. Probably more than any other society, we revere technological innovation, we seldom seek to limit its effects on other areas of society, and we have developed complex institutions to assure its persistence and acceleration. And, most important, because of the almost unchallenged role of technology in our society, our attitudes toward it spread into other areas of life, coloring our views on change in whatever area it occurs. This country closely approximates the ideal type of unrestrained and undirected technological change which pervades all areas of life; and in so far as other nations wish to or are in fact becoming more like us, the adaptations of American youth may augur similar trends elsewhere.

Our almost unqualified acceptance of technological innovation is historically unusual. To be sure, given a broad definition of technology, most major social and cultural changes have been accompanied, if not produced, by technological advances. The control of fire, the domestication of animals, the development of irrigation, the discovery of the compass—each innovation has been followed by profound changes in the constitution of society. But until recently technological innovation has been largely accidental and usually bitterly resisted by the order it threatened to supplant. Indeed, if there has been any one historical attitude toward change, it has been to deplore it. Most cultures have assumed that change was for the worse; most individuals have felt that the old ways were the best ways. There is a certain wisdom behind this assumption, for it is indeed true that technological change and its inevitable social and psychological accompaniments produce strains, conflicts, and imbalances among societies as among individuals. Were it not for our own and other modern societies, we might ascribe to human nature and social organization a deep conservatism which dictates that changes shall be made only when absolutely necessary and after a last-ditch stand by what is being replaced.

But in our own society in particular, this attitude no longer holds. We value scientific innovation and technological change almost without conscious reservation.[5] Even when scientific discoveries make possible the total destruction of the world, we do not seriously question the value of such discoveries. Those rare voices who may ask whether a new bomb, a new tail fin, a new shampoo, or a new superhighway might not be better left unproduced are almost invariably suppressed before the overwhelming conviction that "you can't stop the clock." And these attitudes extend beyond science and technology, affecting our opinions of every kind of change—as indeed they must if unwillingness to bear the nontechnological side effects of technological innovation is not to impede the latter. Whether in social institutions, in ideology, or even in individual character, change is more often than not considered self-justifying. Our words of highest praise stress transformation—dynamic, expanding, new, modern, recent, growing, current, youthful, and so on. And our words of condemnation equally deplore the static and unchanging—old-fashioned, outmoded, antiquated, obsolete, stagnating, stand-still. We desire change not only when we have clear evidence that the status quo is inadequate, but often regardless of whether what we have from the past still serves us. The assumption that the new will be better than the old goes very deep in our culture; and even when we explicitly reject such notions as that of Progress, we often retain the implicit assumption that change *per se* is desirable.

Given this assumption that change is good, it is inevitable that institutions should have developed which would guarantee change and seek to accelerate it. Here as in other areas, technology leads the way. Probably the most potent innovating institution in our society is pure science, which provides an ever-increasing repertoire of techniques for altering the environment. An even greater investment of time and money goes into applied science and technology, into converting abstract scientific principles into concrete innovations relevant to our industrialized society. The elevation of technological innovation into a profession, research and development, is the high point of institutionalized technological change in this country and probably in the world. And along with the institutionalized change increasingly goes planned obsolescence, to assure that even if the motivation to discard the outmoded should flag, the consumer will have no choice but to buy the newest and latest, since the old will have ceased to function.

But the most drastic strains occur only at the peripheries of purely technological innovation, because of changes in other social institutions which follow in the wake of new commodities and technologies. Consider the effects of the automobile, which has changed patterns of work and residence, transformed the countryside with turnpikes and freeways, all but destroyed public transportation, been instrumental in producing urban blight and the flight to the suburbs, and even changed techniques of courtship in America. Further examples could be adduced, but the point is clear: unrestrained technological change guarantees the continual transformation of other sectors of society to accommodate the effects and requirements of technology. And here, too, our society abounds with planning groups, special legislative committees, citizens' movements, research organizations and community workers and consultants of every variety whose chief task is, as it were, to clean up after technologically induced changes, though rarely if ever to plan or coordinate major social innovations in the first place. Thus, citizens' committees usually worry more about how to relocate the families dispossessed by new roadways than about whether

new roads are a definite social asset. But by mitigating some of the more acute stresses indirectly created by technological change, such organizations add to social stability.

One of the principal consequences of our high regard for change and of the institutionalization of innovation is that we have virtually assured not only that change will continue, but that its pace will accelerate. Since scientific knowledge is growing at a logarithmic rate, each decade sees still more, and more revolutionary, scientific discoveries made available to industry for translation into new commodities and techniques of production.[6] And while social change undoubtedly lags behind technological change, the pace of social innovation has also increased. An American born at the turn of the century has witnessed in his lifetime social transformations unequaled in any other comparable period in history: the introduction of electricity, radio, television, the automobile, the airplane, atomic bombs and power, rocketry, the automation of industry in the technological area, and equally unprecedented changes in society and ideology: new conceptions of the family, of the relations between the sexes, of work, residence, leisure, of the role of government, of the place of America in world affairs. We correctly characterize the rate of change in terms of self-stimulating chain reactions —the "exploding" metropolis, the "upward spiral" of living standards, the "rocketing" demands for goods and services. And unlike drastic social changes in the past (which have usually resulted from pestilence, war, military conquest, or contact with a superior culture), these have taken place "in the natural course of events." In our society at present, "the natural course of events" is precisely that the rate of change should continue to accelerate up to the as-yet-unreached limits of human and institutional adaptability.

The effects of this kind of valued, institutionalized, and accelerating social change are augmented in American society by two factors. The first is the relative absence of traditional institutions or values opposed to change. In most other industrialized nations, the impact of technology on the society at large has been limited by pre-existing social forces —aristocratic interests, class cleavages, or religious values— opposed to unrestrained technological change. Or, as in the case of Japan, technological changes were introduced by semifeudal groups determined to preserve their hegemony in the new power structure. Technologically induced changes have thus often been curbed or stopped when they conflicted with older institutions and values, or these pretechnological forces have continued to exist side by side with technological changes. The result has been some mitigation of the effects of technological innovation, a greater channeling of these changes into pre-existing institutions, and the persistence within the society of enclaves relatively unaffected by the values of a technological era.[7] But America has few such antitechnological forces. Lacking a feudal past, our values were from the first those most congenial to technology—a strong emphasis on getting things done, on practicality, on efficiency, on hard work, on rewards for achievement, not birth, and on treating all men according to the same universal rules.

A second factor which increases the effect of technological change is our unusual unwillingness to control, limit, or guide directions of industrial and social change—an unwillingness related to the absence of institutions opposing innovation. Most rapid changes in the world today involve far more central planning or foreknowledge of goal than we are willing to allow in America. At one extreme are countries like China and Russia, which attempt the total planning of all technological, industrial, and social change. While unplanned changes inevitably occur, central planning means that the major directions of change are outlined in advance and that unplanned changes can frequently be redirected according to central objectives. Furthermore, most underdeveloped nations are aiming at developing a highly technological society; in so far as they succeed, the direction of their changes is given by the model they seek to emulate. Given three abstract types of change—planned, imitative, and unguided—our own society most closely approximates the unguided type. We do little to limit the effects of change in one area of life on other aspects of society, and prefer to let social transformations occur in what we consider a "free" or "natural" way, that is, to be determined by technological innovations. As a result, we virtually guarantee our inability to anticipate or predict the future directions of social change. The Russian knows at least that his society is committed to increasing production and expansion; the Nigerian knows that his nation aims at increasing Westernization; but partly by our refusal to guide the course of our society, we have no way of knowing where we are headed.

The Phenomenology of Unrestrained Technological Change

Man's individual life has always been uncertain: no man could ever predict the precise events which would befall him and his children. In many ways we have decreased existential uncertainty in our society by reducing the possibilities of premature death and diminishing the hazards of natural disaster. But at the same time, a society changing in the way ours is greatly increases the unpredictability and uncertainty of the life situation shared by all the members of any generation. In almost every other time and place, a man could be reasonably certain that essentially the same technologies, social institutions, outlooks on life, and types of people would surround his children in their maturity as surrounded him in his. Today, we can no longer expect this. Instead, our chief certainty about the life situation of our descendants is that it will be drastically and unpredictably different from our own. Few Americans consciously reflect on the significance of social change; as I have argued earlier, the rhetoric with which we conventionally discuss our changing society usually conceals a recognition of how deeply the pace, the pervasiveness, and the lack of over-all direction of change in our society affect our outlooks. But nonetheless, the very fact of living amidst this kind of social transformation produces a characteristic point of view about the past and future, a new emphasis on the present, and above all an altered relationship between the generations which we can call the phenomenology of unrestrained technological change.[8]

The major components of this world view follow from the characteristics of change in this country. First, the past grows increasingly distant from the present. The differences between the America of 1950 and that of 1960 are greater than those between 1900 and 1910; because of the accelerating rate of innovation, more things change, and more rapidly, in each successive decade. Social changes that once would have taken a century now occur in less than a generation. As a result, the past grows progressively more different from the present in fact, and seems more remote and irrelevant psy-

chologically. Second, the future, too, grows more remote and uncertain. Because the future directions of social change are virtually unpredictable, today's young men and women are growing into a world that is more unknowable than that confronted by any previous generation. The kind of society today's students will confront as mature adults is almost impossible for them or anyone else to anticipate. Third, the present assumes a new significance as the one time in which the environment is relevant, immediate, and knowable. The past's solution to life's problems are not necessarily relevant to the here-and-now, and no one can know whether what is decided today will remain valid in tomorrow's world; hence, the present assumes an autonomy unknown in more static societies. Finally, and perhaps of greatest psychological importance, the relations between the generations are weakened as the rate of social innovation increases. The wisdom and skills of fathers can no longer be transmitted to sons with any assurance that they will be appropriate for them; truth must as often be created by children as learned from parents.

This mentality by no means characterizes all Americans to the same degree. The impact of social change is always very uneven, affecting some social strata more than others, and influencing some age groups more than others. The groups most affected are usually in elite or vanguard positions: those in roles of intellectual leadership usually initiate innovations and make the first psychological adaptations to them, integrating novelty with older values and institutions and providing in their persons models which exemplify techniques of adaptation to the new social order. Similarly, social change subjects different age groups to differing amounts of stress. Those least affected are those most outside the society, the very young and the very old; most affected are youths in the process of making a lifelong commitment to the future. The young, who have outlived the social definitions of childhood and are not yet fully located in the world of adult commitments and roles, are most immediately torn between the pulls of the past and the future. Reared by elders who were formed in a previous version of the society, and anticipating a life in a still different society, they must somehow choose between competing versions of past and future. Thus, it is youth that must chiefly cope with the strains of social change, and among youth, it is "elite" youth who feel these most acutely.

Accordingly, in the following comments on the outlooks of American youth, I will emphasize those views which seem most directly related to the world view created by unrestrained change,[9] and will base my statements primarily on my observations over the past decade of a number of able students in an "elite" college. While these young men are undoubtedly more articulate and reflective than most of their contemporaries, I suspect they voice attitudes common to many of their age mates.

Outlooks of Elite Youth

One of the most outstanding (and to many members of the older generation, most puzzling) characteristics of young people today is their apparent *lack of deep commitments to adult values and roles.* An increasing number of young people —students, teenagers, juvenile delinquents, and beats—are alienated from their parents' conceptions of adulthood, disaffected from the main streams of traditional public life, and disaffiliated from many of the historical institutions of our society. This alienation is of course one of the cardinal tenets of the Beat Generation; but it more subtly characterizes a great many other young people, even those who appear at first glance to be chiefly concerned with getting ahead and making a place for themselves. A surprising number of these young men and women, despite their efforts to get good scholarships and good grades so that they can get into a good medical school and have a good practice, nonetheless view the world they are entering with a deep mistrust. Paul Goodman aptly describes their view of society as "an apparently closed room with a rat race going on in the middle."[10] Whether they call it a rat race or not is immaterial (though many do): a surprising number of apparently ambitious young people see it as that. The adult world into which they are headed is seen as a cold, mechanical, abstract, specialized, and emotionally meaningless place in which one simply goes through the motions, but without conviction that the motions are worthy, humane, dignified, relevent, or exciting. Thus, for many young people, it is essential to stay "cool"; and "coolness" involves detachment, lack of commitment, never being enthusiastic or going overboard about anything.

This is a bleak picture, and it must be partially qualified. For few young people are deliberately cynical or calculating; rather, many feel forced into detachment and premature cynicism because society seems to offer them so little that is relevant, stable, and meaningful. They wish there were values, goals, or institutions to which they could be genuinely committed; they continue to search for them; and, given something like the Peace Corps, which promises challenge and a genuine expression of idealism, an extraordinary number of young people are prepared to drop everything to join. But when society as a whole appears to offer them few challenging or exciting opportunities—few of what Erikson would call objects of "fidelity"—"playing it cool" seems to many the only way to avoid damaging commitment to false life styles or goals.

To many older people, this attitude seems to smack of ingratitude and irresponsibility. In an earlier age, most men would have been grateful for the opportunities offered these contemporary young. Enormous possibilities are open to students with a college education, and yet many have little enthusiasm for these opportunities. If they are enthusiastic at all, it is about their steady girl friend, about their role in the college drama society, about writing poetry, or about a weekend with their buddies. Yet, at the same time, the members of this apparently irresponsible generation are surprisingly sane, realistic, and level-headed. They may not be given to vast enthusiasms, but neither are they given to fanaticism. They have a great, even an excessive, awareness of the complexities of the world around them; they are well-read and well-informed; they are kind and decent and moderate in their personal relations.

Part of the contrast between the apparent maturity and the alienation of the young is understandable in terms of the phenomenology of unrestrained change. For the sanity of young people today is partly manifest in their awareness that their world is very different from that of their parents. They know that rash commitments may prove outmoded tomorrow; they know that most viewpoints are rapidly shifting; they therefore find it difficult to locate a fixed position on which to stand. Furthermore, many young men and women sense that their parents are poor models for the kinds of lives they

themselves will lead in their mature years, that is, poor exemplars for what they should and should not be. Or perhaps it would be more accurate to say, not that their parents are poor models (for a poor model is still a model of what not to be), but that parents are increasingly irrelevant as models for their children. Many young people are at a real loss as to what they should seek to become: no valid models exist for the as-yet-to-be-imagined world in which they will live. Not surprisingly, their very sanity and realism sometimes leads them to be disaffected from the values of their elders.

Another salient fact about young people today is their relative *lack of rebelliousness* against their parents or their parents' generation. Given their unwillingness to make commitments to the "adult world" in general, their lack of rebellion seems surprising, for we are accustomed to think that if a young man does not accept his parents' values, he must be actively rejecting them. And when the generations face similar life situations, emulation and rejection are indeed the two main possibilities. But rebellion, after all, presupposes that the target of one's hostility is an active threat: in classical stories of filial rebellion, the son is in real danger of being forced to become like his father, and he rebels rather than accept this definition of himself. But when a young man simply sees no possibility of becoming like his parents, then their world is so remote that it neither tempts nor threatens him. Indeed, many a youth is so distant from his parents, in generational terms if not in affection, that he can afford to "understand" them, and often to show a touching sympathy for their hesitant efforts to guide and advise him. Parents, too, often sense that they appear dated or "square" to their children; and this knowledge makes them the more unwilling to try to impose their own values or preferences. The result is frequently an unstated "gentleman's agreement" between the generations that neither will interfere with the other. This understanding acknowledges a real fact of existence today; but just as often, it creates new problems.

One of these problems appears very vividly in the *absence of paternal exemplars* in many contemporary plays, novels, and films. One of the characteristic facts about most of our modern heroes is that they have no fathers—or, when they do have fathers, these are portrayed as inadequate or in some other way as psychologically absent. Take Augie March or Holden Caulfield, take the heroes of Arthur Miller's and Tennessee Williams' plays, or consider the leading character in the film like *Rebel Without A Cause*. None of them has a father who can act as a model or for that matter as a target of overt rebellion. The same is true, though less dramatically, for a great many young people today. One sometimes even hears students in private conversations deplore the tolerance and permissiveness of their exemplary parents: "If only, just once, they would tell me what *they* think I should do." Young people want and need models and guardians of their development; and they usually feel cheated if they are not available. The gentleman's agreement seldom works.

It would be wrong, however, to infer that parents have suddenly become incompetent. On the contrary, most American parents are genuinely interested in their children, they try hard to understand and sympathize with them, they continually think and worry about how to guide their development. In other, more stable times, these same parents would have been excellent models for their children, nourishing their growth while recognizing their individuality. But today they often leave their children with a feeling of never really having had parents, of being somehow cheated of their birth-right. The explanation is not hard to find; even the most well-intentioned parent cannot now hope to be a complete exemplar for his children's future. A man born in the 1910's or 1920's and formed during the Depression already finds himself in a world that was inconceivable then; his children will live in a world still more inconceivable. It would be unrealistic to hope that they would model their lives on his.

Another aspect of the psychology of rapid change is the *widespread feeling of powerlessness*—social, political, and personal—of many young people today. In the 1930's, there was a vocal minority which believed that society should and, most important, *could* be radically transformed; and there were more who were at least convinced that their efforts mattered and might make a difference in politics and the organization of society. Today the feeling of powerlessness extends even beyond matters of political and social interest; many young people see themselves as unable to influence any but the most personal spheres of their lives. The world is seen as fluid and chaotic, individuals as victims of impersonal forces which they can seldom understand and never control. Students, for example, tend not only to have a highly negative view of the work of the average American adult, seeing it as sterile, empty, and unrewarding, but to feel themselves caught up in a system which they can neither change nor escape. They are pessimistic about their own chances of affecting or altering the great corporations, bureaucracies, and academies for which most of them will work, and equally pessimistic about the possibility of finding work outside the system that might be more meaningful.

Such feelings of powerlessness of course tend to be self-fulfilling. The young man who believes himself incapable of finding a job outside the bureaucratic system and, once in a job, unable to shape it so that it becomes more meaningful will usually end up exactly where he fears to be—in a mean-ingless job. Or, a generation which believes that it cannot in-fluence social development will, by its consequent lack of involvement with social issues, in fact end up powerless be-fore other forces, personal or impersonal, which *can* affect social change. In a generation as in individuals, the convic-tion of powerlessness begets the fact of powerlessness.[11] But, however incorrect, this conviction is easy to comprehend. The world has always been amazingly complex, and with our widening understanding comes a sometimes paralyzing awareness of its complexity. Furthermore, when one's van-tage point is continually shifting, when the future is in fact more changeable than ever before, when the past can pro-vide all too few hints as to how to lead a meaningful life in a shifting society—then it is very difficult to sustain a conviction that one can master the environment.

The most common response to this feeling of helplessness is what David Riesman has called *privatism*. Younger people increasingly emphasize and value precisely those areas of their lives which are least involved in the wider society, and which therefore seem most manageable and controllable. Young men and women today want large families, they are prepared to work hard to make them good families, they often value family closeness above meaningful work, many expect that family life will be the most important aspect of their lives. Within one's own family one seems able to control the present and, within limits, to shape the future. Leisure, too, is far more under the individual's personal control than his public life is; a man may feel obliged to do empty work to earn a living, but he can spend his leisure as he likes.

Many young people expect to find in leisure a measure of stability, enjoyment, and control which they would otherwise lack. Hence their emphasis on assuring leisure time, on spend-ing their leisure to good advantage, on getting jobs with long vacations, and on living in areas where leisure can be well enjoyed. Indeed, some anticipate working at their leisure with a dedication that will be totally lacking in their work itself. In leisure, as in the family, young people hope to find some of the predictability and control that seem to them so absent in the wider society.

Closely related to the emphasis on the private spheres of life is the *foreshortening of time span*. Long-range endeavors and commitments seem increasingly problematical, for even if one could be sure there will be no world holocaust, the future direction of society seems almost equally uncertain. Similarly, as the past becomes more remote, in psychological terms if not in actual chronology, there is a greater tendency to disregard it altogether. The extreme form of this trend is found in the "beat" emphasis on present satisfactions, with an almost total refusal to consider future consequences or past commitments. Here the future and the past disappear completely, and the greatest possible intensification of the present is sought. In less psychopathic form, the same em-phasis on pursuits which can be realized in the present for their own sake and not for some future reward is found in many young people. The promise of continuing inflation makes the concept of a nest egg obsolete, the guarantee of changing job markets makes commitment to a specialized skill problematical, the possibility of a war, if seriously enter-tained, makes all future planning ridiculous. The conse-quence is that only the rare young man has life goals that extend more than five or ten years ahead; most can see only as far as graduate school, and many simply drift into, rather than choose, their future careers. The long-range goals, post-poned satisfactions, and indefinitely deferred rewards of the Protestant Ethic are being replaced by an often reluctant hedonism of the moment.

A corollary of the emphasis on the private and the present is the *decline in political involvement* among college youth. To be sure, American students have never evinced the intense political concerns of their Continental contemporaries, and admittedly, there are exceptions, especially in the "direct-action" movements centered around desegregation. But the general pattern of political disengagement remains relatively unchanged, or if anything has become more marked. Those familiar with elite college students in the 1930's and in the late 1950's contrast the political activity of a noisy minority then with the general apathy now before world problems of greater magnitude. Instead of political action, we have a burgeoning of the arts on many campuses, with hundreds of plays, operas, poems, and short stories produced annually by college students. Underlying this preference of aesthetic to political commitment are many of the outlooks I have mentioned: the feeling of public powerlessness, the emphasis on the private and immediate aspects of life, the feeling of disengagement from the values of the parental generation. But most important is the real anxiety that overtakes many thoughtful young people when they contemplate their own helplessness in the face of social and historical forces which may be taking the world to destruction. It is perhaps sig-nificant that Harvard students began rioting about Latin diplomas the evening of a relatively underattended rally to protest American intervention in Cuba, a protest to which most students would have subscribed. So high a level of anxiety is generated by any discussion of complex international relations, the possibilities of nuclear war, or even the complicated issues of American domestic policies, that all but the extraordinarily honest or the extraordinarily masochistic prefer to release their tensions in other ways than in political activity. And in this disinvolvement they are of course supported by the traditional American myth of youth, which makes it a time for panty raids but not for politics.

In general, then, many college students have a kind of *cult of experience,* which stresses, in the words of one student, "the maximum possible number of sense experiences." Part of the fascination which the beat generation holds for college students lies in its quest for "kicks," for an intensification of present, private experiences without reference to other people, to social norms, to the past or the future. Few college students go this far, even in the small group that dresses "beat," rides motorcycles, and supports the espresso bars; for most, experience is sought in ways less asocial than sex, speed, and stimulants. But travel, artistic and expressive experience, the enjoyment of nature, the privacy of erotic love, or the company of friends occupy a similar place in the hierarchy of values. Parallel with this goes the search for self within the self rather than in society, activity or commitment, and a belief that truth can be uncovered by burrowing within the psyche. The experience sought is private, even solipsistic; it involves an indifference to the beckonings of the wider society. To be sure, Teddy Roosevelt, too, was in his way a seeker after experience; but unlike most contemporary American youths, he sought it in frantic extroversion, in bravado and heroic action; and its rewards were eventual public acclaim. But for most college students today, T.R. and the values of his era have become merely comic.

Youth Culture and Identity

Many of these outlooks of youth can be summed up as a sophisticated version of the almost unique American phenomenon of the "youth culture,"[12] that is, the special culture of those who are between childhood and adulthood, a culture which differs from both that of the child and that of the adult. To understand the youth culture, we must consider not only the increasing gap between the generations but the discontinuity between childhood and adulthood.[13] Generational discontinuities are gaps in time, between one *mature* generation and the next; but age group discontinuities are gaps between different age groups at the *same* time. The transition from childhood to adulthood is never, in any society, completely continuous; but in some societies like our own there are radical discontinuities between the culturally given definitions of the child and of the adult. The child is seen as irresponsible, the adult responsible; the child is dependent, the adult is independent; the child is supposedly unsexual, the adult is interested in sex; the child plays, the adult works, etc. In societies where these age-group discontinuities are sharpest, there is usually some form of initiation rite to guarantee that everyone grows up, that the transition be clearly marked, and that there be no backsliding to childish ways.

But in our society we lack formalized rites of initiation into adulthood; the wan vestiges of such rites, like bar mitzvah, confirmation, or graduation-day exercises, have lost most of their former significance. Instead, we have a youth culture, not so obviously transitional, but more like a waiting period, in which the youth is ostensibly preparing himself for adult responsibilities, but in which to adults he often seems to be armoring himself against them. Of course, the years of the youth culture are usually spent in acquiring an education, in high school, college, vocational or professional training. But it would be wrong to think of the youth culture as merely an apprenticeship, a way of teaching the young the technical skills of adulthood. For the essence of the youth culture is that it is not a rational transitional period—were it one, it would simply combine the values of both childhood and adulthood. Instead, it has roles, values, and ways of behaving all its own; it emphasizes disengagement from adult values, sexual attractiveness, daring, immediate pleasure, and comradeship in a way that is true neither of childhood nor of adulthood. The youth culture is not always or explicitly anti-adult, but it is belligerently *non*-adult. The rock'n'roller, the Joe College student, the juvenile delinquent, and the beatnik, whatever their important differences, all form part of this general youth culture.

To understand this subculture we must consider its relation to both the discontinuities between age groups and the discontinuities between generations. I have noted that young people frequently view the more public aspects of adult life as empty, meaningless, a rat race, a futile treadmill; only in private areas can meaning and warmth be found. Childhood contrasts sharply with this image: childhood is seen as (and often really is) a time for the full employment of one's talents and interest, a time when work, love, and play are integrally related, when imagination is given free play, and life has spontaneity, freedom, and warmth. Adulthood obviously suffers by comparison, and it is understandable that those who are being rushed to maturity should drag their feet if this is what they foresee. The youth culture provides a kind of way-station, a temporary stopover in which one can muster strength for the next harrowing stage of the trip. And for many, the youth culture is not merely one of the stops, but the last stop they will really enjoy or feel commitment to. Thus, the youth culture is partially a consequence of the discontinuity of age groups, an expression of the reluctance of many young men and women to face the unknown perils of adulthood.

But the gap between childhood and adulthood will not explain why in our society at present the youth culture is becoming more and more important, why it involves a greater and greater part of young men and women's lives, or why it seems so tempting, compared with adulthood, that some young people increasingly refuse to make the transition at all. Rock'n'roll, for example, is probably the first music that has appealed almost exclusively to the youth culture; catering to the teenage market has become one of the nation's major industries. And, as Riesman has noted, the very word "teenager" has few of the connotations of transition and growing up of words like "youth" and "adolescent," which "teenager" is gradually replacing.[14]

The youth culture not only expresses youth's unwillingness to grow up, but serves a more positive function in resolving generational discontinuities. Erik H. Erikson would characterize our youth culture as a psychosocial moratorium on adulthood, which provides young people with an opportunity to develop their identity as adults.[15] One of the main psychological functions of a sense of identity is to provide a sense of inner self-sameness and continuity, to bind together the past, the present, and the future into a coherent whole; and the first task of adolescence and early adulthood is the achievement of identity. The world "achieve" is crucial here, for identity is not simply given by the society in which the adolescent lives; in many cases and in varying degrees, he must make his own unique synthesis of the often incompatible models, identifications, and ideals offered by society. The more incompatible the components from which the sense of identity must be built and the more uncertain the future for which one attempts to achieve identity, the more difficult the task becomes. If growing up were merely a matter of becoming "socialized," that is, of learning how to "fit into" society, it is hard to see how anyone could grow up at all in modern America, for the society into which young people will some day "fit" remains to be developed or even imagined. Oversimplifying, we might say that socialization is the main problem in a society where there are known and stable roles for children to fit into; but in a rapidly changing society like ours, identity formation increasingly replaces socialization in importance.

Even the achievement of identity, however, becomes more difficult in a time of rapid change. For, recall that one of the chief tasks of identity formation is the creation of a sense of self that will link the past, the present, and the future. When the generational past becomes ever more distant, and when the future is more and more unpredictable, such continuity requires more work, more creative effort. Furthermore, as Erikson emphasizes, another of the chief tasks of identity formation is the development of an "ideology," that is, of a philosophy of life, a basic outlook on the world which can orient one's actions in adult life. In a time of rapid ideological change, it seldom suffices for a young man or woman simply to accept some ideology from the past. The task is more difficult; it involves selecting from many ideologies those essential elements which are most relevant and most enduring. Such an achievement takes time, and sometimes the longest time for the most talented, who usually take the job most seriously.

The youth culture, then, provides not only an opportunity to postpone adulthood, but also a more positive chance to develop a sense of identity which will resolve the discontinuity between childhood and adulthood on the one hand, and bridge the gap between the generations on the other. Of course, a few young men and women attempt to find an alternative to identity in other-direction. Unable to discover or create any solid internal basis for their lives, they become hyperadaptable; they develop extraordinary sensitivity to the wishes and expectations of others; in a real sense, they let themselves be defined by the demands of their environment. Thus, they are safe from disappointment, for having made no bets on the future at all, they never have put their money on the wrong horse. But this alternative is an evasion, not a solution, of the problem of identity. The other-directed man is left internally empty; he has settled for playing the roles that others demand of him. And role-playing does not satisfy or fulfill; letting the environment call the shots means having nothing of one's own. Most young people see this very clearly, and only a few are tempted to give up the struggle.

There is another small group, the so-called beats and their close fellow-travelers, who choose the other alternative, to opt out of the System altogether and to try to remain permanently within the youth culture. In so doing, some young people are able to create for themselves a world of immediate, private and simple enjoyment. But leaving the System also has its problems. The search for self which runs through the youth culture and the beat world is not the whole of life, and to continue it indefinitely means usually renouncing

attainments which have been traditionally part of the definition of a man or a woman: intimacy and love for others; personal creativity in work, ideas, and children; and that fullness and roundedness of life which is ideally the reward of old age. So, though many young people are tempted and fascinated by the beat alternative, few actually choose it.

The vast majority of young people today accept neither the other-directed nor the beat evasion of the problem of identity. In many ways uncommitted to the public aspects of adult life, they are willing nonetheless to go through the motions without complete commitment. They have a kind of "double consciousness," one part oriented to the adult world which they will soon enter, the other part geared to their version of the youth culture. They are not rebellious (in fact they like their parents), but they feel estranged and distant from what their elders represent. They often wish they could model themselves after (or against) what their parents stand for, but they are sensible enough to see that older people are often genuinely confused themselves. They feel relatively powerless to control or to influence the personal world around them, but they try to make up for this feeling by emphasizing those private aspects of life in which some measure of predictability and warmth can be made to obtain. They often take enthusiastic part in the youth culture, but most of them are nonetheless attempting to "graduate" into adulthood. And though many hesitate on the threshold of adulthood, they do so not simply from antagonism or fear, but often from awareness that they have yet to develop a viable identity which will provide continuity both within their lives and between their own, their parents', and their future children's generations. And in each of these complex and ambivalent reactions young people are in part responding to the very process of unrestrained change in which they, like all of us, are involved.

Evaluations and Prospects

In these comments so far I have emphasized those attitudes which seem most directly related to the stresses of unrestrained change, neglecting other causal factors and painting a somewhat dark picture. I have done this partly because the more sanguine view of youth—which stresses the emancipations, the sociological understandability of youth's behavior, the stability of our society despite unprecedented changes, and the "adaptive" nature of youth's behavior—this more encouraging view has already been well presented.[16] But furthermore, if we shift from a sociological to a psychological perspective and ask how young people themselves experience growing up in this changing society, a less hopeful picture emerges. Rightly or wrongly, many young people experience emancipations as alienations; they find their many freedoms burdensome without criteria by which to choose among equally attractive alternatives; they resent being "understood" either sociologically or psychologically; and they often find the impressive stability of our society either oppressive or uninteresting. Furthermore, what may constitute an "adaptation" from one sociological point of view (e.g., the American Indian's regression in the face of American core culture) may be not only painful to the individual but disastrous to the society in the long run. A sociological and a psychological account of youth thus give different though perhaps complementary pictures, and lead to different evaluations of the outlook of American youth. Despite the stability of American society and the undeniable surfeit of opportunities and freedoms available to young people today, many of youth's attitudes seem to me to offer little ground for optimism.

The drift of American youth, I have argued, is away from public involvements and social responsibilities and toward a world of private and personal satisfactions. Almost all young people will eventually be *in* the system—that is, they will occupy occupational and other roles within the social structure—but a relatively large number of them will never be *for* the system. Like the stereotypical Madison Avenue ad-man who works to make money so that he can nourish his private (and forever unrealized) dream of writing a novel, their work and their participation in public life will always have a somewhat half-hearted quality, for their enthusiasms will be elsewhere—with the family, the home workshop, the forthcoming vacation, or the unpainted paintings. Their vision and their consciousness will be split, with one eye on the main chance and the other eye (the better one) on some private utopia. This will make them good organizational workers, who labor with detachment and correctness but without the intensity or involvement which might upset bureaucratic applecarts. And they will assure a highly stable political and social order, for few of them will be enough committed to politics to consider revolution, subversion, or even radical change. This orientation also has much to commend it to the individual: the private and immediate is indeed that sphere subject to the greatest personal control, and great satisfaction can be found in it. The "rich full life" has many virtues, especially when contrasted with the puritanical and future-oriented acquisitiveness of earlier American generations. And I doubt if commitment and "fidelity" will disappear; rather, they will simply be transferred to the aesthetic, the sensual, and the experiential, a transfer which would bode well for the future of the arts.

Yet the difficulties in this split consciousness seem to me overwhelming, both for the individual and for the society. For one, few individuals can successfully maintain such an outlook. The man who spends his working day at a job whose primary meaning is merely to earn enough money to enable him to enjoy the rest of his time can seldom really enjoy his leisure, his family, or his avocations. Life is of a piece, and if work is empty or routine, the rest will inevitably become contaminated as well, becoming a compulsive escape or a driven effort to compensate for the absent satisfactions that should inhere in work. Similarly, to try to avoid social and political problems by cultivating one's garden can at best be only partly successful. When the effects of government and society are so ubiquitous, one can escape them only in the backwaters, and then only for a short while. Putting work, society, and politics into one pigeonhole, and family, leisure and enjoyment into another creates a compartmentalization which is in continual danger of collapsing. Or, put more precisely, such a division of life into nonoverlapping spheres merely creates a new psychological strain, the almost impossible strain of artificially maintaining a continually split outlook.

Also on the demerit side, psychologically, is the willful limitation of vision which privatism involves, the motivated denial of the reality or importance of the nonprivate world. Given the unabating impact of social forces on every individual, to pretend that these do not exist (or that, if they do exist, have no effect on one) qualifies as a gross distortion of reality. Such blindness is of course understandable: given

the anxiety one must inevitably feel before a volatile world situation, coupled with the felt inability to affect world events, blinders seem in the short run the best way to avoid constant uneasiness. Or similarly, given the widespread belief that work is simply a way of earning a living, refusal to admit the real importance to one's psychic life of the way one spends one's working days may be a kind of pseudo-solution. But a pseudo-solution it is, for the ability to acknowledge unpleasant reality and live with the attendant anxiety is one of the criteria of psychological health. From a psychological point of view, alienation and privatism can hardly be considered ideal responses to social change.

From a social point of view, the long-range limitations of these "adaptations" seem equally great. Indeed, it may be that, through withdrawal from concern with the general shape of society, we obtain short-run social stability at the price of long-run stagnation and inability to adapt. Young people, by exaggerating their own powerlessness, see the "system," whether at work, in politics, or in international affairs, as far more inexorable and unmalleable than it really is. Consider, for example, the attitude of most American youth (and most older people as well) toward efforts to direct or restrain the effects of social change. Partly by a false equation of Stalinism with social planning, partly on the assumption that unrestrained social change is "natural," and partly from a conviction that social planning is in any case impossible, young people usually declare their lack of interest. Apart from the incorrectness of such beliefs, their difficulty is that they tend to be self-confirming in practice. Given a generation with such assumptions, social changes will inevitably continue to occur in their present haphazard and unguided way, often regardless of the needs of the public. Or again, it seems likely that if any considerable proportion of American students were to demand that their future work be personally challenging and socially useful, they would be able to create or find such work and would revolutionize the quality of work for their fellows in the process. But few make such demands. Or, most ominous of all, if the future leaders of public opinion decide that they can leave the planning of foreign policy to weapons experts and military specialists, there is an all too great chance that the tough-minded "realism" of the experts will remain unmitigated by the public's wish to survive.

In short, an alienated generation seems too great a luxury in the 1960's. To cultivate one's garden is a stance most appropriate to times of peace and calm, and least apposite to an era of desperate international crisis. It would be a happier world than this in which men could devote themselves to personal allegiances and private utopias. But it is not this world. International problems alone are so pressing that for any proportion of the ablest college students to take an apolitical stance seems almost suicidal. And even if world problems were less horrendous, there is a great deal to be done in our own society, which to many, young and old, still seems corrupt, unjust, ugly, and inhuman. But to the extent that the younger generation loses interest in these public tasks, remaining content with private virtue, the public tasks will remain undone. Only a utopia can afford alienation.

In so far as alienation and privatism are dominant responses of the current college generation to the stresses of unrestrained change, the prospects are not bright. But for several reasons, I think this prognosis needs qualification. For one, I have obviously omitted the many exceptions to the picture I have sketched—the young men and women who have the courage to confront the problems of their society and the world, who have achieved a sense of identity which enables them to remain involved in and committed to the solution of these problems. Furthermore, for most students alienation is a kind of *faute de mieux* response, which they would readily abandon, could they find styles of life more deserving of allegiance. Indeed, I think most thoughtful students agree with my strictures against privatism, and accept withdrawal only as a last resort when other options have failed. But, most important, I have omitted from my account so far any discussion of those forces which do or might provide a greater sense of continuity, despite rapid change. Discussion of these forces may correct this perhaps unnecessarily discouraged picture.

Throughout this account, I have suggested that Americans are unwilling to plan, guide, restrain, or coordinate social change for the public good. While this is true when America is compared with other industrialized nations, it is less true than in the past, and there are signs that many Americans are increasingly skeptical of the notion that unrestrained change is somehow more "free" or more "natural" than social planning. We may be beginning to realize that the decision not to plan social changes is really a decision to allow forces and pressures other than the public interest to plot the course of change. For example, it is surely not more natural to allow our cities to be overrun and destroyed by the technological requirements of automobiles than to ask whether humane and social considerations might not require the banning or limiting of cars in major cities. Or to allow television and radio programming to be controlled by the decisions of sponsors and networks seems to many less "free" than to control them by public agencies. If we are prepared to guide and limit the course of social change, giving a push here and a pull there when the "natural" changes in our society conflict with the needs of the public, then the future may be a less uncertain prospect for our children. Indeed, if but a small proportion of the energy we now spend in trying to second-guess the future were channelled into efforts to shape it, we and our children might have an easier task in discovering how to make sense in, and of, our changing society.

I have also neglected the role that an understanding of their situation might play for the younger generation. Here I obviously do not mean that students should be moralistically lectured about the need for social responsibility and the perversity of withdrawal into private life. Such sermonizing would clearly have the opposite effect, if only because most young people are already perfectly willing to abandon privatism if they can find something better. But I do mean that thoughtful students should be encouraged to understand the meaning and importance of their own stage in life and of the problems which affect them as a generation. The emphasis on individual psychological understanding which characterizes many "progressive" colleges can provide only a part of the needed insight. The rest must come from an effort to end the pluralistic ignorance of the stresses confronting all members of the current younger generation. Here colleges do far too little, for courses dealing with the broad social pressures that impinge on the individual often deliberately attempt to prevent that personal involvement which alone gives insight. But one can imagine that a concrete understanding of the psychosocial forces that affect a generation might have some of the same therapeutic effects on the more reflective members of the generation that insight into psychodynamic forces can give the thoughtful individual.

And finally, I have underplayed the importance that values and principles can and do play in providing continuity amid rapid change. If one is convinced that there are guiding principles which will remain constant—and if one can find these enduring values—life can be meaningful and livable despite rapid change. But here we need to proceed cautiously. Technologies, institutions, ideologies, and people—all react by extremes when faced with the fear of obsolescence. Either they firmly insist that *nothing* has changed and that they are as integrally valid as ever before or—and this is equally disastrous—they become so eager to abandon the outmoded that they abandon essential principles along with the irrelevant. Thus, parents who dimly fear that they may appear "square" to their children can react either by a complete refusal to admit that anything has changed since their early days or (more often) by suppressing any expression of moral concern. The second alternative seems to me the more prevalent and dangerous. An antiquated outlook is usually simply ignored by the young. But person or institution that abandons its essential principles indirectly communicates that there are no principles which can withstand the test of time, and thus makes the task of the young more difficult.

Yet the bases for the continuity of the generations must of necessity shift. Parents can no longer hope to be literal models for their children; institutions cannot hope to persist without change in rite, practice, and custom. And, although many of the essential principles of parents, elders, and traditional institutions can persist, even those who seek to maintain the continuity of a tradition must, paradoxically, assume a creative and innovating role. We need not only a rediscovery of the vital ideals of the past, but a willingness to create new ideals—new values, new myths, and new utopias—which will help us to adapt creatively to a world undergoing continual and sweeping transformations. It is for such ideals that young people are searching: they need foundations for their lives which will link them to their personal and communal pasts and to their present society but which at the same time will provide a trustworthy basis for their futures. The total emulation or total rejection of the older generation by the young must be replaced by a recreation in each generation of the living and relevant aspects of the past, and by the creation of new images of life which will provide points of constancy in a time of rapid change.

REFERENCES

1. An earlier version of parts of this paper was presented at the Annual Conference of Jewish Communal Services, May 1961, and was published in *The Journal of Jewish Communal Services* (Fall 1961).

2. It need hardly be added that our society's capacity for innovation and change is also one of its greatest strengths.

3. Among the other major factors creating stresses for American youth are (1) the discontinuities between childhood and adulthood, especially in the areas of sex, work, and dependency; (2) the great rise in the aspirations and standards of youth, which create new dissatisfactions; and (3) the general intellectual climate of skepticism and debunking, which makes "ideological" commitment difficult. In this essay, however, I will concentrate on the stresses created by social change.

4. One should not confuse static with stable societies. American society is extremely stable internally despite rapid rates of change. Similarly, other societies, though relatively static, are unstable internally.

5. Unconsciously, however, most Americans have highly ambivalent feelings about science and technology, usually expressed in the myth of the (mad) scientist whose creation eventually destroys him.

6. See Walter Rosenblith, "On Some Social Consequences of Scientific and Technological Change," *Dædalus* (Summer 1961), pp. 498–513.

7. Obviously, the existence of institutions and values opposed to technological change in a technological society is itself a major source of social and individual tension.

8. Other types of social change also have their own characteristic world views. In particular, the mentality of elite youth in underdeveloped countries now beginning industrialization differs from that in transitional countries like Japan, where technological and pretechnological elements coexist. American society probably comes closest to a "pure" type of exclusively technological change.

9. Once again I omit any discussion of other sources of strain on youth (see reference 3). Furthermore, I do not mean to suggest that these outlooks are the only possible responses to unrestrained change, or that they are unaffected by other historical and social forces in American life.

10. Paul Goodman, *Growing Up Absurd*. New York: Random House, 1960.

11. It is ironic that this generation, which is better prepared than any before it, which knows more about itself and the world and is thus in a better position to find those points of leverage from which things can be changed, should feel unable to shape its own destiny in any public respect.

12. Talcott Parsons, "Age and Sex Grading in the United States," reprinted in Parsons, *Essays in Sociological Theory, Pure and Applied* (Glencoe, Illinois: The Free Press, 1949). The beginnings of a youth culture are appearing in other highly industrialized countries, which suggests that this institution is characteristic of a high degree of industrialization.

13. Ruth Benedict, "Continuities and Discontinuities in Cultural Conditioning," in Clyde Kluckhohn and Henry A. Murray (eds.), *Personality in Nature, Society, and Culture*. New York: Norton, 1948.

14. David Riesman, "Where is the College Generation Headed?" *Harper's Magazine*, April 1961.

15. Erik H. Erikson, "The Problem of Ego Identity," in *Identity and the Life Cycle*, published as vol. I, no. 1 of *Psychological Issues* (1959). See also his "Youth: Fidelity and Diversity," in this issue.

16. Talcott Parsons, "Youth in the Context of American Society," in this issue.

40

ROBERT COLES

The Words
and Music of
Social Change

OXFORD, OHIO, is a town of about ten thousand located about forty miles north of Cincinnati. Gentle hills are nearby, and farms and roads go a long way before meeting other ones. The people in rural Ohio are white, conservative, and generally prosperous. They vote Republican. They want their children to get educated, though not "too educated," by which they mean a lot of philosophy and poetry and leftist political science or sociology. True to its name, Oxford claims Miami University and Western College for Women, both of which were founded well back in the nineteenth century, and both of which (so I heard from a doctor in the town) occasionally stimulate the "wrong ideas" in students. "They read everything these days," I can remember him saying. A second later he pointedly added something else: "and they're not fussy about who they let use their buildings."

Yes, indeed, in June of 1964 Western College for Women had offered its entire campus to the Student Non-Violent Coordinating Committee and CORE and God knows who else—for God knows what purpose. The year 1964 right now seems like much more than five years in the past, perhaps five times five years. Yet for all the changes since then the historical significance of the Mississippi Summer Project of 1964 cannot be questioned: A decade of sporadic, lonely, and occasionally fierce social struggle—most of it connected with southern racial problems that arose as a result of the Supreme Court's decision of 1954—had finally become a political crisis of national significance. Black youths who for years had been hunted down by the police and called "delinquent" or "psychopathic" by judges (and sent away for psychiatric observation as well as imprisonment) were now leaders and heroes to hundreds of middle-class white college students—and those students took their ideals seriously. They came to Oxford, Ohio, because of those ideals, and after two weeks of orientation they would go to Mississippi because of those ideals.

Within a few days, however, three young men, who had left Oxford well before the rest of us, were found missing and immediately presumed dead. "They're dead, they're absolutely dead," I was told by Stokely Carmichael, with whom I shared the responsibility for a seminar rather wryly and with mock pretense called "methods and techniques of nonviolence." Then Stokely Carmichael believed in nonviolent protest—and believed that yet another demonstration, yet another summer's blood, would bring "freedom, oh delicious freedom, freedom at last," as one song

302

put it. Then, even the death of three comrades was somehow a beginning and not an end, a measure of success rather than a failure. Then I could hear this, record this—on a tape which now can only be considered a document of sorts from another era: "*They killed them, but they can't kill the summer, and what we're going to do this summer. They can't kill our spirit, only our bodies. They'll find out what they did when they murdered our people, our brothers. They'll find that they made us stronger, that we'll beat them sooner, because of what they've done. The whole nation will rally round—but even more important, we'll rally round.*"

Well, how did they "rally round"? Did they—the leaders of the project—ask me to talk with people, analyze their obviously increased sense of fear and gloom? Did they suggest a "group" or two, perhaps a bit of "sensitivity training," as it is put by all those "group leaders"? Did they call in advisers—political scientists and social scientists and doctors and lawyers—so that those several hundred young men and women would feel better advised, better protected? Did they rush to Washington, to the newspapers and magazines, to the television cameras?

In fact, they did worry about the collective mood of their new recruits, many of whom had never been south—and now had to face the distinct possibility that a first trip might be a last one. They also wondered about morale, about everyone's morale, about the ways people affect one another when they feel sad and anxious and in a way suspended—not at home, not in Mississippi, "just waiting," which were the words one heard again and again from youths terribly hurt by the sudden loss of three good friends, under conditions that the mind could only imagine, and know to have been as awful as any fantasy could possibly be. And finally, the young civil rights workers knew how self-conscious things would have to be: The press didn't have to be sought out, nor the cameras; the entire county had become involved in that project. Again, in Stokely Carmichael's words: "*We'll have to show them, show them we're not afraid, we won't pull back, we'll go there, and stay there and outlast them; show them they can't scare us.*"

As we now know, they were not scared, or at least private fears never became a public display of terror, or something else like T. S. Eliot's "compromise, complacency and confusion." How did they manage? How did they dare, continue to dare? Again, in Eliot's word (yes, in this context, Eliot) how could they "presume" —presume to go on, to believe there was any justifiable "going on" in the face of such brute force, such longstanding power, now instantly and arbitrarily summoned? Choices there were: to reconsider, to retreat, to "regroup," to wait and only later go south— and, above all, to consult with advisers, all sorts of knowledgeable and experienced and well-trained people, who I can remember appeared as if out of nowhere, whether or not asked, to have their say, to express fear or worry or, occasionally, a bit of hope.

Suddenly, though, in a couple of days, something quite surprising and wonderful and (I can only use the word) awesome happened. Suddenly hundreds of young Americans became charged with new energy and determination. Suddenly I saw fear turn into toughness, vacillation into quiet conviction. Suddenly waves of emotion swept over that land-locked town of Oxford—to the point that even the doctor I mentioned at the start of this essay became shaken, touched, affected, and, in the end, very much moved. What, how, why—those are the words invoked by observers like me, however "involved" or "participant" or whatever we are. For a while I wanted to banish all the questions, all the analytic propositions and scientific explorations that my nicely trained mind could not help raising with itself. Yet eventually I realized how needlessly protective I was—of students, black and white, whose words and deeds and purposes could quite definitely tolerate any scrutiny I felt driven to make.

"*How did we do it?*" I had asked him how he and others had converted a grim piece of news into an unforgettable occasion, an almost spectacular kind of moral and philosophical experience for an entire midwestern town, and he replied right off by asking himself my question. In a way, the earnest way he did so should have been my clue, but as it turned out I didn't need one, because he was prepared to go on: "*We never thought we had anything to 'do.' We had to get going, and we decided the best way to get going was to get going.*"

I knew there was more to say, because I had been with him and others at Oxford all along. I had in fact seen and heard a powerful and lovely and stirring spectacle (that is the word) take place over a span of two days. Still, he was right; it had developed, grown, almost bloomed, and if guile had helped things along, the unself-conscious, direct, spontaneous character of the activities and meetings—which in fact were *rites*—cannot be denied. So, I asked him simply to tell me what had occurred. I knew and he knew that I knew the facts. I had been part of the scene. But I felt his account would tell me something else—not facts, not data, not even clues to over-all "attitudes" or emotional states. I suppose I believed that the effort of narrative can be revelatory (not revealing), and even redemptive (not therapeutic). I suppose I believed that in talking, in telling, we could not so much clarify as be properly amazed and surprised and, yes, even stunned. In this century, among the West's intelligentsia, the look backward has become such a sober and serious matter. We are puzzled or troubled. We try to find the first causes of our bewilderment, our present pain. But perhaps old sorrows can indeed make themselves felt later—but in new assertions of pride and wonder and hope, as I discovered in Oxford, Ohio, when I saw tired, hurt victims of the civil rights movement: *"If things had fallen apart there'd have been no Summer Project, no Selma, nothing. They'd have known they could scare us, make us back down. There'd have been no civil rights laws—on voting and all the rest. I know you can't two years later say that, say it was one point in time that was so important; but I can say no other moment was more important, that I know.*

"We thought about what to do, and then we fell to arguing a lot. Finally we decided we should become religious, real religious. We decided we should go to church—and until then we didn't even know where the chapel was on that campus. We decided we had to get together, really get together. We decided we all had to stop and think, that's what, that's what we kept saying, stop and think and figure out the meaning of things. It was as if we wanted everyone to become philosophical—and face it, real head-on: to risk their lives or not to risk their lives; to fight or surrender; to know what's important, really important, and stand up for it, or run home and say later, later—because it's too dangerous now.

"That's the kind of thing we wanted them to think about, the kind we thought about, the few of us sitting up through the night wondering what to do. And we started asking each other what to say, what to do, what to read in the church, what to sing. We wanted each volunteer to stop and think—but feel close to the next person, who would be doing the same thing. We wanted to have silence, so people could ask themselves things, and we wanted a lot of talking, too—a lot of music and arms locked together, all that you know—so that people wouldn't be scared, at least not too scared."

Well, I knew the rest. I took part in the rest. I heard the folk songs. I heard the poems, the selections from John Donne and Shakespeare and Dostoevsky and Thoreau and Tolstoy and W. H. Auden. I heard the phonographs play Beethoven and Brahms and Berlioz. I saw several hundred young men and women—black and white, rich and poor, northern and southern—form themselves into a huge circle, hands held together or arms locked into one another. I saw that circle close in on itself and then expand. I saw it break up into smaller circles: to dance and embrace and shout words of sadness and determination and anger and outrage and pity and vengeance and most of all soreness, in all the senses of that old and powerful word.

In between the public moments, the times when we were all

together, all listening or singing or praying or reciting, we went off in two's and four's and six's to wonder and be afraid and straighten up suddenly and say yes, not no. Then, too, the writers and artists and composers appeared, as if out of nowhere. I was astonished at the sight of those books—among people told to come with very little, to travel light, to bring only essentials. Essentials they brought: *The Plague, Crime and Punishment, Light in August, The Mind of the South, All the Kings Men,* the poems of Wallace Stevens or W. C. Williams or W. H. Auden. In a moment of fear, of decision, of social struggle, I saw books, inert books (and symphonies and post cards from this or that museum) become—well, if it has to be said that way, "relevant" and "useful." In those desperate moments, when actually more than the outcome of a Summer Project hung in balance, what can loosely be called the "humanities" had an emphatic and remarkable effect on a large group of bewildered, mourning, hesitant activists—who then wanted and needed wisdom, not knowledge, a sense of moral purpose rather than "goals" or "programs" or "data" or "interpretations."

In a way, as an observer and a friend, I found myself taken aback. The Bible and the Classics figured prominently in my life. My parents—correctly I believe—had little faith that some combination of technological ingenuity, socialist politics, and psychoanalytic discovery would put us all within sight of the New Jerusalem. By the same token, they urged upon me an ethical code grounded in the past, the distant past. I came to college familiar with Jeremiah and Isaiah; with Matthew, Mark, and Luke; indeed with St. John's apocalyptic Revelations; and I came there grounded in years and years of Latin and Greek. In contrast, most—though not all—of the white college students in that Mississippi Summer Project had spent a good deal of time weighing the "meaning," the "message," the "value" of books I simply (and all too naïvely) considered novels, or poems, or "contemporary literature," pure if not so simple.

So, as I look back and think about it all, I have to conclude that for a long time I felt closer to the black youths from the rural South than many of the northern students. For example, I favored the Supreme Court's 1954 decision (striking down the legal fiction called "separate-but-equal" schools) because what was right—ethically, philosophically, religiously, *humanly*—had to prevail. It seemed almost (and literally) blasphemous that the Court had to bulwark its decision with all sorts of psychological and sociological testimony from people like me. Many times during our night-long talks and arguments I heard the Supreme Court's wisdom upheld as modern, as sophisticated; as tied to discoveries made here or there, and written up in this or that book—only to hear in reply (from a young black "fieldworker," a civil rights activist) an outburst that came across almost like a gospel-song. Here is one cry, recorded in Hattiesburg: *"You all have your books, and you tell me I've got to read* The Plague *(is it?) and something else, the one with the long title about 'praising men,' and the poems you have. But to me it's in plain sight what has to be done and I don't need anyone telling me from a book. My book, it's the Bible. When I was a little kid, my mother would tell us we should listen to what the Book says, and someday, if we're lucky, we'd get a chance to do something, and then the Bible would tell us how to behave and do it right. Maybe—I admit it—maybe you need a lot more than the Bible today; but as I hear some of you talk—well, I say to myself, they've got their bibles and I've got mine, and when you come right down to it, there might not be too much difference. The guy who wrote* The Plague, *he must have been sweating about some of these things; like Matthew and Mark did, they surely did. And maybe the one thing the summer has taught me is: with different people, you get different saints that they listen to. In fact, I don't believe there's a man alive who doesn't have at least one saint he listens to, even if we'd call him a devil, not a saint. I'll bet over in the Klan meeting, over there across town, they're quoting somebody, yes sir.*"

His closing verb had summarized a lot of that summer. We had all been quoting people left and right, day and night. Lines or whole stanzas from Auden or Spender had been underlined, or paragraphs from Agee and Camus bracketed. Songs were sung not only for "release" or to achieve solidarity, but to say something, to declare, to affirm and sing out.

Still, in the face of that experience, and others like it, if less dramatic, I hear the humanities questioned. Are they of any value, of any possible interest to today's students? Yes, it is nice to read a novel sometimes, and listen to a symphony; but the world is full of immediate problems and enormous challenges, all of which requires from young people an almost single-minded sense of competence and purpose. And, of course, some who claim to speak for literature and art can be impossible: deliberately arrogant, aloof, condescending, priggish, stuffy, and all the rest. Writers and artists sweat and suffer and finally manage a lucid moment here and there—only to be worked over by cold and mannered pedants and declared their property. No wonder many people, even among the well-to-do, are put off or walk away in disgust and anger. Yet in spite of everything—the fake and self-appointed connoisseurs, the smug literary coteries and the petty, artistic salons, the schools that thrive on jealousy and exclusiveness and hauteur and vengeance— the world's Melvilles and Faulkners, its Balzacs and Tolstoys and Picassos continue to confront us with everything, with pain and suffering and tenderness and love, with moral choices and ethical conflicts and most of all with an effort toward coherence, toward a vision that inspires, that summons, that makes us, at least from time to time, a little more than we usually are, than we possibly can be for very long. Perhaps what I am trying to say can be best said by someone else. Here is what one leader of the Mississippi Summer Project said to me in Greenville, right near the great mythic river, in late July of 1964: "*Well, we did it, I don't know how, but we did. We all were scared. Who wouldn't be after what they did in Neshoba County, so fast—like a challenge to us. You ask where it came from, the guts it took to stay in Oxford, and then drive down here. I don't know. You find it, you find it in people— and I guess you call it guts or courage or things like that. You're scared, but you've asked yourselves some questions and find the answers. You know, it's like living in a novel or a play this whole summer is. Everything is bigger, bigger than usual—the way writers picture things they write.*"

Yet, four years ago in Mississippi during one of those interminable "soul sessions" uncannily and unself-consciously used by civil rights workers to weaken fear and trembling, I heard another message, this time an outcry: *"Whatever we do, it'll be the white man who will benefit the most. We'll ask for school desegregation and they'll get better schools. We'll say that we get no medical care at all, and they'll get health insurance and more medical schools. We'll criticize the values of this society, and they'll start asking themselves what they really believe in. The Negro may come out of all this with the vote, but it'll be white people again who really win. They'll have better schools and better doctors and better everything because we helped wake them up. Our pain made them look at themselves, and then they said, 'Here, boy, here's a band-aid'—while they went rushing off to the hospital to try and get their own sickness cured."*

Of course I knew he was "upset" then—because a freedom house had been dynamited the night before. I also knew how *complicated* things are. I could allow him his stark, polemic rhetoric —and go on to remind myself how much he had omitted from his "analysis." Yet I could not forget the important point he was making. America's present-day political and racial unrest has strengthened the hand of all sorts of social and educational critics. We in the upper-middle-class academic and professional world have indeed been asked to look both inward and outward—asked once again to look at what we are doing and for whom. Our assumptions and values have indeed been questioned. Our purposes have been attacked. We have been called narrow-minded, parochial, self-centered. We are not "involved"; our interests and work are not "relevant." We are race-bound, class-bound. We are crusty and snobbish. We are dying.

All those charges have to be answered. Here I can only list some ideas and feelings I have acquired during ten years of what I suppose could be called "field work"—done by a child psychiatrist in the South and the North, among Appalachian families, migrant farm families, and ghetto families.

I have learned to question a number of medical and psychiatric tenets I had never before doubted. I have learned to give "ordinary" people more credit for courage, guile, discretion, and, yes, those "higher things" like sensibility, restraint, tact, generosity. I have learned to draw upon Ellison's *Invisible Man* instead of a book called *The Mark of Oppression*, which offers "in depth"—of course! —psychiatric case studies of the Negro. I have learned that one does not have to be a political or social or philosophical "romantic" to comprehend and appreciate the kind of truth that binds a Faulkner to a Tolstoy, an Agee to a Bernanos, a Simon Weil to an Orwell.

I think that more than anything else I have learned to *know* what social scientists know, but *see* what a Eudora Welty, a Flannery O'Connor, a Richard Wright, a Robert Penn Warren, a Walker Percy demand and suggest and hint and urge one like me to see. What a far from tragic poet has called "the things of this world" defies all categories, man-made and inborn.

Above all, in Roxbury's ghetto, and among people grimly and all too easily and condescendingly dismissed as the "backlash" I continue to see evidence of both hope and failure. I hear strong language that is unharnessed. I see visions, valuable and imaginative visions, that are on the point of being crushed or abandoned. I see children paint poetry and put to word the landscapes of their minds. I watch them come home from school—tired and bored and ready in a back alley to reclaim their humanity, their right to test themselves and learn about one another.

And on the other side of town, "across town" as the children put it, I hear college students and college teachers speak and think in language that on good days can perhaps cause a resigned smile. Ghetto children need and crave coherence, a sense of what the world is truly about. But students and graduate students and professors can stand a few lessons too. Clear, direct, and strong language is no luxury, no sign of literary talent. Our words reveal our thoughts. Cloudy minds and murky disciplines need more than a few hundred editorial assistants to "clean things up."

We the enlightened cram our children with facts and figures. We ask our teachers to be sensitive, to understand psychology, child development, the nature of prejudice, the facts of "group experience." We offer "the new math," and we crowd our classrooms with teaching machines to make French easier and (I suppose, soon) Chinese possible. But I talk with and teach college students who do not know how to struggle for a straight thought and put such a victory down on paper. They may know that they can't "write," but they do not know that they have been denied what they must (and can) have, a mind that works—lives and breathes rather than digests facts, theories, and "data."

I hear from some that Henry James or T. S. Eliot is reactionary; or Carson McCullers merely odd in a clever and powerful way. If you would know America, take courses in "race relations" and political theory. Know the social system, the power structure, the latent this and the unconscious that. And know the facts, man, the facts—who owns what and who is bigger than whom. Yet I believe I find the whole world in the letters of Van Gogh, not to mention his paintings; in a story by Flannery O'Connor; in one of Eliot's quartets; in a "decadent" novel by that great, curious, stubborn, long-winded, ambitious, shrewd observer and artist Henry James. I believe that ghetto children and suburban children can learn the most important "facts" that can possibly be learned from Rembrandt's "Life of Christ," from his canvasses and from the Scripture that he brings alive: how long man has suffered and how much man can do to redeem himself, to win a little ground from life's built-in ironies, ambiguities, and terrors—enemies far stronger than particular men or even social systems.

Finally, I believe that we can actively struggle with the world, but also sit back and wonder at things, understand them and be amused or scornful at how "it all" works out, comes to pass, whatever. And I believe that in "culturally deprived" and "culturally disadvantaged" ghetto children we in medicine and law and business and education, we right in the middle of the universities, see much more of ourselves than we dare realize. All one need do is read the themes, the papers, the reports, the journals, go to the movies, watch television, and hear the talk in clubs and parlors to know how far we have come from our own language, from the logic and dignity of words, from the writer's vision, the artist's (or artisan's) craft, the theologian's or philosopher's or anyman's puzzled, hungry, alarmed, hopeful, skeptical search—for whatever scrap of sense and sensibility can be and must be found, "world without end."

But whatever troubles "us," the well-off and supposedly well-educated, we still have all of "them" to trouble us. They just don't learn how to read very well. They seem to have their own music, which we find and treasure—out of our sophisticated interest in everything, everywhere, however "primitive" or "parochial." Yes, in the Delta, in Appalachia, out west on reservations, they have their jazz and their folk songs, their crafts and ballads and myths and rites—but how, exactly how, are they going to become more literate, more industrious, more like us: able to read and understand Max Weber's *The Protestant Ethic and the Spirit of Capitalism*, but, most of all, *feel* the book's truth—that is, remember it as an experience out of one's life?

At this point, with such questions in mind, I have to get very specific and, God forbid, talk about "educational materials" that I have met up with—seen, heard sung, watched being used—again, down in Mississippi, but also up north in the ghetto of a large city. In 1965 I saw a Head Start program get under way, but a most unusual one: hundreds of small children from sharecropper cabins all over Mississippi's Delta were suddenly confronted with schools that meant business, schools that were not meant to be a mere formality, a half-gesture of "separate-but-equal" education, but schools that had behind them—oh, I suppose it could be called a "philosophy," though I would like to call it a burning sense of conviction. Here is how one of the teachers described the effort she and others were making: "*We believe we can reach these little kids, and be reached by them. We believe that they can learn—learn a million things—if we keep believing that they can learn. The trouble is that for too long their teachers have been convinced that they're hopeless. (A lot of them never even go to school more than a day or two a week, and they drop out when they're about ten). And the trouble is that a lot of the teachers, the more sophisticated ones—the outsiders who come here—keep on dwelling on how bad things are in the state, and how peculiar and different these kids are. You know: they have a special culture, and they don't trust you, or understand you, and all the rest. Well, they do have a special culture. It's different, the way they live. That's for sure. But they are children, and they can learn, and they can desire to learn. You have to forget yourself, and stop trying to impose on them all you've gone through, all the rote memory you had to accept, all the business of speaking clearly and learning the alphabet and reading the books your parents read—the Dick and Jane books that are handed down from one generation to the other. You have to get around words. Remember, black people were slaves—still are, in many respects. They were told to keep quiet, to mind their every step, to obey, obey, obey. They were denied the right to have a family, to vote—to build up a social and political tradition. They were kept from books and magazines and newspapers. Their children were kept ignorant and poor. They were called 'uppity' if they spoke out, even spoke at all. No wonder they learned to be quiet, to fear words and distrust talk. No wonder they don't have books—most of them are lucky to eat half-well. But they are men and women, and they see the world and respond to it—and from that comes a whole culture. I mean 'culture' in the sense of style of looking at the world, in the sense of a particular form and structure to one's vision, one's feelings about things.*

"You—you people talk about 'cultures' and 'sub-cultures' as if men are only what they do and think: they live here and pray there and have this custom or that one. But the poorest sharecroppers developed secret, clever things: musical rhythms, sayings, songs. You can call it folk music and of course jazz; but the point is to recognize that it isn't just you, the outsiders, who 'appreciate' such things, who see the beauty and subtlety in them. Poor, illiterate blacks sung and spoke their way to—to jazz, to the blues, to a rich tradition that we love to enjoy on our long-playing records. And to make a long story short: we believe that these children can learn, can learn like thousands and thousands of blacks have learned, learned every day—even though they'd be found on the bottom of every I.Q. test in America. We believe they see and hear and listen and feel things going on inside them and look outside themselves and take stock of the world and figure out how they have to act and what they have to say and how the world is run and who runs it—all of which is learning, I'll tell you, sad learning. So, we go ahead and do things, with all that in mind, I guess."

I spent a summer (1965) watching what she and others like her and hundreds of Mississippi's black children (ages three to six) all did, together. I have to admit it, I was surprised—as were others like me, who came from all over the country to observe, inspect, study, whatever, and left, invariably, scratching their puzzled heads. Children from rural cabins were learning all sorts of things: first how to own and wear clothes; then, how to eat food and enjoy it and come to believe that there will be yet another meal, yes sir and for real; and finally, how to do things and make things and look at things (and at one another) and, in sum, breathe life into the body's senses and the mind's already developing sensibilities. Paints, crayons, dances, movies, walks, exercises—all of that and more enabled children to become alert and delightfully self-conscious. But one child told me something I hope I never forget, particularly when I congratulate myself and others on a Head Start Project well done, or any other achievement: *"You go to the Head Start place and they want you to see everything and tell it to the teacher—just like my little sister does when she comes shouting at me and pulling on me, to tell me that she saw a bird up there, and did I see it."* Her sister was then two years old, not quite eligible for Head Start. Does anyone really believe that "preliterate" and "illiterate" people don't learn, learn, learn—from the beginning of life on?

The schools I visited in Mississippi had at last caught up with the possibilities that exist in all children, even the children of sharecroppers. In Boston's ghetto, in Appalachia, in migrant labor camps, I have seen young, idealistic (sober, not starry-eyed) youths do similar things: such as give cameras to "culturally deprived" children, who then take pictures and movies—that we all might not have expected, might not have looked for or dreamed possible, from "them," from "poor them." I know that many photographers or movie directors would be fascinated by what such boys and girls have done, though I am not so sure about any number of thoroughly accredited and certified teachers.

Can there really be any doubt that the "humanities" mean everything to children—whose eyes and ears are still alive, have yet to be killed. Elizabeth Bowen knew that "death of the heart" is, to use the expression, a "cross-cultural phenomenon," as anyone knows who lives near rich and well-educated parents, whose children have learned how to glut themselves with facts and utterly dread a mere suggestion, an unanswerable question, a little bit of mystery. By the same token, poor and illiterate children die every moment—in the end spiritually, if not earlier because of hunger, malnutrition, and untreated diseases of all sorts. Yet how many people are really hopeless, really damned outright and forever? In 1965 I watched young black children from Holmes County, Mississippi, sit around a teacher and listen to her as she read some of William Faulkner's pastoral writing. Yes, a lot went unnoticed; indeed, a lot was bothersome or thoroughly unclear. But every once in a while—and, I noticed, with increasing frequency as the minutes followed one another—a word or a phrase or an observation struck the right chord: in a child here, another one over there, and from time to time in all of us. And last year, I heard students at Harvard—who already love records like "The Original Sonny Boy Williamson" or "The Blues of Alabama" or "The Sound of the Delta"—marvel at some photographs taken by a group of children from Boston's ghetto. They're amazing, we all thought. They remind one of postwar Italian movies—you know, *Open City* and *Bicycle Thief*—where violence is everywhere; yet the lives portrayed were meant to show that beauty lives on—in people crushed by wars, revolution, and a history of virtual slavery and poverty. It took an artist like DeSica to pull all that together, the sadness and misery with the stubborn, lovely pride and the hope that never quite disappears.

For generations writers and artists and musicians—the men and women who *make* the humanities—have done that, have tried to give life and coherence to our ambiguous, ironic fate on this earth. For generations to come it will be the same: People will live, and some of them will write about it all, sing about it, draw and paint it, capture it on film. Certainly those who live life (whatever kind of life) and those who use their senses and then their minds to record and comment on life, in all its variety and complexity, have no quarrel with one another, are not "alienated" from one another, do not naturally feel "irrelevant" to one another. But in between them stand us—the mediators, the scholars and educators and teachers and just plain citizens—with our own ideas about what is possible, appropriate, suitable, "right" or "wrong" for children, and of course for writers and artists, too. I fear the rub is there, where the writer, say, in all his clever and calculated and summoning childishness is kept away from his audience, the child and the child in us, by censors of all sorts, who often enough are murderers, pure and simple. In the words of that Head Start teacher I quoted: "*Some teachers, some people, they don't really like writers and artists, so they turn them into dust, and make the kids try to eat the dust, and if the kids start vomiting— well, it just goes to show you that the writers are no-good, or*

*not suitable for such kids, or don't speak their language, the right
language. Can you beat that for dishonesty?"* I fear the answer is no.

Yet, teachers can be different. They can in fact learn with their
students, offer them fire, spirit, and force; offer them ideas and
doubts and questions; offer them a willingness to experiment, admit error, take risks and chances. Writers, artists, composers—all
of them mean to teach, to enliven; even as the rest of us, young
and old, crave the breath of life that their stories, pictures, and
songs all offer. If Tolstoy or Faulkner or Mozart or Big Joe Williams,
the bluesman from Mississippi's Delta, cannot bring professors and
students, older people and youths together, make them one and
all readers and listeners, human beings who share and respond to
something that transcends time and space, then who and what possibly can?

This question of Theodore Roethke's was rhetorical:

> Stupor of knowledge lacking inwardness—
> What book, O learned man, will set me right?

He knew that no book can provide the Word, that any book,
however lovely and even exalted, can be inadequate to life's awful
moments. But as a poet he persisted; he wrote his words, "words
for the wind," and he hoped they would inform, excite, alarm,
deliver courage and something one can only call a moment of
quietness, a truce for a brief spell in the wars we all know. I
believe that the winds he enriched naturally seek us out in classrooms as well as in a field, a hill, a place lonely and apart. Do we
hear—we together, we in those classrooms? We can hear. *Do* we,
though? Or does the life of a man like Roethke, his vitality, become his lyrics, scare us to—oh, in fact, scare us to death?

They changed rock, which changed the culture, which changed us

By Jeff Greenfield

They have not performed together on stage for more than eight years. They have not made a record together in five years. The formal dissolution of their partnership in a London courtroom last month was an echo of an ending that came long ago. Now each of them is seeking to overcome the shadow of a past in which they were bound together by wealth, fame and adulation of an intensity unequaled in our culture. George Harrison scorns talk of reunion, telling us to stop living in the past. John Lennon told us years ago that "the dream is over."

He was right: When the Beatles broke up in 1970 in a welter of lawsuits and recriminations, the sixties were ending as well—in spirit as well as by the calendar. Bloodshed and bombings on campus, the harsh realities beneath the facile hopes for a "Woodstock nation," the shabby refuse of counterculture communities, all helped kill the dream.

What remains remarkable now, almost 20 years after John Lennon started playing rock 'n' roll music, more than a decade after their first worldwide conquest, is how appealing this dream was; how its vision of the world gripped so much of a generation; how that dream reshaped our recent past and affects us still. What remains remarkable is how strongly this dream was triggered, nurtured and broadened by one rock 'n' roll band of four Englishmen whose entire history as a group occurred before any of them reached the age of 30.

Their very power guarantees that an excursion into analysis cannot fully succeed. Their songs, their films, their lives formed so great a part of what we listened to and watched and talked about that everyone affected by them still sees the Beatles and hears their songs through a personal prism. And the Beatles themselves never abandoned a sense of self-parody and put-on. They were, in Richard Goldstein's phrase, "the clown-gurus of the sixties." Lennon said more than once that the Beatles sometimes put elusive references into their songs just to confuse their more solemn interpreters. "I am the egg man," they sang, not "egghead."

Still, the impact of the Beatles cannot be waved away. If the Marx they emulated was Groucho, not Karl, if their world was a playground instead of a battleground, they still changed what we listened to and how we listened to it; they helped make rock music a battering ram for the youth culture's assault on the mainstream, and that assault in turn changed our culture permanently. And if the "dream" the Beatles helped create could not sustain itself in the real world, that speaks more to our false hopes than to their promises. They wrote and sang songs. We turned it into politics and philosophy and a road map to another way of life.

Jeff Greenfield is a writer whose most recent book, "No Peace, No Place," deals with the rise of rock 'n' roll.

314

41

The Beatles grew up as children of the first generation of rock 'n' roll, listening to and imitating the music of Little Richard, Larry Williams, Chuck Berry, Elvis Presley, and the later, more sophisticated sounds of the Shirelles and the Miracles. It was the special genius of their first mentor, Brian Epstein, to package four Liverpool working-class "rockers" as 'mods," replacing their greasy hair, leather jackets, and on-stage vulgarity with jackets, ties, smiles and carefully groomed, distinctive haircuts. Just as white artists filtered and softened the raw energy of black artists in the nineteen-fifties, the Beatles at first were softer, safer versions of energetic rock 'n' roll musicians. The words promised they only wanted to hold hands; the rhythm was more insistent.

By coming into prominence early in 1964, the Beatles probably saved rock 'n' roll from extinction. Rock in the early nineteen-sixties existed in name only; apart from the soul artists, it was a time of "shlock rock," with talentless media hypes like Fabian and Frankie Avalon riding the crest of the American Bandstand wave. By contrast, the Beatles provided a sense of musical energy that made successful a brilliant public-relations effort. Of course, the $50,000 used to promote the Beatles' first American appearance in February, 1964, fueled some of the early hysteria; so did the timing of their arrival.

Coming as it did less than a hundred days after the murder of John Kennedy, the advent of the Beatles caught America aching for any diversion to replace the images of a flag-draped casket and a riderless horse in the streets of Washington.

I remember a Sunday evening in early February, standing with hundreds of curious collegians in a University of Wisconsin dormitory, watching these four longhaired (!) Englishmen trying to be heard over the screams of Ed Sullivan's audience. Their music seemed to me then derivative, pleasant and bland, a mixture of hard rock and the sounds of the black groups then popular. I was convinced it would last six months, no more.

The Beatles, however, had more than hype; they had talent. Even their first hits, "I Want to Hold Your Hand," "She Loves You," "Please Please Me," "I Saw Her Standing There," had a hint of harmonies and melodies more inventive than standard rock tunes. More important, it became immediately clear that the Beatles were hipper, more complicated, than the bovine rock stars who could not seem to put four coherent words together.

In the spring of 1964, John Lennon published a book, "In His Own Write," which, instead of a ghost-written string of "groovy guides for keen teens," offered word plays, puns and black-humor satirical sketches. A few months later came the film "A Hard Day's Night," and in place of the classic let's-put-on-a-prom-and-invite-the-TeenChords plot of rock movies, the Beatles and director Richard Lester created a funny movie parodying the Beatles's own image.

I vividly recall going to that film in the midst of a National Student Association congress; at that time, rock 'n' roll was regarded as high-school nonsense by this solemn band of student-body presidents and future C.I.A. operatives. But after the film, I sensed a feeling of goodwill and camaraderie among that handful of rock fans who had watched this movie: The Beatles were media heroes without illusion, young men glorying in their sense of play and fun, laughing at the conventions of the world. They were worth listening to and admiring.

The real surprise came at the end of 1965, with the release of the "Rubber Soul" album. Starting with that album, and continuing through "Revolver" and "Sgt. Pepper's Lonely Hearts Club Band," the Beatles began to throw away the rigid conventions of rock 'n' roll music and lyrics. The banal abstract, second-hand emotions were replaced with sharp, sometimes mordant portraits of first-hand people and experiences, linked to music that was more complicated and more compelling than rock had ever dared attempt. The Beatles were drawing on their memories and feelings, not those cut from Tin Pan Alley cloth.

"Norwegian Wood" was about an unhappy, inconclusive affair ("I once had a girl/or should I say/she once had me"). "Michelle" and "Yesterday" were haunting, sentimental ballads, and Paul McCartney dared sing part of "Michelle" in French—most rock singers regarded English as a foreign language. "Penny Lane" used cornets to evoke the suggestion of a faintly heard band concert on a long-ago summer day. Staccato strings lent urgency to the story of "Eleanor Rigby."

These songs were different from the rock music that our elders had scorned with impunity. Traditionally, rock 'n' roll was rigidly structured: 4/4 tempo, 32 bars, with a limited range of instruments. Before the Beatles, rock producer Phil Spector had revolutionized records by adding strings to the drums, bass, sax and guitar, but the chord structure was usually limited to a basic blues or ballad pattern. Now the Beatles, with the kind of visibility that made them impossible to ignore, were expanding the range of rock, musically and lyrically. A sitar—a harpsichord effect—a ragtime piano—everything was possible.

With the release of "Sgt. Pepper" in the spring of 1967, the era of rock as a strictly adolescent phenomenon was gone. One song, "A Day in the Life," with its recital of an ordinary day combined with a dreamlike sense of dread and anxiety, made it impossible to ignore the skills of Lennon and McCartney. A decade earlier, Steve Allen mocked the inanity of rock by reading "Hound Dog" or "Tutti-Frutti" as if they were serious attempts at poetry. Once "Sgt. Pepper" was recorded, Partisan Review was lauding the Beatles, Ned Rorem proclaimed that "She's Leaving Home" was "equal to any song Schubert ever wrote," and a Newsweek critic meant it when he wrote: "'Strawberry Fields Forever' [is] a superb Beatleizing of hope and despair in which the four minstrels regretfully recommend a Keatsian lotus-land of withdrawal from the centrifugal stresses of the age."

"We're so well established," McCartney had said in 1966, "that we can bring fans along with us and stretch the limits of pop." By using their fame to help break through the boundaries of rock, the Beatles proved that they were not the puppets of backstage manipulation or payola or hysterical 14-year-olds. Instead, they helped make rock music *the* music of an entire international generation. Perhaps for the first time in history, it was possible to say that tens of millions of people, defined simply by age, were all doing the same thing: they were listening to rock 'n' roll. That fact changed the popular culture of the world.

■

Rock 'n' roll's popularity had never been accompanied

Beatles rising—Paul McCartney, Ringo Starr, John Lennon, George Harrison in 1963.

by respectability, even among the young. For those of us with intellectual pretenses, rock 'n' roll was like masturbation: exciting, but shameful. The culturally alienated went in for cool jazz, and folk music was the vehicle for the politically active minority. (The growth of political interest at the start of the sixties sparked something of a folk revival).

Along with the leap of Bob Dylan into rock music, the Beatles destroyed this division. Rock 'n' roll was now broad enough, free enough, to encompass every kind of feeling. Its strength had always been rooted in the sexual energy of its rhythms; in that sense, the outraged parents who had seen rock as a threat to their children's virtue were right. Rock 'n' roll made you want to move and shake and get physically excited. The Beatles proved that this energy could be fused with a sensibility more subtle than the "let's-go-down -to - the - gym - and -beat - up - the - Coke -

machine" quality of rock music.

In 1965, Barry McGuire recorded the first "rock protest" song (excluding the teen complaints of the Coasters and Chuck Berry). In his "Eve of Destruction," we heard references to Red China, Selma, Alabama, nuclear war and middle-class hypocrisy pounded out to heavy rock rhythms. That same year came a flood of "good time" rock music, with sweet, haunting melodies by groups like the Lovin' Spoonful and the Mamas and the Papas. There *were* no limits to what could be done; and the market was continually expanding.

The teen-agers of the nineteen-fifties had become the young adults of the nineteen-sixties, entering the professions, bringing with them a cultural frame of reference shaped in good measure by rock 'n' roll. The "youth" market was enormous—the flood of babies born during and just after World War II made the under-25 population group abnor-

mally large; their tastes were more influential than ever before. And because the music had won acceptability, rock 'n' roll was not judged indulgently as a "boys will be boys" fad. Rock music was expressing a sensibility about the tangible world — about sensuality, about colors and sensations, about the need to change consciousness. And this sensibility soon spilled over into other arenas.

Looking back on the last half of the last decade, it is hard to think of a cultural innovation that did not carry with it the influence of rock music, and of the Beatles in particular: the miniskirt, discotheques, the graphics of Peter Max, the birth of publications like Rolling Stone, the "mind-bending" effects of TV commercials, the success of "Laugh-In" on television and "Easy Rider" in the movies— all of these cultural milestones owe something to the emergence of rock music as the most compelling and pervasive force in our culture.

This is especially true of

the incredible spread of drugs —marijuana and the hallucinogens most particularly— among the youth culture. From "Rubber Soul" through "Sgt. Pepper," Beatle music was suffused with a sense of mystery and mysticism: odd choral progressions, mysterious instruments, dreamlike effects, and images that did not seem to yield to "straight" interpretation. Whether specific songs ("Lucy in the Sky with Diamonds," "A Little Help From My Friends") were deliberately referring to drugs is beside the point. The Beatles were publicly recounting their LSD experiences, and their music was replete with antirational sensibility. Indeed, it was a commonplace among my contemporaries that Beatle albums could not be understood fully without the use of drugs. For "Rubber Soul," marijuana; for "Sgt. Pepper," acid. When the Beatles told us to turn off our minds and float downstream, uncounted youngsters assumed that the key to this kind of mind-expansion could be found in a plant or a pill. Together with "head" groups like Jefferson Airplane and the Grateful Dead, the Beatles were, consciously or not, a major influence behind the spread of drugs.

In this sense, the Beatles are part of a chain: (1) the Beatles opened up rock; (2) rock changed the culture; (3) the culture changed us. Even limited to their impact as musicians, however, the Beatles were as powerful an influence as any group or individual; only Bob Dylan stands as their equal. They never stayed with a successful formula; they were always moving. By virtue of their fame, the Beatles were a giant amplifier, spreading "the word" on virtually every trend and mood of the last decade.

They were never pure forerunners. The Yardbirds used the sitar before the Beatles; the Beach Boys were experimenting with studio enhancement first; the Four Seasons were using elaborate harmonies before the Beatles. They were never as contemptuously antimiddle-class or decadent as the Kinks or the Rolling Stones; never as lyrically compelling as Dylan; never as musically brilliant as the Band; never as hallucinogenic as the San Francisco groups. John Gabree, one of the most perceptive of the early rock writers, said that "their job, and they have done it well, has been to travel a few miles behind the avant-garde, consolidating gains and popularizing new ideas."

Yet this very willingness meant that new ideas did not struggle and die in obscurity; instead, they touched a hundred million minds. Their songs reflected the widest range of mood of any group of their time. Their openness created a kind of salon for a whole generation of people, an idea exchange into which the youth of the world was wired. It was almost inevitable that, even against their will, their listeners shaped a dream of politics and lifestyle from the substance of popular music. It is testament both to the power of rock music, and to the illusions which can be spun out of impulses.

∎

The Beatles were not political animals. Whatever they have done since going their separate ways, their behavior as a group reflected cheerful anarchy more than political rebellion. Indeed, as editorialists, they were closer to The Wall Street Journal than to Ramparts. "Taxman" assaults the heavy progressive income tax ("one for you, 19 for me"), and "Revolution" warned that "if you go carrying pictures of Chairman Mao/you ain't gonna make it with anyone anyhow."

The real political impact of the Beatles was not in any four-point program or in an attack on injustice or the war in Vietnam. It was instead in

the counterculture they had helped to create. Somewhere in the nineteen-sixties, millions of people began to regard themselves as a class separate from mainstream society *by virtue of their youth and the sensibility that youth produced.*

The nineteen-fifties had produced the faintest hint of such an attitude in the defensive love of rock 'n' roll; if our parents hated it, it had to be good. The sixties had expanded this vague idea into a battle cry. "Don't trust anyone over 30!"—shouted from a police car in the first massive student protest of the decade at Berkeley—suggested an outlook in which the mere aging process was an act of betrayal, in which youth itself was a moral value. Time magazine made the "under-25 generation" its Man of the Year in 1967, and politicians saw in the steadily escalating rebellion among the middle-class young a constituency and a scapegoat.

The core value of this "class" was not peace or social justice; it was instead a more elusive value, reflected by much of the music and by the Beatles own portrait of themselves. It is expressed best by a scene from their movie "Help!" in which John, Paul, George and Ringo enter four adjoining row houses. The doors open—and suddenly the scene shifts inside, and we see that these "houses" are in fact one huge house; the four Beatles instantly reunite.

It is this sense of communality that was at the heart of the youth culture. It is what we wished to believe about the Beatles, and about the possibilities in our own lives. If there is one sweeping statement that makes sense about the children of the last decade, it is that the generation born of World War II was saying "no" to the atomized lives their parents had so feverishly sought. The most cherished value of the counter-

culture—preached if not always practiced—was its insistence on sharing, communality, a rejection of the retreat into private satisfaction. Rock 'n' roll was the magnet, the driving force, of a shared celebration, from Alan Freed's first mammoth dance parties in Cleveland in 1951, to the Avalon Ballroom in San Francisco, to the be-ins in our big cities, to Woodstock itself. Spontaneous gathering was the ethic: Don't plan it, don't think about it, *do* it—you'll get by with a little help from your friends.

In their music, their films, their sense of play, the Beatles reflected this dream of a ceaseless celebration. If there *was* any real "message" in their songs, it was the message of Charles Reich: that the world would be changed by changing the consciousness of the new generation. "All you need is love," they sang. "Say the word [love] and you'll be free." "Let it be." "Everything's gonna be all right."

As a state of mind, it was a pleasant fantasy. As a way of life, it was doomed to disaster. The thousands of young people who flocked to California or to New York's Lower East Side to join the love generation found the world filled with people who did not share the ethic of mutual trust. The politicization of youth as a class helped to divide natural political allies and make politics more vulnerable to demagogues. As the Beatles found in their own personal and professional lives, the practical outside world has a merciless habit of intruding into fantasies; somebody has to pay the bills and somebody has to do the dishes in the commune and somebody has to protect us from the worst instincts of other human beings. John Lennon was expressing some very painful lessons when he told Rolling Stone shortly after the group's breakup that "nothing happened except we all dressed up . . . the same bas-

tards are in control, the same people are runnin' everything."

He was also being unfair. If the counterculture was too shallow to understand how the world does get changed, the forces that were set loose in the nineteen-sixties have had a permanent effect. The sensuality that rock 'n' roll tapped will never again be bottled up. The vestiges of the communal dream have changed the nature of friendships and life-styles and marriages, in large measure for the better. And with the coming of harder economic times, the idea of abandoning private retreat for shared pleasures and burdens has a direct contemporary practicality.

For me, the final irony is that the Beatles themselves have unconsciously proven the value of communality. As a group, they seemed to hold each other back from excess: McCartney was lyrical, but not saccharine; Lennon was rebellious but not offensive; Harrison's mysticism was disciplined (Ringo was always Ringo, drummer and friend). Now, the sense of control seems to have loosened. Paul and Linda McCartney seem tempted by the chance to become the Steve and Eydie of rock; Lennon is still struggling to free himself from a Fad of the Month mentality; George Harrison's Gospel According to Krishna succeeded in boring much of his audience on his recent concert tour. Perhaps the idea they did so much to spread several years ago is not as dead as all that; perhaps we all need a little help from our friends. The enduring power of that idea is as permanent as any impact their music had on us, even if they no longer believe it.

XII. Reactions to Adolescents and Adolescence

It seems ironic that the two words, adolescence and adolescents, are pronounced almost identically. At first hearing, one is not certain whether to respond to the people of the age period in question or to the period itself. Similarly, one's reactions to adolescents and adolescence may be to contemporary adolescents, to the period of time, or indeed to one's own adolescence. It is this last option, moreover, that colors one's observations of the age group we have been examining in this volume.

No one needs to be told that adolescence can be a period of great upheaval and excitement. No one needs to be told that many adults are delighted to realize that they need never be adolescents again. But many people long for their adolescence and act as if the period had never concluded. They criticize the young and then go ahead and act like them. Or they ask the young to be something that they, the adults, want them to be, rather than accepting adolescents as they are. One might say, in this regard, that because adolescence falls between childhood and adulthood, characteristics of adult and childlike behavior appear in the behavior of adolescents. Thus it is sometimes difficult for adults to realize that the adolescent response to certain circumstances and experiences will be tinged with adult *and* childlike elements.

Still, no matter how a particular adolescent behaves, and no matter how any expert chooses to characterize adolescence, adults often are complicated about their reactions to the young. It seems inevitable, moreover, that in reacting to adolescents, the word "maturity" gets bandied about, frequently in the most scientific sounding ways. One almost begins to believe that we have actually developed instruments to measure the adolescent's level of maturity as we have instruments to measure his or her heart rate or blood pressure. We might pause on this point, because lurking in many sections in this book is the concept of maturity and the degree to which one may justifiably expect adolescents to behave as adults. While we continually preach that adolescents are not adults, and that we must not expect them to behave as adults—indeed we embrace the word *adolescence* because it means something different from childhood and adulthood—we assess them in terms of adult standards. When, as adults, we try to recapture our adolescence, we invariably fall into the trap of perceiving of this period of our lives in terms of who we are at this present point in time. It is difficult, in other words, to look at adolescents in terms of adolescence.

It may well be that examinations of adolescence evoke in those of us who study and write about the young feelings of our own adolescence, or thoughts about our own children, students, or friends. That is, we may end up with personalized accounts rather than discreetly scientific reports. But this may not be a wholly undesirable result if our personalized statements about adolescence first convey the truth of this delicate and complex stage of the life cycle and second honor and enhance the young men and women whose lives are the object of our inquiries.

42

Coming of age in America

By Peter and Jane Davison

"He's a mere child, you're a typical teen-ager, we're sort of middle-aged, she's really getting on, and he's practically dead." How ironic that technological America can accept so vaguely calibrated a continuum to tick off the ages of man. The way we dress now expresses the way we gloss over society's compartmentalization by age and generation. Lately, the young, in rebellion against tailormade conformity, broke out into a revolution of dress, if not ultimately one in fact, and now, like most revolutions, it has become a model for antirevolutionary imitation. A grandmother in St. Petersburg strolls under the palms in a size 16½ duplicate of the double-knit pants suit her daughter-in-law wears while car-pooling her jersey-clad children to school in Mamaroneck — yet their life expectations are as different as chalk and cheese. Now, less than five years after Kent State, college students (boys or girls) dip into their mother's bureau for her Yves Saint Laurent shirt, silk scarf or bulky cardigan. Even at the

Peter and Jane Davison are regarded by their two children as uncanny but not necessarily inimical. He is a poet and editor, whose most recent book is "Walking the Boundaries: Poems 1957-1974."

height of what may be described as the Mannerist Sixties, when inspired originality was the universal cry, the with-it people from Harvard Square to Haight-Ashbury ended up looking like so many interchangeable characters in an all-American ethno-historico-theatrical motley. The laws of costume have a certain leveling inevitability.

The homogenization of the way we look has begun to shatter the merchandising category known as Children's Clothes — yet children's clothes of any kind are a surprisingly recent development in Western civilization. In his fascinating book, "Dress and Society: 1560-1970," Geoffrey Squire states that not until the last decades of the 18th century, under the influence of Rousseau, did it occur to parents to abandon the age-old practice of dressing children like miniature adults. The well-dressed child, with sighs of relief, cast aside knee breeches and corselets to slip into loose trousers and smocks.

This innovation coincided, moreover, with a movement in both adult dress and manners to separate the sexes and intensify the differences between them. This reached its most elaborate and dramatic phase in

the 19th century, the age of vapors and the double standard, when the fabrics as well as the silhouettes of men's and women's clothes reached their extremes of polarization. Who could mistake Scarlett O'Hara for Rhett Butler? Ultimately, all the adult and juvenile categories of dress became part of the Byzantine inventories of the 20th-century department store. In Children's Clothes alone, we had to learn to make our way through 3-6x, Young Subdebs, Older Preps, Junior Chubbettes and other exotic subdivisions. Now in the seventies we seem to be leaving those distinctions of age and sex behind us.

The way we dress, Squire contends, reflects the way we are. Costume is "only a unit in the complete production, which is illuminated by the spirit of the age in which we live." We have moved into an era of democratization, of attempting to dispense with social and economic distinctions, of welcoming cradle-to-grave blue denim "work clothes." We have mass production and mass media and, if you like, a mass mess. Our clothes have followed our customs. As we have blurred or eliminated social differences in the name of equality, ritual distinctions among us have faded. Many changes have been morally and socially beneficial — the abolition of slavery and the relative liberation of women, for example — but enlightened progress has its casualties. We sense uneasily that something has been lost.

Less complicated, confused cultures have been able to preserve a variety of social ceremonies marking the major, irreversible biological/social stages of an individual's life. Although age-old and universal in one form or another, these rituals had no generic name until 1909 when the anthropologist A. L. Van Gennep coined the term "rites of passage."

As Carleton Coon points out in "The Hunting Peoples," a rite of passage is therapeutic both for the "patient" and for those close to him, such as his immediate family. It eases difficult adjustments to change for all concerned. We agree that it provides a boy or girl, man or woman with a navigational fix on his position in the society that surrounds him like a sea. Moreover, it helps reduce the individual's fear of the future; it reassures him with its public announcement that he has changed and must henceforth be regarded differently by society; it keeps the society informed of who has got to what stage of life, and how, accordingly, he should be treated. If rituals are erased or suppressed, an emotional geography haltingly tamed through the millennia is delivered over to wilderness.

To what extent has this happened to us? As a nation we expend ourselves on two rites of passage which we regard as major events in human life: marriages, with their picturesque folkways — like white veils, champagne receptions, engraved announcements and competitive gift-giving — and funerals, with their euphemistic language and cosmetic disguising of the facts of death. (Note that what others do is ritual; what we do is The Way It's Done.) Coming of age is a happening we seem to neglect, certainly in comparison to such cultures as that the Mbuti pygmies of the Ituri Forest, in northwest Zaire.

For several months after their first menstruation, Mbuti girls are segregated in what is called an *elima*

Our sons and daughters emerge from childhood into what? Into that big waiting room that is adolescence in America.

house to undergo an experience something like a summer camp crossed with a slumber party. They sing special *elima* songs, make a lot of noise and are told the facts of life. If any boys approach, the girls beat them with sticks. Eventually, they begin to let certain suitors in, and the wooing is on. At this point the mothers step in and harass the suitors with all sorts of deterrents, from a little more run-of-the-mill stick-beating to throwing particularly unattractive prospects into a stream. The battle of the sexes and generations intensifies, and the boys retaliate by such horseplay as slapping their prospective mothers-in-law with banana skins. Somehow in the melee betrothals are negotiated, whereupon a girl busies herself with prenuptial activities, like painting white clay stars on her buttocks or rings on her breasts. Meanwhile, the boy hunts for a nice large antelope to give to her parents to seal the deal.

To us these carryings-on seem amusing enough, but no more so perhaps than a visiting Mbuti pygmy would find the mummery of a first-class interment at Forest Lawn. It might be instructive to imagine a modern American adaptation of the perky coed rite of passage described above, but the mind boggles at the possibilities for such a living theater hoedown. Think of the by-products. "Celebrate your lovely daughter's coming of age with the all-new Pandora's Box, her very own simulated-gold coffer containing a six months' supply of The Pill! Available in better stores across the country." No, such revels cannot be invented; they have to grow out of the inner needs of a society.

If they do, they work. After weeks of being the center of the Mbuti hullabaloo, you must certainly know (1) that you are no longer the same as before, and (2) that certain new expectations now rest upon you, whether they be signalized by stars on your rear, king-size antelopes or more private and personal engagements, like sex and children.

Our sons and daughters emerge from childhood into what? Into that big waiting room that is adolescence in America. Here the boy or girl puts away childish things and takes up adult concerns and entertainments, but not adult duties. In middle-class America Daddy pays the tuition and the piper, and the principal emotions rise over the rights, not the rites, of passage. It is a terrifying and terrible time, in that no one, neither the parent nor the child, has any way to measure when it will ever end, and what few yardsticks are available keep changing.

Erik H. Erikson wrote in "Childhood and Society," "The adolescent mind is essentially a mind of the moratorium, a psychosocial stage between childhood and adulthood, and between the morality learned by the child, and the ethics developed by the adult. It is an ideological mind — and indeed it is the ideological outlook of a society that speaks most clearly to the adolescent who is eager to be confirmed by his peers, and is ready to be confirmed by the rituals, creeds, and programs which at the same time define what is evil, uncanny, and inimical." Because we as a society have shucked off, one by one, and mostly in the name of ideology, the "rituals, creeds, and programs" that help define the adult, a vacuum remains, and it is filled by the adolescent's peers. Yet how unsatisfactory. How can one pass a test in a course where there is no teacher?

Only a few specific acknowledgments of entrance into an adult community still exist — the bar mitzvahs and first communions of formal but receding religions. The ideologies, however, are all too ready at hand, and new ones keep arriving — old ideas in new disguises — offering panaceas that can be dropped as quickly as they were adopted. "Historically," as C. G. Jung wrote in "The Undiscovered Self," it is chiefly in times of physical, political, economic, and spiritual distress that men's eyes turn with anxious hope to the future, and when anticipations, utopias, and apocalyptic visions multiply." If our adolescents a decade ago gave themselves to the cause of civil rights, how soon they neglected that cause when they became more nearly threatened by the Vietnam war. Once we were out of the war, they turned to the ecological threats posed by technology, and their next cause well may be world famine.

Who would call these causes unworthy? No one. But the adolescent, who is given nothing by society to assure him of first-class membership, has fewer defenses against fads and panics than anyone else. As Jung went on to write, "Resistance to the organized mass can be effected only by the man who is as well organized in his individuality as the mass itself. I realize that this proposition must sound well-nigh unintelligible to the man of today."

Perhaps it sounds less unintelligible now than when it was first written in 1957. No longer militant, the young seem to be turning inward, or at least away from social struggle. Perhaps they have come to suspect that one element in their protests was retribution against their parents for not having provided them with the satisfying "rituals, creeds, and programs" that define the "evil, uncanny, and inimical."

Parents themselves went through a lot in those bitter years of the nineteen-sixties, and they still do. On certain dark winter mornings they recognize themselves as "uncanny"; they can see themselves mirrored in their children's eyes as "inimical." Some of them run away from their lives into divorce, second professions, new homes and surroundings; others take no action but drift into a worrisome limbo — the *Weltschmerz* of a second adolescence, the acknowledged but totally unritualized mid-life crisis, an increasingly familiar neurosis that arises, as much as anything, from the absence of any rite of passage into age. Undeniably, becoming a respected elder reassures one more than simply growing older.

There is nothing new about the feelings of a father in his forties, aware of the waning of his seemingly illimitable sexual powers, watching with rueful amusement the stretching and preening of his 13-year-old son, who is wearing a sleeveless Italian shirt so that no one can avoid noticing the new tufts of hair under his arms. Nor is there anything new about the emotions of a mother, who looks up from the latest magazine article on breast cancer and sees her blossoming braless daughter jounce by, seemingly unaware of the aura she casts. Parents have no doubt always held such feelings about their children, but there were once the compensations of eldership. Those few who survived past middle age gained a certain status in the society; their experience seemed a source of wisdom; the young looked to them for answers to famine, inflation and war, though it may be we still believe in the elders of the Supreme Court as wise and just.

With so few specific rites of passage to mark our adolescent coming of age, clothes have assumed a symbolic importance — or they did so 30 years ago. We girls were children as long as we dressed up in tweed reefers from Best & Co. (just like Princess Margaret Rose's), and patent leather Mary Janes with fine white cotton socks, and a velveteen party dress with heavy white lace at the neck. Only with the first pimple and the first box of sanitary supplies (a euphemism that ranks for quaintness with *sal volatile* and the vapors) did we cast aside the trappings of childhood and harness up in bra, garter belt, "hose" and "heels." Or, as boys, we seemed to change when we traded our curly hair and shorts (after a long battle with our mothers) for crew cuts and long corduroys from J. C. Penney.

When we won these minor battles for status, we knew something significant had happened in our lives, but it hardly constituted adult recognition. We had a feeling that whatever else was wanted had more to do with sex than anyone was letting on. "I see you're growing up," one of those little blue-haired ladies who knew your mother would say, peering through her specs, and we wondered uneasily exactly what she could see. When in the nineteen-sixties one generation dramatized its differences with the preceding one far more overtly than we ever had, there was no question that sex as an issue underlay adult hysteria about long hair and dirty jeans.

Not knowing what the world had a right to expect, we had no idea what to expect from ourselves as semi-adults, except to *keep going*. For a white middle-class child, particularly a boy, this meant an endless slogging upward on the academic and business slopes. No graduation, whether from high school or from college or from graduate school, could replace the rites of passage invented by our "primitive" ancestors. We were herded along through the decades in the increasingly frightening knowledge that next year or next week or even perhaps tomorrow we would be expected to comport ourselves like adults, to be as ruthless and tough as adults, without, of course, making any of the mistakes the older generation had made. The worst of it was that we had no way of judging our own performance, until our children came along to mark us, and we began to fear we had flunked out. We had no ceremony to give us the sense of where we were now in the procession. The occasion never arose when we might taste the pride of public recognition of our achievement, when we might, so to speak, introduce the succession to a cheering populace, "My son, the Prince of Wales, and my daughter, the future Queen of France."

The traditional acknowledgments of coming of age have been very directly, if symbolically, linked with sex and reproduction: the girl is now of an age to bear children; the boy is equipped to father them. In an age of population explosion, years of suspended animation are required of young people, and reproduction is to be prevented, not encouraged. The major difference between adolescence today and 30 years ago is more than that between anxious backseat groping and sexual freedom or coed dorms, far more than that between velveteen dresses and Levi's. Thirty years ago how many of our contemporaries discussed, seriously and as a matter of choice, not having children? Girls never even talked about not marrying, except as one would speak of the possibility of some cataclysm.

Today, even as fashion begins to move away from the unisex effect of the blue denim uniform, educators confer and speculate on the advantages of adrogyny, or at least of the androgynous mind. A recent study at Stanford University seemed to prove that a young mind that balances attributes traditionally viewed as male or female is likely to be more adept at problem solving than one more sexually polarized. The trend in education may be to discourage sexual stereotyping, at least for a time, and probably it is desirable, but we are moving still father away from conceiving of adulthood as a confirmation of our sexual identities, and the biological fact of puberty will continue to lose its traditional social significance.

In the absence of sexually defined rites of passage, some people have groped for substitutes to replace our vanished rituals. Artificial and exclusive subgroups have sprung into being, small communes as well as those societies ordered and financed on a larger scale — the Jesus Freaks and Maharishis and Esalens and Hare Krishnas and Reverend Moons. If an industrial civilization cannot provide us with a purified social order containing those rites of passage and progress which our soul loveth, some of us will feel obliged to turn again, in the American way, and run up a society out of whole cloth to satisfy the heart's desire.

Alas, the record is not encouraging for this do-it-yourself kind of social enterprise. Our New Harmonys, Shakers, Amanas, Amish and Doukhobors don't seem to be much more fertile than the mules they drive, and have a sad way of fading into extinction after a generation or two. For ritual to perform its functions of refreshment, vitalization and renewal, it must truly reflect the human needs and realities of the society that decrees it. What rites would a technological society decree that all members could consent to?

When Freud was asked what a mature adult should be able to do well, his answer was short and awesomely simple: *"Lieben und arbeiten."* To love and to work. The standard is so profound that it can apply to Mbuti pygmies or anyone in America. Whether we are young adolescents seeking reassurance of growth or recidivists in our forties, we would have received little help toward either goal from sex-oriented rites of passage. The discouraging thing about so exalted and rational a goal as Freud's is that it will not admit of the thrill of initiation, the graduate's self-satisfaction, the parents' gratification, the recognition and intensification of a social pattern in which all generations have a set role. Loving and working are somehow left to the individual to learn for himself or herself.

The only rites of passage left are those which each of us must set up for ourselves. There is cause for celebration the first time we say, "No, I won't go to bed with you just because you want me." "Yes, I will go to bed with you because I want you." "No, I won't smoke dope just because everyone else does," "No, I won't follow my parents' pattern of competitive expertise." "No, I won't challenge my parents just because all my peers say it's the thing to do." Simplistic? Perhaps. But such considered assents and refusals, weighed against the demands and bounties of a society that so far has seemed to offer us everything and refuse us nothing, are the only acts by which we can define ourselves, while telling our world that we have at last — at whatever age, 13 or 39 — become adults.

43

THE USES OF IMMATURITY

by Jerome Bruner

In the last centuries, in response to the change of technology, we have come implicitly to the belief that choosing a vocation could be postponed till "later" while one trained the generalist in the skills that would serve in any vocation. But without vocation, intention becomes diluted and learning may fail. The young cry out about irrelevance, which is almost certainly a wrong diagnosis of their troubles. A better one would be "aimlessness."

Occupation is one of the major means whereby human beings integrate intentions toward a long-range goal and embed them in a hierarchical structure that defines priorities. The subjective definition of one's work is surely a major source of one's feeling of authenticity. Quite obviously, the two modes of defining work, the social and the personal, interact.

At one extreme, as Norbert Wiener put it, when work is organized in such a way as to be unfit for human production, the human being rebels or else risks being dehumanized. At the other extreme is the phenomenon of The Calling, where the structure of one's *life* and of one's *work* are indistinguishable.

The decision to delay vocational or job decisions until comparatively late in the life cycle inevitably makes fuzzy one's definition of oneself as an adult. At the very moment the young man or woman is seeking authenticity, the only legitimate role that is open to him is that of student. Youth culture becomes more deeply entrenched, more prolonged, more ideologically in opposition, more "adult" in the sense of being a timeless status.

The result of all this is that enormous difficulties have been generated for the young. Their neuroses are far more likely to revolve around work than around sex. And there has been thunder in those learned councils that debate the best course to follow in rearing the young. The contradictory diagnoses that have been offered for the Hamlet-like conflict of the young about work boggle the imagination.

Education has always been an extrapolation of social, political and economic objectives, and when these could be taken for granted, attention could be focused on appropriate means for achieving implicit goals. Under those circumstances, one could concentrate on requirements built into the nature of man's way of knowing and of learning. But these do *not* enter into the debates that concern us today. They crop up almost as afterthoughts in

Jerome Bruner, long a renowned member of the Harvard faculty, is Watts Professor of Psychology at Oxford University.

the heat of particular episodes of political troubles in academia. There has been emphasis on "spontaneity" and self-initiated learning and "free schools" with individualized curricula. But that is not at the heart of the debate nor does it relate to specific incidents of protest.

I find it hard to believe that the academic arrangements of the school system of the City of New York have much to do with the fact that half its high school students take drugs with a frequency exceeding once-for-kicks, if *The Times'* report can be taken at face value. The problem is in the definition of roles and aims and ideals in the society at large, rather than with the schools.

I cannot escape the conclusion that the first order of business in the transformation of our mode of educating is to revolutionize and revivify the idea of vocation.

There is some deep, unrecognized but anxious sense of impending change that pervades the thinking of students, a feeling of uncertainty about the future. I am not speaking only of the counterculture with its more radical search for new life styles but of a much broader range of the young. They are searching, I think, not only for a sense of what has happened to the world, but what their own role in it is to be. Neither vocational training nor training in the general skills of mind seems to solve their doubts.

An extraordinary isolation develops between the young and the older generation when role models fail. A gap is created not only *between* generations but also in the needs of the young. For one can make a strong case for attachment, observation and demonstration as a unique triad of human processes used by youth in mastering the ways of the adult world.

There is no indication that early attachment is diminished in the contemporary family. But the subculture of the young creates a norm or a style that leads to attachment figures being ignored or rejected by adolescence or before. What eventually takes the place of the deposed competence figure, the classical adult image of skill? At first protest-withdrawal figures: the pop figures of rock and the Timothy Leary prophets who offer heightened subjectivity in place of external control. But gradually there emerges a new form of role bearer: an intermediate generation, young adults and late adolescents, who take over the modeling roles, who set the tone of change, lead protests or run free schools, explore new enterprises or establish communes. Their skills and vocation are dramatically proclaimed, miniaturized to appropriate size and highly personalized. They are often daft, highly romantic

or utopian, even at times absurd. An intermediate generation, nonetheless, is a response to the crisis of a change
rate that outstrips the transition rate from one generation
to the next.

What is most characteristic of the present intermediate generation is its capacity for generating hypotheses
about occupation, about styles of life. It is an important
kind of serious playfulness. Play during early childhood
permits the child to explore combinations of things and
acts that would never be explored if he kept just to reasonable problem solving. It is for this reason that we can
properly speak of play as the serious business of childhood. There is a later form of play, "deep play," that
Jeremy Bentham goes so far as to condemn in his *Theory
of Legislation*. By deep play, Bentham meant play in
which the stakes are so high that it is irrational for men to
engage in it at all—a situation in which the marginal utility of what one stands to win is less than the marginal
utility of what one stands to lose.

What strikes one about the past decade is the enormous increase in the depth of play of adolescents and
young adults—willingness to risk one's preferment in support of conviction or even of convinced whimsy: the professor's son off farming on a remote island, the doctor's
daughter leaving medical school to help start an experimental day-care center, the successful young editor chuck-
ing everything and going off untutored to build a globe-
girdling boat; the myriad modes of "dropping out" to find
oneself.

In a stable society, this would either suggest deep
trouble, structural strain, as our sociologists like to call it,
or at least the emergence of an eccentric fringe who are
refugees from regimentation as were the *fin de siècle* ec-
centrics. But I would like to argue that in our transitional
society, this phenomenon constitutes the very kind of push
toward new occupations and hypotheses about life styles
—to which we were alluding earlier—and that the epi-
demic nature of the support that such actions command
suggests how deep is the yearning for reformulation.

Several volumes have recently appeared proposing
that students take more academic responsibility for their
fellow students. One of them (*The Letter to a Teacher*,
Penguin, 1970), prepared by the schoolchildren of an Italian hill town long stalled in poverty, tells in the words of
former students of a new priest who, recognizing that the
competitive school system had been defeating most of the
children, transforms the school into one where the whole
class assumes responsibility for each of its members mastering items in the curriculum as they come up. The effect
was, of course, electrifying.

But an example is not a proof. A recent work by
Riesman, et al. (*Children Teach Children*, Heron, 1970)
reports on a variety of local experiments in the United
States, involving "cross-age tutoring," the awkward name
for older children helping younger ones. The authors report a considerable increase in the scholastic performance
of the *tutored* children and a *very* considerable increase
among those doing the *tutoring* (a well-known secret
among those who teach). But what is most notable in the
transcripts of interviews in this book is the notable increase in self-worth and group pride among all the parties
involved—including the authors of the book. Schooling
takes on a new significance.

Surely we can take a leaf from the kind of experiments just described. I would strongly urge, knowing full
well the enormous administrative complexities involved,
that we use the system of student-assisted learning from
the start in our schools, that we test achievement *outside*
the context of school, that we treat the process of mastering the culture's devices and disciplines, its amplifiers, as a
communal undertaking.

On the grounds of efficiency all the evidence points to
the superiority of communal effort. On grounds of humane
concern of each man for his brothers, it is surely to be
preferred. And as important, on grounds of tapping the
immediacy of experience of the intermediate generation in
a time of deep perplexity and change, the plan must surely
be taken seriously. For not only would it give an outlet for
ideals but it would also provide an opportunity for responsible participation in communal problems.

But most critically, it is the services of those who are
more skilled that are needed in the extended form of education being proposed. It is from those at work that we
can recruit the "teachers" or at least the aides for helping
with the "returns," the "conversions," the "refreshers." I
do not doubt that a plan of this sort is complicated and
"impossible." I only urge that something of the sort be
tried to find one that is simpler and more manageable.

In various communities in the United States, teen-
aged committees (usually of minorities like blacks and
Chicanos) have formed themselves to dissuade potential
dropouts or to get them back to school. I had the astonishing privilege of spending two days with representatives of
a dozen or so of these groups brought to Washington by
the United States Office of Economic Opportunity to help
set up a network for informing new groups around the
country. It was quite plain after a few hours that what was
needed for those who wished to come back into the system
was precisely the kind of "cross-age" tutoring we have
been discussing. Such a service would be as appropriate
for those who are not dropping out but who cannot wait
for the moment when they can leave without trouble.
There are plenty of places where one could start now.

Alas I realize how far we are from utopian plans
like the ones I have suggested. I also know how far short
of a full account this is. Yet, for all that, I think the future
inclines toward what I am proposing. We are living, I
believe, in a time of deep revolutionary change. Tinkering
with details of school organization without making room
for a means of absorbing the wider revolution into our
ways of educating is surely unworthy of us as a species.

44

PHYLLIS LA FARGE

An Uptight Adolescence

EARLY ADOLESCENCE, perhaps more than other periods in life, feels in memory as if it were uniquely one's own. No one else could have been so tentative, so lyrical, and so despairing by turns. At the time one felt unique, too, perhaps especially in my generation. When I was an adolescent there was far less of a youth culture supporting and generalizing as well as blunting the experience of the individual. I was doubtful that anyone else felt as I did and uncertain in my attempts to interpret the self emerging in me. Enough of this still lingers so that I feel most comfortable if I do not generalize but speak of my own adolescence in specifics.

I was twelve in 1945. For me the end of World War II in Europe came during recess in a girls' private school in New York City. It was announced by the sallow hysteric whose title was Head of the Middle School. That very winter she had disbanded our French class after we had reduced the white Russian emigré teacher to tears once too often. The hysteric thought she could make us guilty enough so that we would sign up for a new French class in a more docile frame of mind. Her strategy failed. No one signed up, not even the class goody-goody, me. We knew that there was no real question of the school's discontinuing French. We waited out a week of extra study halls and sure enough we were back with Mme. T., with her black suit buttoned too tightly over her large breasts, her braids coiled over her ears, and, just in front of her braids, a neatly trimmed fringe of black sideburns.

The end of the war in the Pacific came on an island off the coast of Maine where I was visiting with my mother and my sister. The day was brilliant. My mother and I walked on a path that was a foot-worn trough in the pine mulch, looking at the headlined *Times* we had picked up at the dock. "But it is not the same for us as it is for other people," she said. She meant that the fathers and husbands of others would return, whereas my father, who had died in the war, would not. This is the only time in those years that I can remember her mentioning what she thought grief had done to us—that it had set us apart.

Set apart from my peers and from an important part of my younger life: these sensations of isolation and discontinuity were the strongest experiences of my early adolescence. While the war went on I felt a continuity, even if of an abstract sort, with my father. The newsreels at the 85th Street Translux on Madison Avenue proved that we were still living in the same piece of time in which he had died; in my consciousness the jiggly black and white images (Dresden, Salerno) were of a piece with the event of his death. But when the war was over we were in a new time he had not known.

There were other, more specific discontinuities. A year or so before the end of the war my mother had sold the house in the country where we had lived and taken an apartment in New York where she herself had been raised. We spent most of the summer in my maternal grandmother's Westchester house where my mother had lived as a child. There was continuity but it was with my mother's earlier years (we had spent no more than a few weeks there each year as small children). Continuity with my own and my sister's earlier experience was broken.

My mother's decisions gave me a latter-day Jamesian adolescence. My sister, my mother, and I became the pawns of a beautiful and powerful woman—my grandmother—who found in us an acceptable rationale for continuing to live in a house and in a style which she clung to for reasons of her own. I lived with auras and essences and intimations that I only half understood. I picked up tastes, prejudices, turns of phrase that belonged to the two or three earlier generations who had lived in my grandmother's house and in the other family houses nearby. Auras and tastes which lingered on with the same long half-life of old photographs, old records, old coats and canes in the closets of country houses, old toys in top floor playrooms. Treasures if there is enough going on and if there is not, as there was not for me, then a complex burden, not unlike the burden of foreign parentage, beloved and yet rejected because it appears an impediment to defining oneself in a new land or, as in my case, in one's own time.

I saw no one my own age except my sister all summer and no adults except family. I learned no sports, no crafts. I had a few tennis lessons and a few riding lessons with ludicrous results (it seems improbable that I could have ended up clinging upside down to the neck of a horse but this is what I recall—perhaps the whole business simply felt that way). Everything I attempted was done "cold," that is without the support of other people doing and enjoying it. Performance became synonymous with an unattainable perfection. I withdrew into what I could do—read and swim, paint watercolors. I could have gone to camp if I had wanted (yet as I write it, it seems a paltry solution) but I could least of all have dared what might have freed me. And no one prodded.

I learned to read the few people I was with minutely. Survival seemed to depend—I make it sound conscious but it wasn't—on an understanding of character and motivation. An Argus grew within me (and is with me still). On summer mornings my grandmother ate breakfast in bed and my mother until her nerves drove her out to garden sat in a chair beside the bed reading the *Times*. I, too, spent a few minutes in the room remembering the pleasure I had felt there as a small child, and feeling it no more. In the summer of 1948 I wrote in my diary:

Ga crushes Mummy and fixes everything in her mind. Exasperating but I am still detached enough to be intrigued by the patterned carpet of Ga's bedroom. Ever since the idyllic mornings that I spent crawling on the floor of her bedroom the intricate blue and purple design has fascinated me. I am still young enough to enjoy rolling the hatstand down the paths and halls of my imagination's castle on this carpet.

(I went on to write that the news was bad in the summer of 1948 and that I always read the fashion page and Billy Rose first. The news has become so bad since that I have almost ceased to read it and Billy Rose is dead.)

It was in those years of early adolescence that I think I learned to counter pain with observation, not only of people but things— carpets, plants, language, paintings—and to think even if awkwardly, pompously about my own experience. Characteristic of those years, too, is the "betweenness," the awkward position between a child's pleasures and perceptions and a more adult mode, and the sense of change and changing suggested by the repeated word "still." The first "still" points ahead to a time when I might no longer be able to bear my family situation, in fact, almost insinuates that I expect someday not to be able to bear it. The second "still" harks back to a child's enjoyment. Early adolescence brings not only a sense of change and the changing nature of experience but, perhaps as a result of an awareness of change, an altered perception of time. Time begins to move faster, summers are not as long; the more static "timeless" world of childhood is passing. Ambitious person that I am, I think I began in the twelve to sixteen years to equate the passage of time with some sort of progress. (It took a long time to shake that notion.)

My sister and I became very close; we lived in our heads, at the same time longing for involvement, action, most of all people our own age. Twenty-five years later we are still convinced that for us friends are not what they are for others: to us they still seem benefactions not at all to be taken for granted. "I must build myself a world inside myself," I wrote in a 1947 diary entry which expresses much of what we felt, "a secret place, impenetrable to all but those I love. And yet from this seclusion I love people."

My sister was my ideal. I thought it was better to have curly hair, to be very fair. I valued what she was—absolute, intense, uncompromising—and I knew I could not attain to it; beside her I felt a trimmer. I was still a Roman Catholic (my diaries are full of prayers) but I was already aware that she was more religious than I and this gave her a kind of worthiness I had an inkling I could not hope for. My passion for the events of the day (I was an avid reader of newspapers in my teens) seemed second-rate beside her passion for poetry and the natural world. She became the model for later love. I wonder how often such models grow out of the close affections of early adolescence, taking siblings or friends for models rather than parents.

But I falsify if I suggest only the negative. The longing for the companionship of peers and the chance to do things with people my own age was so overriding that I tended to underrate what I had—and even now risk doing so in writing about those years. I have written recently about my relationship with my mother and do not want to repeat it here except to say that she cared for me so much and was (is) a person of such moral passion and honesty that she gave my life a kind of guarantee.

Important, too, was the experience every summer of a large household and of an extended family of aunts, uncles, great-aunts, all living nearby. I took it so for granted that there was always someone to turn to, family or not family, that I could be bored and confined by what I had (and, true, there was no one my own age). Only later did I value as nearly priceless the sense of a world small enough to perceive it whole, the play of people above and below stairs, with and against each other, the stuff that novels used to be made of—and to continue to feel as I did inarticulately in adolescence that it was experience that fitted me to a time earlier than my own.

It was easy to live in such a world without social consciousness even in the late forties. I thought my relatives snobbish and prejudiced, but I had no concrete alternatives to their point of view beyond a vague liberalism and I would not have known where to turn for other models.

Along with the discontinuities specific to my circumstances came the discontinuities of puberty, the changes in my own body. The changes of adolescent bodies are subject matter for Goldoni or the Marx brothers, if only adolescents could feel that way. I had hips before I had breasts; it seemed cruel mismanagement. My mother, slender, erect, and a puritan in her corseting as well as in the control of her emotions, bought me a girdle. I wore it with a Carter's knit undershirt, the kind with the little string tied about level with breast bone. Cotton knit in contact with other fabrics is bound to roll itself into a little ridge. It is this ridge circumnavigating my hips which I remember above all else from the marriage ceremony of my uncle—this and the little string bow which kept popping out of the slit neck of my dress. It seemed impossible that the entire gathering, absorbed in a high nuptial mass, was not eyeing me.

Self-consciousness about my body and appearance were overwhelming for several years. I did not put it into words, or even think it, but there was always the possibility that my body, like some not quite predictable tyrant, a sort of Ubu Roi, would betray me, that something else would bulge or sweat or all at once sprout hair and so depart from the firm, predictable body of childhood.

It still strikes me as fathomless that when it came I did not recognize the menses for what it was, although it had been explained by my mother and the headmistress at school. Perhaps its gaudiness was too removed from their restrained explanations. (I see the headmistress's earnest, thin-lipped face still as she wrote the Latin derivation on the blackboard. Somehow she got through the entire talk without a single mention of sexuality. Lord knows what she might have said, given the time, the place, and her own nature, but still it seems a feat.) Perhaps it was too abrupt a discontinuity with the body I had always known. Perhaps I had expected menstruation to be accompanied with immediate radical change in the rest of me, that the little girl spending a warm September weekend at her grandmother's would be instantly transformed into an adult woman. Transformation is another, more positive way of stating the discontinuities of early adolescence. It is longed for and feared, signaling as it does changes in, if not the end of the self one knows. Perhaps the fear of transformation explains something else; after my mother's "talk" I remember weeping in a great storm of emotion as I took my before-bed shower and looked down (perhaps in fear? in memory the feeling is one of extreme mortalness) at my still childish body.

In my generation rites of passage were inadequate if there at all.

Yet when I finally did know what had happened to me I felt along with confusion at least a hint of the quiet and private immensity that I knew years later in pregnancy and after the birth of my children.

This is the point: years later. In my time and in my milieu childhood was protracted and protected; the gap between readiness and fulfillment which is characteristic of human animals was at its widest; moreover, sex and birth were remote from those around me (at least as far as I knew). Possibly these factors—extreme in my case but generally present in upper-middle-class families of my generation—added to a fear of transformation and to a longing for it, forcing the young to hold in abeyance what is vital to them, refusing to sanction a chance to assay it. It was done in the name of education and in the name of culture, or rather one kind of culture. Central to this culture is a premise that a certain male bonding is necessary to achievement whether military or intellectual. Bonding takes time—namely the adolescent years. It leaves girls with a long wait, a delayed promise, and all the consequences to development which inaction brings. The current young question the premise on which this culture is founded without entirely knowing that they do so. At the same time that they refuse to keep the sexual in abeyance they whittle away at the protracted childhood which I knew. It is not clear what consequences their behavior will have for the culture they came out of, the one that I was raised in.

Not included in the bonding of young men and denied easy access to the achievement which is the reward for delay and sublimation, yet subjected to the same or greater restraints, upper-middle-class young women of my own and earlier generations were condemned to the juggling act of pretending that they would achieve (how else could one get through a school course that aped a young man's?), acquiring a nonthreatening cultural *batterie de cuisine* ("I have no accomplishments," one diary entry reads), and longing for the encompassing love which attracted doubly, not only as the thing one's heart and body were ready for but as the only goody the culture would give with full approval.

The conflict created by this situation in someone like me was considerable, but it was largely unconscious, expressed in diary entries which now seem mutually exclusive but then did not seem the least bit contradictory. Windy talk about intellectual endeavor, worry about exams, the wish to transfer to a more stimulating school—and then passages about loneliness and the longing for love, essays on what a good mother should be, including this fine sentence which could only have been written by someone very young who had never had a child: "Develop the best in them [your children] in the best possible way and stamp out the bad without seeming aggressive about it." Only once did I record any conflict over the paths that lay open to me. I wince to quote my fifteen-year-old pomposities:

There must be one person who works twenty-four hours a day to bring up children, even when the family has only two. This is the mother's job. If she is absolutely unfitted for it, then she must supply someone who will furnish love, culture, learning, and discipline. There are no substitutes for these, and they must be supplied one way or another. This is an awful thing for me to have to face. I will never want to surrender myself wholly to the job of home-making.

It goes without saying that the example of a relative or family friend who worked would have helped me. (The only one who did was constantly put down by my mother and grandmother for neglecting her children—and they were right about her.) Today I would feel that a woman interested in what at fifteen I airily referred to as the "life of the mind" may do better not to have children, but to judge by the passage quoted above, my character and conditioning were such that even in early adolescence this option was already closed to me.

In saying that sex was remote from my adolescent life I do not mean that I did not think about it all the time. But, inheriting a romantic (and lady-like) tradition, I would have found it impossible to admit it was sex I was thinking of. Instead I called it loneliness, or more disastrously, love (which, of course, I also wanted)—that is, the only love which would have been acceptable to me, especially with my Roman Catholic background and the example of my mother and grandmother's lives: complete, final, culminating in wedlock. This led to rampant fantasy life, designs on several unsuspecting young men, and a long involvement with the first young man who cared for me. I could think of it all as farcical if it didn't still make the palms of my hands sweat. Most of it came later than the early adolescent years. At sixteen I had been no more than kissed, hardly rumpled, although I knew myself on the basis of classmates' intimated experiences (girls in those days did not compare notes) to be backward.

It was another matter if sex was in a book and did not refer to me. I read Balzac's *Droll Stories* and Erich Remarque's *The Arch of Triumph*. There was nothing more so available. I was twenty-two before I found under the counter on the Avenue de l'Opéra all the green-bound books that are now over-the-counter all over the United States—not to mention in your neighborhood theater. My grandmother told me not to read Thornton Wilder's *The Ides of March;* I protested in my diary, "What does an historical novel accomplish if it does not make us aware that though the vestal virgins were virgins the rest of Rome was perfectly normal?"

During the twelve to sixteen years I was apt to think about sex through anxiety about myopia and fat. Puberty brought nearsightedness; all at once I could not see the numbers on the sails of boats on Long Island Sound (the trickster, unpredictable body again). I can remember weeping all the way home from the optician as a new and stronger pair of glasses made the pavement look all at once like a Dubuffet. I never stated it to myself but in fact I believed that "Men seldom make passes at girls who wear glasses." I think I also believed that they never made passes at anyone who weighed over 120 pounds. (I lived, as I still do, on the dubious frontier between gourmandise and gluttony—with a cottage cheese metabolism.) The summer I turned fifteen I lost twenty pounds. It was a ritual, I see now, of sexual eligibility.

I am bitter about the way I and others of my generation were made to feel about physical appearance. There was scarcely an ad I looked at as I was growing up which did not equate the ideal body and the possibility of acceptance by others, especially one's peers. The price in self-hatred was enormous. We were without a counterculture and yet exposed in early adolescence to a post-World War II advertising style at once more blatant and suggestive than anything our parents had known. The sexual criterion was pronounced. Moreover, the ideal was a photograph, or rather a certain photographic style or styles. Mine is a generation that doubted itself in deep ways because we were not photographs. The dieting of WASPS like me was of a piece with noses altered and hair straightened, but of course paltry in comparison. In my case the situation was exacerbated by my particular background. It is the final refinement of having plenty to leave it on your plate, and scorn for gratification can be a by-product of an ethic of control.

Inextricable from worry about fat and glasses was anxiety about social life, and in the upper-class New York milieu in which I was raised that consisted of subscription dances during Christmas and Easter vacations.

A few of my contemporaries knew boys at day school in New York, often through a brother, but I did not. Many of my Jewish classmates had (or appeared to have—I feel uncertain writing about any of this; I tended to see others through a glass, rosily) a better social life because they were part of a more cohesive society with a gregarious allegiance to each other ("Our Crowd") in which families saw to it that parties at home and membership in country clubs supplemented formal social life and brought young people together. Something like this existed in the summer life of latter-day Wharton or Jamesian WASPS but it was spotted around the map of New England. It seems to me that in the city the cohesiveness of an earlier age (my grandmother's youth) had been lost and with it a degree of confidence. The group was too big to know each other and to maintain a sense of scale. And it was no longer quite the same group. To a degree it had been infiltrated, not by robber barons and their offspring as at the turn of the century, but by what my grandmother referred to scornfully as "café society." (She herself was something of an infiltrator, but that is another story and one I had not figured out during those years.) In any case, most boys of this milieu were sent to boarding school so that for most adolescents there was no social contact at all except for the vacations. Some lucky girls knew boys they could write to—"I am writing this under the covers at night by the light of a flashlight," wrote a friend of mine in study hall. The rest relied on their luxuriant fantasy life.

Everything that has been written about the horrors of the college mixer dance could be applied to the subscription dances: the emphasis on superficial attractiveness, the encouragement of puny strategies and aggressive or defensive behavior, the fostering of feelings of inadequacy, almost inevitable at least for the awkward and shy. If anything these dances were worse than college dances because the participants were younger and generally more inept socially. Moreover, the girls had to invite the boys, thus reversing the stance which they were meanwhile learning to assume. And not only one boy but two, so that there would be a stag line.

The evenings began with dinner parties at which perhaps a dozen young people awkwardly battened into formal clothes did what they could to make conversation. One of my cousins always opened by asking girls whether or not they sat facing the drain when taking a bath. Bodies, tyrannical and unpredictable as ever, were just below the surface of the conversation. Suddenly brawny wrists which had thrust three inches in three months (it seemed) out of the sleeves of dinner jackets, Etna-like pimples monopolizing one's consciousness, and in that era of the strapless dress, breasts, too much or too little. I remember falsies, in their own antiseptic way as surreal as the *mamelles de Tiresias*, rising clear out of the bodice of a friend's dress. I admit it happened while she was dancing, but I'm sure they felt unreliable even at the dinner table.

After dinner as many as 350 young people congregated in the semi-darkness of the Plaza ballroom, there to manage as best they could for three hours. The underlying myth said that everyone knew everyone because everyone was from the same milieu. In fact, little clusters of people knew other clusters based on schools attended and summer friendships—and some knew scarcely anyone at all. (My position in relation to all this was particularly difficult since my mother's family was both of the milieu and at the same time half withdrawn from it, or in the case of my mother almost totally withdrawn from it.) There were people who had a good time but they tended to be the most aggressive of the boys and the "stars" among the girls. Myopia is one of my chief memories of those evenings; I could not possibly have considered wearing my glasses. But despite nearsightedness I remember individual dresses, faces, scenes sharply at a more than twenty year distance, so intensely was I keyed up to survive in what I had plunged myself into. I had not been forced to go (my sister refused to); I had chosen to, if one can associate choice with an unrelenting effort to succeed with peers. Conforming and succeeding were inextricable in my adolescence from the desire to overcome a feeling of isolation, half social, half sexual.

My situation, and perhaps the situation of many young adolescents, demanded the comfort of a fantasy self. Hand in hand with the plump, striving, myopic individual the world could see walked a glamorous, seductive ghost socially adept and at the same time lyrical, sensitive; a creature in love with spring rains and spring flowers. Glamor and lyricism are strange companions, but this never struck me; perhaps my unconscious model was the Cecil Beaton photos I had pored over as a child: English beauties in organdy grouped on the grass around the trunk of a stately tree and in the distance ponds, sheep, woods, sunlit mist, and plenty of sward.

It was the ghost who chose the dresses in which to brave the dances: black and green moiré or net embroidered with peacock's eyes. And it was the ghost who began to read poetry, trying with words to flesh out feeling in the most traditional adolescent way.

"Up the airy mountain,/down the rushing glen,/We daren't go a-hunting/for fear of little men." This is where I was just before the twelve to sixteen years began. This was rapidly superseded by Alfred Noyes: "There's a barrel-organ carolling across a golden street/In the City as the sun sinks low."
Or:

> Yes; as the music changes,
>   Like a prismatic glass,
> It takes the light and ranges
>   Through all the moods that pass;
> Dissects the common carnival
>   Of passions and regrets,
> And gives the world a glimpse of all
>   The colours it forgets.

Next came:

> Sabrina fair
>   Listen where thou are sitting
> Under the glassy, cool, translucent wave,
>   In twisted braids of lilies knitting
> The loose train of thy amber-dropping hair,
>   Listen for dear honor's sake,
>   Goddess of the silver Lake
>   Listen and save!

Although there was still room for:

> Over the cobbles he clattered and clashed in the
>   dark inn yard.
> He tapped with his whip on the shutter, but all
>   was locked and barred.
>   (Noyes again)

Then came quantities of Shelley, the songs of Shakespeare, fragments of Keats and Coleridge, and not a single thing from the modern period except:

> A brackish reach of shoal off Madaket—
> The sea was still breaking violently and night
> Had steamed into our North Atlantic Fleet.

I did not read even Yeats until I was in college (I would have loved him; the ghost self was Yeatsian; it stood at the edge of still brown waters and watched the flight of swans, but the water was Long Island Sound and the birds were gulls).

Others have said it, but my generation and my milieu of peers were slow to discover ourselves in our own time. We read Eliot, Pound, Yeats, and Rilke in college. I did not understand *Howl* when it first appeared. It is possible that the fare we were offered in elementary and high school had some influence on our tardiness. Literature, it was implied, had stopped somewhere around 1870. Traditional education has always operated with this sort of gap or lag and for centuries no one expected the present—or the relevant as it is called today—to be formally taught. Interested people picked it up, were part of it. I am not sure now that I believe that the present should be taught, at least in literature, and yet I am bothered by what I was taught in my early teens. Somehow it was not good enough to read three Scott novels and William Cullen Bryant in seventh and eighth grades. Now young people are starved on relevance but we were force-fed the past. Is this one reason we were so slow to put any stock in the validity of our own experience or to find our own way of seeing? Or did our adolescent years come at precisely the moment when everything that has become so apparent since was just beginning to show (the technological juggernaut, the overly rapid rate of change, political powerlessness, the substitution of symbiosis with a pop environment for a relationship with the natural world)? Were we slow because we were frozen, seeing a little and not knowing how to interpret? Whatever the answer, we started out believing that traditional tools would· be adequate to interpret our experience. I think we were the last generation to believe so. When at the very end of the twelve-to-sixteen period it first occurred to me that I might try one day to be a writer, I did not question that I would write novels. I did not, for instance, consider films, as did those five or six years younger than I. (My five-year-old son, on the other hand, dictating his first story, asks, "Is it going to be a book or a show or T.V.?" And when he paints—on long pieces of shelf paper taped to the floor—he asks me to attach the paper to the cardboard tubes of paper towel rolls so that he can make a moving picture.)

For me the transformation of tools and understanding came slowly and is incomplete.

In a certain sense I feel I falsify speaking of early adolescence in terms of discontinuity and transformation, sex and sensibility. What I did was go to school. Whatever my inner sense of discontinuity and isolation, for eight months of the year there was the continuity of school and the daily contact with about twenty other girls.

My sister and I left the apartment at 8:15, walked two blocks to the Spence School and thereupon were enclosed until 3:00 and sometimes 4:00 or 4:30 in a self-contained world housed in a more or less Georgian brick building on East 91st Street. The day began with prayers and announcements (some of the prayers sounded like announcements) and ended with sports. In between came a traditional curriculum traditionally and, in the case of many of the subjects, well taught. (It is easy to denigrate the education the school then offered. There were indeed endless grammar and spelling drills, a good deal of memorization, and, of course, *Ivanhoe,* the *Talisman,* and the *Heart of Midlothian.* But perhaps it is just worth mentioning that somewhere along the line I built a model of an Erie Canal lock, wrote a play about Catherine de Medici, and twice a week painted all afternoon with an excellent teacher. The strictest teacher was the French teacher—successor to the white Russian—yet it was she who would now and then stand on her desk to act out one of La Fontaine's fabels.)

It was a lock-step day, hardly broken by lunch and the free time that followed it, yet it was in this free time and in the afternoons before the hours of homework set in that friendships were formed. It is claimed that, unlike men, women do not need or else are socialized to do without close friendship groups of their own sex. I think, however, that friendships between individual girls can be important and sometimes even durable. I, for instance, count among my closest friends two women whom I first knew in early adolescence and met at school. I notice that although I do not see them very often, I confide in them as I do not in others (and they in me)

as if those early years had created a special trust. We seem to continue conversations we began twenty-five years ago.

It is perhaps only ten years since I had a nightmare that I had
not done my French homework. I can still conjure up the queasy
stomach which I had each morning during those palatable Episcopalian prayers. (There were Jews and Catholics in the school, but
it was taken for granted that tone was at least part of what parents
wanted from the place and tone was Episcopalian.) I have often
wondered whether school meant to my classmates what it meant to
me. I think for many it did not. For me it was an outlet for ambition—the only one available to me—something I could do and succeed at. At the same time there gleamed out at me from the pages
of sturdy textbooks baubles of true interest which I snapped at like
a bower-bird: tidbits about the Renaissance, about the structure of
language and the derivation of words, English history and the structure of plants.

But there was a price for succeeding, or rather a double price.
Doing well set one off as a "brain," winning respect but not the acceptance one craved. Moreover, it pressured one to compete with
one's previous record. One mid-years I wrote a long criticism of the
exam system in my diary, praising intellectual endeavor for its own
sake, but when I got my marks a few days later I recorded that I
was not pleased—at two B's and three A's. Pressuring myself thus
I was tired by the end of the year and wrote:

> Everything is endless. The work pours in; it is only ended by nine
> o'clock. The weather is warmer. My head is fuzzier. I wonder what I
> shall remember from all this hodgepodge . . . I can't remember this year
> at all. I remember Christmas vacation and the Big Snow [that blanketed
> New York in 1947]. I can recall that my hands sweated in English class
> from fear and hatred of Mrs. ———. I know even now that I didn't
> want to go back to school in October. The winter seemed interminable.
> The weekends were and are full of the family and the country but al-
> ways accompanied by a deep down loneliness and lack of anyone to talk
> to my own age.

Perhaps this suggests not only the melodrama of adolescence
and the depression which is the ever-present obverse of natures like
mine but also at least one possible effect of a school such as the one
I attended. The school was a copy of a copy of a copy—that is, it was
a copy of a boy's college prep school and traditional boy's schools
are copies in their picture of authority, their emphasis on competition and team sports of an all-male, more or less anglophile, achieve-
ment-oriented model of society. But girls were supposed *not* to do
what the school prepared them to do, although they were subjected
to a very similar education, minus some math and science, and an
identical set of values (the Episcopalian prayers, the team sports,
the scholastic honor rolls). As I said earlier only the achievement
of marrying well was completely sanctioned. (In an earlier generation it would have been somewhat acceptable to achieve as long as
one eschewed marriage, or at least didn't count on it, but in my
adolescence, which coincided with the "feminine mystique," this
course no longer had any status.) I am not sure that this situation
was a source of conflict for many of my school contemporaries, but
it was for me, not because I put less value on marriage—it was the
only thing I was sure I wanted—but because I placed a value on
school that they in many cases did not. I believed in it. In 1949 I
wrote as follows (and the pomposity in this case seems in direct
proportion to uncertainty):

> Next year I shall have to decide about college. Certainly my opinions

are not those of five years ago. At that time I thought that I would never want to go to college. Now I most probably shall. I am not sure that I want to spend four years because as in the minds of most girls my age is the idea of marriage.

It seems at least possible that I could have contemplated four years of college more positively—and not been so blue at the end of a long winter of being a good girl—if I had had at home or at school any models to lead me to believe that what I was doing had a future for me on its own terms. I think it is quite clear that I thought it was perilous to extend this future even a full four years beyond high school.

As if this situation was not enough to contend with, there was in the air both at home and at school the very WASP and very American ethos (perhaps it has something to do with a pre-sputnik era in education, too) that urged high achievers never to thrust themselves forward. It was not simply a question of being lady-like (men are as affected by this as women): it was a question of being humble and humility was not exactly or only a Christian virtue but a civic one. What's good enough for everyman is good enough for anyone who gets A's, and you're rocking the boat in an un-American way if you don't think so. It was this group of ideas that was hardest for me to accommodate myself to at fifteen and sixteen. I fancied myself an intellectual. An arrogant prig was closer to the point. Nevertheless, the following episode with the school librarian still rankles:

This morning I said something which I suppose is rather rude to Miss C. She asked what books we had gotten out of the library for the Renaissance project and I said I hadn't gotten any. Then afterwards she took me out of the library and told me a lot of things. She said that I was adolescent, having an adolescent's new discovery of brain power and the new feeling of the power of one's own ideas. She said that I was riding too high, not humble enough, and tending towards intellectual snobbery and introspection.

However well founded, it seems typical of my background that the repressive put-down came first rather than any attempt at offering the kind of freedom or challenge which would have forced me to test the wings I thought I had. Why didn't Miss C. show me the books I had been too hoity-toity to discover for myself?

The complete set of signals blipped at girls like me went something like this: achieve if you want to but remember it will set you apart from other girls and make it harder to attract boys. If you achieve prepare to interrupt your achievement at an appropriate (marriageable) age. Achieve but be cool about it; hide it if possible and above all don't claim that achievement has any prerogatives.

Needless to say I didn't articulate these signals to myself. I was not even aware of them; I just did my homework. Nevertheless, I responded to the code—by making rules for myself. There are more rules than there are prayers in my diary. When I first reread the entries before writing this piece the rules appeared ludicrous or pathetic, but I now think they represent a pretty accurate rendering of what it took to do well and at the same time be accepted in the time and the setting I grew up in. For instance:

1. Not to talk too much.
2. Not to be a fix-it.
3. To be sincere without being unwitty, stupid, or a goody-goody.
4. To be kind.
5. To avoid gossip.
6. To work hard.

7. To be friendly without being obnoxious.

8. To be sensitive without being hypersensitive.

9. To cultivate and work toward the right attitude.

Another set included these:

Placate everyone.

Strive for originality.

Early adolescents are assailed with the outer world as never before in their lives, or rather assailed with the sudden importance of succeeding in it, whether this means in work or love or friendship. In my uptight case this meant giving carte blanche to my superego. (I find the admission ignominious.) While others revolted I made rules. I had always wanted to please, not out of virtue, but because I was born cowardly about conflict. The desire to please became much more intense in adolescence and at the same time pleasing was all at once far more complicated.

Rule-making led me to distrust my own perceptions. This was its greatest drawback.

There is a cold and lonely feeling which I get living here this way [I wrote one summer about life at my grandmother's]. It creeps into me from every corner of the house, and I feel it shifting into me from each object that I touch. I sit all day building up hate for the place and the way of life in general.

But then I pulled the rug out from under myself:

This is bad because I suppose there is nothing wrong with it—the atmosphere, I mean. I am thoroughly biased at this point.

Reading old diaries is a particularly blatant form of narcissism. I am glad to say it is not one I had indulged in for many years until writing this piece. It is narcissistic because one is looking for oneself, trying to give one's present a psychic or emotional continuity in the past. I do not catch a clear reflection of myself from my adolescent diary; the elements are there but they do not have the same proportions they have now and the harping on loneliness, the lyricism, the prayers seem part of a self I have not known for a long time. I have a hunch that I might feel more of a piece with the self of childhood if I had a record of it; then I think I made fewer rules, was less ambitious and less bent on acceptance by my peers—and perhaps trusted my perceptions more. Yet if I do recognize myself in the early adolescent I once was it is in this conflict between rules and perception, a conflict which is still with me unresolved. What I perceive most of the time makes me not want to cope (it is probably significant that I use the word cope)—unless writing is coping—but the pattern is set, the sense of obligation is so strong that I can do otherwise only in spurts, and then feel guilty. One of the drawn-out, painful discoveries of adult life has been the discovery that rule-making is incompatible with the kind of writing I admire and that fantasy, the escapist reaction to too much rule-making, is almost equally incompatible. But the point I want to make here is that one's stance in relation to the outer world may be partly innate or created in childhood, but it is in a sense recreated in early adolescence and so strongly set and reinforced by a feeling of the vital importance of others that it is hard if not impossible to change. A lot of the time I am still doing my homework.

We need your advice

Because this book will be revised every two years, we would like to know what you think of it. Please fill in the brief questionnaire on the reverse of this card and mail it to us.

Business Reply Mail

No postage stamp necessary if mailed in the United States

First Class
Permit No. 247
New York, N.Y.

Postage will be paid by

George A. Middendorf
Executive Editor
Harper & Row Publishers Inc.
College Dept.
10 East 53rd St.
New York, NY 10022

Adolescent Psychology

ADOLESCENT PSYCHOLOGY: CONTEMPORARY PERSPECTIVES

I am a _____ student _____ instructor

Term used _____ 19_____

Name_____School_____

Address_____

_____

City_____ State_____ Zip_____

How do you rate this book?

1. Please list (by number) the articles you liked best.

_____ _____ _____ _____ _____

Why? _____

_____

2. Please list (by number) the articles you liked least.

_____ _____ _____ _____ _____

Why? _____

_____

3. Please evaluate the following:

	Excell.	Good	Fair	Poor	Comments
Organization of the book	____	____	____	____	_____
Section introductions	____	____	____	____	_____
Overall Evaluation	____	____	____	____	_____

4. Do you have any suggestions for improving the next edition?

_____

_____

_____

5. Can you suggest any new articles to include in the next edition?

_____

_____

_____

_____

_____

_____

_____

_____

Thank you very much

ATTENTION

Now you may order individual copies of the books in the CONTEMPORARY PERSPECTIVES READER SERIES directly from the publisher.

The following titles are now available:

Readings in ABNORMAL PSYCHOLOGY, Edited by Lawrence R. Allman and Dennis T. Jaffe (ISBN 0-06-043259-4) ($5.95)

Readings in ADOLESCENT PSYCHOLOGY, Edited by Thomas J. Cottle (ISBN 0-06-047057-7) ($7.25)

Readings in ADULT PSYCHOLOGY, Edited by Lawrence R. Allman and Dennis T. Jaffe (ISBN 0-06-047054-2) ($7.95)

Readings in AGING AND DEATH, Edited by Steven H. Zarit (ISBN 0-06-047056-9) ($5.95)

Readings in ECOLOGY, ENERGY AND HUMAN SOCIETY, Edited by William R. Burch, Jr. (ISBN 0-06-047058-5) ($5.95)

Readings in EDUCATIONAL PSYCHOLOGY, Edited by Robert A. Dentler and Bernard J. Shapiro (ISBN 0-06-047083-6) ($5.95)

Readings in HUMAN DEVELOPMENT, Edited by David Elkind and Donna C. Hetzel (ISBN 0-06-047055-0) ($6.95)

Readings in HUMAN SEXUALITY, Edited by Chad Gordon and Gayle Johnson (ISBN 0-06-047084-4) ($5.95)

Readings in SOCIAL PROBLEMS, Edited by Peter M. Wickman (ISBN 0-06-047053-4) ($5.95)

Readings in SOCIAL PSYCHOLOGY, Edited by Dennis Krebs (ISBN 0-06-043772-3) ($5.95)

Readings in SOCIOLOGY, Edited by Ian Robertson (ISBN 0-06-045502-0) ($5.95)

Paperback

Order your copies of any of the above titles by filling in the coupon below.

Please send me:

_____ copies of_____ (ISBN)

_____ copies of_____ (ISBN)

_____ copies of_____ (ISBN)

_____ copies of_____ (ISBN)

My check or money order in the amount of $_____ is enclosed. (Harper & Row will pay the postage and handling.)

_____
Name

_____
Address

_____
City

_____
State   Zip

77 78 79   9 8 7 6 5 4 3 2 1